Treasury
of
Spiritual
Wisdom

· · · · · · · · · · · · · · · ·

Treasury of Spiritual Wisdom

A Collection of 10,000 Inspirational Quotations

Compiled by
Andy Zubko

BLUE DOVE PRESS
SAN DIEGO, CALIFORNIA • 1998

Blue Dove Press Publishes books by and about saints and sages of all religions as well as other inspiring works. For a catalog of books available in books stores write to:

BLUE DOVE PRESS
4204 Sorrento Valley Blvd., Suite K
San Diego, CA 92121
Phone: (619) 623-3330 or 800-691-1008
E-mail: bdp@bluedove.com
website: www.bluedove.com

Third Edition - 1998

Copy and text design:
Brian Moucka, Poppy Graphics
Santa Barbara, California

Original cover art by Kathleen Hession
Cover concept by Richard Polese

Special thanks to Carlene Faucher for her endless patience, effort and skill in the preparation of this edition.

Special thanks to Dr. Lance Nelson, Department of Theological and Religious Studies, University of San Diego, for inspired and unstinting help.

Thanks to Mary Kowit for her significant help with this edition.

ISBN:1-884997-10-4
Printed in Canada

Library of Congress Cataloging in Publication Data:

Treasury of Spiritual Wisdom : a collection of 10,000 powerful
quotations for transforming your life / compiled by Andy Zubko.
        p.   c.m.
ISBN 1-884997-10-4
1. Religion--Quotations, maxims, etc. 2. Conduct of life-quotations,
maxims, etc.   I. Zubko, Andy.
PN6084.R3T75   1996
200--dc20   95-33635
                                   CIP

*This book
is dedicated
to all seekers.*

Table of Contents

Introduction

T his collection of quotes is unusual, even unique, in several respects. First, it spans diverse cultural, religious and wisdom traditions, and includes the thoughts of many people from the East as well as the West. Second, while it contains numerous practical sayings on skillful handling of day to day life, it also contains numerous quotes that are deeply spiritual in nature, conveying the universal insights of saints and sages. Third, the selections were chosen from a stand point of inspiring growth on all levels—physical, mental, emotional and spiritual.

The sayings in this book are taken from a wide variety of men and women, some well-known, others more obscure. Collectively, they represent a broad spectrum of spiritual traditions, including Christian, Jewish, Islamic, Buddhist, Hindu, Native American as well as less familiar traditions. Because some of these quotes are from masters of the spiritual realm, they may take some amount of reflection to "get" their full meaning. Indeed, some of them go beyond the boundaries of the common wisdom of our culture. Readers who encounter entries that baffle them are therefore encouraged in the direction of patient contemplation and occasional revisitation. We believe that doing so may bring special rewards.

Andy Zubko, the compiler and editor of this collection is a dear longtime friend. A natural contemplative and a deeply spiritual being in his own right, Andy had been in the habit of collecting inspirational quotes for many years. When he told me his idea of arranging them by category in book form, it immediately stuck me as a good one. I was doubly convinced when I read a sampling of the quotes, which were both well chosen and extremely profound.

Treasury is not Andy's first success as compiler. In 1981, Andy, in a team effort with four others, helped compile *Peace Pilgrim—Her Life and Work in Her Own Words*. This book was assembled as a loving tribute to the American sage, Peace Pilgrim, who between 1953 until the time of her passing in 1981, walked back and forth across America, on faith, as a witness to both inner and outer peace. Andy, who had been well-acquainted with Peace Pilgrim in the final years of her life and had the opportunity to accompany her on "inspirational-educational" tours to both Alaska and Hawaii, was well qualified to assist in this project. The book quickly become a spiritual classic with over 400,000 copies in print worldwide and translations into several major languages.

In addition to Peace Pilgrim, Andy was deeply influenced by Ramana Maharshi, a great Indian sage who died in the early 1950's. Both Peace Pilgrim and Ramana continue to be guiding lights in Andy's life.

Andy has always adhered to the idea that service to humanity was a vital part of his spiritual path. He left his successful greeting card business to manage an orphanage where he had been a long-time volunteer. In later years he journeyed to Haiti to work with Mother Teresa's nuns, the Sisters of Charity in a free medical clinic. More recently, near his home in rural Northern California, he has worked running a house where the homeless and mentally ill can congregate.

Blue Dove Press is pleased to have the opportunity to offer this exceptional and, I believe, inspired work, compiled as a true labor of love. My hope is that you will benefit from it as much as I have.

Jeff Blom, Publisher

Treasury
of
Spiritual
Wisdom

. . . .

Abundance

God wills us to have everything. As we express life, we fulfill God's law of abundance, but we do this only as we realize that there is good enough to go around—only as we know that all God's gifts are given as freely and fully as the air and the sun....
—*Ernest Holmes*

You can take as much water from the ocean as you are capable of carrying, but if you don't bother to go down to the shore with a pot you get nothing at all.... —*Annamalai Swami*

The great universe is filled with an abundance of all things, filled to over-flowing. All there is, is in her, waiting only for the touch of the right forces to cast them forth.... —*Ralph W. Trine*

Giving is the secret of abundance....
—*Sivananda*

The true wonder of the world is available everywhere, in the minutest parts of our bodies, in the vast expanses of the cosmos, and in the inter-connectedness of these and all things....
—*Michael Stark*

Abundance is knowing that everything you need has already been supplied....
—*Shantidasa*

Man is not the sum total of what he has already, but rather the sum of what he does not yet have, of what he could have.... —*Jean-Paul Sartre*

There is enough in the world for every-one's need; there is not enough for everyone's greed....
—*Mohandas Gandhi*

An abundance mentality springs from internal security, not from external rank-ings, comparisons, opinions, posses-sions, or associations....
—*Stephen R. Covey*

Nature deals with her children gener-ously; man's cup is always full to the brim; and if he chooses to taste of the fine and life-giving essence, he must cast away something of the grosser and less sensitive part of himself....
—*Mabel Collins*

Anyone can count the seeds in an apple; no one can count the apples in a seed.... —*Anonymous*

Supply is infinite, but there must be receptivity....We can have all the supply we will give. But that is where the barri-er is—the unwillingness to give. That is where the lack or limitation is....
—*Joel Goldsmith*

If there is but little water in the stream, it is the fault, not of the channel, but of the source.... —*St. Jerome*

The Abundance of God is like a mighty ocean, so vast you cannot pos-sibly exhaust it or cause a shortage for others. You can go to this inex-haustible ocean with a small cup and bring away only that small cup of bounty and blessing. Or, if you have faith enough, you can take a bucket and bring away a bucketful. It makes no difference to the ocean. Nor does it matter how often you go....abundance is always there.... —*Henry T. Hamblin*

To him that has, more shall be given; but from him that has not, the little that he has shall be taken away....
—*Jesus*

Abundance can be had simply by consciously receiving what already has been given....　*—Sufi saying*

Man individually and collectively is entitled to life in all abundance....El Dorado, a country rich beyond all precedent in gold and jewels, lies at every man's door. Your bonanza lies under your feet. Your luck is already at hand. All is within; nothing is without....　*—Herbert Seibert*

There is enough of everything for everyone....　*—Patricia Sun*

When your Source of supply, both spiritual and temporal, is the Infinite Spirit, your supply is unlimited and inexhaustible: it can never fail. When you realize this great truth, everything becomes changed: you look upon life with different eyes. You can say joyfully: "The Lord is my Shepherd, I shall not want," accepting the literal meaning of the words....
—Henry T. Hamblin

Keep the thought of God's abundance always in mind. If any other thought comes, replace it with that of God's abundance, and bless that abundance. Give thanks constantly, if need be, that the work is done....　*—Baird Spalding*

The universe cannot be miserly. It cannot be wanting. It holds nothing but abundance. It is perfect love, and perfect love is absolute, eternal giving....
—Emmanuel

Abundance consists not so much in material possessions, but in an uncovetous spirit....　*—John Selden*

Abundance is of God; pour into it and it cannot be filled, pour out of it and it cannot be emptied....
—Shantidasa

There is an unvarying law of Divine Supply of temporal necessities which, if obeyed, and complied with, never fails to act. All that we need for our body and for our work is already waiting for our use to fulfill the conditions. The law always acts, it cannot fail....　*—Henry T. Hamblin*

There cannot be a sense of abundance or the experience of prosperity without appreciation. You cannot find beauty unless you appreciate beauty. You cannot find friendship unless you appreciate others. You cannot find love unless you appreciate loving and being loved. If you wish abundance, appreciate life....　*—William R. Miller*

If you approach the ocean with a cup, you can only take away a cupful; if you approach it with a bucket you can take away a bucketful....
—Ramana Maharshi

When you realize there is nothing lacking, the whole world belongs to you....
—Lao-tzu

He who lives in the realization of his oneness with the Infinite Power becomes a magnet to attract to himself a continual supply of whatever things he desires....The one who is truly wise and who uses the forces and powers with which he is endowed; to him the great universe always opens her treasure house....　*—Ralph W. Trine*

Prosperity means that we are able to appreciate and use God's spiritual ideas of abundance....　*—Lowell Fillmore*

Abundance is a natural law of the universe. The evidence of this law is conclusive; we see it on every hand. Everywhere Nature is lavish, wasteful, extravagant. Nowhere is economy observed in any created thing. Profusion is manifested everywhere....　*—Charles Haanel*

Where man sees lack, lack manifests. Where man sees abundance, abundance is supplied.... —*Darwin Gross*

Abundance is scooped from abundance yet abundance remains....
—*Anne Sexton*

Too often we visit the well of divine abundance with a teacup instead of a bucket.... —*Elinor MacDonald*

God is able to provide you with every blessing in abundance....
—Paul of Tarsus

Opulence is the law of the universe, an abundant supply for every need if nothing is put in the way of its coming....
—*Ralph W. Trine*

Acceptance

There is nowhere we need to go and nothing we need to do; we only need be.... —*Margaret R. Stortz*

Acceptance is observation of life and suspension of judgement about whether what is happening is good or bad, right or wrong....
—*Ron Smothermon*

Everything is acceptable as it is and how it is in existence. There is not the slightest desire in nature for it to be otherwise.... —*Ormond McGill*

When God sends rain....rain is my choice.... —*James W. Riley*

You may accept the inevitable with bitterness and resentment or with patience and grace. Mere acceptance is not sufficient.... —*Paul Brunton*

To teach man how to live without certainty and yet without being paralyzed by hesitation is the lesson of learning acceptance.... —*Anonymous*

Let us....learn to accept ourselves—accept the truth that we are capable in some directions and limited in others, that genius is rare, that mediocrity is a portion of almost all of us, but that we can contribute from the storehouse of our skills to the enrichment of our common life.... —*Joshua L. Liebman*

Acceptance is a letting-go process. You let go of your wishes and demands that life can be different. It's a conscious choice.... —*Gary Emery*

Acceptance of one's life has nothing to do with resignation; it does not mean running away from the struggle. On the contrary it means accepting it as it comes....To accept is to say yes to life in its entirety.... —*Paul Tournier*

Of course there is no formula for success except perhaps, an unconditional acceptance of life and what it brings.... —*Arthur Rubinstein*

Some people confuse acceptance with apathy but there's all the difference in the world. Apathy fails to distinguish what can and cannot be helped; acceptance makes the distinction....
—*Arthur Gordon*

The transition from rebellion to acceptance has an extremely important consequence....in which we start seeing life as a training school....to teach us what we need to learn.... —*Piero Ferrucci*

Rowing against the tide is hard and uncertain. To go with the tide and thus take advantage of the workings of the great natural force is safe and easy....
—*Ralph W. Trine*

Be willing to have it so. Acceptance of what has happened is the first step to overcoming the consequences of any misfortune.... —*William James*

Seek not that the things which happen should happen as you wish; but wish the things which happen to be as they are, and you will have a tranquil flow of life.... —*Epictetus*

Action

Most of people's activities are valueless, if not downright destructive. Dom- inated by desire and fear, ceasing to do evil precedes beginning to do good. Hence the need for stopping all activities for a time, to investigate one's urges and their motives.... —*Nisargadatta*

Action springs out of what we fundamentally desire.... —*Harry A. Overstreet*

Never confuse movement with action.... —*Ernest Hemingway*

Creativity is "doing," and it burns itself out; its end is exhaustion.... —*William Gibson*

Action in itself is neither virtuous nor sinful. The error lies in attributing it to our false individuality, when really it emanates from God. So no action is to be discarded. All actions are to be surrendered to Him.... —*Papa Ramdas*

Perpetual motion is the eternal law of life. Like human respiration, it manifests everywhere in attraction and repulsion. Every action provokes a reaction; every reaction is proportional to the action which provoked it.... —*Eliphas Levi*

All human actions....are on principle doomed to failure.... —*Jean P. Sartre*

Man is now only more active—not more happy, nor more wise than he was 6,000 years ago.... —*Edgar A. Poe*

All activities and experiences are equal, for it is not the action that holds importance, but how tuned and aware your attention is while doing it.... —*A Spiritual Warrior*

In our era, the road to holiness necessarily passes through the world of action.... —*Dag Hammarskjöld*

There should be less talk; a preaching point is not a meeting point. What do you do then? Take a broom and clean someone's house. That says enough.... —*Mother Teresa*

Some people have ideas. A few carry them into the world of action and make them happen. These are the innovators.... —*Andrew Mercer*

An action is never good just because it obeys a rule, a custom, or an impulse.... —*Fernando Savater*

The real compensation of a right action is inherent in having performed it.... —*Seneca*

The quality of our expectation determines the quality of our actions.... —*André Grodin*

There is a relationship between prayer and action. Receptive prayer results in an inner receiving, which motivates to right action.... —*Peace Pilgrim*

A man rises or goes down by his own actions; as the builder of a wall, or as digger of a well.... —*Hitopadesa*

Inaction may be the highest form of action.... —*Jerry Brown*

People take action in order to satisfy essential human needs....
—*Abraham Maslow*

Action should culminate in wisdom....
—*Bhagavad-Gita*

All activity of the universe is God at work—not on its periphery but at its heart.... —*Matthew Fox*

Desire is the prompting of all activity. Desire is the urge. No activity arises in those who have attained all desires....
—*Sathya Sai Baba*

A man does not become greater by good action nor inferior by bad action.... —*The Upanishads*

Action is nothing but the movement of energy in consciousness, and it inevitably bears its own fruit....
—*Yoga Vasistha*

The cause of all actions is desire. A desire crops up in your mind for an object. Then you exert to possess the object. Desire is the motive power that keeps up the continuance of life....
—*Sivananda*

Do not be too timid and squeamish about your actions. All life is an experiment.... —*Ralph W. Emerson*

Any activity becomes creative when the doer cares about doing it right, or better.... —*John Updike*

The only way we can be freed from the chain of action and reaction is by not caring for the result....
—*Paramananda*

I think that feelings waste themselves in words; they ought to be distilled into actions, and into actions which bring results.... —*Florence Nightingale*

Fortune of her own accord, takes her abode with the man who is endowed with energy, who is prompt and ready, who knows how to act....
—*Hitopadesa*

The life of action is not incompatible with the life of contemplation, but subordinate to it.... —*Cuthbert Hall*

Steady, determined and purposeful action is one prayer always answered....
—*Norman Thornton*

Act well at the moment, and you have performed a good action to all eternity.... —*John K. Lavater*

Trust only movement. Life happens at the level of events, not of words....
—*Alfred Adler*

Dreaming has its place; inspiration is invaluable; but life is action as well as thought. They get farthest in the realm of character-building who link up thought and action, who do not merely dream, but act upon their noblest imaginings.... —*R. W. Wilde*

Knowing is not enough; we must apply! Waiting is not enough; we must do....
—*Johann W. Goethe*

Between saying and doing many shoes are worn out.... —*Italian saying*

Thought and analysis are powerless to pierce the great mystery that hovers over the world and over our existence, but knowledge of the great truths only appears in action and labor....
—*Albert Schweitzer*

We get to know the things we are attempting to master only by doing them. No amount of teaching or study ever made a craftsman....
—*U. S. Anderson*

The great end of life is not knowledge, but action....   —*Thomas Fuller*

The difference between what we do and what we are capable of doing would suffice to solve most of the world's problems....
—*Mohandas Gandhi*

Think like a man of action, act like a man of thought....   —*Henri Bergson*

When a man acts wisely, he grows old slowly. When he acts unwisely, he grows older and older every day in every way....   —*Fred Van Amburgh*

Do what you can, with what you have, where you are....
—*Theodore Roosevelt*

A man who has to be convinced to act before he acts is not a man of action....
—*Georges Clemenceau*

Activity simply for the sake of activity doesn't provide the satisfaction it promises....   —*Shantidasa*

Good actions ennoble us, and we are the sons of our own deeds....
—*Miguel de Cervantes*

Your thoughts should agree with your words, and the words should agree with your actions. In this world people think one thing, say another thing, and do something else. This is horrible. This is crookedness....   —*Sivananda*

Men's actions depend to a great extent upon fear of loss....   —*John Milhourn*

There is no power greater than right action in the present moment....
—*Yoga Vasistha*

Action to be productive has need of contemplation....   —*Mother Teresa*

Leadership is action, not position....
—*Donald H. McGannon*

The soul of all action is blindness. He who knows, cannot act any longer. Knowing means forgoing action and renouncing passion....   —*Egon Friedell*

The perfect man does nothing, the sage takes no action....   —*Chuang Tse*

Those who are called to the works of the active life would be wrong in thinking that their duty exempts them from the contemplative life....   —*St. Thomas*

The world is imprisoned by its own activity....   —*Hindu saying*

We must know that we have two kinds of happiness in this life, according to two different ways, one good, one best, which lead us thereto: one is the active life, and the other the contemplative....
—*Dante Alighieri*

Our deeds determine us, as much as we determine our deeds....   —*George Eliot*

The result of any action is dependent upon the amount of confidence with which it is done....   —*Sathya Sai Baba*

Where thou hesitatest between two courses of action, always choose the one which leaves thee more alone, more in silence, more in love....
—*Sister Consolata*

Blessed are they who translate every good thing they know into action, for ever higher truths shall be revealed to them....   —*Peace Pilgrim*

He who sees inaction in action and action in inaction, he is intelligent among men; he is a man of established wisdom and a true performer of all actions....   —*Bhagavad-Gita*

Action is the single most effective antidote to depression, anxiety, stress, fear, wrong, guilt and of course, immobility. It is virtually impossible to be depressed and active at the same time.... —*Wayne Dyer*

He who moves not forward goes backward.... —*Johann W. Goethe*

Every act of will is an act of self-limitation. To desire action is to desire limitation.... —*G. K. Chesterton*

Experience is the child of thought, and thought is the child of action. We cannot learn from books.... —*Benjamin Disraeli*

Doing is the great thing. For if, resolutely, people do what is right, in time they will come to like doing it.... —*John Ruskin*

Concern should drive us into action and not into depression.... —*Karen Horney*

Wisdom without action hath its seat in the mouth; but by means of action, it becomes fixed in the heart.... —*Shekel Hakodesh*

For purposes of action nothing is more useful than narrowness of thought combined with energy of will.... —*Henri F. Amiel*

Every action of our lives touches on some chord that will vibrate into eternity.... —*Edwin H. Chapin*

All the beautiful sentiments in the world weigh less than a single lovely action.... —*James Russell Lowell*

If we all did the things we are capable of doing, we would literally astound ourselves.... —*Thomas A. Edison*

He who desires but acts not, breeds pestilence.... —*William Blake*

If the fruits of action do not affect the person, he is free from action.... —*Ramana Maharshi*

Why should we be cowed by the name of Action?...The rich mind lies in the sun and sleeps and is Nature.... —*Ralph W. Emerson*

Every man without passions has within him no principle of action, nor motive to act.... —*Claude A. Helvetius*

I find the great thing in this world is not so much where we stand, as in what direction we are moving.... —*Oliver W. Holmes*

Action alone is just that does not harm either party to a dispute.... —*Mohandas Gandhi*

A little knowledge which you carry into action is more profitable than much knowledge which you neglect to carry out into action.... —*Hermes*

Heaven never helps the man who will not act.... —*Sophocles*

Active natures are rarely melancholy. Activity and sadness are incompatible.... —*Christian Bovee*

When you cannot make up your mind which of two evenly balanced courses of action you should take—choose the bolder.... —*W. J. Slim*

Desire causes our voluntary acts, force our involuntary.... —*Blaise Pascal*

The basis of action is the lack of imagination. It is the last resource of those who know not how to dream.... —*Oscar Wilde*

An ounce of action is worth a ton of theory.... —*Friedrich Engels*

Whatever you do, if you do it sincerely, will eventually become a bridge to your wholeness, a good ship that carries you through the darkness.... —*Carl Jung*

Abandon all action and come to Me for shelter.... —*Krishna*

Only those who do not need to engage in action are happy; they are perfectly content and self contained, and they experience happiness that extends to all the pores of the body.... —*Tripura Rahasya*

Visible deeds do not increase the goodness of the inner life, no matter how numerous.... —*Meister Eckhart*

The only way to know truly is through practical experiment and experience. Theory and speculation, if they are not followed by trial and demonstration, are useless....Knowledge itself is of little or no value if it does not lead to action.... —*Henry T. Hamblin*

The shortest answer is doing.... —*Lord Herbert*

Great thoughts reduced to practice become great acts.... —*William Hazlitt*

The acts of this life are the destiny of the next.... —*Hindu saying*

The actions of men are the best interpreters of their thoughts.... —*John Locke*

Activity is God's medicine; the highest genius is willingness and ability to do hard work.... —*Robert S. MacArthur*

If it is not right, do not do it.... —*Marcus Aurelius*

Unselfish and noble actions are the most radiant pages in the biography of souls.... —*David Thomas*

The end of man is action, and not thought, though it be of the noblest.... —*Thomas Carlyle*

Action is transitory, a step, a blow, the motion of a muscle–this way or that.... —*William Wordsworth*

Nothing is so terrible as activity without insight. Look before you leap is the maxim for the world.... —*Johann W. Goethe*

That action that takes you towards God is right, and that action which takes you away from God is wrong.... —*Papa Ramdas*

We are not to lead events but follow them.... —*Epictetus*

To know and yet not to do is in fact not to know.... —*Wang Yang Ming*

The busy bee has no time for sorrow.... —*William Blake*

Adversity

Bad times have a scientific value. These are occasions a good learner would not miss... —*Ralph W. Emerson*

The only way the Self can manifest is through conflict. To meet one's insoluble and eternal conflict is to meet God, which would be the end of the ego with all its blather.... —*Marie-Louise von Franz*

To have a crisis, and act upon it, is one thing. To dwell in perpetual crisis is another.... —*Barbara G. Harrison*

There is never really anything to be discouraged about, because difficulties are opportunities for inner growth, and the greater the difficulty, the greater the opportunity for growth....
—*Peace Pilgrim*

Adversity is not undesirable. Because, it is only when you are down and out in life that you can realize its true value....
—*Papa Ramdas*

If you yield to adversity, the chances are it will master you, but if you recognize in yourself the power of mastery over conditions, then adversity will yield to you.... —*Ralph W. Trine*

Adversity may call out dormant powers that have never before been suspected.... —*Alice H. Rice*

The bravest sight in the world is to see a great man struggling against adversity.... —*Seneca*

You get tragedy where the tree, instead of bending, breaks....
—*Ludwig Wittgenstein*

Difficulty....is the nurse of greatness—a harsh nurse, who roughly rocks her foster children into strength and athletic proportion.... —*William C. Bryant*

God is a light to our feet. Let us not be troubled by man, for what is man if not a fleeting shadow, a windblown leaf, a fading flower, and vanishing smoke....
—*Olympia Morata*

Tragedy is like a strong acid—it dissolves away all but the very gold of truth.... —*D. H. Lawrence*

The positive and victorious attitude keeps adversity away, while a negative attitude attracts it....
—*Henry T. Hamblin*

You cannot create experience. You must undergo it.... —*Albert Camus*

Men often bear little grievances with less courage than they do large misfortunes.... —*Aesop*

One of the secrets of life is making stepping stones out of stumbling blocks....
—*Jack Penn*

It may serve as a comfort to us, in all our calamities and afflictions, that he who loses anything and gets wisdom by it is a gainer by the loss....
—*Roger L'Estrange*

In many cases stress is caused not by the event itself but rather our response to the event.... —*Robert Eliot*

If we have our own why of life, we shall get along with almost any how....
—*Friedrich W. Nietzsche*

Times of confusion and general adversity have always been a source of great good. Real calamity was ordained as man's perfect mirror, that he may see himself and see how helpless he is without the support of a Supreme Being.... —*Fred Van Amburgh*

A man doesn't realize how much he can stand until he is put to the test. You can stand far more than you think you can. You are much stronger than you think you are....if God is dwelling in your life.... —*Martin Neimoller*

Meet adversity by turning defeat into victory.... —*John A. Schindler*

You cannot direct which way the winds of adversity will blow, but you can adjust your sails.... —*Shantidasa*

Adversity is the first path of truth....
—*George Byron*

The most generous vine, if not pruned, runs out into many superfluous stems and grows at last weak and fruitless; so doth the best man if he be not cut short in his desires, and pruned with afflictions....
—*Joseph Hall*

Extraordinary afflictions are not always the punishment of extraordinary sins, but sometimes the trials of extraordinary graces....
—*Matthew Henry*

Difficulties strengthen the mind, as labor does the body....
—*Seneca*

It is not until we have passed through the furnace that we are made to know how much dross there is in our composition....
—*Charles C. Colton*

Affliction comes to us all, not to make us sad, but sober, not to make us sorry, but wise, not to make us despondent, but by the darkness to refresh us....
—*Henry W. Beecher*

It is a great thing when the cup of bitterness is pressed to our lips, to feel that it is not fate or necessity, but divine love working upon us for good ends....
—*Edwin H. Chapin*

As threshing separates the wheat from the chaff, so does affliction purify virtue....
—*Richard E. Burton*

If you do not hear reason, she will rap you on the knuckles....
—*Benjamin Franklin*

Look at a man in the midst of doubt and danger, and you will learn in his hour of adversity what he really is....
—*Lucretius*

Adversity? It's a tonic, not a stumbling block! Every adversity carries the seed of an equal or greater benefit....
—*Napoleon Hill*

Affliction is a treasure, and scarce is any man who hath enough of it. No man hath affliction enough that is not matured, and ripened by it, and made fit for God by that affliction....
—*John Donne*

All loss, all gain, is particular....it is only the finite that has wrought and suffered; the infinite lies stretched in smiling repose....
—*Ralph W. Emerson*

The afflictions to which we are accustomed do not disturb us....
—*Claudianus*

When written in Chinese the word crisis is composed of two characters. One represents danger and the other represents opportunity....
—*John F. Kennedy*

There is nothing, no tragedy too great, no malady so incurable, that we cannot find something to counteract it if we do not forget to go within....
—*Paramananda*

Many things are learned in adversity which the prosperous man never dreams of....
—*Charles H. Spurgeon*

There's a tremendous amount to be gained through what appears to be adversity. If we don't allow the crisis, these challenges to take place, then we remain fixed in life and never really ripen or mature....
—*Thomas More*

All your sins and sorrows, your fears and anxieties are your own, and you can cling to them or you can give them up....
—*James Allen*

Adversity has the effect of eliciting talents which in prosperous times would have lain dormant....
—*Horace*

Man meets with adversity and fights it tooth and nail, as something evil, not knowing that it is merely a preparation for greater things and a larger and fuller life....　　　—*Henry T. Hamblin*

Fire is the test of gold; adversity of strong men....　　　—*Seneca*

When apparent adversity comes, be not cast down by it, but make the best of it, and always look forward for better things....　　　—*Ralph W. Trine*

Adversity is the trial of principle. Without it a man hardly knows whether he is honest or not....　　　—*Henry Fielding*

I never met a single instance of adversity which I have not in the end seen was for my own good....
　　　—*Alexander M. Proudfit*

We're like tea bags: We don't know our strength until we get into hot water....
　　　—*Bruce Laingen*

The man who is swimming against the stream knows the strength of it....
　　　—*Woodrow Wilson*

Our worst misfortunes never happen, and most miseries be in anticipation....
　　　—*Honoré de Balzac*

Adversity may be used as a stepping stone to better things, or it may be used as an excuse for failure. You can measure your own worth by your reactions to adversity....　　　—*J. M. Jussawalla*

Comfort and prosperity have never enriched the world as much as adversity has. Out of pain and problems have come the sweetest songs, and the most gripping stories....　　　—*Billy Graham*

An undisturbed mind is the best sauce for adversity....　　　—*Plautus*

Heaven sends us misfortunes as a moral tonic....
　　　—*Lady Blessington*

Adversity is the midwife of genius....
　　　—*Napoleon Bonaparte*

The brightest crowns that are worn in heaven have been tried, and smelted, and polished, and glorified through the furnace of tribulation....
　　　—*Edwin H. Chapin*

The greater the obstacle the more glory we have in overcoming it; the difficulties with which we are met are the maids of honor which set off virtue....
　　　—*Jean B. Moliere*

Misfortune is never mournful to the soul that accepts it; for such do always see that in every cloud is an angel's face....　　　—*St. Jerome*

Prosperity best discovers vice; adversity best discovers virtue....Adversity is not without many comforts and hopes....
　　　—*Francis Bacon*

Nature deals us her cruelest blows when she desires us to grow. Once we see the logic of this, we never again will quit in the face of adversity....
　　　—*U. S. Anderson*

Adversity is a severe instructor, set over us by one who knows better than we do ourselves....　　　—*Edmund Burke*

Who is honorable in the sight of the Creator? He who has met with adversity but bravely endures whatever befalls him....　　　—*Solomon Ibn Gabirol*

People need trouble—a little frustration to sharpen the spirit on, toughen it....you have to learn fortitude, endurance....　　　—*William Faulkner*

Difficulties show men what they are. In case of any difficulty God has pitted you against a rough antagonist that you may be a conqueror, and this cannot be without toil....   —*Epictetus*

Calamity is the perfect glass wherein we truly see and know ourselves....
—*William Davenant*

Mishaps are like knives, that either serve us or cut us, as we grasp them by the blade or the handle....
—*James Russell Lowell*

If an obstacle is put in our path, it is only to prevent us from going the wrong way, and to guide us into what is for us the only right path....
—*Henry T. Hamblin*

Adversity can be a great advantage to any man, for it rouses his resources, excites his energies, stimulates his skill, and fires his fortitude....
—*Fred Van Amburgh*

Behold a contest worthy of a god, a brave man matched in conflict with adversity....   —*Seneca*

If a serious calamity occurs, your mind should not be upset. Just keep the mind cool and calm. Have presence of mind. Do not cry over spilt milk....
—*Sivananda*

If there are difficulties in your path, be thankful for them. They will test your capabilities of resistance; you will be impelled to persevere from the very energy of the opposition....
—*William Punshon*

Difficulties are God's errands; and when we are sent upon them we should esteem it a proof of God's confidence— as a compliment from Him....
—*Henry W. Beecher*

As in nature, as in art, so in grace; it is rough treatment that gives souls, as well as stones their luster. The more the diamond is cut the brighter it sparkles....   —*Thomas Guthrie*

It cannot be too often repeated that it is not helps, but obstacles, not facilities, but difficulties, that make men....
—*William Matthews*

Behind every adversity lies a hidden possibility....   —*Sufi Saying*

The ultimate measure of a man is not where he stands in moments of comfort and convenience, but where he stands at times of challenge and controversy....   —*Martin L. King, Jr.*

It is often better to have a great deal of harm happen to one than a little; a great deal may rouse you to remove what a little will only accustom you to endure....   —*Lord Greville*

About the only difference between stumbling blocks and stepping stones is the way you use them....
—*Bernard Meltzer*

The lessons we learn in sadness and from loss are those that abide. Sorrow clarifies the mind, steadies it, forces it to weigh things correctly....
—*Theodore Munger*

The less we parade our misfortunes, the more sympathy we command....
—*Orville Dewey*

The winds and the waves are always on the side of the ablest navigators....
—*Edward Gibbon*

Never rejoice at other people's misfortunes for you cannot know when adversity may come to you....
—*Old Testament*

Nothing befalls a man except what is in his nature to endure....
—*Marcus Aurelius*

It is only from the belief of the goodness and wisdom of a supreme being, that our calamities can be borne in the manner which becomes a man....
—*Henry Mackenzie*

The greatest misfortune of all is not to be able to bear misfortune....
—*Bias of Priene*

We attempt nothing great but from the sense of the difficulties we have to encounter; we persevere in nothing great but from a pride in overcoming them....
—*William Hazlitt*

We become wiser by adversity; prosperity destroys our appreciation of the right....
—*Seneca*

The art of living lies less in eliminating troubles than in growing with them....
—*Bernard Baruch*

No matter how difficult the situation, life can be celebrated....
—*Robert Veninga*

Prosperity is too apt to prevent us from examining our conduct; but adversity leads us to think properly of our state, and so is most beneficial to us....
—*Samuel Johnson*

A great man does not lose his self-possession when he is afflicted; the ocean is not made muddy by the falling in of its banks....
—*Panchatantra*

He that is down needs fear no fall....
—*John Bunyan*

Why in all the affairs of life, do we seem to grow best under adversity?...
—*Manly Hall*

Prosperity is no just scale; adversity is the only balance to weigh friends....
—*Plutarch*

He who has no cross will have no crown....
—*Francis Quarles*

The keenest sorrow is to recognize ourselves as the sole creator of all our adversities....
—*Sophocles*

For trouble is the thing that strong men grow by....
—*H. Bertram Lewis*

If you lose heart when adversity comes, your strength will only be weakness....
—*Old Testament*

Kites rise against, not with the wind. No man ever worked his passage anywhere in a dead calm....
—*John Neal*

Adversities do not make the man either weak or strong, but they reveal what he is....
—*Faith Forsyte*

Sometimes great difficulties are permitted only in order to strengthen the character....
—*Robert Benson*

Adversity is the diamond dust Heaven polishes its jewels with....
—*Robert Leighton*

The weak sinews become strong by their conflict with difficulties...
—*Edwin H. Chapin*

The happy and efficient people in this world are those who accept trouble as a normal detail of human life and resolve to capitalize on it when it comes along. The hiding places of men are discovered by affliction....
—*James Alexander*

All the troubles of man come from his not knowing how to sit still....
—*Blaise Pascal*

Different people must contend with different trials, but adversities in some shape or other come to everyone. Life is a procession of people bearing crosses and when one carries his awkwardly he interferes with his fellow-marchers....
—*R. C. McCarthy*

Paradoxical as it may seem, God means not only to make us good, but to make us also happy, by sickness, disaster and disappointment.... —*Cyrus A. Bartol*

The only way to meet affliction is to pass through it solemnly, slowly, with humility and faith....Then its very ways of misery will divide and become to us a wall, on the right side and the left, until the gulf narrows before our eyes, and we land on the opposite shore....
—*Dinah M. Craik*

Advice

Among the most disheartening and dangerous of....advisors, you will often find those closest to you, your dearest friends, members of your own family, perhaps, loving, anxious, and knowing nothing whatever....
—*Minnie Fiske*

No advice is ever necessary from anywhere.... —*Nisargadatta*

Let me listen to me and not to them....
—*Gertrude Stein*

People have a way of becoming what you encourage them to be—not what you nag them to be....
—*Scudder Parker*

The true secret of giving advice is, after you have honestly given it, to be perfectly indifferent whether it is taken or not.... —*Hannah W. Smith*

We are apt to be very pert at censuring others, where we will not endure advice ourselves.... —*William Penn*

All the advice in the world will never help you until you help yourself....
—*Fred Van Amburgh*

Nobody gives you wiser advice than yourself.... —*Cicero*

Advice is like castor oil, easy enough to give but dreadful uneasy to take....
—*Henry W. Shaw*

To one who knows, it is superfluous to give advice; to one who does not know, it is insufficient.... —*Seneca*

Whoever gives advice to a heedless man is himself in need of advice....
—*Saadi*

The advice of all who are mature in the life of dependence upon God is: When in doubt, wait.... —*Henry T. Hamblin*

Advice is worth what it costs—that is, nothing.... —*Douglas MacArthur*

Nobody has the answer for you. The truth lies in each person. When you give up looking to others to tell simple rights and wrongs, you are left with only the inward search to discover the truth.... —*Jordan & Margaret Paul*

When a man seeks your advice he generally wants your praise....
—*Philip Chesterfield*

Men give away nothing so liberally as their advice....
—*Francois La Rochefoucauld*

I have found the best way to give advice to your children is to find out what they want and then advise them to do it.... —*Harry Truman*

One of the best ways to persuade others is with your ears, by listening to them....
—*Dean Rusk*

When a man has been guilty of any vice or folly, the best atonement he can make for it is to warn others not to fall into the like....
—*Joseph Addison*

Do not advise too much: do the job yourself. This is the only advice you can give to others. Do it and others will follow....
—*Jawaharlal Nehru*

Do not scatter advice without the authority born of practical experience....
—*Sathya Sai Baba*

Giving advice is sometimes only showing our wisdom at the expense of another....
—*Anthony Shaftesbury*

We obey our own destiny best when we listen to our heart....
—*U. S. Anderson*

People do not want advice. Even when they ask for it, they want confirmation. We want to be told we are right....
—*Fred Van Amburgh*

It is easy when we are in prosperity to give advice to the afflicted....
—*Aeschylus*

Whatever advice you give, be brief....
—*Horace*

Unasked advice is a trespass on sacred privacy....
—*Henry S. Haskins*

A good scare is worth more to a man than good advice....
—*Edgar W. Howe*

Seek information, but not from the unreliable; ask for advice but not from the unwise....
—*Mahabharata*

Advice is like snow; the softer it falls the longer it dwells upon, and the deeper it sinks into the mind....
—*Samuel Coleridge*

Harsh counsels have no effect; they are like hammers which are always repulsed by the anvil....
—*Claude A. Helvetius*

All dependence on another is futile, for what others can give others will take away. Only what is your own at the start will remain your own in the end. Accept no guidance but from within....
—*Nisargadatta*

Advice is what we ask for when we already know the answer but wish we didn't....
—*Erica Jong*

Never bother about other people's opinions. Be humble and you will never be disturbed....
—*Mother Teresa*

How is it possible to expect mankind to take advice when they will not so much as take warning?...
—*Jonathan Swift*

I do not ask advice, I rarely give it. If my advice is not often called for, still less is it followed. I know of no public or private business which it has corrected or bettered....
—*Michel Montaigne*

When we ask advice we are usually looking for an accomplice....
—*Marquis De La Grange*

Many receive advice, few profit from it....
—*Publilius Syrus*

He who can take advice is sometimes superior to him who can give it....
—*Karl von Knebel*

Advice is seldom welcome; those who need it most, like it least....
—*Samuel Johnson*

I have often wondered how it is that every man loves himself more than the rest of man, but yet sets less value on his own opinion of himself than on the opinion of others....

—*Marcus Aurelius*

If I wanted to become a tramp, I would seek information and advice from the most successful tramp I could find. If I wanted to be a failure, I would seek advice from men who never succeeded. If I wanted to succeed in all things, I would look around me for those who are succeeding, and do as they do....

—*Joseph M. Wade*

Before giving advice we must have secured its acceptance, or rather, have made it desired....   —*Henry F. Amiel*

We cling to our own point of view, as though everything depended upon it. Yet our opinions have no permanence; like autumn and winter, they gradually pass away....   —*Chuang Tse*

Ambition

Ambition is a mental condition which compels one to work one's self to death in order to live....

—*Anonymous*

He who rides the tiger of ambition is oftentimes afraid to dismount....

—*Chinese proverb*

To be unhappy at home is the ultimate result of all ambition....   —*Ben Johnson*

The ambitious climb up high and perilous stairs, and never care how to come down....   —*Thomas Adams*

Ambition renders the mind restless. If the ambition is not realized, the mind is filled with depression and anxieties. The ambitious man has no peace of mind....   —*Sivananda*

A slave has one master; an ambitious man has many masters....

—*Jean La Bruyere*

When you find God within you, all your ambitions are fulfilled....there is no fulfillment of your ambitions for external things....   —*Papa Ramdas*

It is the constant fault and inseparable evil quality of ambition, that it never looks behind it....   —*Seneca*

Ambition is not a vice of little people....

—*Michel Montaigne*

Ambition is but the evil shadow of aspiration....   —*George MacDonald*

Put personal ambition away from you, and then you will find consolation in living or in dying, whatever may happen to you....   —*Henry F. Amiel*

Ambition is the grand enemy of all peace, inner as well as outer....

—*John Cowper Powys*

Ambition is bubbles on the rapid stream of life....   —*Edward Young*

Ambition breaks the ties of blood and forges the obligations of gratitude....

—*Walter Scott*

Ambition is the avarice of power; and happiness herself is soon sacrificed to that very lust of dominion....

—*Charles C. Colton*

Most of the trouble in the world is caused by people wanting to be important....   —*T. S. Eliot*

Ambition is a lust that is never quenched, but grows more inflamed and madder by enjoyment....
—*Thomas Otway*

Ambition is like love, impatient of delays and rivals....   —*John Denham*

Fling away ambition. By that sin angels fell. How then can man, the image of his Maker, hope to win by it....
—*William Shakespeare*

Ambition and suspicion always go together....   —*Georg C. Lichtenberg*

Ambition is a condition inspired by the wish to be first....   —*Max Gralnick*

Ambition is so powerful a passion in the human breast, that however high we reach we are never satisfied....
—*Niccolo Machiavelli*

Ambition is bondage....
—*Solomon Ibn Gabirol*

Life gets more tranquil when the ambitions die away....   —*Lord Birket*

If we do not encourage our ambition, feed it and strengthen it by vigorous exercise, it will soon die....
—*Orison S. Marden*

Ambition is the senseless chasing of rainbows....   —*Frederick Loewe*

In their hurry to attain some ambition, to gratify the dream of life, men often throw honor, truth, and generosity to the winds....   —*William G. Jordan*

When men's hearts are free from the ambition of earthly power....the light of God shining in them will surely dispel the clouds and create an atmosphere of peace and goodwill....
—*Papa Ramdas*

No ambition is spiritual. All ambitions are for the sake of the "I am." If you want to make real progress you must give up the idea of personal attainment. The ambitions of so-called spiritual teachers are preposterous....
—*Nisargadatta*

Ambition can creep as well as soar....
—*Edmund Burke*

A wise man is cured of ambition by ambition itself; his aim is so exalted that riches, office, fortune and favor cannot satisfy him....
—*Jean La Bruyere*

Discontent follows ambition like a shadow....   —*Henry S. Hawkins*

We have tried the ways of ambition, of self-aggrandizement, of aggressive opportunism, and we have seen the kind of flimsy success to which they lead; we have tasted the bitter poisons they generate, we have known the conflict, the disgust, the inner division, the outer isolation that follow in their wake....   —*Gregory Vlastos*

Nothing is too high for the daring of mortals; we storm heaven itself in our folly....   —*Horace*

Most people would succeed in small things, if they were not troubled with great ambitions....
—*Henry W. Longfellow*

Throw away all ambition beyond that of doing the day's work well....
—*William Osler*

Nothing is so commonplace as to wish to be remarkable....
—*Oliver W. Holmes*

Ambition destroys its possessor....
—*The Talmud*

Though ambition is itself a vice, it is often the parent of virtues....
—*Quintilian*

If you pride yourself on your ambition, take a mental inventory of its ends, and ask yourself whether you desire to attain those personal ends and forego the opportunities of being happy....
—*Walter B. Wolfe*

Ambition plagues her proselytes by keeping them always in show and public, like a statue in a street....
—*Thomas Fuller*

Ambition is the mother of unhappiness and prefers to sulk in corners and dark places. It cannot understand the light of day.... —*St. Bernard*

Ambition has but little reward for all: A little power, a little transient fame, a grave to rest in, and a fading name....
—*William Winter*

It is the ambition of many to live without working. What they desire is a parasitic life, in which they take everything, but give nothing in return. This is against the principle of Life, and those who try to act in this manner bring a blight upon themselves....
—*Henry T. Hamblin*

One of the most difficult lessons for ambitious young people to learn is that when you try to make an impression, that is the impression you make. Those whose center of emotional gravity is deeply embedded are willing to wait quietly in line until they are discovered.... —*Sidney Harris*

Ambition drives people to become false.... —*Anonymous*

Ambition kills spirituality....
—*Paramanada*

Ambition is the first curse: the great tempter of the man who is rising above his fellows. It is the simplest form of looking for a reward....Yet it is a necessary teacher.... —*Mabel Collins*

Ambition for a self-centered motive is very detrimental to spiritual growth....
—*Peace Pilgrim*

Ambition to earn fame in the world, to gain some position of authority over fellow-men, to lead a luxurious life— this can never insure Mental Peace. Mental Peace is the result of quite different attainments....
—*Sathya Sai Baba*

Ambition makes the same mistake concerning power, that avarice makes as to wealth. She begins by accumulating it as a means of happiness, and finishes by continuing to accumulate it as an end.... —*Charles C. Colton*

Ambition has its disappointments to sour us, but never the good fortune to satisfy us.... —*Benjamin Franklin*

Ambition becomes displeasing once it is satisfied.... —*Pierre Corneille*

Anger

There is no passion that so shakes the clarity of our judgement as anger. Things will truly seem different to us when we have quieted and cooled down.... —*Michel Montaigne*

Wrath springs only from thwarted desires.... —*Yukteswar*

It is not what we say that hurts but how we say it.... —*John Gray*

Anger and hatred are the materials from which hell is made....
—*Thich Nhat Hanh*

Always shun whatever makes you angry.... —*Publilius Syrus*

Tremendous energy comes with anger....Do not suppress it: that would only hurt you inside. Do not express it: this would not only hurt you inside, it would cause ripples in your surroundings. What you do is transform it. You somehow use that tremendous energy constructively on a task that needs to be done, or in a beneficial form of exercise....
—*Peace Pilgrim*

Anger is the emotion preeminently serviceable for the display of power....
—*Walter B. Cannon*

The wise conquer by strength, rather than anger. The malevolent fall by their own rage.... —*Tibetan saying*

Anger seeks to separate rather than join, to tear down rather than build up, to gain an advantage rather than to share.... —*Shantidasa*

The wise man does not argue, he remains silent and goes quietly on his path.... —*White Eagle*

You can't be fueled by bitterness. It can eat you up, but it cannot drive you....
—*Benazir Bhutto*

Angry men are blind and foolish, for reason at such a time takes flight and, in her absence, wrath plunders all the riches of the intellect while the judgement remains the prisoner of its own pride.... —*Pietro Aretino*

We must interpret a bad temper as the sign of an inferiority complex....
—*Alfred Adler*

Anger insures that one gives oneself up to one's enemies blindly....
—*Eliphas Levi*

Anger is the seducer of thought. No man can think clearly when his fists are clenched.... —*George J. Nathan*

Anger burns up all that is noble. It is a consuming fire, born of the fires of destruction. At the end, it leaves the victim nothing but a wreck of his better self, burned out, blackened and dead, like forest trees over which a great fire has swept.... —*Julian P. Johnson*

Anger helps straighten out a problem like a fan helps straighten out a pile of papers.... —*Susan Marcotte*

No one has ever talked himself (or anyone else) out of an undesired emotion by hurling insults or by delivering a moral lecture.... —*Nathaniel Branden*

The surest proof that you lack common sense is when you lose your temper and your poise. When in a rage, you reveal your weakness, and "weakness" is not common sense....
—*Fred Van Amburgh*

Expressing anger when you feel angry nearly always makes you angrier....
—*Carol Tavris*

Hesitation is the best cure for anger. The first blows of anger are heavy, but if it waits, it will think again....
—*Seneca*

When a sage is angry, he is no longer a sage.... —*The Talmud*

Strong negative emotions like anger, irritation, and indignation usually, but not always, indicate that our weak spot has been touched consciously or unconsciously.... —*Fritz Kunkel*

An unawakened person uses "anger" as a screen to hide fear, insecurity and a guilty conscience.... —*Ot Lat Nom*

Your anger is nothing more than your anger toward yourself.... —*Ram Dass*

Anger is an affect which is the veritable epitome of striving for power and domination. This emotion reveals very clearly that its objective is to destroy quickly and forcefully any obstruction in the path of its angry victim.... —*Thurman Fleet*

When angry, count to ten before you speak; if very angry, one hundred.... —*Thomas Jefferson*

Anger is momentary madness.... —*Horace*

You will not be punished for your anger, you will be punished by your anger....Let a man overcome anger by love.... —*Gautama Buddha*

Whenever you are angry, be assured that it is not only a present evil, but you have increased a habit, added fuel to a fire.... —*Epictetus*

To be angry is to revenge the faults of others upon ourselves.... —*Alexander Pope*

When you allow thoughts of anger....to exercise sway, they have a corroding and poisoning effect upon the organism; they pull it down, and if allowed to continue will eventually tear it to pieces by externalizing themselves in particular forms of disease.... —*Ralph W. Trine*

A child should gain no respect by anger; when he is quiet let him be offered what was refused when he wept.... —*Seneca*

The angry man always thinks he can do more than he can.... —*Albertano of Brescia*

Angry people are insecure people. Anger becomes a face-saving device to cover up deficiencies of another sort. Don't be fooled by the domineering character of an angry person. Know that during moments of anger there dwells a poor self-image.... —*Shantidasa*

God turns his back on those who quarrel among themselves.... —*Mohandas Gandhi*

What causes conflicts and quarrels among you? Do they not spring from the aggressiveness of your bodily desires? You want something which you cannot have....you are envious and cannot attain your ambitions, and so you quarrel and fight.... —*Paul of Tarsus*

For he who gives no fuel to fire puts it out, and likewise he who does not in the beginning nurse his wrath and does not puff himself up with anger takes precautions against it and destroys it.... —*Plutarch*

Oppose not rage while rage is in its force, but give it a while and let it waste.... —*William Shakespeare*

Anger is....an alarm system, signaling the presence of nothing more than fear. It tells us we are working at cross-purposes to our own happiness, fearing the loss of something more than we enjoy the experience of having it.... —*Jesse Jennings*

When a man's desire is not gratified and when someone stands in the way of its fulfillment, he gets angry.... —*Sivananda*

Angry outbursts tend to produce angry responses.... —*Leland F. Wood*

There is no enemy more vicious than your own anger.... —*Sathya Sai Baba*

The best response you can give to anger is silence.... —*Shantidasa*

When angry, or afflicted with any negative emotion, take time to be alone with God. Do not talk with people who are angry; they are irrational and cannot be reasoned with. If you or they are angry, it is best to leave and pray.... —*Peace Pilgrim*

For every minute you are angry you lose sixty seconds of happiness.... —*Ralph W. Emerson*

Anger may aptly be compared to cancer. It is, in fact, mental carcinoma. In its effects it is more deadly to the mind than cancer is to the body.... —*Julian P. Johnson*

Anger is the most futile emotion one can experience. It is totally negative and feeds on one's irrational, vindictive and punitive nature. It accomplishes nothing but a wider rift between persons, a growing dissatisfaction with self, and empty feeling where loving understanding ought to be.... —*Louise Doud*

Anger is the wind which blows out the lamp of the mind.... —*Robert Ingersoll*

Anger is a form of fear and evidence of the need of defense.... —*Fred Van Amburgh*

Anger is the most impotent of passions. It effects nothing as it goes about, and hurts the one who is possessed by it more than the one against whom it is directed.... —*Edward Clarendon*

Anger is quieted by a gentle word just as fire is quenched by water.... —*Jean P. Camus*

Anyone who conducts an argument by appealing to authority is not using his intelligence.... —*Leonardo da Vinci*

Anger is a symptom, a way of cloaking and expressing feelings too awful to experience directly—hurt, bitterness, grief and, most of all, fear.... —*Joan Rivers*

He who angers you, conquers you.... —*Elizabeth Kenny*

Be not hasty in your spirit to be angry; for anger rests in the bosom of fools.... —*Old Testament*

Anger begins in folly, and ends in repentance.... —*Pythagoras*

Human nature is so constituted that if we take absolutely no notice of anger or abuse, the person indulging in it will soon weary of it and stop.... —*Mohandas Gandhi*

Nothing on earth consumes a man more completely than the passion of resentment.... —*Friedrich W. Nietzsche*

There is no sin or wrong that gives a man such a foretaste of hell in this life as anger and impatience.... —*Catherine of Siena*

Rage is anger that has been shame bound. Shame-bound-anger grows in intensity over the years. It is like a ravenous wolf held captive in the basement.... —*John Bradshaw*

Consider how much more you suffer from your anger and grief, than from the very things for which you are angry and grieved.... —*Marcus Aurelius*

Frequent fits of anger produce in the soul a propensity to be angry, which oftentimes ends in a bad temper, bitterness, and morosity; then the mind becomes ulcerated, peevish, and grumbling, and is wounded by the least occurrence....   —*Plutarch*

A man is not wise until he is able to control his passions....   —*Sufi proverb*

Anger is a brief period of lunacy; the most practical way of dealing with anger is to avoid people when they are angry; the worst possible reaction to anger is to respond with anger....
                          —*Shantidasa*

Whenever you hold resentment toward another, you are bound to that person or condition by an emotional link that is stronger than steel....
                    —*Catherine Ponder*

Anger comes to us because we lose contact with God. When we keep in constant contact with God, there is no room for us to be angry....Anger means lack of love....   —*Papa Ramdas*

Sometimes we think that when we are excited and angry we exhibit strength. It is the weak person who yields to these lower emotions....
                      —*Paramananda*

Argument is the worst sort of conversation....   —*Jonathan Swift*

Every angry thought makes it a little easier to get angry the next time, and a little more likely....
                    —*Eknath Easwaran*

An angry man opens his mouth and closes his eyes....   —*Cato the Elder*

Attempt not to placate a man at the time of his rage....   —*Simon Eleazar*

He best keeps from anger who remembers that God is always looking at him....   —*Plato*

Many people lose their tempers merely from seeing you keep yours....
                      —*Frank M. Colby*

He whose face is inflamed with anger shows the evil spirit burns within him....   —*The Zohar*

When a man is wrong and won't admit it, he gets angry....
                  —*Thomas Haliburton*

Anger leads to hatred, to scapegoats, to violence, to destruction....
                      —*Jesse Jackson*

Anger and intolerance are the twin enemies of correct understanding....
                  —*Mohandas Gandhi*

When one obeys anger in his life he will reap only pain and anguish. No one can follow the habit of anger and make any progress on the spiritual path....   —*Paul Twitchell*

Anger repressed can poison a relationship as surely as the cruelest words....
                    —*Joyce Brothers*

Life appears to me too short to be spent in nursing animosity or registering wrong....   —*Charlotte Bronte*

From anger arises delusion; from delusion loss of memory is caused. From loss of memory, the discrimination facility is ruined, and from the ruin of discrimination he perishes....
                    —*Bhagavad-Gita*

The intoxication of anger, like that of the grape, shows us to others, but hides us from ourselves....
                    —*Charles C. Colton*

Men often make up in wrath what they want in reason.... —*William Alger*

Only the ignorant man becomes angry. The wise man understands.... —*Indian proverb*

The angry person is never in the right even when right.... —*Shantidasa*

Anger begins with madness, and ends with regret.... —*Abraham Hasdai*

If a man cannot control his temper, how much less can he control others.... —*Solomon Ibn Gabirol*

To rule one's anger is well; to prevent it is still better.... —*Tryon Edwards*

Anger concealed hardens into revenge.... —*Edward Bulwer-Lytton*

If the anger of another person rises, the wise man lets the contest end.... —*Plutarch*

Anger is brief madness, and unchecked, becomes protracted madness, bringing same and even death.... —*Petrarch*

Anxiety

Loss gives rise to anxiety when the loss is either impending or thought to be temporary. Anxiety contains a kernel of hope. But when loss appears to be permanent, anxiety—protest—gives way to depression—despair.... —*Judith Viorst*

Anxiety is the price of freedom.... —*Sören Kierkegaard*

Anxiety is the dread of nothingness.... —*Martin Heidegger*

Anxiety is a word of unbelief or unreasoning dread. We have no right to allow it. Full faith in God puts it to rest.... —*Horace Bushnell*

So long as we believe in our heart of hearts that our capacity is limited and we grow anxious and unhappy, we are lacking in faith. One who truly trusts in God has no right to be anxious about anything.... —*Paramananda*

Anxiety is the mark of spiritual insecurity.... —*Thomas Merton*

There are three marks of a superior man: being virtuous, he is free from anxiety; being wise, he is free from perplexity; being brave, he is free from fear.... —*Confucius*

Anxiety is a thin stream of fear trickling through the mind. If encouraged, it cuts a channel into which all other thoughts are drained.... —*Arthur S. Roche*

Anxiety is the poison of human life; the parent of many sins and more miseries.... —*Hugh Blair*

Anxiety in the heart....causes depression, but a good word makes it glad.... —*Old Testament*

Anxiety looks at things and makes you concerned about, even obsessed, with things that seem impossible. It tries to get you to worry, to brood about your problems and needs. It gets your eyes off God.... —*Anonymous*

Take not anxious thought as to the results of your work nor of your work. If you are doing all that you can, the results, immediate or eventual, are not your affair at all.... —*Bolton Hall*

Nothing in life is more unspeakable than the unnecessary anxiety which we endure....   —*Benjamin Disraeli*

The misfortunes hardest to bear are those which never come....
            —*James Russell Lowell*

The crosses which we make for ourselves by over-anxiety as to the future are not Heaven-sent crosses. We tempt God by our false wisdom, seeking to forestall His arrangements....
            —*Francois Fenelon*

We suffer more in imagination than in reality....   —*Seneca*

Why does such a simple thing as keeping busy help to drive out anxiety? Because of a law....that it is utterly impossible for any human mind, no matter how brilliant, to think of more than one thing at any given time....
            —*Dale Carnegie*

Anxiety is the rust of life, destroying its brightness and weakening its power. A childlike and abiding trust in Providence is its best preventive and remedy....   —*Tryon Edwards*

Anxiety is the malady of our time....
            —*Aldous Huxley*

Anxiety is caused by disapproval either of oneself or by others. The disapproval may not actually occur; anxiety can occur even with the anticipation of disapproval....   —*John & Muriel James*

Anxiety is the worst demon in life....
            —*Berthold Auerbach*

God did not make us to be eaten by anxiety, but to walk erect, free, unafraid in a world where there is work to do, truth to seek, love to give and win....   —*Joseph Newton*

We worry away our lives, fearing the future, discontent with the present, unable to take in the idea of dying, unable to sit still....   —*Lewis Thomas*

There is no such thing as pure pleasure; some anxiety always goes with it....
            —*Ovid*

Do not push a wagon as you will only raise dust about yourself; do not think of all your anxieties; you will only make yourself ill....   —*Shih King*

He who foresees calamities suffers them twice over....   —*Beilby Porteous*

Anxiety is fear of one's self....
            —*Wilhelm Stekel*

Beware of anxiety....there is nothing that so much troubles the mind, strains the heart, distresses the soul and confuses the judgement....
            —*William B. Ullathorne*

Suffering itself does less afflict the senses than the anticipation of suffering....
            —*Quintilian*

One of the most useless of all things is to take a deal of trouble in providing against dangers that never come....
            —*William Jay*

Be not anxious about what you have, but about what you are....
            —*Pope Gregory I*

Nothing in the affairs of man is worthy of great anxiety....   —*Plato*

Anxiety springs from the desire that things should happen as we wish rather than as God wills....
            —*Anonymous*

No anxiety can change the course of things ordained....   —*Papa Ramdas*

No grand inquisitor has in readiness such terrible tortures as has anxiety and no spy knows how to attack more artfully the man he suspects, choosing the instant when he is weakest; nor knows how to lay traps where he will be caught and ensnared as anxiety knows how, and no sharp-witted judge knows how to interrogate, to examine the accused, as anxiety does, which never lets him escape....
—*Sören Kierkegaard*

The pursuit of wisdom leads to tranquility, the pursuit of wealth, to anxiety.... —*Shantidasa*

In whatever areas anxiety or timidity are dominant, there we are supine and incapable.... —*David Seabury*

Do you wish to live in tension? By no means. No one who is in a state of fear or sorrow or tension is free, but whoever is delivered from sorrows or fears or anxieties, he is at the same time delivered from servitude.... —*Epictetus*

Apathy/Inertia

Laziness grows on people; it begins in cobwebs and ends in iron chains.... —*Charles Buxton*

All that is necessary to break the spell of inertia and frustration is this: Act as if it were impossible to fail. This is the talisman, the formula, the command of right-about-face....
—*Dorthea Brande*

Were it not for the leaping and twinkling of the soul, man would rot away in his greatest passion, idleness....
—*Carl Jung*

Beware of creating paralysis by analysis.... —*Edwin & Sally Kiester*

Stagnation is not a desirable state. Through struggle we develop strength....
—*Papa Ramdas*

In idleness there is perpetual despair....
—*Thomas Carlyle*

Even when you're on the right track, you'll get run over if you just sit there.... —*Will Rogers*

To "decide not to decide" is still a decision.... —*Gerald G. May*

Instead of tackling the most important priorities that would make us successful and effective in life, we prefer the path of least resistance and do things simply that will relieve our tension, such as shuffling papers and majoring in minors.... —*Denis Waitley*

Put off for one day and ten days will pass.... —*Korean proverb*

Delay is the deadliest form of denial....
—*C. Northcote Parkinson*

Be not afraid of growing slowly, be afraid of standing still....
—*Chinese proverb*

I would rather attempt to do something great and fail, than attempt to do nothing and succeed.... —*Robert Schuller*

Iron rusts from disuse; stagnant water loses its purity and, in cold, water becomes frozen; even so does inaction sap the vigor of the mind....
—*Leonardo da Vinci*

Idleness is the bane of body and mind, the muse of naughtiness, the chief author of all mischief, one of the seven deadly sins.... —*Richard E. Burton*

Idleness is the wellspring and root of all vice....　　　*—Thomas Bacon*

There are only two mistakes one can make along the road to truth: not going all the way, and not starting....
　　　　　　　—Gautama Buddha

The man who makes no mistakes does not usually make anything....
　　　　　　　—W. C. Magee

The force that opposes determination is inertia. Inertia is not a static thing; it is a dynamic force. Like any force, it tends to magnify itself and gain momentum until or unless it is superseded by another force stronger than itself....
　　　　　　　—Alan Cohen

The great thing in this world is not so much where we stand, as in what direction we are moving....
　　　　　　　—Oliver W. Holmes

There is something worse than a difficulty. It is inertia. If you try to escape difficulties, you decay....
　　　　　　　—Herbert Casson

It is the greatest of all mistakes to do nothing because you can only do a little. Do what you can....
　　　　　　　—Sydney Smith

The greatest mistake a man can make is to be afraid of making one....
　　　　　　　—Elbert Hubbard

Nothing will ever be attempted if all possible objections must be first overcome....　　　*—Samuel Johnson*

The procrastinating man is ever struggling with ruin....　　　*—Hesiod*

The worst robber, the greatest thief is the roaming vagabond—procrastination....　　　*—Fred Van Amburgh*

The worst thing one can do is not to try, to be aware of what one wants and not give in to it, to spend years in silent hurt wondering if something could have materialized—and never knowing....　　　*—David Viscott*

Idleness is the rust that attaches itself to the most brilliant metals....
　　　　　　　—Voltaire

There is no more miserable human being than one in whom nothing is habitual but indecision. Fully half of the time of such a man goes to the deciding, or regretting of matters....
　　　　　　　—William James

To be happy we must keep busy. Idleness soon becomes dreary and tiresome. If you keep busy enough, you won't have time to think and worry about yourself....　　　*—George Byron*

Fear in its various guises is at the bottom of procrastination....
　　　　　　　—Edwin C. Bliss

Don't procrastinate. Delays can make a job seem bigger than it really is—and thinking about what you haven't done steals time from the job you have before you....　　　*—Bernice Strawn*

If you're doing nothing, you're doing wrong....　　　*—Lord Mountbatten*

Science may have found a cure for most evils, but it has found no remedy for the worst of them all—the apathy of human beings....　　　*—Helen Keller*

Procrastination is just another way of concealing cowardice....
　　　　　　　—Shantidasa

Nothing wilts faster than laurels that have been rested on....
　　　　　　　—Carl Rowan

From its very inaction, idleness ultimately becomes the most active cause of evil.... —*Charles C. Colton*

Never put off for tomorrow what you can do today.... —*Philip Chesterfield*

Given the choice between action and delay, people will generally delay.... —*Robert Grudin*

With the majority the ship of thought is allowed to "drift" upon the ocean of life. Aimlessness is a common vice, and such drifting must not continue for him who would steer clear of catastrophe and destruction.... —*James Allen*

To do nothing is in every man's power.... —*Samuel Johnson*

Immature people tend to be apathetic, they tend to place material values above spiritual values.... —*Peace Pilgrim*

If you wish a man not to do a thing you had better get him to talk about it; for the more men talk, the more likely they are to do nothing else.... —*Thomas Carlyle*

Procrastination is the thief of time.... —*Edward Young*

Procrastination is the fear of success.... —*Denis Wheatley*

The idle get irritable, grow indifferent, go to seed mentally and physically. An idle mind becomes flabby as does an idle body....It is much better to make mistakes doing something, than to make the mistake of doing nothing.... —*Fred Van Amburgh*

Atheism

A man may believe in all the churches in the world; he may carry in his head all the sacred books ever written; he may baptize himself in all the rivers of the earth—still if he has no perception of God, I would class him with the rank atheist.... —*Vivekananda*

An atheist is a man who believes himself an accident.... —*Francis Thompson*

I cannot conceive how a man could look up into the heavens and say there is no God.... —*Abraham Lincoln*

A little philosophy inclineth a man's mind to atheism; but depth in philosophy bringeth men's minds about to God.... —*Francis Bacon*

There are no atheists in life rafts.... —*Eddie Rickenbacker*

The absolute affirmation of evil is the denial of God, since God is the supreme and absolute source of life.... —*Eliphas Levi*

An atheist may be simply one whose faith and love are concentrated on the impersonal aspects of God.... —*Simon Weil*

We find out the most terrible form of atheism, not in the militant and passionate struggle against the idea of God himself, but in the practical atheism of everyday living, in indifference and torpor.... —*Nikolay Berdyayev*

There is really no such thing as an atheist. Atheists think they exist, but in God's reality they do not exist.... —*Peace Pilgrim*

Atheism is not a constructive idea—it is an infernal institution, designed to bring about destitution and despair....
—*Fred Van Amburgh*

Those who deny God are denying themselves and their glory....
—*Sathya Sai Baba*

No one has ever died an atheist....Few men are so obstinate in their atheism, that a pressing danger will not compel them to the knowledge of a divine power....
—*Plato*

Nobody talks so constantly about God as those who insist there is no God....
—*Heywood Brown*

An atheist is a man who has no invisible means of support....
—*John Buchan*

The worst moment for an atheist is when he feels grateful and doesn't know who to thank....
—*Wendy Ward*

Atheism is the death of hope, the suicide of the soul....
—*Anonymous*

Atheists put on a false courage in the midst of their darkness and misapprehensions, like children who when they fear to go in the dark, will sing or whistle to keep up their courage....
—*Alexander Pope*

Atheism is the source of all iniquities....
—*Philo*

Selfishness is the only real atheism....
—*Israel Zangwill*

People who tell me there is no God are like a six-year-old saying that there is no such thing as passionate love. They just haven't experienced Him yet....
—*William Alfred*

Whoever considers the study of anatomy can never be an atheist....
—*Edward Herbert*

Atheism is a sign of strength, but only up to a point....
—*Blaise Pascal*

In a way, the greatest praise of God is his denial by the atheist who thinks creation is so perfect it does not need a creator....
—*Marcel Proust*

My atheism....is true piety towards the universe and denies any gods fashioned by men in their own image....
—*George Santayana*

The pious man and the atheist always talk of religion; the one of what he loves, and the other of what he fears....
—*Baron de Montesquieu*

The soul of man does not thrive on godlessness....
—*Harry Wolfson*

Men of earth have branded themselves atheists...and there are no atheists, man may become antagonistic, but in a true sense he never becomes an atheist. Impossible....
—*Frater Achad*

I do not see the difference between avowing that there is no God, and implying that nothing definite can for certain be known about Him....
—*John H. Newman*

Atheism thrives where religion is most debated....
—*Welsh proverb*

You don't find atheists in the country; you can't watch a field of wheat ripple and ripen without deep beliefs and without feeling that you're a small part of something pretty big and lasting....
—*Chester Charles*

No man hates God without first hating himself....
—*Fulton J. Sheen*

Every criminal is an atheist, though he doesn't always know it....
—*Honoré de Balzac*

The conflict between persons who accept God and deny God and those who declare that God is to be found in this place and those who affirm that he can be found nowhere is never ending.... —*Sathya Sai Baba*

Awakening/ Awareness

A religious awakening which does not awaken the sleeper to love has aroused him in vain.... —*Jessamyn West*

Awareness and happiness are exactly the same thing.... —*Vernon Howard*

Our true nature does not have to be found; it is present at all times, and we need only abide in its unconditioned awareness.... —*A Spiritual Warrior*

The greatest part of mankind....may be said to be asleep, and that particular way of life which takes up each man's mind, thoughts and actions, may be very well called his particular dream.... —*William Law*

Most are asleep as to their spiritual destiny, but they will one day awaken to it.... —*Darwin Gross*

To see, to hear, means nothing. To recognize (or not to recognize) means everything.... —*André Breton*

When a man wakes up to see how little he is, he has by that very awakening found out how great he is. When he learns that he is nothing, he has in that process discovered that he is everything.... —*Sheldon Shepard*

To those who are awake, there is one ordered universe, whereas in sleep each person turns away from the world to one of his own.... —*Heraclitus*

Those who are awake live in a state of constant amazement.... —*Jack Kornfield*

The aim of life is to live, and to live means to be aware, joyously, drunkenly, serenely, divinely aware.... —*Henry Miller*

The man who is aware of himself is henceforth independent.... —*Virginia Woolf*

There is a difference between awakening and deliverance: The former is sudden, thereafter deliverance is gradual.... —*Shen Hui*

A being whose awareness is totally free, who does not cling to anything, is liberated.... —*Ram Dass*

Watchfulness....is the vital need, for he who does not watch is soon overwhelmed. The steerman need only sleep a moment and the vessel is lost.... —*Epictetus*

Awakening, or enlightenment, or liberation is nothing, absolutely nothing other than perceiving profoundly, deeply, intuitively that what we are—that-which-is-here-now—is the absolute absence of whatever is imaginable or recognizable.... —*Nisargadatta*

To be taught is nothing; everything is in man, awaiting to be awakened.... —*Paracelsus*

An aware person is in tune with all the powers of God and makes them his own.... —*Donald Curtis*

O my blessed beloved, awake! Why do you sleep in ignorance?... —*Kabir*

The most powerful agent in character building is the awakening of the true self to the fact that man is a spiritual being.... —*Ralph W. Trine*

Awakening cannot take place so long as the idea persists that one is a seeker.... —*Ramesh Balsekar*

Our original....Nature is, in highest truth, devoid of any atom of objectivity. It is void, omnipresent, silent, pure; it is glorious and mysterious peaceful joy —and that is all. Enter deeply into it by awakening yourself.... —*Huang Po*

Only when you awaken do you realize you were dreaming.... —*John Wareham*

With awareness, the mystery is perceived....Without awareness we live only in a world of our own illusion.... —*A Spiritual Warrior*

Life is a series of awakenings.... —*Sivananda*

A thing cannot observe itself. A thing identified with itself cannot see itself, because it is the same as itself; and cannot have a standpoint apart from itself, from which to observe itself.... —*George I. Gurdjieff*

What we usually call human evolution is the awakening of the divine nature within us.... —*Peace Pilgrim*

If I were to begin life again, I should want it as it was. I would only open my eyes a little more.... —*Jules Renard*

Awareness means the capacity to see a coffeepot and hear the birds sing in one's own way and not the way one was taught.... —*Eric Berne*

He who dreams must be awakened, and the deeper the man is who slumbers, or the deeper he slumbers, the more important it is that he be awakened, and the more powerfully must he be awakened.... —*Sören Kierkegaard*

When man awakens, he finds that he is part of the one great Reality and he realizes his union with all things.... —*Paramananda*

How many people eat, drink, and get married; buy, sell, and build; make contracts and attend to their fortune; have friends and enemies, pleasures and pains, are born, grow up, live and die— but asleep!... —*Joseph Joubert*

There is no end to the beauty for the person who is aware. Even the cracks between the sidewalk contain geometric patterns of amazing beauty.... —*Matthew Fox*

No single event can awaken within us a stranger totally unknown to us. To live is to be slowly born.... —*Antoine de Saint-Exupery*

Deep within us all there is an amazing inner sanctuary....a holy place, A Divine Center, a speaking voice, to which we may continually return. Eternity is at our hearts, pressing upon our time-worn lives, warning us with intimations of an astounding destiny, calling us home to Itself to be awakened.... —*Thomas Kelly*

You have not known what you are, you have slumbered upon yourself all your life....Whoever you are! Claim your own.... —*Walt Whitman*

The real voyage of discovery consists not in seeking new landscapes but in having new eyes.... —*Marcel Proust*

Compared with what we ought to be, we are only half awake. We are making use of only a small part of our physical and mental resources. Stating the thing broadly, the human individual thus lives far within his limits. He possesses powers of various sorts which he habitually fails to use.... —*William James*

Man does not evolve, he awakens.... —*Darwin Gross*

The spiritual journey does not consist in arriving at a new destination where a person gains what he did not have, or becomes what he is not. It consists in the dissipation of one's own ignorance concerning oneself and life, and the gradual growth of that understanding which begins the spiritual awakening. The finding of God is a coming to one's self.... —*Aldous Huxley*

The millions are awake enough for physical labor; but only one in a million is awake enough for effective intellectual exertion, only one in a hundred million to a poetic or divine life. To be awake is to be alive....We must learn to reawaken and keep ourselves awake, not by mechanical means, but by an infinite expectation of the dawn.... —*Henry D. Thoreau*

It's the awareness....of how you are stuck, that makes you recover.... —*Fritz Perls*

Of course you have work to do in this world. Your first job is to awaken your own divine nature. You can do that by putting yourself into inspirational circumstances and looking within and waiting in receptive silence for answers from within.... —*Peace Pilgrim*

Every Awakened man or woman knows that the object of life is to realize God.... —*Papa Ramdas*

Beauty

Though we travel the world to find the beautiful we must carry it within us or we find it not.... —*Ralph W. Emerson*

Beauty is one of those rare things that does not lead to the doubt of God.... —*Jean Anouilh*

There is but one essence of beauty and that is joy. A truly beautiful person is always joyful.... —*Shantidasa*

Passing beauties are only the fugitive reflections of the eternal....All beauty alters and all life melts away; in short, everything passes with marvelous rapidity; beautiful Helen (of Troy) has become a toothless skull, then a handful of dust, then nothing.... —*Eliphas Levi*

There is no physical barrier to experiencing yourself as beautiful, only your belief.... —*Harold H. Bloomfield*

A thing of beauty is a joy forever....Beauty is truth—truth, beauty—that is all ye know on earth, and all ye need to know.... —*John Keats*

Beauty you may have with you always, if you will but plant beauty in your heart.... —*Fred Van Amburgh*

God's beauty is expressed whenever man of earth so desires to seek for it. It shall not be difficult for man to behold beauty, when he beholds the beauty of God within his own consciousness.... Beauty is everywhere to he or she who would behold it. When God reigns supreme in the consciousness of man, the tiniest blade of grass speaks of God's beauty.... —*Frater Achad*

The thing which we speak of as beauty does not have to be sought in distant lands....It is here about us or it is nowhere....　　　　　*—Allen Tucker*

True beauty must come, must be grown, from within....
　　　　　—Ralph W. Trine

We are living in a world of beauty, but few of us open our eyes to see it....
　　　　　—Lorado Taft

Beauty fades, but a good name endures....　　　*—Apocrypha: Ahikar*

The concept of beautiful and ugly is an individual concept....　　*—Yogi Bhajan*

Physical beauty plays a bizarre and central role in our concepts of love....
　　　　　—Robert C. Solomon

It is wisest and best to fix our attention on the beautiful and the good, and dwell as little as possible on the evil and false....　　　*—Richard Cecil*

Beauty is not caused. It is....
　　　　　—Emily Dickinson

Beauty is merely the spiritual making itself known sensuously....
　　　　　—Georg W. Hegel

What is beautiful? Whatever is perceived joyfully is beautiful. Bliss is the essence of beauty....　　*—Nisargadatta*

Never lose an opportunity of seeing anything that is beautiful; for beauty is God's handwriting—a wayside sacrament. Welcome it in every fair face, in every fair sky, in every fair flower, and thank God for it as a cup of blessing....
　　　　　—Ralph W. Emerson

Things are beautiful if you love them....
　　　　　—Jean Anouilh

Beauty, unaccompanied by virtue, is a flower without perfume....
　　　　　—French proverb

Nature is painting for us, day after day, pictures of infinite beauty if only we have eyes to see them....
　　　　　—John Ruskin

The best part of beauty is that which no picture can express....
　　　　　—Francis Bacon

The most natural beauty in the world is honesty and moral truth. For all beauty is truth....　　*—Anthony Shaftesbury*

What is beautiful is good, and who is good will soon also be beautiful....
　　　　　—Sappho

We ourselves possess Beauty when we are true to our own being; ugliness is in going to another order; knowing ourselves, we are beautiful; in self-ignorance, we are ugly....　　　*—Plotinus*

If you look for ugliness, you will find it everywhere. When you look for beauty, you will find that everywhere....
　　　　　—Narayana

Everything that is true is beautiful....
　　　　　—Eliphas Levi

An appearance of delicacy, and even fragility, is almost essential to beauty....
　　　　　—Edmund Burke

God is beautiful and He loves beauty....
　　　　　—Mohammed

Beauty is God's handwriting....
　　　　　—Charles Kingsley

Beauty and her twin brother Truth require leisure and self-control for their growth....
　　　　　—Rabindranath Tagore

The criterion of true beauty is that it increases upon examination; if false, that it lessens.... —*Fulke Greville*

We are conscious of beauty where there is a harmonious relationship between something in our nature and the quality of the object which delights us.... —*Blaise Pascal*

True beauty consists of purity of heart.... —*Mohandas Gandhi*

In all ranks of life the human heart yearns for the beautiful; and the beautiful things that God makes are his gift to all alike.... —*Harriet Beecher Stowe*

Beauty is in the eye of the beholder.... —*Margaret W. Hungerford*

What is beautiful is a joy for all seasons and a possession for all eternity.... —*Oscar Wilde*

Beauty is the mark God sets on virtue.... —*Ralph W. Emerson*

Belief

Belief is our own exercise, and thus it will always be subject to doubt and its reverse—unbelief or no belief. In other words, belief is not stable.... —*Bernadette Roberts*

Believe! No storm harms a man who believes.... —*Ovid*

Believe in poverty and you will be poor. Believe in wealth and you will be rich. Believe in love and you will have love. Believe in health and you will be healthy.... —*Napoleon Hill*

The word "belief" is difficult for me. I don't believe, I must have a certain reason for a certain hypothesis. Either I know a thing, and then know it—I don't need to believe in it.... —*Carl Jung*

What distinguishes the majority of men from the few is their inability to act according to their beliefs.... —*Henry Miller*

To believe is to be strong. Doubt cramps energy. Belief is power.... —*Frederick W. Robertson*

A belief is like a guillotine, just as heavy, just as light.... —*Franz Kafka*

We are incredibly heedless in the formation of our beliefs, but find ourselves with an illicit passion for them when anyone proposes to rob us of their companionship. It is obviously not the ideas themselves that are dear to us, but our self-esteem that is threatened.... —*James Harvey*

We never believe enough in ourselves.... —*Martin Gray*

Believe that life is worth living, and your belief will help create that fact.... —*William James*

We can be victimized by our beliefs.... —*Judy Tatelbaum*

He does not believe that does not live by his belief.... —*Thomas Fuller*

As our beliefs actually change, so do our experiences.... —*Carol Sheffield*

If we believe in magic, we'll live a magical life. If we believe our life is defined by narrow limits, we've suddenly made those beliefs real.... —*Anthony Robbins*

You are what you are by what you believe.... —*Oprah Winfrey*

A belief system carries with it an element of doubt, while knowing does not. The only way we can successfully do away with our belief systems is to turn them into knowing....
—*Michael Eldridge*

Anything you believe will limit you in one way or another....
—*Stephen H. Wolinsky*

You must recognize yourself for what you are, not what you believe yourself to be.... —*Shantidasa*

To effectively change yourself, you must believe yourself capable of changing and you must have no beliefs which prevent that change....
—*Paul E. Wood*

Upon this little word *belief* hang all your sorrows and joys....
—*James Allen*

To believe with certainty, we must begin with doubting....
—*Stanislaus I*

To believe in the things you see and touch is no belief at all; but to believe in the unseen is a triumph and a blessing.... —*Abraham Lincoln*

Remember that what you believe will depend very much upon what you are.... —*Noah Porter*

The essence of belief is the establishment of habit.... —*Charles S. Pearce*

All belief that does not make us more happy, more free, more loving, more active, more calm, is, I fear, a mistaken and superstitious belief....
—*John K. Lavater*

There is a golden thread that makes life work. That thread can be named in a single word: belief.... —*Claude Bristol*

Whether you believe you can do a thing or whether you believe you cannot, you are right both times.... —*Henry Ford*

One person with a belief is equal to a force of ninety-nine who only have interests.... —*John S. Mill*

The mole burrowing in the earth cannot see the stars, for it is blind; so a man who does not believe in God concerning the temporal, equally cannot believe concerning the eternal....
—*St. Mark, the Ascetic*

Men tend to have the beliefs that suit their passions.... —*Bertrand Russell*

Men often become what they believe themselves to be. If I believe I cannot do something, it makes me incapable of doing it. But when I believe I can, then I acquire the ability to do it even if I didn't have it in the beginning....
—*Mohandas Gandhi*

Men easily believe what they wish to believe.... —*Julius Caesar*

Do not believe in anything simply because you have heard it. Do not believe in traditions because they have been handed down for many generations. Do not believe in anything because it is spoken and rumored by many. Do not believe in anything simply because it is found written in your religious books. Do not believe merely on the authority of your teachers and elders.... —*Gautama Buddha*

A belief is not true because it is useful.... —*Henri F. Amiel*

Nothing is so easy as to deceive one's self; for what we wish, that we readily believe.... —*Demosthenes*

Do what you believe in and believe in what you do. All else is a waste of energy and time.... —*Nisargadatta*

A man can believe a considerable deal of rubbish, and yet go about his daily work in a rational and cheerful manner.... —*Norman Douglas*

Belief is not truly belief while doubt can still touch it.... —*Karlfried G. Durckheim*

There are two ways to slide easily through life; to believe everything or to doubt everything; both ways save us from thinking.... —*Alfred Korzybski*

Believe that you have it, and you have it.... —*Erasmus*

The thing always happens that you really believe in and the belief in a thing makes it happen. And I think nothing will happen until you thoroughly and deeply believe in it.... —*Frank L. Wright*

By believing passionately in something that still does not exist, we create it. The nonexistent is whatever we have not sufficiently desired.... —*Nikos Kazantzakis*

Maturity of mind is best shown in slow belief.... —*Baltasar G. Morales*

One does not have to believe everything one hears.... —*Cicero*

Nothing splendid has ever been achieved except by those who dared believe that something inside of them was superior to circumstance.... —*Bruce Barton*

A belief is not merely an idea the mind possesses; it is an idea that possesses the mind.... —*Robert Bolton*

Nothing is so firmly believed as that which we least know.... —*Michel Montaigne*

Believe you can and you can. Believe you will and you will. See yourself achieving, and you will achieve.... —*Gardner Hunting*

A consistent man believes in destiny, a capricious man in chance.... —*Benjamin Disraeli*

Beliefs have the power to create and the power to destroy.... —*Anthony Robbins*

No iron chain, or outward force of any kind, could ever compel the soul of man to believe or to disbelieve.... —*Richard Carlile*

Everyone believes very easily whatever he fears or desires.... —*Jean La Fontaine*

Why crawl with beliefs when with a little more effort you can soar by knowing?... —*Shantidasa*

Every man prefers belief to the exercise of judgement.... —*Seneca*

If you are not careful, beliefs can stifle you.... —*Stuart Wilde*

A man's most valuable trait is a judicious sense of what not to believe.... —*Euripides*

Whatsoever things you desire, believe and you shall have them.... —*Jesus*

To believe in the Tao is easy; to keep the Tao is difficult.... —*Lao-tzu*

Men and civilizations live by their beliefs and die when their beliefs pass into doubt.... —*Philip Lee Ralph*

There are a great many truths which we do not deny, and which nevertheless we do not fully believe....
—*James W. Alexander*

It is easier to believe than to doubt....
—*Everett Martin*

To accomplish great things, we must not only act but also dream, not only plan but also believe....
—*Anatole France*

It is always easier to believe than to deny. Our minds are naturally affirmative....
—*John Burroughs*

Belief consists in accepting the affirmations of the soul, unbelief, in denying them....
—*Ralph W. Emerson*

All unbelief is the belief of a lie....
—*Horatius Bonar*

A man lives by believing something, not by debating and arguing about many things....
—*Thomas Carlyle*

The practical test of a belief is the real test of its soundness....
—*James A. Froude*

Believe as though you are, and you will be....
—*Ernest Holmes*

There is everything we need laid up for us in the Divine Providence, but if we do not believe it, it remains outside our experience....
—*Henry T. Hamblin*

We do not easily believe what we cannot see....
—*John Dryden*

Where belief is painful, we are slow to believe....
—*Ovid*

I believe in the sun even when it is not shining. I believe in love even when I do not feel it. I believe in God even when He is silent....
—*Anonymous*

Body

In vain we penetrate more deeply the secrets of the structure of the human body. We shall not dupe nature; we shall die as usual....
—*Bernard de Fontenelle*

The body is made for the soul to express it....
—*Jean Mouroux*

This body is an instrument or servant of the Soul, and not its prison....
—*Sivananda*

Death is a shadow that always follows the body....
—*English proverb*

You are not your body. It is just something you wear for a while, because living in the earthplane is infinitely more meaningful and more involved if you are encased in its trappings and subject to its rules....
—*P. M. H. Atwater*

So long as you identify yourself as the body, your experience of pain and sorrow will increase day by day....If you take yourself as the body, it means you have forgotten your true Self....and sorrow results for the one who forgets himself....
—*Nisargadatta*

Don't pay too much attention to the body. If you worry about the well-being of your body, you identify with it more and more. Look upon it as a useful vehicle: maintain it, fuel it properly and repair it if it breaks down, but don't become attached to it....
—*Annamalai Swami*

The soul is a guest in our body, deserving of our kind hospitality....
—*Hillel*

The body has one fault, that the more people pamper it, the more its wants are made known.... —*Teresa of Avila*

The body exists, by nature, in a condition of well-being. It is a place to observe the world from. It is a physical representation of you, and it is not you.... —*Ron Smothermon*

Our bodies change and in the end crumble. It is a house of clay. But inside there is a spiritual duplicate.... —*Malcolm J. MacLeod*

Give the body the attention it deserves, but not more....When you cultivate the attitude that you are the body, the body will demand from you more food, more variety in food, more attention to appearance and physical comfort.... —*Sathya Sai Baba*

The true ascetic does not gratify the body; but he cares well for the body that he may advance the spiritual life. Cared for, it is a better vessel for truth.... —*Gautama Buddha*

He will be the slave of many masters who is his body's slave.... —*Seneca*

Every man is the builder of the temple called his body—we are all sculptors and painters, and our material is our flesh and blood and bones. Any nobleness begins at once to refine a man's features.... —*Henry D. Thoreau*

The human body has one ability not possessed by any machine—the ability to repair itself.... —*George W. Crile*

Everything in this world is transitory and fleeting....No man was ever born who could stop his body from changing constantly. Body is the name of a series of changes.... —*Paramananda*

This body is mortal, always gripped by death, but within it dwells the immortal Self.... —*The Upanishads*

A strong body and a bright, happy or serene countenance can only result from the fine admittance of thoughts of joy and goodwill and serenity into the mind.... —*James Allen*

So long as we are attached to the body and external objects, we shall never know true peace.... —*Papa Ramdas*

Do not neglect this body. This is the house of God; take care of it. Only in this body can God be realized.... —*Nisargadatta*

I have visited in my wanderings shrines and other places of pilgrimage. But I have not seen another shrine like my own body.... —*Saraha*

The body dies but the spirit is not entombed.... —*Dhammapada*

Even as a man puts off his worn-out clothes and puts on new ones, even so the Self casts off old bodies and takes up new ones.... —*Bhagavad-Gita*

To identify oneself with the body and yet seek happiness, is like attempting to ford a lake on the back of an alligator.... —*Ramana Maharshi*

How can I, who knows the body to be perishable and the soul to be imperishable, mourn over the separation of body from the soul?... —*Mohandas Gandhi*

The body and the mind are so closely connected that not even a single word or thought can come into existence without being reflected in the personality and health of the individual.... —*John Prentiss*

People make the mistake of identifying themselves with their body, then if something happens to a person's body, they think something has happened to the person. When you think about it, that's as ridiculous as saying that if something happens to the clothing I'm wearing, something has happened to me. Our body is just what we wear....We need to take care of it, but it's not who we are....
—*H. Frederick Vogt*

Our minds have unbelievable power over our bodies.... —*André Maurois*

Flesh is merely a lesson. We learn it and pass on.... —*Erica Jong*

All of us have mortal bodies, composed of perishable matter, but the soul lives forever: it is a portion of the Deity housed in our bodies....
—*Flavius Josephus*

We should be very grateful to have a limited body....If you had a limitless life it would be a real problem for you....
—*Shunryu Suzuki*

The body without the spirit is dead....
—*Paul of Tarsus*

Our bodies are but dust, but they bring praise to Him that formed them....
—*Alexander Punshon*

So great a power is there of the soul upon the body, that whichever way the soul imagines and dreams that it goes, thither doth it lead the body....
—*Marcus Agrippa*

The body is a workhouse of the soul....
—*Henry G. Bohn*

A healthy body is a guest-chamber for the soul; a sick body is a prison....
—*Francis Bacon*

Any good practical philosophy must start out with the recognition of our having a body.... —*Lin Yutang*

My body is merely a clay structure; today it is here, tomorrow it shall be gone.... —*Peace Pilgrim*

The body, a perishable cage of flesh and bones, we are identified with it, we cling to it, we love it, we are attached to it.... —*Chidananda*

As a monastery be content with the body, for the bodily substance is the palace of divinity.... —*Marpa*

Identifying ourselves with the body is putting the cart before the horse and is why we stumble in life....
—*Ramana Maharshi*

Man is divine. But he is not aware of his own divinity. He mistakenly thinks he is this little body. But he is not this body....Man is something infinite, immutable and eternal....
—*Sathya Sai Baba*

Men cling to and gratify the flesh as though it were going to last forever....
—*James Allen*

The body is not a home but an inn and that only briefly.... —*Seneca*

(Our body is) a thing of shreds and patches, borrowed unequally from good and bad ancestors and a misfit from the start....
—*Ralph W. Emerson*

There is no wealth greater than the health of the body....
—*Old Testament*

Things divine cannot be obtained by those whose intellectual eye is directed to the body.... —*Proclus*

Many people treat their bodies as if they were rented from Hertz—something they are using to get around in but nothing they genuinely care about understanding....
—*Chungliang Al Huang*

You are not the body, you are only wearing your body; you are that which activates the body....   —*Shantidasa*

If anything is sacred the human body is sacred....   —*Walt Whitman*

Forego not the sublimely spiritual for the lowly physical....
—*Shem Tob Falaquera*

There is nothing the body suffers that the soul does not profit by....
—*George Meredith*

Verily, there is no freedom from pleasure and pain for one while he dwells in the body....   —*The Upanishads*

The body is the soul's house. Shouldn't we take care of our house that it doesn't fall into ruin?...   —*Philo*

The body is a tabernacle in which the transmissible human spirit is carried for a while, a shell for the immortal seed that dwells in it and has created it....   —*George Santayana*

Good men spiritualize their bodies....
—*Benjamin Whichcote*

Believe not that man consists of flesh, skin and veins. The real part of man is his soul, and the things just mentioned are only outward coverings. They are only veils, not the real man....
—*The Zohar*

There are no souls without bodies. God alone is wholly without body....
—*Goffried Leibniz*

Heavy thoughts bring on physical maladies; when the soul is oppressed so is the body....   —*Martin Luther*

God made the human body, and it is the most exquisite and wonderful organization which has come to us from the divine hand....   —*Henry W. Beecher*

This body, which you love so much, is time bound....Treat the body like a visitor or guest which has come and must go....   —*Nisargadatta*

Cause & Effect

To have love towards another human being is a blessing and to have anger towards him is a curse....
—*Annamalai Swami*

The seed never explains the flower....
—*Edith Hamilton*

If men spit upon the ground, they spit upon themselves....   —*Chief Seattle*

The one who shares will never be lacking, for his or her storehouse will always be full of love, and will receive abundant love to perpetually replenish it....   —*A Spiritual Warrior*

A human being fashions his consequences as surely as he fashions his goods or his dwelling. Nothing that he says, thinks, or does is without consequences....   —*Norman Cousins*

Mankind cares nothing for you until you have shown that you care for mankind....   —*Ralph W. Trine*

No good ending can be expected in the absence of the right beginning. It is too late....   —*I Ching*

A harmonious action produces its harmonious counterpart. A discordant action necessitates a reaction and will look ill-regulated but will be, in reality, a balancing one. If you fight violence with violence, you will perpetuate violence; but if you oppose it with strength of meekness, you will enable meekness to triumph and violence will be broken....   *—Eliphas Levi*

People who spit into the wind are defying the workings of cause and effect....
—Shantidasa

Man (is) the sole and absolute master of his own fate forever. What he has sown in the times of his ignorance, he must inevitably reap; but when he attains enlightenment, it is for him to sow what he chooses and reap accordingly....   *—Geraldine Coster*

In this world everything changes except good deeds and bad deeds; these follow you as the shadows follow the body....   *—Ruth Benedict*

Nothing in all Nature is more certain than the fact that no single thing or event can stand alone. It is attached to all that has gone before it, and it will remain attached to all that will follow it. It was born of some cause, and so it must be followed by some effect in an endless chain....   *—Julian P. Johnson*

Not in the heavens above, nor in the farthest reaches of the sea, nor by transporting yourself to the remotest valleys of the mountains, will you be able to hide from the consequences of your own evil actions. Likewise, certain are the blessings growing out of your good actions....   *—Gautama Buddha*

A perfect cause must produce a perfect effect....   *—Ernest Holmes*

In all human affairs there are efforts, and there are results, and the strength of the effort is the measure of the result. Chance is not....
—James Allen

The law of cause and effect is inexorable and unrelenting. You reap a harvest of suffering, poverty, pain and sorrow, because you have sown the seed of evil in the past. You reap a harvest of plenty and bliss owing to your sowing of seeds of good....   *—Sivananda*

The cause is hidden, but the result is known....   *—Ovid*

A vacuum cannot exist in nature. An empty space is immediately filled by something else. And this law is effective on all levels. If what you give is luminous, radiant, beneficial, in return you will receive elements of the same quality, with the same luminous, radiant quintessence. But if you emanate something filthy, you will at once be filled with filth....
—Omaraam M. Aivanhov

A great flame follows a little spark....
—Dante Alighieri

Whoso casteth a stone on high, casteth it on his own head....Whoso diggeth a pit shall fall herein; and he that setteth a trap shall be taken therein. He that worketh mischief, it shall fall upon him, and he shall not know whence it cometh....   *—Old Testament*

If you help others, you will be helped, perhaps tomorrow, perhaps in one hundred years, but you will be helped. Nature must pay off the debt....it is a mathematical law and all life is mathematics....   *—George I. Gurdjieff*

Sin does not always bear its painful fruit unto the sinner, here on earth, at once; but circling, it reacts unfailingly, and cuts the sinner's very roots of being; and often it inflicts the consequence upon the children and grandchildren too....   —*Manu*

Never goes a sin without its due return; and deeds of noble goodness, or dire sin, bear their just fruit, here, in this very life. Never is there escape from consequence, because the Great Judge dwells within each heart....
                              —*Mahabharata*

Cause and effect, means and ends, seed and fruit, cannot be severed; for the effect already blooms in the cause, the end pre-exists in the means, the fruit in the seed....You cannot do wrong without suffering wrong....
                              —*Ralph W. Emerson*

One who knows the cause knows the effect. But the cause of human effects is the heart....   —*Thomas Aquinas*

The seed of God is in us. Given an intelligent farmer and a diligent farmhand, it will thrive and grow up to God whose seed it is and, accordingly, its fruit will be God-nature. Pear seeds grow into pear trees; nut seeds into nut trees, and God-seed into God....   —*Meister Eckhart*

To treat effect while ignoring cause is not the appropriate remedy for any social malady. Any person of wealth can uplift the poor and downtrodden for a period of time, but genuine healing lies in working with cause, the upliftment of the spirit....   —*Anonymous*

Thoughts of lack manifest as limitation. Thoughts of abundance manifest as success and happiness. Failure and success are but two ends of the same stick....   —*Ernest Holmes*

Nothing happens by chance. Every occurrence has its cause from which it follows by necessity....   —*Democritus*

No man in the world ever attempted to wrong another without being injured in return—some way, somehow, some time. Nature keeps her books admirably; she puts down every item, she closes all accounts finally, but she does not always balance them at the end of the month....   —*William G. Jordan*

We sow our thoughts, and we reap our actions; we sow our actions, and we reap our habits; we sow our habits, we reap our characters; we sow our characters and reap our destiny....
                              —*C. A. Hall*

There is always a close and intimate relationship between the end we aim at and the means adopted to attain it....
                              —*Jawaharlal Nehru*

The whole of human life is cause and effect; there is no such thing in it as chance, nor is there even in all the wide universe....Let him never forget that whatever he may get for himself at the expense of someone else....will by a law equally subtle, equally powerful, be turned into ashes in his very hands....
                              —*Ralph W. Trine*

The present condition continues nothing more than the past, and what is found in the effect was already in the cause....   —*Henri Bergson*

We are both the cause and the effect of ourselves. Our world was, is, and always will be what we made, make, or will make of it....   —*Guy L. Playfair*

Good and evil do not befall men without reason. Heaven sends them happiness or misery according to their conduct....   —*Confucius*

No man, who continues to add something to the material intellect and moral well-being of the place in which he lives, is left living without proper reward.... —*Booker T. Washington*

Heaven will permit no man to secure happiness by crime.... —*Vittorio Alfieri*

God is the free cause of all things.... —*Baruch Spinoza*

For every action, there is an equal and opposite reaction. If you push hard on the world, the world pushes back on you. If you touch the world gently, the world will touch you gently in return.... —*Paul Hewitt*

Beware of spitting into the wind.... —*Friedrich W. Neitzsche*

Wise is the man who seeks the cause of things....If the market goes up, or if the market goes down, there is a cause. If business is good, or not so, there is a cause. If you are ill, there is a cause.... —*Fred Van Amburgh*

Wisdom is the faculty of knowing what will be the effect of a cause.... —*Alfred A. Montapert*

Our personal dispositions are as window panes through which we see the world either as rosy or dull. The way we color the glasses we wear is the way the world seems to us.... —*Fulton J. Sheen*

Good thoughts and actions never produce bad results; bad thoughts and actions can never produce good results. This is but saying that nothing can come from corn but corn, nothing from nettles but nettles.... —*James Allen*

The one who strives for effect is always fooled more than he succeeds in fooling others. The man and the woman of true insight can always see the causes that prompt, the motives that underlies the acts of all with whom he or she comes in contact.... —*Ralph W. Trine*

The consequences of bad thought or action cannot be avoided; they are the invisible police, the unseen avengers, that accept no gifts, that hear no prayers, that no cleverness can deceive.... —*Robert Ingersoll*

In this world whatever is gained is gained only by self-effort; where failure is encountered, it is seen that there has been a slackness in self-effort.... —*Yoga Vasistha*

He who injures others is sure to be injured by them in return.... —*Chuang Tse*

One generation plants trees while another gets the shade.... —*Chinese proverb*

The world is a looking glass, and gives back to every man the reflection of his own face. Frown at it, and it will in turn look sourly upon you; laugh at it and with it, and it is a jolly, kind companion.... —*William M. Thackeray*

It is foolish to be surprised when a fig tree produces figs.... —*Marcus Aurelius*

The game of life is a game of boomerangs. Our thoughts, deeds, and words return to us sooner or later, with astounding accuracy.... —*Florence S. Shinn*

You can do anything in this world if you're prepared to take the consequences.... —*Somerset Maugham*

The man who has no inner life is a slave of his surroundings, as the barometer is the obedient servant of the air....
—*Henry F. Amiel*

There is a certain interval between sowing and reaping. Therefore we must not lose belief in the reward....
—*St. Mark, the Ascetic*

God does not play dice with the universe....
—*Albert Einstein*

A grain thrown into good ground brings forth fruit; a principle thrown into a good mind brings forth fruit. Everything is created and conducted by the same Master: the root, the branch, the fruits—the principles, the consequences....
—*Blaise Pascal*

Chance is a word void of sense, nothing can exist without a cause....
—*Voltaire*

Do not blame karma, or anybody else, for what you are. You can undo what has been done, through the exercise of a....determined will....
—*Papa Ramdas*

All life is a boomerang. We receive what we give....
—*Shirley MacLaine*

Take away the cause, and the effect ceases....
—*Miguel de Cervantes*

A thought of anger or hatred sends arrows from the mental factory towards the person aimed at, hurts the individual, sets up discord and disharmony in the thought-world, and comes back again to the sender and harms the sender also....
—*Sivananda*

Every seed bears its fruit; the fruit of good deeds is sweet, that of others is always bitter; always remember that....
—*Allan Kardec*

He who asks questions cannot avoid the answers....
—*Oriental proverb*

The notion of causation is one of the first lessons we learn from experience....
—*John H. Newman*

The law, "Whatsoever a man sows that he shall also reap," is inscribed in flaming letters upon the portal of Eternity, and none can deny it, none can cheat it, none can escape it....
—*James Allen*

Nothing exists from whose nature some effect does not follow....
—*Baruch Spinoza*

There is an old saying that though the mills of the gods grind slowly, yet they grind exceedingly fine. That is only another way of saying that one can never escape his own karma....
—*Julian P. Johnson*

Humanity, it seems, always treats the physical effects, not the spiritual causes—lust, greed, selfishness. Humanity always ends up treating the effects—not the cause. To treat the causes would change lifestyles—even this civilization itself! And that humanity is unwilling to do....
—*Michael A. Sydner*

Through the law of cause and effect we choose our destiny. Moreover, we are our own prophets for we constantly project our future state by the seeds we plant in the present....
—*Cheryl Canfield*

There is no place in the universe, no mountain, no sky, no heaven where one does not undergo the consequences of actions performed by oneself....
—*Yoga Vasistha*

No effect is ever the effect of a single cause, but only a combination of causes....
—*Herbert Samuel*

In nature there are neither rewards or punishments—there are consequences.... —*Robert Ingersoll*

God is the cause, everything else is the effect.... —*Shantidasa*

A wicked man who reproaches a virtuous one is like one who looks up and spits at heaven; the spittle soils not the heaven but comes back and defiles his own person.... —*Gautama Buddha*

God is not to be fooled; a man reaps what he sows. If he sows seed in the field of his lower nature, he will reap from it a harvest of corruption, but if he sows in the field of spirit, the spirit will bring him a harvest of eternal life.... —*Paul of Tarsus*

If we are loving we are likely to have love in return, but if we show harsh and critical attitudes we are certain to provoke resentment and opposition so we get what we ask for.... —*Leland F. Wood*

Change

Consider how hard it is to change yourself, and what little chance you have of trying to change others.... —*Jacob M. Braude*

The world never stands still. It is a constant becoming. The face of the earth—as well as the face you see in the mirror—offers clear evidence that all is flux and change.... —*Robert Collier*

The most powerful thing you can do to change the world, is to change your own beliefs about the nature of life, people, reality, to something more positive....and begin to act accordingly.... —*Shakti Gawain*

A living thing is distinguished from a dead thing by the multiplicity of changes at any moment taking place in it.... —*Herbert Spencer*

The direction of change to seek is not in our four dimensions: it is getting deeper into what we are, where you are, like turning up the volume on the amplifier.... —*Thaddeus Golas*

Only that which is real never changes.... —*Shankara*

Whenever we decide to change, we meet resistance. We are always challenged to see if we are serious.... —*Andrew Matthews*

The wheel of change moves on, and those who were down go up and those who were up go down.... —*Jawaharlal Nehru*

The things that come into being change continuously.... —*Augusto Roa Bastas*

A change of heart is the essence of all other change and is brought about by re-education of the mind.... —*Emmeline Pethich-Lawrence*

Not everything that is faced can be changed, but nothing can be changed until it is faced.... —*James Baldwin*

All things change, creeds and philosophies and outward systems—but God remains!... —*Mrs. Humphry Ward*

All is change, all yields its place and goes.... —*Euripides*

All things which have a soul change, and possess in themselves a principle of change, and in changing move according to the law and to the order of destiny.... —*Plato*

The absurd man is he who never changes....   —*Auguste Barthelemy*

All our resolves and decisions are made in a mood or frame of mind which is certain to change....
          —*Marcel Proust*

Your life is not going to change until you change, and the only way you can really change is to stop changing....
          —*Anonymous*

Some people change when they see the light; others when they feel the heat....
          —*Caroline Schroeder*

Resisting change is as futile as resisting the weather....   —*Warren Bennis*

All changes are taking place in the universe as willed by the divine. Changes are due to the very fact that this manifestation is not permanent. It is ever-changing. But the Spirit underlying the universe is eternal and changeless....   —*Papa Ramdas*

Everything is destined to change except God and the spark of God within....
          —*Peace Pilgrim*

Change man and you change society. Try to change society without the inner change in man, and confusion will be the sole result. And each conscious individual is solely responsible for making changes in himself....
          —*George Trevelyan*

When something seems to change in the world....it is really you that is changing....   —*Deepak Chopra*

If you want to truly understand something, try to change it....   —*Kurt Lewin*

It's only forms that change, not essence....   —*Ram Dass*

Change requires energy. It usually doesn't take any more energy to change than you have been expending maintaining yourself in the old patterns, but initially it feels like it is taking more energy....   —*Paul E. Wood*

When faced with the choice between changing and proving there's no need to do so, most people get busy on the proof....   —*John K. Galbraith*

It is only change that is at work here....
          —*I Ching*

There is nothing that stands fast, nothing fixed, nothing free from change, among the things which come into being, neither among those in heaven nor among those on earth. God alone stands unmoved....   —*Hermes*

God, give us the serenity to accept what cannot be changed, the courage to change what should be changed, and the wisdom to know the difference....
          —*Reinhold Niebuhr*

If you don't like something about yourself, change it. If you can't change it, then accept it....   —*Ted Shackelford*

There are no quick fixes that can permanently change your life....
          —*Sonya Friedman*

It is useless and futile to try to change other people. The only person I can change is myself....   —*William Curtiss*

In this world everything changes, everything decays. Youth becomes old age, health becomes sickness, beauty becomes disease....   —*Muktananda*

Perhaps man, having remade his environment, will turn around at last and begin to remake himself....
          —*Will Durant*

He who expects to change the world will be disappointed; he must change his view. When this is done, the tolerance will come, forgiveness will come and there will be nothing he cannot bear.... —*Hazrat Inayat Khan*

Change, indeed is painful, yet ever needful.... —*Thomas Carlyle*

All things must change to something new, to something strange.... —*Henry W. Longfellow*

No one can persuade another to change. Each of us guards a gate of change that can only be unlocked from the inside. We cannot open the gate of another, either by argument or by emotional appeal.... —*Marilyn Ferguson*

It is only the wisest or the very stupidest who cannot change.... —*Confucius*

Change is always more complicated then most of us imagine....Even when you are highly motivated to change, it is difficult to do so. Years have gone into building who we are, and worse than anything it is scary to rearrange our parts.... —*Melvyn Kinder*

Consistency is contrary to nature.... —*Aldous Huxley*

Change is life. Without change there would be no growth, no understanding, no relating and no surprises. We are by nature changing beings. Still we seem to fear and resist it more than any other aspect of life.... —*Leo Buscaglia*

Change is one thing, progress is another.... —*Lord Russell*

God will not change the condition of men, until they change what is in themselves.... —*Koran*

A permanent state of transition is man's most noble condition.... —*Juan R. Jimenez*

Change seems to happen when you have abandoned the chase after what you want to be (or think you should be) and have accepted—and fully experienced—what you are.... —*Janette Ramwater*

In a higher world it is otherwise; but here below to live is to change, and to be perfect is to change often.... —*John H. Newman*

Only the changeable can be thought of and talked about. The unchangeable can only be realized in silence.... —*Nisargadatta*

Everything subject to time is liable to change.... —*Joseph Albo*

There is a strict rule in spiritual life that every change, each experience, comes only when the person is ripe.... —*Lucy Cornellssen*

Other people do not have to change for us to experience peace of mind.... —*Gerald Jampolsky*

The change of one simple behavior can affect other behaviors and thus change many things.... —*Jean Baer*

The main dangers in this life are the people who want to change everything....or nothing.... —*Lady Astor*

We are restless because of change, but we would be frightened if change were stopped.... —*Lyman L. Bryson*

Any change, even a change for the better, is always accompanied by drawbacks and discomforts.... —*Arnold Bennett*

We must all obey the great law of change. It is the most powerful law of the universe.... —*Edmund Burke*

Some pessimists would say that no one changes, that a leopard never changes his spots. But in fact everyone is changing every day either for better or for worse.... —*Alan L. McGinnis*

You never have to change what you see, only the way you see it.... —*Thaddeus Golas*

Everything is changing; God alone is changeless.... —*Teresa of Avila*

Observe constantly that all things take place by change, and accustom thyself to consider that the nature of the Universe loves nothing so much as to change....The Universe is change.... —*Marcus Aurelius*

Change is our ally.... —*Willard Wirtz*

Let no one disturb you, let nothing frighten you. Everything passes away except God.... —*Theresa of Lisieux*

Nothing that exists perishes, but men are in error when they call the changes which take place 'destructions' and 'deaths.'... —*Hermes*

Progress is impossible without change; and those who cannot change their minds cannot change anything.... —*George B. Shaw*

Change means movement, movement means friction, friction means heat, and heat means controversy.... —*Saul Alinsky*

The wood does not change the fire into itself, but the fire changes the wood into itself. So we are changed into God, that we shall know Him as He is.... —*Meister Eckhart*

Such is the state of life that none are happy but by the anticipation of change.... —*Samuel Johnson*

Anytime you sincerely want to make a change, the first thing you must do is raise your standards.... —*Anthony Robbins*

The world hates change; yet it is the only thing that has brought progress.... —*Charles F. Kettering*

Most of the change we think we see in life is due to truths being in and out of favor.... —*Robert Frost*

The more things change, the more they remain the same.... —*Alphonse Karr*

Weep not that the world changes—did it keep a stable, changeless state, it would be cause enough to weep.... —*William C. Bryant*

Change is not made without inconvenience, even from worst to best.... —*Richard Hooker*

It's the most unhappy people who most fear change.... —*Mignon McLaughlin*

The man who never alters his opinion is like a man standing in water, and breeds reptiles in his mind.... —*William Blake*

It is sufficiently clear that all things are changed and nothing really perishes, and the sum of matter remains absolutely the same.... —*Francis Bacon*

Times of change are times of fearfulness and times of opportunity. Which they may be for you depends upon your attitude toward them.... —*Ernest C. Wilson*

Know that it is the image that changes; the true Self never moves or changes....
—*Vachaka Kovia*

We can change, slowly and steadily, if we set our will to it....
—*Robert Benson*

All things change, nothing perishes....
—*Ovid*

The desire to change the direction of your life is one of the surest signs of grace....For a while you may not know the direction in which to go. But you will know without doubt that the direction you have been going in is wrong....
—*Eknath Easwaran*

Change in all things is sweet....
—*Aristotle*

We ought not to progress in life by a series of violent jerks, but should learn to navigate our lives upon the flowing stream of change. By being amenable and adaptable we should cease to resent either life or conditions, and seek to "change" them by changing ourselves....
—*Ronald Beesley*

Times change and we change with them....
—*Raphael Holinshed*

The unforgiving mind rigidly sees the past and future as the same and is resistant to change. It does not want the future to be different from the past....
—*Gerald Jampolsky*

We must always change, renew, rejuvenate ourselves; otherwise, we harden....
—*Johann W. Goethe*

The only thing in life you can really count on is change....
—*Anonymous*

To deny change is to deny the only single reality....
—*Leo Buscaglia*

Change is resisted when we do not have a voice in the change....
—*Mason Horton*

Keep the currents moving. Don't let your life stagnate....
—*John Burroughs*

We are on the verge of the new age, a whole new world. Human consciousness, our mutual awareness, is going to make a quantum leap. Everything will change....All this is going to happen just as soon as you're ready....
—*Paul Williams*

Truth, as a general rule, is severely resisted by the worldly. It oftentimes advocates an unwanted change and change for many people is an uncomfortable inconvenience. The support of custom, the security of tradition does not enjoy being rattled or placed in jeopardy....
—*Shantidasa*

Today is not yesterday. We ourselves change. How then, can our works and thoughts....continue always the same?...
—*Thomas Carlyle*

There is no sin punished more by nature than the sin of resistance to change....
—*Anne Morrow Lindbergh*

Three things make people want to change. One is that they hurt sufficiently. They have beat their heads against the same wall so long that they decide they have had enough....Another thing that makes people want to change is a slow type of despair called ennui, or boredom....A third thing that makes people want to change is the sudden discovery that they can....
—*Thomas Harris*

Nothing ever is, but is always becoming....
—*Plato*

Everything in life that we really accept undergoes a change....
—*Katherine Mansfield*

The moment you start moving in the direction of accomplishment, you will find that life will accommodate you....
—*Jack Addington*

All is flux, nothing stands still. Nothing endures but change....You could not step twice into the same river, for other waters are ever flowing onto you. There is nothing permanent except change.... —*Heraclitus*

If you do not change direction, you may end up where you are heading....
—*Lao-tzu*

You do not alter God by your prayers; you do not have to change God's will or make God change His mind towards you, but only to become changed yourself, in order to be made at-one, or brought in tune, with the good that God has prepared for you....
—*Henry T. Hamblin*

Intolerance, uncharitable judgement of other people, censorious criticism, disparagement of other people's efforts....all these things indicate resistance to change.... —*Ronald Beesley*

In this world of change naught which comes stays, and naught which goes is lost.... —*Ann S. Swetchine*

You are not here to change the world, the world is here to change you....
—*Shantidasa*

Everything that seems to us imperishable tends toward its destruction....
—*Marcel Proust*

The ripple effect describes how a minor change in behavior or attitude can have a major effect.... —*Joyce Brothers*

The wheel of Providence is always in motion.... —*Philip Henry*

Whatever you consider yourself to be changes from moment to moment. Nothing is constant.... —*Nisargadatta*

Is any man afraid of change? What can take place without change?...
—*Marcus Aurelius*

Change your mind and change your life.... —*Anonymous*

Are you willing to be sponged out, erased, cancelled, made nothing? Are you willing to be made nothing? Dipped into oblivion? If not, you will never really change....
—*D. H. Lawrence*

Character

The most powerful agent in character-building is the awakening to the true self, to the fact that man is a spiritual being—nay, more, that I, this very eternal I, am a spiritual being, right here and now, at this very moment, with the God-powers which can be quickly called forth....
—*Ralph W. Trine*

Characters live to be noticed. People with character notice how they live....
—*Nancy Moser*

To keep your character intact you cannot stoop to filthy acts. It makes it easier to stoop the next time....
—*Katherine Hepburn*

Character is like a tree and reputation like its shadow. The shadow is what we think of it; the tree is the real thing....
—*Abraham Lincoln*

The reputation of a thousand years may be determined by the conduct of one hour....
—*Japanese proverb*

In this world a man must either be an anvil or hammer....
—*Henry W. Longfellow*

Character builds slowly, but it can be torn down with incredible swiftness....
—*Faith Baldwin*

Trifles often uncover a man's character best because with trifles, one is apt to be more easily caught off guard....
—*Shantidasa*

In the pursuit of wealth or knowledge or reputation, circumstances have power to mar the wisest schemes, but where character is the prize, no chance can rob us of success....
—*Frederich Robertson*

If you want success in life, if you want to influence others, if you want to progress well in the spiritual path and if you wish to have God-realization, you must possess an unblemished, spotless character. The quintessence of man is his character....
—*Sivananda*

As fire when thrown into water is cooled down and put out, so also a false accusation when brought against a man of the purest character, boils over and is at once dissipated and vanishes....
—*Cicero*

No one can climb out beyond the limitations of his own character....
—*John Morley*

Your character is the result of your conduct....
—*Aristotle*

No change of circumstance can repair a defect of character....
—*Ralph W. Emerson*

Character is much easier kept than recovered....
—*Thomas Paine*

Every man has an atmosphere which is affecting every other. So silent and unconsciously is this influence working, that man may forget it exists....
—*William G. Jordan*

A man's own character is the arbiter of his fortune....
—*Publilius Syrus*

Character is not made in a crisis—it is only exhibited....
—*Robert Freeman*

Character is what you are in the dark....
—*Dwight L. Moody*

The man of character bears the accidents of life with dignity and grace, making the best of the circumstances....
—*Aristotle*

Character is simply a habit long continued....
—*Plutarch*

Character is the final decision to reject whatever is demeaning to oneself or to others and with confidence and honesty choose what is right....
—*Arthur Trudeau*

You cannot dream yourself into character; you must hammer and forge one for yourself....
—*James Froude*

Character is constructed in the midst of the tempests of the world....
—*Johann W. Goethe*

A man of character finds a special attractiveness in difficulty, since it is by coming to grips with difficulty that he can realize his potentialities....
—*Charles de Gaulle*

Character is the result of two things—mental attitude and the way we spend our time....
—*Elbert Hubbard*

Life is not....for mere passing pleasure, but for the highest unfoldment that one can attain to, the noblest character that one can grow.... —*Ralph W. Trine*

Integrity includes but goes beyond honesty. Honesty is telling the truth—in other words, conforming our words to reality. Integrity is conforming reality to our words—in other words, keeping promises and fulfilling expectations....
—*Stephen R. Covey*

If I keep my good character, I shall be rich enough.... —*Platonicus*

Character is best tested by our reaction to adversity and temptation. It requires real character to go on when the going is difficult.... —*J. M. Jussawalla*

The grand aim of man's creations is the development of a grand character—and a grand character is....the product of probationary discipline....
—*Austin Phelps*

Many men build character as cathedrals were built, the part nearest the ground finished; but that part which soars toward heaven, the turrets and the spires, forever incomplete....
—*Henry W. Beecher*

The noblest contribution which any man can make for the benefit of posterity is that of good character....
—*Robert C. Winthrop*

It is when a man ceases to do the things he has to do and does the things he likes to do, that the character is revealed.... —*Lin Yutang*

Be more concerned with your character than your reputation, because your character is what you really are, while your reputation is merely what others think you are.... —*John Wooden*

You can't give character to another person, but you can encourage him to develop his own by possessing one yourself.... —*Artemus Calloway*

Let us not say, Every man is the architect of his own fortune; but let us say, Every man is the architect of his own character.... —*George Boardman*

Choices lead to action; action forms habits; habits solidify into character....If character grows out of the spiritual vision of oneness and brotherliness, it will lead us to ultimate union with the infinite.... —*Sathya Sai Baba*

There is nothing by which men display their character so much as in what they consider ridiculous....
—*Johann W. Goethe*

The best characters are made by vigorous and persistent resistance to evil tendencies.... —*Henry M. Dexter*

It takes character to stay in one place and be happy there....
—*Elizabeth C. Dunn*

Character is like a tree—it will always fall in the direction it leans....
—*Shantidasa*

Character cannot be counterfeited, nor can it be put on and cast off as if it were a garment to fit the whim of the moment. Day by day we become what we do. This is the supreme law and logic of life....
—*Madame Chiang Kai-shek*

Character is built out of circumstances. From exactly the same materials one man builds palaces, while another hovels.... —*George H. Lewes*

High aims form high character....
—*Tryon Edwards*

Character is a strange blending of flinty strength and pliable warmth....
—*Robert Schaffer*

A man may die, but his character remains. His thoughts remain. It is the character that gives real force and power to man. Character is power....
—*Sivananda*

No man, for any considerable period, can wear one face to himself, and another to the multitude, without finally getting bewildered as to which may be the true....
—*Nathaniel Hawthorne*

Character is that which lives and abides, and is admired long after its possessor has left the earth....
—*John Todd*

Character is what God and the angels know of us; reputation is what men and women think of us....
—*Horace Mann*

Our character is but the stamp on our souls of the free choices of good and evil we have made through life....
—*John C. Geikie*

No amount of ability is of the slightest avail without honor....
—*Andrew Carnegie*

When wealth is lost, nothing is lost; when health is lost, something is lost; when character is lost, all is lost....
—*German proverb*

The aphorism, "As a man thinketh in his heart, so he is," embraces the whole of man's being. It is so comprehensive that it reaches out to every condition and circumstance of life. A man is literally what he thinks. His character is the sum of his thoughts....
—*James Allen*

Character is the governing element of life, and is above genius....
—*Frederick Saunders*

If you wish to know the character of a man, confer upon him a little authority....
—*Shantidasa*

Character is the spiritual house in which we live....
—*Faith Baldwin*

As the sun is best seen at its rising and setting, so man's native dispositions are clearest seen when they are children, and when they are dying....
—*Robert Boyle*

There is a broad distinction between character and reputation, for one may be destroyed by slander, while the other can never be harmed save by the possessor....
—*Josiah Holland*

Fame is a vapor, popularity an accident, riches take wings, those who cheer today will curse tomorrow, only one thing endures—character....
—*Horace Greeley*

Character may be manifested in the great moments, but it is made in the small ones....
—*Phillips Brooks*

Character is the total of thousands of small daily strivings to live up to the best that is in us....
—*Arthur Trudeau*

Character isn't built on ease, success, a million dollars or a happy life. Mainly through pain, sorrow and adversity are the bricks fashioned which can erect an enduring edifice....
—*Alfred A. Montapert*

Character is that which can do without success....
—*Ralph W. Emerson*

A man's character is his guardian divinity....Character is destiny....
—*Heraclitus*

Talent develops in quiet, character in the torrent of the world....
—*Johann W. Goethe*

A man never discloses his own character so clearly as when he describes another's....
—*Jean P. Richter*

Character is the ability to carry out a good resolution long after the emotion of the moment has passed....
—*Cavett Robert*

A man's reputation is the opinion people have of him; his character is what he really is....
—*Jack Miner*

Out of our beliefs are born deeds. Out of our deeds we form habits; out of our habits grow our character; and on our character we build our destinations....
—*Dean H. Hancock*

A man's true estate of power and riches, is to be himself; not in his dwelling, or position or external relations, but in his own essential character....
—*Henry W. Beecher*

There is nothing more esteemed than a....decision of character. I like a person who knows his own mind and sticks to it; who sees at once what, in given circumstances, is to be done, and does it....
—*William Hazlitt*

To be worth anything, character must be capable of standing firm upon its feet in the world of daily work, temptation and trial....
—*Samuel Smiles*

It is our duty to compose our character, not to compose books; and to win, not battles and provinces, but order and tranquility for our conduct of life....
—*Michel Montaigne*

Integrity has no need of rules....
—*Albert Camus*

The encrusted character cannot be melted: it is too late. It has been fused, and has hardened again. It cannot be fused again. It must all be broken away....
—*Robert Benson*

Character is the sum of what a person has left after losing everything else....
—*Shantidasa*

There is nothing so fatal to character as half-finished tasks....
—*David L. George*

You can tell the character of every man when you see how he receives praise....
—*Seneca*

Charity

One should never expect any other reward from charity than the satisfaction it gives....
—*Darryl F. Zanuck*

The white man knows how to make everything, but he does not know how to distribute it....
—*Sitting Bull*

Expect no reward for an act of charity. Expecting something in return leads to a scheming mind....
—*Kyong Ho*

There are two kinds of charity, remedial and preventive. The former is often injurious in its tendency; the latter is always praiseworthy and beneficial....
—*Tryon Edwards*

God reveals Himself to man, in man and by man. His true worship is Charity. Dogmas and rites alter and succeed one another; charity does not change and its power is eternal....
—*Eliphas Levi*

Charity is the power of defending that which we know to be indefensible....
—*G. K. Chesterton*

How shall we expect charity toward others, when we are uncharitable to ourselves?...
—*Thomas Browne*

Charity is neither weak nor blind. It is essentially prudent, just, temperate and strong....
—*Thomas Merton*

Be careful not to parade your good deeds before men to attract their attention; by doing so you will lose all reward....when you give alms do not have it trumpeted before you....
—*Jesus*

Our strength will be found in our charity....
—*Betty J. Eadie*

There is only one way of being charitable to another and that is quietly, with no strings attached....
—*Shantidasa*

That charity is bad which takes from independence its proper pride, and from mendacity its proper shame....
—*Robert Southey*

Money spent on ourselves may be a millstone about the neck; spent on others it may give us wings like eagles....
—*Roswell Hitchcock*

Charity is never lost: it may meet with ingratitude, or be of no service to those on whom it was bestowed, yet it ever does a work of beauty and grace upon the heart of the giver....
—*Conyers Middleton*

Charity begins at home....
—*Terence*

The charities that soothe, and heal, and bless, lie scattered at the feet of men like flowers....
—*William Wordsworth*

The charitable man has found the path of salvation. He is like a man who plants a sapling and thereby has shade, the flowers, and the fruit in future years....
—*Gautama Buddha*

If you can't feed a hundred people, then feed just one....
—*Mother Teresa*

Be charitable and indulgent to everyone but yourself....
—*Joseph Joubert*

Did universal charity prevail, earth would be a heaven, and hell a fable....
—*Charles C. Colton*

In charity there is no excess; neither angel nor man come in danger of it....
—*Francis Bacon*

The charity that hastens to proclaim its good deeds ceases to be charity, and is only pride and ostentation....
—*William Hutton*

The charities of life are worth more than all ceremonies....Charity is that which equals all the other commandments....
—*The Talmud*

True charity is the desire to be useful to others with no thought of recompense....
—*Emanuel Swedenborg*

Charity is the pure gold which makes us rich in eternal wealth....
—*Jean P. Camus*

When a needy person stands at your door God himself stands at his side....
—*Hebrew proverb*

Charity is, indeed, a great thing, and a gift offered, and when it is rightly ordered, likens us to God himself, as far as that is possible; for it is charity that makes the man....
—*John Chrysostom*

Charity is love; not all love is charity....
—*Thomas Aquinas*

One act of charity will teach us more of the love of God than a thousand sermons.... —*Frederick W. Robertson*

To feel much for others, and little for ourselves; to restrain our selfish, and exercise our benevolent affections, constitutes the perfection of human nature.... —*Adam Smith*

The greatest pleasure I know is to do a good action by stealth, and to have it found out by accident....
—*Charles Lamb*

He who bestows his goods upon the poor, shall have as much again, and ten times more.... —*John Bunyan*

The more is given the less the people will work for themselves, and the less they work the more the poverty will increase.... —*Leo Tolstoy*

Benevolence is allied to few vices; selfishness to fewer virtues....
—*Henry Home*

The poor man's charity is to wish the rich man well.... —*Anonymous*

Charity is injurious unless it helps the recipient to become independent of it.... —*John D. Rockefeller*

To give alms is nothing unless you give thought also....A little thought and a little kindness are often worth more than a great deal of money....
—*John Ruskin*

The man who refuses to live within his means, but seeks to be supplemented by charity, must not be helped....
—*The Talmud*

The best way to do good to ourselves is to do it to others; the right way to gather is to scatter.... —*Seneca*

Nothing is more pleasing to God than a open hand and a closed mouth....
—*Francis Quarles*

Good deeds ring clear through heaven like a bell.... —*Jean Paul Richter*

The highest charity of all occurs when we have become so pure and perfect we become mediums of God's love in such a way that His love passes through us without our knowing, or without knowingly having done a thing....
—*Bernadette Roberts*

Where there is charity and wisdom, there is neither fear nor ignorance....
—*Francis of Assisi*

Charity is a virtue of the heart, and not of the hands.... —*Joseph Addison*

If you don't have charity in your heart, you have the worst kind of heart trouble.... —*Bob Hope*

Charity is patient, is kind, feels no envy, is never perverse or proud or insolent; it has no selfish aims, cannot be provoked, does not brood over an injury; it takes no pleasure in wrongdoing but rejoices over victory of the truth.... —*Mother Teresa*

Charity brings to life again those who are spiritually dead....
—*Thomas Aquinas*

Charity is giving someone bread, not a lecture.... —*Anonymous*

True charity is always gentle as well as benevolent, for it consists as much in the manner of doing kindness as in the deed itself.... —*Allan Kardec*

The task of feeding the hungry, quenching the thirsty, clothing the naked and healing the sick shows magnanimity of character. But it must be remembered that such charity is only a temporary measure.... —*Shantidasa*

Charity with a smile shows the donor's character.... —*Nachman of Bratslav*

Give work rather than alms to the poor. The former drives out indolence, the latter industry.... —*Tryon Edwards*

The more charity, the more peace....
—*Hillel*

He that giveth to the poor, lendeth to the Lord.... —*Thomas Browne*

To pity distress is but human; to relieve it is Godlike.... —*Horace Mann*

Your charity is not genuine if your words, no matter how true, are not charitable.... —*Jean P. Camus*

Charity is the queen of virtues. As the pearls are held together by the thread, thus the virtues by charity; and as the pearls fall when the thread breaks, thus the virtues are lost if charity diminishes.... —*Padre Pio*

The noblest charity is to prevent a man from accepting charity; and the best alms are to show and to enable a man to dispense with alms....
—*The Talmud*

Children

Parents wonder why the streams are bitter, when they themselves have spoiled the fountain....
—*John Locke*

Nothing you do for your children is ever wasted. They seem not to notice us, hovering, averting our eyes, and they seldom offer thanks, but what we do for them is never wasted....
—*Garrison Keillor*

Death cannot be hidden from children. The parent who tries to protect a child from the experience of death is only adding confusion and anxiety to an already difficult world....
—*Robert W. Buckingham*

Teach the child that it will not have to worry over the future; that it will not have to lie, cheat, steal, murder or take any advantage of its fellow human beings in order to receive its share of the good things of life....
—*Alfred Lawson*

If you think you are your body, then you think that your children's bodies are extensions of your body. But they are a gift, just like your body is a gift. We don't own them, nor can we control them.... —*Stephen Levine*

Children are like little plants. If they grow too close together, they become thin and sickly and never attain maximum growth. We need room to grow....
—*Peace Pilgrim*

Children learn about their world through their play....
—*Susan Partnow*

It's easier for a father to have children than for children to have a real father....
—*Pope John XXIII*

What is a neglected child? He is a child not planned for, not wanted. Neglect begins, therefore, before he is born....
—*Pearl Buck*

If we could all remain children and not grow up at all, it would be such a happy world....   —*Ramana Maharshi*

One of the most obvious facts about grown-ups to a child is that they have forgotten what it is like to be a child....
—*Randall Jarrell*

You can do anything with children if you only play with them....
—*Otto von Bismarck*

One of the most responsible things you can do as an adult is become more of a child....   —*Wayne Dyer*

A clever child brought up with a foolish one can itself become foolish....
—*Georg C. Lichtenberg*

When dealing with the unknown, children are often bewildered by the fact that their parents do not know all the answers....   —*Edgar N. Jackson*

The mother who gives up her life for her children does them no kindness but rather burdens them with the legacy of a life unlived....   —*Janet Falldron*

Even a minor event in the life of a child is an event of that child's world and thus a world event....   —*Gaston Bachelard*

The mother-child relationship is paradoxical and, in a sense, tragic. It requires the most intense love on the mother's side, yet this very love must help the child grow away from the mother and become fully independent....   —*Erich Fromm*

A child is a reflection of God....
—*Nityananda*

Healthy children will not fear life if their elders have integrity enough not to fear death....   —*Erik H. Erikson*

We have no power to fashion our children as suits our fancy; as they are given by God, so must we have them and love them....   —*Johann W. Goethe*

A child must learn very early to realize that failing is a part of living. To lead him to believe otherwise is to deny reality....   —*Louis Binstock*

It is the attitude of a child that is necessary before we can enter the kingdom of heaven....For then we realize that of ourselves we can do nothing, but that it is only as we realize that is the Divine life and power working within us....that we are or can do anything....
—*Ralph W. Trine*

If a child lives with approval, he learns to live with himself....
—*Dorothy Law Nolte*

Give a little love to a child and you get a great deal back....   —*John Ruskin*

At every step the child should be allowed to meet the real experience of life; the thorns should never be plucked from the roses....   —*Ellen Key*

Your children are not your children. They are the sons and daughters of Life's longing for itself. They come through you but not from you. And though they are with you yet they belong not to you....   —*Kahlil Gibran*

Every child comes with the message that God is not yet discouraged of man....   —*Rabindranath Tagore*

So long as one does not become simple like a child, one does not get divine illumination. Forget all the worldly knowledge that you have acquired and become as ignorant as a child, and then you will get the divine wisdom....   —*Ramakrishna*

A child who is protected from all controversial ideas is as vulnerable as a child who is protected from every germ. The infection, when it comes—and it will come—may overwhelm the system, be it the immune system or the belief system.... —*Jane Smiley*

Limiting a child's behavior does not mean that we should be discourteous to them.... —*Walter C. Alvarez*

Except ye become as a little child ye shall not enter the kingdom of heaven.... —*Jesus*

Children are so beautiful....They're so original, so independent. They're everything you wish adults were. But adults are consistently herd-minded, conformant, subject to group pressure. They're moving in the wrong direction. They're moving away from individualism toward the herd.... —*Allen Funt*

Up to a certain age the child has a perfect trust in its parents to supply it with food, clothing and shelter. When it is obliged to provide for itself the trouble begins....Then it trusts hardly anything. That may be the cause of all our trouble, wakefulness included.... —*Prentice Mulford*

With children we must mix gentleness with firmness. They must not always have their own way, but they must not always be thwarted.... —*Charles Spurgeon*

The child must know that he is a miracle, a miracle that since the beginning of the world there hasn't been, and until the end of the world there will not be another child like him. He is a unique thing, a unique thing from the beginning until the end of the world.... —*Pablo Casals*

The great man is he who does not lose his child's heart.... —*Menicus*

It is the child who is full and the man who is empty, empty as an empty gourd and as an empty barrel. Now then, children, go to school. And you men, go to the school of life. Go and learn how to unlearn.... —*Charles Peguy*

In every man there is a child hidden—it wants to come out.... —*Friedrich W. Nietzsche*

You are children of the living God. What then is your inheritance? Is it less than the Fathers? It cannot be.... —*Frater Achad*

Children are God's apostles—sent forth day by day, to preach of love, and hope and peace.... —*James Russell Lowell*

A child is not your ego, it is not a pet dog in the house, it is not a substitute for love. A child has nothing to do with that. A child is born to you so that you can prepare him to face time unto eternity.... —*Yogi Bhajan*

Man is most nearly himself when he achieves the seriousness of a child at play.... —*Heraclitus*

One of the sad things about growing up is that as adults we often lose our ability to pretend, to imagine. To the young child, imagination is a magic door that leads to thrills, excitement and happiness.... —*Eric Butterworth*

This is a truth that children know: If you want joy, go back to your creative enthusiasm. Refuse to make life work of anything you cannot fill with magic.... —*David Seabury*

There are two lasting bequests we can hope to give our children. One of these is roots; the other, wings....
—*Hodding Carter*

Never fear spoiling children by making them happy. Happiness is the atmosphere in which all good affections grow.... —*Ann Liza Bray*

If you don't teach the ox to plow when he is young, it will be difficult to teach him when he is grown.... —*Midrash*

Childhood and genius have the same master-organ in common—inquisitiveness.... —*Edwin Bulwer-Lytton*

When we are no longer children, we are already dead....
—*Constantin Brancusi*

Sometimes we're so concerned about giving our children what we never had growing up, we neglect to give them what we did have growing up....
—*James Dobson*

A child becomes an adult when he realizes that he has a right not only to be right but also to be wrong....
—*Thomas Szasz*

What God is to the world, parents are to their children.... —*Philo*

A child is as sensitive to outside influences and forces as a seismograph is sensitive to an earthquake which is ten thousand miles away....
—*Luther Burbank*

Children live in a world of imagination and feelings. They invest the most insignificant object with any form they please, and see in it whatever they wish to see.... —*Adam Oehlenschlager*

Zen is to have the heart and soul of a little child.... —*Takuan*

As a child learning to walk falls a thousand times before he can stand, and after that falls again and again until at last he can walk, so are we as little children before God....
—*Hazrat Inayat Khan*

The joy of raising children is the joy of giving. This is giving in the purest form. You don't give with any ulterior motive involved—you just do it for the child.... —*Gary Emery*

What is childhood but a series of happy delusions?... —*Sydney Smith*

Children who are not loved in their very beginnings do not know how to love themselves.... —*Marion Woodman*

Be guided by children's questions, for they will teach you, and they will not be content with half-truths. It is true you cannot answer them all, for children ask questions which nobody can answer.... —*Froebel*

What is a child? An experiment. A fresh attempt to produce the just man....that is to make humanity divine....And if you should try to shape this new being in your idea of a godly man or a godly woman, you will destroy its own holiest expectation and perhaps create a monster.... —*George B. Shaw*

Do not confine your children to your own learning, for they were born of another time.... —*Hebrew proverb*

Children need love, especially when they do not deserve it....
—*Harold S. Hubert*

If children grew up according to early indications, we should have nothing but geniuses.... —*Johann W. Goethe*

The first duty to children is to make them happy. If you have not made them so, you have wronged them. No other good they may get can make up for that.... —*Charles Buxton*

After all, what is God? An eternal Child playing an eternal game in the eternal garden.... —*Aurobindo Ghose*

Hard words bruise the heart of a child.... —*Henry W. Longfellow*

Society wants kids to grow up more quickly. It offers them rewards for being more and more adultlike in their behavior rather than childlike. Adults need to reassure them that play—their own unique, imaginative play—is something to be valued.... —*Fred Rogers*

Grown men may learn from very little children, for the hearts of little children are pure, and therefore, the Great Spirit may show to them many things which older people miss.... —*Black Elk*

When childhood dies, its corpses are called adults.... —*Brian Addiss*

God sends children for another purpose than merely to keep up the race—to enlarge our hearts and to make us unselfish and full of kindly sympathies and affections.... —*Mary Howitt*

Children are naturally spiritual....Children are naive mystics....
—*John Bradshaw*

Know for certain that Nature is wonderfully simple; and that the characteristic mark of a childlike simplicity is stamped upon all that is true and noble in Nature.... —*Michael Sendivogius*

If you can't hold children in your arms, please hold them in your heart....
—*Mother Clara Hale*

You cannot teach a child to take care of himself unless you will let him try to take care of himself. He will make mistakes and out of these mistakes will come his wisdom....
—*Henry W. Beecher*

Words are more powerful than perhaps anyone suspects, and once deeply engraved in a child's mind, they are not easily eradicated.... —*May Sarton*

Of all people, children are the most imaginative.... —*Thomas B. Macaulay*

Feel the dignity of a child. Do not feel superior to him, for you are not....
—*Robert Henri*

When I was a child, I spoke as a child, I understood as a child, I thought as a child. When I became a man, I put away childish things.... —*Paul of Tarsus*

To endure is the first thing that a child ought to learn, and that which he will have most need to know....
—*Jean J. Rousseau*

The best way to make children good is to make them happy....
—*Oscar Wilde*

You can learn many things from children. How much patience you have, for instance.... —*Franklin P. Jones*

Children should grow up in the awareness of the brotherhood of man and the Fatherhood of God....
—*Sathya Sai Baba*

Give me the children until they are seven and anyone can have them afterwards.... —*Francis Xavier*

Children enjoy the present because they have neither a past nor a future....
—*Jean La Bruyere*

Children are the creatures of example—whatever surrounding adults do, they will do....　　　　*—Josiah Warren*

The greatest gifts you can give your children are the roots of responsibility and the wings of independence....
　　　　　　　　　　—Denis Waitley

Children require guidance and sympathy far more than instruction....
　　　　　　　　　　—Anne Sullivan

In praising or loving a child, we love and praise not that which is, but that which we hope for....
　　　　　　　　—Johann W. Goethe

Whatever parent gives his children good instruction, and sets them at the same time bad example, may be considered as bringing them food in one hand, and poison in another....
　　　　　　　　　　—John Balguy

Mothers give sons permission to be a prince but the father must show him how....Fathers give daughters permission to be princesses, but the mothers must show them how. Otherwise, both boys and girls will grow up and always see themselves as frogs....
　　　　　　　　　　—Eric Berne

The conscience of children is formed by the influences that surround them....
　　　　　　　　—Jean Paul Richter

Choice

We cannot lead a choiceless life. Every day, every moment, every second, there is a choice. If it were not so, we would not be individuals....　　　*—Ernest Holmes*

Far too often the choices reality proposes are such as to take away one's choice for choosing....　　　*—Jean Rostand*

The great tragedy of humankind lies in its apparent freedom of choice. Our choices are endless, but also beyond the ability of most to distinguish between what is correct and what is absurd....In truth, there is no choice but one—to rely upon God to make our choices....
　　　　　　　　　　—Shantidasa

If you limit your choices only to what seems possible or reasonable, you disconnect yourself from what you truly want, and all that is left is compromise....　　　　*—Robert Fritz*

By choosing we learn to be responsible. By paying the price of our choices we learn to make better choices....
　　　　　　　　　—Marsha Sinetar

The only limit put on choice is that it cannot serve two masters....
　　　　　　　—A Course In Miracles

We choose our joys and sorrows long before we experience them....
　　　　　　　　　—Kahlil Gibran

Whenever we bemoan our destiny on Earth and complain of our ill-fortune, we are railing against our own choice; not the choice of some arbitrary god or gods who have done us a bad turn....For we have what we have chosen and earned....　　　*—Stewert C. Easton*

Always there is a desire to accept some things and reject others. Who is making this choice, and with what wisdom?...
　　　　　　　　　　—Gerald May

Our greatest power is the power of choice; our greatest freedom lies in the exercise of our power of choice....
　　　　　　　　　—William Curtis

Fate chooses our relatives. We choose our friends.... —*Jacques Bossuet*

The power to define is the power to choose.... —*Michael O'Neal*

Happiness and love are just a choice away.... —*Leo Buscaglia*

Before man is life and death, good and evil, and that which he shall choose shall be given him....
—*Old Testament*

Life is a series of choices and nobody can stop you from making your choices....People punish themselves by making wrong choices. Constantly, enlightenment is being offered to them, but they refuse to accept it. Therefore, people are being taught by problems that are set before them, since they refuse to make right choices voluntarily.... —*Peace Pilgrim*

One does not decide in favor of one thing without deciding against another: Nothing is ever achieved or gained without giving up something....
—*U. S. Anderson*

If you choose you are free; if you choose you need blame no man—accuse no man. All things will be at one according to the mind of God....
—*Epictetus*

The power of choosing good and evil is within the reach of all.... —*Origen*

Whatever you choose will become your experience when you believe in your choice and have faith in the ability of Life to fulfill your desires....
—*Jack Addington*

Life is a series of choices and sometimes your only choice is what your attitude will be.... —*Shantidasa*

God impels nobody, for He will have no one saved by compulsion....God has given free will to men that they may choose for themselves, either the good or the bad.... —*Hans Denck*

Everything can be taken from a man but one thing; the last of human freedoms—to choose one's attitude in any given set of circumstances, to choose one's own way.... —*Victor Frankl*

Choose always the way that seems best, however rough it may be; custom will soon render it easy and agreeable....
—*Pythagoras*

Life is a perpetual choice between endless pairs of rival ills. Right choice, which will bring most happiness and least pain....is a choice inspired by the Spirit.... —*Bhagavan Das*

Life is change....Growth is optional. Choose wisely.... —*Karen K. Clark*

We do not choose the day of our birth nor may we choose the day of our death, yet choice is the sovereign faculty of the mind.... —*Thornton Wilder*

No power impels us forcibly either to good or to evil.... —*St. Mark, the Ascetic*

Know how to choose well. Most of life depends thereon. It needs good taste and correct judgement, for which neither intellect nor study suffices....
—*Baltazar Gracian*

Happiness is a choice. Reach out for it at the moment it appears, like a balloon drifting seaward in a bright blue sky....
—*Adair Lara*

There is a small choice in rotten apples.... —*William Shakespeare*

You don't get to choose how you're going to die, or when. You only decide how you're going to live. Now....
—*Joan Baez*

The free will of man holds a place midway between the divine Spirit and the inordinate desires of the body....
—*St. Bernard*

Man is fully responsible for his nature and his choices.... —*Jean-Paul Sartre*

It is the choices you make that are wrong. To imagine that some little thing—food, sex, power, fame—will make you happy is to deceive yourself.... —*Nisargadatta*

God asks no man whether he will accept life. That is not the choice. You must take it. The only choice is how....
—*Henry W. Beecher*

Life is an endless creative experience and we are making ourselves every moment by every decision we make....
—*Kent Nerburn*

When choices are taken away, a perfect path remains.... —*Bo Lozoff*

Choice of attention—to pay attention to this and ignore that—is to the inner life what choice of action is to the outer. In both choices man is responsible for his choice and must accept the consequences.... —*W. H. Auden*

He who does anything because it is custom, makes no choice.... —*John S. Mill*

This choice of ours, the choice between an alliance with God or a conflict, is not made once and for all and in a moment. It is a choice that we have to be making always....
—*Arthur Clutton-Brock*

The strongest principle of growth lies in the human choice.... —*George Eliot*

It is in our power to choose the better, and likewise to choose the worst....
—*Hermes*

Man has two roads always before him. And he must choose between them. Two roads before his eyes, two destinies. And at each step there is a new crossing.... —*Martin Grey*

Nature gives man corn but he must grind it; God gives man a will, but he must make the right choices....
—*Fulton J. Sheen*

The power of choice must involve the possibility of error—that is the essence of choosing.... —*Herbert Samuel*

Always choose the right thing, for brief is your choice. It is like a moment, but it is also eternity.... —*Anonymous*

If a man does not keep pace with his companions, perhaps it is because he hears a different drummer. Let him step to the music he hears, however measured or far away....
—*Henry D. Thoreau*

Man is made or unmade by himself....By the right choice and true application of thought, man ascends to the Divine Perfection. By the abuse and wrong application of thought, he descends below the level of the beast. Between these two extremes are all the grades of character, and man is their maker and master....—*Baird Spalding*

The power of choice. You have it. But you forfeit it when you imagine that you can choose for others. You can't. But you can choose for yourself—from hundreds of exciting, happiness-producing alternatives....
—*Harry Browne*

Destiny is not a matter of chance; it is a matter of choice; it is not a thing to be waited for, it is a thing to be achieved....
—*William J. Bryan*

"Many are called but few are chosen." Who makes the choice?...only the ones who are called.... —*Frater Achad*

Those who fail to make choices when they have the opportunity are not necessarily backing away from the choices. They may simply not recognize that a choice does exist.... —*Gordon P. Miller*

I discovered I always have choices and sometimes it's only a choice of attitudes.... —*Judith Knowlton*

Life is a series of choices and as all ideas in this manifested universe are divided as opposites, we can choose the negative ego approach or the positive spiritual approach....From the negative ego approach we learn that we will suffer until we balance our actions and bring our lives into harmony with the laws that govern the universe. This is called the law of hard knocks or karma. With the positive spiritual approach we choose to live in obedience to God's will, to live in harmony with universal laws without being pushed into it. This can be called the school of grace....
—*Cheryl Canfield*

Conscience

Conscience is the most perfect mirror ever made—the one looking glass that cannot be broken....
—*Fred Van Amburgh*

When we know the truth in our own consciences, it is unnecessary to be troubled about anything else....
—*Madeleine de Scudery*

The conscience interprets life honestly and realistically; the same cannot be said about the ego.... —*Shantidasa*

Real human progress depends upon a good conscience.... —*Albert Einstein*

Everyone's conscience....is between God and themselves, and it belongs to none other.... —*Margaret Cavendish*

Conscience is the perfect interpreter of life.... —*Karl Barth*

The one thing that doesn't abide by majority rule is a person's conscience....
—*Harper Lee*

There is no witness so dreadful, no accuser so terrible as the conscience that dwells in the heart of every man....
—*Polybius*

The voice of conscience is so delicate that it is easy to stifle it: but it is also so clear that it is impossible to mistake it.... —*Madame de Staël*

If you compromise with your own conscience, you will weaken your conscience. Soon your conscience will fail to guide you and you will never have real wealth based on peace of mind....
—*Napoleon Hill*

A man that will enjoy a quiet conscience must lead a quiet life....
—*Philip Chesterton*

Whenever conscience speaks with a divided, uncertain, and disputed voice, it is not the voice of God. Descend still deeper into yourself, until you hear nothing but a clear, undivided voice, a voice which does away with doubt and brings with it persuasion, light and serenity.... —*Henri F. Amiel*

When conscience is our friend, all is peace; but if once offended, farewell to the tranquil mind....
—*Mary W. Montagu*

A quiet conscience makes one so serene....
—*George Byron*

Cowardice asks, Is it safe? Expediency asks, Is it politic? Vanity asks, Is it popular? but Conscience asks, Is it right?...
—*Alexander Punshon*

The foundation of true joy is in the conscience....
—*Seneca*

Be the master of your will, and the slave of your conscience....
—*Yiddish saying*

I simply want to please my own conscience, which is God....
—*Mohandas Gandhi*

Conscience, as a mentor, the guide and compass of every act, leads ever to happiness. When the individual can stay alone with his conscience and get its approval, without knowing force or specious knowledge, then he begins to know what real Happiness is....
—*William G. Jordan*

Blind is he who sees not his conscience; lame is he who wanders from the right way....
—*Anthony of Padua*

The Inner Guide, who works in everybody, does not tolerate other influences than His own. And he certainly knows best....
—*Lucy Cornellssen*

The torture of a bad conscience is the hell of a living soul....
—*John Calvin*

Conscience is that great beacon of light God sets in all....
—*Robert Browning*

A disciplined conscience is a man's best friend. It may not be his most amiable, but it is his most faithful monitor....
—*Austin Phelps*

Conscience is God's presence in man....
—*Emanuel Swedenborg*

I am more afraid of my own heart than of the pope and all his cardinals. I have within me the great pope, Self....
—*Martin Luther*

Conscience, the higher mind, awoke in me, shook me and questioned: "Think —careless one! Who are you? Whose are you? I ask you: Why are you here?"...
—*Zoroaster*

Conscience is called the adversary, because it always opposes our evil will; it reminds us of what we ought to do but do not, and condemns us if we do something we ought not....
—*Abba Dorotheus*

Conscience is the royalty and prerogative of every private man....
—*John Dryden*

Conscience warns us as a friend before it punishes us as a judge....
—*Leszczynski Stanislaw*

Conscience and reputation are two things. Conscience is due to yourself, reputation to your neighbor....
—*Augustine*

The testimony of a conscience is the glory of the good man; have a good conscience and thou shalt have gladness....
—*Thomas à Kempis*

Trust that man in nothing who has not a conscience in everything....
—*Laurence Sterne*

The truth is not so much that man has a conscience, as that conscience has man.... —*Isaac Dorner*

Conscience is a sacred sanctuary, where God alone has the right to enter and judge.... —*Lamennais*

The unknown is an ocean. What is conscience? The compass of the unknown.... —*Joseph Cook*

Conscience is God to all mortals.... —*Menander*

Conscience is the voice of the soul, as passions are the voice of the body. No wonder they contradict each other.... —*Jean J. Rousseau*

The paradoxical—and tragic—situation of man is that his conscience is weakest when he needs it the most.... —*Eric Fromm*

A good conscience is a continual feast.... —*Richard E. Burton*

If you are honest with yourself, conscience will make known your character.... —*Edward Payson*

A good conscience is to the soul what health is to the body; it preserves constant ease and serenity within us, and more than countervails all the calamities and afflictions which can befall us without.... —*Joseph Addison*

Conscience is nothing else but the echo of God's voice within the soul.... —*E. B. Hall*

Conscience is the root of all free courage; if a man would be brave, let him obey his conscience.... —*James F. Clark*

In matters of conscience, the law of majority has no place.... —*Mohandas Gandhi*

There is a difference between him who does no misdeeds because of his own conscience and he who is kept from wrongdoing because of the presence of others.... —*The Talmud*

A man's conscience and his judgement are the same thing.... —*Thomas Hobbes*

Man's conscience is the oracle of God.... —*George Byron*

There is always a voice saying the right thing to you somewhere, if you'll only listen for it.... —*Thomas Hughes*

The only religion is conscience in action.... —*Henry D. Lloyd*

Conscience emphasizes the word "ought."... —*Joseph Cook*

Conscience: the soft whisper of God in man.... —*Edward Young*

God leaves to our conscience the choice of the road we decide to follow, and the liberty of yielding to one or other of the opposing influences that act upon us.... —*Allan Kardec*

Consciousness

There's something queer about describing consciousness: whatever people mean to say, they just can't seem to make it clear....How could anything seem so close, yet always keep beyond our reach?... —*Marvin Minsky*

The chief delusion of man is his conviction that there are other causes at work in his life than his own states of consciousness. All that happens to him, all that is done by him, comes to him as a result of his states of consciousness....
—*Paul Twitchell*

A lake that is absolutely calm gives to you a perfect reflection. The moment it becomes disturbed in the least, the reflection is distorted; and if the agitation is increased, the reflection will be completely lost. Your consciousness is the lake.... —*James B. Schafer*

Consciousness reigns but doesn't govern.... —*Paul Valery*

A person is but consciousness. Even if a hundred bodies perish, consciousness does not perish. Consciousness is like space, but it exists as if it is the body. The infinite appears to be divided into infinite parts, with and without form. This is because countless particles of experiences shine within that consciousness.... —*Yoga Vasistha*

There is no world, there are no men, there are no women, there is no sin, and there is no illusion. What we see is nothing but the supreme play of cosmic consciousness.... —*Anonymous*

Mystical consciousness is a state of insight into the depths of truth unplumbed by the discursive intellect.... —*William James*

It is impossible that consciousness can ever come to an end. Hence, there must be rebirth. Otherwise, what happens to the....individual soul after it shakes off the physical body? It must exist in a different form of consciousness suited to its further growth into greater fullness.... —*Sivananda*

We live, breath, and die by a miracle, one phase of existence not being any more than another, for consciousness is our true nature.... —*A Spiritual Warrior*

There is nothing about any level of consciousness that is right or wrong, good or bad, pure or evil....
—*Ken Keyes, Jr.*

The crisis is in our consciousness, not in the world.... —*J. Krishnamurti*

In the long run, no one can retain what does not belong to him by right of consciousness, nor be deprived of that which is truly his by the same supreme title.... —*Emmet Fox*

There is no coming into consciousness without pain.... —*Carl Jung*

Science's biggest mystery is the nature of consciousness.... —*Nick Herbert*

Any addiction is a falling into unconsciousness.... —*Marion Woodman*

Consciousness is all there is, and whatever appears or happens is merely a movement of consciousness....Consciousness is where God abides....
—*Ramesh Balsekar*

All that befalls a man, all that is done by him, all that comes from him, happens as a result of his state of consciousness.... —*Darwin Gross*

Everything exists in Consciousness, and Consciousness exists in Everything.... —*Vayu-Purana*

There is individual consciousness and from there, group consciousness and then we reach universal consciousness. The aim of man is to reach universal consciousness.... —*Yogi Bhajan*

There is only one consciousness, equally distributed everywhere. You, through illusion, give it unequal distribution. (There is) no distribution, no everywhere.... —*Ramana Maharshi*

Consciousness is the way emptiness knows itself.... —*Stephen H. Wolinsky*

There can be nothing but consciousness. Tell me any place where there is no consciousness; there is no place beyond consciousness. Or can anyone prove in any manner anything outside consciousness? Consciousness is inescapable.... —*Tripura Rahasya*

God's Garment, Nature, changes hues and forms, moment to moment, tireless, ceaselessly; His Consciousness continues ever the same.... —*Sankhya-yoga*

When games and gratifications quickly cease to satisfy, the pilgrim can make rapid progress in consciousness.... —*Sunyata*

Consciousness is never experienced in the plural, only in the singular.... —*Erwin Schrodinger*

The unconsciousness of man is the consciousness of God.... —*Henry D. Thoreau*

Consciousness means freedom from attachment....You realize that the only thing you have to do is to keep yourself really straight, and then do whatever it is you do.... —*Baba Ram Dass*

Modern physics has eliminated the notion of substance....Mind is the first and most direct thing in our experience....I regard consciousness as fundamental....I regard matter as a derivation of Consciousness.... —*Arthur Eddington*

The world is painted on your screen of consciousness and is entirely your private world....Once you realize that the world is your own projection, you are free of it.... —*Nisargadatta*

All consciousness reacts to recognition favorably.... —*Anonymous*

Little ought you to care who you are; the urgent thing is what you will be. The being that you are is but an unstable, perishable being, which eats of the earth and which the earth some day will eat; what you will be is an idea of you in God, the Consciousness of the universe.... —*Miguel de Yunamunojugo*

Our understanding is limited by the perspective of our consciousness and, in most cases, our consciousness is lens-like. It distorts reality by narrowing down the picture.... —*Vilayat I. Khan*

Consciousness of our powers increases them.... —*Luc de Clapiers Vauvenargues*

I shall now state clearly the profound secret....Understand that when the ego dies and the real Self is realized as the One reality, then there remains only that real Self, which is pure Consciousness.... —*Ramana Maharshi*

When you have achieved the consciousness that God is in you, with you, for you, that awareness must reshape every thought, word and deed, and make you wish good, speak good, and do good.... —*Sathya Sai Baba*

That consciousness perishes at the time of death of the physical body is a childish idea. Consciousness is eternal and it persists beyond death. In man the consciousness is veiled by mind and matter. Therefore, he is not able to realize his essential, divine nature.... —*Sivananda*

When we quit thinking primarily about ourselves and our own self-preservation, we undergo a truly heroic transformation of consciousness....
—*Joseph Campbell*

When a man has true knowledge, he feels everything is filled with consciousness.... —*Ramakrishna*

What you appear to be is the outer body; what you are is consciousness....
—*Nisargadatta*

Contentment

Man is the only animal that can be bored, who can be discontented, that can feel evicted from paradise.... —*Erich Fromm*

Neither circumstances nor surroundings can bring contentment. Only by fitting ourselves to meet conditions as they are, calmly and courageously, may we hope to reconcile ourselves to our position and conditions of life....
—*Fred Van Amburgh*

Contentment with the divine will is the best remedy we can apply to misfortunes.... —*William Temple*

It is far more important to be content with what is actually happening than to get upset over what might be happening but isn't.... —*John Heider*

If you remain utterly content, you may easily escape the grasp of harm. Pleasures entwined by desire beget trouble at every step.... —*Tibetan saying*

A man is content if he can find happiness in simple pleasures....
—*Thomas Malloy*

Contentment is a modest, prudent spirit; and....for the most part she avoids the high places of the earth, where the sun burns and the tempests beat, and leads her favorites along quiet vales to sequestered fountains....
—*Catharine M. Sedgwick*

Contentment can never make you idle. It is a Sattvic (pure) virtue that propels man towards God. It gives strength of mind and peace. It checks unnecessary and selfish exertions. It opens the inner eye of man and moves his mind towards divine contemplation....
—*Sivananda*

All the discontented people I know are trying sedulously to be something they are not, to do something they cannot do.... —*David Grayson*

Contentment has the ability to squeeze out of every situation all the good there is to get.... —*Shantidasa*

We can never be fully satisfied but in God.... —*Tryon Edwards*

A man whose heart is not content is like a snake which tries to swallow an elephant.... —*Chinese proverb*

You traverse the world in search of happiness which is within the reach of every man; a contented mind confers it all.... —*Horace*

No one can be poor that has enough, nor rich, that covets more than he has.... —*Seneca*

Never coddle a malcontent....
—*Peter Baida*

The best way to lead a peaceful life is to be content with the situation in which God places us. We seek changes and the result is we get into a worse hole than the previous one.... —*Papa Ramdas*

Contentment is natural wealth, luxury is artificial poverty.... —*Socrates*

Contentment is a pearl of great price, and whosoever procures it at the expense of ten thousand desires makes a wise and happy purchase....
—*John Balguy*

I am always content with what happens; for I know that what God chooses is better than what I choose....
—*Epictetus*

A contented mind is the greatest blessing a man can enjoy in this world....
—*Joseph Addison*

You never know what is enough unless you know what is more than enough....
—*William Blake*

He who with little is well content is rich indeed as a king; and a king, in his greatness, is poor as the peddler, when his kingdom sufficeth him not....
—*Shekel Hakoodesh*

We are made for God and will be dissatisfied until we have God in our hearts.... —*Augustine*

In whatever state I find myself, I have learned to be content....
—*Paul of Tarsus*

Contentment consists not in adding more fuel, but in taking away some fire; not in multiplying of wealth, but in subtracting men's desires....Generally those who boast most of contentment have least of it. Their very boasting shows they want something and basely beg it, namely commendation.... —*Thomas Fuller*

When we have not what we like, we must like what we have....
—*Bussy-Rabutin*

Discontent in most people's lives is caused by wishing they were something which they are not. They are unhappy because they compare their own life with other people's, and in that comparison they apparently find a lot wanting.... —*Ronald Beesley*

Contentment gives a crown, where fortune hath denied it.... —*John Ford*

Blessed is he who expects nothing, for he shall never be disappointed....
—*Alexander Pope*

The world is full of people looking for spectacular happiness while they snub contentment.... —*Doug Larson*

Our discontent is from comparison: were better states unseen, each man would like his own.... —*John Norris*

Flow with whatever may happen and let your mind be free: Stay centered by accepting whatever you are doing. This is the ultimate.... —*Chuang Tse*

He who doesn't accept the conditions of life sells his soul....
—*Charles Baudelaire*

What is contentment? To renounce all craving for what is not obtained unsought and to be satisfied with what comes unsought, without being elated or depressed ever by them—this is contentment.... —*Yoga Vasistha*

Divine discontentment is born of the spirit. It is the will toward freedom and life, not the discontent of the desirous ego that seeks its own aggrandizement, or the discontent of the child who clamors for small satisfactions. It is the discontent that will not let a man rest until he has found the creative meaning of his own individualized life....
—*Francis G. Wickes*

If a man is not content in the state he is in, he will not be content in the state he would be in.... —*Erskine Mason*

When a man is contented with himself and his resources, all is well. When he undertakes to play a part on the stage, and to persuade the world to think more about him than they do themselves, he has gotten into a track where he will find nothing but briars and thorns, vexation and disappointment.... —*William Hazlitt*

Happiness comes out of contentment and contentment always comes out of service.... —*Yogi Bhajan*

There are two brands of discontent: the brand that merely fosters greed and snarling and back-biting, and the brand that inspires greater and greater effort to reach the desired goal.... —*B. C. Forbes*

Let him who has enough ask for nothing more.... —*Horace*

He knew not God and worshiped not, who displayed not contentment with his fortune and daily bread.... —*Saadi*

Learn to be pleased with everything; with wealth, so far as it makes us beneficial to others; with power, for not having much to care for; and with obscurity, for being unenvied.... —*Plutarch*

There is no wealth more satisfying than contentment. Eat your fill; you cannot eat more. If you are forced to eat more, it becomes torture.... —*Sathya Sai Baba*

Discontent is like ink poured into water, which fills the whole fountain full of blackness.... —*Owen Felltham*

He who has known the contentment of being contented will always be content.... —*Lao-tzu*

If you have a contented mind, you have enough to enjoy life with.... —*Plautus*

The fountain of contentment must spring up in the mind, and he who has so little knowledge of human nature as to seek happiness by changing anything but his own disposition, will waste his life in fruitless efforts and multiply the grief he proposes to remove.... —*Samuel Johnson*

We are never more discontented with others than when we are discontented with ourselves. The consciousness of wrongdoing makes us irritable, and our heart in its cunning quarrels with what is outside of it, in order that it may deafen the clamor within.... —*Henry F. Amiel*

Contentment is the Philosopher's Stone, that turns all it touches to gold.... —*Benjamin Franklin*

It's not doing what you like that's important—it's liking what you do.... —*Eric Butterworth*

Riches are not from abundance of worldly goods, but from a contented mind.... —*Mohammed*

If all our misfortunes were laid in one common heap, where everyone must take an equal portion, most people would be content to take their own and depart.... —*Socrates*

Place yourself in the middle of the stream of power....place yourself in the full center of that flood; then you are without effort impelled to....a perfect contentment.... —*Ralph W. Emerson*

When we cannot find contentment in ourselves, it is useless to seek it elsewhere....
—*Francois La Rochefoucauld*

A man's discontent is his worst evil....
—*George Herbert*

To the contented, even poverty is joy. To the discontented, even wealth is a vexation....
—*Ming Lum Paou Keen*

Contentment....comes as the infallible result of great acceptances, great humilities—of not trying to make ourselves this or that....but of surrendering ourselves to the fullness of life—of letting life flow through us....
—*David Grayson*

Nothing is so bitter that a calm mind cannot find comfort in it....
—*Seneca*

Courage

Courage is the price that Life extracts for granting peace....
—*Amelia Earhart*

If you don't place your foot on the rope, you'll never cross the chasm. Life is a risk. Change and chance are constants....
—*Liz Smith*

The weak in courage are strong in cunning....
—*William Blake*

We could never learn to be brave and patient if there were only joy in the world....
—*Helen Keller*

It takes great courage to break with one's past history and stand alone....
—*Marion Woodman*

A hero is no braver than an ordinary man, but he is brave five minutes longer....
—*Ralph W. Emerson*

Courage is grace under pressure....
—*Ernest Hemingway*

To persevere, trusting in what hopes one has, is courage. The coward despairs....
—*Euripides*

Courage is fear that has said its prayers....
—*Anonymous*

A man of courage is also full of faith....
—*Cicero*

To see what is right and not do it, is want of courage....
—*Confucius*

A coward flees backward, away from new things; a man of courage flees forward, in the midst of new things....
—*Jacques Maritain*

Courage consists not in hazarding without fear, but being resolutely minded in a just cause....
—*Plutarch*

Courage and perseverance have a magical talisman, before which difficulties disappear and obstacles vanish....
—*John Quincy Adams*

The principal act of courage is to endure and withstand dangers doggedly rather than to attack them....
—*Thomas Aquinas*

Courage leads starward, fear towards death....
—*Seneca*

Courage is not the absence of fear but the ability to carry on with dignity in spite of it....
—*Scott Turow*

Nothing but courage can guide life....
—*Luc de Clapiers Vauvenargues*

To be loved, and to love, need courage; the courage to judge certain values as of ultimate concern—and to take the jump and stake everything on these values....
—*Erich Fromm*

Until the day of his death, no man can be sure of his courage....
—*Jean Anouilh*

Fortune favors the bold....
—*Virgil*

Talk courage, think courage, act courageously. The opposite course will surely cause you to have more mental burdens than you can carry....
—*Fred Van Amburgh*

Courage is almost a contradiction in terms. It means a strong desire to live taking the form of a readiness to die....
—*G. K. Chesterton*

Never undertake anything for which you wouldn't have the courage to ask the blessings of heaven....
—*Georg C. Lichtenberg*

Courage is fear holding on a minute longer....
—*George S. Patton*

If you are afraid of water, you cannot cross the river even by boat. If you are afraid of fire, you cannot even cook a meal. For anything to be done, first you must have courage....
—*Nityananda*

Courage is doing what you're afraid to do. There can be no courage unless you're scared....
—*Eddie Rickenbacker*

Courage is resistance to fear, mastery of fear, not absence of fear....
—*Mark Twain*

When there is no adversary, what avails thy courage?...
—*Rumi*

Perfect courage means doing unwitnessed what one would be capable of doing before the whole world....
—*Francois La Rochefoucauld*

Courage is contagious: When brave men take a stand, the spines of others are stiffened....
—*Billy Graham*

Courage is the first of human qualities because it is a quality which guarantees the others....
—*Winston Churchill*

A man with outward courage dares to die; A man with inward courage dares to live....
—*Lao-tzu*

A man without courage is like a dead man. Life without courage is no life....
—*Babaji*

Courage is very important. Like a muscle, it is strengthened by use....
—*Ruth Gordon*

A decent boldness ever meets with friends....
—*Homer*

A great deal of talent is lost to the world for the want of a little courage....
—*Sydney Smith*

We must build dikes of courage to hold back the flood of fear....
—*Martin L. King, Jr.*

Life shrinks or expands in proportion to one's courage....
—*Anais Nin*

If the creator had a purpose in equipping us with a neck, he surely meant us to stick it out....
—*Arthur Koestler*

Have courage to use your own reason! That is the motto of enlightenment....
—*Immanuel Kant*

One man with courage makes a majority....
—*Andrew Jackson*

You cannot discover new horizons unless you have the courage to lose sight of the shore....   —*Anonymous*

Courage may be taught, as a child is taught to speak....   —*Euripides*

The greatest test of courage on earth is to bear defeat without losing heart....
—*Robert Ingersoll*

There is nothing in the world so admired as a man who knows how to bear unhappiness with courage....
—*Seneca*

Death

There is but one freedom, to put oneself right with death. After that everything is possible. I cannot force you to believe in God. Believing in God amounts to coming to terms with death. When you have accepted death, the problem of God will be solved—and not the reverse....
—*Allbert Camus*

We survive death regardless of whether we have been good or bad. We survive with memory, personality, and capacity for recognition....   —*Arthur Ford*

Death is going from one room to another, ultimately to the most beautiful room....   —*Mendel of Kotzk*

In reality, there is no death because you are not the body. Let the body be there or not be there, your existence is always there; it is eternal....   —*Nisargadatta*

It is difficult to accept death in this society because it is unfamiliar. In spite of the fact that it happens all the time, we never see it....
—*Elisabeth Kubler-Ross*

Death is the temporary end of a temporary phenomenon....
—*Gautama Buddha*

Death is always the great trial. The void that suddenly opens under our feet. It is useless to flee it. We must learn to face it. And also to get around it....
—*Martin Grey*

Death as finality or extinction is only a concept of thought, and has no reality. Our spiritual essence will continue to flow with the whole and ever change and evolve. Thus, through the death of form we evolve and find renewal. In form our energy radiates outward, and we relate to this energy vibrating around us; but in death of form, our energy radiates inward as we go back into the center of our essence....
—*A Spiritual Warrior*

Death as the termination of life is the greatest lie which has been perpetrated upon mankind. For the truth is that it is quite impossible to kill YOU. Only the body can die. The real YOU, as an individual consciousness which dwells within that body, is entirely beyond death....   —*Ormond McGill*

Death is nothing at all. I have only slipped away into the next room. I am I and you are you. Whatever we were to each other, that we are still....
—*Henry S. Holland*

The tragedy of death....is separation, but even separation may not be permanent....   —*Elizabeth Gray Vining*

Life is the entrance; death is the exit....
—*Bahya Ibn Pakuda*

It is the duty of a doctor to prolong life. It is not his duty to prolong death....
—*Thomas Horder*

Death cancels everything but truth, and strips a man of everything but genius and virtue. It is a sort of natural canonization. It makes the meanest of us sacred—it installs the poet in his immortality, and lifts him to the skies....   —*William Hazlitt*

People so often give up in death and that is a pity. Death is not a tragedy to be feared, but actually it is an opportunity for transformation....
                    —*Sogyal Rinpoche*

No university will teach you how to live so that when the time of dying comes, you can say: "I lived well, I do not need to live again."...   —*Nisargadatta*

The dead are indeed happy, having gotten rid of the incubus of the body; the dead do not grieve. Do men fear sleep? No, they court it and prepare for it....   —*Ramana Maharshi*

We should teach our children to think no more of their bodies when dead, then they do of their hair when cut off, or of their old clothes when they are done with them...
                    —*George Macdonald*

Thinking and talking about death need not be morbid; they may be quite the opposite. Ignorance and fear of death overshadow life, while knowing and accepting death erases this shadow....
                    —*Lily Pincus*

Death is not a deplorable event; it is the journey's end, the owner getting out of the car when the time is up and the goal is reached. It is a consummation, a happy conclusion, or at least it ought to be, if only all are wise enough to treat it as such and be prepared for it....
                    —*Sathya Sai Baba*

Death? Why the fuss about death. Use your imagination, try to visualize a world without death....Death is an essential condition of life, not an evil....
                    —*Charlotte P. Gilman*

Death, when we consider it closely, is the true goal of our existence. I have formed during the last few years such close relations with this best and truest friend of mankind, that this image is not only no longer terrifying to me, but is indeed very soothing and consoling! And I thank my God for graciously granting me the opportunity....of learning that death is the key which unlocks the door to our true happiness....
                    —*Wolfgang A. Mozart*

Death is the liberator of him whom freedom cannot release, the physician of him whom medicine cannot cure, and the comforter of him whom time cannot console....   —*Charles C. Colton*

The call of death is a call of love. Death can be sweet if we answer to the affirmative, if we accept it as one of the great eternal forms of life and transformation....   —*Hermann Hesse*

Death is a part of life not to be shunned or dreaded or feared, but to be welcomed with a glad and ready smile when it comes in its own good way and time....   —*Ralph W. Trine*

The wise man is never surprised by death: he is always ready to depart....
                    —*Jean La Fontaine*

Never say about anything, "I have lost it," but only "I have given it back." Is your child dead? It has been given back. Is your wife dead? She has been returned....   —*Epictetus*

Death is a doorway to another reality....
—*Barbara Harris*

The calls of death are always for the best, for we are solving problems there as well as here; and one is sure to find himself where he can solve his problems best.... —*The Aquarian Gospel*

Sleep is temporary death. Death is longer sleep. Why should one desire continuance of body shackles? Let the man find out his undying Self and be immortal.... —*Ramana Maharshi*

In death is always a new life....
—*Amar Jyoti*

Death is the last adventure....
—*Daniel Brinkley*

The fear of death is indeed the pretense of wisdom, and not real wisdom, being a pretense of knowing the unknown; and no one knows whether death, which men in their fear apprehend to be the greatest evil, may not be the greatest good.... —*Plato*

Only the dead are free, the chain is broken....but perhaps they miss their chains?... —*Eva-Lisa Manner*

What is death? Either a transition or an end. I am not afraid of coming to an end, this being the same as never having become; nor of transition, for I shall never be in confinement quite so cramped anywhere else as I am here....
—*Seneca*

Death has no terror for the righteous man.... —*Allan Kardec*

We must die! These words are hard, but they are followed by a great happiness: it is in order to be with God that we die.... —*Francis de Sales*

The first sign of love to God is not to be afraid of death, and to be always waiting for it. For death unites the friend to his friend—the seeker to the object which he seeks.... —*Al-Ghazzali*

Death will always be among us. We shall never escape it. Dying is part of the process of living. We must not fear it. We must not hide it. We must not ignore it. We must not deny it. Death is.... —*Robert W. Buckingham*

Death is a release from the impressions of the senses, and from the desires that make us their puppets, and from the vagaries of the mind, and from the hard service of the flesh....
—*Marcus Aurelius*

Death is the enlightener. The essential thing concerning it must be that it opens the closed eyes, draws down the veil of blinding mortality, and lets the man see spiritual things....
—*Phillips Brooks*

Death is nothing to fear; the body will go, for it is part of the manifestation, but our spirit is the undying essence of the absolute. There is no non-existence, death is just the miraculous, wonderous release of our spirit into a further journey of unfoldment, an evolution within the realm that is our home.... —*A Spiritual Warrior*

Death is nothing more than changing gears in the journey of life....
—*Hubert van Zeller*

The dead are not dead; life's flag is never furled: they passed from world to world.... —*Edwin Markham*

I see clearly that there are two deaths: to cease loving and being loved is unbearable. But to cease to live is of no consequence.... —*Voltaire*

If you want to die happily, learn to live; if you would live happily, learn to die....
—*Celio Calgagnini*

When we come to realize that death that crushes is but the tender clasp of God that loves, it loses all its terror....
—*Vincent McNabb*

Do not seek death. Death will find you. But seek the road which makes death a fulfillment....   —*Dag Hammarskjöld*

It is worth dying to find out what life is....   —*T. S. Eliot*

Come death, if you will: you cannot divide us; you can only unite us....
—*Franz Grillparzer*

Man loses nothing by death, but is still a man in all respects, although more perfect than when in the body....
—*Emanuel Swedenborg*

Death would be terrifying if there were not alongside it resplendent immortality....   —*Adrien-Emanuel Roquette*

After you die, you wear what you are....
—*Teresa of Avila*

When we attempt to imagine death, we perceive ourselves as spectators....
—*Sigmund Freud*

When you die you lose your body. That is all there is to it. Nothing else is lost....
—*P. M. H. Atwater*

I think of death as some delightful journey that I shall take when all my tasks are done....   —*Ella Wheeler Wilcox*

King Tety has not indeed died. He has become a glorious one in the sky; he abides in continuity....
—*Royal Egyptian Tomb, 2500 B.C.*

Most of us act like a child in the dark when we talk of death. To dispel that fear, we turn on a light....
—*JoAnn Kelley Smith*

The thought of death should slip from our consciousness altogether....
—*Ernest Holmes*

The attitude toward death is changing....No longer is it something to be feared, but rather a giving of ourselves to God....   —*Clifford Howell*

You fear death because you identify with the body. If you identified with the reality which activates the body you wouldn't be so attached to the clay garment—the body....   —*Peace Pilgrim*

Death teaches us to live; it gives us a boundary to map our living within. Death's hammer breaks through the mirror separating us from light....
—*David Meltzer*

Death is a delightful hiding-place for weary men....   —*Herodotus*

Death....means no more to me than what a caterpillar experiences when it sheds its old skin and emerges into the full light of a new day as a butterfly....
—*David Manners*

If death did not exist, there would be an unbearable accumulation of memories. People come and go, the memories are wiped out therefore, there is a sense of balance....   —*Nisargadatta*

Death does not come with a trumpet....
—*Danish proverb*

Death is not the end. It is the beginning. No one you are close to ever dies. There is life everlasting; there is no such thing as death....Death is not a termination but a transition....   —*George Anderson*

There is no death, because the wand of truth can change the driest bones to living things, and bring the loveliest flowers from stagnant ponds, and turn the most discordant notes to harmony and praise....　*—The Aquarian Gospel*

Death is no death if it raises us in a moment from darkness to light, from weakness to strength, from sinfulness into holiness....　*—Charles Kingsley*

Dying is easy work compared with living. Dying is a moment's transition; living, a transaction of years....
—Maltbie D. Babcock

Death is the quick transition to life in another form; the putting off of the old coat and the putting on of a new; a passing not from light to darkness but from light to light, according as we have lived here....　*—Ralph W. Trine*

In the democracy of the dead, all men are equal. The poor man is as rich as the richest, and the rich man as poor as the pauper. The creditor loses his usury, and the debtor is acquitted of his obligation. There, the proud man surrenders his dignity; the politician his honors, the worldling his pleasures; the invalid needs no physician; the laborer rests from toil. The wrongs of time are redressed; injustice is expiated, and the irony of fate is refuted....
—Anonymous

Death....is that stake one puts up in order to play the game of life....
—Jean Giraudoux

We are all equal in the presence of death....　*—Publilius Syrus*

Each man must die alone....
—Blaise Pascal

Death knocks impartially at the door of the poor man's shop and the prince's palace....　*—Horace*

Death in itself is nothing; but we fear to be we know not what, we know not where....　*—John Dryden*

No one who is fit to live need fear to die....To us here, death is the most terrible word we know. But when we have tasted its reality, it will mean to us birth, deliverance, a new creation of ourselves....　*—George S. Merriam*

Death is but another phase of the dream that existence can be material....Man, tree, and flower are supposed to die; but the fact remains that God's universe is spiritual and immortal....
—Mary Baker Eddy

Our fear of death is like our fear that summer will be short, but when we have had our swing of pleasures, our fill of fruit, and our swelter of heat, we say we have had our day....
—Ralph W. Emerson

Death cannot kill what never dies....
—Thomas Traherne

Asking why you have to die is like asking why you have to grow up physically as well as spiritually. It is all part of the human experience and upon death you go into a freer living....　*—Peace Pilgrim*

The fear of death is the most unjustified of all fears, for there's no risk of accident for someone who's dead....
—Albert Einstein

Do not allow death to disturb you, do not let the demise of flesh be the cause of pain or anguish. It is merely riddance of your vehicle, the sloughing off of your clothes.　*—Shantidasa*

Every man knows he will die, but no man wants to believe it....
> —*Yiddish saying*

Death is simply a shedding of the physical body, like the butterfly coming out of a cocoon. It is a transition into a higher state of consciousness, where you continue to perceive, to understand, to laugh, to be able to grow, and the only thing you lose is something you don't need anymore....your physical body. It's like putting away your winter coat when spring comes....
> —*Elisabeth Kubler-Ross*

How foolish to cling to life when God has ordained otherwise....
> —*Jorge Manrique*

The only thing we can take with us from this life is the good that we have done to others.... —*Betty J. Eadie*

Death is a black camel that kneels at every man's door....
> —*Turkish proverb*

To be born is to begin to die; the end is linked to the beginning....
> —*Manilus*

Life is a great surprise, I do not see why death should not be a greater one....
> —*Vladimir Nabokov*

We think of death as ending, let us rather think of death as beginning and that more abundantly. We think of losing, let us think of gaining. We think of parting, let us think of meeting. We think of going away, let us think of arriving.... —*Norman Macleod*

The event of death is always astonishing; our philosophy never reaches, never possesses it; we are always at the beginning of our catechism; always the definition is yet to be made. What is death?... —*Ralph W. Emerson*

Man's knowledge that he has to die is also man's knowledge that he is above death.... —*Paul Tillich*

Death is the bright side of life....
> —*Alfred L. Tennyson*

I often feel that death is not the enemy of life, but it is our friend, for it is the knowledge that our years are limited, which makes them so precious....
> —*Joshua Liebman*

Death is not to be feared. It is a friend. No man dies before his hour. The time you leave behind was no more yours than that which was before your birth and concerneth you no more. Make room for others as others have done for you. Like a full-fed guest, depart to rest.... —*Michel Montaigne*

Death does not end all. Death does not mean total annihilation. Death does not end the chain or sequence. The working agent, the Soul in the body, does not and cannot die with the death of the body. Man's Soul is immortal. Just as a person lays aside his overcoat, so also he lays aside the physical body at death.... —*Sivananda*

Were we to live forever, then indeed people would not feel the pity for things. Truly the beauty of life is its uncertainty.... —*Yoshida Kenko*

To have a peaceful death and be able to move from this existence to another, one needs to be free from all human relationships.... —*JoAnn Kelley Smith*

Death is a friend of ours; and he that is not ready to entertain him is not at home....Happy is he who dies before he calls for death to take him away....
> —*Francis Bacon*

Death is an event whereby the body disappears in one way or another—buried or cremated—and the breath in the body ceases and mingles with the air outside, and consciousness which had trapped itself within a body (and had identified itself with it) is released and becomes the universal consciousness, like a drop of rain water falling in the river....
    —Ramesh Balsekar

Death is not the end of things. Death can be spoken only of the body. The soul is eternal, undying and indestructible. Every death wrung out by the fire of a lofty ideal liberates the soul into the knowledge of its immortality—a kingdom of absolute peace and bliss....
    —Papa Ramdas

Death....is but a passing through a dark entry, out of one little dusky room in our Father's house into another that is far and large, lightsome and glorious, and divinely entertaining....
    —McDonald Clarke

Death becomes a marker, a motivator for living one's limited time fully....
    —David K. Reynolds

Death is a law, not a punishment....
    —Jean-Baptiste Dubos

Death is not the final accounting. It is merely a time to take inventory of ourselves....
    —Anonymous

Dying is hard under any circumstances, but dying in the familiar surroundings at one's home with those you love and who love you, can take away much of the fear....
    —Elisabeth Kubler-Ross

The things we now esteem fixed shall, one by one, detach themselves, like ripe fruit, from our experience, and fall....
    —Ralph W. Emerson

It is through death, the daily dying, that the soul has a gradual rising to the consciousness of God. It is a gradual liberation and self-discovery of the divine germ within the self. Physical death is an insignificant thing, about as significant as the breaking of a string....
    —Paul Twitchell

In the last analysis it is our conception of death which decides our answers to all the questions that life puts to us....
    —Dag Hammarskjöld

When death is imminent, we open our hearts quickly and wide....
    —Hazel B. André

Suicide may be regarded as an experiment—a question which man puts to Nature, trying to force her to an answer. The question is this: What change will death produce in a man's existence and in his insight into the nature of things? It is a clumsy experiment to make; for it involves the destruction of the very consciousness which puts the question and awaits the answer....
    —Arthur Schopenhauer

Death is not an evil, for it liberates from all evils, and if it deprives man of any good thing it also takes away his desire for it....
    —Giacomo Leopardi

To die is only to be as we were before we were born; yet no one feels any remorse or regret, or repugnance, in contemplating this last idea. It is rather a relief and disburdening of the mind....
    —William Hazlitt

To die is landing on some distant shore....
    —John Dryden

One should depart from life as Ulysses parted from Nausicaa—blessing it rather than in love with it....
    —Friedrich W. Nietzsche

Death is considered to be a traumatic experience, but understand what happens. That which has been born, the knowledge "I Am," will end. That knowledge which was limited by this body will then become unlimited, so what is to be feared?...

—*Nisargadatta*

The truest end of life is to know that life never ends....Death is no more than a turning us over from time to eternity....

—*William Penn*

Just as one must learn the art of killing in training for violence, so one must learn the art of dying in the training of non-violence....

—*Mohandas Gandhi*

O man, do not be afraid of death at all. Thou art immortal. Death is not the opposite of life. It is only a phase of life. Life flows on ceaselessly. The fruit perishes but the seed is full of life. The seed dies but a huge tree grows out of the seed. The tree perishes but it becomes coal which has rich life. Water disappears but it becomes the invisible steam which contains the seed of new life. The stone disappears but it becomes lime which is full of new life. The physical sheath only is thrown but life persists....

—*Sivananda*

All we have thought of as adventure in this world pales beside the most exciting adventure of all: our return to Real Reality....

—*Iris Belhayes*

There is no such thing as death. In nature nothing dies. From each sad remnant of decay some forms of life arise....

—*Charles Mackay*

Death no longer seems the final end it used to be, but rather the entrance to a new and free existence which includes all space and time....

—*Charles Lindbergh*

If you ask, does a man live beyond death, I answer No, not in any sense comprehensible to the mind of man which itself dies at death, and if you ask, does a man altogether die at death, I answer No, for what dies is what belongs to this world of form and illusion....

—*Gautama Buddha*

The knowledge that we will die burns out our attachments to the dignified madness of our socially constructed existence. Death is an ally that helps us to release our clinging to social position, material accumulation, and superficial desires as a source of ultimate security....

—*Duane Elgin*

Inexorable—that is what death is like. We hide and run away from it; we use every trick and illusion we know to fend it off. But death will find us, whatever corner of the world we run to....

—*Piero Ferrucci*

Nothing can happen more beautiful than death....

—*Walt Whitman*

Death is no enemy of man; it is a friend who, when the work of life is done, just cuts the cord that binds the human boat to earth, that it may sail on smoother seas....

—*Matheno*

When you take the wires of a cage apart, you do not hurt the bird, but you help it. You let it out of prison. How do you know that death does not help me when it takes the wires of my cage down?—that it does not release me, and put me into some better place and better condition of life?...

—*Randolph S. Foster*

Think not disdainfully of death, but look upon it with favor for Nature wills it like all else....Look for the hour when the soul shall emerge from its sheath....

—*Marcus Aurelius*

Death is only pushing aside the portiere and passing from one room to another....I think of death as a glad awakening from this troubled sleep which we call life; as an emancipation from the world which, beautiful though it be, is still a land of captivity....
—*Lyman Abbott*

If at the death of your body you are a mere hoarder of things, you will be tied to those things by bonds and chains (of thought), which, though invisible, are as real as chains of iron....
—*Prentice Mulford*

We should not fear death, for then we cease to live fully now....
—*Doris Webster Havice*

Among all the passions inflicted from without, death holds first place....Consequently, when a person conquers death and things directed to death, this is a most perfect victory....
—*Thomas Aquinas*

Men fear death as children fear to go into the dark; and as that natural fear in children is increased with tales, so is the other....
—*Francis Bacon*

Death? Translated into the heavenly tongue, that word means life....
—*Henry W. Beecher*

How do I know that the love of life is not a delusion after all? How do I know but that he who dreads death is not as a child who has lost his way and does not know his way home?...
—*Chuang Tse*

The end of everything that is born is death....construction must result in destruction of that which is constructed. It is a law of nature that birth ends in death and death leads to birth....
—*Sathya Sai Baba*

Do not grudge your brother his rest. He has at last become free, safe and immortal....Your brother has not lost the light of day, but has obtained a more enduring light. He has not left us, but has gone before us....
—*Seneca*

To meet death not only as an event at the end of life but as an ever-present ingredient in the life process itself is the final goal to be sought....
—*J. Bruce Long*

Death is not a foe, but an inevitable adventure....
—*Oliver Lodge*

After your death you will be what you were before your birth....
—*Arthur Schopenhauer*

As a well-spent day brings happy sleep, so life well used brings happy death....
—*Leonardo Da Vinci*

Dissolution of the body is no more than sleep. Just as a man sleeps and wakes up, so is death and birth. Death is like sleep. Birth is like waking up. Death brings promotion to a new and better life. A man of discrimination and wisdom is not afraid of death. He knows that death is the gate of life. Death to him is no longer a skeleton bearing a sword to cut the thread of life, but rather an angel who has a golden key to unlock for him the door to a wider, fuller and happier existence....
—*Sivananda*

We should weep for men at their birth, not at their death....
—*Baron de Montesquieu*

Life is eternal and love is immortal; and death is only a horizon; and a horizon is nothing save the limit of our sight....
—*Rossiter Raymond*

We cannot tell. We do not know. But whether death is an end or the beginning, we must not fear. For death is perfect rest and peace. The dead do not suffer....   —*Robert Ingersoll*

We understand death for the first time when he puts his hand upon one whom we love....   —*Madame de Staël*

There is no death. They only truly live who pass into the life beyond, and see this earth as but a school preparative for higher ministry....
    —*John Oxenham*

Nature invented death that there might be new life....   —*Johann W. Goethe*

We cannot rationally feel sorry for the departed person....because as dead he is completely insensitive to all such things as any piece of earth or non-living matter. He is just exactly as nonexistent as he was before birth and conception....   —*Corliss Lamont*

Death is only an old door set in a garden wall....   —*Nancy Byrd Turner*

There is no need to be fearful of death. It is nature's way to recycle superfluous trash. The body becomes food for the worms and the spirit ascends to heavenly planes....   —*Anonymous*

The spirit of man, which God inspired, cannot together perish with this corporeal clod....   —*John Milton*

On the day of his death, a man feels he has lived but a single day....
    —*The Zohar*

It is impossible that anything so natural as death, so necessary, and so universal as death should ever have been designed as an evil to mankind....
    —*Jonathan Swift*

The person who loves God is not afraid of death because it's looking into the face of God....   —*Ignatius Loyola*

Although I want to live and labor as long as God lets me, I consider the moment of my death as the most precious of my life....
    —*Friedrich von Schiller*

Death, so called, is a thing which makes men weep, and yet a third of life is passed in sleep....   —*George Byron*

I find it is natural to believe that death is not a disastrous sundown but rather a spiritual sunrise, ushering in the unconjectured splendors of immortality....   —*Archibald Rutledge*

Death holds terrors for us. This is because we think we are merely physical bodies subject to birth, growth, decay and death. To shed this fear we must realize that we are immortal and that even if the body perishes we are not going to perish. Only when fear leaves our hearts we shall remain in peace....   —*Papa Ramdas*

Death is the greatest of all human blessings....   —*Plato*

The tomb is not a blind alley; it is a thoroughfare. It closes on the twilight, it opens on the dawn....
    —*Victor Hugo*

Everything science has taught me—and continues to teach me—strengthens my belief in the continuity of our spiritual existence after death....
    —*Werner von Braun*

It is only in the face of death that man's self is born....   —*Augustine*

Think not disdainfully of death, but look on it with favor; for even death is one of the things that Nature wills....
    —*Ptolemy*

At the death of every living being the spirit returns to the world of spirits and the body to the world of bodies. But only the bodies change in the process. The world of spirit is a single spirit standing like a light in back of the world of bodies and shining through each individual that comes into existence as through a window....

—*Aziz Nasifi*

Death....Why worry one's head over a thing that is inevitable? Why die before one's death?... —*Mohandas Gandhi*

Readiness for death is that of character rather than occupation. It is right living which prepares for safe or even joyous dying.... —*Jacques Bossuet*

Living is death; dying is life. On this side of the grave we are exiles, on that, citizens; on this side orphans, on that, children; on this side, captives, on that, freeman; on this side disguised, unknown, on that, disclosed and proclaimed as the sons of God....

—*Henry W. Beecher*

The living all find death unpleasant, men mourn over it. And yet, what is death, but the unbending of the bow and its return to its case; what is it but the emptying of the corporal envelope?... —*Chuang Tse*

People fear death because what happens at death is unknown. However....I look forward to the change called death as life's last great adventure....

—*Peace Pilgrim*

The Aramaic word for death translates: "not here present elsewhere." This ancient concept of death best describes the near-death experience and what happens to those who go through it. These people were present—elsewhere.... —*P. M. H. Atwater*

Death does not exist. There must be another life. The contrary would even be more impossible....

—*Robert Muller*

What better can the Lord do for man than take him home when he has done his work?... —*Charles Kingsley*

The fear of death keeps us from living, not from dying.... —*Paul Roud*

The dead take to the grave, clutched in their hands, only what they have given away.... —*DeWitt Wallace*

One of the most common errors is the notion that pain and dying are inseparable companions. The truth is that they rarely go together. Occasionally, the act of dissolution is a painful one, but this should be the exception to the general rule.... —*Edward Clarke*

Somebody should tell us, right from the start of our lives, that we are dying. Then we might live life to the limit, every minute of the day....There are only so many tomorrows....

—*Michael Landon*

Death is a punishment to some, to some a gift, and to many a favor....

—*Seneca*

If you love others, let them know it while they live. Tributes after death never equal one encouraging smile or one friendly handclasp while the loved one is living....

—*Fred Van Amburgh*

Of all the things that move man, one of the principle ones is the terror of death....The idea of death, the fear of it, haunts the human animal like nothing else.... —*Ernest Becker*

The loss of friends by the transition we call death will not cause sorrow to the soul that has come into this higher realization....that there is no such thing as death, for each one is not only a partaker, but an eternal partaker, of this Infinite Life. He knows that the mere falling away of the physical body by no means affects real soul life....
— *Ralph W. Trine*

What is death? A mask. Turn it and be convinced. See, it does not bite....
— *Epictetus*

A man's dying is more the survivor's affair than his own....
— *Thomas Mann*

What is death at most? It is a journey for a season: a sleep longer than usual. If thou feared death, thou shouldest also fear sleep.... — *John Chrysostom*

Death is but a casting-off of old clothes.... — *Sathya Sai Baba*

Death is a great adventure, but none need go unconvinced that there is an issue to it. The man of faith may face it as Columbus faced his first voyage from the shores of Spain....that the sea has another shore....
— *Harry E. Fosdick*

Bodies are like pillowcases. It doesn't matter whether they remain or drop off.... — *Ramakrishna*

To be afraid of death is like being afraid of discarding an old worn-out garment.... — *Mohandas Gandhi*

Death is not a period but a comma in the story of life.... — *Amos J. Traver*

Death is no more traumatic than taking off an old coat....
— *Eknath Easwaran*

Never is the undying Self born nor does it die; never did it come to be nor will it come not to be: Unborn, eternal, everlasting is the primordial Self. It is not slain when the body is slain....
— *Bhagavad-Gita*

Whatever state of being one calls to mind at the end upon leaving aside his body, to that very state he attains, always being in that state....
— *Tibetan Book of the Dead*

Death is but a new birth into a new state. Death is not to be feared, any more than birth. When the body ceases to be, the spirit emerges, free and unencumbered. I shall be richer all my life for this sorrow.... — *Shirley H. Jeffrey*

The premeditation of death is the premeditation of liberty. As a person has learned how to die he has learned how not to be a slave....
— *Michel Montaigne*

Death strikes without notice: the young and the old, the well and the sickly, the high and the low, the rich and the poor. It is no respecter of persons. There is no lasting peace as long as the person is still in the body. Therefore, one should not place any trust in a life which is sustained by so uncertain a thing as breathing in and out....
— *J. Bruce Long*

People are afraid to die, because they do not know what is death....the moment you know your real being, you are afraid of nothing. Death gives freedom and power.... — *Nisargadatta*

Death is transition. Our body dies and it breaks correspondence with our physical environment. But our life is in the spirit, and this life is eternal. Life never dies. Bodies cease, but life is eternal.... — *Alfred A. Montapert*

Death: where the changing mist of doubts will vanish at a breath, and the mountain peaks of truth will appear....
—*Rabindranath Tagore*

Death is the final stage of growth in this life. There is no total death. Only the body dies. The self or the spirit, or whatever you may wish to label it, is eternal. You may interpret this in any way that makes you comfortable....
—*Elisabeth Kubler-Ross*

The moment comes when the great nurse, death, takes man, the child, by the hand and quietly says, "It is time to go home. Night is coming. It is your bedtime, child of earth. Come; you're tired. Lie down at last in the quiet nursery of nature and sleep. Sleep well. The day is gone. Stars shine in the canopy of eternity."...
—*Joshua Liebman*

Is there any doctrine of immortality that can say anything more simple yet definite about man's fate after death? He has come from and returns to God....
—*Hermann Cohen*

Know that the body is like a garment. Go seek the wearer of the garment....You are such that without the material body you have a spiritual body; do not, then, dread the going forth of the soul from the body....Your fear of death is really fear of yourself; see what it is from which you are fleeing!...
—*Rumi*

Men fear death only because death is the ending of sense pleasures....
—*Anonymous*

Let death be daily before your eyes, and you will never entertain any abject thought, nor too eagerly covet anything....
—*Epictetus*

The foolish fear death as the greatest of evils, the wise deserve it as a rest after labors and the end of ills....Death is not only not an evil but a good thing....
—*St. Ambrose*

Death for those who understand it is immortality, but for those unenlightened ones, who do not understand it, it is death....
—*St. Antony the Great*

The meaning we find in life cannot be separated from the meaning we give death. Seen from the outside, death is an end—from the inside, a beginning. Properly died, death is a total release: letting ourselves go, letting ourselves sink, letting ourselves fade into nothingness and fuse with the fullness of eternity....
—*Karlfried G. Durckheim*

It is not hard to die. It is harder, a thousand times harder, to live....
—*Henry W. Beecher*

Nothing is dead. People feign themselves dead, and endure mock funerals and mournful obituaries. And there they stand, looking out the window, sound and well in some strange new disguise....
—*Ralph W. Emerson*

Life is going forth, death is returning home....
—*Lao-tzu*

At the time of death, the mind forgets the existing body and enters into another body. Whether you will it or not, what is designed to happen will certainly happen as ordained by God. Hence, it is advisable to leave all sorrows to God and live in peace....
—*Lakshmana*

The fear of death is more to be dreaded then death itself....
—*Publilius Syrus*

Not by lamentations and mournful chants ought we to celebrate the funeral of a good man, but by hymns, for in ceasing to be numbered to mortals, he enters upon the heritage of a diviner life....
—*Plutarch*

Death is a tax the soul must pay for having a name and form....
—*Hazrat Inayat Khan*

Alas for those who never sing but die with all their music in them....
—*Oliver W. Holmes*

I like to compare the change called death to that of going to sleep at night and losing consciousness, but awakening again in the morning to full consciousness without any suffering or without any violation of nature's laws....
—*H. Spenser Lewis*

The goal of all life is death....
—*Sigmund Freud*

Death opens unknown doors. It is most grand to die....
—*John Masefield*

Death used to announce itself in the thick of life but now people drag on so long, it sometimes seems that we are reaching the stage when we have to announce ourselves to death....
—*Ronald Blythe*

Nobody is born or dies at any time; it is the mind that conceives its birth and death and its migration to other bodies and other worlds....
—*Yoga Vasistha*

A dying man needs to die as a sleeping man needs to sleep, and there comes a time when it is wrong, as well as useless, to resist....
—*Stewart Alsop*

Don't be afraid your life will end; be afraid it will never begin....
—*Grace Hanson*

Death....is no more than passing from one room into another. But there's a difference for me, you know. Because in that other room I shall be able to see....
—*Helen Keller*

Death is a debt we all must pay....
—*Euripides*

Death is for many the gate of hell; but we are inside on the way out, not on the outside on the way in....
—*George B. Shaw*

Death is one of life's many illusions, drawing our attention to the perishing and makes us lose sight of the permanent and imperishable....
—*Erik Plamstierna*

There is no evil in life to the man who is thoroughly convinced that to be deprived of life is not evil; to be ready to die frees us from bondage and thralldom....
—*Michel Montaigne*

When death comes, he respects neither age nor merit. He sweeps from this earthly existence the sick and the strong, the rich and the poor, and should teach us to live to be prepared for death....
—*Andrew Jackson*

Why do we dread death so much? Death is our redeemer....We should thankfully enjoy its blessed wine....
—*Solomon Ibn Gabirol*

A solemn funeral is inconceivable to the Chinese mind....
—*Lin Yutang*

Death, when it approaches, ought not to take one by surprise. It should be part of the full expectancy of life....
—*Muriel Spark*

Weep not for him who departs from life, for there is no suffering beyond death....
—*Palladas*

They that love beyond the world, cannot be separated. Death cannot kill what never dies. Nor can Spirits ever be divided that love and live in the same Divine Principle.... —*William Penn*

We weep when we are born, not when we die!... —*Thomas B. Aldrich*

Death is only the servant who opens the door when Providence rings the bell, and ushers you into a larger building.... —*George H. Hepworth*

The gods conceal from men the happiness of death, that they may endure life.... —*Lucan*

The end of birth is death; the end of death is birth; this is ordained.... —*Edwin Arnold*

We only die once and the great mystery is in knowing what it is going to be like. How can we possibly prepare for it? The answer is that death exists within life. Life is just a series of changes. All the little deaths that occur within life are teaching us to let go.... —*Sogyal Rinpoche*

Life and death are one thread, the same line viewed from different sides.... —*Lao-tzu*

Death consists chiefly in getting rid of a worn-out husk which is left behind, much in the same way as the chrysalis sheath of a moth or as the husks of a growing bud or bulbs are peeled off.... —*Paul Twitchell*

If life must not be taken too seriously— then so neither must death.... —*Samuel Butler*

If some people died, and others did not die, death would indeed be a terrible affliction.... —*Jean La Bruyere*

Death is common in the world. Everyone in it must one day or other doff the physical part of living. Hence, it is not at all proper to be afraid of it....While the body perishes, the Spirit is immortal. We are here to realize we are the spirit. Body is only a vesture, a mask, or a vehicle, impermanent and transitory.... —*Papa Ramdas*

While I thought that I was learning how to live, I have been learning how to die.... —*Leonardo Da Vinci*

Death is an illusion....What people call death is the intensification and reinvigoration of life.... —*Abraham I. Kook*

There awaits men at death what they do not expect or think.... —*Heraclitus*

Death has nothing terrible which life has not made so....this world is the land of dying; the next is the land of living.... —*Tryon Edwards*

Death is a beautiful liberation into freer life. The limiting clay garment, the body, is put aside. The self-centered nature goes with you to learn and grow on the disembodied side of life, and then returns here into a suitable clay garment and suitable circumstances to learn the lessons we need to learn.... —*Peace Pilgrim*

When you stop learning, stop listening, stop looking and asking questions, then it is time to die.... —*Lillian Smith*

I will be dead in a few months. But it hasn't given me the slightest anxiety or worry. I always knew I was going to die.... —*B. F. Skinner*

Death is experienced only once; but he who fears it dies each minute.... —*Solomon Rubin*

I regard death as a friend, a valet who helps one off with ones's physical plane overcoat when it is worn out or in any other way no longer usable....
—*George S. Arundale*

No man who is fit to live need fear to die. To us here, death is the most terrible thing we know. But when we have tasted its reality it will mean to us birth, deliverance, a new creation of ourselves. It will be what health is to the sick man; what home is to the exile; what the loved one given back is to the bereaved.... —*Thomas Fuller*

Once you accept your own death, all of a sudden you are free to live. You no longer care about your reputation....you no longer care except so far as your life can be used tactically to promote a cause you believe in.... —*Saul Alinsky*

Death is just a distant rumor to the young.... —*Andy Rooney*

There are some odd things about human dying....that don't fit at all with the notion of agony at the end. People who almost die but don't, and then recover to describe the experience, never mention anguish or pain, or even despair; to the contrary, they recall a strange feeling of tranquility and peace.... —*Lewis Thomas*

There is no suffering for him who has finished his journey, and abandoned grief, who has faced himself on all sides, and thrown off all fetters....
—*Dhammapada*

Are you afraid you don't know how to die? Don't worry. Nature will take care of that for you.... —*Marco Vassi*

At death, if at any time, we see ourselves as we are, and display our true characters.... —*Robert Benson*

After death, the soul goes to the next world bearing in mind the subtle impressions of its deeds, and after reaping their harvest returns again to this world of action.... —*The Upanishads*

To pass from midnight to noon on the sudden, to be decrepit one minute and all spirit and activity the next, must be a desirable change. To call this dying is an abuse of language....
—*Jeremy Taylor*

We are but tenants and....shortly, the great Landlord will give us notice that our lease has expired....
—*Joseph Jefferson*

The act of dying is one of the acts of life.... —*Marcus Aurelius*

Death....is a transition from one state of being to another. The lowly silkworm, after weaving his silken shroud, is transformed into a radiant butterfly....
—*Charles F. Alsop*

To die will be an awfully big adventure.... —*James M. Barrie*

Every man faces two deaths and not just one. There is the biological event marked by mortuaries and monuments. But there is also the personal event, the spiritual death, which often goes unnoticed.... —*Carl Micholson*

Death is merely a change of clothing....We are what we are....
—*André Luiz*

To fear death....is nothing other than to think oneself wise when one is not; for it is to think one knows what one does not know. No man knows whether death may not even turn out to be the greatest of blessings for a human being; and yet people fear it as if they knew for certain that it is the greatest of evils.... —*Socrates*

Death is a golden key that opens the palace of eternity.... —*John Milton*

When man departs this life, he divests himself of all the veils which cover him.... —*The Zohar*

As soon as a man comes to life, he is immediately old enough to die.... —*Der Ackermon aus Böhmen*

Nothing can be accomplished after death in the way of spiritual liberation unless it is at least begun during this life.... —*Santon ki Shiksha*

Death is the certain end of all pain, and all capacity to suffer pain. Of all the things that man thinks of as evils, this is the last.... —*Johann G. Fichte*

O death, where is thy sting? O grave, where is thy victory?... —*Paul of Tarsus*

Death is to put off a garment. For the body is about the soul as a garment; and after laying this aside for a short time by means of death, we shall resume it again with the more splendor.... —*John Chrysostom*

Death is like an arrow that is already in flight, and your life lasts only until it reaches you.... —*Hermes*

Whoever is interested in life is particularly interested in death.... —*Thomas Mann*

Let me tell you as one who has witnessed many deaths, that in my experience I have never seen one that was unhappy.... —*Leslie D. Weatherhead*

Science has found that nothing can disappear without a trace. Nature does not know extinction. All it knows is transformation.... —*Werner von Braun*

My present experience is that Eternal Life does not begin after death, but that we start living it now; only it is masked by our daily cares, and it is only on contact with death, perhaps, that we discover it. God is not a God of the dead, but of the living, since for him they are all living.... —*Theo Bovet*

A man abandons worn-out clothes and acquires new ones, so when the body is worn out a new one is acquired by the self, who lives within.... —*Bhagavad-Gita*

To die is a debt we must all of us discharge....The dead have no tears, and forget all sorrow.... —*Euripides*

The secret of the world is that all things subsist and do not die, but only retire a little from sight and afterwards return again.... —*Ralph W. Emerson*

Death is but a sharp corner near the beginning of life's procession down eternity.... —*Ayscough*

Birth and death are like ships: why do we rejoice over a ship setting out on a journey when we know not what she may encounter on the seas? We should rejoice when the ship returns safely to the port.... —*Midrash Tanhuma*

This life is only a prelude to eternity. For that which we call death is but a pause, in truth, a progress into life.... —*Seneca*

On the day when death will knock at thy door, what will you offer him? I will set before my guest the full vessel of my life. I will never let him go with empty hands.... —*Rabindranath Tagore*

The body is nothing but a covering over our soul, and when it is gone we are not dead; just as we do not think that we are dead when our coat is worn out, or if someone tears our shirt. The moment when a person dies is the only moment when he feels he is dead. The impression of this dying condition, the hopelessness of the doctor, the sorrow and grief of the family cause this impression. After death, as he recovers from this, he gradually finds himself alive....for the great burden has been removed.... —*Hazrat Inayat Khan*

Death *(Last Words)*

The hour I have long wished for is now come.... —*Teresa of Avila*

Dear me! I must be turning into a god.... —*Vespasian*

Why do you weep? Did you think I should live forever?...*(last days)*
—*Louis XIV*

I want to meet my God awake....
(refused drugs on deathbed)
—*Maria Theresa*

I have been dying for twenty years, now I am going to live....
—*James D. Burns*

I am a broken machine. I am ready to go.... —*Woodrow Wilson*

Let us be kinder to one another....
—*Aldous Huxley*

There is no reality to my sickness. There is no reality to my death....
—*Milarepa*

Let us cross the river and rest in the shade.... —*Stonewall Jackson*

It's been very interesting....
—*Mary Wortly Montagu*

If this is death, it is easier than life....
—*Robert L. Stevenson*

I go from a corruptible to an incorruptible crown, where no disturbance can take place....*(last words on scaffold)*
—*Charles I England*

Why fear death? It is the most beautiful adventure in life....*(last words before going down on the Lusitania)*
—*Charles Frohman*

Dying is a wild night and a new road....
(night of death) —*Emily Dickinson*

This is the last of earth! I am content....
—*John Quincy Adams*

Now comes the mystery....
—*Henry W. Beecher*

I shall hear in heaven....
—*Beethoven (who was deaf)*

I leave this world without a regret....
—*Henry D. Thoreau*

Do let me die in peace....
—*Voltaire*

Light, light, the world needs more light.... —*Johann W. Goethe*

I am going to that country which I have all my life wished to see....
—*William Blake*

This is not the end of me....
—*Henry C. Bonnerman*

If I had the strength to hold a pen, I would write down how easy and pleasant it is to die.... —*William Hunter*

Turn up the lights; I don't want to go home in the dark.... —*O. Henry*

God will forgive me; that's his business.... —*Heinrich Heine*

It is very beautiful over there.... —*Thomas Edison*

Midnight strikes. One more step towards the grave.... *(last words in diary)* —*Henri F. Amiel*

Depression/Despair

You can be healed (of depression) if every day you begin the first thing in the morning to consider how you will bring a real joy to someone else.... —*Alfred Adler*

The biggest disease today is not leprosy or tuberculosis, but rather the feeling of being unwanted.... —*Mother Teresa*

The attitude of unhappiness is not only painful, it is mean and ugly.... —*William James*

Unhappiness is best defined as the difference between our talents and our expectations.... —*Edward de Bono*

Man's unhappiness....comes of his greatness; it is because there is an Infinite in him, which, with all his cunning, he cannot quite bury under the finite.... —*Thomas Carlyle*

It is ironic that man should feel such a painful void inside of himself when he lives in a world of so many things....but which apparently cannot fill the heart.... —*John Powell*

Whenever you feel dissatisfied with life and the way things are going....if we just wait a little while, we will eventually see that the way God is doing things is the right way, the best way, and (in the final analysis) the only way.... —*Elinor MacDonald*

When the thickness of anger is repressed, it thins, spreading out into a cloud of despair.... —*Anonymous*

Men who are unhappy, like men who sleep badly, are always proud of the fact.... —*Bertrand Russell*

Don't let life discourage you: everyone who got where he is had to begin where he was.... —*Richard Evans*

Almost anything carried to a logical extreme becomes depressing.... —*Ursula K. LeGuin*

Depression is a disorder of mood, so mysteriously painful and elusive....as to verge close to being beyond description.... —*William Styron*

Despair is the price one pays for setting oneself an impossible aim.... —*Graham Greene*

We seldom think of what we have but always of what we lack.... —*Arthur Schopenhauer*

No one can ever gain strength by brooding over his weakness.... —*Paramananda*

Depression is rage spread thin.... —*Paul Tillich*

Noble deeds and hot baths are the best cures for depression.... —*Dodie Smith*

Helplessness leads to panic, and panic leads to depression....
—*Martin E. P. Seligman*

The essence to remove from yourself is every hint of the bitter blackness of depression. The fundamental reason why people are far from God is because of depression....   —*Rabbi Nachman*

Despondency is ingratitude; hope is God's worship....   —*Henry W. Beecher*

When we close our cheerful hearts, we shut the sunshine in. When we draw down the shades, we darken our spirits. The dejected, depressed, damp-spirited men—the melancholy, dumpy people have had, and always will have, a hard time of it....   —*Fred Van Amburgh*

In separation from God is man's greatest misery....   —*Mohandas Gandhi*

Depression occurs when you are not being yourself. You're probably doing things you don't want to do....
—*Eda LeShan*

Misery is not absence of happiness, but limited happiness. For as happiness recedes misery pours in....
—*Tripura Rahasya*

It is certainly wrong to despair; and if despair is wrong, hope is right....
—*John Lubbock*

Gloom is an epidemic disease. All those who come in contact with gloomy people are immediately affected. A gloomy man should cover his face when he comes out....
—*Sivananda*

Depression is the inability to construct a future....   —*Rollo May*

When I am depressed, somewhere deep inside, I know that I am denying the Presence of God....
—*Gerald Jampolsky*

A self-pitying life is a doomed life. Only the life which deliberately picks up and starts over again is victorious....
—*James G. Gilkey*

Melancholy is born of self-importance....   —*Nancy D. Potts*

There is nothing more insidious than that solacing self-pity which would rather bear a woe than induce the anguish which its removal requires. Worse still, if an individual identifies himself as an underling, continually stating, "I can't win," he diminishes his power to achieve, crippling himself against all future endeavor....
—*David Seabury*

Sadness usually results from one of the following causes—either when a man does not succeed, or is ashamed of his success....   —*Seneca*

Self-pity gets you nowhere. One must have the adventurous daring to accept oneself as a bundle of possibilities and undertake the most interesting game in the world—making the most of one's best....   —*Harry E. Fosdick*

We are unhappy only when we want things other than they are....
—*Lucy Cornellssen*

Pity was invented by the weak....
—*Mendele M. Seforim*

Gloom and sadness are poison to us....
—*Madame Sevigne*

Despair is the damp of hell, as joy is the serenity of heaven....   —*John Donne*

Depression cannot exist in the presence of God....
—*Shantidasa*

God allows us to experience the low points of life in order to teach us lessons we could not learn in any other way. The way to learn these lessons is not to deny the feelings but to find the meanings underlying them....
—*Stanley Lindquest*

By sadness you destroy the divine image in your soul. God is joy....
—*Lombez*

To be melancholy is to be forever thinking of oneself.... —*Comtesse Diane*

When the clouds of depression start gathering, we must do something constructive to dispel them. The mind that can contemplate goodness will be prepared for such emergencies and provide some safety valve for the occasion.... —*Lowell R. Ditzen*

Never despair, but if you do, work on in despair.... —*Edmund Burke*

Despair is the offspring of fear, of laziness, and of impatience; it argues a defect of spirit and resolution, and often of honesty too....
—*Jeremy Collier*

Despondency is not a state of humility. On the contrary, it is a vexation and despair of a cowardly pride; nothing is worse.... —*Francois Fenelon*

Man is only miserable as far as he thinks himself so....
—*Jacopo Sannazaro*

One must never despair if something is lost to one, a person or a joy or a happiness; everything comes back again more gloriously.... —*Rainer M. Rilke*

Despair is the rejection of God within oneself....
—*Antoine de Saint-Exupery*

We have no more right to put our discordant states of mind into the lives of those around us and rob them of their sunshine and brightness than we have to enter their houses and steal their silverware.... —*Julia Mosileton*

What poison is to food, self-pity is to life.... —*Oliver C. Wilson*

The mass of men lead lives of quiet desperation. What is called resignation is confirmed desperation....
—*Henry D. Thoreau*

Sometimes sadness and sorrow wash the eyes with the tears of a more perfect understanding....
—*Fred Van Amburgh*

He that despairs measures Providence by his own little contracted model and limits infinite power to finite apprehension.... —*Robert Smith*

A lot of what passes for depression these days is nothing more than a body saying that it needs work....
—*Geoffrey Norman*

He who despairs wants love and faith, for faith, hope and love are three torches which blend their light together, nor does one shine without the other....
—*Pietro Metastais*

Misery acquaints man with strange bedfellows....
—*William Shakespeare*

Sorrows are like thunderclouds. Far off they look black, but directly over us merely gray.... —*Jean Paul Richter*

Sorrow is a form of self-pity....
—*Robert F. Kennedy*

When a person drowns himself in negative thinking he is committing an unspeakable crime against himself....
—*Maxwell Maltz*

The great enemy of the soul is not trial but sadness, which is the bleeding wound of self-love....
—*William B. Villathorne*

In depression we look for evidence of anger behind the saddened aspect...
—*Albert Rothenberg*

It is impious in a good man to be sad....
—*Owen D. Young*

Keep aloof from sadness for sadness is a sickness of the soul. Life has, indeed, many ills, but the mind that views every object in its most cheering aspect, and every doubtful dispensation as replete with latent good, bears within itself a powerful and perpetual antidote.... —*Lydia Sigourney*

The best thing for being sad is to learn something.... —*T. H. White*

As high as we have mounted in delight, in our dejection do we sink as low....
—*William Wordsworth*

We wear the chains we forge in life....
—*Charles Dickens*

What we call despair is often only the painful eagerness of unfed hope....
—*George Eliot*

People ruled by the mood of gloom attract to them gloomy things. People always discouraged and despondent do not succeed at anything, and live only by burdening someone else....
—*Ralph W. Trine*

It is impossible for that man to despair who remembers his Helper is omnipotent.... —*Jeremy Taylor*

Look at the discontented, gloomy, melancholy and ill-tempered men or women, and you see in their faces proof of this silent force of their unpleasant thought, cutting, carving, and shaping them to present expression.... —*Prentice Mulford*

Every day can be a blue day to you, every night just another night of misery; you produce in your daily life these very things by constantly impressing wrong ideas upon your mind.... —*Norman V. Peale*

Through depression we not only drag ourselves down but we drag others down with us....One who is melancholy has no right to touch another person's life.... —*Paramananda*

A morose, gloomy man cannot attract and influence people. He is an infectious parasite amidst society. He spreads gloom everywhere....
—*Sivananda*

The cause of your misery is not in your outer life; it is in you, as your ego. You impose limitations on yourself and then make a vain struggle to transcend them.... —*Ramana Maharshi*

If a melancholic person broods over his misery, he is sure to become even more miserable, instead of recognizing his misery as unfounded.... Melancholy, as every other wrong attitude, is due to a false mental starting point....
—*Hans-Ulrick Rieker*

Some people are sad because certain things are not present and sadder because other things are present....
—*Narayana*

Melancholy sees the worst of things—as they may be, and not as they are. It looks upon a beautiful face, and sees a grinning skull.... *—Christian Bovee*

Melancholy is a symptom of on-coming sickness.... *—Nahman Bratzlav*

Although others may feel sorry for you, never feel sorry for yourself—it has a deadly effect on spiritual well-being. "Before the eyes can see they must have lost the power to shed tears."...
—Peace Pilgrim

When any fit of....gloominess or perversion of the mind lays hold upon you, make it a rule not to publish it by complaints but exert your whole care to hide it. By endeavoring to hide it, you will drive it away.... *—Samuel Johnson*

Do not appraise your disappoint-ments too quickly. Disappointment is often good luck in disguise—often Providence piloting your boat through the channel of circum-stance....
—Fred Van Amburgh

Sadness is so ungrateful....
—Han Suyin

You have no responsibility to join gloomy people or even be around them. Surround yourself with happy faces—people who are interested in growing and enjoying.... *—Wayne Dyer*

There are men who are like malarious swamps, poisonous, depressing and weakening by their presence. They make heavy, oppressive and gloomy the atmosphere of their own homes.... And there are other men who seem like the ocean; they are constantly bracing, stimulating, giving new drafts of tonic life and strength by their very presence.... *—William G. Jordan*

Make not a close friend of a melancholy, sad person. He will be sure to increase your adversity and decrease your good fortune. He goes always heavily loaded, and you must bear half.... *—Francois Fenelon*

Despair is the absolute extreme of self-love.... *—Thomas Merton*

Desire

Want is a growing giant whom the coat of have was never large enough to cover....
—Ralph W. Emerson

When all the desires that surge in the heart are renounced, the mortal becomes immortal. When all the knots that strangle the heart are loosened, the mortal becomes immortal....
—The Upanishads

Without desire, there is nothing to possess. Without attachment, there is nothing to bind....With each desire and attachment, we forge a chain, link by link, to anchor us to the world of form, thought and concept....
—A Spiritual Warrior

It's very important to get your desires centered so you will desire only to do God's will for you. You can come to a point of oneness of desire, just to know and do your part in the Life Pattern. When you think about it, is there anything else as really important to desire?... *—Peace Pilgrim*

The more one yields to desire, the more insatiable it will become....
—Mahabharata

Desire never ceases its demands. It doesn't let a man rest, day or night....It never relents, nor does it slacken its chains or cease to apply the lash, even though the poor victim lies weak and spent upon his death bed. Even then a desire to live....still holds on....
—Julian P. Johnson

Desire tells us, each time, "Now get thou this, and then you shall be happy."...The fact is, desire is a bottomless pit which can never fill up, or like the all-consuming fire which burns the fiercer, the more we feed it....
—Lakshmana Sarma

Man is insatiable for power; he is infantile in his desires and, always discontented with what he has, loves only what he has not....
—Joseph de Maistre

All desires can cause you trouble, even spiritual ones....   *—Annamalai Swami*

We cannot be free of nagging desires through suppression. This is like trying to keep a rubber boat beneath the water. But we remove compulsive desires altogether by understanding their nature....   *—Vernon Howard*

Pleasure is beguiling; it has a dangerous tendency to take over....
—Fernando Savater

There is no calamity greater than lavish desires....   *—Lao-tzu*

Every attachment is a sign of our insuficiency....A truly happy being is a solitary being....   *—Jean J. Rousseau*

If men could regard the events of their lives with more open minds, they would frequently discover that they did not really desire the things they failed to obtain....   *—André Maurois*

The lust for comfort, that stealthy thing that enters the house a guest, then becomes a host, and then a master....
—Kahlil Gibran

Do not become attached to the things you like; do not maintain an aversion to the things you dislike. Sorrow, fear and bondage come from likes and dislikes....   *—Gautama Buddha*

The deepest human urge is the desire to be important....   *—John Dewey*

The letter of the law deals with the acts of man; the spirit of the law takes note of his desires....   *—The Aquarian Gospel*

To identify with any desire keeps you separate from God....   *—Vivekananda*

Man's many desires are like the small metal coins he carries about in his pocket. The more he has, the more they weigh him down....   *—Sathya Sai Baba*

People who constantly find new disguises for their desires can easily lie to themselves....   *—Hans-Ulrich Rieker*

Where desire is, there is no bliss; where bliss is, there is no desire....
—Sivananda

The more you find yourself yielding to desires, the more dominant desire becomes in your life....   *—Anonymous*

We cannot see everything as divine because we have got a mind which is obsessed with desires. Desires debar us from the vision of the Divine in each and everyhing....   *—Papa Ramdas*

Gratification of one desire or one set of desires merely gives rise to another....
—Ramesh Balsekar

Desire is the creator; desire is the destroyer.... —*Hari Das Baba*

Desire blinds us, like the pickpocket who sees only the saint's pockets.... —*Jack Kornfield*

Wherever there is desire, association with it brings endless misery.... —*Gampopa*

Be very careful what you set your heart upon, for you will surely have it.... —*Ralph W. Emerson*

The great and difficult victory, the conquering of the desires of the individual soul, is a work of ages....but when you have found the beginning of the way, the star of your soul will show its light.... —*Mabel Collins*

What makes a man unhappy? When he has a desire and it is not satisfied. It does not matter what the desire is.... —*Yogi Bhajan*

Because creation is finished, what you desire already exists....Be still and know that you are that which you desire to be, and you will never have to search for it.... —*Darwin Gross*

Nothing troubles you for which you do not desire.... —*Cicero*

We are what we desire to be. We can be what we wish to be. If we make a plan of our lives and desire that plan to be fulfilled, we will become that. Desire to be great and you will be. Desire to kill and you can also kill. Mind will work to fulfill desire, no matter what the desire is.... —*Walter Russell*

The passionate are like men standing on their heads; they see all things the wrong way.... —*Plato*

If thou wilt make a man happy, add not unto his riches but take away from his desires.... —*Epicurus*

The fewer desires, the more peace.... —*Thomas Wilson*

Lust is the captivity of the reason and the enraging of passions.... —*Jeremy Taylor*

The discipline of desire is the background of character.... —*John Locke*

Impossible desires are punished in the desire.... —*Philip Sidney*

Destiny has two ways of crushing us— by refusing our wishes and by fulfilling them.... —*Henri F. Amiel*

When I say a man has no desire I mean that he does not disturb his inner well-being with likes and dislikes. He accepts things as they are and does not try to improve upon them.... —*Chuang Tse*

Love becomes lust the moment you make it a means for the satisfaction of animal needs.... —*Mohandas Gandhi*

What a mistake to suppose that the passions are the strongest in youth. The passions are not stronger, but the control over them is weaker.... —*Edward Bulwer-Lytton*

My belief is that to have no wants is divine.... —*Socrates*

The satisfaction which results from gratified desire is brief and illusionary, and is always followed by an increased demand for gratification. Desire is insatiable as the ocean, and clamors louder and louder as its demands are attended to.... —*James Allen*

Desires are innumerable, insatiable and unconquerable. Enjoyment cannot bring satisfaction. It is a mistake to think so. Enjoyment only fans a desire....Enjoyment strengthens, increases and aggravates a desire....
—*Sivananda*

The marvelous things about human beings is that we are perpetually reaching for the stars. The more we have, the more we want. And for this reason, we never have it all.... —*Joyce Brothers*

Our passions are like convulsive fits, which though they make us stronger for a time, leave us weaker ever after....
—*Jonathan Swift*

Other desires perish in their gratification, but the desire of knowledge never.... —*Alfred E. Housman*

When all desire is surrendered but the desire to function as God wills, the way is opened before you....
—*Amy & Evarts Loomis*

Don't think about desires and how to get rid of them. Just be still and quiet and all your doubts and desires will vanish.... —*Lakshmana*

In moderating, not in satisfying desires, lies peace.... —*Reginald Heber*

In the light of eternity we should see that what we desired would have been fatal to us, and that what we would have avoided was essential to our well-being.... —*Francois Fenelon*

Our desires always disappoint us; for though we meet with something that gives us satisfaction, yet it never thoroughly answers our expectations....
—*Francois La Rochefoucauld*

There are two tragedies in life. One is not to get your heart's desire. And the other is to get it.... —*George B. Shaw*

Desires go on increasing and burning more fiercely as they are fed....The more you yield to desire, the more dominant it becomes in your life. It does not matter the desire—the more you try to satisfy desire, the more you become captivated and enslaved by it....
—*Ramana Maharshi*

Desire never ceases to pray even though the tongue be silent....
—*Augustine*

Attainment often lessens ambition, and possessions frequently paralyze interest. We are always wanting something, and seldom satisfied when we get it....
—*Fred Van Amburgh*

We should not even desire rewards for our actions. He who looks to rewards will become a slave to such rewards....
—*Julian P. Johnson*

Every desire bears its death in its very gratification. Curiosity languishes under repeated stimulants, and novelties cease to excite surprise, until at length we do not even wonder at a miracle.... —*Washington Irving*

It would not be better for mankind if they were given their desires....
—*Heraclitus*

Desires are like a forest fire....consuming and destroying everything....
—*Philo*

It should be an indispensable rule in life to contract our desires to our present condition, and whatever may be our expectations, to live within the compass of what we actually possess....
—*Joseph Addison*

Man is greater than all the objects of his desire.... —*Rabindranath Tagore*

A man who has had his way is seldom happy, for generally he finds that the way does not lead very far on this earth of desires which can never be fully satisfied.... —*Joseph Conrad*

When a man's desires are boundless, his labors are endless. They will set him a task he can never go through, and cut out work he can never finish. The satisfaction he seeks is always absent and the happiness he aims at is ever at a distance.... —*John Balguy*

I have made it my habit to alter my desires rather than the order of the world.... —*Rene Descartes*

He who expects much will be disappointed; yet disappointment seldom cures us of expectations.... —*Samuel Johnson*

Every desire is insatiable, and therefore is always in want.... —*Sextus, the Pythagorean*

The one who has come into the realization of the higher life no longer has the desire for the accumulation of enormous wealth, any more than he has a desire for any other excess.... —*Ralph W. Trine*

Who clings faithfully to God desires nothing for himself.... —*Itzikl of Radvil*

By annihilating the desires, you annihilate the mind. Every man without passions has within him no principle of action, nor motive to act.... —*Claude Helvetius*

Where there is desire there is no fullness.... —*Chidananda*

Desires and inspirations after the holy are the only ones as to which the human soul can ever be assured that they will never meet with disappointment.... —*Marcia Macintosh*

It is not good to suppress desires as that gives them more strength. It is much better to surrender them all to God.... —*Saradamma*

All experiences which loom out of contact with the five senses are the sources of sorrow only. All these desires should be abandoned without reserve.... —*Bhagavad-Gita*

Who is the greater conqueror? One who with vast armies invades territories and subdues kingdoms, or one who conquers his own desires, his own senses? He is the greater conqueror who has subdued himself, who has conquered his own desires, subdued his own senses.... —*Gautama Buddha*

Our duty is to be useful, not according to our desires but according to our powers.... —*Henri F. Amiel*

Attachment is real death. Non-attachment is eternal life. Attachment brings manifold miseries. Non-attachment brings manifold bliss. Attachment contracts the heart. Non-attachment expands the heart ad infinitum.... —*Sivananda*

There cannot be self-restraint in the absence of desire.... —*Rumi*

Desire is the region of hell, and all torments are centered there. The giving-up of desire is the realization of heaven, and all delights await the pilgrim there.... —*James Allen*

He who is utterly without desire has a happiness that ages not.... —*Santi-deva*

It is difficult to overcome one's passions, and it is impossible to satisfy them....　　　—*Marguerite De la Sabiere*

If you did not desire your present position, you would not be doing everything possible to maintain it....
　　　　　　　　　　　—*Leo Tolstoy*

A life is either all spiritual or not spiritual at all. No man can serve two masters. Your life is shaped by the end you live for. You are made in the image of what you desire....　　　—*Thomas Merton*

When desire is quenched, peace is found....　　　　　　　—*Paul Brunton*

It is better to desire the things we have than to have the things we desire....
　　　　　　　　　　—*Henry Van Dyke*

The thirst of desire is never filled, nor fully satisfied....　　　　　　　—*Cicero*

A person who represses all his ambitions and wishes and denies any reality to them is on the road to misery. The person, on the other hand, who consciously renounces unrealizable and unworthy desires, has straightened himself by daring to face life as it is and making clear to himself why he has chosen that course of action....
　　　　　　　　　—*Joshua L. Liebman*

It is much easier to suppress a first desire than to satisfy those that follow....　　—*Francois La Rochefoucauld*

The soul....by reason of desire had become the principal accomplice in her own captivity....Desires are only the lack of something: and those who have the greatest desires are in a worse condition than those who have none or very slight ones....　　　　　　—*Plato*

What is strong? The man who can control his passions....　　　—*Ben Zoma*

All suffering is born of desire....Give up desire for pleasure and you will not know what is pain....Only contentment can make you happy—desires fulfilled breed more desires....　　　　　—*Nisargadatta*

Desire of having is the sin of covetous....　　　—*William Shakespeare*

It is with our passions, as it is with fire and water, they are good servants but bad masters....　　—*Roger L'Estrange*

Covetousness is the root of all evil, the ground of all vice....
　　　　　　　　　—*Leonard Wright*

Indulging in one's desires in the hope of transcending them is like attempting to extinguish a fire by pouring kerosene on it....　　　—*Lakshmana*

To live for the physical, mental and sensual pleasure is like building a home on quicksand, or trying to cross a stream on the back of a crocodile, believing it to be a tree trunk....　—*Sankaracharya*

The man who wants everything is apt to end by being in want of everything....　　　—*George H. Hepworth*

Just as children are not born without a mother, so passions and desires are not born without wandering thoughts....
　　　　　　　　　—*Isaac of Syria*

The desire of power in excess caused the angels to fall; the desire of knowledge in excess caused man to fall....
　　　　　　　　　—*Francis Bacon*

Desire grows in strength if you follow it, but dies if you turn from it and abstain....Desire is slavery; renunciation is freedom....　　　—*Hermes*

All passions contain an element of sadness.... —*Jonathan Eibeschutz*

When one renounces selfish desires, his love expands into the farthest region of the universe until he becomes aware of cosmic love.... —*Sathya Sai Baba*

As a bird tied by the leg, when it starts to rise upwards, is pulled back to earth by the string, so the mind which has not yet attained desirelessness....is pulled back to the earth by desires.... —*St. Maximus*

When you most seek, and most anxiously desire, you will never find if you seek for yourself, not even in the most profound contemplation; but only in deep humility and submission of heart.... —*John of the Cross*

Everything that the deep soul within thee craveth shall surely come to thee by straight or winding passages.... —*Ralph W. Emerson*

The easiest thing of all is to deceive oneself; for what a man wishes, he generally believes to be true.... —*Demosthenes*

Limited in his nature, infinite in his desires, man is a fallen god who remembers heaven.... —*Alphonse de Lamartine*

Madness lies in every passion.... —*Robert Benson*

We would often be sorry if our wishes were granted.... —*Aesop*

They who are possessed by desire suffer much and enjoy little, as the ox that drags the cart gets by on a morsel of grass.... —*Santi-deva*

Most of us die wishing we could live again, so many mistakes committed, so much left undone.... —*Nisargadatta*

Everything belongs to the man who wants nothing....He has God. That is enough. Now he is ready to come back into the world. He is washed clean of desires, now he can form new ones, from a new center and a new motive....The fullest and most complete life comes out of the most completely empty life.... —*E. Stanley Jones*

From the deepest desire often ensues the deadliest hate.... —*Socrates*

Sexual desire is not love....mutual desire does not make things better. It only means that each of the two persons is treating the other as a means of self-satisfaction.... —*John Macmurray*

Of all longings and desires none is stronger than sex. Sex as a desire has no equal. Rely upon the Oneness. No one is able to become a follower of the Way if he accepts dualism.... —*Gautama Buddha*

A life devoted to the interests and enjoyments of this world, spent and wasted in the slavery of earthly desires, may be truly called a dream.... —*William Law*

Know this: the object you crave is perishable and transient in itself. How then can lasting peace be derived from it?... —*Papa Ramdas*

The man who seeks one, and but one thing in life may hope to achieve it, but he who seeks all things, wherever he goes, only reaps from the hopes which he sows, a harvest of barren regrets.... —*Edward Bulwer-Lytton*

Sensual pleasure is tantalizing. There is enchantment only as long as a person does not possess the object. He exerts hard. His mind is full of anxiety. He is under despondency as to whether he will secure the object or not. The moment he is in possession of the object, the charm vanishes. He finds that he is entangled....   —*Sivananda*

Before we set our hearts too much upon any thing, let us examine how happy those are who already possess it....   —*Francois La Rochefoucauld*

When the gods want to punish us, they grant our desires....
—*Ancient Greek saying*

A full investigation into Truth will extinguish your desires at once, and the extinction of desires will restore your mind to rest....   —*Yoga Vasishtha*

When a man is always occupied with the cravings of desire and ambition, and is eagerly striving to satisfy them, all his thoughts must be mortal....But he who has been earnest in the love of knowledge and wisdom....must have thoughts immortal and divine....
—*Plato*

It is not good to be too free. It is not good to have everything one wants....
—*Blaise Pascal*

The heart detached has no desire for anything nor has it anything to be delivered from....   —*Meister Eckhart*

Worldly desires are like columns of sunshine radiating through a dusty window, nothing tangible, nothing there....   —*Nahman Bratzlav*

When the one thought of God saturates your mind, naturally all other desires will disappear from it....   —*Papa Ramdas*

Devil

To see the devil it is necessary to make oneself up like the devil and then look in the mirror....
—*Eliphas Levi*

What people call Satan, the Devil, the Black Forces, etc., is simply ignorance of the true Self....
—*Ramana Maharshi*

If you reflect upon the devil long enough, his horns will seem to appear on everyone you meet....
—*Anonymous*

The devil is an egotist....
—*Johann W. Goethe*

Man can hardly even recognize the devils of his own creation....
—*Albert Schweitzer*

Anyone who lives for any length of time in a state of bitterness, resentment, anger, or hostilty is living with demons....   —*Elinor MacDonald*

It is no good casting out devils. They belong to us and we must accept them and be at peace with them....
—*D. H. Lawrence*

We cannot look for a devil to blame. There isn't any....   —*Joel Goldsmith*

What is the demon? Your own mind. It is not outside, this demon is inside; that complicates the battle. You have to go into yourself....   —*Chidananda*

Many weapons invented by great teachers of mankind for use against the devil have been taken hold of by the devil himself....   —*K. Swaminathan*

The only devil from which men must be redeemed is self, the lower self. If man would find his devil he must look within; his name is self....

—*The Aquarian Gospel*

If the devil does not exist, and man has therefore created him, he has created him in his own image and likeness....

—*Fyodor Dostoyevsky*

God is good, there is no devil but fear; nothing can harm us, the Universe is planned for our good....

—*Elbert Hubbard*

Hell or the devil has no abiding place except in man's mortal mind. Both of them are just wherever man places them. I never saw the devil in any man, save he brought him there himself....

—*Baird Spalding*

When the devil is called the God of this world, it is not because he made it, but because we serve him with our worldliness.... —*Thomas Aquinas*

The devil is a myth, hence he exists and continues to be active. A myth is a story which describes and illustrates in dramatic form certain deep structures of reality.... —*Denis de Rougemont*

The only real devil that exists in this or any other world is the man whose business is that of making devils....

—*Napoleon Hill*

The devil is in whatever tries to master you. If you do not resist, he will temporarily master you....Resist the devil and he will flee from you....

—*Prentice Mulford*

Stand up to the devil and he will turn and run. Come close to God and God will come close to you....

—*New Testament*

The devil is compromise....

—*Henrik Ibsen*

The Devil hunts down those who are frightened of him, and flees those who resist him boldly. The art of chaining up demons is to do good and fear nothing.... —*Eliphas Levi*

When once we believe in the Sovereignty of God, satanic influence becomes a thing of the past. Evil can only affect us through our own evil. Evil has power only on its own plane: it has no part in the Divine Providence....

—*Henry T. Hamblin*

Egotism is the most persistent and obstinate devil in us, and unless we receive help from God we cannot conquer the devil.... —*Ramakrishnananda*

Discipline

If you have mastered yourself, nature will obey you.... —*Eliphas Levi*

Be gentle to all and stern with yourself.... —*Teresa of Avila*

When you learn to discipline your mind, you become master of your mind rather than your mind being master of you.... —*Ormond McGill*

If you are doing things you know you shouldn't do and don't really want to do, you certainly lack discipline....

—*Peace Pilgrim*

Discipline is a quality. You start with a little bit of it, you submit yourself to authority and a job and a goal, and you learn a bit more about discipline....

—*Charles E. Jones*

What makes a man a good artist, a good sculptor, a good musician? Practice. What makes a man a good linguist, a good stenographer? Practice. What makes a man a good man? Practice. Nothing else.... —*Henry Drummond*

He who cannot obey himself will be commanded. This is the nature of living creatures....
—*Friedrich W. Nietzsche*

The only worthy discipline is self-discipline.... —*Wayne Dyer*

If you cannot command your own soul, how can I give you enlightenment how to do so?... —*Marjorie Bowen*

A horse that resists the reins, a car without brakes and a person with no self-control, are all equally headed for disaster.... —*Sathya Sai Baba*

The man who refuses to submit to discipline is like a river that overflows its banks, thereby destroying the means by which it could reach the sea....Fortunately, it is not left entirely to us to discipline ourselves. Life does it for us....
—*Alice H. Rice*

Self-discipline does within while you do without.... —*Denis Waitley*

If self-control were easy to obtain, we'd end up accomplishing nothing at all....
—*Marvin Minsky*

Most powerful is he who has himself in his own power.... —*Seneca*

Not to have control over the senses is like sailing in a rudderless ship, bound to break into pieces on coming in contact with the very first rock....
—*Mohandas Gandhi*

Discipline is the ability to carry out a resolution long after the mood has left you. The mountain of soul-achievement and mastery of life cannot be scaled by the faint of heart. Without discipline, you won't make it to the mountain top.... —*Susan Smith Jones*

The difference between a savior and a sinner is this: that the one has perfect control of all the forces within him; the other is dominated and controlled by them.... —*James Allen*

No man is free who cannot command himself.... —*Pythagoras*

No conflict is so severe as his who labors to subdue himself....
—*Thomas à Kempis*

Self-discipline is your golden key; without it, you cannot be happy....
—*Maxwell Maltz*

The superior man is uncontaminated by pleasure, unharmed by pain, untouched by any insult, feeling no wrong, not overpowered by passion, dyed deep with justice, accepting with all his soul everything which is assigned to him as his portion....
—*Marcus Aurelius*

Self-conquest is the greatest of victories.... —*Plato*

The most precious of all possessions is power over ourselves; power to withstand trial, to bear suffering; to confront danger; power over pleasure and pain; power to follow our convictions....
—*John Locke*

He that cannot decidedly say "No" when tempted to evil is on the highway to ruin.... —*Joel Hawes*

To change an undesirable trait, you must zero in on exactly what it is you need to change....   —*Joyce Brothers*

Carpenters bend wood; fletchers bend arrows; wise men fashion themselves....
—*Gautama Buddha*

Without consistency there is no moral strength....   —*John J. Owen*

I consider that the greatest discovery of my life is this: I have learned that within me resides the power to control my own moods....   —*Wright Field*

Discipline divorced from wisdom is not true discipline, but merely the meaningless following of custom, which is a disguise for ignorance....
—*Rabindranath Tagore*

There never has been, and cannot be, a good life without self-control; apart from self-control, no good life is imaginable....   —*Herbert Spencer*

One must train oneself, by small and frequent efforts, to dominate one's feelings....   —*Alexis Carrel*

It is not possible to discipline ourselves so effectively if out of touch with the world, as while pursuing the world-life with wisdom....   —*Manu*

Discipline is learnt in the school of adversity....   —*Mohandas Gandhi*

Conquer thyself. Till thou hast done this, thou art a slave....
—*Robert Burton*

One of the most important, but one of the most difficult things for a powerful mind, is to be its own master....
—*Joseph Addison*

There is no king like him who is king of himself....   —*St. Cadoc*

Self-control confers contentment....
—*Samhita*

Such power there is in clear-eyed self-restraint....   —*James Russell Lowell*

He who reigns within himself and rules his passions, desires and fears is more than a king....   —*John Milton*

I never suspected that....there were specific disciplines and ways of seeing the world I had to master before I could awaken to a simple, happy, uncomplicated life....   —*Dan Millman*

Nothing gives one person so much advantage over another as to remain cool and unruffled under all circumstances....   —*Thomas Jefferson*

Above everything, you must command yourself, and your true self is not your wildly roving thoughts....
—*Berthold Auerbach*

Nothing exterior shall ever take command of me....   —*Walt Whitman*

Learn to say no. It will be of more use to you than to be able to read Latin....
—*Charles H. Spurgeon*

Self-knowledge and self-improvement are very difficult for most people. It usually needs great courage and long struggle....   —*Abraham Maslow*

If you would learn self-mastery, begin by yielding yourself to the One Great Master....   —*Johann Lobstein*

Common-sense is the fundamental factor in all spiritual disciplines. No rule is an eternal rule. Rules change from place to place, time to time and from one condition to another condition....
—*Sivananda*

Man must be disciplined, for he is by nature raw and wild....
—*Immanuel Kant*

The disciplined man masters thoughts by stillness and emotions by calmness....
—*Lao-tzu*

People who have learned to control themselves, who do not live on the surface of their being, but who reach down into the depths, where, in the stillness, the voice of God is heard....are not affected by the thousand and one storms and tempests....
—*Orison S. Marden*

Our own inner child has to be disciplined in order to release its tremendous spiritual power....
—*Marion Woodman*

Self-control may be developed, precisely the same manner as we tone up a weak muscle—by little exercises day by day....
—*W. G. Jordan*

When reason is not the master, the senses usually swing back and forth....
—*Maximus*

It is one thing to praise discipline, and another thing to submit to it....
—*Miguel de Cervantes*

Subdue the animal within you; conquer every selfish uprising, every discordant voice; transmute the base metals of your selfish nature into the unalloyed gold of Love....
—*James Allen*

The control man has secured over nature has far outrun his control over himself....
—*Ernest Jones*

The virtue of all achievement is victory over oneself. Those who know this victory can never know defeat....
—*A. J. Cronin*

Strength doesn't come from physical capacity. It comes from an indomitable will....
—*Mohandas Gandhi*

Mistake, error, is the discipline through which we advance....
—*William E. Channing*

Cheerfulness is the rich and satisfying result of strenuous discipline....
—*Edwin P. Whipple*

Be kings, not slaves, of your passions....
—*Raphael Elijah*

We go all wrong by too strenuous a resolution to go all right....
—*Nathaniel Hawthorne*

He that has not mastery over his inclinations, he that knows not how to resist the importunity of present pleasure or pain....is in danger of never being good for anything....
—*John Locke*

Who has a harder fight than he who is striving to overcome self?...
—*Thomas à Kempis*

Man has six organs to serve him, and he is master only of three. He cannot control his eye, ear or nose, but he can his mouth, hand and foot....
—*Amora Levi*

The first and best victory is to conquer self. To be conquered by self is, of all things, the most shameful and vile....
—*Plato*

There never has been, and cannot be, a good life without self-control....
—*Leo Tolstoy*

Whoever preaches absence of discipline is an enemy of progress....
—*Max Nordau*

Exercise, exercise your powers; what is difficult will finally become routine....
—*Georg C. Lichtenberg*

No one is free who is not master of himself.... —*William Shakespeare*

Doubt

It is the human condition to question one god after another; one appearance after another; or better, one apparition after another, always pursuing the truth of the imagination....
—*Alain LeSage*

Despair is an expression of the total personality, doubt only of thought....
—*Sören Kierkegaard*

The doubter's dissatisfaction with his doubt is as great and widespread as the doubt itself.... —*Jan DeWitt*

Doubt is really a groping ignorance....
—*Eliphas Levi*

Doubt destroys. Faith builds....
—*Robert Collier*

Hidden doubts and fears build walls around you.... —*Paul Williams*

There is no greater hell than doubts....
—*Amar Jyoti*

God gave us faith. The devil introduced doubt.... —*Fred Van Amburgh*

We do not listen to and do not follow this voice within our own souls, and so we become a house divided against itself. We are pulled this way and that, and we are never certain of anything....
—*Ralph W. Trine*

Doubt is the vestibule through which all must pass before they can enter the temple of wisdom....
—*Charles C. Colton*

Indecision, doubt and fear. The members of this unholy trio are closely related; where one is found, the other two are close at hand.... —*Napoleon Hill*

If a man will begin with certainties, he shall end in doubts, but if he will be content to begin with doubts, he shall end in certainties.... —*Francis Bacon*

Doubts are more cruel than the worst of truths.... —*Jean B. Moliere*

Doubts arise because of the absence of surrender.... —*Ramana Maharshi*

Doubt is like a little germ which gets lodged in the heart and infects the whole being.... —*Paramananda*

When you doubt, abstain....
—*Zoroaster*

Let go of the things of which you are in doubt for the things in which there is no doubt.... —*Mohammed*

The intelligence of a doubting person dwindles; wherever he looks, he sees nothing but doubt....
—*Nityananda*

Doubt is brother devil to despair....
—*John B. O'Reilly*

Skepticism is slow suicide....Skepticism is unbelief in cause and effect....
—*Ralph W. Emerson*

There is no weariness like that which arises from doubting—from the perpetual jogging of unfixed reason....
—*Robert Smith*

Doubt of whatever kind, can be ended by Action alone.... —*Thomas Carlyle*

Doubt is not a pleasant condition, but certainty is an absurd one.... —*Voltaire*

Never doubt that a small group of thoughtful, committed citizens can change the world; indeed, it's the only thing that ever has....
—*Margaret Mead*

Doubt grows with knowledge....
—*Johann W. Goethe*

The end of doubt is the beginning of repose.... —*Petrarch*

Doubt is the disease of this inquisitive, restless age. It is the price we pay for our advanced intelligence and civilization—the dim light of our resplendent day. But as the most beautiful night is born of darkness, so the faith that springs from conflict is often the strongest and best....
—*Robert J. Turnbull*

Doubt indulged soon becomes doubt realized.... —*Francis R. Havergal*

They who have conquered doubt and fears have conquered failure. Their every thought is allied with power, and all difficulties are bravely met and wisely overcome.... —*James Allen*

Where doubt is, there truth is—it is her shadow.... —*Gamaliel Bailey*

If you wait for the perfect moment when all is safe and assured, it may never arrive. Mountains may never be climbed, races won, nor happiness achieved.... —*Maurice Chevalier*

It is only by doubting that we eventually come to the truth.... —*Cicero*

Doubt is hell in the human soul....
—*Madam Gasparin*

A fanatic is a man who consciously overcompensates a secret doubt....
—*Aldous Huxley*

If you would be a real seeker of the truth, it is necessary at least once in your life to doubt, as far as possible, all things.... —*Rene Descartes*

With most people, doubt about one thing is simply blind belief in another.... —*Georg C. Lichtenberg*

To know much is often the cause of doubting more.... —*Michel Montaigne*

When you have constant communion with God, a constant receiving from within, there is never any doubt; you know your way.... —*Peace Pilgrim*

Our doubts are traitors, and make us lose the good we oft might win by fearing to attempt....
—*William Shakespeare*

The important thing is not to stop questioning.... —*Albert Einstein*

Doubt comes in the window when inquiry is denied at the door....
—*Benjamin Jowett*

Doubt is a greater mischief than despair.... —*John Denham*

Doubt is the beginning, not the end of wisdom.... —*George Ileo*

Man never encounters a mountain greater than doubt. Doubt is a deceiver. It is as a thief in the night. Remove it....do not let it come nigh your dwelling. Never doubt. Learn to say and learn to mean it, "I am the all of everything good."... —*Frater Achad*

Doubting is truly a component of man's worst nature. It clips the wings of joy; it dampens enthusiasm, it tarnishes hope. Such men cannot attain the goal even at the end of a thousand births....   —*Sathya Sai Baba*

When you are in doubt, be still, and wait. When doubt no longer exists for you, then go forward in courage....   —*White Eagle*

As long as there is a material body, you are carrying doubt. Do not despise your doubting. That is the human condition. When there is no more doubt, you do not need to be human....   —*Emmanuel*

The supreme fall of falls is this, the first doubt of one's self....
—*Comtesse de Gasparin*

Dreams

Most of the things we think of today as hard, practical and even indispensable were once merely dreams....   —*Carroll Carroll*

Dream delivers us to dream and there is no end to illusion....
—*Ralph W. Emerson*

If a man advances confidently in the direction of his dreams to live the life he has imagined, he will meet with success unexpected in common hours....
—*Henry D. Thoreau*

Hold fast to dreams for if dreams die, life is a broken-winged bird that cannot fly....   —*Langston Hughes*

Within our dreams and aspirations we find our opportunities....
—*Sue A. Ebaugh*

Dream lofty dreams, and as you dream, so shall you become. Your Vision is the promise of what you shall one day be, your Ideal is the prophecy of what you shall at last unveil....   —*James Allen*

Without dreams, the illusion is gone....
—*A Spiritual Warrior*

We've removed the ceiling above our dreams. There are no more impossible dreams....   —*Jesse Jackson*

Dreams are so important in one's life, yet when followed blindly they can lead to the disintegration of the soul....
—*Maria Campbell*

Whatever you can do or dream you can, begin it. Boldness has genius, power, and magic in it. Begin it now....
—*Johann W. Goethe*

One of the characteristics of the dream is that nothing surprises us in it. With no regret, we agree to live in it with strangers, completely cut off from our habits and friends....   —*Jean Cocteau*

It can be a very dangerous thing to go in search of a dream for the reality does not always match it....   —*Gracie Fields*

We grow through our dreams. All great men and women are dreamers....
—*Woodrow Wilson*

Great dreams contain inexhaustible truths, and orient us, like runes, toward our futures....Great dreams are like wells that never run dry....
—*Michael Grosso*

Dreams are real while they last. Can we say more of life?...   —*Havelock Ellis*

Too many dreams are cast by the wayside in deference to opinion and tradition....   —*Alan Cohen*

Man is the garden in which this only begotten Son of God sleeps. We awaken this Son by lifting our imagination up to heaven and clothing men in godlike stature.... —*Darwin Gross*

Have a dream and believe in it. Strong dreams always come true.... —*Robert Muller*

Dreams retain the infirmities of our character.... —*Ralph W. Emerson*

High on the wall, in the castle of your dreams of success, hangs the picture of what you want to be. Always keep that picture hanging there. See yourself where you intend to be. Night and day dream of what you intend to do and what you intend to be, for your dreams interpret your intentions always. All successes are, at first, dreams.... —*Fred Van Amburgh*

If you can dream it, you can do it.... —*Walt Disney*

The greatest achievement was at first and for a time a dream. The oak sleeps in the acorn; the bird waits in the egg; and in the highest vision of the soul, a waking angel stirs. Dreams are the seedlings of realities.... —*James Allen*

Tens of thousands of forests lie dormant within the dreams of one acorn.... —*Anonymous*

One-pointedness is the ability to exclude from your mind all thoughts but the one you want to be possessed by. It is the power to concentrate on your dream until it has become more than a dream.... —*Robert Collier*

If you can imagine it, you can achieve it. If you can dream it, you can become it.... —*William A. Ward*

If you have built castles in the air, your work need not be lost; that is where they should be. Now put the foundations under them.... —*Henry D. Thoreau*

Waiting and hoping are the whole of life, and as soon as a dream is realized it is destroyed.... —*Giancarlo Menotti*

When your heart's dream becomes a burning desire to achieve and accomplish its specific purpose, the entire cosmos opens its doors to you.... —*Lloyd Littlepage*

You must learn to turn your....dreams into exactly expressed targets. Once you have done so, and know just where you are heading, you are then in a position to see immediately an opportunity when it comes your way.... —*R. J. Heathorn*

Take time to dream—it is hitching your wagon to a star.... —*Irish prayer*

Existence would be intolerable if we were never to dream.... —*Anatole France*

All that we see or seem is but a dream within a dream.... —*Edgar A. Poe*

All men dream—but not equally. Those who dream by night in the dusty recesses of their minds wake in the day to find it was vanity: but the dreamers of the day are dangerous men, for they may act their dreams with open eyes, to make it possible.... —*T. E. Lawrence*

Nothing happens unless first a dream.... —*Carl Sandburg*

Dreaming is an act of pure imagination, attesting in all men a creative power.... —*Frederick H. Hedge*

Dreams are true while they last, and do we not live in dreams?...
—*Alfred L. Tennyson*

The years forever fashion new dreams when old ones go. God pity the one-dream man....　　—*Robert Goddard*

Waking life is a dream controlled....
—*George Santayana*

How can you determine whether at this moment we are sleeping, and all our thoughts are a dream: or whether we are awake, and talking to one another in the waking state....　　—*Plato*

Dream big dreams, then put on your overalls and go out and make the dreams come true....
—*Fred Van Amburgh*

It may be those who do most, dream most....　　—*Stephen Leacock*

Nothing so much convinces me of the boundlessness of the human mind as its operations in dreaming....
—*William B. Clulow*

Dreams are the touchstones of our character....　　—*Henry D. Thoreau*

Man is a dream of a shadow....
—*Pindar*

The dreamers are the saviors of the world. As the visible world is sustained by the invisible, so men, through all their trials and sins and sordid vocations, are nourished by the visions of their solitary dreamers....
—*James Allen*

Most dreams represent either wanderings on the psychic realm or illusions produced by physical, mental or emotional stresses, and should be promptly forgotten....　　—*Peace Pilgrim*

Kill a dream and the dreamer dies too....　　—*Leonard M. Foley*

Duality

People wish to swim and at the same time keep one foot on the ground....
—*Marcel Proust*

Joy is at its keenest when contrasted with sorrow, courage at its height when it follows fear, faith at its noblest when it grows from doubt....
—*Alice H. Rice*

Duality is not real, because reality is the opposite of eternity. Without duality there is no perception....
—*Sivananda*

You cannot alter your shadow except by altering yourself....It is the same with life: outward circumstances are merely what we are within, and can be altered only as we ourselves become inwardly changed....
—*Henry T. Hamblin*

Upon the battlefield of the human soul two masters are ever contending for the crown of supremacy, for the kingship and dominion of the heart: the master of self, called also the "prince of this world," and the master of Truth, called also the Father God....　　—*James Allen*

If you stand straight, do not fear a crooked shadow....　　—*Chinese proverb*

Each of us can feel a dual life within ourselves. The struggle of the mind against the conscience; of unmanly desire against noble feelings; in a word, of the brute against the intelligent creature....　　—*Eliphas Levi*

All suffering begins with a notion of duality. As long as this duality-consciousness is strongly fixed in the mind, one cannot give real help to other people. If one realizes one's non-dual nature and becomes peaceful within, one becomes a fit instrument to help others.... —*Annamalai Swami*

There is no fruit which is not bitter before it is ripe.... —*Publilius Syrus*

The sense of duality vanishes completely once you realize your identity with God. You and He become one. The drop becomes one with the ocean.... —*Papa Ramdas*

The maker fused duality in all; sorrow and joy foremost of all these pairs.... —*Manu*

They only who love God with a steadfast mind can cross the ocean of duality, and they who rise above this dualness, they only know God as the One Sole Truth.... —*Bhagavad-Gita*

Man is as full of potentiality as he is of impotence.... —*George Santayana*

When the Reality is experienced, there is no duality at all.... —*Sathya Sai Baba*

All behavior consists of opposites....Learn to see things backward, inside out, and upside down.... —*Lao-tzu*

In the world duality always exists.... —*Nisargadatta*

The world and Reality are negations of each other. They cannot be seen simultaneously.... —*Ramana Maharshi*

The exterior man may be undergoing trials, but the interior man is quite free.... —*Meister Eckhart*

Yin and yang, male and female, strong and weak, rigid and tender, heaven and earth, light and darkness, thunder and lightning, cold and warmth, good and evil....the interplay of opposite principles constitutes the universe.... —*Confucius*

Where there is much light, the shadow is deep.... —*Johann W. Goethe*

The mind stream on two rival currents flows, heading to virtue and vice.... —*Yogi Bhashya*

We cannot possibly imagine the variety of contradictions in every heart.... —*Francois La Rochefoucauld*

The rose and the thorn, and sorrow and gladness are linked together.... —*Saadi*

Man was made for joy and woe; and when this we rightly know, safely through the world we go.... —*William Blake*

The world is made of pairs of opposites; all things occur in pairs of two and two....Two birds of wondrous plumage rest awhile on the curious tree of bodied life; One eats the sweet-sour fruits with eager greed, and suffers many ills in consequence; the other looks on compassionately.... —*The Upanishads*

Good and evil; altruism and egotism; both are inherent in each living thing.... —*Shankaracharya*

There is in reality neither truth nor error, neither yes nor no, nor any distinction whatsoever, since all—including the contraries—is One.... —*Chuang Tse*

To the man of God right and wrong are alike.... —*Divani Shamsi Tabriz*

Two people have been living in you all of your life. One is the ego, garrulous, demanding, hysterical, calculating; the other is the hidden spiritual being, whose still voice of wisdom you have only rarely heard or attended to....
—*Sogyal Rinpoche*

If there be light, then there is darkness; if cold, then heat; if height, depth also; if solid, then fluid; hardness and softness; roughness and smoothness; calm and tempest; prosperity and adversity; life and death.... —*Pythagoras*

A hair's breadth divides heaven from hell. Both are ever present in us. Now the one prevails, now the other....
—*Bhagavan Das*

Everything is plain and easy to the earnest; it is the double-minded who find difficulties.... —*John H. Newman*

Each of us can feel a dual life within ourselves. The struggle of the mind against the conscience; of unmanly desire against noble feelings; in a word, of the brute against the intelligent creature.... —*Eliphas Levi*

Our mind is placed between two entities, each suggesting what belongs to it: one virtue, the other vice; that is between an angel and a demon. But the mind has the power and strength to follow or oppose which it wills....
—*Maximus*

Negations serve to glorify positives. Thus death glorifies immortality, ignorance glorifies wisdom, misery glorifies bliss, night glorifies dawn....
—*Sathya Sai Baba*

Humility is the root of honor, lowliness the foundation of loftiness; the world's weakest overcomes the world's hardest.... —*Lao-tzu*

No man can serve two masters; for either he will hate the one and love the other; or else he will hold to one, and despise the other. You cannot serve God and Mammon.... —*Jesus*

Two men look out through the same bars; one sees the mud, and one the stars.... —*Frederick Langbridge*

As long as you are concerned about what you do, that is dualistic....
—*Shunryu Suzuki*

It's as though we have two selves or two natures or two wills with two contrary viewpoints....Your lower self sees you as the center of the universe—your higher self sees you as a cell in the body of humanity.... —*Peace Pilgrim*

Every man, in reality, is two men. The man he is, and the man he could be....
—*Earl Nightingale*

The Masters say that the soul has two faces. The higher one always sees God, the lower one looks downward and informs the senses....
—*Meister Eckhart*

The greatest flood has soonest ebb; the sorest tempest, the most sudden calm; the hottest love the coldest end; and from the deepest desire often ensues the deadliest hate.... —*Socrates*

By passion for the pairs of opposites, by those twin snares of like and dislike, all creatures live bewildered, save some few who, quit of sins, holy in act, informed, freed from the opposites, and fixed in faith, cleave unto God....
—*Bhagavad-Gita*

There are two souls in my own breast, and one is determined to beat down the other.... —*Johann W. Goethe*

Good and evil are merely conceptional and relative. What is good for one may be bad for another. There are no fixed standards, but only those set by the mind.... —*Papa Ramdas*

For everything you have missed, you have gained something else; and for everything you gain, you lose something.... —*Ralph W. Emerson*

Are there two entities in the human body? Yes and No. They seem two, but they become one.... —*Paramananda*

In the external universe there is ceaseless turmoil, change, and unrest; at the heart of all things there is undisturbed repose; in this deep silence dwelleth the Eternal. Man partakes of this duality, and both the surface change and disquietude, and the deep-seated eternal abode of Peace are contained within him.... —*James Allen*

It is innocence that is full and experience that is empty. It is innocence that wins and experience that loses. It is innocence that is young and experience that is old. It is innocence that grows and experience that wanes. It is innocence that is born and experience that dies. It is innocence that knows and experience that does not know.... —*Charles Peguy*

I contradict myself. I am large. I contain multiples.... —*Walt Whitman*

Good is that which makes for unity; evil is that which makes for separation.... —*Aldous Huxley*

Anyone who serves God will discover sooner or later that the great hinderance to his work is not others but himself. He will discover that his outward man and his inward man are not in harmony, for both are tending toward opposite directions.... —*Watchman Nee*

Ego/Vanity

To be egotistic is to be blind to the needs, and the reality, of others.... —*Robert Mueller*

The ego cannot be blamed for its ignorance of reality, it specializes in fantasy....The ego cannot gain spiritual maturity through fantasy, and thus all the problems of relating between persons arise.... —*A Spiritual Warrior*

The ego is like a crooked tree. If you catch it when it is small, it is easy to tie to a stick and straighten out. If you wait till it has grown big, it is far more difficult to control.... —*Saradamma*

An inflated consciousness is always egocentric and conscious of nothing but its own existence. It is incapable of learning from the past, incapable of understanding contemporary events, and incapable of drawing right conclusions about the future. It is hypnotized by itself and therefore cannot be argued with. It inevitably dooms itself to calamities that must strike it dead.... —*Carl Jung*

When you are governed by your ego, you are selfish and materialistic, but insofar as you follow the promptings of your higher self, you will see things realistically and find harmony within yourself and others.... —*Peace Pilgrim*

The tendency of the ego to be humble is like the tendency of water to flow uphill.... —*Anonymous*

Your ego is an event and not a thing, and it is in a continual state of flux; it changes a thousand times each day and takes a thousand forms.... —*Ormond McGill*

Any true gentility mellows the ego, not by weakening its strength but by diminishing its arrogance, its false exclusiveness, its pretense of ultimacy.... —*Adrian van Kaan*

All pruning of the ego is of little use, for as one fault is removed a new one springs out of latency.... —*Paul Brunton*

The ego is just like a ghost. It has no real form of its own....Identifying oneself with the body and mind results in ignorance of the Self. This is how the ego takes birth. Detaching ourselves and disengaging from the body and the mind results in the death of the ego.... —*Annamalai Swami*

Flattery is counterfeit money which, but for vanity, would have no circulation.... —*Francois La Rochefoucauld*

The more you prune a plant, the more it grows. So too the more you seek to annihilate the ego, the more it will increase. You should seek the root of the ego and destroy it.... —*Ramana Maharshi*

The ego is like an iceberg. Ninety percent of it is underwater. As we observe it, the submerged begins to move into the light of observation, and melts in the light of awareness.... —*Meher Baba*

In a futile quest for pleasure, the ego resembles a dancing horse on a carousel; around and around the ego travels, up and down on the merry-go-round of life.... —*Shantidasa*

Vanity will set a crown upon its own head and wonder why all men do not rush to acknowledge it king. It will bray like an ass and imagine itself singing in a grand opera.... —*Julian P. Johnson*

Egolessness is impersonality. Personality seems to be something, and impersonality nothing. But that's because we do not easily see that personality is limitation to a body, while impersonality is the absence of limitation....Impersonality is Consciousness undiminished.... —*Lakshmana Sarma*

All....striving is a function of the ego, dissatisfied with what actually is, needing to become, to reaffirm its existence as a real thing.... —*Karl Sperber*

One may understand the cosmos, but never the ego; the self is more distant than any star.... —*G. K. Chesterton*

The ego has convinced us that we need it—not only that we need it, but that we are it.... —*Ram Dass*

The ego is a self-satisfying historian which seeks only that information that agrees with it, rewrites history when it needs to, and does not even see the evidence that threatens it.... —*Anthony G. Greenwald*

Self-centeredness....takes two forms: Thinking too well of one's self and thinking too ill....It is harder to cure the latter than the former.... —*Alice H. Rice*

To the one devoid of ego, the whole world is a heaven of rest, a realm of peace and a kingdom abounding in all happiness. He who has no ego and who has surrendered himself to God is the master of every power and force.... —*Sivananda*

We tell you this: We are doing the impossible. We are teaching ourselves to be human.... —*Martha Courto*

Nothing seems to happen exactly as its ego desires. It is simply the mind clouded over by impure desires, and impervious to wisdom, which stubbornly persists in thinking of "me" and "mine."... —*Gautama Buddha*

The problem is that the ego can convert anything to its own use, even spirituality. Ego is constantly attempting to acquire and apply the teachings of spirituality for its own benefit.... —*Chögyam Trungpa*

Intrinsically, there is no ego—it is something that we ourselves create.... —*Roshi P. Kapleau*

The ego-life is not life but death.... —*K. Swaminathan*

Self-realization is the great goal of living, but where the ego is, realization is not.... —*Robert S. Ellwood*

The ego is like an empty glass that dips itself into the ocean and after emerging filled to the brim, cries out: "This is me!"... —*Anonymous*

To sum up all in a word: Nothing has separated us from God but our own will, or rather our own will is our separation from God.... —*William Law*

The greed to possess things that you see is caused by egotism. Love all things as expression of God's glory, but do not delude yourself into the belief that possessing them will make you happy.... —*Sathya Sai Baba*

Let no one think he has been appointed the Savior.... —*Johann W. Goethe*

Half of the harm that is done in the world is due to people who want to feel important.... —*T. S. Eliot*

Think of a vast ocean filled with water on all sides. A jar is immersed in it. There is water both inside and outside the jar; but the water does not become one unless the jar is broken....What is the jar? It is I-consciousness—the ego. When the I disappears, what is, remains.... —*Ramakrishna*

The ego has the power of making imaginative forms which can be used in the world of purification or made....to magnify fears, passions and powers.... —*Ray Mitchell*

Egotism erects its center in itself; love places it out of itself in the axis of the universal whole.... —*Friedrich von Schiller*

When a man is wrapped up in himself he makes a pretty small package.... —*John Ruskin*

Vanity is an inordinate desire for the notice, approval, or praise of others....Vanity is always a mark of inferiority. All exaggerated attitudes of superior knowledge, wisdom, authority and morality are unmistaken indicators of the opposite qualities. They are the most obvious attempts to pose as superiority, weakness masquerading as strength.... —*Thurman Fleet*

Of all the foolish vices, vanity is the foolishest.... —*Fred Van Amburgh*

We do not content ourselves with the life we have in ourselves; we desire to live an imaginary life in the minds of others, and for this purpose we endeavor to shine.... —*Blaise Pascal*

Just about the most useless desire we can have is the desire to impress other people.... —*Vernon Howard*

It is the admirer of himself, and not the admirer of virtue, who thinks himself superior to others.... —*Plutarch*

Our limited self is the wall separating us from the self of God....It is being dead to self that is the recognition of God.... —*Hazrat Inayat Khan*

The source of our actions resides in an unconscious propensity to regard ourselves as the center, the cause and the conclusion of time.... —*E. M. Cioran*

Vanity of vanities; all is vanity.... —*Ecclesiastes*

The ego thinks from a small standpoint in the center. It thinks outward. It seeks to know by groping in the unknown, attempting to rationalize what it finds there. Since infinite space surrounds it, it is impossible for it to ever grow into great understanding.... —*U. S. Anderson*

All suffering surely revolves around egotism and egotism is the sole cause of mental distress.... —*Yoga Vasistha*

The most overrated thing in the world is your opinion of yourself....the more you think yourself spiritual....the more the ego deflates itself.... —*Raymond C. Barker*

Intolerance itself is a form of egoism, and to condemn egoism intolerantly is to share it.... —*George Santayana*

We are so vain that we even care for the opinion of those we don't care for.... —*Marie Von Ebner-Eschenbach*

The way of the ego is to have us forget about God by getting and attaching ourselves to people and things.... —*Gerald Jampolsky*

The ego endlessly pulls us from one burning desire to another. Somehow the ego wishes to impose its will on events, to pretend that its needs, its plans are the most important, that it knows all, and knows what is best for us.... —*A. Haji*

It is the ego that is the great bar to spiritual progress. If you want ego, then you can't have God. If you want God, then you must be crowned with humility.... —*Paramananda*

The ego frightens us in innumerable ways: with death, with pain, with loneliness.... —*Lily Benatar*

Keep God in remembrance until your self is forgotten.... —*Shams Tabriz*

Egotism: the art of seeing in yourself what others cannot see.... —*George Higgins*

All unhappiness is due to the ego. With it comes all your trouble. If you would deny the ego and scorch it by ignoring it you would be free.... —*Ramana Maharshi*

The root of all discontent is self-love.... —*James F. Clarke*

Men are just like animals so long as they are subject to the ego.... —*The Upanishads*

The ego, the lower nature, is of persistent character. It struggles fiercely not to die. The ego lives by denying what is real, conveniently ignoring truth in the process.... —*Shantidasa*

The ego is....primarily engaged in its own defense and the furtherance of its own ambitions. Everything that interferes with it must be repressed.... —*Jack Sanford*

The ego is simply the ignorance that limits the real Self to a single body out of a multitude of bodies, all of which are its own creation....We need to realize in all its implications the fact that the ego itself is the source of all the evil that besets life....

—*Lakshmana Sarma*

Self-love is the greatest of all flatters....

—*Francois La Rochefoucauld*

Man seeks something which will give him a brief moment of satisfaction; and his ego will often follow the most tortuous paths to obtain this moment....

—*Hans-Ulrick Rieker*

The great corrupter of public man is the ego....Looking at the mirror distracts one's attention from the problem.... —*Dean Acheson*

The only thing which a man must renounce if he wishes to attain the Supreme Truth is the notion of individuality—nothing else....A man who is entirely free from the ego-sense is the happiest man in the world. Because, he has found God—absolute existence, consciousness and bliss—in place of the ego.... —*Papa Ramdas*

He that falls in love with himself will have no rivals....

—*Benjamin Franklin*

It is a curious fact that of all the illusions that beset mankind, none is quite so curious as that tendency to suppose that we are mentally and morally superior to those who differ from us in opinion.... —*Elbert Hubbard*

It must be remembered that even though the ego is the individual's inaccurate concept of himself, it seems to be what he is.... —*Fritz Kunkel*

Praising an egotist is like pouring water on a drowning man....

—*Anonymous*

Egoism makes one see glory in petty achievements, happiness in trivial acquisitions, joy in temporary authority over others. But, the Immortal in him is awaiting discovery to confer bliss and liberation from birth and death....

—*Sathya Sai Baba*

The self-centered nature is a very formidable enemy and it struggles fiercely to retain its identity. It defends itself in a cunning manner and should not be regarded lightly....

—*Peace Pilgrim*

There is nothing contrary to God in the whole world, nothing that fights against him, but self-will....

—*Ralph Cudworth*

One of the ego's favorite paths of resistance is to fill you with doubt....

—*Ram Dass*

Healing only comes from that which leads the patient beyond himself and beyond his entanglements with ego....

—*Carl Jung*

It is characteristic of the ego that it takes all that is unimportant as important and all that is important as unimportant.... —*Meher Baba*

The best way of seeing divine light is to put out your own little candle....

—*English proverb*

The ego will always be able to find ways to keep the aspirant busy in self-improvement, thus binding him to the fact that the self is still there behind all improvements. For why should the ego kill itself?... —*Paul Brunton*

When the ego fights, God must go; when God fights, the ego must go....
—*Ramakrishnananda*

An egotist will always speak of himself, either in praise or censure; but the modest man ever shuns making himself the subject of his conversation....
—*Jean La Bruyere*

God is nearer to you than anything else, yet because of the screen of egotism you cannot see him....
—*Ramakrishna*

Many could forego heavy meals, a full wardrobe, a fine house....it is the ego they cannot forego....
—*Mohandas Gandhi*

The ego's idea of staying in the present is to continue whatever it is doing at all costs....   —*Hugh Prather*

The fullest possible enjoyment is to be found by reducing your ego to zero....
—*G. K. Chesterton*

When the ego-life dissolves and dies in silence, then one lives the life supreme of pure awareness....   —*Vachaka Kovia*

Truth cannot be achieved or possessed by the ego....   —*Sunyata*

The ego is really our weakness, the way our disbelief in ourselves shows in life. When we give up fighting for it and determine to discipline it, we are on our way toward being ourselves and mature individuals....   —*Alfred Ulher*

Ego is another synonym for limitation....   —*Anonymous*

Ego is only an illusion caused by your ignorance. The ignorance is removed by Self-enquiry....   —*Papa Ramdas*

Emotions

The emotions may be endless. The more we express them, the more we may have to express....
—*E. M. Forster*

When you look at things emotionally, you will not see them clearly; when you perceive things spiritually, you will understand....   —*Peace Pilgrim*

Many worthy causes have been lost because they were founded on emotion instead of facts....
—*Whitney S. Seymour, Jr.*

The principal use of prudence, of self control, is that it teaches us to be masters of our emotions....
—*Rene Descartes*

Emotions are more intense forms of feelings. The feeling of sadness may build into grief, the feeling of irritation can become a fierce rage. The distinguishing characteristic of emotion is that it dominates our attention and cannot be ignored, while a feeling can remain in the backround of awareness....   —*John Welwood*

One of the most prevalent problems of modern times is emotional immaturity. A surprising number of people act like little children walking around in grown-up bodies....
—*Elinor MacDonald*

Most relate to the world by their emotions, which means they know only the unreality of illusion—this world of emotion is the world of duality, of love and hate, of joy and sorrow. All emotions are relative to themselves, and last only as long as the supporting thought is maintained....
—*A Spiritual Warrior*

Life is a tram of moods like a string of beads, and as we pass through them they prove to be many colored lenses which paint the world in their own hue....
—*Ralph W. Emerson*

Since emotions are few and reasons are many, the behavior of a crowd can be more easily predicted than the behavior of one person can....
—*Isaac Asimov*

Our emotions can take us to God or they can take us to hell....
—*Alan Cohen*

Thought is deeper than all speech, feeling deeper than all thought....
—*Christopher Cranch*

Good emotions are the best medicine....
—*John A. Schindler*

Emotions are like waves. Watch them come and go on the vast ocean of existence....
—*Hindu proverb*

We become our own enemy when we are thrown out of balance by anger, hatred, grief or any other intense emotion. We are for the time being obsessed by something alien....
—*Paramananda*

The belief that we're responsible for others' feelings makes addicts out of us all. As long as we operate from this belief, our ability to feel good is tied to the feelings of others....
—*Jordan & Margaret Paul*

In sports as in child rearing, marital arguments, or tantrums, the same laws of learning apply: when an emotion is encouraged and the rules permit it, it is perpetuated, not "drained."...An emotion without social rules of containment and expression is like an egg without a shell: a gooey mess....
—*Carol Tavris*

When negative emotions are running high, one rarely makes the best decisions....
—*Anonymous*

In the march toward Truth, anger, selfishness, hatred, naturally give way, for otherwise Truth would be impossible to attain. A man who is swayed by negative emotions may have good enough intentions, may be truthful in word, but he will never find the truth....
—*Mohandas Gandhi*

Emotions should be servants, not masters—or at least not tyrants....
—*Robert Benson*

We have lost confidence in reason because we have learned that man is chiefly a creature of habit and emotion....
—*John Dewey*

The most beautiful and profound emotion we can experience is the sensation of the mystical. It is the sower of all true art and science. He to whom this emotion is a stranger, who can no longer wonder and stand rapt in awe, is as good as dead....
—*Albert Einstein*

The taste for emotion may become a dangerous taste; we should be very cautious how we attempt to squeeze out of human life more ecstasy and paroxysm than it can well afford....
—*Sidney Smith*

We are all human beings. We have emotions. Men and women just express them differently. That is the difference between us. Women want to talk about their emotions, whereas men want to privately deal with them and think them through....
—*John Gray*

To be calm and well poised is to be the center of power. The weak are those who have no control of their feelings and emotions....
—*Leon DeSeblo*

Emotion, whether of ridicule, anger, or sorrow, whether used at a puppet show, a funeral, or a battle, is your grandest of levelers. The man who would always be superior should be always apathetic....

—*Edward Bulwer-Lytton*

Passion of any kind is a bad counselor....   —*Paul Brunton*

Resentment is warmed-over anger. Anxiety is warmed-over fear. Self-pity is nothing more than warmed-over grief. Warmed-over feelings happen when there isn't anything better to do....

—*Roberta Jean Bryant*

The strongest and most fantastic fact about negative emotions is that people actually worship them....

—*P. D. Ouspensky*

Emotions....become more violent when expression is stilted....   —*Philo*

By starving emotions we become humorless, rigid and stereotyped; by repressing them we become literal, reformatory and holier-than-thou; encouraged, they perfume life; discouraged, they poison it....

—*Joseph Collins*

When a man is prey to his emotions, he is not his master....   —*Baruch Spinoza*

Hatred, envy, malice, jealousy and fear all have children. Any bad thought breeds others, and each of these goes on and on, ever repeating until our world is peopled with their offspring....

—*Ralph W. Trine*

If negative emotions produce negative chemical changes in the body, wouldn't the positive emotions produce positive chemical changes?...

—*Norman Cousins*

All emotions are pure which gather you and lift you up; that emotion is impure which seizes only one side of your being and so distorts you....

—*Rainer M. Rilke*

Emotion which does not lead to and flow out in right action is not only useless, but it weakens character, and becomes an excuse for neglect of effort....   —*Tryon Edwards*

Emotions are the color of life; we would be drab creatures indeed without them. But we must control these emotions or they will control us....

—*John M. Wilson*

When you feel yourself in the grip of an emotion such as jealousy or anger or sorrow, detach yourself from it. Take a step back. When you do that, you can allow the emotion to run through you without causing negative thoughts or actions....   —*Gary Zukav*

It is difficult for an appeal to the mind and the intellect to go far. Most people unfortunately do not think. They feel and act according to their feelings....

—*Jawaharlal Nehru*

Joy or bitterness is largely an outcome of the cultivation and guidance of emotions. While this applies to all personal relationships, it is especially weighty in marriage. Emotional attitudes may be either the positive and constructive emotions of love and trust, or the negative and potentially destructive emotions of fear and hatred....   —*Leland F. Wood*

The man who is involved in the surface phenomena of life is mainly a creature caught up in the constantly changing emotions of life....   —*Papa Ramdas*

Enemy

No one will attack a person unless he appears to be an enemy....
—*Lao-tzu*

One of the most time consuming things is to have an enemy.... —*E. B. White*

You can discover what your enemy fears most by observing the means he uses to frighten you.... —*Eric Hoffer*

Man is wise....when he recognizes no greater enemy than himself....
—*Marguerite of Navarre*

It is hard to fight an enemy who has outposts in your head....
—*Sally Kempton*

The hand that holds the whip over our heads is most often our own....
—*Harvey Eagan*

It pays to know the enemy—not the least because at some time you may have the opportunity to turn him into a friend.... —*Margaret Thatcher*

Build your adversary a golden bridge over which to retreat.... —*Sun Tzu*

If we could read the secret history of our enemies we shall find in each man's sorrow and suffering enough to disarm all hostility....
—*Henry W. Longfellow*

Why should we love our enemies? Our enemy is our greatest friend. Those who speak ill of me, exposing my weakness, do me the greatest good....
—*Vinobe Bhave*

No one is to be called an enemy; all are your benefactors, and no one does you harm. You have no enemy except yourselves.... —*Francis of Assisi*

Our only enemies are those inside ourselves. They are our weaknesses and vices, our lower passions and intellectual deformities. It is better to fight them than other men.... —*Paul Brunton*

The enemy has no definite name, though in a certain degree we all know him. He who puts always the body before the spirit, the dead before the living; who makes things only in order to sell them; who has forgotten that there is such a thing as truth, and measures the world by advertisement or by money.... —*Gilbert Murray*

We live happily indeed, not hating those who hate us. Among men who hate us we dwell free from hatred!...We live happily indeed, though we call nothing our own! We shall live like the bright gods, feeding on happiness! Victory breeds hatred, for the conquered is unhappy. He who has given up victory and defeat, he, the contented, is happy.... —*Gautama Buddha*

The most discouraging, destroying and wretched enemies that can exist....are negative thoughts....
—*Fred Van Amburgh*

Your enemy is your greatest teacher....
—*Buddhist saying*

No man is your enemy; no man is your friend. All alike are your teachers. Your enemy becomes a mystery that must be solved, even though it takes ages, for man must be understood. Your friend becomes a part of yourself, an extension of yourself, a riddle hard to read. Only one thing is more difficult to know—your own heart....
—*Mabel Collins*

Our enemies, are our outward consciences....   *—William Shakespeare*

The desire-nature is your worst foe. It is very difficult to be armed against it, since, firstly, it is an internal foe....
—Ray Mitchell

Never disregard what your enemies say. They may be severe, they may be prejudiced, they may be determined to see only in one direction, but still in that direction they see clearly. They do not speak all the truth, but they generally speak the truth from one point of view; so far as that goes, attend to them....   *—Benjamin Haydon*

Better a thousand enemies outside the house than one inside....
—Arabian proverb

It is the enemy who can truly teach us to practice the virtues of compassion and tolerance....   *—Dalai Lama*

We should never make enemies, if for no other reason, because it is so hard to behave toward them as we ought....
—Ray Palmer

A wise man gets more use from his enemies than a fool from his friends....
—Baltasar Gracian

Man's chief enemy is his own unruly nature and the dark forces pent up within him....   *—Earnest Jones*

Luxury is more deadly than any foe....
—Juvenal

In the degree that we become enemies to the highest and best within us, do we become enemies to all....
—Ralph W. Trine

There is no little enemy....
—Benjamin Franklin

It is much safer to reconcile an enemy than to conquer him; victory may deprive him of his poison, but reconciliation, of his will....   *—Owen Felltham*

We have to learn to be our own best friend because we fall too easily into the trap of being our own worst enemies....   *—Roderick Thorp*

The fire you kindle to destroy your enemy often burns you first....
—Anonymous

My worst enemies are more valuable to me than my best friends....
—Martin Luther

In spite of all the awful evidence of history that nearly every man who has ever lived allows himself to be split up into two enemy camps, to wage a continuous war, mild or violent, on himself, it need not happen....
—James T. Mangan

The fine and noble way to destroy a foe is not to kill him; with kindness you may so change him that he shall cease to be so; then he's slain....
—Charles Alleyn

Beware of no man more than yourself; we carry our worst enemies within us....   *—Charles H. Spurgeon*

Heat not a furnace for your foe so hot that it will singe yourself....
—William Shakespeare

Men of sense often learn from their enemies....   *—Aristophanes*

The greatest enemy of the modern world is boredom. Despite all appearances, mankind is bored. We no longer know what to do with ourselves. Hence....the disorderly turmoil of individuality pursuing conflicts and egotistical aims....   *—Teilhard de Chardin*

Love your enemies, bless them that curse you, do good to them that hate you, and pray for them which spitefully use you and persecute you.... —*Jesus*

Pay attention to your enemies, for they are the first to discover your mistakes.... —*Antishenes*

None but myself ever did me any harm.... —*Napoleon Bonaparte*

If you want enemies, excel others; if friends, let others excel you.... —*Charles C. Colton*

None but one can harm you, none but yourself are your greatest foe; he that respects himself is safe from others: he wears a coat of mail that none can pierce.... —*Henry W. Longfellow*

Most people are their own worst enemies—unconsciously bent on self-destruction.... —*Hans Selye*

Conquer your mind and your senses. These are your real enemies.... —*Sivananda*

In order to have an enemy, one must be somebody.... —*Ann S. Swetchine*

I am persuaded that he who is capable of being a bitter enemy can never possess the necessary virtues that constitute a true friend.... —*William Melmoth*

Flatterers are the worst kind of enemies.... —*Tacitus*

Everyone is his own enemy.... —*St. Bernard*

Love your enemy not because he is your enemy but because beneath his enmity is the eternal fact of brotherhood.... —*Harold Marshall*

To "love your enemies" means to forgive them, and to return good for evil and by doing so you become their superior.... —*Allan Kardec*

Those who hate you don't win unless you hate them and then you destroy yourself.... —*Richard M. Nixon*

When the heart becomes pure, necessarily your enemy must become your friend.... —*Papa Ramdas*

Energy

One of the chief causes of fatigue is boredom....Our fatigue is often caused not by work, but by worry, frustration and resentment....We rarely get tired when we are doing something interesting and exciting.... —*Dale Carnegie*

It is astonishing....how much energy the body is capable of pouring out and then replenishing. That is a magical act, because you never really understand where all that energy comes from.... —*Robert Bly*

Energy is increased in solitude....If you are filled with the energy of the Self, that energy flows out of you and nourishes everyone in your vicinity. You don't have to direct this power outwards....this energy will flow of its own accord.... —*Annamalia Swami*

You are tired because of your mental conflicts. You are antagonistic toward too many things in your environment. Too much of the time you are a house divided against itself, and this inner conflict is an exhausting and sometimes frightening experience.... —*Elinor MacDonald*

When thoughts of concern for the past and of apprehension for the future are dropped, a tremendous energy is freed for use in the present moment....
—A Spiritual Warrior

Fatigue makes cowards of us all....
—Vince Lombardi

The senses are thieves who steal the energy of the Self.... *—Arunagirinatha*

Energy is wasted enormously when one gets angry. The whole nervous system is shattered by an outburst of anger....
—Sivananda

When you have found inner peace, you are in constant contact with the source of universal energy and cannot be tired....You have endless energy....
—Peace Pilgrim

The greater part of the fatigue from which we suffer is of mental origin....
—J. A. Hadfield

Vitality shows in not only the ability to persist, but in the ability to start over....
—F. Scott Fitzgerald

Creative words generate energy; negative words drain out energy....
—Robert Schuller

As energy runs down, there's a loss of order, which is the real meaning of entropy.... *—Vilayat I. Khan*

The body is consuming energy when tense and restoring energy when it is relaxed.... *—John Lust*

Energy levels are determined by feelings: depression saps energy, enthusiasm creates even more energy....
—Anonymous

You can sense energy to the degree your heart is open and loving....
—Sanaya Roman

One of the common causes of exhaustion in the nervous is inability to make a decision quickly and then stick to it....
—W. C. Alvarez

Surrender refreshes and regenerates. Failure to surrender strains and wearies.... *—Piero Ferrucci*

There is no genius in life like the genius of energy.... *—Donald G. Mitchell*

Success is speedy for the energetic....
—Pantanjali

Enthusiasm is the emblem of energy. Enthusiasm tells you where you are today, and predicts where you will be tomorrow. Without enthusiasm you are simply chasing the rainbow promise that recedes as you pursue....
—Fred Van Amburgh

Energy can do anything that can be done in the world....
—Johann W. Goethe

Human energy is low and the Divine Energy is without limit. You are God. You are the Divine Energy. When you do the Divine work, your energy grows.... *—Sathya Sai Baba*

The longer I live, the more deeply am I convinced that that which makes the difference between one man and another—between the weak and the powerful, the great and the insignificant—is energy—invisible determination....
—Charles Buxton

Love the moment, and the energy of that moment will spread out beyond all boundaries.... *—Corita Kent*

The battle to keep up appearance unnecessarily, the mask—whatever name you give creeping perfectionism —robs us of our energies....
—*Robin Worthington*

He alone has energy who cannot be deprived of it.... —*John K. Lavater*

Every time you don't follow your inner guidance, you feel a loss of energy, loss of power, a sense of spiritual deadness.... —*Shakti Gawain*

Energy is like a muscle; it grows stronger through being used....
—*Prabhavananda*

By anger one loses his energy....Anger transmuted into Love becomes an energy so powerful as to move the whole world.... —*Sivananda*

If anything is to be done, let a man do it, let him attack it vigorously!...
—*Gautama Buddha*

In....silence we find a new energy and a real unity. God's energy becomes ours, allowing us to perform things well....
—*Mother Teresa*

Recharging ourselves with endless energy is accomplished simply by consciously thinking of those qualities we know as joy, happiness, enthusiasm, inspiration and ecstasy....
—*Cheryl Canfield*

Think of it, how simple it is to know that the joy of achievement recharges you with a balancing energy for the next achievement. If you have no joy or happiness in your work, finding it to be a drudgery instead, you will find fatigue from the constant devitalizing draining of energy.... —*Walter Russell*

To hate fatigues....
—*Jean Rostand*

Cosmic energy enters any man who will receive it. It flows into his every action, transforming all he touches. But it cannot come in save as it flows out....
—*Dave Seabury*

You have endless energy only insofar as you are working for the good of the whole. As soon as you start working for your selfish little self, it's gone. That's the secret of it.... —*Peace Pilgrim*

The most exhausting thing in life is being insincere. This is why so much social life is exhausting....
—*Anne Morrow Lindbergh*

Energy is Eternal Delight....
—*William Blake*

The universe is energy that responds to expectations.... —*James Redfield*

Once we open up to the flow of energy within our body, we also open up to the flow of the energy in the universe....
—*Wilhelm Reich*

Enlightenment

Those who really seek the path to Enlightenment dictate terms to their mind. They then proceed with strong determination....
—*Gautama Buddha*

There is no difference between an enlightened man and an ignorant one. What makes the difference, is that the one realizes it, while the other is kept in ignorance of it.... —*Hui-Neng*

Enlightenment is characterized by the pure inner light. This creation emerges from nothing, it dissolves in nothing, its nature is void, it does not exist....
—*Yoga Vasistha*

Enlightenment is "being," and it grows; its end is serenity.... —*William Gibson*

Enlightenment must come little by little, otherwise it would overwhelm.... —*Idries Shah*

The spirit enlightens whom it chooseth.... —*Hindu proverb*

There are many paths to enlightenment. Be sure to take the one with a heart.... —*Lao-tzu*

Enlightenment is the natural condition of life after you strip the unnatural heavy and dark conditions away.... —*Ron Smothermon*

Enlightenment is simply waking up and recognizing the illusion of life for what it is.... —*Shantidasa*

To the enlightened man....whose consciousness embraces the universe, to him the universe becomes his "body."... —*Lama Govinda*

You are destined for enlightenment. Cooperate with your destiny, don't go against it, don't thwart it. Allow it to fulfill itself.... —*Nisargadatta*

Everyone will become enlightened. Some before others. But everyone will. There is no way it won't happen. But all need inspiration in order to find their way.... —*Iris Belhayes*

Inner peace is also enlightenment, a state where your life is governed by the God-centered nature, as opposed to the self-centered nature.... —*Peace Pilgrim*

If you are enlightened, you are not free, as some people say, but you are freedom itself. Not like a bird in the sky, but like the sky itself.... —*Walter A. Keers*

Since I received enlightenment in the infinite wonders of truth I have always been cheerful and laughing.... —*Hung Chou*

If a man is free from sin, his mind and heart must be opened to the influence of enlightenment.... —*The Talmud*

God realization does not begin in a cave high atop the Himalayas. It begins in the pots and pans of the kitchen. Treat all of your tasks, however small, as opportunities to see God and serve Him.... —*Sivananda*

Everything that I have written seems to me like straw, in comparison with the things that I have seen and that have been revealed to me.... —*Thomas Aquinas*

Words are a distraction to enlightenment. Getting rid of conceptual thinking means enlightenment.... —*Ramesh Balsekar*

Enlightenment is not an attainment; it is a realization. When you wake up, everything changes and nothing changes. If a blind man realizes that he can see, has the world changed?... —*Dan Millman*

Enlightenment is the highest good. Once you have it, nobody can take it away from you.... —*Siddharameshwar*

Before enlightenment, I chopped wood and carried water; after enlightenment, I chopped wood and carried water.... —*Zen saying*

You may have expected that enlightenment would come ZAP! instantaneous and permanent. This is unlikely. After the first "ah ha" experience, it can be thought of as the thinning of a layer of clouds.... —*Ram Dass*

The Wisdom of Enlightenment is inherent in every one of us. It is because of the delusion under which our mind works that we fail to realize it ourselves, and that we have to seek the advice and the guidance of enlightened ones....   —*Hui-Neng*

The attainment of enlightenment from ego's point of view is extreme death....
                    —*Chögyam Trungpa*

In proportion as men become enlightened in regard to spiritual things, they attach less value to material things....
                    —*Allan Kardec*

Enlightenment cannot be attained, nor forced. It can only happen....It can appear only when it is given a vacant space to appear in....
                    —*Nisargadatta*

A person who says, "I'm enlightened" probably isn't....   —*Ram Dass*

The reason why so few people find enlightenment is because they have free will and punish themselves by making wrong choices. Constantly, enlightenment is being offered to them, but they refuse to accept it. Therefore they are being taught problems that are set before them, since they refuse to make choices voluntarily....   —*Peace Pilgrim*

Enthusiasm

Enthusiasm is the greatest asset in the world. It is nothing more or less than faith in action....
                    —*Henry Chester*

Enthusiasm makes the difference!...
                    —*Charles E. Jones*

Enthusiasm is not a thing which some possess and others lack. All persons have it potentially, but only a few are able to express it....
                    —*William W. Atkinson*

Enthusiasm changes the quality of the job because it changes people....
                    —*Norman V. Peale*

Look at everything as though you were seeing it for the first or last time. Then your time on earth will be filled with glory....   —*Betty Smith*

Without enthusiasm, every task is difficult....   —*Anonymous*

If we find nothing of interest where we are, we are likely to find little of lasting interest where we wish to go....
                    —*Edwin W. Teale*

Enthusiasm is the temper of the mind in which the imagination has got the better of judgement....
                    —*William Warburton*

When you are inspired by some great purpose, some extraordinary project, all your thoughts break their bounds. Your mind transcends limitations, your consciousness expands in every direction, and you will find yourself in a new, great and wonderful world....
                    —*Patanjali*

When a man's willing and eager, God joins in....   —*Aeschylus*

Enthusiasm is that secret and harmonious spirit which hovers over the production of genius....   —*Isaac D'Israeli*

When you go through a day, utterly devoid of enthusiasm, you are like a sluggish little stream of muddy water, flowing its easiest, sluggish, downhill course....   —*Fred Van Amburgh*

Enthusiasm reaches out with joy, for there is nothing depressing about it; it reaches out in faith, for there is no fear in it; it reaches out with acceptance, for there is no doubt in it; it reaches out as a child for there is no uncertainty about it.... —*Ernest Holmes*

Enthusiasm is the great tool of persuasion....You can do nothing effectively without enthusiasm....
—*Napoleon Hill*

Your enthusiasm is not dead; it merely hides below your cynical practicality....
—*David Seabury*

Enthusiasm is the genius of sincerity; and truth accomplishes no victories without it....
—*Edward Bulwer-Lytton*

Every great and commanding movement in the annals of the world is a triumph of enthusiasm....
—*Ralph W. Emerson*

Nothing great or new can be done without enthusiasm. Enthusiasm is the flywheel which carries your saw through the knots in the log....
—*Harvey Cushing*

Enthusiasm gives life to what is invisible.... —*Madame de Staël*

Great designs are not accomplished without enthusiasm of some sort. It is the inspiration of everything great....
—*Christian Bovee*

Enthusiasm is the father of excellence.... —*Bruce A. Johnson*

We act as though comfort and luxury were the chief requirements of life, when all we need to make us happy is something to be enthusiastic about....
—*Charles Kingsley*

If you can give your son or daughter only one gift, let it be enthusiasm....
—*Bruce Barton*

Be enthusiastic till it thrills you. Display it, radiate it, till it infects all those around you.... —*Homi Kharas*

All noble enthusiasms pass through a feverish stage, and grow wiser and more serene.... —*William E. Channing*

Every man loves what he is good at....
—*Thomas Shadwell*

The worst bankrupt is the person who has lost enthusiasm. Let one lose everything but enthusiasm and that person will again come through to success....
—*H. W. Arnold*

Enthusiasm always exaggerates the importance of important things and overlooks the deficiencies....
—*Hugh S. Tigner*

Opposition always inflames the enthusiast, never converts him....
—*Johann von Schiller*

A man without judgement is like a car without brakes, but a man without enthusiasm is like a car without a motor.... —*Judith Lane*

Enthusiasm, like measles, mumps and the common cold, is highly contagious.... —*Emory Ward*

Zeal without knowledge is fire without light.... —*Thomas Fuller*

Enthusiasm is the thing which makes the world go round. Without its driving power, nothing worth doing has ever been done. Love, friendship, religion, altruism, devotion to career or hobby, —all these, and most of the other good things of life, are forms of enthusiasm.... —*Robert H. Schauffler*

No person who is enthusiastic about his work has anything to fear from life. All the opportunities in the world are waiting to be grasped by people who are in love with what they're doing....
—*Sam Goldwyn*

Earnestness is enthusiasm tempered by reason.... —*Blaise Pascal*

Apathy can only be overcome by enthusiasm, and enthusiasm can only be aroused by two things: first, an ideal which takes the imagination by storm; and second, a definite intelligible plan for carrying the ideal into practice....
—*Arnold Toynbee*

None are so old as those who have outlived enthusiasm....
—*Henry D. Thoreau*

There can be no success without enthusiasm. The secret of a full life is lots of enthusiasm, the kind that keeps you fighting and winning over all obstacles —and enjoying every minute of it....
—*Alfred Krebs*

Enthusiasm is one of life's greatest qualities, but it must be practiced to become a dominant factor in one's life....There is real magic in enthusiasm. It spells the difference between mediocrity and accomplishment....
—*Norman V. Peale*

Enthusiasts soon understand each other.... —*Washington Irving*

The world belongs to the enthusiast who keeps cool.... —*William McFee*

Enthusiasm is one thing that can't be feigned.... —*Jerome S. Gross*

Fires can't be made with dead embers, nor can enthusiasm be stirred by spiritless men.... —*James Baldwin*

The Greeks have given us one of the most beautiful words of our language, the word "enthusiasm"—a god within. The grandeur of the acts of men is measured by the inspiration from which they spring. Happy is he who bears a God within.... —*Louis Pasteur*

Enthusiasm is more catching than the measles. So are indifference and lack of enthusiasm.... —*Les Giblin*

The successful reformers are those who are seeking not so much to "make people good" as to share an enthusiasm....
—*Charles A. Bennett*

The sense of this word among the Greeks affords the noblest definition of it; enthusiasm signifies "God in us."...
—*Madame de Staël*

The prudent man may direct a state, but it is the enthusiast who regenerates it....Nothing is so contagious as enthusiasm.... —*Edward Bulwer-Lytton*

Envy/Jealousy

When envy consumes us, we are unable to love, unable to appreciate others. Envy opens the floodgates to our darkest emotions and our most mean-spirited inclinations....
—*Melvyn Kinder*

Envy always implies conscious inferiority wherever it resides.... —*Pliny*

All envy is proportionate to desire; we are uneasy at the attainments of another.... —*Samuel Johnson*

Jealousy, that dragon that slays love under the pretense of keeping it alive....
—*Havelock Ellis*

Though jealousy be produced by love, as ashes are by fire, yet jealousy extinguishes love as ashes smother the flame.... —*Marguerite of Navarre*

Immature people are jealous because they do not know they are just as important as anyone else, with just as much potential, and with a job in the divine plan.... —*Peace Pilgrim*

Envy is the desire to possess something you don't have; jealousy is the fear of losing something you don't possess.... —*Anonymous*

Nothing is more capable of troubling our reason and consuming our health, than secret notions of jealousy in solitude.... —*Aphra Behir*

To jealousy, nothing is more frightful than laughter.... —*Francoise Sagan*

Jealousy is indeed a poor medium to secure love, but it is a secure medium to destroy one's self-respect.... —*Emma Goldman*

Envy's a coal coming hissing hot from hell.... —*Philip J. Bailey*

When men are full of envy they disparage everything, whether it be good or bad.... —*Tacitus*

Jealousy lives upon doubts. It becomes madness or ceases entirely as soon as we pass from doubt to certainty.... —*Francois La Rochefoucauld*

There is a time in every man's education when he arrives at the conviction that envy is ignorance.... —*Ralph W. Emerson*

Envy shooteth at others, but hitteth and woundeth herself.... —*Gabriel Harvey*

Jealousy is based on a feeling of inadequacy and a lack of self-worth....The best way to handle the jealousy is to concentrate on loving yourself.... —*Louise L. Hay*

Envy slays itself by its own arrows.... —*Anonymous*

Jealousy is like fire; it eats up goodness, just as fire consumes fuel.... —*Sivananda*

Jealousy is more self-love than love.... —*Francois La Rochefoucauld*

Never try to please an envious person.... —*Luc de Clapiers Vauvenargues*

A man that has no virtue in himself ever envies virtue in others; for men's minds will either feed upon their own good, or upon other's evil.... —*Francis Bacon*

It is not love that is blind but jealousy.... —*Lawrence Durrell*

When envy is in your heart, your neighbor's hens will look like turkeys, and your neighbor's cabin like a castle. Envy enlarges everything.... —*Fred Van Amburgh*

Our knowledge of what the richer than ourselves possess, and the poor do not, has never been more widespread. Therefore, envy, which is wanting what others have, and jealousy, which is not wanting others to have what one has, have never been more widespread.... —*John Fowles*

Jealousy is the injured lover's hell.... —*John Milton*

Envy has a thousand eyes, but none with correct vision.... —*Issachar Hurwitz*

Jealousy sees things always with magnifying glasses which make little things large; of dwarfs, giants, of suspicions, truths.... —*Miguel de Cervantes*

If we but knew how little some enjoy of the great things that they possess, there would not be much envy in the world.... —*Edward Young*

If you believe that God pervades everything that He has created, you must believe that you cannot enjoy anything that is not given by Him, and seeing that He is the Creator of his numberless children, it follows that you cannot covet anybody's possessions.... —*Mohandas K. Gandhi*

Jealousy is the sister of love, as the devil is the brother of angels.... —*Stanislas Bouttlers*

It would be an error to try to build the Kingdom of Heaven upon envy. For nothing that is founded on envy can thrive; it must have another root.... —*Paracelsus*

Jealousy is the fear or apprehension of superiority; envy, our uneasiness under it.... —*William Shenstone*

Envy has no other quality but that of detracting from virtue.... —*Livy*

Envy is simply being angry at being left out of the happiness of others.... —*Hans-Ulrick Rieker*

Jealousy is a manifestation of an inferiority complex; it is born of self-love, begotten by weakness, and it lives on doubt.... —*Fred Van Amburgh*

No man can ever know his own garden who is always looking over the wall.... —*Fulton J. Sheen*

Envy ought to have no place allowed it in the heart of man; for the goods of this present world are so vile and low that they are beneath it; and those of the future world are so vast and exalted that they are above it.... —*Charles C. Colton*

Envy is its own torturer.... —*Danish proverb*

Envy is the enemy of happiness.... —*John H. Crowe*

Envy requires keeping your eyes off yourself and focused on others.... —*Melvyn Kinder*

Base envy withers at another's joy, and hates the excellence it cannot reach.... —*James Thomson*

As a moth gnaws a garment, so does envy consume a man.... —*John Chrysostom*

Jealousy is another canker that consumes man. It is nothing but petty-mindedness.... —*Sivananda*

Evil

Good is great and real; hence, its opposite, evil, must be small and unreal.... —*Mary Baker Eddy*

Imaginary evils are incurable.... —*Marie von Ebner Eschenbach*

Evil does exist, but we do not have to accept it as an inevitable fact of life.... —*Paramananda*

One can only think of spoiling others after one has spoiled oneself.... —*Ramana Maharshi*

Evil is merely a mask—a dysfunction....
—*Wendy Kaminer*

When God is everywhere, how can there be a place for evil? There are changes and they sometimes appear evil. Everything is at work. Only God knows what He is about....
—*Yoga Swami*

We need to realize in all its implications the fact that the ego itself is the source of all the evil that besets life. But to most inquirers the ego is dear as life itself, because they think it is themselves, and do not want to lose it. They would rather suffer all the ills of life than be happy without it....
—*Lakshmana Sarma*

In the eyes of God there is no evil. We suffer because of our ego....What, after all, is right and wrong? That which takes you towards God is right and that which takes you away from God is wrong. There is no question of right and wrong for one who has realized God....   —*Papa Ramdas*

Nothing which is naturally inevitable can possibly be evil. Winter, night, death are not evils. They are the natural transitions from one day to another day, from autumn to spring, from one life to another life....   —*Eliphas Levi*

Evil and negative conditions cannot be overcome by fighting them, or endeavoring to alter them, anymore than one can alter one's shadow by trying to cut it into a different shape with a pair of shears....   —*Henry T. Hamblin*

Whenever evil befalls us, we ought to ask ourselves, after the first suffering, how we can turn it into good. So shall we take occasion, from one bitter root, to raise perhaps many flowers....
—*Leigh Hunt*

Much in man's world looks evil and ugly to us because we are seeing everything in an unfinished state of evolution....   —*Elinor MacDonald*

There is no explanation for evil. It must be looked upon as a necessary part of the order of the universe; to ignore it is childish, to bewail it senseless....
—*Somerset Maugham*

If one is plotting evil he always uses pleasant words. When a hunter sees the game he sings a sweet song to lure it....
—*Tibetan saying*

The evil you know is better than the evil you don't know....
—*Russian proverb*

He who passively accepts evil is as much involved in it as he who helps to perpetuate it....   —*Martin L. King, Jr.*

Sin....has been made not only ugly but passé. People are no longer sinful, they are only immature or underprivileged or frightened or, more particularly, sick....   —*Phyllis McGinley*

Do not resist the wicked person: If someone strikes you on one cheek, turn the other....   —*Jesus*

Sin and evil are nothing less than our inability to love....
—*Thomas M. MacDonald*

Really good and evil are one and the same, and are in our mind. When the mind is tranquil neither good nor evil affects it....We must find we are beyond good and evil....   —*Vivekananda*

Only by contrast with evil could I have learned to feel the beauty of truth and love and goodness....   —*Helen Keller*

Evil....can never pass away, for there must always be an opposite to good. It has no place in heaven, so of necessity it haunts the mortal nature of this earthly sphere. Therefore, we ought to escape from earth to heaven as quickly as we can; and the way to escape is to become like God, as far as possible; and the way to become like Him is to become holy, good and wise....

—*Plato*

Evil is a screen which hides the truth....

—*Hindu saying*

The belief in a supernatural power of evil is not necessary; men alone are quite capable of every wickedness....

—*Joseph Conrad*

If evil existed, this would mean God created it. Such a thing is impossible. If there were two equal powers, they would neutralize each other. What we see as evil is not ultimately real but is simply a result of the creative power of thought....　　—*Shirley Briggs*

Negativity has within it the seeds of its own destruction....　　—*Emmanuel*

There is no evil that does not offer inducements. Avarice promises money; luxury, a varied assortment of pleasure; ambition, a purple robe and applause. Vices tempt you by the rewards which they offer....　　—*Seneca*

For every thousand hacking at the leaves of evil, there is one striking at the root....　　—*Henry D. Thoreau*

There is only one good—knowledge, and one evil—ignorance....　　—*Socrates*

In our obsession with original sin, we have forgotten original innocence....

—*Pope Innocent*

Evil has an appetite for falsity, and eagerly seizes it as truth....

—*Emanuel Swedenborg*

For as long as the root of wickedness is hidden, it is strong, but when it is recognized it is dissolved....

—*Gospel of Phillip*

Do not fight evil directly—bypass it!...

—*The Talmud*

There is a great difference between resisting the negative force and renouncing it. When you resist this dark force, or what man calls evil, you give the subject attention and growth. When you renounce evil you take your attention from it and give your attention to what you want....

—*Darwin Gross*

The coward only threatens when he is safe....　　—*Johann W. Goethe*

The greatest cure for disharmony is the knowledge that it is not from God, and that God never did create it....

—*Baird Spalding*

Distrust all men in whom the impulse to punish is powerful....

—*Friedrich W. Nietzsche*

To see and listen to the wicked is already the beginning of wickedness....

—*Confucius*

Often our greatest crimes are those we don't realize....　　—*Eliphas Levi*

In the huge mass of evil as it rolls and swells, there is ever some good working toward deliverance and triumph....

—*Thomas Carlyle*

We believe at once in evil; we only believe in good upon reflection. Is not this sad?...　　—*Madam Deluzy*

Remember that the sin and shame of the world are your sin and shame for you are part of it. The soiled garment you shrink from touching may have been yours yesterday, may be yours tomorrow. Therefore, be wary lest too soon you fancy yourself something apart from the masses....

—*Mabel Collins*

Evil is evil because it is unnatural....

—*Frederick W. Robertson*

Forces of evil have power only on their own plane: they can affect us only through our own evil, or thought and receptiveness to evil....

—*Henry T. Hamblin*

The use of evil will create more evil....

—*Fridtjof Nansen*

Evil is not a reality, but it is an obsession. It has come with the ego. It will disappear along with the ego....

—*Papa Ramdas*

The only evil there is, is the belief in a self-hood or a condition separate and apart from God....   —*Joel Goldsmith*

Evil can never survive, though for a time it may seem to triumph. It is only a question of our endurance and patience....   —*Paramananda*

In the world there is nothing absolutely bad. Know, moreover, evil is only relative....   —*The Masnavi I Ma'Naui*

If an evil person falls in a well, what should be done? Pull him out. Do not think that the bad will always be bad; lead them to the right road....

—*Nityananda*

The first way to avoid an evil, is to know it, and to know the cause and occasion of it....   —*Benjamin Whichcote*

Fighting any adverse condition only increases its power over us....

—*Ernest Holmes*

Evil is antagonism with the entire creation....   —*Johann H. Zschokke*

In their immaturity, the people of the world have been attempting to overcome evil with more evil and they have multiplied the evil. Evil can only be overcome by good....   —*Peace Pilgrim*

There is but one way to worship God: it is to be devoid of evil....It is the height of evil not to know God....   —*Hermes*

Good has but one enemy, the evil; but the evil has two enemies, the good and itself....   —*Johannes von Muller*

It matters not what our evils are....hardness of heart, covetousness, wrath, pride and ambition. Our remedy is always one and the same, always at hand, always certain and infallible....

—*William Law*

As sure as God is good, so surely there is no such thing as necessary evil....

—*Robert Southle*

The exit of evil works the entrance of virtue....   —*Philo*

We cannot do evil to others without doing it to ourselves....

—*Joseph Desmahis*

There is nothing evil save that which perverts the mind and shackles the conscience....   —*St. Ambrose*

All punishment in itself is evil....

—*Jeremy Bentham*

Those who do evil in the open light of day—men will punish them. Those who do evil in secret—God will punish them....   —*Kwang Tze*

Much that we call evil is really good in disguise; and we should not quarrel rashly with adversaries not yet understood, nor overlook the mercies often bound up in them....
—*Thomas Browne*

All evils are negations....
—*Maimonides*

Whatever good you have is all from God. Whatever evil, all is from yourself....
—*Koran*

No man chooses evil because it is evil; he only mistakes it for happiness, the good he seeks....
—*Mary Wollstonecraft*

Evil consists in destroying life, doing it injury, hindering its development....
—*Albert Schweitzer*

This would be the most extreme of ills —not to be conscious of the presence of evil. For this is the condition of people who no longer want to rise....
—*Synesius*

The most evil is done by people who never make up their minds to be either good or evil....
—*Hannah Arendt*

Evil is not an actual substance, but absence of good; just as darkness is nothing but absence of light....
—*Abba Evagrius*

If we rightly estimate what we call good and evil, we shall find it lies in comparison....
—*John Locke*

Even in evil, that dark cloud that hangs over creation, we discern rays of light and hope, and gradually come to see, in suffering and temptations, proofs and instruments of the sublimest purposes of wisdom and love....
—*William E. Channing*

The greatest penalty of evil-doing is to grow into the likeness of bad men....
—*Plato*

The basic formula for all sin is: frustrated or neglected love....
—*Franz Werfel*

Every evil thought or deed or hatred, or any other thought or reaction if it is controlled, will be laid in our favor. It is not that we lose by thus restraining ourselves; we are gaining infinitely more than we suspect....
—*Vivekananda*

The man who has no wound on his hand may touch poison with his hand, for poison cannot affect a man with no open wound. Neither is there evil for the man free of evil....
—*Buddhist saying*

It is not sufficient to deny or ignore evil; it must be understood. It is not enough to pray to God to remove the evil; you must find out why it is there, and what lesson it has for you. It is of no avail to fret and fume and chafe at the chains that bind you; you must know how and why you are bound....
—*James Allen*

Non-cooperation with evil is as much a duty as cooperation with good....
—*Mohandas Gandhi*

The root of evil is attachment which has sprung from the seed called desire —the primal cause of ignorance....
—*Papa Ramdas*

The lives of the best of us are spent in choosing evils....
—*Junius*

Belief in a cruel God makes a cruel man....
—*Thomas Paine*

Without evil the All would be incomplete. For most or even all forms of evil serve the Universe....Vice itself has many useful sides.... —*Plotinus*

Idleness leads first to boredom, then to mischief, and eventually to evil....
—*Anonymous*

It is a law of our humanity that man must know good through evil. No great principle ever triumphed but through much evil. No man ever progressed to greatness and goodness but through mistakes.... —*Frederick W. Robertson*

Ill deeds are doubled with an evil word.... —*William Shakespeare*

In every evil thought there is a spark of divinity, which has sunk to a very low degree, and begs to be elevated....
—*Joseph Opatoshu*

Most of the evil that man has inflicted upon man has come through people feeling quite certain about something which, in fact, was false....
—*Lord Russell*

The only intrinsic evil is lack of love....
—*John Robinson*

We need not reach out to tear down that which is evil because nothing which is contrary to God's laws can endure. All not-good things in the world are transient, containing within themselves the seeds of their own destruction.... —*Peace Pilgrim*

Evil is good perverted....
—*Henry W. Longfellow*

Evil is like poison ivy; the more you scratch, the more it itches, and the more it spreads.... —*A. Nicolas*

People who seek evil in others, find it. This applies to nations as well as individuals.... —*Jawaharlal Nehru*

Evil is not being, it is a hole in being, a lack. That is why there can be no absolute evil.... —*Yves M. Congar*

Evil is that which makes for separateness.... —*Aldous Huxley*

Evil is neither person, place, nor being, but simply a belief, an illusion of material sense.... —*Mary Baker Eddy*

Evil is that which God does not will....
—*Emil Brunner*

Evil has no substance of its own, but is only the defect, excess, perversion, or corruption of that which has substance.... —*John H. Newman*

The first lesson of history is that evil is good.... —*Ralph W. Emerson*

If you believe that evil is at work, that is, malicious forces uncontrolled by God, then you are sure to act wrongly by forcing the issue instead of waiting for Divine Wisdom to open a better way.... —*Henry T. Hamblin*

Example

W e must be the change we wish to see in the world....
—*Mohandas Gandhi*

Few things are harder to put up with than the annoyance of a good example.... —*Mark Twain*

To set a lofty example is the richest bequest a man can leave behind....
—*Samuel Smiles*

A rogue is not an eternal rogue. A prostitute is not an eternal prostitute. Put these people in the company of saints. They will be newly molded and will be transformed into saints with virtuous qualities.... —*Sivananda*

If you see anybody fallen by the wayside and lying in the ditch, it isn't much good climbing into the ditch and lying by his side.... —*H. R. L. Sheppard*

Be a pattern to others, and all will go well: for as a whole city is affected by the promiscuous passions of great men, so it is likewise reformed by their moderation.... —*Cicero*

Let us preach without preaching, not by words but by example, by the catching force, the sympathetic influence of what we do.... —*John H. Newman*

People never improve unless they look to some standard or example higher and better than themselves....
—*Tryon Edwards*

You think absolute consistency is possible; prove it by example. Don't preach what you do not practice....
—*Nisargadatta*

Nothing is so infectious as example....
—*Charles Kingsley*

Live with wolves and you will soon learn to howl.... —*Spanish proverb*

One watch set right will do to set many by; one that goes wrong may be the means of misleading a whole neighborhood; and the same may be said of example.... —*Lewis W. Dilyn*

A good example is always the best sermon, the most effective teacher....
—*Anonymous*

Precept is instruction written in the sand. The tide flows over it, and the record is gone. Example is graven on the rock, and the lesson is not soon lost.... —*William E. Channing*

We can only change others through example.... —*Peace Pilgrim*

My advice is to consult the lives of other men, as one would a looking glass, and from thence fetch examples for imitation.... —*Terence*

Children have never been very good at listening to their elders, but they have never failed to imitate them....
—*James Baldwin*

None preach better than the ant, and she says nothing....
—*Benjamin Franklin*

From the loving example of one family, a whole state may become loving; from the ambition and perseverance of one man, the whole state may be thrown into a rebellion. Such is the nature of influence.... —*Confucius*

No reproof or denunciation is so perfect as the silent influence of a good example.... —*Maturin Ballou*

One thorn of experience is worth a whole wilderness of warning....
—*James Russell Lowell*

Old people like to give good advice, as solace for no longer being able to provide bad examples....
—*Francois La Rochefoucauld*

We reform others unconsciously acting uprightly.... —*Hebrew proverb*

Example is the school of mankind, and they will learn at no other....
—*Edmund Burke*

Example • 140 • *Example*

People seldom improve when they have no model but themselves to copy after....
—*Oliver Goldsmith*

Men trust rather their eyes than their ears. The effect of precepts is, therefore, slow and tedious, while that of examples is summary and effectual....
—*Seneca*

There is transcendent power in example. We reform others subconsciously, when we walk uprightly....
—*Ann S. Swetchine*

We are all of us more or less echoes, repeating involuntarily the virtues, the defects, the movements, and the characters of those among whom we live....
—*Jean Joubert*

I have ever deemed it more honorable and more profitable, too, to set a good example than to follow a bad one....
—*Thomas Jefferson*

Do not take the example of another as an excuse for your wrongdoing....
—*Eknath Easwaran*

I am satisfied that we are less convinced by what we hear than by what we see....
—*Herodotus*

Example is a lesson that all men can read....
—*Gilbert West*

The only rational way of education is to be an example—if you can't help it, a warning example....
—*Albert Einstein*

One example is more valuable....than twenty precepts written in books....
—*Roger Ascham*

For each man to be a standard unto himself is excellent for the good, but for the bad it is the worst of all things....
—*Homer*

In no way can we so effectively hasten the dawning of the inner consciousness of another, as by showing forth the divinity within ourselves simply by the way we live. By example and not by precept. By living not by preaching. By doing not by professing....
—*Ralph W. Trine*

It is no use walking anywhere to preach unless our walking is our preaching....
—*Francis of Assisi*

Make small commitments and keep them. Be a light, not a judge. Be a model, not a critic. Be part of the solution, not part of the problem....
—*Stephen R. Covey*

There is no real excellence in all this world which cannot be separated from right living....
—*David S. Jordan*

He who lives well is the best preacher....
—*Miguel de Cervantes*

Even when walking in a party of three I can always be certain of learning from those I am with. There will be good qualities that I can select for imitation and bad ones that will teach me what requires correction in myself....
—*Confucius*

A frightened captain makes a frightened crew....
—*Lister Sinclair*

Example is not the main thing in influencing others. It is the only thing....
—*Albert Schweitzer*

No one can become another, even by following exactly what another is doing....
—*Muni Swamy*

Example is always better than precept. Live an ideal life and by doing so, change the heart of others....
—*Papa Ramdas*

Failure/Mistake

There are occasions when it is undoubtedly better to incur loss than to make gain.... —*Plautus*

When we begin to take our failures nonseriously, it means we are ceasing to be afraid of them. It is of immense importance to learn to laugh at ourselves.... —*Katherine Mansfield*

It is in our faults and failings, not in our virtues, that we touch one another and find sympathy.... —*Jerome K. Jerome*

Failure will never overtake you if your determination to succeed is strong enough.... —*Og Mandino*

Thinking like a winner means not always having to defeat someone else. It means being able to grow from a situation in which you fail to meet your goal.... —*Wayne Dyer*

Defeat does not finish a man—quit does. A man is not finished when he is defeated. He's finished when he quits.... —*Richard M. Nixon*

The basic causes of failure in life are: Lack of objectives, lack of steadfastness of purpose or a resolute plan to fulfill the objectives.... —*A. V. Deshmane*

The only failure a man ought to fear is failure to cleaving to the purpose he sees to be best.... —*George Eliot*

A series of failures may culminate in the best possible result.... —*Gisela Richter*

Failure is impossible.... —*Susan B. Anthony*

To understand how something works, it helps to know how it can fail.... —*Marvin Minsky*

Defeat is a school in which truth always grows strong.... —*Henry W. Beecher*

Losers visualize the penalties of failure. Winners visualize the rewards of success.... —*Rob Gilbert*

Picture yourself vividly as defeated and that alone will make victory impossible.... —*Harry E. Fosdick*

You only fail if you quit trying.... —*Edgar Cayce*

There are thousands to tell you it cannot be done, there are thousands to prophesy failure. There are thousands to point out to you, one by one, the dangers that await to assail you. But just buckle in with a bit of a grin, just take off your coat and go to it; Just start to sing as you tackle the thing that "cannot be done," and you'll do it.... —*Edgar Guest*

Do not brood over failures, defects and mistakes. They will weaken your "will."...Just reflect for a while why you have failed in the attempt and try to be careful in the second attempt.... —*Sivananda*

There is no failure except in no longer trying. There is no defeat save your own inherent weakness of purpose.... —*Richard Pape*

Even after the greatest defeats, the depressing thought of being a failure is best combated by taking stock of all your past achievements.... —*Hans Selye*

If you can learn to learn from failure, you'll go pretty much where you want to go.... —*Arthur Gordon*

Any action that is conceived in the ego and entered into for egotistical purposes, if not doomed to failure from the onset, can result in only mediocre success.... —*U. S. Anderson*

Being defeated is often a temporary condition. Giving up is what makes it permanent... —*Marilyn vos Savant*

Failure is often God's own tool for carving some of the finest outlines in the character of his children.... —*Thomas Hodgkin*

He who hopes to avoid all failure and misfortune is trying to live in a fairyland; the wise man realistically accepts failures as a part of life and builds a philosophy to meet them and make the best of them.... —*Wilferd A. Peterson*

What is defeat? Nothing but education; nothing but the first step to something better.... —*Wendell Phillips*

Failure is instructive. The person who really thinks, learns quite as much from his failures as from his successes.... —*John Dewey*

A failure is a man who has blundered and then is not able to cash in on the experience.... —*Elbert Hubbard*

Failures are divided into two classes— those who thought and never did, and those who did and never thought.... —*John C. Salak*

It is only when everything, even love, fails, that with a flash, man finds out how vain, how dream-like is this world.... —*Vivekananda*

Most people fail not because they lack ability, intelligence, or opportunity, but they fail because they don't give it all they've got.... —*Norman V. Peale*

Our highest hopes are often destroyed to prepare us for better things. The failure of the caterpillar is the birth of the butterfly; the passing of the bud is the becoming of the rose; the death or destruction of the seed is the prelude to its resurrection as wheat. It is at night, in the darkest hours, those preceding dawn, that plants grow best, that they most increase in size.... —*William G. Jordan*

Failure comes only when we forget our ideals and objectives and principles and begin to wander away from the road that leads to their realization.... —*Jawaharlal Nehru*

In God's economy, nothing is wasted. Through failure, we learn a lesson in humility which is probably needed, painful though it is.... —*Bill Wilson*

Only those who dare to fail greatly can ever achieve greatly.... —*Robert F. Kennedy*

Through humiliation and despair, failure and mistakes, the ego may be crushed to the ground.... —*Paul Brunton*

Failure never hurt anybody. It is fear of failure that kills you....You got to go down the alley and take those chances.... —*Jack Lemmon*

Sometimes noble failure serves the world as faithfully as a distinguished success.... —*Edward Dowden*

You always pass failure on the way to success.... —*Mickey Rooney*

When an archer misses the mark, he turns and looks for the fault within himself. Failure to hit the bulls-eye is never the fault of the target. To improve your aim—improve yourself.... —*Gilbert Arland*

There is only one real failure in life that is possible, and that is not to be true to the best one knows....
—*Frederic W. Farrar*

The failures and reverses which await men and one after another sadden the brow of youth—add a dignity to the prospect of human life, which no Arcadian success would do....
—*Henry D. Thoreau*

Many a man fails because he never tries.... —*Norman MacEwan*

Failures always overtake those who have the power to do, without the will to act.... —*James Ellis*

Men heap together the mistakes of their lives and create a monster they call Destiny.... —*John O. Hobbs*

There are some defeats more triumphant than victories....
—*Michel Montaigne*

Man thinks he can fail; man thinks he is failing, man thinks he has failed. Man thinks others are failing and that others have failed him. This is not true. What we have called failure is but the unfolding experiences that have brought us to this present time....
—*Sue Sikking*

I have found that failure is a far better teacher than success....
—*Bernard M. Baruch*

I never blame failure—there are too many complicated situations in life—but I am absolutely merciless towards lack of effort....
—*Francis Scott Key*

There is no cure for failure, except success; it is failure that gives success its value.... —*Walter Winchell*

It is defeat that turns bone to flint and gristle to muscle, and makes men invincible....Do not then be afraid of defeat. You are never so near victory as when defeated in a good cause....
—*Henry W. Beecher*

Failure changes for the better, success for the worse.... —*Seneca*

Failure is not external. It means something is disordered within....
—*Paramananda*

We mount to heaven on the ruins of our cherished schemes, finding our failures were successes....
—*Amos B. Alcott*

Defeat never comes to any man until he admits it.... —*Josephus Daniels*

Failures come to all of us. No matter how hard we try sometimes, things will go wrong....Do not be discouraged because of failures; begin over....
—*Ida S. Taylor*

The way to succeed is to double your failure rate.... —*Thomas Watson*

Whether we stumble, or whether we fall, we must only think of rising again and going on in our course....
—*Francois Fenelon*

There is no failure except in no longer trying. There is no defeat except from within, no really insurmountable barrier save our own inherent weakness of purpose.... —*Elbert Hubbard*

We learn wisdom from failure much more than from success. We often discover what will do by finding out what will not do, and probably he who never made a mistake never made a discovery.... —*Samuel Smiles*

Failure and frustration are in the written pages of everyone's record....
—*Marian Anderson*

The surest recipe for failure is to try to please everyone....   —*Anonymous*

I am not discouraged, because every wrong attempt discarded is another step forward....   —*Thomas A. Edison*

Whenever one finds oneself inclined to bitterness, it is a sign of emotional failure....   —*Bertrand Russell*

Failure is just another word for learning....failure can lead us in new directions....   —*Lois Wolfe-Morgan*

A failure establishes only this, that our determination to succeed was not strong enough....   —*Christian Bovee*

Some of your greatest advances you have judged as failures, and some of your deepest retreats you have evaluated as success....
—*A Course In Miracles*

A fool often fails because he thinks what is difficult is easy, and a wise man because he thinks what is easy is difficult....   —*John C. Collins*

Failure is only postponed success....
—*Herbert Kaufman*

What would you attempt to do if you knew you could not fail?...
—*Robert Schuller*

When you speak of failure, you attract failure. When you speak of success, you attract success....   —*Napoleon Hill*

I cannot give you a formula for success, but I can give you the formula for failure—which is: try to please everybody....
—*Herbert B. Swope*

Failure is not fatal; victory is not success....   —*Tony Richardson*

While one person hesitates because he feels inferior, the other is busy making mistakes and becoming superior....
—*Henry Link*

The biggest contributor to failure is a poor self-image....   —*Will Munson*

If you aim high enough, there is even some glory in failure....
—*Fred Van Amburgh*

No man ever became great or good except through many and great mistakes....   —*William Gladstone*

Though all men fail you, and all material sources fail, God is the same, yesterday and today, and forever; and if you put your trust in God within, you can never fail, because God, by nature, can never fail you....   —*Henry T. Hamblin*

The shame is never in having failed—the shame is only in not having tried....
—*Andrew Matthews*

Mistakes are the portals of discovery....
—*James Joyce*

Strong people make as many and as ghastly mistakes as weak people. The difference is that strong people admit them, laugh at them, learn from them. This is how they become strong....
—*Richard Needham*

If thou art a man, admire those who attempt great things, even though they fail....   —*Seneca*

Without divine assistance I cannot succeed; with it I cannot fail....
—*Abraham Lincoln*

He who fears being conquered is sure of defeat....   *—Napoleon Bonaparte*

Good people are good because they've come to wisdom through failure....
   —William Saroyan

Failure is one of God's educators. It is experience leading man to higher things; it is the revelation of a way, a path hitherto unknown to us. The best men in the world....look back with serene happiness on their failure....
   —William G. Jordan

We are all of us failures—at least, the best of us are....   *—James M. Barrie*

Failure teaches you that you can't count on winning. It provides you with a chance to learn how to deal with defeat....   *—Wess Roberts*

There is always another chance....This thing called "failure" is not the falling down but staying down....
   —Mary Pickford

Failure generally takes the path of least persistence....   *—Anonymous*

An occasional mistake is inevitable, but our mistakes are rarely all that important, and never as disastrous as our minds make them out to be....
   —C. H. Teear

If I were asked to put into one word the greatest cause of failure I would say "negativity." This habit of seeing the ills of life and ignoring the forces leading to accomplishment is far too universal....   *—David Seabury*

Any man may make a mistake, but none but the fool will continue in it....
   —Cicero

We must never forget that disobedience to God's laws brings disaster, although people eventually do learn by their own mistakes....   *—Peace Pilgrim*

The road to wisdom? Well, it's plain and simple to express: Err and err and err again but less and less and less....
   —Piet Hein

Experience is the name so many people give to their mistakes....   *—Oscar Wilde*

From error to error one discovers the entire truth....   *—Sigmund Freud*

Unreasonable haste is the direct road to error....   *—Moliere*

If you shut your door to all errors, truth will be shut out....
   —Rabindrinath Tagore

It is a mistake to look too far ahead. Only one link in the chain of destiny can be handled at a time....
   —Winston Churchill

An expert is someone who knows some of the worst mistakes that can be made in his subject and how to avoid them....
   —Werner Heisenberg

Every great mistake has a halfway moment, a split second when it can be recalled and perhaps remedied....
   —Pearl Buck

There is no fool like the fool who will continue to kick the rubbish of his mistakes along the path ahead of him, and then be compelled to stumble over these mistakes a second time....
   —Fred Van Amburgh

Of course we make mistakes; it's how we learn. We're all in training. Life can be difficult; what an opportunity....
   —Dan Millman

Experience enables you to recognize a mistake when you make it again....
—*Franklin P. Jones*

If the first button of a man's coat is wrongly buttoned, all the rest will be crooked.... —*Giordano Bruno*

The sages do not consider that making no mistake is a blessing. They believe rather that the virtue of man lies in his ability to correct his mistakes and continue to make a new man of himself....
—*Wang Yang Ming*

No persons are more frequently wrong, than those who will not admit they are wrong... —*Francois La Rochefoucauld*

Mistakes are your best teachers....
—*Sivananda*

Mistakes are lessons of wisdom....
—*Hugh White*

Whenever you meet a misfortune, put it into your past. Keep your mind upon future achievement, and you will find that mistakes of the past often work to fill the future with good....
—*Napoleon Hill*

People are failures, not because they are stupid, but because they are not sufficiently impassioned....
—*Burt Struthers*

A full and candid admission of one's mistakes should make proof against its repetition.... —*Mohandas Gandhi*

You need the ability to fail. I'm amazed at the number of organizations that set up an environment where they do not permit their people to be wrong. You cannot innovate unless you are willing to accept some mistakes....
—*Charles Knight*

The only man who never makes a mistake is the man who never does anything.... —*Theodore Roosevelt*

All failures are apparent, not real. Every slip, every fall, every return to selfishness is a lesson learned, an experience gained, from which a golden grain of wisdom is extracted....
—*James Allen*

There is no height to which you cannot climb; no difficulty which you cannot overcome; no failure which cannot be retrieved.... —*Henry T. Hamblin*

There is no such thing as failure for people who have done their best....
—*Anonymous*

Failure is, in a sense, the highway to success, insomuch as every discovery of what is false leads us to seek earnestly after what is true, and every fresh experience points out some form of error which we shall afterward carefully avoid.... —*John Keats*

Failure is the opportunity to begin again more intelligently....
—*Henry Ford*

A man carries his success or failure with him: it is not dependent upon outside conditions.... —*Ralph W. Trine*

Faith

It is the heart which experiences God, and not reason. This, then, is faith: God felt by heart, not by reason....
—*Blaise Pascal*

Neither reproaches nor encouragements are able to revive a faith that is waning.... —*Nathalie Sarraute*

When you rely upon the invisible world there is no place for anything, however small, as a provision....
—*Kitab-Ilahi*

Faith is a function of the heart. It must be enforced by reason. The two are not antagonistic as some think. The more intense one's faith is, the more it whets one's reason. When faith becomes blind it dies.... —*Mohandas Gandhi*

Faith is no faith which is not tried....
—*Katherine Zell*

Nothing in life is more wonderful than faith—the one great moving force which we can never weigh in the balance nor test in the laboratory....
—*William Osler*

There is no greater God than faith....
—*Nityananda*

If you repeat anything constantly and generate enough faith to believe that what you are saying is correct, your mind will become what you are repeating.... —*Annamalai Swami*

What is the use of having faith? It is to connect the soul with God. And what is the object of connecting man with God? That he may become like God....
—*Henry Drummond*

Faith is one of the powers of youth and doubt is a symptom of senility....
—*Eliphas Levi*

In truth, there is no real conflict between faith and reason....
—*Lakshmana Sarma*

The test of our faith is our willingness to suffer for it....The supreme test of faith comes in our belief in a life hereafter.... —*Alice H. Rice*

The most meager hope is nearer the truth than the most rational despair....
—*Charles Wagner*

Faith is not only the means to God, but the end.... —*Bernadette Roberts*

Faith is acknowledging that you know nothing.... —*Anonymous*

All the strength and force of man comes from his faith in things unseen.... —*J. F. Clarke*

Faith receives; love gives. No one will be able to receive without faith. No one will be able to give without love....
—*Gospel of Philip*

The principal part of faith is patience....
—*George MacDonald*

Faith is a dynamic power that breaks the chain of routine.... —*Helen Keller*

One doesn't discover new lands without consenting to lose sight of the shore for a very long time.... —*André Gide*

Faith is the belief in the unknown. Faith heals, faith creates, faith works wonders, faith moves mountains. Faith is the searchlight for God-finding....
—*Sivananda*

An emotionally healthy person is committed to a principle higher than himself: he has faith....
—*Sue Wahlroos*

Faith worships at the shrine of one not seen; but doubt must see her God....
—*The Aquarian Gospel*

To leap across an abyss, one is better served by faith than doubt....
—*William James*

Faith is the temple of virtues.....
—*Amar Jyoti*

If a man wishes to be sure of the road he treads on, he must close his eyes and walk in the dark.... —*John of the Cross*

It is impossible to live a life of faith without prayer—continual prayer. It is only through persistence and perseverance in prayer that our faith can be maintained.... —*Henry T. Hamblin*

Faith remains a matter of personal experience, like chocolate ice cream, a day in autumn and greenness.... —*John Powell*

If you do not expect the unexpected you will not find it, for it is not reached by search or trial.... —*Heraclitus*

Faith is better understood as a verb than a noun, as a process than a possession. It is an on-again, off-again rather than once-and-for-all. Faith is not sure where you're going but going anyway... —*Frederick Buechner*

If one is willing to trust himself fully to the Law, the Law will never fail him. It is the halfhearted trusting to it that brings uncertain, and so, unsatisfactory results.... —*Ralph W. Trine*

If you have faith as a grain of a mustard seed, you shall say unto the mountain, "Remove hence to yonder place," and it shall remove and nothing will be impossible to you.... —*Jesus*

Faith is the biggest and best thing in a man's life. Faith is power. Doubt is weakness.... —*Fred Van Amburgh*

Cease today to merely hope. Stop daydreaming. Forget about wishing, and remember to formulate the consciousness which corresponds with what you truly desire in life.... —*Frank Richelieu*

Faith supplies staying power....Anyone can keep going when the going is good, but some extra ingredient is needed to keep you fighting when it seems that everything is against you.... —*Norman V. Peale*

Faith argues not, thinks not, reasons not.... —*Sivananda*

Hope springs eternal in the human breast.... —*Alexander Pope*

Man must be arched and buttressed from within, else the temple wavers to dust.... —*Marcus Aurelius*

Faith is the consciousness of a reservoir too deep for earthly droughts to run dry.... —*Anonymous*

Divine bounty and provision never fail if we only hang on long enough with faith. If we cast ourselves upon God, entirely and completely, then God has to deliver us, because God can never fail anyone who trusts entirely.... —*George Muller*

Hope is the pillar that holds up the world, the dream of a waking man.... —*Pliny the Elder*

Faith is the substance of things hoped for, the evidence of things not seen.... —*Paul of Tarsus*

Faith begins as an experiment and ends as an experience.... —*W. R. Inge*

Our dependence upon God ought to be so entire and absolute that we should never think it necessary, in any kind of distress, to seek out human consolations.... —*Thomas à Kempis*

It is necessary to the happiness of man that he be mentally faithful to himself.... —*Thomas Paine*

I have lived eighty-six years. I have watched men climb up to success, hundreds of them, and of all the elements that are important for success, the most important is faith... —*James Gibbons*

There is no medicine like hope, no incentive so great, and no tonic so powerful, as expectation of something tomorrow... —*Orison S. Marden*

Faith....looks upward and decries objects remote; but reason can discover things only near, and sees nothing that is above her.... —*Francis Quarles*

Faith comes about in a collision of the unending passion for Truth and the failure to attain it by one's own means.... —*Abraham J. Heschel*

Fear knocked at the door. Faith answered.... —*Irish proverb*

The whole course of things goes to teach us faith. We need only obey. There is guidance for each of us, and by lowly listening we shall hear the right word.... —*Ralph W. Emerson*

Faith is not something to be sought after. Faith is something to be discovered within ourselves.... —*Norma Hawkins*

A faith that varies with differing conditions of life is no faith at all.... —*Anonymous*

Faith can grow only by long cultivation and careful attention.... —*Sathya Sai Baba*

Faith is positive, enriching life in the here and now. Doubt is negative, robbing life of glow and meaning. So though I do not understand immortality, I choose to believe.... —*Webb B. Garrison*

Blind faith should be turned into rational faith. Faith without understanding is only blind faith. Devotion is the development of faith. Knowledge is the development of devotion. Faith leads to the final spiritual experience. Whatever a person strongly believes in, that he experiences and becomes.... —*Sivananda*

All things are possible until they are proved impossible—and even the impossible may only be so as of now.... —*Pearl S. Buck*

Faith is a simple childlike belief in a Divine Friend who solves all problems that come to us.... —*Helen Keller*

When proof is possible, faith becomes impossible! And when proof is impossible, faith becomes possible!... —*Robert Schuller*

By the power of faith every enduring work is accomplished. Faith in the Supreme; faith in the over-ruling Law; faith in your work, and in your power to accomplish that work—here is the rock upon which you must build if you would achieve, if you would stand and not fall.... —*James Allen*

Faith is a belief in things that your senses have not experienced and your mind does not understand, but you have touched them in other ways and have accepted them. It is easy for one to speak of faith; it is another thing to live it.... —*Peace Pilgrim*

In the midst of winter I found within me an invincible summer.... —*Albert Camus*

With faith a man is never alone, never forsaken....Faith is one of the forces by which men live, and the total absence of it means collapse.... —*William James*

Faith is the bird that sings when the dawn is still dark....
—*Rabindranath Tagore*

If you have faith in God, or man, or self, say so. If not, push back upon the shelf of silence all your thoughts, till faith shall come....
—*Ella Wheeler Wilcox*

The man of faith must burn his boats behind him every day of his life. Indeed, he needs no boats, because....he walks on the sea of experience upheld by invisible forces....
—*Henry T. Hamblin*

Directed faith makes every thought crackle with power. You can rise to limitless heights impelled by lifting forces of your mighty new self-confidence....
—*Napoleon Hill*

Be faithful to your love and you will be recompensed beyond measure....
—*Albert Schweitzer*

Faith is the subtle chain that binds us to the infinite.... —*Elizabeth O. Smith*

God never fails His devotees in the hour of trial. The condition is that there must be a living faith and the uttermost reliance on Him. The test of faith is that having done our duty we must be prepared to welcome whatever He may send—joy as well as sorrow, good luck as well as bad....
—*Mohandas Gandhi*

Faith....is the resolve to live as if certain things were true, in the confident assurance that they are true, and that we shall one day find out for ourselves that they are true.... —*W. R. Inge*

In the midst of sorrow, faith draws out the sting of every trouble, and takes out the bitterness from every affliction....
—*Richard Cecil*

Faith moves mountains, but you have to keep pushing while you are praying.... —*Mason Cooley*

Logic and cold reason are poor weapons to fight fear and distrust. Only faith and generosity can overcome them.... —*Jawaharlal Nehru*

Faith is believing where we cannot prove.... —*Alfred L. Tennyson*

Faith without works is like a bird without wings; though she may hop about on earth, she will never fly to heaven....
—*J. Beaumont*

Faith is a rare flower of inestimable value. It must be cultivated in the garden of your heart. It must be watered daily with the water of sincerity. The weeds of doubts and misgivings should be totally eradicated. Then faith will strike deep root, blossom and bear the fruit of devotion quickly....
—*Sivananda*

In actual life every great enterprise begins with and takes its first forward step in faith.... —*August von Schlegel*

If our faith is real, it must encroach upon our life.... —*Karl Barth*

Faith is not a thing which one "loses," we merely cease to shape our lives by it.... —*George Bernaos*

Faith is the door through which we enter the supernatural order. It opens to heaven.... —*Abbot Chapman*

Faith is devotion to God....
—*Jacob Katz*

Hope lives in ignorance, open-eyed. Faith is built upon our knowledge of our life.... —*Robert L. Stevenson*

No black cloud can settle down and overshadow the faith of a good man. In his darkest hour, the true man can see a rift in the clouds, and there find a rainbow of hope.... —*Fred Van Amburgh*

Faith not based on understanding is worse than atheism....
—*Judah L. Gordon*

Faith is the root of all blessings. Believe, and you shall be saved; believe, and your needs must be satisfied; believe, and you cannot but be comforted and happy.... —*Jeremy Taylor*

Faith does nothing alone—nothing of itself, but everything under God, by God, through God.... —*John Stoughton*

Many of us say that we have faith, and that we believe that our supply will manifest, yet at the same time make arrangements in case it does not appear....We say we are going to be victorious, yet we make preparations for defeat. The life of faith cannot be lived in this way.... —*Henry T. Hamblin*

Faith is the capacity of the soul to perceive the abiding....in the transitory, the invisible in the visible....
—*Leon Baeck*

Faith has need of the whole truth....
—*Teilhard de Chardin*

Where is the law that says all things are not possible? No such law exists. Everything is possible to one who understands that limits created by humans can be dispensed with....
—*David Manners*

Faith must have adequate evidence, else it is mere superstition....
—*Archibald A. Hodge*

Faith is the root of all good works....
—*Daniel Wilson*

Faith is to believe, on the word of God, what we do not see, and its reward is to see and enjoy what we believe....
—*Augustine*

Faith expressed in action is a sure means of realization....Faith is not blind. It is the willingness to try....
—*Nisargadatta*

He who has no faith in himself can never have faith in God....
—*Vivekananda*

All the scholastic scaffolding falls, as a ruined edifice, before one single word –faith.... —*Napoleon Bonaparte*

Faith is like a fond mother who can never fail to save her trusting son from dangerous situations....
—*Tripura Rahasya*

There is a thing the world calls disappointment but there is no such word in the dictionary of faith.... —*John Newton*

Let us never lose faith in human nature, no matter how often we are deceived.... —*Chauncey M. Depew*

Act as if you had faith and in time faith will take hold of you.... —*Sufi saying*

Only the person who has faith in himself is able to be faithful to others....
—*Erich Fromm*

Things of God that are marvelous are to be believed on a principle of faith, and not to be pried into by reason....
—*Samuel Gregory*

A faith that cannot survive collusion with the truth is not worth many regrets.... —*Arthur C. Clarke*

I do not pray for success. I ask for faithfulness.... —*Mother Teresa*

As soon as a man rejects all visible help and human hope, and follows after God with faith and a pure heart, grace straightaway follows after him and reveals its power in help of various kinds....
—*Isaac of Syria*

Faith is like love: it cannot be forced. As trying to force love begets hatred, so trying to compel....belief leads to unbelief....
—*Arthur Schopenhauer*

Faith is an invisible and invincible magnet, and attracts to itself whatever it fervently desires and calmly and persistently expects....
—*Ralph W. Trine*

Life is God's novel. Let Him write it....
—*Isaac Bashevis Singer*

Faith is an excitement and an enthusiasm: it is a condition of intellectual magnificence to which we must cling as to treasure, and not squander in the small coin of empty words....
—*George Sand*

In spiritual matters, faith is the very essence. Doubt shakes the foundations of spiritual practices and is therefore to be avoided. Have faith in the wisdom of the ancients; do not pitch your tiny little brain against the intuitions of the saints and their discoveries....
—*Sathya Sai Baba*

It gives me a deep comforting sense that things seen are temporal and things unseen are eternal....
—*Helen Keller*

Faith is the flame that lights the candle of life and without it we are fallow....
—*William R. Miller*

Faith is personal, individual....Faith comes in the finding of one's self. This self-finding establishes a clear realization of one's identity with the eternal....
—*Claude M. Bristol*

Faith is not blind to needs; faith faces reality but sees reality as measured by God, not as measured by man....
—*Anonymous*

Life would not be worth living without faith. Faith in God, faith in ourselves, faith in our fellow men; we should omit none of the three....
—*Ida S. Taylor*

Faith is....an act, an intention, a project, something that makes you, in leaping into the future, go so far, far, far ahead that you shoot clean out of time and right into eternity....
—*Joanna Russ*

Through faith the imagination is invigorated and completed, for it really happens that every doubt mars its perfection. Faith must strengthen the imagination, for faith establishes the will....
—*Paracelsus*

Work without faith is like an attempt to reach the bottom of a bottomless pit....
—*Mohandas Gandhi*

We must embrace the absurd and go beyond everything we have ever known....
—*Janie Gustafson*

Faith is a grand cathedral, with divinely pictured windows. Standing without, you see no glory, nor can imagine any, but standing within, every ray of light reveals a harmony of unspeakable splendors....
—*Nathaniel Hawthorne*

Faith always implies the disbelief of a lesser fact in favor of a greater. A little mind often sees the unbelief, without seeing the belief of large ones....
—*Oliver W. Holmes*

By faith you can move mountains; but the important thing is not to move mountains, but to have faith....
—*Arthur Clutton-Brock*

Without faith a man can do nothing....
—*Henri F. Amiel*

It is cynicism and fear that freezes life; it is faith that thaws it out, releases it, sets it free.... —*Harry E. Fosdick*

Ultimately faith is the only key to the universe. The final meaning of human existence, and the answers to the questions on which all our happiness depends cannot be found in any other way.... —*Thomas Merton*

No ray of sunlight is ever lost, but the green which it wakes into existence needs time to sprout, and it is not always granted to the sower to live to see the harvest. All work that is worth anything is done in faith....
—*Albert Schweitzer*

The only faith that wears well, and holds its color in all weathers, is that which is woven of conviction....
—*James Russell Lowell*

Faith laughs at the shaking of a spear; unbelief trembles at the shaking of a leaf; unbelief starves the soul, faith finds food in famine, and a table in the wilderness.... —*Robert Cecil*

Faith is affirming success before it comes. Faith is making claims to victory before it is achieved....
—*Robert Schuller*

Faith is nothing more or less than the operation of the thought forces in the form of earnest desire, coupled with expectation as to its fulfillment....
—*Ralph W. Trine*

The greatest undeveloped resource in our country is faith.... —*Roger Babson*

Faith declares what the senses do not see.... —*Blaise Pascal*

If faith is lacking, it is because there is too much selfishness, too much concern for personal gain. For faith to be true, it has to be generous and loving. Love and faith go together, they complete each other.... —*Mother Teresa*

The reason why birds can fly and we can't is simply that they have perfect faith, for to have faith is to have wings.... —*James M. Barrie*

Faith is the pencil of the soul that pictures heavenly things....
—*Thomas Burbridge*

Faith is the a-b-c of the realization of God.... —*Hazrat Inayat Khan*

Faith is the wire that connects you to grace, and over which grace comes streaming from God.... —*Anonymous*

Reason is our soul's left hand, Faith her right; by these we reach divinity....
—*John Donne*

Faith is not belief in spite of evidence, but life in scorn of consequences....
—*Kirsopp Lake*

The faith that stands on authority is not faith.... —*Ralph W. Emerson*

A little faith brings your soul to heaven, but a lot of faith will bring heaven to your soul.... —*Dwight L. Moody*

The idea of faith is often misunderstood by people, because they associate it with those who are ignorant, uneducated, and who have no power to investigate for themselves. But faith is not blind belief. It is never well-founded until it is based on experience....
—*Paramananda*

Faith and unfaith can never be equal powers.... —*Alfred L. Tennyson*

At the summit of every noble human endeavor, you will find a steeple pointing toward God....   —*Mack Stokes*

Much knowledge of divine things is lost to us through want of faith....
—*Heraclitus*

Lack of faith in God is the source of most of society's troubles....
—*Albert E. Ribourg*

Our only protection against fear is faith....   —*Ryllis G. Lynip*

Faith and Truth is the same thing—God's side is Truth, our side is Faith....
—*Bernadette Roberts*

Learning to be men and women of faith is like being trained as an athlete. We have to be tested, and our training made more severe, so that our strength and powers of endurance are increased progressively....Every time of testing prepares us for greater adventures in faith....   —*Henry T. Hamblin*

God is there for them that have faith and not for them who have not....
—*Papa Ramdas*

Falsehood

L ying to ourselves is more deeply ingrained than lying to others....
—*Fyodor Dostoyevsky*

Falsehood is so easy; truth so difficult....
—*George Eliot*

If there were no falsehood in the world, there would be no doubt; if there were no doubt, there would be no inquiry; if no inquiry, no wisdom....
—*Walter S. Landor*

One person speaks a falsehood, a hundred repeat it as fact, and soon it becomes a truth....   —*Shantidasa*

Truth is the day of soul, and the night is falsehood. All truth implies falsehood because forms are limited, and all falsehood implies and necessitates a truth in the rectification of the finite by the infinite....   —*Eliphas Levi*

It is falsehood and illusion that always make one suffer—never the truth....
—*Anonymous*

Man cannot play false to his heredity forever. Spawned by the gods, he must return to them....   —*Paul Brunton*

Overcome falsehood with truth....
—*Peace Pilgrim*

A man should blush to think a falsehood; it is a disease of cowards....
—*Charles Johnson*

Once you see the false as false, it is not necessary any further to seek the truth....   —*Nisargadatta*

Whatever is only almost true is quite false and among the most dangerous of errors....   —*Henry W. Beecher*

The telling of a falsehood is like a cut of a sabre; for though the wound may heal, the scar of it will remain....
—*Saadi*

Falsehood, like poison, will generally be rejected when administered alone, but when blended with wholesome ingredients, may be swallowed unperceived....   —*Richard Whatley*

Falsehood often lurks upon the tongue of him, who, by self-praise, seeks to enhance his value in the eyes of others....   —*James G. Bennett*

Falsehoods not only disagree with truths, but usually quarrel among themselves.... —*Daniel Webster*

Falsehood has an infinity of combinations, but truth has only one mode of being.... —*Jean J. Rousseau*

Falsehood may have its hour, but it has no future.... —*Francois D. Pressense*

Falsehood is never so successful as when she baits her hook with truth, and no opinions so falsely mislead us as those that are not wholly wrong.... —*Charles C. Colton*

Fraud and falsehood only dread examination. Truth invites it.... —*Thomas Cooper*

You cannot play with the animal in you without becoming wholly animal, play with falsehood without forfeiting your right to truth, play with cruelty without losing your sensitivity of mind. He who wants to keep his garden tidy doesn't reserve a plot for weeds.... —*Dag Hammarskjöld*

Falsehood is a refuge, an asylum for the cruel, the violent, for consummate animals. What begins in a lie ends in a blasphemy.... —*Abraham J. Heschel*

The most dangerous of all follies is perverted wisdom.... —*Eliphas Levi*

Fame

There is not in the world so toilsome a trade as the pursuit of fame.... —*Jean La Bruyere*

Fame is a fickle food upon a shifting plate.... —*Emily Dickinson*

Most people who have attained inner peace are not famous.... —*Peace Pilgrim*

Man in blessing others finds his highest fame.... —*Sara J. Hale*

One of the drawbacks of Fame is that one can never escape from it.... —*Nellie Melba*

Fame always brings loneliness. Success is as ice cold as the north pole.... —*Vicki Baum*

Those who make fame and the opinion of others their life's goal are always panting after it like a thirsty dog. They never find peace.... —*Martin Grey*

Fame has also this great drawback, that if we pursue it we must direct our lives in such a way as to please the fancy of men, avoiding what they dislike and seeking what is pleasing to them.... —*Baruch Spinoza*

Fame is sometimes like unto a kind of mushroom, which Pliny recounts to be the greatest miracle in nature because growing and having no root.... —*Thomas Fuller*

Good fame is like a fire; when you have kindled it, you may easily preserve it; but if you extinguish it, you will not easily kindle it again.... —*Francis Bacon*

Fame is but the empty noise of madmen.... —*Epictetus*

We all want to be famous people, and the moment we want to be something we are no longer free.... —*J. Krishnamurti*

Fame is a flippant lover.... —*Wole Soyinka*

Fame is nothing but an empty name....
—*Charles Churchill*

Fame is what you have taken; character is what you give; when to this truth you waken, then you begin to live....
—*Bayard Taylor*

Everyone has a lurking wish to appear considerable in his native place....
—*Samuel Johnson*

Love of fame is the last thing even the wise give up....
—*Tacitus*

Let us satisfy our own consciences, and trouble not ourselves by looking for fame....If we deserve it, we shall attain it; if we deserve it not, we cannot force it....
—*Seneca*

Men think highly of those who rise rapidly in the world, whereas nothing rises quicker than dust, straw and feathers....
—*Augustus & Julius Hare*

The is no road of flowers leading to glory....
—*Jean La Fontaine*

Fame is an empty bubble....
—*James Grainger*

In fame's temple there is always to be found a niche for rich dunces, importunate scoundrels, or success butchers of the human race....
—*Johann G. Zimmerman*

Fame to the ambitious, is like saltwater to the thirsty—the more one gets, the more one wants....
—*Emil Ebers*

Glory is fleeting, but obscurity is forever....
—*Napoleon Bonaparte*

What is fame? A many-colored cloak, without warmth, without protection....
—*Berthold Auerbach*

Fate and circumstances seize only the ignorant; the wise have learned to be free from both. Fame and rest are utter opposites....
—*Richard Steele*

Fame is an epitaph that must be brief; and fortunately, the epitaph cannot be all told on the tombstone....
—*Fred Van Amburgh*

Fame is like a river, that beareth up things light and swollen, and drowns things weighty and solid....
—*Francis Bacon*

Worldly fame is but a breath of wind that blows now this way, and now that, and changes name as it changes direction....
—*Dante Alighieri*

Popularity? It's glory's small change....
—*Victor Hugo*

The desire for fame tempts even noble minds....
—*Augustine*

What a heavy burden is a name that has become too famous....
—*Voltaire*

He who seeks to gain fame and reputation shall lose it; he who does not seek fame and reputation shall gain it....
—*The Talmud*

Fame—a few words upon a tombstone, and the truth of those not depended upon....
—*Christian Bovee*

Who are these by whom you wish to be admired? Are not these men whom you generally describe as mad? Why do you want them? Do you want to be admired by madmen?...
—*Epictetus*

No true and permanent Fame can be founded except in labors which promote the happiness of mankind....
—*Charles Sumner*

All fame is dangerous: Good bringeth envy; bad, shame.... —*Thomas Fuller*

All people have the common desire to be elevated in honor, but all people have something still more elevated in themselves without knowing it....
—*Mencius*

Fame is proof that people are gullible....
—*Ralph W. Emerson*

Fate/Destiny

Our fate is matched by the total freedom we have to react to our fate. It is as if we were dealt a hand of cards. Once we have them, we are free to play them as we choose....
—*Thomas Sowell*

Of course, fortune has its part in human affairs, but conduct is really much more important....
—*Jeanne Detourbey*

Sometimes our fate resembles a fruit tree in winter. Who would think that these branches would turn green again and blossom, but we hope it, we know it.... —*Johann W. Goethe*

If you would know the meaning of destiny, understand that it is not a map of where you are going to go. Rather, it is where you will go if you will flow with existence without a struggle....
—*Ormand McGill*

Failure or success seems to have been allotted to men by their stars. But they retain the power of wriggling, of fighting with their star or against it, and in the whole universe, the only interesting movement is this wriggle....
—*E. M. Forster*

By cultivating free will, one can conquer fate.... —*Ramana Maharshi*

Chance is the pseudonym of God when he did not want to sign....
—*Anatole France*

Fate! There is no fate. Between the thought and the success God is the only agent....Fate is not the ruler, but the servant of Providence....
—*Edward Bulwer-Lytton*

Fate is only a name for the final result of all our efforts.... —*Sivananda*

Nothing is predestined; there is nothing that cannot be avoided. And if indeed, there are "matters hidden by the gods," you need only remember: what beckons is the creative power of the unknown.... —*Ralph Blum*

The greater part of our happiness or misery depends on our dispositions and not on our circumstances....
—*Martha Washington*

Destiny is not a matter of chance; it is a matter of choice. It is not a thing to be waited for; it is a thing to be achieved....
—*William J. Bryan*

When one was born one had no choice, nor does one have a choice when faced with imminent "death." In between birth and death, however, man considers himself the master of his destiny. If only one gave some quiet thought to the matter, one would surely find that almost every significant event in one's life has had an enormous element of "chance" or "coincidence" in it....
—*Ramesh Balsekar*

Nothing comes by chance, for in all the world there is no such thing as chance.... —*Ralph W. Trine*

Whatever limits us we call Fate....
—Ralph W. Emerson

No matter the barbs of fate that frustrate you, no matter how stacked against you the cards of fortune....There is a liberating law in the universe, and you can become the highest of the high, wisest of the wise.... *—U. S. Anderson*

The doctrine of chance is the bible of the fool.... *—William G. Simms*

Men at sometime are masters of their fate. The fault....is not in the stars, but in ourselves....that we are underlings....
—William Shakespeare

Chance is a word void of sense; nothing can exist without a cause.... *—Voltaire*

Chance is the nickname for Providence.... *—Nicolas Chamfort*

To everything there is a season and a time for every purpose under heaven....a time to be born and a time to die; to plant and pluck up; to kill and to heal; to break down and build up; to weep and to laugh; to keep silent and to speak; to love and to hate; a time of war and a time of peace.... *—Old Testament*

The harder you work, the luckier you get.... *—Gary Player*

Fate is the friend of the good, the guide of the wise, the tyrant of the foolish, the enemy of the bad.... *—William R. Alger*

There is a Divine Plan behind everything, and if we allow ourselves to be used by that unseen Force....many things can happen in a mysterious, miraculous way. If we interfere with that Plan by introducing our own plan, the egocentric plan, tension will be created.... *—Satchidananda*

When good befalls a man he calls it Providence, when evil, fate....
—Knut Hamsun

By the word chance we merely express our ignorance of the cause of any fact or effect—not that we think that chance was itself the cause.... *—Henry Fergus*

The thoughtless, the ignorant, and the indolent, seeing only the apparent effects of things and not the things themselves, talk of luck, of fortune, and chance.... *—James Allen*

How a person masters his fate is more important than what his fate is....
—Wilhelm von Humboldt

I don't believe in circumstances. The people who get on in this world are the people who get up and look for circumstances they want.... *—George B. Shaw*

Nothing splendid has ever been achieved except by those who dared believe that something inside them was superior to circumstance....
—Bruce Barton

We do not know what is really good or bad fortune.... *—Jean J. Rousseau*

There is no such thing as chance; and what seems to us the merest accident springs from the deepest source of destiny.... *—Johann von Schiller*

Chance usually favors the prudent man.... *—Joseph Joubert*

People generally think that it is the world, the environment, external relationships, which stand in one's way, in the way of one's good fortune....And at bottom it is always man himself that stands in his own way....
—Sören Kierkegaard

Fate, destiny and luck—these are weak apologies for our own faults....
—*Fred Van Amburgh*

Luck is being ready for the chance....
—*J. Frank Dobie*

Depend not upon fortune, but on conduct....
—*Publilius Syrus*

We are the makers of our own lives. There is no such thing as fate. Our lives are the result of our previous actions, our karma, and it naturally follows that, having been ourselves the makers of our karma, we must also be able to unmake it....
—*Vivekananda*

There is no Fate....Man is the creator of his destiny....
—*Elias Auerbach*

The true adventurer goes forth aimless and uncalculating to meet and greet unknown fate....
—*O. Henry*

Fate leads the willing and drags along the unwilling....
—*Seneca*

Destiny is but a phrase of the weak human heart—the dark apology for every error, the strongest and virtuous admit no destiny....
—*Edward Bulwer-Lytton*

Chance is always powerful. Let your hook be always cast. In the pool where you least expect it, will be a fish....
—*Ovid*

We make our fortunes, and we call them fate....
—*David Alroy*

Chance works for us when we are good captains....
—*George Meredith*

The road is predestined, but the way we walk it, the attitude with which we bear our fate, can be a great influence over events....
—*Richard Beer-Hoffmann*

A strong belief in fate is the worst kind of slavery; on the other hand there is a comfort in the thought that God will be moved by our prayers....
—*Epicurus*

If man lets destiny rule him, destiny more than willingly obliges....
—*Deepa Kodikal*

Fault-finding

Criticism is futile because it puts a man on the defensive, and usually makes a man strive to justify himself....
—*Dale Carnegie*

You show respect for another man's opinions by never telling him he is wrong....
—*Anonymous*

Do not measure yourself short with the yardstick of judgement by measuring the frailties of your fellow man....
—*Frater Achad*

Be wary of experts—you don't need to be a shoemaker to know that your shoes fit tight....
—*Shantidasa*

Everybody is unique. Compare not yourself with anybody else lest you spoil God's curriculum....
—*Baal Shem Tov*

Correcting oneself is correcting the whole world. The sun is simply bright. It does not correct anyone. Because it shines, the whole world is full of light. Transforming yourself is a means of giving light to the whole world....
—*Ramana Maharshi*

Whoever is aware of his own failings will not find fault with the failings of other men....
—*James Ross*

A new idea is delicate. It can be killed by a sneer or a yawn; it can be stabbed to death by a quip and worried to death by a frown on the right man's brow....
—*Charles Brower*

Love in the making sees faults; love in the fulfillment sees none. Seeing faults is like cutting love into pieces, murdering love....   —*Papa Ramdas*

The girl who cannot dance says the band can't play....   —*Yiddish proverb*

Any time you make another person wrong, you have created evil and have prepared the way for the overt acting out of that evil....   —*Ron Smothermon*

Don't complain about the snow on your neighbor's roof, when your own doorstep is unclean....   —*Confucius*

You have in yourself all the faults which you scorn in others....
—*Will Durant*

No man can justly censure or condemn another, because indeed no man truly knows another....   —*Thomas Brown*

So long as we are full of self we are shocked at the faults of others. Let us think often of our own sin, and we shall be lenient to the sins of others....
—*Francois Fenelon*

We endeavor to make a virtue of the faults we are unwilling to correct....
—*Francois La Rochefoucauld*

How much time a man gains who does not look to see what his neighbor says, or does or thinks, but only what he does himself....   —*Marcus Aurelius*

The faultfinder will find faults even in Paradise....   —*Henry D. Thoreau*

Do not blame men when they err, but purify your own heart. Do not get angry when the world forgets the Way, and ceases to abide by the law. But look for the fault in yourself. The root of all evil is in yourself....
—*Julian P. Johnson*

Vulgar people take huge delight in the faults and follies of great men....
—*Arthur Schopenhauer*

Never throw mud. You may miss your mark. And you will certainly have dirty hands....   —*Joseph Parker*

The more you try to prove how wrong the other person is—in terms of either lateness or impatience—the more the other person needs to persist in proving how right he or she is....
—*Harold Bloomfield*

It requires no thought, no consideration, no character, no talent to be a fault-finder....It is much easier to find fault then to find ways to help....How easy to be critical and how hard to be correct. How easy to find fault with others and how hard to mend our own ways....   —*Fred Van Amburgh*

Overlook the greatest fault of another, but do not partake of it yourself in the smallest degree....
—*Hazrat Inayat Khan*

Faults of the head are punished in this world, those of the heart in another....
—*Charles C. Colton*

See everything: overlook a good deal; correct a little....   —*Pope John XXIII*

If you are pleased at finding faults, you are displeased at finding perfections....
—*John K. Lavater*

Never complain about bad environments. Create your own mental world wherever you remain and wherever you go. There are some difficulties and disadvantages wherever you go....God has placed you there to grow quickly....
—*Sivananda*

Every person should have a special cemetery lot in which to bury the faults of friends and loved ones....
—*Anonymous*

And why do you behold the mote that is in your brother's eye, and do not consider the beam in your own eye....
—*Jesus*

It is far better to know our weaknesses and failings than to point out those of others.... —*Jawaharlal Nehru*

Faults are thick where love is thin....
—*James Howell*

If instead of seeing faults in others, we look within ourselves, we are loving God.... —*Meher Baba*

To hear complaints is wearisome alike to both the wretched and the happy....
—*Samuel Johnson*

Ten thousand of the greatest faults in our neighbors are of less consequence to us than one of the smallest in ourselves.... —*Richard Whatley*

He who complains, sins....
—*Francis de Sales*

The disease of men is this: that they neglect their own field, and go weed the fields of others, and what they require from others is great, while what they lay upon themselves is light....
—*Mencius*

The narrow-minded man thinks and says: "This man is one of us; this one is not, he is a stranger." To the man of noble soul the whole of mankind is but one family.... —*Hitopadesa*

When you are offended at any man's fault, turn to yourself and study your own failings. Then you will forget your anger.... —*Epictetus*

As far as possible one should not interfere in the affairs of others....
—*Ramana Maharshi*

You will find it less easy to uproot faults than to choke them by gaining virtue.... —*John Ruskin*

This life is not for complaint, but for satisfaction.... —*Henry D. Thoreau*

Faults, mustard seed small, of others, you see well; your own, as large as a melon, you see not.... —*Mahabharata*

To attempt to correct others while one's own virtue is clouded is to set one's own virtue a task for which it is inadequate.... —*Kwang Tze*

Speak evil of no one....
—*Mohammed*

Anyone can blame; it takes a specialist to praise.... —*Konstantin Stanislavsky*

The most savage controversies are those about matters as to which there is no good evidence either way....
—*Bertrand Russell*

The faults of others we see easily; our own are very difficult to see. Our neighbor's faults we winnow eagerly, as chaff from grain; our own we hide away....
—*Dhammapada*

How much easier it is to be critical than to be correct.... —*Benjamin Disraeli*

Stop complaining about the management of the universe. Look around for a place to sow a few seeds of happiness.... —*Henry Van Dyke*

Let us look at our own faults, and not other people's. We ought not to insist on everyone following in our footsteps, nor to take upon ourselves to give instructions in spirituality when, perhaps, we do not even know what it is.... —*Theresa of Lisieux*

One of the distinguishing differences between a big man and a petty one frequently is the ability to take criticism and profit by it instead of getting indignant, stewed-up and resentful.... —*Douglas Lurton*

The real fault is to have faults and not to amend them....When you have faults, do not fear to abandon them.... —*Confucius*

Nothing is easier than fault-finding. No talent, no self-denial, no brains, no character is required to set up in the grumbling business.... —*Alfred A. Montapert*

It is the nature of love not to perceive a fault; once there is evidence of finding fault, love has ceased to be.... —*Anonymous*

When you feel the urge to criticize and condemn the other fellow, crawl into some cave, do some shouting and then listen to the echo. That will teach you how disagreeable the thing sounds.... —*Fred Van Amburgh*

A man only begins to be a man when he ceases to whine and revile, and commences to search for the hidden justice which regulates his life.... —*James Allen*

We should correct our own faults by seeing how uncomely they appear in others.... —*Francis Beaumont*

Fair play is primarily not blaming others for anything that is wrong with us.... —*Eric Hoffer*

You yourselves make or mar your lives. Still you are busy blaming and finding fault with everybody in the world for your sufferings. You fail to probe within and remove the seed of discontent which is in your mind.... —*Papa Ramdas*

Every one is eagle-eyed to see another's faults and deformity.... —*John Dryden*

It is a barren kind of criticism which tells you what is not.... —*Rufus W. Griswold*

No man should be judged by others here in this life, for good or for evil that they do. Nevertheless, deeds may lawfully be judged, but not the men.... —*Thomas à Kempis*

It is much easier to find fault than to overlook a fault.... —*Anonymous*

Quarrels would not last long if the fault were only on one side.... —*Francois La Rochefoucauld*

Worrying about the faults of others is an unnecessary addition to the worry we have over our own faults.... —*Hazrat Inayat Khan*

I see no fault committed by others that I have not committed myself.... —*Johann W. Goethe*

When we condemn other people, we generally indirectly mean to flatter ourselves.... —*John S. Blackie*

The world is full of wooden people who are always doing their best to whittle others down....   —*Puzant K. Thomajan*

When you feel like finding fault with somebody or something, stop for a moment and think; there is very apt to be something wrong within yourself....
—*J. J. Reynolds*

When any fit of gloominess or perversion of mind lays hold of you, make it a rule not to publish it by complaints, but exert your whole care to hide it. By endeavoring to hide it, you will drive it away....   —*Samuel Johnson*

He that fancies himself very enlightened because he sees the deficiencies of others, may be very ignorant, because he has not studied his own....
—*Edward Bulwer-Lytton*

Those who look well after their own consciences rarely fall into the sin of judging others....   —*Jean P. Camus*

Deal with the faults of others as gently as with your own....
—*Chinese proverb*

Whatever one of us blames in another, each one will find in his own heart....
—*Seneca*

Another's "fault" is certainly a most valuable gift to me. It is a mirror which allows me to choose another reflection....   —*Hugh Prather*

For man to find fault with his fellow man is to find fault with God. God is faultless. Man cannot find fault with God. For if he endeavors to find fault with God, he is but finding fault with himself....   —*Frater Achad*

Love sees no faults....
—*Thomas Fuller*

Regarding that which happens in harmony with nature, we ought to blame neither gods, for they do nothing wrong either voluntarily or involuntarily, nor men, for they do nothing wrong except unconsciously. Consequently, we shall blame no one....
—*Marcus Aurelius*

The flies seek filth, the bees seek honey. I will shun the habit of the flies and follow that of the bees. I will refrain from finding faults in others and only look for the good which is in them....
—*Hindu vow*

Finding fault with others, developing skill at discovering weakness and inconsistency in others, will begin to eat into your peace of mind. If you keep it up forever, it will eventually rob you of all the joys of life....
—*James Mangan*

If he who carefully picks holes in the character of others would but expend the same skill upon himself, what could prevent him from breaking through the bonds of ignorance....
—*Anonymous*

Do you never look at yourself when you criticize another person?...
—*Plautus*

In the degree that we hold a person in the thought of evil or of error, do we suggest evil and error to him....and so in this way we may be sharers in the very evil-doing in which we hold another in thought....   —*Ralph W. Trine*

It is only imperfection that complains of what is imperfect. The more perfect we are, the more gentle and quiet we become towards the defects of others....
—*Francois Fenelon*

He censures God who quarrels with the imperfection of men....
—*Edmund Burke*

Always remember that a person that you find fault with a great deal, will finally rebel.... —*E. W. Howe*

Everything that irritates us about others can lead us to an understanding of ourselves.... —*Carl Jung*

Men always try to make virtues of their weaknesses.... —*H. L. Mencken*

The mystery of existence is the connection between our faults and our misfortunes.... —*Madame de Staël*

Fear

We should not let our fears hold us back from pursuing our hopes.... —*John F. Kennedy*

Where there is hate there is fear and where there is fear there is hate....
—*Papa Ramdas*

Two sturdy asses bind the will of man; their names are fear and unbelief. When these are caght and turned aside, the will of man will know no bounds....
—*The Aquarian Gospel*

Never fear uncertainty. There is never anything to fear in uncertainty. Fear arises because men want to be certain according to their terms, but these terms are all wrong. It is quite possible to have a thousand uncertainties and not have a single fear....
—*Vernon Howard*

Almost all fear is fear of the unknown. Therefore, what's the remedy? To become acquainted with the thing you fear.... —*Peace Pilgrim*

We promise according to our hopes and perform according to our fears....
—*Francois La Rochefoucauld*

No passion so effectively robs the mind of all its powers of acting and reasoning as fear.... —*Edmund Burke*

Fear is not a good teacher. The lessons of fear are quickly forgotten....
—*Mary C. Bateson*

Fear is only an illusion. It is the illusion that creates the feeling of separateness—the false sense of isolation that exists only in your imagination....
—*Jeraldine Sanders*

Do the thing you fear and the death of fear is certain.... —*Ralph W. Emerson*

Fear is not created by the world around us, but in the mind....
—*Elizabeth Gawain*

What do you have to fear? Nothing. Whom do you have to fear? No one. Why? Because whoever has joined forces with God obtains three great privileges: omnipotence without power, intoxication without wine, and life without death.... —*Francis of Assisi*

Your greatest gift lies beyond the door named fear.... —*Sufi saying*

Man imagines that it is death he fears, but what he fears is the unforeseen....What man fears is himself, not death.... —*Antoine de Saint-Exupery*

Fear is fatal....
—*Harry Houdini*

Happy is the man who has trampled underfoot his fears and can laugh at the approach of all-subduing death....
—*Virgil*

If we have respect for all created things and treat all human beings with love and respect....we are spared the need to live in fear or tension.... —*Babaji*

The best way to confront your fears is to stop avoiding the situation you're most afraid of.... —*David D. Burns*

There are two kinds of people: those who are paralyzed by fear, and those who are afraid but go ahead anyway....
—*Brooke Knapp*

Nothing in life is to be feared, only understood.... —*Marie Curie*

The fear of death is merely an extension of the fear of the unknown....
—*Robert W. Buckingham*

Fear is the main source of superstition, and one of the main sources of cruelty. To conquer fear is the beginning of wisdom.... —*Bertrand Russell*

To him who is in fear, everything rustles.... —*Sophocles*

As children tremble and fear everything in the blind darkness, so we in the light sometimes fear what is no more to be feared than the things children in the dark hold in terror and imagine will come true.... —*Lucretius*

Fear exists wherever an other exists....
—*The Upanishads*

The only thing we have to fear is fear itself.... —*Franklin D. Roosevelt*

Fear is more disgraceful than failure....
—*Robert Schuller*

Keep your fears to yourself, but share your courage with others....
—*Robert L. Stevenson*

If a man harbors any sort of fear, it....makes him landlord to a ghost....
—*Lloyd Douglas*

Of all the liars in the world, sometimes the worst are your own fears....
—*Rudyard Kipling*

From the body of one guilty deed, a thousand ghostly fears and haunting thoughts proceed....
—*William Wordsworth*

There is nothing so bad and so dangerous in life as fear....
—*Jawaharlal Nehru*

Fear is a trick, a sham, a sleight of hand. It is illusion.... —*Emmanuel*

Fear comes from uncertainty. When we are absolutely certain, whether of our worth or worthlessness, we are almost impervious to fear.... —*Eric Hoffer*

Find out what a person fears most and that is where he will develop next....
—*Carl Jung*

The one permanent emotion of the inferior man is fear, fear of the unknown, the complex, the inexplicable. What he wants beyond everything else is safety....
—*Napoleon Bonaparte*

Fears are caused by a misuse of imagination.... —*Herbert Casson*

To permit fear to possess you is suicidal and worse. A human full of fear puts a blight on everything and everybody....
—*Fred Van Amburgh*

Fear builds walls to bar the light....
—*Israel Baal Shem Tov*

Fear is an emotion. Emotions come wholly from within, and have only the strength we allow them....
—*John M. Wilson*

The first duty of man is that of subduing fear.... —*Thomas Carlyle*

Our greatest enemies are not wild beasts or deadly germs but fears that paralyze throughout, poison the mind, and destroy character....
—*Ryllis G. Lynip*

Fear makes the wolf bigger than he is....
—*German proverb*

When we feel alone or isolated from God, it is ours to know that it was not God who turned away but we through some form of petulance or fear....
—*Margaret Stortz*

Fear is the sand in the machinery of life.... —*E. Stanley Jones*

People who enjoy life and radiate their happiness fear nothing. Fear never has led, and never will lead, a man victoriously in any phase of life....
—*George M. Adams*

This is the most effective way of dealing with our fears—we must begin to do the very thing we are afraid of doing. No man has ever learned to swim by refusing to get wet....
—*Robert Moore*

Fear is an acid which is pumped into one's atmosphere. It causes mental, moral and spiritual asphyxiation, and sometimes death—death to energy and all growth.... —*Horace Fletcher*

Faith in yourself and faith in God are the key to the mastery of fear....
—*Harold Sherman*

Fear is a greater evil than the evil itself.... —*Francis de Sales*

Most of our fears are built around a sense of mortality, a sense that physical death is the end of our existence....
—*H. Frederick Vogt*

Taking a new step, uttering a new word, is what people fear most....
—*Fydor Dostoyevsky*

If you do not come face to face with your fears, you will come to find yourself always running away from them.... —*Anonymous*

It is better to suffer the worst at once than to live in perpetual fear of it....
—*Julius Caesar*

We fear our highest possibility (as well as our lowest one). We are generally afraid to become that which we can glimpse in our most perfect moments.... —*Abraham Maslow*

The only fear you need have is the fear of not standing by the thing you believe to be right. Take your stand and hold it, then come what will....
—*Susan B. Anthony*

It is human nature to fear that which is not ordinary; it is godlike to love the unordinary.... —*Shantidasa*

He has not learned the lesson of life who does not every day surmount a fear.... —*Ralph W. Emerson*

Let nothing disturb you. Let nothing frighten you. Everything passes away except God.... —*Teresa of Avila*

The most dramatic and usually the most effective remedy for fear is direct action.... —*William Burnham*

Fear makes strangers of people who should be friends....
—*Shirley MacLaine*

Fear and love can never be experienced at the same time. It is always our choice as to which of these emotions we want.... —*Gerald Jampolsky*

Fear is confusion....Decisions made from fear will always bring more confusion.... —*Maya Sarada Devi*

Since fear is unreasonable, never try to reason with it. So called "positive thinking" is no weapon against fear. Only positive faith can rout the black menace of fear and give life a radiance.... —*Marion Hilliard*

Fear is the tax conscience pays to guilt.... —*George Sewell*

You gain strength, courage and confidence by every experience in which you really stop to look fear in the face.... —*Eleanor Roosevelt*

Worry is a form of fear, and all forms of fear produce fatigue. A man who has learned not to fear will find the fatigue of daily life enormously diminished....
—*Bertrand Russell*

All my fears and cares are of this world; if there is another, an honest man has nothing to fear from it....
—*Robert Burns*

What we fear we tend to develop an unreasonable hatred for—so we come to hate and fear. This not only injures us psychologically and aggravates world tensions, but through such negative concentration we tend to attract the things which we fear....
—*Peace Pilgrim*

What governs man is the fear of truth....
—*Henri F. Amiel*

Fear always springs from ignorance....
—*Ralph W. Emerson*

He who fears being defeated is sure of defeat.... —*Napoleon Bonaparte*

Forgiveness

Never does the human soul appear so strong as when it forgives revenge, and dares forgive an injury....
—*Edwin H. Chapin*

Forgiveness is not for the forgiven but for the sake of the forgiver....
—*Anonymous*

An apology is the superglue of life. It can repair just about everything....
—*Lynn Johnston*

Forgiveness is the freedom to make wrong choices.... —*Lewis B. Smedes*

Forgiving someone is solid proof of your intent to live your life now, while you have it.... —*Ron Smothermon*

How unhappy is he who cannot forgive himself.... —*Publilius Syrus*

Any man can seek revenge; it takes a king or prince to grant a pardon....
—*Arthur J. Rehrat*

To be forgiven is not enough; we must put an end to the very need to be forgiven.... —*Bernadette Roberts*

To be really sorry for one's errors is like opening the door of Heaven....
—*Hazrat Inayat Khan*

Forgiveness is the grace that wipes away all thoughts of judgement....
—*Shantidasa*

When a deep injury is done us, we can never recover until we forgive....
—*Alan Paton*

A man must learn to forgive himself....
—*Arthur D. Ficke*

When we forgive others for the wrongs done to us, it is not the human heart that forgives. It is the divine quality revealed in the heart.... —*Papa Ramdas*

It is hardest to forgive ourselves....
—*Judy Tatelbaum*

We cannot love unless we have accepted forgiveness, and the deeper our experience of forgiveness is, the greater is our love.... —*Paul Tillich*

When Christ says, "Forgive your enemies," it is not for the sake of the enemy, but for one's own sake that he says so.... —*Oscar Wilde*

He is a very green hand at life who cannot forgive any mortal thing....
—*Robert L. Stevenson*

We pardon as long as we love....
—*Francois La Rochefoucauld*

Forgiveness is primarily for our own sake so that we no longer carry the burden of resentment. But to forgive does not mean we allow injustice again.... —*Jack Kornfield*

Not to forgive is to be imprisoned by the past, by old grievances that do not permit life to proceed with new business.... —*Robin Casarjian*

We find it difficult to forgive only because we like our sense of condemnation....As long as we can condemn another, we can feel superior to him....
—*Maxwell Maltz*

Love is an act of endless forgiveness....
—*Peter Ustinov*

True forgiveness must be extended not only to others, but also to ourself, and sometimes, in our limited understanding, to the God who we mistakenly believe has singled us out for harsh treatment....
—*Elinor MacDonald*

When you go to bed at night, have for your pillow three things—love, hope and forgiveness. And you will awaken in the morning with a song in your heart.... —*Victor Hugo*

The narrow soul knows not the godlike glory of forgiving.... —*Nicholas Rowe*

If you want to see the brave, look at those who can forgive....
—*Bhagavad-Gita*

The effects of forgiveness are cumulative. As we forgive, we are forgiven....
—*Katherine Gould*

If you haven't forgiven yourself something, how can you forgive others?... —*Dolores Huerta*

I have been all things unholy; if God can work through me, he can work through anyone.... —*Francis of Assisi*

Decide to forgive: For resentment is negative; resentment is poisonous; resentment diminishes and devours the self.... —*Robert Muller*

It is in vain for you to expect, it is impudent for you to ask of God forgiveness for yourself if you refuse to exercise this forgiving temper to others.... —*Benjamin Hoadly*

Without forgiveness life is governed by....an endless cycle of resentment and retaliation.... —*Robert Assagioli*

It is easier to forgive an enemy than to forgive a friend....   —*William Blake*

Humanity is never so beautiful as praying for forgiveness, or else forgiving another....
—*Jean Paul Richter*

A forgiving spirit is by its very nature a unifying force. It can remove the barriers of separation between peoples and nations and weld them together in peace and goodwill; something that legislation with the help of armies can never accomplish....   —*Charles R. Loss*

Forgiveness is another word for letting go....   —*Matthew Fox*

Those who do not forgive others burn the bridge over which they must pass, for everyone has need to be forgiven....
—*Anonymous*

Forgiveness saves the expense of anger, the cost of hatred....   —*Hannah More*

It is more noble to forgive than to revenge an injury....
—*Benjamin Franklin*

Forgiveness is eminently a divine virtue. The moment the forgiving nature enters into your life, depend on it: God has revealed Himself in you....
—*Papa Ramdas*

He who forgives, ends the quarrel....
—*African proverb*

To be wronged is nothing unless you continue to remember it....
—*Confucius*

To err is human; to forgive, divine....
—*Alexander Pope*

We must be willing to forgive without limit even as God forgives; otherwise we cannot be forgiven....
—*Nels F. S. Ferre*

Little vicious minds abound with anger and revenge, and are incapable of feeling the pleasure of forgiving their enemies....   —*Philip Chesterfield*

To forgive our enemies, yet hope that God will punish them, is not to forgive enough....   —*Thomas Browne*

In pardoning we rise above those who insult us....   —*Napoleon Bonaparte*

"I can forgive, but I cannot forget," is only another way of saying, "I will not forgive."...   —*Henry W. Beecher*

There is no need for God to forgive, for God has never held man in account. God has never judged man....
—*Frater Achad*

In order to learn forgiveness, man must first learn tolerance....
—*Hazrat Inayat Khan*

The unforgiving mind sees itself as innocent and others as guilty. It thrives on conflict and on being right, and it sees inner peace as its enemy. It perceives everything as separate....
—*Gerald Jampolsky*

Forgiveness is eternal and ever available. What a load is dropped from the shoulders of personal responsibility, when we realize that the Eternal Mind holds naught against anybody....
—*Ernest Holmes*

Forgive others. Do it not only for their sake, but for your own. If you don't, you will feel within you a nauseating resentment, destroying you from within....   —*Maxwell Maltz*

In this life, if you have anything to pardon, pardon quickly. Slow forgiveness is little better than no forgiveness....   —*Arthur W. Pinero*

If you forgive others their failings, your heavenly Father will forgive yours; but if you do not forgive others, your Father will not forgive your failings either....   —*Jesus*

Only the brave know how to forgive. A coward never forgives. It is not his nature....   —*Robert Muller*

To understand everything means to forgive everything....   —*French proverb*

Here is a mental treatment guaranteed to cure every ill that flesh is heir to: sit for half an hour every night and mentally forgive everyone against whom you have any ill will or antipathy....   —*Charles Fillmore*

The best way to get even is to forget....
                    —*Anonymous*

He who has not forgiven an enemy has not yet tasted one of the most sublime enjoyments of life....   —*John K. Lavater*

You must forgive those who transgress against you before you can look to forgiveness from God....   —*The Talmud*

Be the first to forgive, to smile and take the first step, and you will see happiness bloom....Be always the first. Do not wait for others to forgive, for by forgiving, you become the master of fate, the fashioner of life, the doer of miracles. To forgive is the highest, most beautiful form of love. In return you will receive untold peace and happiness....   —*Robert Muller*

Forgiving ourselves dissolves all kinds of unhealthy attitudes—about ourselves and about the other. We are released from brutal self-downing when we stop criticizing others....   —*Marsha Sinetar*

In heaven the only art of living is forgetting and forgiving....
                    —*William Blake*

Forgive, forget. Bear with the faults of others as you would have them bear with yours. Be patient and understanding. Life is too short to be vengeful or malicious....
                    —*Phillips Brooks*

The remedy for wrongs is to forget them....   —*Publilius Syrus*

Somehow we've come to believe that forgiveness is hard, a conflict-ridden challenge that we will have to fight to do.... What a joke we play on ourselves! The joke is that we are so slow in realizing that forgiveness is anything but a heavy, difficult step to take. Instead, it's light-hearted, joyful, simple, and, most of all, fun!...
                    —*Ruth Hanna*

There is no condition for forgiveness....
                    —*Paul Tillich*

If anyone will take these two words to heart and use them for his own guidance, he will be almost without sin and will lead a very peaceful life. These words are bear and forbear....
                    —*Epictetus*

On the wings of forgiveness is carried all other wisdom....   —*Honey J. Rubin*

Forgiveness does not originate from a position of weakness, but is a consequence of strength....
                    —*Anonymous*

There is no limit to which you can forgive those who have wronged you....
                    —*Papa Ramdas*

Freedom

You can't separate peace from freedom because no one can be at peace unless he has freedom....
—*Malcolm X*

You are already free. Only you have to know and realize this truth....
—*Sivananda*

Freedom is not a goal, it is the supreme awareness of who you are....Freedom is found once all concepts are thrown away, and one stands alone in the present moment to find the depth of meaning inherent in their spirit....
—*A Spiritual Warrior*

You cannot parcel out freedom in pieces because freedom is all or nothing....
—*Tertullian*

Free will is the power of choosing good and evil....
—*Origen*

If the bird does like its cage, and does like its sugar, and will not leave it, why keep the door so very carefully shut?...
—*Olive Schreiner*

When you enslave someone—you are enslaved....
—*Louise Nevelson*

Freedom is not for the timid....
—*Vijaya L. Pandit*

Freedom is not a philosophy, nor is it an idea—it is a stirring of conscience that causes us to utter, at certain moments, one of two monosyllables: Yes or No....
—*Octavio Paz*

Freedom means the right to be different, the right to be oneself....
—*Ira Eisenstein*

The only freedom which deserves the name is that of pursuing our own good in our own way, so long as we do not attempt to deprive others of theirs, or impede their efforts to obtain it....
—*John S. Mill*

Freedom can only come from God, and that can take place only as an activity within your own consciousness....
—*Joel Goldsmith*

Remember that to change your mind and follow him who sets you right is to be none the less free than you were before....
—*Marcus Aurelius*

The invisible chains are always stronger than the visible ones....
—*Anonymous*

Do you think you are not free? You are free, but you do not know that you are free—and it is your not knowing that you are free that is your limitation and your imprisonment. Realize your freedom and you are free....
—*Vilayat I. Khan*

A man's only freedom is his freedom to deal with his impressions, to accept one, to reject another....
—*Epictetus*

Wherever the spirit of God is, there is freedom....
—*Paul of Tarsus*

Freedom is a new religion....
—*Heinrich Heine*

Freedom and forgiveness are indissolubly linked. Not to forgive is to be at war with ourselves, for we are freed according to our capacity to forgive....
—*Darwin Gross*

In the last analysis, our only freedom is the freedom to discipline ourselves....
—*Bernard M. Baruch*

Freedom: there's none unless you know the Self. But if you know the truth, then you are free....   —*The Upanishads*

Freedom is freedom from worry. Having realized that you cannot influence results, pay no attention to your desires and fears. Let them come and go....   —*Nisargadatta*

Men are freest when they are most unconscious of freedom....
—*David H. Lawrence*

Most people do not wish to be free. They would prefer to moan and chafe about how impossible it is to give up their various enslavements to possessions, food, drink, smoking, and so forth. It is not that they can't give them up–they really don't want to give them up....   —*Peace Pilgrim*

No one is free who is a slave to the flesh....   —*Seneca*

We find freedom when we find God; we lose it when we lose Him....
—*Paul E. Sherer*

God's service spells freedom....
—*Judah Halevi*

One has to be on guard against the misunderstanding of the idea of freedom by many who....seem to think it means the freedom to do what one likes, and especially the freedom to be licentious. Real freedom is very different from this and comes from a higher level....   —*D. T. Suzuki*

At the end of the way is freedom. Till then, patience....   —*Gautama Buddha*

There are two freedoms: the false, where a man is free to do what he likes; the true, where a man is free to do what he ought....   —*Charles Kingsley*

But what is freedom? Rightly understood, a universal license to be good....
—*Hartly Coleridge*

Man is really free only in God, the source of his freedom....
—*Sherwood Eddy*

Freedom is just another word for nothing left to lose....   —*Janis Joplin*

No man is free until he is free at the center. When he lets go there, he is free indeed. When the self is renounced, then one stands utterly disillusioned, apart, asking for nothing....If anything comes to him, it is all sheer gain. Then life becomes one constant surprise....
—*E. Stanley Jones*

There are no galley slaves in the royal vessel of love–every man works his oar voluntarily....   —*Jean P. Camus*

Man is condemned to be free; because once thrown into the world, he is responsible for everything he does....
—*Jean-Paul Sartre*

None are more hopelessly enslaved than those who falsely believe they are free....   —*Johann W. Goethe*

Our freedom can be measured by the amount of things we can walk away from...   —*Vernon Howard*

You have freedom to do right or wrong. Clearly you can go astray, for the road is not fenced. You can make mistakes, you can fall into sin....
—*Charles Eliot*

A human being is always a prisoner of something. The only freedom is within ourselves....   —*Robert Mueller*

You have freedom when you're easy in the harness....   —*Robert Frost*

Everybody has the right to freedom without interference from anyone else....Nobody has the power to judge what is good for another person's conscience....   —*Paul Twitchell*

You are only free when you know the truth and care not that other people know that you know....   —*Anonymous*

There can be no freedom without the freedom to fail....   —*Eric Hoffer*

Liberty is not without, but within. It is in the heart, or it does not exist. No one is free from external constraint. But man may remain free in the midst of the severest privations....
—*Paul Tournier*

Those who deny freedom to others deserve it not for themselves....
—*Abraham Lincoln*

The price of freedom is responsibility, but it is a bargain, because freedom is priceless....   —*Hugh Downs*

To enjoy freedom we have to control ourselves....   —*Virginia Woolf*

Who, then, is free? The wise man who commands his passions, who fears not want, nor death, nor chains, firmly resisting his appetites and despising the honors of the world, who relies wholly on himself....   —*Horace*

Freedom comes from human beings, rather than from laws and institutions....   —*Clarence Darrow*

To be free from everything is to be—nothing. Only nothing is quite free, and freedom is abstract nothingness....
—*F. H. Bradley*

You are your own jailer....
—*Farid Attar*

No man is free who cannot command himself; liberty exists in proportion to wholesome restraint....
—*Daniel Webster*

He only has freedom who ideally loves freedom himself and is glad to extend it to others. He who cares to have slaves must chain himself to them. He who builds walls to create exclusion for others, builds walls across his own freedom....   —*Rabindranath Tagore*

Freedom is not truly freedom while constraint can still limit it....
—*Karlfried G. Durckheim*

Freedom is the absolute right of all....to seek permission for their action only from their own conscience and reason....   —*Mikhail A. Bakunin*

Every virtuous man is free....
—*Philo*

Freedom is not worth having if it does not connote freedom to err....
—*Mohandas Gandhi*

As long as you keep a person down, some part of you has to be down to hold him down, so it means you cannot soar as you might otherwise....
—*Marian Anderson*

Freedom is nothing but a chance to be better....   —*Albert Camus*

The more I understand about myself, the more I understand about the world. The more I understand about my world, the freer I am from it....
—*Donald Curtis*

Freedom is a mirage on the desert. If you reach the place it seemed to be, you will find it dry, because being free means that you are no longer needed or loved by others....
—*Josephine Lowman*

Freedom is a need of the soul, and nothing else. It is a striving toward God, that the soul strives continually after a condition of freedom....
—*Whittaker Chambers*

Perfect freedom is reserved for that man who lives by his own work and in that work does what he wants to do....
—*R. G. Collingwood*

Freedom is recreated year by year in hearts wide open on the Godward side....   —*James Russell Lowell*

God wills us to be free....He wills not only that we should be free in power, but that we should be free in its exercise....   —*Jacques Bossuet*

Anything you strive to hold captive will hold you captive and if you desire freedom you must give freedom....
—*Peace Pilgrim*

No man is free who is not master of himself....Is freedom anything else than the power of living as we choose?...
—*Epictetus*

When we are a free and open channel for Divine provision to flow through us to others, then abundance flows to us, and the freer we become the more freely does God's bounty come....
—*Henry T. Hamblin*

Most people are afraid of freedom because it means they must be prepared to stand or fall entirely by their own decisions....   —*Ronald Beesley*

The worst thing about slavery is that eventually the slaves get to like it....
—*Aristotle*

The freer you feel yourself in the presence of another, the more free he is....   —*John K. Lavater*

If a person could understand all the horror of the lives of ordinary people who are turning round in a circle of insignificant interests....if they could understand what they are losing, they would understand that there can only be one thing serious—to escape the general law, to be free....
—*George I. Gurdjieff*

Your freedom to choose a positive attitude is the treasure God will let no one take from you....   —*Robert Schuller*

Let me not be tied down to property or praise and I shall be free. Free from the nagging ache of envy. Free from the hurts of resentment. Free to love all and forgive all. Free to do and say what is right, regardless of the unpopularity. Free to wander everywhere as inspiration guides me....   —*Francis of Assisi*

Freedom is the power to create out of nothing, the power of the spirit to create out of itself....
—*Nikolay Berdyayev*

What is freedom? It means not being a slave to any circumstance, to any restraint, to any chance....   —*Seneca*

Nearly all men are slaves....because of the inability to say the word "No." To be able to speak that word and to live alone, are the two means to preserve one's freedom....   —*Sebastien Chamfort*

Man is free at the moment he wishes to be....   —*Voltaire*

The path of freedom is blocked much more by those who wish to obey than by those who wish to command....
—*M. D. Petre*

Liberty is the one thing you can't have unless you give it to others....
—*William A. White*

Freedom is only an opportunity, it is not in itself a goal. It simply gives you the opportunity to do whatever you want....an opportunity to find a definition for yourself....　　*—Osho*

Freedom is what you do with what's been done to you....　　*—Jean-Paul Sartre*

You don't have to reconstruct the social order; you don't have to overpower the villains; you don't have to reeducate the world....All you have to do is to use your sovereign power of choice to release yourself from those who would keep you in bondage....
　　—Harry Browne

What do you suppose will satisfy the soul, except to walk free and own no superior....　　*—Walt Whitman*

Man never fastened one end of a chain around the neck of his brother, that God did not fasten the other end round the neck of the oppressor....
　　—Alphonse de Lamartine

Freedom is the right to choose: the right to create for yourself the alternatives of choice. Without the possibility of choice and the exercise of choice, a man is not a man but a member, an instrument, a thing....
　　—Archibald MacLeish

No one can grant freedom to anyone else....　　*—Marilyn Ferguson*

A man who is really free never feels harshness; he is never disturbed by outer conditions....　　*—Paramananda*

Freedom will cost you the mask you have on, the mask that feels so comfortable and is so hard to shed off, not because it fits so well but because you have been wearing it so long....
　　—Florinda Donner

Friendship

The firmest friendships have been formed in mutual adversity, as iron is most strongly united with the fiercest flame....　　*—Charles C. Colton*

A friend is one who knows you as you are, understands where you've been, accepts who you've become, and still gently invites you to grow....
　　—Anonymous

To let friendship die away by negligence and silence is certainly not wise. It is voluntarily to throw away one of the greatest comforts of this weary pilgrimage....　　*—Samuel Johnson*

Be a friend to thyself, and others will be so too....　　*—Thomas Fuller*

Real friendship is exchanging secrets, rolling over like a puppy and exposing the soft underbelly....　　*—Adair Lara*

Meetings and partings, handclasps and farewells, loving nearness and grieving tears—these are the lot of friendship on earth....　　*—Anna Brown Lindsay*

The wise man, the true friend, the finished character we seek everywhere and only find in fragments....
　　—Ralph W. Emerson

We can be our own best friends or we can be our own worst enemies....
　　—Ralph W. Trine

Two may talk together under the same roof for many years, yet never really meet; and two others at first speech are old friends....　　*—Mary Catherwood*

I have discovered the ultimate goal in life is to be your own best friend—and only after you have befriended yourself, can you become a friend to others....
—*Shantidasa*

Taking friendship for granted is one of the surest ways of ending them. Unless nourished, they tend to wither and die. Unless we earnestly desire its continuance we should never start a friendship any more than we would a love affair....
—*Alice H. Rice*

Friendship inspires and enriches the life of those who come together....
—*Vimala Thakar*

A true friend is more to be esteemed than kinfolk....
—*Cicero*

All people in the world are not friends to all other people. Some people who pose as friends prove to be no friends at all in the hour of need. But he who sees the Self in all, has no desires of his own whatsoever, is the friend of all, at all times, and in all circumstances....
—*Tapovan Maharaj*

Friendship is a sheltering tree....
—*Samuel T. Coleridge*

It is easy enough to be friendly to one's friends. But to befriend the one who regards himself as your enemy is the quintessence of all religion. The other is merely business....
—*Mohandas Gandhi*

Wishing to be friends is quick work, but friendship is a slow ripening fruit....
—*Aristotle*

Friendship is almost always the union of a part of one mind with a part of another; people are friends in spots....
—*George Santayana*

No man can be called friendless when he has God and the companionship of books....
—*Elizabeth B. Browning*

Life has no blessing like a prudent friend....
—*Euripides*

If you have just one or two spiritual friends with whom you can share your highest aspirations, you should consider yourself richly blessed....
—*Kriyananda*

Bad company is loss, and good company is gain....In company with the wind the dust flies heavenward; if it joins water, it becomes mud and sinks....
—*Tulsi Das*

Tell me what company you keep, and I'll tell you who you are....
—*Cervantes*

There is no separateness between two genuine friends....
—*Nisargadatta*

When two people relate to each other authentically and humanly, God is the electricity that surges between them....
—*Martin Buber*

If you make friends with people who are without character, your own character will tarnish as well....
—*Anonymous*

A friend cannot not be known in prosperity....
—*Ecclesiastes*

We need old friends to help us grow old and new friends to help us stay young....
—*Letty Cottin Pogrebin*

He who is his own friend, is a friend to all....
—*Seneca*

Fate chooses your relations, you choose your friends....
—*Abbey J. Delille*

A friend is a gift you give yourself....
—*Robert L. Stevenson*

The use of friendship for selfish motive is like mixing bitter poison with sweet rose syrup.... —*Hazrat Inayat Khan*

If there is any one secret of success, it lies in the ability to get the other person's point of view and see things from his angle as well as your own.... —*Henry Ford*

You can make more friends in two months by becoming interested in other people than you can in two years by trying to get other people interested in you.... —*Dale Carnegie*

No man is happier on this earth than he who has a friend with whom he can talk, with whom he can live, with whom he can have a friendly chat.... —*Hitopadesa*

Friendship is equality.... —*Pythagoras*

There can be no friendship where there is no freedom. Friendship loves Free Air; and will not be forced in straight and narrow enclosures.... —*William Penn*

The only way to have a friend is to be one.... —*Ralph W. Emerson*

A friend is, as it were, a second self.... —*Cicero*

Radiate friendship and it will be returned tenfold.... —*Henry P. Davidson*

Of all the things which wisdom provides to make life entirely happy, much the greatest is the possession of friendship.... —*Epicurus*

In the degree that we become friends to the highest and best within us, do we become friends to all.... —*Ralph W. Trine*

A word, a smile, and the stranger at your elbow may become an interesting friend. All through life we deny ourselves stimulating fellowship because we are too proud or too afraid to unbend.... —*D. C. Peattie*

Friendships are fragile things, and require as much care in handling as any other fragile and precious thing.... —*Randolph S. Bourne*

A true friend is the gift of God, and he only who made hearts can untie them.... —*Robert South*

We cannot tell the precise moment when friendship is formed. As in filling a vessel drop by drop, there is at last a drop which makes it run over; so in a series of kindnesses there is at last one which makes the heart run over.... —*James Boswell*

True friendship comes when silence between two people is comfortable.... —*Dave T. Gentry*

Friendship is one mind within two bodies.... —*Aristotle*

No friendship can cross the path of our destiny without leaving some mark on it forever.... —*Francois Mauriac*

Two persons cannot long be friends if they cannot forgive each other's little failings.... —*Jean La Bruyere*

All men have their frailties; and whoever looks for a friend without imperfections will never find what he seeks. We love ourselves notwithstanding our faults, and we ought to love our friends in like manner.... —*Cyrus the Great*

Friendship is seldom lasting but between equals.... —*Samuel Johnson*

Friendship that flows from the heart cannot be frozen by adversity, as the water that flows from the spring cannot congeal in winter....   —*James F. Cooper*

There is a magnet in your heart that will attract true friends. That magnet is unselfishness, thinking of others first....
    —*Paramahansa Yogananda*

Be slow to fall into friendship; but when thou art in, continue firm and constant....   —*Socrates*

Companionship may be one of the most effective ways of staying off treadmills. Our friends are often the ones who remind us when we've gone astray....   —*Melvyn Kinder*

Old friends are best. King James used to call for his old shoes; they were easiest on his feet....   —*John Selden*

Hospitality consists of a little fire, a little food, and immense quiet....
    —*Ralph W. Emerson*

The reward of friendship is itself. The man who hopes for anything else does not understand what true friendship is....   —*Alfred of Aievaulx*

Friendship is to feel as one while remaining two....   —*Ann S. Swetchine*

I used to think that friendship meant happiness: I have learned that it means discipline. Seek how we may, we shall never find a friend without faults, imperfections, traits and ways that vex, grieve, annoy us. Strive as we will, we ourselves can never fully fulfill the ideal of us that is in our friend's mind: we inevitably come short of it....
    —*Anna Brown Lindsay*

The essence of true friendship is to make allowance for another's little lapses....   —*David Storey*

Friendship with oneself is all-important, because without it one cannot be friends with anyone else in the world....
    —*Eleanor Roosevelt*

Wise company will make you also wise; from vicious friends you cannot but gather vice....   —*Sufi saying*

Be friends with all men, but in your thoughts remain alone....
    —*Isaac of Syria*

When two people become friends they establish between themselves a relation of equality. There is and can be no functional subservience to the other....
    —*John Macmurray*

A friend is a person with whom you dare to be yourself....   —*Frank Crane*

You cannot take more from a friendship than you are willing to put back into it....   —*Anonymous*

A real friend is one who walks in when the rest of the world walks out....
    —*Walter Winchell*

Our chief want in life is somebody who can make us do what we can. This is the service of a friend....
    —*Ralph W. Emerson*

It is difficult to say who does you the most mischief, enemies with the worst intentions, or friends with the best....
    —*Edward Bulwer-Lytton*

False friends are like a shadow, keeping close to us while we walk in the sunshine, but leaving us the instant we cross into the shade....
    —*Christian Bovee*

No one is your real friend except your virtues....   —*Muni Swamy*

Friendship is so much more than a word, a handshake, and a smile. It's the ability to see the inner beauty in someone.... —*Vonda K. Van Dyke*

The company of just and righteous men is better than wealth and a rich estate.... —*Euripides*

We love ourselves notwithstanding our faults, and we ought to love our friends in like manner.... —*Cyrus the Great*

Most friendships worth their salt are those nourished in human struggle.... —*Robert Veninga*

Friendships are those fruits gathered from trees planted in the rich soil of love, and nurtured with tender care and understanding. These trees are never subjected to drought.... —*Alma L. Weixelbaum*

Nothing gives such a blow to friendship as detecting another in an untruth. It strikes at the root of our confidence ever after.... —*William Hazlitt*

A friend to everyone is often a friend to nobody; or else, in his simplicity, he robs his family to help strangers, and so becomes brother to a beggar.... —*Charles H. Spurgeon*

Friendship is love minus sex and plus reason.... —*Mason Cooley*

So-called friends are in reality enemies. You will not find in this whole universe a single friend without egotism. Your true friend in need, He who is sincerely attached to you, is God, who lives within your heart.... —*Sivananda*

Friendships require commitment if they are to grow.... —*John Bradshaw*

The true friend seeks to give, not to take; to help, not to be helped; to minister, not to be ministered unto.... —*William Rader*

There can be no friendship without confidence, and no confidence without integrity.... —*Samuel Johnson*

There is no possession more valuable than a good and faithful friend.... —*Socrates*

Genius

An expert is one who does not have to think. He knows.... —*Frank L. Wright*

Genius is no more than childhood recaptured at will.... —*Charles Baudelaire*

There is no great genius without some touch of madness.... —*Seneca*

Thousands of geniuses live and die undiscovered—either by themselves or by others.... —*Mark Twain*

Genius is only the power of making continuous efforts.... —*Elbert Hubbard*

Genius springs from the soul that dares to drink at the fountains of inspiration in the garden of God.... —*Fenwick Holmes*

Genius....means little more than the faculty of perceiving in an unhabitual way.... —*William James*

The great secret of genius is to carry the spirit of the child into old age.... —*Thomas Huxley*

The first and last thing which is required for genius is the love of truth.... —*Johann W. Goethe*

Genius finds its own road, and carries its own lamp.... —*Robert A. Willmott*

Everyone is born a genius, but the process of living de-geniuses them.... —*Buckminster Fuller*

Genius is only a superior power of seeing.... —*John Ruskin*

A man of genius makes no mistakes. His errors are volitional and are the portals of discovery.... —*James Joyce*

Genius, that power which dazzles mortal eyes, is oft but perseverance in disguise.... —*Henry Austin*

Genius must be born; it can never be taught.... —*John Dryden*

When the true genius appears in the world, you may know him by this sign, that the dunces are all in confederacy against him.... —*Jonathan Swift*

Genius does what it must, and talent does what it can.... —*Edward Bulwer-Lytton*

That which we call genius has a great deal to do with courage and daring, a great deal to do with nerve....unexplored spaces do not frighten them as much as they frighten those around them. This is one of the secrets of their power.... —*Nathaniel Branden*

Genius is gold in the mine, talent is the miner who works and brings it out.... —*Lady Blessington*

Genius on earth is God giving Himself. Whenever a masterpiece appears, a distribution of God is taking place.... —*Victor Hugo*

The highest genius is willingness and ability to do hard work.... —*Robert S. MacArthur*

Genius is infinite painstaking.... —*Henry W. Longfellow*

Geniuses reach their goal with one step, whereas common minds must be led to it through a long row of object-ives.... —*Moses Mendelssohn*

One of the strongest characteristics of genius is the power of lighting its own fire.... —*John Foster*

Common sense is genius in homespun.... —*Alfred N. Whitehead*

A genius is one who stands at both ends of a perspective.... —*Elbert Hubbard*

Genius learns only from itself, talent chiefly from others. Genius learns from nature, from its own nature; talent learns from art.... —*Arnold Schoenberg*

Genius is the energy which collects, combines, amplifies, and animates.... —*Samuel Johnson*

With the stones we cast at them, geniuses build new roads for us.... —*Paul Eldridge*

Genius is the ability to reduce the complicated to the simple.... —*C. W. Ceran*

Good sense travels on well-worn paths; genius, never. And that is why the crowd, not altogether without reason, is so ready to treat great men as lunatics.... —*Cesare Lombroso*

Mediocrity is self-inflicted. Genius is self-bestowed.... —*Walter Russell*

Constant effort and frequent mistakes are the stepping-stones of genius....
—*Elbert Hubbard*

The essence of genius is to know what to overlook....   —*William James*

Genius is an infinite capacity for taking pains....   —*Jane Hopkins*

The greatest genius will not be worth much if he pretends to draw exclusively from his own resources....
—*Johann W. Goethe*

What is called genius is the abundance of life or health....   —*Henry D. Thoreau*

To believe your own thought; to believe that what is true for you in your private heart is true for all men—this is genius....   —*Ralph W. Emerson*

Patience is a necessary ingredient of genius....   —*Benjamin Disraeli*

Genius is one percent inspiration and ninety-nine percent perspiration....
—*Thomas Edison*

Genius is patience....
—*Georges L. Buffon*

Giving

M en of noblest dispositions think themselves happiest when others share their happiness with them....
—*William Duncan*

The generous man is always just, and the just who is always generous, may, unannounced, approach the throne of heaven....   —*John K. Lavater*

Generosity lies less in giving much than in giving at the right moment....
—*Jean La Bruyere*

Have no desire to acquire more (with the thought that you can have more to give), what you have is sufficient; the amount of money given is of no importance, the amount of love given is....   —*A Spiritual Warrior*

God loves a cheerful giver. She gives most who gives with joy....
—*Mother Teresa*

It is one of the beautiful compensations of this life that no one can sincerely try to help another without helping himself....   —*Charles D. Warner*

The hoarder, who is anxiously worried about losing something, is, psychologically speaking, the poor impoverished man, regardless of how much he has. Whoever is capable of giving of himself is rich....   —*Erich Fromn*

The best thing to give your enemy is forgiveness; to an opponent, tolerance; to a friend, your heart; to your child, a good example; to your father, deference; to your mother, conduct that will make her proud of you; to your self, respect; to all men, charity....
—*Sivananda*

You must give if you want to receive. Let the center of your being be one of giving, giving, giving. You can't give too much, and you will discover you cannot give without receiving....
—*Peace Pilgrim*

Blessed are those who can give without remembering and take without forgetting....   —*Melvin Schleeds*

There is no happiness in having or in getting, but only in giving....
—*Henry Drummond*

You can't give what you haven't got....
—*Latin proverb*

Supply is not getting; supply is giving. The bread that you cast upon the water is the bread that comes back to you....
—*Joel Goldsmith*

It is in giving oneself that one receives....　—*Francis of Assisi*

Be generous, not wasteful; give, not indiscriminately....　—*Mahabharata*

Your giving is sacred and therefore should be kept secret. It is wise to give quietly with no strings attached....
—*Catherine Ponder*

Give, and it shall be given unto you, good measure, pressed down....and running over....For with the same measure you give to others it shall be measured to you again....　　—*Jesus*

The very act of giving, with its apparent loss, tends to throw us upon Spirit and makes us depend upon God for supply....　—*Henry T. Hamblin*

Man only keeps that which he gives away....　　—*Ancient proverb*

Money giving is a very good criterion of a person's mental health. Generous people are rarely mentally ill people....
—*Karl Menninger*

Generosity gives help rather than advice....
—*Luc de Clapiers Vauvenargues*

Giving begins with an open heart and ends with an open hand....
—*Anonymous*

Unhappiness is the hunger to get; happiness is the hunger to give....
—*William G. Jordan*

The person who gives of himself and his substance, no matter how little, opens the door for life to pour in, not only compensating him for his gift, but increasing the gift. The more one gives the more that a person is able to receive....　—*Jack Addington*

We can only give what we have in our purse....　　—*Henri F. Amiel*

The wise man does not lay up his treasures. The more he gives to others, the more he has for his own....
—*Lao-tzu*

Rings and jewels are not gifts, but apologies for gifts. The only gift is a portion of thyself....
—*Ralph W. Emerson*

To receive more, we must give out what we receive....For it is by giving that we set in operation the unfailing law of measure for measure. With no thought of receiving, it is impossible to avoid receiving, for the abundance you have given is returned to you in fulfillment of the law....　—*Baird Spalding*

Cast thy bread upon the waters; for thou shall find it after many days....
—*Old Testament*

I have found that there is a tremendous joy in giving....　　—*William Black*

Love gives for the joy of giving, attachment gives for the return that may come....　—*Paramananda*

The more you love, the more you'll find that life is good and friends are kind, for only what we give away enriches us from day to day....
—*Helen Steiner Rice*

Examples are few of men ruined by giving....　　—*Christian Bovee*

Giving of ourselves for the betterment of the less fortunate is the cheapest and most effective therapy available today. To deny ourselves the joy of giving is to deny our basic needs....
—*John C. Cornelius*

Most of the joy of living comes out of true giving—giving without strings attached.... —*Gary Emery*

You can give of your talent, you can give of your possessions, or you can give of yourself. For God's sake, give something.... —*Cleveland Amory*

The real test of a man is not: How much has he got? The measure of a man is: How much does he give that he can afford to give.... —*Fred Van Amburgh*

Trees bend low with ripened fruit; clouds hang down with gentle rain; Noble men bow graciously. This is the way of generous things.... —*Bhartrihari*

When you give something to your brother, to your sister, you lose nothing. You gain whenever your brother and sister gain because your brother and sister are also your own Self.... —*Shantidasa*

Every gift, though it be small, is in reality great if given with affection....
—*Pindar*

Almost always the most indigent are the most generous....
—*Leszezynski Stanislaw*

In giving, the purpose is not to fulfill another person's expected desires, but to share what is in our capacity, and give it with love and joy....
—*A Spiritual Warrior*

The giver is greater than the gift....
—*Eknath Easwaran*

The soul lives forever by giving, not receiving. This is the grand paradox. You get most by giving most. Conversely, by receiving much you impoverish yourself. By selfish accumulation you become bankrupt....
—*Julian P. Johnson*

Our true acquisitions lie only in our charities; we gain only as we give....
—*William Simms*

If you are not generous with a meager income, you will never be generous with abundance.... —*Harold Nye*

The gift is most of the giver and comes back most to him.... —*Walt Whitman*

Fill yourselves first and then only will you be able to give to others....
—*Augustine*

The truly generous is the truly wise, and he who loves not others, lives unblest.... —*Henry Home*

It is more blessed to give than to receive.... —*Paul of Tarsus*

God has the power to give and to take away; but if anything is taken away it is only to make room for something far better.... —*Henry T. Hamblin*

In the sphere of material things, giving means being rich. Not he who has much is rich, but he who gives much....
—*Erich Fromm*

(To) take something from yourself, to give to another, that is humane and gentle and never takes away as much comfort as it brings.... —*Thomas More*

In this world it is not what we take up, but what we give up, that makes us rich.... —*Henry W. Beecher*

We get what we give, no more, no less, and let us remember that every time we put up a fence we shut out more than we shut in....
—*John H. Randall*

We should give as we would receive, cheerfully, quickly, and without hesitation; for there is no grace in a gift that sticks to the fingers.... —*Seneca*

He who gives freely is apt to grow richer in heart, though he grows poorer in purse... —*George H. Hepworth*

You can't live a perfect day without doing something for someone who will never be able to repay you....
—*John Wooden*

The manner of giving is worth more than the gift.... —*Pierre Corneille*

A bit of fragrance always clings to the hand that gives you roses....
—*Chinese proverb*

The generous heart is the happy heart.... —*Ida S. Taylor*

It is not what we give, but what we share, for the gift without the giver is bare.... —*James Russell Lowell*

We must possess love before we can give.... —*Mother Teresa*

They who scatter with one hand, gather with two, not always in coin, but in kind. Nothing multiplies so much as kindness.... —*John Wray*

He gives little who gives with a frown; he gives much who gives little with a smile.... —*The Talmud*

When I give, I give myself....
—*Walt Whitman*

He that gives all, though but little, gives much, because God looks not at the quantity of the gift, but to the quality of the givers.... —*Francis Quarles*

Do not limit what you give, limit what you take.... —*Napoleon Hill*

Give to the world the best you have and the best will come back to you....
—*Anonymous*

Giving requires good sense....
—*Ovid*

We enjoy thoroughly only the pleasure that we give.... —*Alexandre Dumas*

Giving is most blessed and most acceptable when the donor remains completely anonymous....
—*Maimonides*

You do not have to be rich to be generous. If you have the spirit of true generosity, a pauper can give like a prince.... —*Corinne U. Wells*

Blessed are they who give without expecting even thanks in return, for they shall be abundantly rewarded....
—*Peace Pilgrim*

To receive everything, one must open one's hands and give....
—*Taisen Deshimaru*

If you would take, you must first give....
—*Lao-tzu*

Complete possession is proved only by giving. All you are unable to give possesses you.... —*André Gide*

If the sun were asked why he is giving light, if it could speak to us, he would answer that it is his nature to do so....We must be like the sun.... This is the purpose of life.... —*Papa Ramdas*

Goals

You can't get anywhere unless you know where to start from and where to go.... —*Lionel Barrymore*

Our supreme goal should be a state of mind in which invisible things are of more importance than the visible.... —*Alice H. Rice*

If you don't know where you are going, you will probably wind up somewhere else.... —*Laurence J. Peter*

Perfection of means and confusion of goals seem to characterize our age.... —*Albert Einstein*

No one has attained his goal without action.... —*Bhagavad-Gita*

If one sets up fantasy goals, then it follows that they will experience fantasy victories and fantasy defeats, the inevitable pendulum swing within the world of desire....The goal of God is the reality of yourself; you are within God, and God is within you.... —*A Spiritual Warrior*

Know what you want to do—then do it. Make straight for your goal and go undefeated in spirit to the end.... —*Ernestine Schumann-Heink*

Goals are simply tools to focus your energy in positive directions, they can be changed as your priorities change, new ones added, and others dropped.... —*O. Carl Simonton*

The goal of life is to become one with the Eternal....You cannot reach the goal without leading a righteous life and without possessing a pure heart.... —*Sivananda*

Let him that would move the world first move himself.... —*Socrates*

Man forgets that the ultimate goal in life—if such it can be called—is not "becoming" something but "non-becoming" or "non-living."... —*Ramesh Balsekar*

If the will knows not what to will, it will not be able to will.... —*Lao-tzu*

Most of humanity drifts with the tides, letting the ebb and flow of life take them where it will. They are living flotsam and jetsam; lacking resolve and direction, they frequently find themselves cast upon unfriendly, barren shores.... —*Robert Collier*

The knowledge of having chosen an ultimate objective gives direction and emphasis to the days of one's years.... —*Oveta Hobby*

You must know for which harbor you are headed if you are to catch the right wind to take you there.... —*Seneca*

Not having a goal is more to be feared than not reaching a goal.... —*Robert Schuller*

One does not begin life in emptiness with a goal of constant attainment; nor is life an urn to be continually filled with superfluous goals.... —*Shantidasa*

If you have no goals, your thoughts will take you toward what you think about most.... —*Andrew Matthews*

The reason most people never reach their goals is that they don't define them, or ever seriously consider them as believable or achievable.... —*Denis Waitley*

Security is a game in which the final goal is never quite in reach....

—Laurence Martin

Our goal and purpose is to bring our lives into harmony with God's will....

—Peace Pilgrim

Life is not an end in itself. Your goal is not conformed to this material world in which your body is living. Your goal goes beyond this world of appearances. Your goal is the attainment of Divine Perfection, which is the nature of absolute peace and joy....

—Chidananda

The goal of human life is to realize God. If people praise or blame you, if they honor or insult you....if your body stands or falls—never move an inch from your principles or from your ideals.... *—Brahmananda*

It must be borne in mind that the tragedy of life does not lie in not reaching your goals, the tragedy lies in not having any goals to reach....

—Benjamin I. Mays

You must have long-range goals to keep you from being frustrated by short-range failure.... *—Charles C. Noble*

Goals are absolutely essential, for goals give meaning to life.... *—Victor Frankl*

There is no goal to be reached. There is nothing to be attained. You are the Self. You exist always....

—Ramana Maharshi

All human beings, though they may seem to be walking on divergent paths, are all marching to one goal, and that goal is Self-realization....

—Bhagavad-Gita

We are already the goal of our own search.... *—Stephen H. Wolinsky*

Seeking means to have a goal; but finding means to be free, to be receptive, to have no goal....

—Hermann Hesse

The Goal of life is God-realization....

—Sivananda

Not every end is a goal. The end of a melody is not its goal; but nevertheless, if the melody had not reached its end it would not have reached its goal either.... *—Friedrich W. Nietzsche*

The happiest days are found in struggling toward a goal, not in any attainment..... *—Anonymous*

God

A single spirit fills infinity. It is that of God, whom nothing limits or divides, who is everywhere entire and nowhere confined.... *—Eliphas Levi*

Either God is everything or there is no God. If God is, God is. If God isn't, God isn't. Your beliefs do not determine what is and what isn't....

—Ron Smothermon

Once you've seen the face of God, you see the same face on everyone you meet.... *—Deng Ming-Dao*

When you lose God, it is not God who is lost.... *—Anonymous*

It is difficult to know why God reveals Himself to some and plays the game of hide-and-seek with others....

—Papa Ramdas

We have but a little knowledge of God....We are like bats who cannot look up in the light of the sun....
—*Caterina Cibo*

No man can ever know God until he consciously becomes ONE with God. Anything short of that is more or less speculative, imaginary, visionary, and imperfect.... —*Julian P. Johnson*

We learn that God is, that He is in me, and that all things are shadows of Him.... —*Ralph W. Emerson*

The description that God is egoless may seem to be a poor one. It conveys no sense to the ego-ridden mind. People want to be told that God dwells somewhere in the sky, in a world of great splendor, surrounded by wonderful beings....Even to understand that God dwells in their own hearts, men take time.... —*Lakshmana Sarma*

There is one thing God cannot do—He cannot separate Himself from the soul.... —*Yoga Swami*

God does not pay at the end of every week, but he pays.... —*Ann of Austria*

In essence, the life of God and the life of man are identically the same, and so are one. They differ not in essence, in quality; they differ in degree....
—*Ralph W. Trine*

We give God the name of good: it is only by shortening it that it becomes God.... —*Henry W. Beecher*

The helping of man by man is God....
—*Ancient Greek saying*

The eye with which I see God is the same eye by which God sees me....
—*Meister Eckhart*

If you are simple and truthful, seeing God is easier than anything else in the world.... —*Prabhushri*

If man is not made for God, why is he happy only in God? If man is made for God, why is he opposed to God?...
—*Blaise Pascal*

Everywhere you look in science, it becomes the harder to understand the universe without God....
—*Robert Herrman*

When the veil is removed, God can be experienced everywhere in full....
—*Sathya Sai Baba*

If we have any conception of what God is, certainly it should be changing and expanding as we ourselves grow and change.... —*Bernadette Roberts*

I cannot imagine a God who rewards and punishes the objects of His creation, whose purposes are modeled after our own—a God, in short, who is a reflection of human frailty....
—*Albert Einstein*

God in the depths of us receives God who comes to us; it is God contemplating God.... —*Jan van Ruysbroeck*

God never uses a cookie cutter to create.... —*Dom Stephen*

God is no fairy story, no wishful thinking, no joke, no ancient legend. ....God is real. God is.
—*P. M. H. Atwater*

God is a gold wire on which gold beads of His own manifestation are strung....
—*Jnaneshwar Maharaj*

God is a sea of infinite substance....
—*John of Damascus*

Do you need proof of God? Does one light a torch to see the sun?...
—*Chinese proverb*

I could not say I believe. I know! I have had the experience of being gripped by something that is stronger than myself, something that people call God....
—*Carl Jung*

God is like a mirror. The mirror never changes but everyone who looks at it sees a different face....
—*Midrash Tanhama*

God is simple, everything else is complex. Do not seek absolute values in the relative world of Nature....
—*Paramahansa Yogananda*

Do not despise the world, for the world too is God....   —*Mohammed*

The most basic thing you can say about God is that God is love....
—*C. Alan Anderson*

If you put God first in your life, everything else will fall into place....
—*Anonymous*

God is an experience, and no one knows God until he has had that experience....   —*Joel Goldsmith*

Let us be Gods and then help others to be Gods....   —*Vivekananda*

Nothing exists save God....
—*Sufi saying*

To men's eyes God has many faces, and each one swears that the one he sees is the only true God. Yet they are all wrong, for all are true....   —*Anana*

Why should God need us, unless it were to give us His love?...
—*Henri Bergson*

God is very near the simple, innocent, guileless, unselfish, loving child—unconsciously; or, better, supra-consciously....   —*Bhagavan Das*

God is concealed from the mind but revealed in the heart....   —*Anonymous*

All things proclaim the existence of God....   —*Napoleon Bonaparte*

Man is a god in ruins....
—*Ralph W. Emerson*

Do you know God? Do you know there is a power greater than ourselves which manifests itself within us as well as everywhere else in the universe? This I call God. Do you know what it is to know God, to have God's constant guidance, a constant awareness of God's presence?...   —*Peace Pilgrim*

Man can cease to become man, and become God; but man cannot be God and man at the same time....
—*Plotinus*

We can know what God is not, but we cannot know what He is....   —*Augustine*

You are related to God as a drop of water is related to the ocean. The drop and the ocean are not different, they are essentially the same. Except for one thing—you cannot sail a ship in a drop of water and you can sail a billion ships in the ocean....   —*Shantidasa*

Man appoints, and God disappoints....
—*Miguel de Cervantes*

God is not omnipotent, omniscient, and omnipotent—you are. If you think that there is God and you, the doors of heaven are shut...   —*Walter Starcke*

God is not like a fish or vegetables that you can buy Him for a price....
—*Sarada Devi*

God is a light that is never darkened....
—*Francis Quarles*

We are, in the hands of God, like blocks of marble in the hands of sculptors....
—*Alphonsus Liguori*

What does God do all day long? God lies in a maternity bed giving birth....
—*Meister Eckhart*

God is Spirit, and they that worship Him must worship in spirit and truth....
—*New Testament*

He alone grasps God who does not grasp Him. Anyone who understands God does not know Him....
—*Hindu saying*

God is day—night, winter—summer, love—hate, war—peace, abundance—want, heat—cold, death—life, youth—age, waking—asleep, creation—destruction....
—*Heraclitus*

Belief in a cruel God makes a cruel man....
—*Thomas Paine*

The acceptance of the omnipresence of God leads to a very profound conclusion. You cannot be APART from Him under any circumstances, for otherwise it would mean there are some places where He is not present....which naturally, is absurd....
—*Mouni Sadhu*

God is a circle whose center is everywhere, and its circumference nowhere....
—*Empedocles*

God alone is good and perfect....
—*Anandamayi Ma*

Until a man has found God, and been found by God, he begins at no beginning, he works to no end....
—*Herbert G. Wells*

We cannot tell of what God is; we can only tell "what God is not."...
—*The Zohar*

God is man minus his desires....
—*Sathya Sai Baba*

When people are loving, brave, truthful, charitable, God is present....
—*Harold Kushner*

The ancient hieroglyphic for God was the figure of an eye upon a sceptre, to denote that he sees and rules all things....
—*John M. Barker*

The eternal, unchangeable Lord, who is formless and attributeless, who is absolute knowledge and absolute bliss, evolves the whole universe out of Himself, plays with it, and again withdraws it into Himself....
—*Srimad Bhagavatam*

We cannot go where God is not, and where God is, all is well....
—*Anonymous*

Once you accept the evidence of God—however you define Him....then you are caught forever with His presence in the center of all things....
—*Morris West*

I gave in and admitted that God was God....   *(upon relinquishing atheism)*
—*C. S. Lewis*

God must not be thought of as a physical being, or having any kind of body. He is pure mind. He moves and acts without needing any corporeal space, or size, or form, or color, or any other property of material....
—*Origen*

God to me, it seems, is a verb not a noun, proper or improper....
—*Buckminster Fuller*

The kingdom of God is not imminent but immanent; it is not "among you," suddenly about to break like a thunderstorm, but "within you," ready to be expressed the moment you understand your latent common nature.... —*Gerald Heard*

Don't bargain with God....
—*Jewish proverb*

The simplest person who in his integrity worships God, becomes God....
—*Ralph W. Emerson*

Everyone is in a small way the image of God.... —*Marcus Manilius*

Whoever finds God becomes wholly God; and unto God there is no other God. Where the sun shines, can there be a night?... —*Sufi saying*

God is the only reality....
—*Archie Canfield*

Wherever you turn is God's face....
—*Mohammed*

Belief in God is acceptance of the basic principle that the universe makes sense, that there is behind it an ultimate purpose.... —*Carl W. Miller*

God is that which has no definition....
—*Joseph Albo*

God's delight is in the communication of Himself, His own happiness to everyone according to his or her capacity. He does everything that is good, righteous, and lovely for its own sake, because it is good, righteous and lovely....—*William Law*

I had a thousand questions to ask God; but when I met Him they all fled and didn't seem to matter....
—*Christopher Morley*

Man without God is a bubble in the sea, a single grain of sand on an infinite beach.... —*Pincus Goodblatt*

Because you cannot see Him, God is everywhere.... —*Yasunari Kawabata*

God created man in His Image and likeness, and then man returned the compliment and created God in his own image and likeness....
—*Jean J. Rousseau*

We cannot get away from God, though we can ignore Him....
—*James E. Cabot*

If you say that God is good, great, blessed, wise or any such thing, the starting point is this: God is....
—*Bernard of Clairvaux*

God is always here and now; God does not know distance. And if we fail to make contact with God, it is we who have distanced ourselves from God....
—*Shantidasa*

All power comes from God....
—*Jacques B. Bossuet*

We lump together all things that are beyond the capacity of all of us collectively to understand—and one name we give to all those things together is God.... —*Peace Pilgrim*

An idea about God is not God....
—*Leo Tolstoy*

The sun only shines, just as God only loves.... —*John Powell*

The deepest need of men is not food and clothing and shelter, important as they are. It is God....
—*Thomas R. Kelly*

Some people treat God like they do a lawyer; they go to Him only when they are in trouble.... —*Anonymous*

God is the greatest democrat the world knows, for He leaves us free to make our own choice between good and evil.... —*Mohandas Gandhi*

God has created the world in play....It is God Himself who is sporting in the form of man.... —*Ramakrishna*

Four veils hide God from us: solids, liquids, gases, and light. Lift these veils and find God everywhere, in everything.... —*Paramahansa Yogananda*

The people most separated from God are the ascetics by their asceticism, the devotees by their devotion, and the knowers by their knowledge.... —*Bayazid al-Bistami*

God is the great magician who can, by His touch, transmute even the basest life into a golden consciousness full of His light, power and joy.... —*Papa Ramdas*

God is the indwelling, not the transient, cause of all things.... —*Baruch Spinoza*

On the day I first really believed in God, for the first time life made sense to me and the world had meaning.... —*Dag Hammarskjöld*

It is easy to understand God as long as you don't try to explain Him.... —*Joseph Joubert*

What is needed is to see God in everything, and to receive everything directly from His hands, and no intervention of second causes.... —*Catherine Marshall*

God is over all things, under all things; outside all, within but not enclosed; without but not excluded; alone but not raised up; below but not depressed; wholly above, presiding; wholly beneath, sustaining; wholly without, embracing; wholly within, filling.... —*Hildebert of Lavardin*

God is a blank sheet upon which nothing is found but what you yourself have written.... —*Martin Luther*

God outside us is an hypothesis; God inside us is an experience.... —*Harry E. Fosdick*

God becomes man, that man might become God.... —*St. Athanasius*

God enters a private door to every individual.... —*Ralph W. Emerson*

When asked where God is, people point towards the sky or some far distant region; that is why He is not manifesting Himself. Realize that He is in you, with you, behind you, before you and all around you; and He can be seen and felt everywhere.... —*Sathya Sai Baba*

If God made us in His image, we have certainly returned the compliment.... —*Voltaire*

God is a fountain flowing into itself.... —*St. Dionysius*

God is a reality of spirit....God cannot....be conceived of as an object, not even as the very highest object. God is not to be found in the world of objects.... —*Nikolay Berdyayev*

We turn to God for help when our foundations are shaking, only to learn that it is God who is shaking them.... —*Charles C. West*

A man with God is always in the majority....　　　—*John Knox*

You are a principal work, a fragment of God Himself, you have a part of Him. Why then are you ignorant of your high birth?...You bear God about with you, poor wretch, and know it not....
　　　—*Epictetus*

No man can build a bridge to God. But God never forces man to cross the bridge that He builds for him....
　　　—*Nels F. S. Ferre*

The entire effort of our Soul is to become God. This effort is as natural to man as that of flying is to birds....
　　　—*Marsilio Ficino*

Whatever your belief about the nature of God, God becomes to you what you believe Him to be. If you think God is cruel, punishing, vindictive and that He sends sickness, pain and suffering, you will live in fear, dread and guilt. These negative attitudes will create every opportunity to demonstrate God's wrath. If you believe that God is love, wisdom and beauty, you will live in happy expectation and joy–that will attract wondrous transformation in your life....　　　—*Cheryl Canfield*

You're God in your universe....
　　　—*Werner Erhard*

God is a superior reasoning power....revealed in the incomprehensible universe....　　　—*Albert Einstein*

There is nothing we can give God that He does not have already; nothing we can do for God that He cannot do better....　　　—*Bernadette Roberts*

Metaphysics begins and ends with God....　　　—*John S. Erigena*

God is omnipresent—which simply means you cannot be where God is not....　　　—*Peace Pilgrim*

The only God to worship is the human soul in the human body....
　　　—*Vivekananda*

Nothing is void of God; He Himself fills His work....　　　—*Seneca*

We are—because God is!...
　　　—*Emanuel Swedenborg*

God is the sum of all possibilities....
　　　—*Isaac Bashevis Singer*

What a privilege and how enjoyable it would be to live and walk in a world where we meet only Gods. In such a world you can live....For in the degree that we come into higher realization do we see only the God in each human soul....When God speaks to God, then God responds, and shows forth as God....　　　—*Ralph W. Trine*

The Blessed Trinity....can be best understood as the Omnipresence, Omnipotence, and Omniscience of the Universal Mind, God....
　　　—*Baird Spalding*

The things which are impossible with men are possible with God....　　　—*Jesus*

God does not dwell in a body, so we cannot define Him in a material way. God is a spirit....　　　—*Billy Graham*

If there exists a good and wise God, then there also exists a progress of mankind toward perfection....　　　—*Plato*

God gives us always strength enough, and sense enough, for everything He wants us to do....　　　—*John Ruskin*

When man shall see God, he shall see himself and not until then....
—*Frater Achad*

God sleeps in minerals, awakens in plants, walks in animals, and thinks in man.... —*Sanskrit saying*

Each man enters into God so much as God enters into him.... —*Henri F. Amiel*

Every man is a divinity in disguise, a god playing the fool....
—*Ralph W. Emerson*

Where God is, all agree....
—*Henry Vaughan*

Even we may become gods walking about in the flesh.... —*Athanasius*

The mind that wishes to behold God must itself become God.... —*Plotinus*

God does not stop creating, but always creates and begins to create....For creatures are always in the process and beginnings of their creation....
—*Meister Eckhart*

Think of God as a divine ocean and you as one drop with free will. You can choose to remain separate from the ocean—but you won't be happy. You can choose to be part of the ocean, in which case you have given up your free will, but you will be delightfully happy.... —*Peace Pilgrim*

God has two dwellings: one in heaven and the other in a meek and thankful heart.... —*Izaak Walton*

God generates beings and sends them back over and over again, until they return to Him.... —*Koran*

Wherever there are no limits, where Infinity and Eternity and Immortality exist, that is where God is....
—*Omraam M. Aivanhov*

God's Will

The strength of man consists in finding out the way in which God is going, and going in that way too....
—*Henry W. Beecher*

Not an atom moves except by God's will.... —*Ramana Maharshi*

There is nothing great, there is nothing holy, there is nothing wise, there is nothing fair, but to depend wholly upon God, like a child does and can do only what is bidden....
—*Jeanne-Marie Guyon*

Life has taught me that it knows better plans than we can imagine, so I try to submerge my own desires....into a calm willingness to accept what comes....
—*Julia Seton*

I am like a pencil in (God's) hand. That is all. He does the thinking. He does the writing. The pencil has nothing to do with it. The pencil has only to be allowed to be used.... —*Mother Teresa*

We must follow, not force providence....
—*William Shakespeare*

There is a reason for everything; nothing happens without the permission of God....
—*Allan Kardec*

Learn to will what God wishes, and everything you want will certainly happen.... —*Eliphas Levi*

To understand the workings of God's will, you have to submit yourself to it unreservedly. Then you come to know that everything happens by His will, and for good.... —*Papa Ramdas*

Whatever the universal nature assigns to any man at any time is for the good of that man at the time....
—*Marcus Aurelius*

God is our owner, we are His property; His providence works for our good....
—*Immanuel Kant*

Some who have no knowledge of the subject, say that to surrender to the will of God is an act of weakness. They should try it and see for themselves. They would then find that they had taken on "a man's job," and there is no life that calls for so much courage and faith as that which seeks to be led according to the will of God....
—*Henry T. Hamblin*

The will of God is always good....
—*Ernest Holmes*

Those people who are not governed by God will be ruled by tyrants....
—*William Penn*

There is a divine plan behind everything, and if we allow ourselves to be used by that Unseen Force, as good instruments, many things can happen in a mysterious, miraculous way....
—*Satchidananda*

He is truly very learned, who does the will of God, and forsakes his own will....
—*Thomas à Kempis*

We may rest assured that nothing whatever happens on Earth without God's permission....
—*Alphonsus Liguori*

Most of the near perfect actions or performances, and almost all the works of creativity, happen in this state of egolessness, when the tenet "Thy Will be Done" is actually put into practice....
—*Ramesh Balsekar*

You choose yourself to be a receiver of spiritual truth when you surrender your will to God's will. We all have the same potential. God is revealed to all who seek—God speaks to all who will listen. When you surrender your will to God's will you enter a very busy life— and a very beautiful one....
—*Peace Pilgrim*

Do not say, regarding anything, "I am going to do that tomorrow," but only, "if God will."...
—*Koran*

Whatever Heaven ordains is best....
—*Confucius*

God does not will that we abound in knowledge, but that we lovingly and humbly submit ourselves in all things to His will....
—*Henry Suso*

God gives the perfect blueprint for each upcoming experience and we either wisely go along with God's plan or we foolishly refuse to follow His lead....
—*C. Alan Anderson*

A tragic mistake that is often made by orthodox religious people is to assume that the Will of God for them is bound to be something very dull and un-inviting, if not positively unpleasant. The truth is that the Will of God for us always means greater freedom, greater self-expression, wider and newer and brighter experience....
—*Emmet Fox*

Live in the world like a dead leaf. As a dead leaf is carried by the wind into a house or on the roadside and has no choice of its own, so let the wind of the Divine Will blow you wherever it chooses....
—*Ramakrishna*

Desire and pray always that God's will be perfectly fulfilled in you....
—*Thomas à Kempis*

Remember that you are an actor in a play, and of such sort as the Author chooses, whether long or short. If it be His good pleasure to assign you the part of a beggar, a ruler, or a simple citizen, it is yours to play the role fitly. For your business is to act well the part assigned you; to choose it, is Another's....
—*Epictetus*

True worship of God consists quite simply in doing God's will, but this sort of worship has never been to man's taste.... —*Sören Kierkegaard*

If we are in a hole, the Way begins in the hole. The moment we set our face in the same direction as His, we are walking with God.... —*Helen Wodehouse*

In His will is our peace....
—*Dante Alighieri*

Do God's will as if it were your will, and God will accomplish your will as if it were His own.. —*Rabbi Gamaliel*

It is not within the law of God that man should live in poverty, destitute. It is God's Will that man should have plenty, heaped up, pressed together and running over.... —*Frater Achad*

He who strives to reach and to accomplish the divine will, will be tried to the very uttermost; and this is absolutely necessary, for how else could one acquire that sublime patience without which there is no real wisdom, no divinity?... —*James Allen*

You must recognize, you must realize yourself as one with the Infinite Spirit. God's will is then your will; your will is God's will, and "with God all things are possible."... —*Ralph W. Trine*

The very best and utmost attainment in this life is to remain still and let God act and speak in thee....
—*Meister Eckhart*

We should ask nothing and refuse nothing, but leave ourselves in the arms of divine Providence without wasting time in any desire, except to will what God wills of us....
—*Francis de Sales*

Perfect conformity to the will of God is the sole sovereign and complete liberty.... —*Jean H. D'Aubigne*

Most people try to fit God into their plans instead of allowing themselves to fit into God's plan.... —*Anonymous*

Divine guidance often comes when the horizon is the blackest....
—*Mohandas Gandhi*

Divine Will prevails at all times and under all circumstances. There is no need to tell God your requirements. He knows them Himself and will look after them.... —*Ramana Maharshi*

If we make God's will our law, then God's promise shall be our support and comfort, and we shall find every burden light, and every duty a joy....
—*Tryon Edwards*

Restrain every wish that is not referred to God's will; banish all eager desires, all anxiety; desire only the will of God; seek Him alone and supremely, and you will find peace....—*Francois Fenelon*

I would consider being in harmony with God's will a much higher state than just loving God. However, loving God is good.... —*Peace Pilgrim*

To do God's will is the only science that gives us rest....
—*Henry W. Longfellow*

To a good man to serve the will of God, it is in the truest and best sense to serve himself.... —*John Smith, the Platonist*

No servant of God can be more than a channel or instrument. God works through His servants. They do not work for God, but God through them. God raises up His own instruments, guides them, trains them, and, if found worthy, uses them....
—*Henry T. Hamblin*

God moderates all at His pleasure....
—*Francois Rabelais*

Divine Will is all powerful. God wills, and everything comes into being that very second. Man wills, but it takes a long time for attaining a thing or materialization of the desired object as his will is weak.... —*Sivananda*

The highest peace which the soul can enjoy is to know itself as much as possible united with God's will....
—*Angelus Silesius*

True peace consists in not separating ourselves from the will of God....
—*Thomas Aquinas*

For with God, to will is to accomplish, inasmuch as, when He wills, the doing is completed in the self-same moment as the willing.... —*Hermes*

Holiness consists in doing God's will joyfully.... —*Mother Teresa*

The essence of true holiness consists in conformity to the nature and will of God.... —*Samuel Lucas*

If you learn to see God in all things, you will learn to love them according to His will, not your own self-will....
—*Gerald Vann*

God's will for us is not some set of instructions independent of our choices, but works through those choices.... —*Jesse Jennings*

If the concept of God has any validity or use, it can only be to make us larger, freer, and more loving....
—*James Baldwin*

Nothing comes to pass but what God appoints. Our fate is decreed, and things do not happen by chance, but every man's portion of joy and sorrow is predetermined.... —*Seneca*

The study of God's word, for the purpose of discovering God's will, is a secret discipline which has formed the greatest characters....
—*James W. Alexander*

God is the master of scenes; we must not choose which part we shall act; it concerns us only to be careful that we do it well.... —*Jeremy Taylor*

He who serves God after God's will shall be rewarded accordingly to his own will; but he who prays to God according to his own will shall not be answered in accordance with his own will, but after God's will.... —*Tauler*

It is not everyone who says to me "Lord! Lord!" who will get into the Kingdom of Heaven, but only those who do the will of my Father.... —*Jesus*

Everything in this life has to be paid for. We can only give our signature to the credit bill: "His will shall be done.".... —*Lucy Cornellssen*

It is perfectly true that everything in the world happens by God's will alone. His power is invincible. To submit to this power means to permit it to work in and through us irresistibly....resistance to the divine will and power means frustration and misery....
—*Papa Ramdas*

If only you will find out the thing God intends you to do, and will do it, you will find that all doors will open to you; all obstacles in your path will melt away; you will be acclaimed a brilliant success.... —*Emmet Fox*

It is the will of God that we surrender our wills....Yield completely to God and then be satisfied.... —*Meister Eckhart*

Man finds it hard to get what he wants, because he does not want the best; God finds it hard to give, because He would give the best, and man will not take it.... —*George Macdonald*

It is best to trust in God, not in our dim reasoning and uncertain conjectures.... —*Philo*

The superior man lives quietly and calmly, waiting for the will of Heaven, while the average man does what is full of risk, looking out for turns of luck.... —*Confucius*

God's will is always being done, whether we like it or not.... —*Sunyata*

While we live here, we must not so much seek to enjoy God, but rather to do His will.... —*Teresa of Avila*

There is not in the world a kind of life more sweet and delightful than that of a continual walk with God. Those only can comprehend it who practice and experience it.... —*Brother Lawrence*

Nothing has separated us from God but our own will, or rather our own will is our separation from God.... —*William Law*

It is for us to make the effort. The result is always in God's hands.... —*Mohandas Gandhi*

Oh, the great folly of those who resist the will of God! They must of necessity endure afflictions, because no one can prevent the accomplishment of the Divine decrees. They must suffer without deriving any benefit from their trials.... —*Alphonsus Liguori*

By the law of God, given by Him to humanity, all men are free, are brothers, and are equals.... —*Guiseppe Mazzini*

The longer I live....the more I am content to let unseen powers go on their way with me and mine without question or distrust.... —*John Burroughs*

The surest method of arriving at a knowledge of God's eternal purpose about us is to be found in the right use of the present moment.... —*Frederick W. Faber*

Life is nothing but a play and a pretense, and His will must be done, however we rebel at it.... —*Robert Benson*

Man proposes, but God disposes.... —*Thomas à Kempis*

Complete surrender does imply that you should have no desire of your own, that God's will alone is your will and you have no will of your own.... —*Ramana Maharshi*

The highest knowledge which man can attain is the longing for peace, that our will becomes one with the infinite Will.... —*Albert Schweitzer*

The will of God is the measure of things.... —*St. Ambrose*

Do nothing by self-will but rather conform to heaven's will, and everything will be done for you.... —*Lao-tzu*

God understands His own plan, and He knows what you want a great deal better than you do. What you call hindrances, obstacles, discouragements, are probably God's opportunities.... —*Horace Bushnell*

Golden Rule

W hat is unpleasant to thyself, that do not do unto thy neighbor. This is the whole law. All else is exposition.... —*Hillel*

"Do not do to others what you would not have them do to you" is one of the most fundamental principles of ethics. But it is equally justifiable to state: Whatever you do to others, you also do to yourself.... —*Erich Fromm*

Treat your inferiors as you would be treated by your betters.... —*Seneca*

It is not fair to ask of others what you are not willing to do yourself.... —*Eleanor Roosevelt*

If each of us were to realize that whatsoever he does to another he does in effect to himself, through the law of reciprocal action, this world would become a happy and peaceful place.... —*Robert Mueller*

Others will mostly treat you the way you treat yourself.... —*Mohammed Moussa*

Do not do unto others what would not be good for yourself.... —*The Magi*

In everything do to others as you would have them do to you, for this is the law of the prophets.... —*Jesus*

Think about others as you would wish them to think about you.... —*Emmet Fox*

This is the way of peace—overcome evil with good, and falsehood with truth, and hatred with love. The Golden Rule would do equally well. There is nothing new about that except the practice of it.... —*Peace Pilgrim*

That nature is good which refrains from doing unto another whatsoever is not good for itself.... —*Zoroastrian saying*

The Golden Rule: "Do unto others as you would have others do unto you," often-times creates a conflict. All people are different and respond differently to certain stimuli. One person's delight can be another person's poison.... —*Shantidasa*

Do not do to others as you would not like done to yourself; so there will be no murmuring against you in the country, and none in the family; your public life will arouse no ill-will nor your private life any resentment.... —*Confucius*

Do not to others what you do not wish done to yourself; and wish for others too what you desire and long for, for yourself—this is the whole of righteousness, heed it well.... —*Mahabharata*

Give to every other human being every right that you claim for yourself—that is my doctrine.... —*Thomas Paine*

The Golden Rule means we should do unto others as we would wish them to do unto us if our positions were reversed.... —*Napoleon Hill*

Pity the misfortunes of others; rejoice in the well-being of others; help those who are in want; save men in danger; rejoice at the success of others; and sympathize with their reverses, even as though you were in their place....
—*Tai-Shang*

Judge not your neighbor till thou art in his situation....　　—*The Mishnah*

We should behave to the world as we wish the world to behave to us....
—*Aristotle*

The Golden Rule is not a religion; it is the expression of religion....
—*Charles L. Allen*

What is hateful to you, do not to your fellow men. That is the entire Law; all the rest is commentary....
—*The Talmud*

The golden rule of conduct is mutual toleration, seeing that we will never all think alike and that we shall always see Truth in fragments and from different angles of vision....　—*Mohandas Gandhi*

The Golden Rule works like gravitation....　　　　　　—*C. F. Dole*

The free market is in accordance with the Golden Rule. We advance ourselves as we help others. The more we help others, the more we receive in return....
—*Percy Greaves*

Regard your neighbor's gain as your own gain, and your neighbor's loss as your own loss....
—*T'ai Shang Kan Ying P'ien*

He that does good to another does good also to himself, not only in the consequence but in the very act. For the consciousness of well-doing is in itself ample reward....　　　　—*Seneca*

You are told you should love your neighbor as yourself; but if you love yourself measly, childishly, timidly, even so shall you love your neighbor. Learn therefore to love yourself with a love that is wise and healthy, that is large and complete....
—*Maurice Maeterlinck*

Try to do to others as you would have them do to you and do not be discouraged if they fail sometimes. It is much better that they should fail than that you should....　—*Charles Dickens*

No one of you is a believer until he desires for his brother what he desires for himself....　　　　—*Sunnah*

Behave to your servants as you desire God to behave to you....　　—*Philo*

The Golden Rule as applied to governmental matters is yet to come, and when it comes, then and only then, will the future of nations be sure....
—*Lajos Kossuth*

Desire nothing for yourself which you do not desire for others....
—*Baruch Spinoza*

Our conscience teaches us it is right, our reason teaches us it is useful, that men should live according to the Golden Rule....　—*W. Winwood Reade*

We have committed the Golden Rule to memory; let us now commit it to life....
—*Edwin Markham*

There is a law that man should love his neighbor as himself. In a few hundred years, it should be as natural to mankind as breathing or the upright gait....　　　　—*Alfred Adler*

Don't do for others what you wouldn't think of asking them to do for you....
—*Josh Billings*

Do not do unto others as you would that they should do unto you. Their tastes may not be the same....
—*George B. Shaw*

Good

The Infinite Goodness has such wide arms that it takes whatever turns to it.... —*Dante Alighieri*

If you see good in people, you radiate a harmonious loving energy which uplifts those who are around you. If you can maintain this habit, this energy will turn into a steady flow of love....
—*Annamalai Swami*

Our original nature is purely good. It is not possible to add anything to this original state.... —*Wang Ying Ming*

If you affirm the positive, the negatives will drop off by themselves....
—*Ramana Maharshi*

Goodness is the only investment that never fails.... —*Henry D. Thoreau*

There is only one sole and veritable power on earth as there is in Heaven: it is that of goodness. The righteous are the only masters of the world....
—*Eliphas Levi*

Riches and power are but gifts of blind fate, whereas goodness is the result of one's own merits.... —*Heloise*

The life of a good man is a continual prayer.... —*Charlotte Lennox*

By the presence of good, evil is cast out, just as by the presence of light, the darkness disappears.... —*Ernest Holmes*

Every good that you do, every good that you say, every good thought you think, vibrates on and on and never ceases. The evil remains only until it is overcome by good, but the good remains forever.... —*Peace Pilgrim*

It is said that good cometh out of evil. This is perfectly true. Every circumstance in life, when viewed from the right angle, proves to be for good. We appreciate the true value of life only when we have tasted the bitterness of the experience which beset it....
—*Papa Ramdas*

Few persons have courage enough to appear as good as they really are....Most people confuse greatness with power, despite the fact that greatness has nothing to do with power....
—*Julius Charles*

When we oppose good, we are hurt, not by evil, but we hurt ourselves. We bring calamity upon ourselves through being out of step with life....
—*Henry T. Hamblin*

There is no one good or bad, only your actions have an effect that is equal and opposite. You cannot get away from Newton's third law.... —*Yogi Bhajan*

The measure of mental health is the disposition to find good everywhere....
—*Ralph W. Emerson*

The only good is knowledge and the only evil ignorance.... —*Socrates*

Doing good to others is not a duty. It is a joy, for it increases your own health and happiness.... —*Zoroaster*

The broadminded only see the goodness in people and in things; the narrowminded only perceive the evil....
—*Chinese parable*

Let no man think lightly of good, saying in his heart, "it will not benefit me." As by the falling of raindrops a jar of water is filled, so the wise man becomes full of good, even though he collects it little by little....
—*Gautama Buddha*

All good things which exist are the fruits of originality....   —*John S. Mill*

True goodness springs from a man's heart. All men are born good....
—*Confucius*

The work an unknown good man has done is like a vein of water flowing hidden underground, secretly making the ground green....   —*Thomas Carlyle*

To the good man nothing that happens is evil....   —*Plato*

I have often said that a person who wishes to begin a good life should be like a man who draws a circle. Let him get the center in the right place and keep it so and the circumference will be good....   —*Meister Eckhart*

To be doing good is man's most glorious task....   —*Sophocles*

You should make an attempt to find good in whatever you see. Whether you see good or bad you must regard it as good....   —*Sathya Sai Baba*

It is good to win; it is good to lose. It is good to have; it is also good to give....
—*Robert A. Johnson*

What a sublime doctrine it is, that goodness cherished now is eternal life already entered on....
—*William E. Channing*

Great and good are seldom the same man....   —*Thomas Fuller*

Wise men appreciate all men, for they see the good in each and know how hard it is to make anything good....
—*Baltazar Gracian*

One becomes good by good action and bad by bad action....
—*The Upanishads*

I came into this world, not chiefly to make this a good place to live in, but to live in it, be it good or bad....
—*Henry D. Thoreau*

Nothing is too good to be true, nothing is too wonderful to happen, nothing is too good to last, when you look to God for your good....
—*Florence Scovel Shinn*

Little progress can be made by merely attempting to repress what is evil; our great life lies in developing what is good....   —*Calvin Coolidge*

The good should be grateful to the bad—for providing the world with a basis for comparison....   —*Sven Halla*

The power generated of ten minds for good is superior to that of ten thousand minds acting on a lower motive. But it is a silent power. It moves in mysterious ways. It is noiseless. It makes no show of open opposition. It uses no methods of effort through tongue or arm or physical force....
—*Prentice Mulford*

At a simple level, good is that which helps people—evil is that which hurts people. At a higher level, good is that which is in harmony with divine purpose—evil is that which is out of harmony with divine purpose....
—*Peace Pilgrim*

A good man is the ripe fruit our earth holds up to God....   —*John Milton*

It is very difficult to know exactly what good should come out of a particular situation. To attempt to manipulate circumstances so your idea of good can come about, is to let the ego play God—and that, as you know, can and does backfire....   —*Neem Karoli Baba*

There is only one way for a man to be true to himself. If he does not know what is good, a man cannot be true to himself....   —*Tse-sze*

The greatest good for man is to become conformable to the will of God....
                —*Thomas Aquinas*

Do not waste yourself in rejections nor bark against the bad, but chant the beauty of the good....
                —*Ralph W. Emerson*

Good people are good because they've come to wisdom through failure....
                —*William Saroyan*

Waste no time arguing what a good man should be. Be one....
                —*Marcus Aurelius*

No evil can come to a good man either in life or after death....   —*Socrates*

Goodness is easier to recognize than to define....   —*W. H. Auden*

He that does good for good's sake, seeks neither praise nor reward....
                —*William Penn*

A self-realized being cannot help benefiting the world. His very existence is the highest good....
                —*Ramana Mahrashi*

The fundamental idea for good is thus that it consists in preserving life, favoring it, in wanting to bring it to its highest value....   —*Albert Schweitzer*

Good things are not done in a hurry....
                —*German aphorism*

The substance of God consisteth in nothing else but goodness....
                —*Boethius*

Goodness is to be seen in its perfection only when man's virtue is fortified against desire....   —*Hermes*

Wicked men obey from fear; good men from love....   —*Aristotle*

All things work together for good to them that love God....   —*New Testament*

A good man does good merely by living....   —*Edward Bulwer-Lytton*

If you believe that God overrules all things for good, and only permits apparently evil happenings for our good and the achievement of great ends unbeknown to you, then all is well. All is well because you believe in the Sovereignty of God....
                —*Henry T. Hamblin*

Goodness consists not in the outward things we do, but in the inward thing we are. To be good is the great thing....
                —*Edwin H. Chapin*

The tendency of man's nature to good is like the tendency of water to flow downwards....   —*Menicus*

He that is good is free, though he be a slave; he that is evil is a slave, though he be a king....   —*Augustine*

According to the sum total of our thoughts, we are either attracting good to us or repelling it from us....
                —*Ernest Holmes*

No amount of good deeds can make us good persons. We must be good before we can do good....
—*Chester A. Pennington*

It is the greatest good to the greatest number which is a measure of right and wrong....　—*Jeremy Bentham*

There is a spark of good in everybody, no matter how deeply it may be buried....　—*Peace Pilgrim*

The greatest amount of good we can do in this world lies not in what we say or in the opinions we advance, but in what we are, the atmosphere we carry with us....　—*Paramananda*

When good people....cease their vigilance and struggle, then evil men prevail....　—*Pearl S. Buck*

The highest good is not something visible, but that which is felt within the heart....　—*Samuel Luzzatto*

A man who claims to know what is good for others is dangerous....
—*Nisargadatta*

The good is that which is closer to God and the bad is that which is farther from Him. Bad is therefore a lower degree of good....　—*Israel Bal Shem Tov*

Grace

Grace is not something outside of you. In fact, your very desire for grace is due to grace that is already working in you....Grace is the Self. It is not something to be acquired. All that is necessary is to know its existence....
—*Ramana Maharshi*

Grace is not something special; it is really universal; it is the only power for good there is, and all alike participate in its goodness; but the ego interferes and discounts its work....
—*Lakshmana Sarma*

Water flows from a higher level to the lower levels. God's grace too is like that. It flows down to those who are bent low with humility....　—*Sathya Sai Baba*

The breeze of grace is always blowing on you. You have to open the sails and your boat will move forward....
—*Ramakrishna*

You do not acquire Grace, you become a part of It; you do not accept Grace, It accepts you....　　—*Anonymous*

The way of grace is mysterious. You struggle for it and you do not get it. Sometimes, without any struggle, you get it. Its working is governed by something beyond all laws. It is not bound by any rules, regulations or conditions....　—*Papa Ramdas*

Most people have many desires which they want to fulfill. But some rare people tell God: "I want nothing. Make me desireless, that is my only desire." Such a one will be a fit instrument to receive grace....The one who will get the most grace is the one who is completely desireless....　—*Annamalai Swami*

If you go near a tree you will get shade; if you go near a fire you will be relieved of coldness; if you go to the river and drink, your thirst will be quenched; if you go near God you will get His grace. If you do not go near and do not receive His grace, is it the fault of God?...　—*Kaivalya Navanitam*

Grace says you have nothing to give, nothing to earn, nothing to pay....
—*Charles Swindoll*

We cannot get grace from gadgets....
—*J. B. Priestley*

The Grace is always there for the asking, always in abundance, but is the seeker capable of receiving it?...
—*Nisargadatta*

With blessing everything is possible....
—*Rabindranath Tagore*

Grace is the absence of everything that indicates pain or difficulty, hesitation or incongruity....　—*William Hazlitt*

Grace is something you can never get but only be given....
—*Frederick Buechner*

Grace represents that God is always reaching toward people....
—*Peace Pilgrim*

No man has a right to expect blessings from God if he through greed and covetousness blocks the pathway down which God's blessings march....
—*John E. Haggai*

All that one can do is to prepare oneself to be ready to receive when the time comes....　　　　—*Mahadevan*

Grace is the power of Truth that vanquishes untruth....　—*Sufi saying*

What is grace? I know until you ask me; when you ask me, I do not know....
—*Augustine*

Do not fall into the trap of trying to force some results. Don't forget we do not deserve anything. Everything is a gift—spontaneous or not at all....
—*Lucy Cornellssen*

Grace is a certain beauty of the soul, which wins the divine love....
—*Thomas Aquinas*

Grace is always sufficient, provided we are ready to cooperate with it. If we fail to do our share, but rather choose to rely on self-will and self-direction, we shall not only get no help from the graces bestowed us, we shall actually make it impossible for further graces to be given....　　　　—*Aldous Huxley*

As heat is opposed to cold, and light to darkness, so grace is opposed to sin. Fire and water may as well agree in the same vessel, as grace and sin in the same heart....　　—*Thomas B. Brooks*

Though we can't always see it at the time, if we look upon events with some perspective, we see things always happen for our best interests. We are always being guided in a way better than we know ourselves....
—*Satchidananda*

If one lives a long time immersed in God's grace, there stretches across one's soul a calm which nothing can destroy....　　　　—*Anonymous*

We must empty ourselves if we are to be filled. When the mind has poured out all its thoughts, a vacuum is created. But this can only last for a few seconds. Then a mysterious influx of divine life will enter....
—*Paul Brunton*

The little word "grace" is like a small window that opens out on to a great landscape....　—*Alexander Maclaren*

There is nothing but God's grace. We walk upon it; we breathe it; we live and die by it....　—*Robert L. Stevenson*

Cheap grace is the grace we bestow upon ourself....Costly grace is the treasure hidden in the field; for the sake of it a man will gladly go and sell all that he has....　—*Dietrich Bonhoeffer*

God is spreading grace around in the world like a five-year-old spreads peanut butter: thickly, sloppily, eagerly.... —*Donna Schaper*

The world is charged with the grandeur of God.... —*Gerard M. Hopkins*

The word "Grace" in an ungracious mouth, is profane....
—*William Shakespeare*

Is it an easy thing to receive the grace of God? One must altogether renounce egotism; one cannot see God as long as one feels, "I am the doer."...
—*Ramakrishna*

The amount of grace which one receives is proportional to the degree to which one surrenders. If you surrender completely, then you will receive enough grace to realize the Self....
—*Lakshmana*

Grace is a word which is pregnant with so much divine power and glory that it defies definition. In brief, it may be described as, the love and power of God. Such a love is ever pouring on all mankind, nay, on all creation, because this love and power dwells in and permeates all animate and inanimate objects.... —*Papa Ramdas*

The sure sign of grace is....the desire to go against all selfish desires....
—*Eknath Easwaran*

Like a lighted lamp, God's Grace spreads all round, on all who approach Him and love to be near him; but if you interpose a shade which shuts out the light from you, you have only yourself to blame if Grace does not shine....
—*Sathya Sai Baba*

In space come the grace....
—*John Heywood*

Grace comes into the soul, as the morning sun into the world: first a dawning, then a light, and at last the sun in his full and excellent brightness.... —*Thomas Adams*

Grace can only be attained by approaching God with empty hands and an empty heart....
—*Anonymous*

Grace is the mastery of truth, the teacher of discipline, the light of the heart, the comforter of affliction, the banisher of sorrow, the nurse of devotion.... —*Thomas à Kempis*

Grace strikes us when we are in great pain and restlessness. It strikes us when we walk through the dark valley of a meaningless and empty life....
—*Paul Tillich*

God is not partial. His grace is on all, the good and the evil, just as rains fall equally on all places. Whoever tills the land reaps the harvest....
—*Turiyananda*

Grace binds you with far stronger cords than the cords of duty or obligation can bind you. Grace is free, but when once you take it you are bound forever to the Giver.... —*E. Stanley Jones*

The grace of God supplies the void and where there is less nature there is more grace.... —*Francis de Sales*

A positive reality is put into a person who receives grace....
—*Thomas Aquinas*

The growth of grace is like the polishing of metals. There is first an opaque surface; and by and by, you see a spark darting out, then a strong light; till at length it sends back a perfect image of the sun that shines upon it....
—*Edward Payson*

God giveth grace unto the lowly....
—*Old Testament*

Destiny is the same as grace. Accept life as it comes and you will find it a blessing.... —*Nisargadatta*

God's grace is the oil that fills the lamp of love.... —*Henry W. Beecher*

God's grace never descends upon a man who is a slave to lust....
—*Mohandas Gandhi*

Knowledge is folly unless it is guided by grace.... —*George Hubert*

As the eye of the body cannot see unless it is helped by the brightness of light, so, neither can a man, even if he is most righteous, have righteousness unless he is helped by the eternal light.... —*Augustine*

Grace is God's love in action for those who don't deserve it....
—*Robert Schuller*

God is able to make all grace abound toward you.... —*New Testament*

Gratitude

Wise men count their blessings; fools, their problems....
—*Anonymous*

Don't drown the man who taught you to swim....Do not kick down the ladder by which you climbed....
—*C. H. Spurgeon*

To be upset over what you don't have....is to waste what you do have....
—*Ken Keyes, Jr.*

Gratitude is the bottom line of happiness.... —*Lewis B. Smedes*

The more we thank God for the blessings we receive, the more we open the way for further blessings....
—*Betty J. Eadie*

There is an inherent law of mind that we increase whatever we praise. The whole of creation responds to praise and is glad. Animal trainers pet and reward their charges with delicacies for acts of obedience; children grow with joy and gladness when they are praised. Even vegetation grows better for those who love it....
—*Charles Fillmore*

If you can't have what you want, be grateful for what you have. Keep thinking constantly of all the big things you have to be thankful for instead of complaining about the little things that annoy you.... —*Dale Carnegie*

Appreciate life instead of resisting it....
—*Judy Tatelbaum*

To stand on one leg and prove the existence of God is a very different thing from going down on one's knees and thanking Him....
—*Sören Kierkegaard*

A thankful heart is not only the greatest virtue, but the parent of all other virtues.... —*Cicero*

If anyone could tell you the shortest, surest way to all happiness and perfection, he must tell you to make a rule to yourself to thank and praise God for everything that happens to you. For it is certain that whatever calamity happens to you, if you thank and praise God for it, you turn it into a blessing.... —*William Law*

God has no need for our worship. It is we who need to show our gratitude for what we have received....
—*Thomas Aquinas*

An attitude of gratitude is most salutary.... —*Ernest Holmes*

When we are grateful for the good we already have, we attract more good into our life. On the other hand, when we are ungrateful, we tend to shut ourselves off from the good we might otherwise experience....
—*Margaret Stortz*

I thank God for my handicaps, for through them, I have found myself, my work and my God....
—*Helen Keller*

None is more impoverished than the one who has no gratitude....Gratitude is a currency that we can mint for ourselves, and spend without fear of bankruptcy.... —*Fred Van Amburgh*

Gratitude is one of the great positive emotions because it creates magnetism....A magnet is that which draws things to itself; therefore, by giving heartfelt thanks for all the good we now have, through the magnetism that gratitude creates, we will start attracting more good into our daily life.... —*Elaine Hibbard*

An attitude of gratitude ensures that our attention is on what we want. As we see ourselves living abundantly and richly, and recognize what we already have, we set up a flow of good things coming our way....
—*Andrew Matthews*

When you arise in the morning, think of what a precious privilege it is to be alive—to breathe, to think, to enjoy, to love.... —*Marcus Aurelius*

Blessings are oftentimes not valued till they are gone.... —*Thomas Fuller*

A grateful thought toward Heaven is itself a prayer.... —*Rudolph Block*

Gratitude is a vaccine, an antitoxin, and an antiseptic.... —*John H. Jowett*

If the only prayer you say in your entire life is "Thank you," that will suffice.... —*Meister Eckhart*

The more you express outwardly your gratitude and thankfulness for what you have, the more you change your molecular vibration away from the dense energy into finer levels.... —*Sanaya Roman*

Seeing a glass half empty is resentment; seeing it half full is gratitude....
—*Anonymous*

He enjoys much who is thankful for a little; a grateful mind is both a great and happy mind.... —*Thomas Secker*

The people who are successful are those who are grateful for everything they have....Giving thanks for what we have, always opens the door for more to come, and ungratefulness always closes the door.... —*Alan Cohen*

Gratitude is the least articulate of the emotions, especially when it is deep....
—*Felix Frankfurter*

Nothing more detestable does the earth produce than the ungrateful man.... —*Ausonius*

The spirit of melancholy would often take its flight from us if only we would take up the song of praise....
—*Phillip B. Power*

The gratitude of most men is nothing but a secret desire to receive greater benefits....
—*Francois La Rochefoucauld*

Nothing is more honorable than a grateful heart.... —*Seneca*

Thanksgiving was never meant to be shut up in a single day....
—*Robert C. Linter*

The lack of gratitude shuts out the light of Divine Intelligence....
—*Arlin C. Hauser*

Gratitude is the fruit of great cultivation.... —*Samuel Johnson*

Would you know who is the greatest saint in the world? It is not he who prays most or fasts most; it is not he who lives most, but it is he who is always thankful to God....
—*William Law*

Words of praise, gratitude, or thanksgiving expand, set free, and in every way radiate energy....You can praise a weak body into strength; a fearful heart into peace and trust; shattered nerves into poise and power; a failing business into prosperity and success; want and insufficiency into supply and support....
—*Charles Fillmore*

It is impossible to be negative while we are giving thanks....
—*Donald Curtis*

Gratitude to God makes even a temporal blessing a taste of heaven....
—*William Romaine*

No one is as capable of gratitude as one who has emerged from the kingdom of the night.... —*Elie Wiesel*

Unconditional gratitude is a powerful activity allowing ourselves to be grateful for whatever happens in our life.... —*Jesse Jennings*

Reflect upon your present blessings, of which every man has many; not on your misfortunes, of which all men have some.... —*Charles Dickens*

Most people don't realize the good they had until they lose it, and by then it's too late.... —*Anonymous*

In every circumstance we must look upwards. Whether someone does good to us or we suffer harm from anyone, we must look upwards and thank God for all that befalls us....
—*Abba Dorotheus*

Gratitude is the memory of the heart....
—*Jean B. Massieu*

You thank God for the good things that come to you, but you don't thank him for the things that seem to be bad; that is where you go wrong....
—*Ramana Maharshi*

The person who has stopped being thankful has fallen asleep in life....
—*Robert L. Stevenson*

Praise expands everything. People, plants, children, animals, even inanimate things, respond to praise. I cannot tell you how, but try it for yourself. If you want more of anything, praise and give thanks and you shall have it.... —*Sue Sikking*

Let us adore God with thanksgiving for words of gratitude are the only offering God accepts.... —*Hermes*

When you drink from the stream, remember the source....
—*Chinese proverb*

To create something new, or to keep receiving more of something you have already gotten, get some paper and pens and write a thank you to the Universe.... —*Sanaya Roman*

Give thanks for all things. All things great and small, good, bad, for all things are for a purpose. If you are faced with a problem, give thanks, for there are no problems; there is an answer. Just ask the Father within.... —*Ann Herbstreith*

In the deepest night of trouble and sorrow God gives us so much to be thankful for that we need never cease on singing.... —*Samuel T. Coleridge*

Praise is the best auxiliary to prayer.... —*Herman Melville*

Man's chief work is to praise God.... —*Augustine*

Gratitude is the fairest blossom which springs from the soul and the heart of man knoweth none more fragrant.... —*Hosea Ballou*

Gratitude is one of the chief graces of human existence and is crowned in heaven with a consciousness of unity.... —*Ernest Holmes*

Gratitude to God should be habitual.... —*Charles Simmons*

If you never learned the lesson of thankfulness, begin now. Sum up your mercies; see what provision God has made for your happiness, what opportunities for your usefulness, and what advantages for your success.... —*Ida S. Taylor*

The worship most acceptable to God comes from a thankful and cheerful heart.... —*Plutarch*

Ungratefulness is the very poison of manhood.... —*Philip Sidney*

Gratitude is what opens the spiritual doors to all the blessings. Everything becomes clear, you see, you feel, you live.... —*Omraam M. Aivanhov*

Some people complain because God put thorns on roses, while others praise Him for putting roses among thorns.... —*Anonymous*

Gratitude is from the same root word as "grace" which signifies the free and boundless mercy of God.... —*Willis P. King*

Gratitude is the sign of noble souls.... —*Aesop*

Ingratitude is the soul's enemy....Like a hot, parching wind, it dries up the wellspring of holiness, the dew of mercy, and the streams of grace.... —*St. Bernard*

Greatness

Those who aspire to greatness must humble themselves.... —*Lao-tzu*

Greatness consists not in the holding of some future office, but really consists in doing great deeds with little means and the accomplishment of vast purposes from the private ranks of life.... —*Russell H. Conwell*

Those who suppress the thought "I am great" by not paying any attention to it....are great. Those who say "I am great" are small people.... —*Sivabhoga Saram*

True greatness is to be free of thoughts.... —*Ramana Maharshi*

We are very near to greatness: one step and we are safe: can we not take the leap?... —*Ralph W. Emerson*

Our greatest weaknesses are always the flip side of our greatest strengths.... —*Judith Sills*

The first element of greatness is fundamental humbleness.... —*Margot Asquith*

There can be no greatness in things. Things cannot be great. The only greatness is unselfish love.... —*Henry Drummond*

Man is great only when he is kneeling.... —*Pius XII*

There never was yet a truly great man that was not at the same time truly virtuous.... —*Benjamin Franklin*

We can do no great things—only small things with great love.... —*Mother Teresa*

The great man always thinks of virtue; the common man thinks of comfort.... —*Confucius*

What is greatness? Greatness is when you have found out that you are not great, but everything else is.... —*Yogi Bhajan*

The world knows nothing of its greatest men.... —*Henry Taylor*

Great men never make bad use of their superiority; they see it, and feel it, and are not less modest; the more they have, the more they know their own deficiencies.... —*Jean J. Rousseau*

A great man is one who can have power and not abuse it.... —*Henry L. Doherty*

Greatness lies in being useful while you live.... —*Fred Van Amburgh*

Greatness lies not in being strong, but in the right using of strength.... —*Henry W. Beecher*

It is the test of greatness in a man that he should be able to see greatness in others, and give them ungrudging credit for it.... —*John Ruskin*

Everything great is not always good, but all good things are great.... —*Demosthenes*

The great men of the earth are but marking stones on the road of humanity.... —*Giuseppe Mazzini*

He is the great man who uses earthenware dishes as if they were silver; and he is equally great who uses silver as if it were earthenware.... —*Seneca*

Nothing can be truly great which is not right.... —*Samuel Johnson*

Pure, clean, void, tranquil, breathless, selfless, endless, undecaying, steadfast, eternal, unborn, independent, he abides in his own greatness.... —*The Upanishads*

Some are born great; some achieve greatness; and some have greatness thrust upon them.... —*William Shakespeare*

He is the greatest man who is the servant of all.... —*Sivananda*

The greatest man is nobody.... —*Chuang Tse*

If any man seeks for greatness, let him forget greatness and ask for truth, and he will find both....   —*Horace Mann*

Great men undertake great things because they are great, and fools because they think them easy.... —*Luc de Clapiers Vauvenargues*

He who stays not in his littleness, loses his greatness....   —*Francis de Sales*

A great man is only an actor playing out his ideal.... —*Friedrich W. Nietzsche*

Most people confuse greatness with power, despite the fact that greatness has nothing to do with power.... —*Anonymous*

The greatest....is to bear defeat without losing heart....   —*Robert Ingersoll*

No life ever grows great until it is focused, dedicated, disciplined.... —*Harry E. Fosdick*

The great of this earth are not only simple but accessible.... —*Isaac F. Marcosson*

Great souls are those which have less passion and more virtue than common souls....   —*Francois La Rochefoucauld*

The greatest joy in life is service. The greatest power in life is love. The greatest battle in life is the battle against oneself. The greatest enemy that man of earth shall ever know is in his own thinking. The greatest poverty that man of earth shall ever know is impoverished thinking; and the greatest blessing man shall ever know is the blessings of spiritual riches.... —*Frater Achad*

Greatness of spirit consists not in soaring high and in pressing forward, but in knowing how to adapt and limit oneself.... —*Michel Montaigne*

The great are only great because we are on our knees. Let us rise up.... —*Pierre Proudhon*

Every calling is great when greatly pursued....   —*Oliver W. Holmes*

Nothing can make a man truly great but being truly good, and partaking of God's holiness....   —*Matthew Henry*

True greatness is often unrecognized.... —*Russell H. Conwell*

It is a grand mistake to think of being great without goodness.... —*Benjamin Franklin*

A great man never loses the simplicity of a child....   —*Confucius*

There is as much greatness of mind in acknowledging a good turn, as in doing it....   —*Seneca*

To be great is to be misunderstood.... —*Ralph W. Emerson*

Great souls care only for what is great....   —*Henri F. Amiel*

Grief

Once the candle of hope is extinguished, the road is all downhill....   —*Ken Olson*

The true way to mourn the dead is to take care of the living who belong to them....   —*Edmund Burke*

The root cause of man's grief and delusion is the identification of the Soul with the body. Fear of death paralyzes him because he is ignorant of the Soul's true nature. The wise perform their duties in the world, cherishing always the knowledge of the Soul's deathlessness.... —*Nikhilananda*

Tears are sometimes an inappropriate response to death. When life has been lived completely honestly, completely successful, or just completely, the correct response to death's perfect punctuation mark is a smile.... —*Julie Burchill*

Misery is due to the great multitude of discordant thoughts that prevail in the mind. If all the thoughts be replaced by one single thought, there will be no misery.... —*Ramana Maharshi*

Do not stand at my grave and weep; I am not there. I do not sleep. I am a thousand winds that blow. I am the diamond glints on snow. I am the sunlight on ripened grain. I am the gentle autumn's rain. When you awaken in the morning's hush, I am the swift uplifting rush of quiet birds in circled light. I am the soft stars that shine at night. Do not stand at my grave and cry; I am not there. I did not die.... —*Stephen Cummins*

The deep pain that is felt at the death of every friendly soul arises from the feeling that there is in every individual something which is inexpressible, peculiar to him alone, and is, therefore, absolutely and irretrievably lost....
—*Arthur Schopenhauer*

To be faithful to those who are dead is not to seclude yourself in sorrow....
—*Martin Grey*

The dead have no tears, and forget all sorrow.... —*Euripides*

If you harbor grief, and give your sorrows vent, they will grow greater every day. They will absorb your very life until at last you will be naught but grief, wet down with bitter tears....
—*The Aquarian Gospel*

Let us not weep for those who have gone away when their lives were at full bloom and beauty. Who are we that we should mourn them and wish them back?... —*Helen Keller*

Grief drives men into habits of serious reflection, sharpens the understanding and softens the heart.... —*John Adams*

To spare oneself from grief at all cost can be achieved only at the price of total detachment.... —*Erich Fromm*

Grieve not; though the journey of life be bitter, and the end unseen, there is no road which does not lead to an end.... —*Hafiz*

Grief is a wound that needs attention in order to heal.... —*Judy Tatelbaum*

One of the chores of grief involves going over and over in one's mind the circumstances that led to the death, the details of the death itself....Since every death diminishes us a little, we grieve—not so much for the dead as for ourselves.... —*Lynn Caine*

It is the peculiarity of grief to bring out the childish side of man....
—*Victor Hugo*

Let us not lament too much the passing of our friends. They are not dead but simply gone before us along the road which all must travel.... —*Antiphanes*

Let the weeping cease; let no one mourn again. These things are in the hands of God.... —*Sophocles*

Do not grieve over your own troubles: you would not have them if you did not need them. Do not grieve over the troubles of "others;" there are no others....
—*Bolton Hall*

He who is dead and gone, honor with remembrance, not with tears....
—*John Chrysostom*

We rejoice over a birth and mourn over a death. But we should not. For when a man is born, who knows what he will do or how he will end? But when a man dies, we may rejoice—if he left a good name and this world in peace....
—*The Midrash Tanhama*

Do not mourn over dying things: look to the east, give your heart to the future. The trees have fallen, but the shoots remain. Reach out your arms to bless those yet to be born....
—*Victor de Laprade*

The wise man, knowing his true nature, transcends all grief....
—*The Upanishads*

We enjoy some gratification when our good friends die; for though their death leaves us in sorrow, we have the consolatory assurance that they are beyond the ills by which in this life even the best of men are broken down or corrupted....
—*Augustine*

Do not grieve over that which does not merit grief. Joy and sorrow are of the world. You are a conscious being. Nothing can affect you. Arise! Be awake!...
—*Natchintanai*

Why grieve for him from whom all grief has gone?...
—*Cato*

Weep not for him who departs from life for there is no suffering beyond death....
—*Palladas*

There is no grief which time does not lessen and soften....
—*Cicero*

Grief is selfish. It is indulged in for self-gratification, not for love. Cosmic man knows the beauty and unreality of death....
—*Walter Russell*

To grieve at any loss, be it of friend or property, weakens mind and body. It is no help to the friend grieved for. It is rather an injury; for our sad thought must reach the person, even if passed to another condition of existence, and is a source of pain to that person....
—*Prentice Mulford*

The loss of friends by the transition we call death will not cause sorrow to the soul that has come into the higher realization, for he knows there is no such thing as death, for each of us is not only a partaker, but an eternal partaker, of this Infinite Life....
—*Ralph W. Trine*

To grieve at death is wrong. Any sorrow is a selfish, misinformed sorrow. One grieves at their own loss and not for the one passed on....
—*Anonymous*

Nowhere has it been convincingly proved that expressing grief has universal therapeutic value....
—*Norman Klein*

The first and necessary step of grief is discovering what you have lost. The next step is discovering what is left, what is possible....
—*John Schneider*

Waste not fresh tears over old griefs....
—*Euripides*

The world is afflicted with death and decay; therefore the wise do not grieve, knowing the terms of the world....
—*Buddhaghosa*

No one is so bereaved, so miserable, that he cannot find someone else to succor, someone who needs friendship, understanding and courage more than he. The unselfish effort to bring cheer to others will be the beginning of a happier life for ourselves....
—*Helen Keller*

It is dangerous to abandon one's self to the luxury of grief; it deprives one of courage, and even of the wish for recovery.... —*Henry F. Amiel*

When grief is fresh, every attempt to divert only irritates. You must wait till it be digested, and then amusement will dissipate the remains of it....
—*Samuel Johnson*

The greatest griefs are those we cause ourselves.... —*Sophocles*

There are moods in which we court suffering, in the hope that here, at least, we shall find reality, sharp peak and edges of truth. But it turns out to be scenic—painting and counterfeit. The only thing grief has taught me is to know how shallow it is....
—*Ralph W. Emerson*

Grief and mourning have to do with being abandoned and with loss. They are the natural consequences of the loss of boundaries.... —*Stanley Keleman*

Every substantial grief has twenty shadows, and most of them shadows of your own making.... —*Sydney Smith*

Grief is a matter of relativity; the sorrow should be estimated by its proportion to the sorrower; a gash is as painful to one as an amputation to another.... —*Francis Thompson*

There is no grief in the presence of God.... —*The Zohar*

No man should be held responsible for the words he utters in grief....
—*The Talmud*

The truly wise mourn neither for the dead nor for the living....
—*Bhagavad-Gita*

Why mourn the dead? They are free from bondage. Mourning is the chain forged by the mind to bind itself to the dead.... —*Ramana Maharshi*

Death is inevitable to every born individual. Similarly, birth is inevitable to every dead person. Why do you grieve over inevitable happenings?...
—*Lakshmana*

Sorrow's best antidote is employment....
—*Edward Young*

Do not count your tears of pain; do not pore over your griefs. Let them pass through your mind, as birds fly through the sky.... —*Sathya Sai Baba*

All grief begins with a loss, but if nothing is ever lost in the universe, what is there to grieve?...
—*Anonymous*

When you live across the road from a cemetery, you cannot grieve for everyone.... —*Welsh proverb*

There is no greater grief than to remember days of joy when misery is at hand.... —*Dante Alighieri*

Excess of grief for the dead is madness; for it is an injury to the living, and the dead know it not.... —*Xenophon*

If you love the life that clings to the body, then you grieve when the body dies. Avoid this grief by truly loving That, the Self, for there is no pain of parting from this life behind all life....
—*Murunganar*

Grief is itself a medicine....
—*William Cowper*

Grief is a tree that tears for its fruit....
—*Philemon*

Grief teaches the steadiest minds to waver.... —*Sophocles*

Nothing becomes offensive so quickly as grief. When fresh, it finds someone to console it, but when it becomes chronic, it is ridiculed, and rightly....
—*Seneca*

Growth

Not to go back is somewhat to advance. And men must walk, at least, before they dance....
—*Alexander Pope*

The human way of growing is unique; it has no rules, and can occur in many ways.... —*Marsha Sinetar*

We cannot stand still. We must grow. We must keep on improving ourself. This is life's main issue. All the experiences of life are for the purpose of making us more wonderful....
—*Elinor MacDonald*

Everyone has to learn to grow through experience. You might as well be a puppet on a string if you don't want to find your own way, your own direction.... —*George Anderson*

All that is human must retrograde if it does not advance.... —*Edward Gibbon*

In the transformation and growth of all things, every bud and feature has its proper form.... —*Fritjof Capra*

Pain is the price we pay for growing....
—*Alice H. Rice*

We are all in the process of growth, a continual evolution—some very quickly and pronounced, others more slow and steady, but all are changing, growing and evolving....we are here to share in the blossoming of consciousness....
—*A Spiritual Warrior*

Spiritual growth may be measured by a decrease of afflictive emotions and increase of love and compassion for others.... —*Chagdud Tulku*

Nothing grows well in the shade of a big tree.... —*Constantin Brancusi*

No smallest atom of our moral, mental or physical structure can stand still a year. It grows—it must grow; nothing can prevent it.... —*Mark Twain*

All growth is a leap in the dark, a spontaneous unpremeditated act without benefit of experience.... —*Henry Miller*

True growth is a process which one allows to happen rather than causes to happen.... —*Gerald May*

We grow by leaving behind our comfortable old beliefs....
—*Meredith Young-Sowers*

I learned if you don't take a risk, you don't grow. If you don't grow, you can't be satisfied, you can't be happy....
—*Phyllis George*

Growing up means accepting our fundamental aloneness....
—*John Bradshaw*

The moment a man begins to think for himself, that moment he begins to grow.... —*Fred Van Amburgh*

Every human being on this earth is born with a tragedy, and it isn't original sin. He's born with the tragedy that he has to grow up. A lot of people don't have the courage to do that....
　　　　　　　　—*Helen Hayes*

You will not grow if you sit in a beautiful flower garden, but you will grow if you are sick, if you are in pain, if you experience losses, and if you do not put your head in the sand, but take the pain and learn to accept it, not as a curse or punishment, but as a gift to you with a very, very specific purpose....　　—*Elisabeth Kubler-Ross*

All growth that is not towards God is growing to decay....
　　　　　　　—*George Macdonald*

Step by step is the law of growth. God does not expect the acorn to be a mighty oak before it has been a sapling....　　—*George E. Carpenter*

All growth....is the result of risk taking....　　　　—*Jude Wanniski*

There are two ways in which we can grow and learn. One way is by our own mistakes. The other way is to simply be willing to do the harmonious thing without being pushed into it....
　　　　　　　　—*Peace Pilgrim*

The two great laws of life are growth and decay. When things stop growing they begin to die. This is true of men, business or nations....　　　—*Charles R. Gow*

Everything that is great in life is the product of slow growth; the newer, and greater, and higher, the nobler the work, the slower is the growth, the surer is its lasting success. Mushrooms attain their full power in a night; oaks require decades....　—*William G. Jordan*

When the fruit grows, the petals drop off themselves....So when divinity in you increases, the weakness of humanity will vanish....　　—*Ramakrishna*

Everybody wants to be somebody; nobody wants to grow....
　　　　　　　—*Johann W. Goethe*

When you see the value of continued growth, the circumstances around you become stepping stones....
　　　　　　—*Clyde M. Narrimore*

The great thing about life is that as long as we live we have the priviledge of growing....　　—*Joshua L. Liebman*

I am still learning....
　　　　　　—*Michelangelo's motto*

All spiritual growth takes place as a gradual harmonious unfolding. It happens automatically. As you live up to your highest light, acting on your inspirations, more and more light comes to you. There is no hurry or impatience to get anything; it comes as you are ready....　　—*Cheryl Canfield*

There can be no end in the sense of a full stop to the soul's growth in the loving knowledge of God....
　　　　　　　　—*Bede Frost*

Either we grow or we pay more for staying the same....　—*Norman Mailer*

Change and growth take place when a person has risked himself and dares to become involved with experimenting with his own life....　—*Herbert Otto*

What does not increase, decreases....
　　　　　　　　　—*Hillel*

In this well ordered universe, the perfect vehicle for our spiritual growth and unfoldment is exactly our present situation....　　—*Sevakram*

What we need for the turning point in the process of growing up is when you discover the core strength within you that survives all hurt.... —*Max Lerner*

Progress and growth are impossible if you always do things the way you've always done things.... —*Wayne Dyer*

We find comfort among those who agree with us—growth among those who don't.... —*Frank Clark*

Life is movement; life is action; life is progression; life is growth. We must ever move forward; we must ever expand....Everything moves forward. No matter what it is in which we may be engaged, we must go forward. The stream that dashes gaily on its way to the sea is bright and clear and pure. Not so the stagnant pool, that is filled with impurity and is unpleasant both to sight and sense of smell....
—*Henry T. Hamblin*

Helping other people grow can become life's greatest joy....
—*Alan Loy McGinnis*

Growth for the sake of growth is the ideology of the cancer cell....
—*Edwin Abbey*

Like plants, we do much of our growing in the darkness, because we are too lazy or stubborn or unconcerned to grow in the light....
—*Elinor MacDonald*

It does not matter how slowly you go so long as you do not stop....
—*Confucius*

Growth cannot be had without first death; gain cannot be realized without a corresponding loss. Always must opposites occur together, one rises high that the other might fall....
—*Shantidasa*

Growing means growing pains: it means changing.... —*Charles E. Jones*

Often we seek to grow or change ourselves by adjusting the external aspects of our lives....We all too often forget that permanent or real change only comes when the center of our being, our inner drives and motivations, undergoes transformation....
—*Errol Strider*

A thousand things advance; nine hundred and ninety-nine retreat, that is progress.... —*Henri F. Amiel*

It matters little where a man may be at this moment; the point is whether he is growing.... —*George Macdonald*

Keep on sowing your seeds; for you never know which will grow—perhaps it all will.... —*Old Testament*

Habits

The habit of being happy enables one to be freed, or largely freed, from the domination of outward conditions.... —*Robert L. Stevenson*

Curious things, habits. People themselves never knew they had them....
—*Agatha Christie*

All useless habits are wasted expenditures of energy, and....should be dropped quickly and completely....
—*A Spiritual Warrior*

Your habits can be your friends or your enemies; they can help you or hurt you.... —*Maxwell Maltz*

Habits change into character....
—*Ovid*

After the mind has become accustomed to create a certain routine of thought, it likes to go on creating....in exactly the same way. It always loves its own way, and it can never believe that any other way is quite as good as its own....Mind adores routine.... —Julian P. Johnson

Men's natures are alike; it is their habits that carry them far apart....
—Confucius

Disgust is half the battle in the conquest of neurotic habits....
—David Seabury

Organisms repeat responses that have brought satisfaction in the past; often these responses persist even when they no longer bring satisfaction....
—Walter Anderson

As long as habit and routine dictate the pattern of living, new dimensions of the soul will not emerge....
—Henry Van Dyke

Pavlov's experiments with dogs were the first proof that habits were the result of preconditioned responses to given stimuli, and that those habits would continue even when the situation no longer remained exactly the same.... —David Abrahamsen

Have you ever fully realized that life is, after all, merely a series of habits, and that it lies entirely within one's own power to determine just what that series shall be?... —Ralph W. Trine

Tension is a habit. Relaxing is a habit. And bad habits can be broken, good habits formed.... —Dale Carnegie

People allow themselves to be slaves of their bad habits and society's bad habits, but they also have free will. If they wish, they can be free....
—Peace Pilgrim

The American overtension, jerkiness and breathlessness and intensity and agony of expression....are bad habits, nothing more or less....
—William James

We are what we repeatedly do. Excellence then, is not an act, but a habit.... —Aristotle

We seldom get rid of an evil merely by understanding its causes....and for all our insight, obstinate habits do not disappear until replaced by other habits....No amount of confession and no amount of explaining can make the crooked plant grow straight; it must be trained upon the trellis by the gardener's art.... —Carl Jung

Habits are like a cable. We weave a strand of it every day and soon it cannot be broken.... —Horace Mann

Our habits, our addictions, our devotions, are either stepping stones or stumbling blocks....
—Fred Van Amburgh

Men cling to the opinions of habits....
—Maimonides

If you have been in the habit of inviting negative thoughts—jealousy, envy, resentment, and self-pity—think of these as intruders in your mind. The old Chinese saying fits here: "You cannot stop the birds of the air from flying over your head, but you need not let them nest in your hair."...
—Floyd & Eve Corbin

Nothing is stronger than habit....
—Anonymous

One can get rid of habits only with considerable difficulty. Once....habits are formed, it takes quite some time to get out of them.... —Nisargadatta

Habits have been given for your strengthening, but they cease to be purposeful when you become subservient to them....No one is a master who is slave to his own inventions....
—*Alan Cohen*

Habits rule the unreflecting herd....
—*William Wordsworth*

Sometimes the hardest habit to curtail is the habit of trying too hard....
—*Mary Bond*

A bad habit never disappears miraculously; it's an undo-it-yourself project.... —*Abigail Van Buren*

As a single footstep will not make a path on the earth, so a single thought will not make a pathway in the mind. To make a deep physical path, we walk again and again. To make a deep mental path, we must think over and over the kind of thoughts we wish to dominate our lives....
—*Henry D. Thoreau*

A nail is driven out by another nail; habit is overcome by habit....
—*Erasmus*

Habit becomes a sort of second nature, which supplies a motive for many actions....Great is the power of habit....
—*Cicero*

Whenever you are angry, be assured that it is not only a present habit, but that you have increased a habit, and added fuel. If you desire not to have an angry temper, then, do not feed the habit. Give it nothing to help its increase.... —*Epictetus*

We cannot in a moment, get rid of habits of a lifetime....
—*Mohandas Gandhi*

Habits are the daughters of action, but they then nurse their mother, and produce beautiful daughters after her image, but far more beautiful and prosperous.... —*Jeremy Taylor*

Habit converts luxurious enjoyments into dull and daily necessities....
—*Aldous Huxley*

Habit, if not resisted, soon becomes necessity.... —*Augustine*

A neurotic thought pattern repeats itself with monotonous regularity....
—*Thomas Troward*

The man who interferes with another's habits has the worst one....
—*Henry S. Hawkins*

Any act often repeated soon forms a bait, and habit allowed, steadily gains strength.... —*Tryon Edwards*

Habits are first cobwebs, then cables....
—*Spanish proverb*

The absurd habit of trying to do many things at once is a great cause of confusion, frustration and nervousness....
—*Maxwell Maltz*

It is very important to realize that we are creatures of habit. Every time we think a certain way, seek a certain good, use a given motive, a habit is forming and deepening in us. Like a groove that is being furrowed, each repetition adds a new depth to the habit.... —*John Powell*

Bad habits of thought and action lessen as spiritual growth progresses....
—*Peace Pilgrim*

The chains of habit are too weak to be felt until they are too strong to be broken.... —*Samuel Johnson*

An elephant can be tethered by a thread—if he believes he is captive. If we believe we are chained by habit or anxiety, we are in bondage. And this bondage may be based on trivial concern....   —*John H. Crowe*

Habit is either the best of servants or the worst of masters....
                    —*Nathaniel Emmons*

It seems, in fact, as though the second half of a man's life is made up of nothing but the habits he has accumulated during the first half....
                    —*Fyodor Dostoyevsky*

The daily habit of wishing everybody well, of feeling like wishing everybody God-speed, ennobles character, and beautifies and enriches life....
                    —*Orison S. Marden*

The only habits you never conquer are the ones you put off doing something about....   —*Wess Roberts*

Habit will reconcile us to everything but change....   —*Charles C. Colton*

Habit is the fly-wheel of civilization....
                    —*Henry James*

Building up character is building up of habits. The changing of character is a changing of habits. Habit is second nature. Character is first nature....
                    —*Sivananda*

The habit of viewing things cheerfully, and of thinking about things hopefully, may be made to grow in us like any other habits....   —*Samuel Smiles*

Once a habit demands something and its request is not fulfilled, the next time you will find it weaker. But once you fulfill its will, the next time you will find it fall on you with much greater force....   —*Isaac of Syria*

In early childhood you may lay the foundation of poverty or riches, industry or idleness, good or evil, by the habits to which you train your children....   —*Lydia Sigourney*

Habit is habit, and not to be flung out the window by any man, but coaxed downstairs a step at a time....
                    —*Mark Twain*

Habits work more constantly and with greater force than reason....
                    —*John Locke*

I have fixed the habit in my mind that I never raise a glass of water to my lips without asking God's blessings, never seal a letter without putting a word of prayer under the seal, never take a letter from the post without a brief sending of my thoughts heavenward, never change classes in the lecture room without a minute's petition for the cadets who go out and for the cadets who come in....
                    —*Stonewall Jackson*

The mind is slow to unlearn what it has been long in learning....   —*Seneca*

The underlying cause of all weakness and unhappiness in man has always been, and still is, weak habit-of-thought....
                    —*Horace Fletcher*

I call that mind free which resists bondage of habit, which does not mechanically repeat itself and copy the past, which does not live on old virtues, which does not enslave itself to precise rules....   —*William E. Channing*

As snowflakes gather, so our habits are formed....   —*Thomas Bentham*

Nothing is in reality either pleasant or unpleasant by nature; but all things become so through habit....
                    —*Epictetus*

When habit is once formed, impulse is powerless against it....
—*George B. Cheever*

The blame that people put upon others for their own behavior is created from....mental habit. We cannot do differently, even if we wished, because most of us choose the path that our minds have established, unless a new impulse comes in from spirit....
—*Paul Twitchell*

All habits increase their power by repetition; resentment begets more resentment and love begets even more love.....
—*Anonymous*

Habit and character are closely interwoven, habit becoming, as it were, second nature....
—*Maimonides*

Habits are to the soul what the veins and arteries are to blood, the courses in which it moves....
—*Horace Bushnell*

Who stoops too often will remain bent....
—*Leon Harrison*

Habit is a hard mistress....
—*Ludwig Boerne*

We first make our habits, and then our habits make us....All habits gather by unseen degrees....
—*John Dryden*

Any action repeated frequently will become habit, and it will remain habit until the mind is reprogrammed to eliminate the habit....
—*Lois Wolfe-Morgan*

We can change, slowly and steadily, if we set our will to it....
—*Robert Benson*

In a thousand ways, our actions today are conditioning our possible actions tomorrow....
—*Norman G. Shidle*

If we would know who is the most degraded and wretched of human beings, look for a man who has practiced a vice so long that he curses it and yet clings to it....
—*William Paley*

Habits are so assumed; but when we endeavor to strip them off, it is being flayed alive....
—*William Cowper*

No habit has any real hold on you other than the hold you have on it....
—*Gardner Hunting*

Instead of being slaves to bad habits, why not be servants to good habits?...
—*Fred Van Amburgh*

Good habits are so much easier to give up than bad habits....
—*Somerset Maugham*

Habit is stronger than reason....
—*George Santayana*

We stuff ourselves into little habitual ways of doing things....and then if we do not get to do it our way, or if someone comes along who wants to do it differently, we get irritable and we become a nuisance to ourselves and those around us....
—*Hilda Charlton*

Happiness

When one door of happiness closes, another opens; but often we look so long at the closed door, that we do not see the one which has opened for us....
—*Helen Keller*

If you ever find happiness by hunting for it, you will find it, as the old woman did her lost spectacles, safe on her nose all the time....
—*Josh Billings*

If you want happiness for an hour—take a nap. If you want happiness for a day—go fishing. If you want happiness for a month—get married. If you want happiness for a year—inherit a fortune. If you want happiness for a lifetime—help someone else. If you want eternal happiness—know yourself....
—*Chinese proverb*

People who postpone happiness are like children who try chasing rainbows in an effort to find the pot of gold at the rainbow's end....Your life will never be fulfilled until you are happy here and now.... —*Ken Keyes, Jr.*

Much of the unhappiness of human life is a result of the undue importance attached by man to the things of the world; vanity, disappointed ambition, and cupidity make up no small part of his troubles.... —*Allan Kardec*

Most happiness is overlooked because it doesn't cost anything....
—*William Ogden*

A man is happy so long as he chooses to be happy and nothing can stop him....
—*Alexander Solzhenitsyn*

Happiness is an endowment and not an acquisition. It depends more upon temperament and disposition than environment.... —*John J. Ingalls*

The most exciting happiness is the happiness generated by forces beyond your control.... —*Ogden Nash*

It isn't necessary to search for happiness in far places. It is everywhere around you and about you....
—*Maurice Maeterlinck*

It's pretty hard to tell what does bring happiness. Poverty and wealth have both failed.... —*Kim Hubbard*

Human love does not lead us to real happiness or enable us to give happiness to others.... —*Papa Ramdas*

This is happiness: to be dissolved into something completely great....
—*Willa Cather*

Happiness is a by-product of an effort to make someone else happy....
—*Gretta B. Palmer*

Happiness must never be your chief aim. Only seeking a more spiritual goal shall we find happiness—along the way.... —*Alice H. Rice*

Nearly all mankind is more or less unhappy because nearly all do not know the true Self. Real happiness abides in Self-knowledge alone. All else is fleeting. To know one's Self is to be blissful always.... —*Ramana Maharshi*

If you want to be happy, be....
—*Leo Tolstoy*

If one thinks one is happy, that is enough to be happy....
—*Mme. de La Fayette*

There is no duty we so underrate as the duty of being happy....
—*Robert L. Stevenson*

Ask yourself whether you are happy, and you cease to be so.... —*John S. Mill*

We can never build happiness on the misery of other people....
—*Constance Warren*

Happiness is the sole satisfactory answer I have found in the sea of puzzles, questions, mysteries, turmoils and competing claims in which we bathe....Happiness is triumph of life; pessimism is its defeat....
—*Robert Mueller*

There is no more mistaken path to happiness than worldliness, revelry, high life.... —*Arthur Schopenhauer*

True happiness is of a retired nature, and an enemy to pomp and noise; it arises, in the first place, from the enjoyment of one's self, and, in the next, from the friendship and conversation of a few select friends....
—*Joseph Addison*

To be obliged to beg our daily happiness from others bespeaks a more lamentable poverty than that of him who begs his daily bread....
—*Charles C. Colton*

The foolish man seeks happiness in the distance; the wise man grows it under his feet.... —*James Oppenheim*

A happy person is not a person in a certain set of circumstances but rather a person with a certain set of attitudes.... —*Hugh Downs*

True happiness is to understand our duties toward God and man; to enjoy the present, without being anxious about the future; not to amuse ourselves with hopes and fears, but to rest satisfied with what we have....
—*Seneca*

Happy is he who is good to others; miserable is he who expects good from others.... —*Eknath Easwaran*

The secret of happiness is this: Let your interests be as wide as possible, and let your reactions to the things and persons that interest you be as far as possible friendly rather than hostile....
—*Bertrand Russell*

Man cannot come in contact with God without feeling happiness....
—*Paramananda*

Seek not happiness too greedily, and be not fearful of unhappiness....
—*Lao-tzu*

Happiness grows at our own firesides, and is not to be picked in strangers' gardens.... —*Douglas Jerrold*

Most people ask for happiness on condition. Happiness can only be felt if you don't set any conditions....
—*Arthur Rubinstein*

If your happiness depends on what somebody does....you do have a problem.... —*Richard Bach*

Happiness is mostly a by-product of doing what makes us feel fulfilled....
—*Benjamin Spock*

A happiness that is sought for ourselves alone can never be found....
—*Thomas Merton*

If happiness can be man's for a moment, it can be man's forever....
—*Frater Achad*

Happiness is not a matter of events; it depends upon the tides of the mind....
—*Alice Meynell*

The foolish seek happiness over the horizon; the wise find it under their feet.... —*Anonymous*

Happiness is basically the awareness of that which is good, but since God is the Creator and Source of all good, true happiness, in its deepest sense, is the awareness of God. The search for happiness is the search for God....
—*Elinor MacDonald*

There is only one way to happiness and that is to cease worrying about things which are beyond the power of our will.... —*Epictetus*

Many persons have a wrong idea of what constitutes true happiness. It is not attained through self-gratification but through fidelity to a purpose....
—*Helen Keller*

The supreme happiness of life is the conviction that we are loved; loved for ourselves, or rather, loved in spite of ourselves.... —*Victor Hugo*

Happiness is a butterfly, which, when pursued, is always just beyond your grasp, but which, if you will set down quietly, may alight upon you....
—*Nathaniel Hawthorne*

Would you rather be right or happy?...
—*Gerald Jampolsky*

The secret of happiness is renunciation....
—*Andrew Carnegie*

Realize that happiness can never be found in the mere rearrangement of exterior conditions.... —*Vernon Howard*

Talk happiness. The world is sad enough without your woes. No path is wholly rough; look for the places that are smooth and clear....
—*Ella Wheeler Wilcox*

Happiness is like a sunbeam, which the least shadow intercepts, while adversity is often as the rain of spring....
—*Chinese proverb*

We take greater pains to persuade others that we are happy, than in endeavoring to be so ourselves....
—*Oliver Goldsmith*

The world is a relative place of good and evil. Remember this point at all times. Try to live happily in any place, under any condition. You will become a strong and dynamic personality. This is a great secret.... —*Sivananda*

Anything you're good at contributes to happiness.... —*Bertrand Russell*

Set happiness before you as an end, no matter in what guise of wealth, or fame, or oblivion even, and you will not attain it. But renounce it and seek the pleasure of God, and that instant is the birth of your own....
—*Arthur S. Hardy*

Nothing is more fatal to happiness than the remembrance of happiness....
—*André Gide*

Unless a person is happy, he cannot bestow happiness on others....
—*Ramana Maharshi*

Happiness is manna; it is to be gathered in grains, and enjoyed every day. It will not keep; it cannot be accumulated; nor have we got to go out of ourselves or into remote places to gather it, since it has rained down from Heaven, at our very door....
—*Tryon Edwards*

Happiness irradiates and makes you look younger.... —*Robert Muller*

The grand essentials to happiness in this life are something to do, something to love, and something to hope for....
—*Joseph Addison*

Happiness is the greatest paradox in Nature. It can grow in any soil, live under any conditions. It defies environment. It comes from within....
—*Norman V. Peale*

A cloudy day is no match for a sunny disposition..... —*William A. Ward*

Two people can travel side by side, and one will always be happy and the other always sad.... —*Narayana*

The superior man is always happy....
—*Confucius*

Nothing in this universe....has by itself an absolute ability to give you happiness. All things have a certain utilitarian value. They are useful but they cannot give you happiness....
—*Chidananda*

He only is happy as well as great who needs neither to obey nor command in order to be something....
—*Johann W. Goethe*

To continue to be whatever we happen to be makes in the long run for the greatest human happiness....
—*Harry A. Wolfson*

The search for happiness is one of the chief sources of unhappiness....
—*Eric Hoffer*

To find out what one is fitted to do and to secure an opportunity to do it is the key to happiness....　—*John Dewey*

What happiness is, no one can say for another. But no one, I am convinced, can be happy who lives only for himself....　—*John Mason Brown*

The haunts of happiness are varied, but I have more often found her among little children, home firesides, and country houses more than anywhere else....　—*Sydney Smith*

Knowledge of God is the consummation of happiness....　—*Philo*

All men desire happiness. They do not know exactly what is meant by happiness, but they desire it just the same....　—*James T. Mangan*

There may be Peace with Joy, and Joy with Peace, but the two combined make Happiness....　—*James B. Tweedsmuir*

Do not place your happiness in distant lands or in grandly imagined tasks; do well what you can do, until you can do greater things as well....
—*Will Durant*

If only we wanted to be happy it would be easy; but we want to be happier than other people, which is difficult, since we think them happier than they are....
—*Charles Montesquieu*

Here is the secret of happiness: Forget yourself and think of others....
—*Paramananda*

There is no happiness higher than tranquility....　—*Gautama Buddha*

If there were in the world today any large number of people who desired their own happiness more than they desired the unhappiness of others, we could have paradise in a few years....
—*Bertrand Russell*

Happiness is your nature. It is not wrong to desire it. What is wrong is seeking it outside when it is inside....
—*Ramana Maharshi*

Remember that happiness is the way of travel—not a destination....
—*Roy M. Goodman*

Happiness is within us, and it is ours, but we are always superimposing our own inner joy onto something outside and thinking it comes from there....
—*Muktananda*

Happiness is living by inner purpose, not by outside pressures....
—*David Augsberger*

Happiness does not depend upon what we have, but it does depend on how we feel towards what we have....
—*W. D. Hoard*

Nothing can make you happier than you are. All search for happiness is misery and leads to more misery. The only happiness worth the name is the natural happiness of conscious being....
—*Nisargadatta*

Happiness is no other than soundness and perfection of the mind....
—*Marcus Aurelius*

The happiness which we receive from ourselves is greater than that which we receive from our surroundings....The world in which a man lives shapes itself chiefly by the way in which he looks at it.... —*Arthur Schopenhauer*

I am a happy man because I have renounced happiness.... —*Jules Renard*

Unhappiness is the hunger to get; happiness is the hunger to give....
—*William G. Jordan*

Supreme happiness consists in self-content; that we may gain this self-content we are placed upon this earth and endowed with freedom, we are tempted by our passions and restrained by conscience.... —*Jean J. Rousseau*

It is not easy to find happiness in ourselves, and it is not possible to find it elsewhere.... —*Agnes Repplier*

There are three occasions for true happiness....the surplus of energy....the cessation of pain....the absolute certainty one is partaking of the will of God.... —*Isak Dinesen*

Happiness depends upon what lies between the soles of the feet and the crown of your head....
—*Honoré de Balzac*

The truly happy man is always a fighting optomist.... —*Walter B. Wolfe*

Men and women are rushing hither and thither in the blind search for happiness, and cannot find it; nor ever will until they recognize that happiness is already within them and round about them, filling the universe, and that they, in their selfish searching, are shutting themselves out from it....
—*James Allen*

Happiness comes not from without but from within. It comes not from the power of possession but from the power of appreciation....
—*J. Walter Sylvester*

Happiness consists not in having, but of being, not of possessing, but of enjoying. It is the warm glow of a heart at peace with itself....
—*Norman V. Peale*

To be happy, we must not be too concerned with others....
—*Albert Camus*

Every man ought to begin with himself, and make his own happiness first, from which the happiness of the whole world would at last unquestionably follow.... —*Johann W. Goethe*

Happiness is the way station between too little and too much....
—*Channing Pollak*

The greatest happiness you can have is knowing that you do not necessarily require happiness....
—*William Saroyan*

If a man is unhappy, remember that his unhappiness is his own fault, for God made all men to be happy....
—*Epictetus*

A great obstacle to happiness is to expect too much happiness....
—*Bernard Fontanelle*

Happiness is not in circumstances, but in ourselves. It is not something we see, like a rainbow, or feel, like the heat of the fire. Happiness is something we are.... —*John B. Shearen*

The happiest people seem to be those who have no particular cause for being happy except that they are so.... —*William R. Inge*

Few things are needed to make a wise man happy, but nothing can satisfy the fool—and this is the reason why so many of mankind are miserable.... —*Francois La Rochefoucauld*

If God told you exactly what it is you were to do, you would be happy doing it, no matter what it was. What you are doing is what God wants you to do. Be happy.... —*Werner Erhard*

As long as we structure our lives in a way where our happiness is dependent upon something we cannot control, then we will experience pain.... —*Anthony Robbins*

Happiness, like an old friend, is inclined to drop in unexpectedly—when you're working hard on something else.... —*Ray Inman*

When people seek excessive entertainment and amusement what are they doing but confessing their lack of happiness and their need to forget this fact?... —*Paul Brunton*

The pursuit of happiness is a most ridiculous phrase; if you pursue happiness you'll never find it.... —*C. P. Snow*

What is your happiness worth when you have to strive and labor for it? True happiness is spontaneous and effortless.... —*Nisargadatta*

Happiness is a habit—cultivate it.... —*Elbert Hubbard*

Happiness is a quality of mind. It is something we possess within....If we do not have it within, nothing outside can give it to us.... —*Paramananda*

The only way for a man to be always happy is to submit to God's will and, leaving everything to Him, be content with the condition in which He places him.... —*Papa Ramdas*

Whoever possesses God is happy.... —*Augustine*

The secret of happiness is freedom, and the secret of freedom is courage.... —*Gilbert Murray*

Happiness is neither without us nor within us. It is in God, both without us and within us.... —*Blaise Pascal*

Happiness? It is an illusion to think that more comfort means more happiness. Happiness comes of the capacity to feel deeply, to enjoy simply, to think freely, to risk life, to be needed.... —*Storm Jameson*

I am more and more convinced that our happiness or unhappiness depends more on the way we meet the events of life than on the nature of those events themselves.... —*Alexander Humboldt*

The happiness of your life depends upon the quality of your thoughts.... —*Marcus Aurelius*

Happiness has no limits....To be happy, to possess eternal life, to be in God, to be saved—all these are the same.... —*Henry F. Amiel*

Perfect happiness is the absence of the striving for happiness.... —*Chuang Tse*

My creed is this: Happiness is the only good. The time to be happy is now. The place to be happy is here. The way to be happy is to make other people happy....
—*Robert Ingersoll*

Happiness is not a state to arrive at, but a manner of traveling....
—*Margaret Lee Runbeck*

Happiness is the one sense that matters. Happiness is abiding enthusiasm. Happiness is single-mindedness. Happiness is whole-heartedness....
—*Samuel M. Shoemaker*

A happy life must be to a great extent a quiet life, for it is only in an atmosphere of quiet that true joy can live.... —*Bertrand Russell*

Happiness consists largely in not wanting something that is out of your reach.... —*Robert C. Edwards*

The happy man is he that knows the world and cares not for it....
—*Joseph Hall*

To enjoy true happiness we must travel into a very far country, and even out of ourselves.... —*Thomas Browne*

Happiness comes more from loving than being loved; and often when our affection seems wounded it is only our vanity bleeding.... —*J. E. Buckrose*

Happiness depends not on things around us, but on our attitude....
—*Alfred A. Montapert*

Happiness is a perfume you cannot pour on others without getting a few drops on yourself....
—*Ralph W. Emerson*

There is no way to happiness; happiness is the way.... —*Wayne Dyer*

Love for life is the fundamental ingredient of all recipes for happiness....Happiness is the peak fulfillment of life. It is a human's own doing, his greatest power and liberty. Happiness is not external to man, it is a genial force in him. It cannot be elsewhere.... —*Robert Muller*

Happiness is the meaning and the purpose of life, the whole aim and end of human existence....
—*Aristotle*

We have been accustomed to thinking that we have to get something from outside us in order to be happy, but in truth it works the other way: we must learn to contact our inner source of happiness and satisfaction and flow it outward to share with others—not because it is virtuous to do so, but because it really feels good....
—*Shakti Gawain*

My present happiness is all I see. I see all things as I would have them be....
—*Gerald Jampolsky*

The ingredients of happiness are so simple that they can be counted on one hand. First of all, happiness must be shared. Selfishness is its enemy; to make another happy is to be happy one's self. It is quiet, seldom found for long in crowds, most easily won in moments of solitude and reflection. It comes from within, and rests most securely on simple goodness and clear conscience.... —*William Ogden*

We have no more right to consume happiness without producing it than to consume wealth without producing it.... —*George B. Shaw*

Happiness is not being pained in body or troubled in mind....
—*Thomas Jefferson*

Happy the man who, unknown to the world, lives content with himself in some retired nook....　　—*Nicolas Boileau*

Happiness is a process of radiation, not absorption. No need to seek for happiness. Happiness is within. Happiness is the only thing where the more you give, the more you possess. Pleasure can be bought at a price. Happiness is priceless....　　—*Fred Van Amburgh*

Happiness is the grace of being permitted to unfold....all the spiritual powers planted in us....　—*Franz Werfel*

The world is so full of a number of things, I'm sure we should all be happy as kings....　　—*Robert L. Stevenson*

Real happiness is not dependent on external things. The pond is fed from within. The kind of happiness that stays with you is the happiness that springs from inward thoughts and emotions....　　—*William L. Phelps*

Very little is needed to make a happy life. It is all within yourself, in your way of thinking....　—*Marcus Aurelius*

He who waits for God fails to understand that he possesses Him. Believe that God and happiness are one, and put all that happiness in the present moment....　　—*André Gide*

What can be added to the happiness of a man who is in health, out of debt, and has a clear conscience....　—*Adam Smith*

Happiness sneaks in through a door you didn't know you left open....
　　　　　　—*John Barrymore*

Happy the man who early learns the wide chasm that lies between his wishes and his powers....
　　　　　　—*Johann W. Goethe*

One of the surest ways to find happiness for yourself is to devote your energies toward making someone else happy. Happiness is an elusive, transitory thing. And if you set out in search for it, you will find it evasive. But if you try to bring happiness to someone else, then it comes to you....
　　　　　　—*Clement Stone*

The happiest place to live in is just inside your income....　—*Anonymous*

Happiness is the realization of God in the heart. Happiness is the result of praise and thanksgiving, of faith, of acceptance; a quiet tranquil realization of the love of God....　　—*White Eagle*

Happiness and success in life do not depend upon our circumstance but on ourselves....　　—*John Lubbock*

Happiness is possible even in pain and suffering. But pleasure only can never create happiness....　　—*Paul Tillich*

Why do people worship God? For happiness. Why do people get married? For happiness. Why do people divorce? For happiness. Everything is done in the name of and for happiness. Still there is no happiness....　—*Yogi Bhajan*

During my whole life I have not had twenty-four hours of happiness....
　　　　　　—*Prince Bismarck*

Happiness is the voice of optimism, of faith, of simple, steadfast love. No cynic or pessimist can be really happy. A cynic is a man who is morally nearsighted, and brags about it...
　　　　　　—*William G. Jordan*

Most people are about as happy as they make up their minds to be....
　　　　　　—*Abraham Lincoln*

About ninety percent of the things in our lives are right and about ten percent are wrong. If we want to be happy, all we have to do is to concentrate on the ninety percent that are right and ignore the ten percent that are wrong.... —*Dale Carnegie*

Happiness comes most to persons who seek her the least and think least about it. It is not an object to be sought; it is a state to be induced. It must follow, not lead. It must overtake you, and not you overtake it.... —*John Burroughs*

Happiness? That's nothing more than health and a poor memory.... —*Albert Schweitzer*

If we want to know what happiness is we must seek it, not as if it were a pot of gold at the end of the rainbow, but among human beings who are living richly and fully the good life.... —*Walter B. Wolfe*

All men wish to be happy, but are dull at perceiving exactly what is that makes people happy.... —*Seneca*

The happiness we receive from ourselves is greater than that which we obtain from our surroundings.... —*Metrodorus*

Happiness in this world, when it comes, comes incidentally. Make happiness the object of pursuit, and it leads us on a wild-goose chase, and is never attained.... —*Nathaniel Hawthorne*

Many people push a burden of inexplicable sadness through half a lifetime....and try to believe they are happy.... —*Peter Stoler*

Happiness doesn't come from doing what we like to do but liking what we do.... —*Wilfred Peterson*

The happy people are those who are producing something; the bored people are those who are consuming much and producing nothing.... —*William R. Ingle*

To be without some of the things you want is an indispensable part of happiness.... —*Bertrand Russell*

Happiness is not a reward—it is a consequence. Suffering is not a punishment—it is a result.... —*Robert Ingersoll*

Man is meant for happiness, and this happiness is in him, in the satisfaction of the daily needs of his nature.... —*Leo Tolstoy*

I have diligently numbered the days of pure and genuine happiness which have fallen on my lot; they amount to fourteen.... —*Abd-El-Raham*

Happiness is essentially a state of going somewhere, wholeheartedly, one-directionally, without regret or reservation.... —*William H. Sheldon*

You don't need the approval of other people to be happy.... —*Anonymous*

Everyone must learn the secret of happiness which consists of refusing to shed tears for anything less than God.... —*Sathya Sai Baba*

Happiness has no existence nor value in itself, as an object which we can pursue and attain as such. It is no more than the sign, the effect, the reward....of appropriately directed action.... —*Teilhard de Chardin*

Your happiness or misery depends on your state of mind and not upon your external conditions or circumstances.... —*Papa Ramdas*

Hatred

Hatred cannot last unless it is continuously nourished and stimulated....   —*Edmund A. Brasset*

The price of hating other human beings is loving oneself less....   —*Eldridge Cleaver*

Hate gets going, it goes round, it gets older and tighter and older and tighter, until it holds a person inside it like a fist holds a stick....   —*Ursula K. LeGuin*

If you want to see the heroic, look at those who can love in return for hatred....   —*Bhagavad-Gita*

Hate traps us by binding us too tightly to our adversary....   —*Milan Kundera*

Hatred is a feeling which leads to the extinction of values....
—*José Ortega y Gasset*

Our first duty is not to hate ourselves....
—*Vivekananda*

Hate injures the hater not the hated....
—*Peace Pilgrim*

The one person perhaps in the world whom you most dislike is the very one to whom you are attaching yourself by a hook that is stronger than steel. Is this what you wish?...   —*Emmet Fox*

Meet hatred with hatred and you degrade yourself. Meet hatred with love and you not only elevate yourself but also the one who bears you hatred....
—*Ralph W. Trine*

Hating people is like burning down your own house to get rid of a rat....
—*Harry E. Fosdick*

Hate the sin and love the sinner....
—*Mohandas Gandhi*

Hate is self-punishment....
—*Hosea Ballou*

Hatred is the vice of narrow souls; they feed it with all their littleness, and make it the pretext of base tyrannies....
—*Honoré de Balzac*

Love, friendship, respect, do not unite people as much as a common hatred for something....   —*Anton Chekhov*

If I wanted to punish an enemy it should be by fastening on him the trouble of constantly hating somebody....   —*Hannah More*

No man, even for his body's sake, can afford to indulge in hatred. It is like repeated doses of poison....
—*Florence Scovel Shinn*

Hatred is the madness of the heart....
—*George Byron*

If you hate a person, you hate something in him that is part of yourself. What isn't part of ourselves doesn't disturb us....   —*Hermann Hesse*

A malicious man drinks his own poison, for malice is mental, moral and physical suicide....
—*Fred Van Amburgh*

Revenge is the poor delight of little minds....   —*Juvenal*

Don't hate, it's too big a burden to bear....   —*Martin L. King, Sr.*

No one hates God without first hating himself....   —*Fulton J. Sheen*

Men hate what they cannot understand....
—*Moses Ibn Ezra*

We hate someone because we do not know them; and we will not know them because we hate them....
—*Charles C. Colton*

One does not hate as long as one has a low esteem of someone, but only when one esteems him as an equal or superior.... —*Friedrich W. Nietzsche*

Hatred is never anything but fear—if you feared no one you would hate no one.... —*Hugh Downs*

Heaven has no rage like love to hatred turned.... —*William Congreave*

Hatred is the coward's revenge for being intimidated....
—*George B. Shaw*

There is no phenomenon which contains so much destructive feeling as moral indignation, which permits....hate to be acted out under the guise of virtue.... —*George J. Nathan*

Never in this world can hatred be stilled by hatred; it will be stilled only by non-hatred—this is the law eternal....
—*Gautama Buddha*

If you hate your enemies, you will contract such a vicious habit of mind that it will break out upon those who are your friends, or those who are indifferent to you.... —*Plutarch*

When our hatred is violent, it sinks us even beneath those we hate....
—*Francois La Rochefoucauld*

The pure, unadulterated love of one person can nullify the hatred of millions.... —*Mohandas Gandhi*

Hatred....is anger which has been allowed to dwell in the mind until it has hardened like so much cement....
—*Napoleon Hill*

Hate and fear breed a poison in the blood, which if continued, affects eyes, ears, nose and the organs of digestion. Therefore, it is not wise to hear and remember the unkind things others might say about you.... —*Pythagoras*

I shall never permit myself to stoop so low as to hate any man....
—*Booker T. Washington*

It is dangerous and harmful to be guided in our life's course by hatreds and aversions, for they are wasteful of energy and limit and twist the mind and prevent it from perceiving the truth.... —*Jawaharlal Nehru*

Hating another is hating oneself, scorning another is but scorning oneself.... —*Bhagavad-Gita*

Hatred is an eternity withdrawn from love.... —*Ludwig Boerne*

Put hatred into the world and we make it a literal hell.... —*Ralph W. Trine*

He that hates his brother is in darkness, and walks in darkness, and knows not where he goes, because that darkness has blinded his eyes....
—*Paul of Tarsus*

Health

The foundation of success in life is good health; that is the substratum of fortune; it is also the basis of happiness. A person cannot accumulate a fortune very well when he is sick. He has no ambition; no incentive; no force.... —*P. T. Barnum*

I was never in a hurry in my life. He lives long who enjoys life and bears no jealousy of others, whose heart harbors no malice or anger, who sings a lot and cries a little, who rises and retires with the sun, who likes to work, and who knows how to rest....*(166-year-old-man)*
—*Shirali Mislimov*

If you want to enjoy health, start this very moment to cleanse your consciousness of all wrong thinking and rid it of every thought except the thought of LOVE....
—*James B. Schafer*

Our ignorance in attaining health lies chiefly in not knowing what to put in our stomachs.... —*Lillian Taylor*

Your body has natural healing capacities that nobody in the field of medicine can pretend ultimately to understand. If you break a bone it will heal itself. All the doctor does is make sure the pieces of the bone are properly set back together.... —*Wayne Dyer*

The art of medicine consists of amusing the patient while Nature cures the disease.... —*Voltaire*

Poor health is not caused by something you don't have; it's caused by disturbing something that you already have. Healthy is not something that you need to get, it's something you have already if you don't disturb it....
—*Dean Ornish*

Extreme remedies are very appropriate for extreme diseases.... —*Hippocrates*

The great secret of medicine, known to doctors but still hidden from the public, is that most things get better by themselves.... —*Lewis Thomas*

To avoid sickness, eat less; to prolong life, worry less.... —*Chu Hui Weng*

Few people can fail to generate a self-healing process when they become genuinely involved in healing others....
—*Theodore I. Rubin*

Body and soul cannot be separated for purposes of treatment, for they are one and indivisible. Sick minds must be healed as well as sick bodies....
—*C. Jeff Miller*

Healing proceeds from the depths to the heights.... —*Carl Jung*

Thousands upon thousands of persons have studied disease. Almost no one has studied health.... —*Adele Davis*

Illness is nothing but an accumulation of foreign matter in the body, and if you want to cure your body you have to clean out that foreign matter. This is the true understanding of health: purity.... —*Omraam M. Aivanhov*

Illnesses hover constantly about us—they are seeds blown by the wind, but they do not take root in the body unless it is ready to receive them....
—*Claude Bernard*

Health and cheerfulness mutually beget each other.... —*Joseph Addison*

There is no physician like a cheerful thought for dissipating the ills of the body.... —*James Allen*

It's supposed to be a professional secret, but I'll tell you anyway. We doctors do nothing. We only help and encourage the doctor within....We are at best when we give the doctor who resides within each patient a chance to go to work.... —*Albert Schweitzer*

Man is ill because he is never still....
—*Paracelsus*

When health is absent, wisdom cannot reveal itself, art cannot become manifest, strength cannot be exerted, wealth is useless and reason is powerless.... —*Herophilies*

There exists in every person a place that is free from disease, that never feels pain, that cannot age or die. When you go to this place, limitations which all of us accept cease to exist. They are not even entertained as a possibility. This is a place called perfect health....
—*Deepak Chopra*

He who has health, has hope; and with hope one has everything....
—*Jewish proverb*

The more I can love everything—the trees, the land, the water, my fellow men, women and children, and myself—the more health I am going to experience and the more of myself I am going to be.... —*Carl Simonton*

To become a thoroughly good man is the first prescription for keeping a sound mind in a sound body....
—*Francis Bacon*

When we begin to trust ourselves more, the body begins to renew itself and becomes healthy and filled with life energy.... —*Shakti Gawain*

Health is certainly more valuable than money because it is by health that money is procured....
—*Samuel Johnson*

Your health is bound to be affected if, day after day, you say the opposite of what you feel, if you grovel before what you dislike and rejoice at what brings you nothing but misfortune....
—*Boris Pasternak*

Half the spiritual difficulties that men and women suffer arise from a morbid state of health.... —*Henry W. Beecher*

Ignorance is disease. Realization is health....What is medicine? God's name.... —*Papa Ramdas*

If you want to be healthy, do not imagine so vain a thing as decrepitude. Make your body perfect by seeing perfection in it. Transient patching-up with lotions and external applications is foolish; the work must be inner transformation.... —*Charles Fillmore*

Give me health and a day, and I will make ridiculous the pomp of emperors....The first wealth is health. Sickness is poor-spirited and cannot serve anyone.... —*Ralph W. Emerson*

The greatest irritant to most people is not a lack of money or status, but ill health. Nothing shines brightly if we do not feel well.... —*Margaret Stortz*

It is health which is real wealth and not pieces of gold and silver....
—*Mohandas Gandhi*

There is no curing a sick man who believes himself in health....
—*Henri F. Amiel*

There are incurable patients but no incurable diseases, for when their causes are removed, the symptoms will disappear like shadows before sunshine and there will be nothing left to cure.... —*J. T. Work*

Every acute disease is not destructive, not an enemy to be dreaded, but a friend and helper if properly treated....
—*Henry Lindlahr*

The secret of longevity largely lies in eating intelligently....
—*Gayelord Hauser*

The secret of health is a pure heart and a well-ordered mind.... —*James Allen*

The greatest force in the human body is the natural drive of the body to heal itself—but that force is not independent of the belief system....Everything begins....with belief. What we believe is the most powerful option of all....
—*Norman Cousins*

Fear kills more than disease....
—*George Herbert*

Talk health. The dreary, never-changing tale of mortal maladies is worn and stale. You cannot charm, or interest, or please by harping on that minor chord, disease.... —*Ella Wheeler Wilcox*

Look to your health and if you have it, praise God and value it next to a good conscience.... —*Izaak Walton*

Everyone should be his own physician. We ought to assist and not force nature. Eat with moderation what agrees with your constitution. Nothing is good for the body but what we can digest. What medicine can produce digestion? Exercise. What will recruit strength? Sleep. What will alleviate incurable ills? Patience.... —*Voltaire*

The truest health is to be able to get along without it.... —*Robert L. Stevenson*

The natural healing force within each of us is the greatest force in getting well.... —*Hippocrates*

Health is the groundwork for all happiness.... —*Leigh Hunt*

Health enables us to serve purpose in our life, but it is not the purpose in life. One can serve purpose with impaired health.... —*Rachel N. Remen*

The causes of health, as the causes of sickness, are very many, but among the forces which we tend to keep us in health, will be a faith which is extended to a real expectation of God's goodness in every department of our being....
—*William Temple*

To wish to be healthy is a part of being healthy.... —*Seneca*

Man can be certified as healthy only when he is fully conscious of his reality and is gladly striving to reach it....
—*Sathya Sai Baba*

All pleasures are tasteless without health. Sickness serves gruel....
—*Fred Van Amburgh*

Among all my patients in the second half of life—that is to say, over thirty-five—there has not been one whose problem in the last resort was not that of finding a religious outlook on life. It is safe to say that every one of them fell ill because he had lost that which the living religions of every age have given their followers, and none of them have been really healed who did not regain his religious outlook.... —*Carl Jung*

Health is not a condition of matter, but of Mind; nor can the material senses bear reliable testimony on the subject of health.... —*Mary Baker Eddy*

A disease is caused whenever a sense of separation from God takes place. It may appear as a dis-eased body, a dis-eased bank account, a dis-eased relationship, but no matter what form it takes, any disease represents exclusion from God.... —*Walter Starcke*

A merry heart does good like medicine.... —*Old Testament*

The time will come when the work of the physician will not be to treat and attempt to heal the body, but to heal the mind, which in turn will heal the body....The true physician will be a teacher; his work will be to keep people well, instead of trying to heal them after sickness.... —_Ralph W. Trine_

Prevention is always preferable to cure.... —_Anonymous_

Say you are well, or all is well with you, and God shall hear your words and make them true.... —_Ella Wheeler Wilcox_

Cheerfulness is the principal ingredient in the composition of health....
—_Arthur Murphy_

Without health life is not life; it is only a state of languor and suffering—an image of death.... —_Francois Rabelais_

If I had my way I'd make health catching instead of disease....
—_Robert Ingersoll_

The greatest mistake a man can make is to sacrifice health for any other advantage.... —_Arthur Schopenhauer_

Most illnesses do not, as is generally thought, come like a bolt out of the blue. The ground is prepared for years, through faulty diets, intemperance, overwork, and moral conflicts, slowly eroding the subject's vitality....
—_Paul Tourier_

Health is the thing that makes you feel that now is the best time of the year....
—_Franklin P. Adams_

He who has health has hope; and he who has hope, has everything....
—_Arabian proverb_

Health is not physical or material but is spiritual. Behind the normal habit of mental and physical action lies a Mind consciously alive with the Life of good— active with the activity of the spirit....
—_William R. Miller_

Nature, time and patience are the three great physicians.... —_Irish proverb_

Health is the greatest of all possessions; a pale cobbler is better than a sick king.... —_Isaac Bickerstaff_

The preservation of health is a duty. Few seem conscious that there is such a thing as physical morality....
—_Herbert Spencer_

An important first step in the process of healing is the removing of value judgements. Being ill is not "bad" and being well is not "good." To judge it— and yourself—is a mistake....
—_David Koffman_

Health is so necessary to all duties, as well as the pleasures of life, that the crime of squandering it is equal to folly.... —_Samuel Johnson_

Health is the soul that animates all the enjoyments of life, which fade and are tasteless without it....
—_William Temple_

We live longer than our forefathers; but we suffer more, from a thousand artificial anxieties and cares....
—_Edward Bulwer-Lytton_

Arise and accept an antidote to ward off old age and death; it is the knowledge that all wealth and prosperity, all pleasures and enjoyments are harmful to us unless devoted to the good of others; they tend only to sicken and enervate our frames....
—_Yoga Vasistha_

The first duty of a physician is that he should do the sick no harm....
—*Hippocrates*

There is this difference between two temporal blessings—health and money; money is the most envied, but the least enjoyed; health is the most enjoyed, but the least envied.... —*Charles C. Colton*

Think health, talk health, visualize health and better health will be your reward.... —*Paavo Airola*

Heart

Whatever comes from the heart quietly touches every other heart.... —*Anonymous*

Keep your heart above the world, and you will not be troubled by the changes in it.... —*Brilliana Harley*

Nothing is impossible to a valiant heart.... —*Jeanne d'Albret*

The only thing that makes one place more attractive....than another is the quality of heart in it.... —*Jane W. Carlyle*

This is the wonderful thing about the pure in heart—they do see God.... —*Corra M. Harris*

When you stop believing in your heart you are but a sterile vessel wandering in the wilderness.... —*Francis Hegmeyer*

Man is nothing when his heart is empty.... —*Martin Gray*

God wants the heart.... —*The Talmud*

To avoid being fascinated by men and women we must never give our whole heart to changeable and perishable individualities. Let us love the immortal virtues and eternal flower of beauty which we see in transient creatures.... —*Eliphas Levi*

When the heart speaks, glory itself is an illusion.... —*Napoleon Bonaparte*

When man has purified his heart by faith, he needs no middleman to intercede. He is on friendly terms with God.... —*The Aquarian Gospel*

If you keep your heart immersed always in the ocean of divine love, your heart is sure to remain ever full to overflowing with the waters of the divine love.... —*Ramakrishna*

The course of human history is determined, not by what happens in the skies, but by what takes place in the hearts of men.... —*Arthur Keith*

Do not let the ways of the world dismay your heart.... —*Ramayana*

Why do you read many books? It is of no use. The great book is within your heart. Open the pages of this inexhaustible book, the source of all knowledge. You will know everything.... —*Sivananda*

Blessed are the pure in heart for they will see God.... —*Jesus*

When God measures a man, He puts the tape around the heart instead of the head.... —*Anonymous*

If wrinkles must be written upon our brows, let them not be written upon the heart. The spirit should not grow old.... —*James A. Garfield*

The worst prison would be a closed heart.... —*Pope John Paul II*

A pure heart is the end of all religion and the beginning of divinity....
—*James Allen*

Hear this: God can only exist in the heart of man, not elsewhere....
—*Nisargadatta*

The love that pulses in the cave of the heart does not depend on anything outside. It is completely independent....
—*Muktananda*

Is not the heart of man a vast solitude into which nothing penetrates?...
—*Gustave Flaubert*

'Heart' is merely another name for the Supreme Spirit, because He is in all hearts....The entire Universe is condensed in the body, and the entire body in the Heart. Thus the Heart is the nucleus of the whole Universe....
—*Ramana Maharshi*

The heart that breaks open can contain the whole universe.... —*Joanna Macy*

The crisis of our time, as we are beginning slowly and painfully to perceive, is a crisis not of the hands but of the hearts.... —*Archibald MacLeish*

The highest good is a good heart, the greatest evil, an evil heart....
—*Arak Eleazar*

The logic of the heart is absurd....
—*Julie de Lespinasse*

A perfect mind comes from a perfect heart, not the heart known by a doctor's stethoscope but the heart which is the seat of God....
—*Mohandas Gandhi*

In every heart there dwelleth a Sage; only man will not steadfastly believe it.... —*Wang Yang Ming*

It is only with the heart that one can see rightly; what is essential is invisible to the eye....
—*Antoine de Saint-Exupery*

It is more fatal to neglect the heart than the head.... —*Theodore Parker*

The heart has always the pardoning power.... —*Ann S. Swetchine*

What comes from the heart, goes to the heart.... —*Samuel T. Coleridge*

You need seek God neither below nor above. He is no farther away than the door of the heart....
—*Meister Eckhart*

Never, never, never will the intellect possess a monopoly over the heart....
—*Luigi Luzzatti*

The heart sees better than the eye....
—*Hebrew proverb*

If you indeed desire a heart you must earn it.... —*The Wizard of Oz*

The heart has its arguments with which the logic of the mind is not acquainted.... —*Blaise Pascal*

What the heart has once owned and had, it can never lose....
—*Henry W. Beecher*

The same heart beats in every human breast.... —*Matthew Arnold*

The heart of a good man is the sanctuary of God in this world....
—*Madame Necker*

The heart is stretched through suffering, and enlarged....
—*Thomas R. Kelly*

Many flowers open to the sun, but only one follows him constantly. Heart, be thou the sunflower; not only open to receive God's blessings, but constant in looking to him....

—*Jean Paul Richter*

The human heart....opens only to the heart that opens in return....

—*Maria Edgeworth*

The heart sometimes finds out things that reason cannot....   —*Robert Benson*

Know that the greatest things which are done on earth are done within, in the hearts of faithful souls....

—*Louis de Montfort*

The heart is the best logician....

—*Wendell Phillips*

Where your treasure is, there will your heart be also....   —*Jesus*

A kind heart is a fountain of gladness, making everything in its vicinity to freshen into smiles....

—*Washington Irving*

Open the doors of your heart, so that the Sun may shine through and disinfect the vices therein and illumine its corners....   —*Sathya Sai Baba*

When your heart is full of God, naturally there is no other thought in it. That is renunciation—to have no desire for anything in the world....

—*Papa Ramdas*

The spirit of life....dwells in the secret chamber of the heart....

—*Dante Alighieri*

Even the poorest heart has some jewel on which it hangs....   —*Karl E. Franzos*

Enter into your heart and labor in the presence of God who is always present there to help you. Fix your loving attention upon Him without any desire to feel or hear anything of God....

—*John of the Cross*

God has created us for Himself, and our heart cannot be quieted until it finds repose in Him....   —*Augustine*

The heart of a wise man should resemble a mirror which reflects every object without being affected in any way....   —*Confucius*

Man's heart is the central point and heaven the circumference....

—*Shabistari*

When the heart is won, the understanding is easily convinced....

—*Charles Simmons*

I am seated in the hearts of all....

—*Bhagavad-Gita*

God's rendezvous with man takes place in the heart....   —*Anonymous*

In a full heart there is room for everything, and in an empty heart there is room for nothing....

—*Antonio Porchia*

A man has many skins in himself, covering the depths of his heart. Man knows so many other things: he does not know himself....Go into your own ground and learn to know yourself....

—*Meister Eckhart*

The heart of man is older than his head....   —*Frederick W. Ziegler*

Great hearts send forth steadily the secret forces that incessantly draw great events....   —*Ralph W. Emerson*

We must alter our lives in order to alter our hearts, for it is impossible to live one way and pray another....
—*William Law*

The heart of humanity has strings in all hearts.... —*Eliphas Levi*

Prayer enlarges the heart....
—*Mother Teresa*

The heart of the fool is in his mouth, but the mouth of the wise man is in his heart.... —*Benjamin Franklin*

Our heart is in heaven, our home is not here.... —*Reginald Heber*

Only when the heart becomes purified through the practice of spiritual disciplines does a man attain to wisdom....
—*Ramakrishna*

Let him who desires to see God wipe his mirror and cleanse his heart....
—*Richard of Saint-Victor*

When we know how to read our own hearts, we acquire wisdom of the hearts of others.... —*Denis Diderot*

God has two dwellings: one in heaven and the other in a meek and thankful heart.... —*Izaak Walton*

Surely a man has come to himself only when he has found the best that is in him, and has satisfied his heart with the highest achievement he is fit for. It is only then that he knows what his heart demands.... —*Woodrow Wilson*

Only where the heart is, can the treasure be found.... —*James M. Barrie*

The world's battlefields are in the heart.... —*Henry W. Beecher*

Find the god in your own heart and you will understand by direct intuition what all the great teachers, real mystics, true philosophers and inspired men have been trying to tell you by the tortuous method of using words....
—*Paul Brunton*

To give one's heart is to give all....
—*Mohandas Gandhi*

Nothing is less in our power than the heart and, far from commanding, we are forced to obey it....
—*Jean J. Rousseau*

The path of the heart is the path of power.... —*Douglas Bloch*

Great ideas come from the heart....
—*Luc de Clapiers Vauvenargues*

All great discoveries are made by men whose feelings run ahead of their thinking.... —*C. H. Parkhurst*

Your heart attaches itself again and again to objects. You have to know how to keep the connection with your origins.... —*Ilahi Nama*

There never was any heart truly great....that was not also tender and compassionate.... —*Robert South*

As a man thinketh in his heart, so he is.... —*Old Testament*

God and the devil are fighting....and the battleground is the heart of man....
—*Fyodor Dostoyevsky*

The heart of man and the bottom of the sea are unfathomable....
—*Jewish proverb*

The heart....is of itself but little, yet great things cannot fill it....
—*Thomas Dekker*

God conceals himself from the mind of man, but reveals himself to the heart....
—*The Zohar*

It is the heart that perceives God and not the reason.... —*Blaise Pascal*

Trust your heart....Never deny it a hearing. It is the kind of house oracle that often foretells the most important.... —*Baltasar Grecian*

A pure heart is one that is unencumbered, unworried, uncommitted and which does not want its own way about anything but which, rather, is submerged in the loving will of God....
—*Meister Eckhart*

Each heart is a world. You find all within yourself that you find without. The world that surrounds you is the magic glass of the world within you....
—*John K. Lavater*

Though a wealthy man with a large estate has many rooms in which to dwell, he has one favorite sitting room in which he delights in being. The Lord loves to dwell in the chamber of the heart of man.... —*Ramakrishna*

The person who attaches more importance to externals than to the heart is a narrow-minded spirit....
—*Allan Kardec*

Hearts are like flowers; they remain open to the softly falling dew, but shut up in the violent downpour of rain....
—*Jean Paul Richter*

All God wants of man is a peaceful heart.... —*Meister Eckhart*

The greatness of man does not lie in his vast riches, exalted position, and name and fame, but in the qualities of the heart. If his heart is pure, free, forgiving, compassionate and humble, then he is great.... —*Papa Ramdas*

Heaven & Hell

Heaven cannot be a place where we go when we die. If there were such a place, it wouldn't be heaven any longer after we got there....Heaven is a state of mind.... —*Elinor MacDonald*

The "kingdom of Heaven" is a condition of the heart—not something that "comes upon the earth" or "after death.".... —*Friedrich W. Nietzsche*

Heaven, the treasury of everlasting joy.... —*William Shakespeare*

The mind is its own place, and in itself can make a heaven of hell, and a hell of heaven.... —*John Milton*

The "Kingdom of Heaven" is in the heart of those who realize God and the whole purpose of life is to make God a reality. Verily, it is simpler to find a way to Heaven than to find one's way on earth.... —*Hazrat Inayat Khan*

Better to go to Heaven in rags than to go to Hell in embroidery....
—*Thomas Fuller*

There is no hell. Hell is only what the ego has made of the present. The belief in hell is what prevents you from understanding the present....
—*A Course In Miracles*

Heaven is a palace with many doors, and each may enter in his own way....
—*Hindu saying*

God is in heaven. That heaven is in your heart. You will find Him there. But you have to purify your heart first.... —*Sivananda*

Heaven is lost merely for the lack of perception of harmony. Hell is a phantom abode of our morbid perceptions. Heaven and Hell are states of consciousness.... —*Ernest Holmes*

The Kingdom of Heaven is perfect trust, perfect knowledge, perfect peace. All is music, sweetness, and tranquility. No irritations, no bad tempers, no harsh words, no suspicions, no lust, and no disturbing elements can enter there....It is literally true that when men die they "go to heaven and hell," in accordance with their deeds. But the heaven and hell are in this world....
—*James Allen*

Hell is synonymous with suffering; but....not a furnace.... —*Allan Kardec*

Imagine heaven requiring love for everyone, no exceptions, and you having the capacity to make it happen.... —*Wayne Dyer*

We do not drift to Heaven. It is necessary to take command of the helm, face the winds of adversity....We must visualize our goal, chart our way, then hold to the course at all hazards....
—*Alice H. Rice*

A guilty conscience is a hell on earth, and points to one beyond....
—*Francis Beaumont*

He who offends against Heaven has none to whom he can pray....Heaven means to be one with God....
—*Confucius*

The kingdom of heaven is not isolation of good from evil. It is the overcoming of good from evil....
—*Alfred N. Whitehead*

Heaven and hell can both be found here and now as well as in the hereafter.... —*Morton T. Kelsey*

The door to Hell is locked from the inside.... —*James A. Pike*

There seems to be the same difference between hell, purgatory, and heaven as between despair, uncertainty, and assurance.... —*Martin Luther*

Hell has three doors: lust, anger and greed.... —*Bhagavad-Gita*

There is no heaven but clarity, no hell except confusion.... —*Jan Struther*

We make our own heaven or our own hell, and the only heaven or hell that will ever be ours is that of our own making.... —*Ralph W. Trine*

If men believe....that this present earth is the only heaven, they will strive all the more to make heaven of it....
—*Arthur Keith*

Heaven is like an egg and the earth is like the yolk of an egg....
—*Chang Heng*

A full stomach is heaven; the rest is luxury.... —*Chinese proverb*

The net of heaven has large meshes and yet nothing escapes it.... —*Lao-tzu*

Earth has no sorrow that Heaven cannot heal.... —*Thomas Moore*

The true heaven is everywhere, even in the very place you stand and go....
—*Jakob Böhme*

I believe in heaven and hell—on earth....
—*Abraham L. Feinberg*

Hell is not to love anymore....
—*George Bernaos*

A good man is influenced by God himself, and has a kind of divinity within him; so it may be a question whether he goes to heaven, or heaven comes to him....   —*Seneca*

Realize heaven is a perfect state of consciousness, a perfect world here on earth now, and all we need to do is accept it....   —*Baird Spalding*

Earth cannot escape heaven. Flee it by going up, or flee it by going down, heaven still invades earth, energizes it, makes it sacred. All hiding places reveal God. If you want to escape God, He runs in your lap. For God is at home. It is we who have gone out for a walk....
—*Meister Eckhart*

Heaven is but the vision of fulfilled desire. And hell the shadow from a soul on fire....   —*Omar Khayyam*

We can gain the Kingdom of Heaven by having the Kingdom of Heaven in our hearts....   —*Elbert Hubbard*

Hell is nothing but self-will, and if there be no self-will there would be no Devil and no hell....   —*Theologica Germanica*

The existence of heaven or hell, or whatever it is, is on this earth only....
—*Nisargadatta*

Discover the joy in the now, some of the peace in the here, some of the love in me and thee which go to make up the kingdom of heaven on earth....
—*Anne Morrow Lindbergh*

Heaven and hell are inward states. Sink into self and all its gratifications, and you sink into hell; rise above self into that state of consciousness which is the utter denial and forgetfulness of self, and you enter heaven....
—*James Allen*

The only thing I could say for sure is that hell means separation from God....
—*Billy Graham*

Hell is the ego with its own satisfied wishes....   —*Fulton J. Sheen*

One's joy is one's heaven and one's sorrow is one's hell....
—*Sathya Sai Baba*

Heaven is doing good from good-will; hell is doing evil from ill-will....
—*Emanuel Swedenborg*

The miles to heaven are but few and short....   —*Samuel Rutherford*

The kingdom of heaven is within you....
—*Jesus*

If the way to heaven be narrow, it is not long; and if the gate be strait, it opens into endless life....
—*William Beveridge*

Heaven and hell are states of being. Heaven is being in harmony with God's will; hell is being out of harmony with God's will. You can be in either state on either side of life. There is no permanent hell....Heaven is only one thought away....   —*Peace Pilgrim*

Love is heaven, and heaven is love....
—*Walter Scott*

We talk about Heaven being so far away. It is within speaking distance to those who belong there....
—*Dwight D. Moody*

When you first learn to love hell, you will be in heaven....   —*Thaddeus Golas*

All the way to heaven is heaven....
—*Catherine of Siena*

Put hatred into the world and we make it a literal hell. Put love into the world and heaven with all its beauties and glories becomes a reality....
—*Ralph W. Trine*

Nothing is farther than the earth from heaven; nothing is nearer than heaven to earth.... —*Julius and Augustas Hare*

It is possible for one person to be living in heaven and another in hell and both be living under the same roof....
—*Anonymous*

Let us imagine a crossroads with one sign on the right pointing "to heaven" and another on the left pointing to "lectures on heaven." The Easterner would turn right and go straight to heaven, when the Westerner would turn left and attend the lectures....
—*Amaury de Riencourt*

You have your paintbrush and colors. Paint paradise, and in you go....
—*Nikos Kazantzakis*

Heaven is under our feet as well as over our heads....When you travel to the Celestial City, carry no letters of introduction—When you knock, ask to see God—none of the servants....
—*Henry D. Thoreau*

What is hell? I maintain that it is the suffering of being unable to love....
—*Fyodor Dostoyevsky*

To appreciate heaven well 'tis good for a man to have some fifteen minutes of hell.... —*Will Carleton*

A fool's paradise is a wise man's hell....
—*Thomas Fuller*

You carry heaven and hell with you....
—*Ramana Maharshi*

Really good minds seem to have ....dissipated the clouds which concealed the heaven from view, and they thus disclose to themselves and to us a clear and blissful world of everlasting repose.... —*Jean Paul Richter*

We are all sons of heaven, wandering in a strange country, homesick for our God-self, our true self....
—*Ernest Wilson*

Hell is truth seen too late—duty neglected in its season....
—*Tryon Edwards*

It is humility alone that makes the unpassable gulf between heaven and hell.... —*William Law*

One path leads to paradise, but a thousand to hell.... —*Hebrew proverb*

If you are not allowed to laugh in heaven, I do not want to go there....
—*Martin Luther*

There is no hell but selfhood, no Paradise but selflessness....
—*Sa'idibn Abi'l-Khayr*

Heaven is the place where the donkey finally catches up with his carrot; hell is the eternity while he waits for it....
—*Russell Green*

Every man is received in heaven who receives heaven in himself while in the world, and he is excluded who does not.... —*Emanuel Swedenborg*

Hell is the stiff resistance to what is. Heaven is loving openness. Hell is resistance. Heaven is acceptance....
—*Stephen Levine*

The foundation of heaven and hell is laid in men's own souls....
—*John Smith, the Platonist*

To reach the port of heaven we must sail sometimes with the wind and sometimes against it–but we must sail, and not drift nor lie in anchor....
　　　　　　　—Oliver W. Holmes

There is no Hades; but all is full of God and Divine Beings....　　*—Epictetus*

Every person is the maker of his own heaven and hell....
　　　　　　　—Elinor MacDonald

I would rather be in hell and possess God, than be in the kingdom of heaven without God....　　　　*—Tauler*

Heaven is perfection of all that can be said or thought....　　*—James Shirley*

The idea that a good God would send people to a burning Hell is utterly damnation to me. The ravings of insanity. Superstition gone to seed....
　　　　　　　—Luther Burbank

Heaven lies about us in our infancy....
　　　　　　　—William Wordsworth

Those who know what causes hell have found the way to the heaven of truth....
　　　　　　　—Muruganar

If there be a hell upon earth it is to be found in a melancholy man's heart....
　　　　　　　—Robert E. Burton

A mind enlightened is heaven; a mind darkened is hell....　　*—Chinese proverb*

Heaven would hardly be heaven if we could define it....
　　　　　　　—William E. Biederwolf

Love of heaven is the only way to heaven....　　*—John H. Newman*

The kingdom of heaven is not a place, but a state of mind....
　　　　　　　—John Burroughs

Heaven is not to be looked upon only as a reward, but as the natural effect of a religious life....　　*—Joseph Addison*

Paradise is where I am....
　　　　　　　—Voltaire

The kingdom of heaven is like unto a merchantman, seeking goodly pearls, who when he had found one pearl of great price, went and sold all that he had, and bought it....　　*—Jesus*

Here & Now

Tomorrow's life is too late. Live today....　　*—Martial*

Real generosity towards the future lies in giving all to the present....
　　　　　　　—Albert Camus

Not living in the present is a form of denial. It's easier to live in the past or future because then you don't have to be responsible for the present....
　　　　　　　—Jane Hendrix

Look forward and be hopeful, look backward and be thankful, look downward and be helpful, look upward and be humble....　　*—Anonymous*

Don't think about the future. Just be here now. Don't think about the past. Just be here now....　　*—Ram Dass*

Seize today and put as little trust as you can in tomorrow....　　*—Horace*

We are within a mystery, a dream of the moment, and the epitome of life is to live ever present within it. Our past illusions and fantasies are not relative to the present moment....Here and now is where all the mystery lies hidden....
　　　　　　　—A Spiritual Warrior

If we know that we are now at the point where we have always wanted to be, we will be there....because we are never there but always here, now!...
　　　　　　　　　　—Paul Twitchell

True happiness is....to enjoy the present, without anxious dependence upon the future....　　　*—Seneca*

All that is required to feel that here-and-now happiness is a simple, frugal heart....　　　*—Nikos Kazantzakis*

Only in a hut built for the moment can one live without fear....
　　　　　　　　　—Kamo no Chomei

Always hold fast to the present hour. Every state of duration, every second, is of infinite value....
　　　　　　　　　—Johann W. Goethe

It isn't the experience of today that drives men mad. It is the remorse for something that happened yesterday, and the dread of what tomorrow may disclose....　　*—Robert Jones Burdette*

Today is yesterday's pupil....
　　　　　　　　　—Thomas Fuller

The present time has one advantage over every other—it is our own....
　　　　　　　　　—Charles C. Colton

The future is purchased by the present....　　*—Samuel Johnson*

Every moment is a golden one for him who has the vision to recognize it as such....　　　*—Henry Miller*

Doing the best at the moment puts you in the best place for the next moment....
　　　　　　　　　—Oprah Winfrey

Today's today. Tomorrow, we may be ourselves gone down the drain of eternity....　　　*—Euripides*

Never agonize over the past or worry over the future. Live this day and live it well....　　　*—Peace Pilgrim*

One should learn from the past but one should not live in the past. My concern is to look to the future, learn from the past and deal with the present....
　　　　　　　　　—George Fernandes

Memories of the past and anticipation of the future exist only now, and thus to try to live completely in the present is to strive for what already is the case....　　　*—Alan Watts*

He who has governed the world before I was born shall take care of it likewise when I am dead. My part is to improve the present moment....　*—John Wesley*

Forget the past. Don't brood over it. Don't plan too much for the future. Try to move through the present serenely unaffected. Then you will experience the peace that is ever present....
　　　　　　　　　—Chidananda

As yesterday is history, and tomorrow may never come, I have resolved from this day on, I will do all the business I can honestly, have all the fun I can reasonably, do all the good I can willingly, and save my digestion by thinking pleasantly....
　　　　　　　　　—Robert L. Stevenson

You should not waste a moment of today on the rottenness of yesterday....
　　　　　　　　　—Ralph W. Emerson

The art of life is to live in the present moment, and to make that moment as perfect as we can by the realization that we are the instruments and expression of God Himself....　　*—Emmet Fox*

Light tomorrow with today....
　　　　　—Elizabeth B. Browning

Now is the time to be doing, now is the time to be stirring, now is the time to amend myself....
—*Thomas à Kempis*

No matter what looms ahead, you can eat today, enjoy the sunlight today, mix good cheer with friends today; enjoy it and bless God for it. Do not look back on happiness—dream of it in the future.... —*Henry W. Beecher*

I am not afraid of tomorrow, for I have seen yesterday and I love today....
—*William A. White*

Today is the only time we can possibly live. Let's not turn it into a physical and mental hell by aimless worry about the future. Let's also stop fretting over the blunders we made yesterday....
—*Dale Carnegie*

I've shut the door on yesterday and thrown the key away. Tomorrow holds no fear for me, since I have found today.... —*Vivien Larrimore*

The present is passed over in the race for the future; the here is neglected in favor of the there. Enjoy the moment, even if it means merely a walk in the country.... —*Anne Morrow Lindbergh*

We have lived today by what truth we can get today and be ready tomorrow to call it falsehood.... —*William James*

The art of enjoying every minute is to deal with only one minute at a time....
—*Hilary Worth*

Realization is a moment by moment happening....There is no coming and going, no birth and death, there is only right now and right here. But no one can say what "here" is, or tell you what time is "now"....
—*A Spiritual Warrior*

Hold every moment sacred. Give each clarity and meaning, each the weight of thine awareness, each its true and due fulfillment.... —*Thomas Mann*

Do not waste your strength in grieving over the past or squander all your energy to encompass the future. Do the real things of today and let the rest go undone.... —*William S. Sadler*

Nothing today need conform to anything of yesterday....
—*Jesse Jennings*

The present is the necessary product of all the past, the necessary cause of all the future.... —*Robert Ingersoll*

The farther backward you can look, the farther forward you can see....
—*Winston Churchill*

The time is now, the place is here. Stay in the present. You can do nothing to change the past, and the future will never come exactly as you plan or hope for.... —*Dan Millman*

We must live today: he who lives tomorrow never lives. If you want to live today, live for God, in whom yesterday and tomorrow are naught but today.... —*Marsilio Ficino*

Never regret yesterday. Life is in you today, and you make your tomorrows....
—*L. Ron Hubbard*

I can feel guilty about the past, apprehensive about the future, but only in the present can I act. The ability to be in the present moment is a major component of mental wellness....
—*Abraham Maslow*

Live in the present. Do the things that need to be done. Do all the good you can each day. The future will unfold....
—*Peace Pilgrim*

Live neither in the past nor in the future, but let each day's work absorb all your interest, energy and enthusiasm. The best preparation for tomorrow is to do today's work superbly well....
—*William Osler*

One can best serve God with whatever one is doing at the present moment....
—*Hasidic saying*

One day at a time—this is enough. Do not look back and grieve over the past, for it is gone; and do not be troubled about the future, for it has not yet come. Live in the present, and make it so beautiful that it would be worth remembering....
—*Ida Scott Taylor*

Expecting is the greatest impediment to living. In anticipation of tomorrow, it loses today....
—*Seneca*

He who thinks to reach God by running away from the world, when and where does he expect to meet him?...We are reaching him here in this very spot, now at this very moment....
—*Rabindranath Tagore*

Nothing is worth more than this day....
—*Johann W. Goethe*

Each day comes bearing its gifts. Untie the ribbons....
—*Ann Ruth Schabacker*

To live with God is to live always in the present, with him who is the eternal Now....
—*John A. T. Robinson*

It is cheap generosity which promises the future in compensation for the present....
—*J. A. Spencer*

Shallow men speak of the past, wise men of the present, and fools of the future....
—*Mme. de Deffand*

One of the most tragic things I know about human nature is that all of us tend to put off living. We are all dreaming of some magical rose garden over the horizon—instead of enjoying the roses that are blooming outside our windows today....
—*Dale Carnegie*

Today is a new day. You will get out of it just what you put into it....
—*Mary Pickford*

Why fret for the future or dream of the past? My here-and-now spirit has treasure so vast. It covers forever, eternity's tone. Yet is caught in one moment, a world of its own....
—*E. Cole Ingle*

As I get older I become aware of the folly of this perpetual reaching after the future, and of drawing from tomorrow, and from tomorrow only, a reason for the joyfulness of today....
—*William H. White*

Look to this day!...For yesterday is but a dream and tomorrow is only a vision, but today well lived makes every yesterday a dream of happiness and tomorrow a vision of hope....
—*Kalidasa*

If we are ever to enjoy life, now is the time—not tomorrow, nor next year, nor in some future life after we have died....Today should always be our most wonderful day....
—*Thomas Dreier*

Our main business is not to see what lies dimly at a distance, but to do what lies clearly at hand....
—*Thomas Carlyle*

Yesterday is a cancelled check; tomorrow is a promissory note; today is the only cash you have—spend it wisely....
—*Kay Lyons*

Sufficient it is to know that the way we lived our yesterday has determined for us our today. And, again, when the morning with its fresh beginning comes, all tomorrows should be tomorrows, with which we have nothing to do. Sufficient to know that the way we live our today determines our tomorrow.... —*Ralph W. Trine*

Any man can fight the battles of today. Any woman can carry the burdens of just one day. Any man can resist the temptations of today....
—*Robert Jones Burdette*

The present moment....has several dimensions....the present of things past, the present of things present, and the present of things future....
—*Augustine*

Let each one examine his thoughts, and he will find them all occupied with the past and the future. We scarcely ever think of the present, and if we think of it, it is only to take light from it to arrange the future.... —*Blaise Pascal*

Those who live in the future always appear selfish to those who live in the present.... —*Ralph W. Emerson*

Very few men....live at present, but are providing to live another time....
—*Jonathan Swift*

We often try to banish gloom and despondency of the present by speculating upon our chances of success in the future—a process that leads us to invent a great many unreal hopes....
—*Arthur Schopenhauer*

The 'past' is only a memory and the 'future' is only a hope. It is only the 'present,' the now, that means anything to us, as presence is what we are...
—*Nisargadatta*

The moment you want to make progress is the moment you become an eternal beginner. The dawn is the beginning of a new day: it stymbolizes hope, illumination and perfection. Every day the dawn plays the role of the beginner. It begins its journey at daybreak and ends its journey in the infinite sun. If you can feel that your whole being—your body, vitality, mind and soul—represents the ever-blossoming dawn, then you will always remain an eternal beginner....
—*Sri Chinmoy*

No mind is much employed upon the present; recollection and anticipation fill up almost all our moments....
—*Samuel Johnson*

The present is a powerful deity....
—*Johann W. Goethe*

Above all, we cannot afford not to live in the present. He is blessed over all mortals who loses no moment of the passing life in remembering the past....
—*Henry D. Thoreau*

Our latest moment is always our supreme moment....
—*Samuel Butler*

Unhappiness exists only as a reflection or regret about the past or as an anticipation or worry toward the future. It does not exist right now, in this moment.. —*Barry N. Kaufman*

Begin to be now what you will be hereafter.... —*Eusebius Hieronymus*

The greatest loss of time is delay and expectation, which depend upon the future. We let go of the present, which we have in our power, and look forward to that which depends upon chance, and so relinquish a certainty for an uncertainty.... —*Seneca*

The load of tomorrow, added to that of yesterday, carried today, makes the strongest falter. We must learn to shut out the future as tightly as the past....
—*William Osler*

Humility

The individual never asserts himself more than when he forgets himself....   —*André Gide*

No one should be our inferior. One who has learned to be inferior will become superior to all....
—*Ramana Maharshi*

If you don't know, you are pure. Not knowing is purity. Then you are humble. If you know, you are not pure....
—*Yoga Swami*

Humility must always be doing its work like a bee making its honey in the hive: without humility all will be lost....
—*Teresa of Avila*

The key to my life is that I am willing to make an ass out of myself....
—*Harry Chapin*

Humble righteousness is nine-tenths of the Egoless State....
—*Lakshmana Sarma*

All streams flow to the ocean because it is lower than they are. Humility gives it its power....   —*Lao-tzu*

Humility is the recognition that what you don't know is more than what you do know....   —*Anonymous*

Go and sit in the last place and then you will be invited to take the first....
—*Jesus*

Never forget the hard times and the early days. Always remember where you came from....
—*David Liederman*

I would rather have men ask why I have no statue than why I have one....
—*Cato the Elder*

It is our emptiness and lowliness that God needs and not our fullness....
—*Mother Teresa*

Looking foolish does the spirit good. The need not to look foolish is one of youth's many burdens; as we get older we are exempted more and more, and float upward heedlessly, singing: "Thanks be to God that I am what I am."...   —*John Updike*

The nail that sticks up will be hammered down....   —*Japanese proverb*

If thou wouldst be exalted, humble thyself before God, who humbles the exalted and exalts the humble....
—*Ahikar*

Earthly crowns are dross to him who looks for a heavenly one....
—*Jane Porter*

Ask too much and it shall be denied you, knock too loudly and it shall not be opened unto you, seek impatiently and you shall not find it....
—*Will Durant*

The richest pearl in the....crown of graces is humility....   —*John M. Good*

The beloved of the Almighty are the rich who have the humility of the poor, and the poor who have the magnanimity of the rich....   —*Saadi*

Stronger by weakness wiser men become....   —*Edmund Waller*

Humility is truth.... —*Erasmus*

It is far more impressive when others discover your good qualities without your help.... —*Judith S. Nartin*

Forgetfulness of self is remembrance of God.... —*Bayazid Al-bistami*

The gods love the obscure and hate the obvious.... —*The Upanishads*

I have found some of the best reasons....for remaining at the bottom simply by looking at the men at the top.... —*Frank Colby*

Humility is the path of immortality. Vanity is the path of births and deaths.... —*Sivananda*

The more you are reduced, the more powerful you become....In humility there is greatness and power.... —*John Panama*

If you are going to bow, bow low.... —*Eastern proverb*

When one says humility, he necessarily implies simplicity; for the two always go hand in hand. The one is born of the other.... —*Ralph W. Trine*

Lowliness is the foundation of loftiness.... —*Lao-tzu*

He who truly knows himself is lowly in his own eyes.... —*Thomas à Kempis*

Humility is indeed only another name for non-egotism.... —*Bhagavan Das*

True humility is not an abject, groveling, self-despising spirit—it is but a right estimate of ourselves as God sees us.... —*Tryon Edwards*

Humility is the highest of all virtues. You can destroy your egotism by developing this virtue alone. You can influence people. You can become a magnet to attract the world. It must be genuine. Feigned humility is hypocrisy.... —*Robert Collier*

The first quality or virtue we have to develop, before we aspire to have God, is humility....You have in fact to unlearn what you have learnt. You must become simple, unsophisticated, and childlike.... —*Papa Ramdas*

Every path that leads to the "kingdom of heaven within" must eventually pass through the valley of humility.... —*Anonymous*

Humility is the eternal fountain of energy.... —*Vimala Thakar*

Humility is the richest jewel you can wear.... —*Paramananda*

God can do great things through the man who doesn't care who gets the credit.... —*Robert Schuller*

The less a man thinks of himself, the more he thinks of his good luck and of all the miraculous gifts of God. For there is no way a man can earn a star, or desire a sunset.... —*Edmond Bordeaux*

Where there is humility and patience, there is neither anger nor vexation.... —*Francis of Assisi*

No need to discount yourself in order to achieve humility; neither can you attain humility by overestimating what you are. Humility is your correct weight; no more, no less.... —*Fred Van Amburgh*

I believe the first test of a truly great man is humility....
—*John Ruskin*

Before honor is humility....
—*Old Testament*

One must be able to strip oneself of all self-deception, to see oneself naked to one's own eyes, before one can come to terms with the elements of oneself and know who one really is....
—*Frances Wickes*

Teach thy tongue to say, "I do not know," and thou shalt progress....
—*Maimonides*

The way to make a good impression on other people is: Never "try" to make a good impression on them. Never act, or fail to act, purely for consciously contrived effect.... —*Maxwell Maltz*

Humility in action is universal consciousness.... —*Yogi Bhajan*

Desire to sow no seed for your own harvesting; desire only to sow that seed the fruit of which will feed the world....
—*Mabel Collins*

Humility, like darkness, reveals the heavenly lights.... —*Henry D. Thoreau*

The bell never rings of itself; unless someone handles or moves it, it is silent.... —*Plautus*

Humility is not weakness; it is the epitome of strength. Humility moves a person away from human, personal weakness and limitation into divine expression, strength and expansion....
—*Donald Curtis*

The less a man thinks or knows about his virtues the better we like him....
—*Ralph W. Emerson*

If two angels were sent down from heaven—one to conduct an empire, and the other to sweep a street—they would feel no inclination to change employments.... —*John Newton*

He who asks of life nothing but the improvement of his own nature, and a continuous good progress towards inner contentment and spiritual submission, is less likely than anyone else to miss and waste life....
—*Henri F. Amiel*

To be humble to superiors, is duty; to equals, is courtesy; to inferiors, is nobleness; and to all, safety; it being a virtue that, for all its lowliness, commandeth those it stoops to....
—*Thomas More*

A man who really understands the strength of his position will never fail to be humble in his apology....
—*Margery Wilson*

The most powerful weapon to conquer evil is humility. For evil does not know at all how to employ it, nor does it know how to defend itself against it....
—*Vincent de Paul*

One who is meek and humble, who regards himself as the lowest of the low can easily swim across the ocean of this world.... —*Maharaj C. Singh*

Modesty and humility are the sobriety of the mind, as temperance and chastity are of the body....
—*Benjamin Whichote*

We ought not to lead events, but to follow them.... —*Epictetus*

Be willing to be a beginner every single morning.... —*Meister Eckhart*

Humility is the acceptance of the possibility that someone else can teach you something else you do not know already, especially about yourself. Conversely, pride and arrogance close the door to the mind....　　*—Arthur Deikman*

Humility should make the possessor realize that he is as nothing....
　　　　　　　—Mohandas Gandhi

Be not arrogant because of your knowledge, but confer with the ignorant man as with the learned....
　　　　　　　—Ptahhotpe

Do not consider yourself to have made any spiritual progress, unless you account yourself the least of all men....Resolve to do the will of others rather than your own. Always choose to possess less rather than more. Always take the lowest plane, and regard yourself as less than others....
　　　　　　　—Thomas à Kempis

No man is humble who does not believe in God....　　*—Fulton J. Sheen*

True humility involves opposites. The truly humble work in silence. Because they do not speak of their accomplishments, credit for them can never be taken away....　　　　*—Lao-tzu*

He who is sincere, though simple, is further advanced on the divine road than he who tries to appear what he is not....　　　　*—Allan Kardec*

A humble person can walk with kings and keep his or her virtue and talk with the crowds and keep the common touch....　　　　*—Anonymous*

Humility is not thinking of ourselves as less than we are, or more than we are, but just as we are....
　　　　　　　—Aubrey P. Andelin

I asked God for strength that I might achieve. I was made weak that I might learn humbly to obey. I asked for health that I might do greater things. I was given infirmity that I might do better things. I asked for riches that I might be happy. I was given poverty that I might be wise. I asked for power that I might have the praise of men. I was given weakness that I might feel the need of God. I asked for all things that I might enjoy life. I was given life that I might enjoy all things. I got nothing that I asked for, but everything I hoped for. Almost despite myself, my unspoken prayers were answered. I am, among all men, most richly blessed....
　　　　—The Prayer of an Unknown
　　　　　　　Confederate Soldier

Only those who feel good about who they are can express humility....
　　　　　　　—Sanaya Roman

Wear your learning like your watch, in a private pocket. Do not pull it out merely to show that you have one. If asked what o'clock it is, tell it, but do not proclaim it hourly and unasked, like the watchman....
　　　　　　　—Phillip D. Stanhope

It is vain to gather virtues without humility; for the spirit of God delights to dwell in the hearts of the humble....
　　　　　　　—Erasmus

Man is humble when the flaming fire of desires has become extinct....
　　　　　　　—Al-Tirmidi

When humility enters a man's soul, he is at last able to perceive that he does not live alone in the world but with millions of brothers, and that hidden in the heart of each is the same animating spirit....　　　　*—U. S. Anderson*

True humility is a great force, and although it works with gentleness, yet it never fails to transform....
—*Paramananda*

If you cannot be the sun, then be the humble planet.... —*Tibetan proverb*

Humbleness is always grace, always dignity.... —*James Russell Lowell*

He that is down needs fear no fall; he that is low, no pride; he that is humble ever shall have God to be his guide....
—*John Bunyan*

Be lowly and humble, only thus can you rise. The lark builds its nest on the ground, but it soars high in the sky....
—*Ramakrishna*

There is nothing more ostentatious than deliberate humility....
—*Alan Watts*

Be humble, and you will remain entire. Be bent, and you will remain straight. Be vacant, and you will remain full....
—*Catholic prayer*

If you are humble, nothing will touch you, neither praise nor disgrace, because you know what you are....
—*Mother Teresa*

Discount the one who immediately starts out to tell you all about his accomplishments or achievements. If they are good and lasting, others will tell you about them....The big man does not have to brag. The little man thinks he must.... —*Fred Van Amburgh*

Of myself I can do nothing; the Father that dwells in me, He does the work....
—*Jesus*

Take the lowest place and you shall reach the highest.... —*Milarepa*

The end of all strife and contention is regret; but the end of humility is strength and possession....
—*Shekel Hakodesh*

The mark of the immature man is that he wants to die nobly for a cause, while the mark of the mature man is that he wants to live humbly for one....
—*J. D. Salinger*

The gate of heaven....is so narrow that it admits only little ones.... —*St. Bernard*

Take your seat a little below your rank, for it is better to be asked to come up than to be told to go down....
—*Tanna Akiba*

A mountain shames a molehill until they are both humbled by the stars....
—*Anonymous*

Humility is a virtue that subdues the hearts of others. A man of humility is a powerful magnet or lodestone....
—*Sivananda*

Do you wish to rise? Begin by descending. You plan a tower that shall pierce the clouds? Lay first the foundation....
—*Augustine*

It often happens that those of whom we speak least on earth are best known in heaven.... —*Nicolas Caussin*

Humility comes....only with maturity....
—*Louis Finklestein*

True humility is contentment....
—*Henri F. Amiel*

Nothing is in vain or without profit to the humble soul: like the bee, it takes its honey from the bitter herbs; it stands always in a state of divine growth, and everything that falls upon it is a dew of Heaven to it....
—*William Law*

If you remember your own nothing-ness, you remember also God's tran-scendence....   —*Philo*

A humble person is generally well-liked and respected because he or she does not challenge others. When the ego is not attacked, not put on guard, it has a hard time gathering strength to attack another....   —*Shantidasa*

Humility is the most excellent cure for anger....   —*Jeremy Taylor*

How ennobling it is to apologize to another when you have been in the wrong, and how doubly thrilling it is— if you can bring yourself to do it—to apologize when you know he is as much in the wrong as you....
                    —*James T. Mangan*

Humility is the surest sign of strength....
                    —*Thomas Merton*

Humility is the first lesson we learn from reflection....
                    —*Johann W. Zimmerman*

Until the ego finally dies, humility alone is good for the spiritual aspir-ant....   —*Ramana Maharshi*

One is only as obedient as one is humble, and one can never be humble if one is not obedient....
                    —*Catherine of Siena*

Humility in itself is nothing but a true feeling of a man's self as he is....God walks with the humble; he reveals himself to the lowly; he gives understanding to the little ones; he discloses his meaning to pure minds, but hides his grace from the curious and proud....   —*Thomas à Kempis*

Humility is to make a right estimate of one's self....   —*Charles Spurgeon*

As life unfolds itself to man the first lesson he learns is humility....
                    —*Hazrat Inayat Khan*

I find hidden, somewhere away in my nature, something that tells me that nothing in the whole world is meaningless, and suffering least of all. That something hidden away in my nature, like a treasure in a field, is Humility....   —*Oscar Wilde*

It is only by forgetting yourself that you draw near God....   —*Henry D. Thoreau*

The Chinese character for humility is also the Chinese character for empti-ness....   —*Anonymous*

It is not a great thing to be humble when you are brought low; but to be humble when you are praised is a great and rare attainment....   —*St. Bernard*

As a dry stick is better disposed for burning than a wet stick, so a humble man is better disposed for faith than a know-it-all....   —*Fulton J. Sheen*

Life is a long lesson in humility....
                    —*James M. Barrie*

The highest goodness is like water. Water is beneficent to all things but does not contend, preferring to gather at the lowest level where others despise....   —*Lao-tzu*

The casting down of our spirits in true humility is but like throwing a ball to the ground, which makes it rebound the higher toward heaven....
                    —*John Mason*

The humble soul is a temple of God, a seat of wisdom....   —*Johann Arndt*

Humility is the seed of contentment....
                    —*Israel M. Kagan*

Humility is to the virtues what the chain is to the rosary: remove the chain, and all the beads escape; take away humility, and all the virtues disappear....
—*The Cure d'Ars*

Man often exults the defeat of another forgetting that, some other time, his own defeat will be the cause of jubilation for others. So, humility in all the conditions of life is the way to enjoy peace....
—*Papa Ramdas*

You should practice humility first toward man and only then toward God. He who despises men has no respect for God....
—*Paracelsus*

Discourses on humility are a source of pride to the vain....
—*Blaise Pascal*

Heaven's gates are not so highly arched as princes' palaces; they that enter there must go upon their knees....
—*John Webster*

My lowliness is my loftiness....
—*Hillel*

In Heaven an angel is nobody in particular....
—*George B. Shaw*

Humility is the most difficult of virtues to achieve; nothing dies harder than the desire to think well of oneself....
—*T. S. Eliot*

Learn to know all, but keep yourself unknown....
—*Sufi saying*

It was pride that changed angels to devils; it is humility that makes men angels....
—*Augustine*

He who knows himself to be insignificant, even among the uncultured and the ignorant, who lives in darkness, shall have the Divine Light dwell within him....
—*Israel Baal Shem Tov*

A modest person is usually admired—if people ever hear of him....
—*Edgar W. Howe*

Sense shines with a double luster when it is set in humility. An able and yet humble man is a jewel worth a kingdom....
—*William Penn*

Humility is the root, mother, nurse, foundation, and bond of all virtue....
—*John Chrysostom*

The voice of humility is God's music and the silence of humility is God's rhetoric....
—*Francis Quarles*

Even if you be otherwise perfect, you fail without humility....
—*The Talmud*

Nothing sets a person so much out of the devil's reach as humility....
—*Jonathan Edwards*

If thou wouldst become a pilgrim on the path of love the first condition is that thou become as humble as dust and ashes....
—*Ansari*

My lowliness raises up God and the lower I humble myself the higher do I exalt God and the higher I exalt God the more gently and sweetly He pours into me His divine gift, His divine influx....
—*Meister Eckhart*

Humility does not cast down the individual, it raises him up....
—*Antoine de Saint-Exupery*

Whosoever shall humble himself....the same is greatest in the kingdom of heaven....
—*Jesus*

He that places himself neither higher nor lower than he ought to do, exercises the truest humility....
—*Charles C. Colton*

A humble man can do great things with uncommon perfection because he is no longer concerned about....his own interests and his own reputation, and therefore he no longer needs to waste his efforts in defending them....
—*Thomas Merton*

One who is well aware that he is humble is no longer humble....
—*Jacob Klatzkin*

True humility makes no pretense of being humble, and scarcely ever utters words of humility....
—*Francis de Sales*

One of the commonest manifestations of vanity is a pretended humility....
—*Julian P. Johnson*

Humility has that low sweet root, from which all heavenly virtues shoot....
—*Thomas More*

These are a few of the ways we can practice humility: Speak as little as possible of oneself. Mind one's own business. Avoid curiosity. Do not want to manage other people's affairs. Accept contradiction and correction cheerfully. Pass over the mistakes of others. Accept blame when innocent. Yield to the will of others. Accept insults and injuries. Accept being slighted, forgotten and disliked. Be kind and gentle even under provocation. Do not seek to be specially loved and admired. Never stand on one's dignity. Yield in discussion even though one is right. Choose always the hardest....   —*Mother Teresa*

Humility is the altar on which God wishes us to offer sacrifices to Him....
—*Francois La Rochefoucauld*

The higher we are placed, the more humbly should we walk....   —*Cicero*

There is no true holiness without humility....   —*Thomas Fuller*

There is but one road to lead to God—humility; all other ways would only lead astray, even were they fenced in with all virtues....   —*Nicolas Boileau*

The science of humility rests upon the knowledge of God and of oneself....
—*William Ullathorne*

There are many people who strive to be pious, but few who yearn to be humble....   —*Anonymous*

He who humbles himself shall be saved; He who bends shall be made straight; He who empties himself shall be filled....   —*Lao-tzu*

Be humble, that you may not be humbled....   —*The Talmud*

The tree laden with fruit always bends low....   —*Ramakrishna*

Hypocrisy

Hypocrisy begins when one is covetous....   —*Sivananda*

If we divine a discrepancy between a man's words and his character, the whole impression of him becomes broken and painful....
—*Charles H. Cooley*

The world consists almost exclusively of people who are one sort and who behave like another sort....
—*Zona Gray*

A bad man is worse when he pretends to be a saint....   —*Francis Bacon*

Hypocrisy in anything whatever may deceive the cleverest and most penetrating man, but the least wide-awake of children recognizes it, and is revolted by it, however ingeniously it may be disguised.... —*Leo Tolstoy*

Let the world know you as you are, not as you think you should be, because sooner or later, if you think you are posing, you will forget the pose, and then where are you?... —*Fannie Brice*

Neither man nor angel can discern hypocrisy, the only evil that walks invisible, except to God alone.... —*John Milton*

Hypocrisy is folly. It is much easier, safer, and pleasanter to be the thing which a man aims to appear, than to keep up the appearance of what he is not.... —*Cecil*

Artful, cunning, crafty people are paralyzed when you refuse to recognize their hypocrisy.... —*Fred Van Amburgh*

Hypocrisy is pretending to be perfect, and in the process, imposing a sense of judgement and guilt on those around you. Hypocrisy is giving everybody the verbal assurance that you are living up to your own standards, when you are really not.... —*Robert H. Schuller*

No man can, for any considerable time, wear one face to himself, and another to the multitude, without finally getting bewildered as to which is the true one.... —*Nathaniel Hawthorne*

The wolf in sheep's clothing is a fitting emblem of the hypocrite. Every virtuous man would rather meet an open foe than a pretended friend who was a traitor at heart.... —*H. F. Kletzing*

One may smile and smile and be a villain still.... —*William Shakespeare*

When you are no longer in danger of being thought of as a hypocrite by your friends, beware of your hypocrisy with God.... —*Oswald Chambers*

I will have nothing to do with a man who can blow hot and cold with the same breath.... —*Aesop*

Where there is much pretense, much has been borrowed—nature never pretends.... —*John K. Lavater*

What hypocrites we seem to be whenever we talk of ourselves. Our words sound so humble while our hearts are so proud.... —*Augustus & Julius Hare*

How can you say to another, "Let me take a speck out of your eye!" Hypocrite! First remove the speck from your own eye, and then you will be able to remove that of your brother.... —*Jesus*

Hypocrisy can afford to be magnificent in its promises; for never intending to go beyond promises, it costs nothing.... —*Edmund Burke*

Hypocrisy is prejudice with a halo.... —*Ambrose Bierce*

Actors are the only honest hypocrites. Their life is a voluntary dream; and the height of their ambition is to be beside themselves.... —*William Hazlitt*

To have one eye glued on the enchanting pleasures of the flesh, and with the other to expect to see a spark of Eternal Bliss, is not only impossible but the height of hypocrisy.... —*Meher Baba*

Hypocrisy is saying one thing and doing another; it is very easy to spot in others and very difficult to find in ourselves.... —*Anonymous*

To thine own self be true, and it shall follow as night the day that thou cannot then be false to any man.... —*William Shakespeare*

A hypocrite is in himself both the archer and the mark, in all actions shooting out his own praise or profit.... —*Thomas Fuller*

No man is a hypocrite in his pleasures.... —*Samuel Johnson*

Ignorance

Most ignorance is the direct result of apathy; people don't know because they don't care to know.... —*Anonymous*

When a stupid man is doing something he is ashamed of, he always declares that it is his duty.... —*George B. Shaw*

There is after all no obligation to answer every passing fool according to his folly.... —*Elias Canetti*

The characteristic of the ignorant man is that he strives to be other than what he is....To the enlightened one, there is none who are ignorant.... —*Yoga Vasistha*

The senses and the mind of man were created out of ignorance. Therefore they move in ignorance and delight in ignorance. They always find joy and peace in falsities. For their nature is ignorance.... —*Sivananda*

Every man takes the limits of his own field of vision for the limits of the world.... —*Arthur Schopenhauer*

People are never so near playing the fool as when they think themselves wise.... —*Mary W. Montagu*

Ignorance is not innocence but sin.... —*Robert Browning*

You are blind until your inner eyes of understanding are open.... —*Archie Canfield*

Ego is only an illusion caused by your ignorance.... —*Papa Ramdas*

All the world over everybody recognizes that he must pay for what he gets. It is only the fool who tries to get something for nothing.... —*Julian P. Johnson*

The ignorant man always adores what he cannot understand.... —*Cesare Lombroso*

The first reason for man's slavery is his ignorance, and above all, his ignorance of himself.... —*George I. Gurdjieff*

Nothing in all the world is more dangerous than sincere ignorance and conscientious stupidity.... —*Martin Luther King, Jr.*

The root of ignorance is the idea that a person is separate from God....Ignorance conceals the existent knowledge just as weeds cover the surface of a pond. Clean the weeds and you have the water.... —*Shirdi Sai Baba*

Only the fool whose mind is deluded by egotism considers himself to be the doer.... —*Bhagavad-Gita*

Ignorance is always indifferent to the truth. Be indifferent and habitually skeptical and you will be rated as ignorant.... —*Fred Van Amburgh*

There is a principle which is a bar against all information, which is proof against all arguments and which cannot fail to keep a man in everlasting ignorance. That principle is contempt prior to investigation.... —*Herbert Spencer*

Man is indeed God playing the fool.... —*Papa Ramdas*

I have always observed that to succeed in the world one should seem like a fool, but be wise.... —*Charles Montesquieu*

I have never met a man so ignorant that I couldn't learn something from him.... —*Galileo Galilei*

A great deal of intelligence can be invested in ignorance when the need for illusion is deep.... —*Saul Bellow*

Better to live alone; with a fool there is no companionship.... —*Buddhist saying*

The world is full of fools; and he who would not wish to see one, must not only shut himself up alone but must break his looking glass.... —*Nicolas Boileau*

Desire is an offspring of ignorance.... —*Sivananda*

Anyone can make a mistake. A fool insists on repeating it.... —*Robertine Maynard*

An ignorant man is, by the very fact of his ignorance, a very dangerous person.... —*Hendrik W. Van Loon*

Fools with bookish knowledge are children with edged weapons; they hurt themselves, and put others in pain. The half-learned is more dangerous than the simpleton.... —*Johann G. Zimmerman*

The recipe for perpetual ignorance is: be satisfied with your opinion and content with your knowledge.... —*Elbert Hubbard*

There is nothing more frightening than ignorance in action.... —*Johann W. Goethe*

Experience is the common schoolhouse of fools and ill men. Men of wit and honesty are otherwise instructed.... —*Erasmus*

Who is ignorant? He who does not educate his children.... —*The Talmud*

Impossible is a word only to be found in the dictionary of fools.... —*Napoleon Bonaparte*

The chief characteristic of folly is that it mistakes itself for wisdom.... —*Luis de Leon*

He is a fool who misjudges good precepts for falsehood.... —*Tripura Rahasya*

A fool can no more see his own folly than he can see his ears.... —*William M. Thackeray*

You can tell a fool from a wise man when you rebuke him; the fool will rebuke you back, the wise man will quietly love you.... —*Anonymous*

Young men think old men fools, and old men know young men to be so.... —*Richard Metcalf*

A fool may be known by six things: anger, without cause; speech, without profit; change, without progress; inquiry, without object; putting trust in a stranger, and mistaking foes for friends....   —*Arabian proverb*

A wise man in the company of those who are ignorant has been compared to a beautiful girl in the company of blind men....   —*Saadi*

The only evil is ignorance....

—*Diogenes*

A fool sees not the same tree that a wise man sees....   —*William Blake*

Ignorant and foolish men, with a labor as vain as it is obstinate, search out the natures of things while they remain in ignorance of the One who is the Author and Maker of themselves and of all things alike....   —*Hugh of Saint-Victor*

Our lives are universally shortened by our ignorance....   —*Herbert Spencer*

There are various routes of escape from responsibility: escape into death, escape into disease, and escape into stupidity. The last is the safest and easiest....   —*Arthur Schnitzler*

It is better to be a beggar than ignorant....   —*Aristippus*

Ignorance is the night of the mind, a night without moon or star....

—*Confucius*

To be overcome by pleasure is ignorance in the highest degree....   —*Plato*

A parable from the mouth of a fool is worthless, for he utters it out of season....   —*Apocrypha: Ben Sira*

There are two kinds of fools: one says, 'This is old, therefore it is good'; the other says, 'This is new, therefore it is better'....   —*William R. Inge*

Fools rush in where angels fear to tread....   —*Alexander Pope*

That which is lacking in the present world is a profound knowledge of the nature of things....   —*Frithjof Schuon*

Ignorance makes you identify yourself with the body and your entire life is centered in and utilized for the satisfaction of your senses—the off-spring of your lower nature. Therefore, rise up and declare that you are immortal spirit full of power, bliss and peace....   —*Papa Ramdas*

There is no slavery but ignorance....

—*Robert Ingersoll*

To be ignorant of one's ignorance is the malady of the ignorant....

—*Amos B. Alcott*

An ignorant man believes the whole universe exists only for him....If, therefore, anything happens to him contrary to his expectations, he at once concludes that the whole universe is evil....   —*Maimonides*

Foolish men mistake transitory semblances for eternal fact, and go astray more and more....

—*Thomas Carlyle*

We should not call our brother a fool; for we ourselves do not know what we are. God alone can judge and know....

—*Paracelsus*

If a man does not struggle hard to realize God, he remains steeped in ignorance....   —*Brahmananda*

To know and yet not to do is in fact not to know.... —*Wang Yang Ming*

Passions, prejudices, fears, neuroses spring from ignorance, and take the form of myths and illusions.... —*Isaiah Berlin*

The greater the ignorance, the greater the dogmatism.... —*William Osler*

If fifty million people say a foolish thing, it is still a foolish thing.... —*Anatole France*

A piece of glass and a diamond are alike to the blind, just as falsehood and truth are both the same to the fool.... —*Anonymous*

It is only evil and ignorance that have many shapes. Truth and wisdom are one and the same.... —*Abbot Lee Lisan*

Let a fool hold his tongue and he will pass for a sage.... —*Publilius Syrus*

Wise men profit more from fools than fools from wise men; for the wise men shun the mistakes of fools, but fools do not imitate the successes of the wise.... —*Marcus Cato*

Ignorance is the primary source of all misery and vice.... —*Victor Cousin*

To act without clear understanding, to form habits without investigation, to follow a path all one's life without knowing where it really leads—such is the behavior of the multitude.... —*Menicus*

The greatest calamity that befalls the heedless is that they are ignorant of their own faults.... —*Hujwiri*

A fool is not aware of his folly.... —*The Talmud*

A fool must now and then be right by chance.... —*William Cowper*

The eternal, blissful and natural state has been smothered by this life of ignorance.... —*Ramana Maharshi*

Those who are blind in this world shall be blind in the next.... —*Koran*

The ignorant man marvels at the exceptional; the wise man marvels at the common.... —*George D. Boardman*

A fool always finds some greater fool to admire him.... —*Nicolas Boileau*

It is better to conceal ignorance than to put it forth into the midst.... —*Heraclitus*

Stubborn and ardent clinging to one's opinion is the best proof of stupidity.... —*Michel Montaigne*

The tragedy of ignorance is its complacency.... —*Robert Quillen*

People oppose things because they are ignorant of them.... —*El-Ghazali*

Most ignorance is vincible ignorance. We don't know because we don't want to know.... —*Aldous Huxley*

Ignorant men raise questions that wise men answered thousands of years ago.... —*Johann W. Goethe*

A man who has never seen the sun cannot be blamed for thinking that no glory can exceed that of the moon.... —*Calderon*

The ultimate result of shielding man from the effects of folly is to fill the world with fools.... —*Herbert Spencer*

It is impossible to defeat an ignorant man in an argument....
—*William G. McAdoo*

Against stupidity the gods themselves struggle in vain....
—*Friedrich von Schiller*

Being ignorant of his true identity, man has evolved to be his own worst enemy. Observing his outside surroundings, man often perceives it as an illusionary foe. A fierce struggle inevitably ensues and the end may be predicted with absolute certainty: man loses, wounding himself in the process....
—*Shantidasa*

The fool says in his heart: "There is no God."...
—*Old Testament*

Better to be unborn than untaught, for ignorance is the root of misfortune....
—*Plato*

Ignorance deprives men of freedom because they do not know what alternatives there are. It is impossible to choose to do what one has never "heard of."...
—*Ralph B. Perry*

Man, ignorant of self, creates his own unhappiness....
—*Paul Brunton*

Ignorance is the beginning of knowledge; knowledge is the beginning of wisdom; wisdom is the awareness of ignorance....
—*William Rotsler*

A fool may have his coat embroidered with gold, but it is a fool's coat still....
—*Antoine Rivarol*

Ignorance or delusion....sets us on the belief that this body of ours is real and makes us forget the all-pervading Divine being whi is the one and only reality. Living in this ignorance, our sole outlook on life becomes one continued service of this unral and perishable body...
—*Papa Ramdas*

Illusions

Everything is vain, hopeless and senseless....
—*Latin saying*

Illusions command themselves to us because they save us pain and allow us to enjoy pleasure instead. We must therefore accept it without complaint when they sometimes collide with a bit of reality against which they are dashed to pieces....
—*Sigmund Freud*

Now the wonderful world is born. In an instant it dies, in a breath it is renewed. From the slowness of our eye and the quickness of God's hand we believe in the world....
—*William Buck*

Each person is a specialist in fantasizing their own illusory world....
—*A Spiritual Warrior*

We suffer primarily not from our vices or our weaknesses, but from our illusions. We are haunted, not by reality, but by those images we have put in place of reality....
—*Daniel J. Boorstin*

When one sees that everything exists as an illusion, one can live in a higher sphere than ordinary man....
—*Gautama Buddha*

Questioning illusions is the first step to undoing them....
—*A Course In Miracles*

Our greatest illusion is disillusion. We imagine that we are disillusioned with life, when the truth is that we have not even begun to live....
—*Paul Brunton*

The real illusion is that we are separate....
—*Ron Smothermon*

This waking life is just a long dream which keeps our attention away from what we really are. If you take the attitude that all the happenings in the world are dream events, your mind becomes tranquil. It is only when you take the dream world to be real that you get agitated....
—*Annamalai Swami*

The greatest illusion is the belief that life has nothing to teach you....
—*Shantidasa*

The universe is illusion merely, not one speck of it real, and we are not only victims....but also captives, bound by the mineral-made ropes of senses....
—*Annie Dillard*

Look upon friends, possessions, wealth, mansions, wives, gifts, and other good fortune, as a dream or a magic show, lasting only a few days....
—*Ashtavakra Gita*

The philosopher laughs, for he alone escapes being duped, while he sees other men the victims of persistent illusion. He is like some mischievous spectator of a ball who has cleverly taken all the strings from the violins, and yet sees musicians and dancers moving and pirouetting before him as though the music were still playing....
—*Henri F. Amiel*

Beware that you do not lose the substance by grasping at the shadow....
—*Aesop*

Illusion exists only for him whose sight is bound.... —*Sankara*

This is a schoolroom of illusion. Do not give permanent reality to temporary things. Once you have learned what you came to learn the illusion can be left.... —*Emmanuel*

The treasures of the earth are but illusive things that pass away....
—*The Aquarian Gospel*

With truth, one cannot live. To be able to live, one needs illusions....
—*Otto Rank*

Worldly enjoyments are fleeting like the flashes of lightning. Human life is ephemeral like the bubble. The vigor of youth is short-lived. All these are illusory in this world.... —*Sivananda*

All that is transitory is only an image....
—*Johann W. Goethe*

The world is an illusion, but it is an illusion which we must take seriously, because it is real as far as it goes....
—*Aldous Huxley*

Truth is simple, but Illusion makes it infinitely intricate. The person is rare who possesses an insatiable longing for Truth; the rest allow Illusion to bind them ever more and more....
—*Meher Baba*

"Passing away" is written on the world and all the world contains....
—*Felicia D. Hemans*

The real illusion is to believe that we are separate from God....
—*Omraam M. Aivanhov*

All phenomena in the world are nothing but the illusory manifestation of the mind and have no reality on their own.... —*Ashvaghosha*

Things are not always what they seem.... —*Phaedus*

We do not exaggerate when we say that life on earth is a mere bubble....
—*Mohandas Gandhi*

Do not hold as gold all that shines as gold....   —*Allain de Lille*

I began to understand that the promises of the world are for the most part vain phantoms, and that to have faith in oneself and become something of worth and value is the best and safest course....   —*Michelangelo*

Human life is an endless illusion....   —*Blaise Pascal*

Pleasure can be supported by illusion, while happiness rests upon truth....   —*Sebastien Chamfort*

People who believe in the reality of the world are really no better than people who build dams to catch the water that they see in a mirage....   —*Annamalai Swami*

The stripping away of illusion and the struggle to find personal reality can be likened to the peeling of an apple. As one peels away the layers of un-reality....eventually only the core remains....   —*Meredith L. Young*

The attainment of an ideal is often the beginning of a disillusion....   —*Stanley Baldwin*

An illusion is nothing but the shadow of God....   —*Anonymous*

A human being is part of the whole, called by us the universe; a part limited by time and space. He experiences himself, his thoughts and feelings as something separated from the rest, a kind of optical illusion of conscious-ness. This delusion is a kind of prison for us, restricting us to our personal desires and to affection for a few persons nearest us. Our task is to free ourselves from this prison....   —*Albert Einstein*

Man's chief delusion is his conviction that there are causes other than his own state of consciousness....   —*Darwin Gross*

The world is an illusion. Why is it unreal? Because none of the knowledge is going to remain permanent, as real knowledge. I had a number of identities; I was a child, I was a boy, I was a teenager, I was a middle-aged man, I was an old man. Like other identities I thought would remain constant, they never remained so. Finally, I became very old....So which identity remained honest with me?...   —*Nisargadatta*

There is no end to illusion. Life is a train of moods like a string of beads, and as we pass through them they prove to be many colored lenses which paint the world their own hue....   —*Ralph W. Emerson*

The phenomena of life can be compared to a dream, a ghost, an air bubble, a shadow, glittering dew, the flash of lightning—and must be contemplated as such....   —*Gautama Buddha*

All illusion is sorry. Only the real Self is true happiness....   —*G. V. Subbaramayya*

Let us watch the divine play on the world stage. People appear on it and disappear from it. The world is a passing show....   —*Papa Ramdas*

Delusion completely overcomes man's sense of right and wrong....   —*Srimad Bhagavatam*

Attachment is the great fabricator of illusions; reality can be attained only by someone who is detached....   —*Simone Weil*

It is a certainty that one cannot live in reality until one has died to illusion....
—*Whitall N. Perry*

Wealth and power pass like a dream, beauty fades like a flower, long life is gone like a wave.... —*William Buck*

Nothing is more hidden from us than the illusion which lives with us day by day, and our greatest illusion is to believe that we are what we think ourselves to be.... —*Henri F. Amiel*

Thus shall you think of all this fleeting world: a star at dawn, a bubble in a stream, a flash of lightning on a summer cloud, a flickering lamp, a phantom, a dream.... —*Hindu sutra*

There is no more dangerous illusion than the fancies by which people try to avoid illusion.... —*Francois Fenelon*

Imagination

Our griefs, as well as our joys, owe their strongest colors to our imaginations. There is nothing so grievous to be borne that pondering upon it will not make it heavier; and there is no pleasure so vivid that the animation of fancy cannot liven it.... —*Jane Porter*

If you wish to advance into the infinite, explore the finite in all directions....
—*Johann W. Goethe*

To visualize is a form of prayer. It is the sending out of a dynamic positive desire which does not have to be put in words.... —*Ambrose Worrall*

The world is but a canvas to our imaginations.... —*Henry D. Thoreau*

Imagination is our ability to see inwardly and picture there that which has not yet appeared outwardly. Imagination is God's gift to us....
—*Donald Curtis*

The first power that meets us at the threshold of the Soul's domain is the power of imagination....
—*Franz Hartmann*

Imagination has always had powers of resurrection that no science can match.... —*Ingrid Bengis*

It is through the imagination that the formless takes form....
—*Darwin Gross*

What is an idea? It is an image that paints itself in my brain....
—*Voltaire*

Imagination grows by exercise, and contrary to common belief, it is more powerful in the mature than in the young.... —*Somerset Maugham*

A prison is never narrow when the imagination can range in it as it will....
—*Marguerite of Navarre*

We are what we pretend to be, so we must be careful about what we pretend to be.... —*Kurt Vonnegut*

Operate out of your imagination, not your memory.... —*Les Brown*

Imagination alone is the life of language. Take away this imaginary relationship between name and object, and you will find that language is dead and useless....
—*Janardan Paramahansa*

The mind, without imagination, would be as useless as an observatory without a telescope.... —*Fred Van Amburgh*

People suffer more in imagination than they do in reality.... —*Anonymous*

The great instrument of moral good is the imagination.... —*Percy B. Shelley*

Imagination is the ruler of our dreams.... —*William B. Clulow*

True imagination is not fanciful daydreaming; it is fire from heaven.... —*Ernest Holmes*

The faculty of imagination is the great spring of human activity, and the principal source of human improvement....Destroy this faculty, and the condition of man will become as stationary as that of the brutes.... —*Dugald Stewart*

We should not ignore the fact that it is left to us either to use or misuse our mind and imagination. One who seeks God and depends upon God, who trains his imagination to correspond with Divine imagination....lives in a condition of peace and harmony.... —*Henry T. Hamblin*

Imagination has the capability to choose pain and disorder in the same measure as it does goodness and order.... —*Anonymous*

Man surrounds himself with true image of himself. Every spirit builds itself a house and beyond its house a world, and beyond its world a heaven.... —*Ralph W. Emerson*

Imagination is more important than knowledge.... —*Albert Einstein*

The highest and best work of imagination is the marvelous transformation that it works in character. Imagine that you are one with the Principle of good, and you will become truly good.... —*Charles Fillmore*

Man consists of body, mind and imagination. His body is faulty, his mind untrustworthy, but his imagination has made him remarkable.... —*John Masefield*

Your imaginings can have as much power over you as your reality, or even more.... —*Charles T. Tart*

The world of reality has its limits; the world of imagination is boundless.... —*Jean J. Rousseau*

Solitude is as needful to the imagination as society is wholesome for the character.... —*James Russell Lowell*

Once you know with abundant certainty that nothing can trouble you but your own imagination, you come to disregard your desires and fears, concepts and ideas, and live by truth alone.... —*Nisargadatta*

Imagination is as good as many voyages—and how much cheaper.... —*George W. Curtis*

Believe that you shall receive and you shall receive.... —*Jesus*

Imagination is the real and eternal world of which this vegetable universe is but a faint shadow....The eternal body of man is the imagination: that is God himself, the Divine Body.... —*William Blake*

Imagination is the first step in creation whether in words or trifles. The mental pattern must always precede the material form.... —*William W. Atkinson*

When the will and imagination are in conflict, the imagination invariably wins the day.... —*Emile Coue*

Imitation

I f the blind lead the blind both shall fall into the ditch....   —*Jesus*

Great bodies of people are never responsible for what they do....
—*Virginia Woolf*

If you live long enough with the lame, you will find yourself walking with a limp....   —*Anonymous*

The faint-hearted and indifferent are those who follow the current of public opinion, and are incapable of any movement by themselves....
—*Eliphas Levi*

There is a time in every man's education when he arrives at the conviction that envy is ignorance; that imitation is suicide; that he must take himself for better or worse as his portion....   —*Ralph W. Emerson*

Remember this: a man flattened by an opponent can get up again. A man flattened by conformity stays down for good....   —*Thomas J. Watson*

Conformity is the jailer of freedom and the enemy of growth....
—*John F. Kennedy*

Man's natural character is to imitate; that of a sensitive man is to resemble as closely as possible the person whom he loves....   —*Marquis de Sade*

Imitation affords only a temporary advantage. Things must be real to endure....He who imitates another most likely lacks individuality....
—*Fred Van Amburgh*

Men nearly always follow the tracks made by others in their affairs by imitation....   —*Niccolo Machiavelli*

Let's not imitate others. Let's find ourselves and be ourselves....
—*Dale Carnegie*

We forfeit our uniqueness by compromising and making concessions, today in this matter, tomorrow in another, according to the dictates of the world—by never contradicting the world, and by always following public opinion....
—*Vincent Van Gogh*

Following along with the crowd is always a sign of immaturity. When you are mature, you live according to your highest light, you lead the way, you are a pioneer....   —*Peace Pilgrim*

The most complete revenge is not to imitate the aggressor....
—*Marcus Aurelius*

We forfeit three-quarters of ourselves in order to be like other people....
—*Arthur Schopenhauer*

He who follows another sees nothing, learns nothing, nay, seeks nothing....
—*William Osler*

The wise man never imitates any action....   —*Bhagavad-Gita*

To admire on principle is the only way to imitate without loss of originality....
—*Samuel T. Coleridge*

Don't drop to the level of others. Let them go on eating dung while you just speak the holy name in your heart....
—*Kabir*

No man ever yet became great by imitation....   —*Samuel Johnson*

Where there is much pretension, much has been borrowed: nature never pretends....It is a poor wit who lives by borrowing the words, decisions, mien, inventions, and actions of others....
—*John K. Lavater*

Most people are other people. Their thoughts are someone else's opinions, their lives a mimicry.... —*Oscar Wilde*

He who imitates evil always goes beyond the example that is set; he who imitates what is good always falls short.... —*Francesco Guicciardini*

We are more than half what we are by imitation. The great point is to choose good models and to study them with care.... —*G. K. Chesterton*

We imitate only what we believe and admire.... —*Robert A. Willmott*

Insist on yourself; never imitate....
—*Ralph W. Emerson*

Everything in this world can be imitated; except truth, for truth that is imitated is no longer truth....
—*Mendel of Kotzk*

To do exactly the opposite is also a form of imitation.... —*Georg C. Lichtenberg*

We fail most frequently when we seek a goal by someone else's path. We stumble most trying to walk the other fellow's way.... —*Norman C. Schidle*

One should respect public opinion insofar as is necessary to avoid starvation and to keep out of prison, but anything that goes beyond this is voluntary submission to an unnecessary tyranny.... —*Bertrand Russell*

There is nothing to be gained by copying others.... —*Polish proverb*

Imitation causes us to leave natural ways to enter into artificial ones; it therefore makes us slaves....
—*Alexander Vinet*

Mediocrity finds reassurance in conformity.... —*Anonymous*

There is a difference between imitating a good man and counterfeiting him....
—*Benjamin Franklin*

Immortality/ Eternity

The average man, who does not know what to do with this life, wants another, one which shall last forever.... —*Anatole France*

You may tell me that my hand and foot are only imaginary symbols of my existence. I could believe you, but you never, never can convince me that the I is not an eternal reality, and that the spiritual is not the true and real part of me.... —*Alfred L. Tennyson*

Let us live as if we were immortal....
—*Aristotle*

Eternity is called whole, not because it has parts, but because it is lacking in nothing.... —*Thomas Aquinas*

Eternity has neither beginning nor end.... —*Eliphas Levi*

Eternity is not something that begins after you are dead. It is going on all the time. We are in it now....
—*Charlotte P. Gilman*

The longing to be so helps make the soul immortal.... —*James Russell Lowell*

We feel and know that we are eternal....
—*Baruch Spinoza*

Man is just a bridge between two eternities, the eternity of nature and the eternity of God....
—*Friedrich W. Nietzsche*

I find it natural to believe that death is not a disastrous sundown but rather a spiritual sunrise, ushering in the unconjectured splendors of immortality...
—*Archibald Rutledge*

Man, tree, and flower are supposed to die; but the fact remains that God's universe is spiritual and immortal....
—*Mary Baker Eddy*

There is no hurry. You are eternal. If you forget something in this life, there will be plenty of time again....
—*Emmanuel*

Expect no greater happiness in Eternity, than to rejoice in God....
—*Benjamin Whichcote*

The man who refuses firmly to entertain the hope of immortality....is no more brave and realistic than a man who refuses to open the door of his dark room and come out into the sunshine....
—*D. G. M. Jackson*

Neither experience nor science has given man the idea of immortality....The idea of immortality rises from the very depths of his soul—he feels, he sees, he knows that he is immortal....
—*Francois Guizot*

The power behind every activity of nature and of man is the power of God. To realize this truth is to be immortal....
—*The Upanishads*

The soul of man is immortal....
—*Benjamin Franklin*

Our own death is indeed unimaginable, and whenever we make the attempt to imagine it we can perceive that we really survive as spectators. Hence....at the bottom no one believes in his own death, or to put the same thing in another way, in the consciousness every one of us is convinced of his own immortality....
—*Sigmund Freud*

Your essence was not born and will not die....
—*Bassui*

Death is not the end; the earthly body vanishes, the immortal spirit lives on with God....
—*Union Prayer Book*

Total annihilation is impossible. We are prisoners of an infinity without outlet, wherein nothing perishes, wherein everything is dispersed but nothing lost. Neither a body nor a thought can drop out of the universe, out of time and space....
—*Maurice Maeterlinck*

Eternity is not the hereafter....This is it. If you don't get it here, you won't get it anywhere....
—*Joseph Campbell*

Everyone carries the proof of immortality within himself, and quite involuntarily....
—*Johann W. Goethe*

Eternity has no end, therefore no beginning; consequently eternity is a circle....
—*Anana*

All men's souls are immortal, but the souls of the righteous are both immortal and divine....
—*Socrates*

Your mind does not know you are immortal, although it may believe if it has been taught. Only through an awakening of your divine nature will you know that you are immortal....
—*Peace Pilgrim*

The sum of all sums is eternity....
—*Lucretius*

If there is anything in me that is of permanent worth and service to the universe, the universe will know how to preserve it.... —*Horace J. Bridges*

The few years we spend on earth are only the first scene in a Divine Drama that extends on into Eternity....
—*Edwin Markham*

Without a belief in personal immortality, religion is like an arch resting on one pillar, or like a bridge ending in an abyss.... —*Max Muller*

Deprived of the hope for immortality, man....is the most wretched being on earth.... —*Moses Mendelssohn*

In the presence of eternity, the mountains are as transient as the clouds.... —*Robert Ingersoll*

It is immortality, and that alone, which amid life's pains....the soul can comfort, elevate and fill.... —*Edward Young*

Immortality, to me, is the continuity of our spiritual existence after death. Since the dawn of history man has believed in immortality....
—*Werner Von Braun*

It is eternity now. I am in the midst of it. It is about me in the sunshine; I am in it, as the butterfly in the light-laden air. Nothing has to come, it is now. Now is eternity; now is the immortal life....
—*Richard Jefferies*

There is only one way to get ready for immortality, and that is to love this life and live it as bravely and faithfully and cheerfully as we can....
—*Henry van Dyke*

The created world is but a small parenthesis in eternity....
—*Thomas Browne*

There can be no purity in anything that is not everlasting.... —*Hermes*

The spirit of man, which God inspired, cannot together perish with this corporeal clod.... —*John Milton*

I believe in immortality....because its denial seems to me to lend the entire race in a hopeless situation....
—*Harry E. Fosdick*

Nothing but beauty and wisdom deserve immortality.... —*Will Durant*

Eternity has no gray hairs. The flowers fade, the heart withers, man grows old and dies, the world lies down in the sepulchre of ages, but time writes no wrinkles on the brow of eternity....
—*Reginald Heber*

What we call eternity may be but an endless series of transitions which men call deaths, abandonments of home, going ever to fairer scenes and loftier heights.... —*Edmund Bulwer-Lytton*

No man can pass into eternity, for he is already in it.... —*Frederic Farrar*

God created man to be immortal, and made him in the image of his own eternity....
—*Apocrypha: Wisdom of Solomon*

In our quiet moments, when we are not relating to traditional thinking patterns, we are certain of our own immortality and of the promise life holds for us. We know that we did not begin at conception, and that we will not end when the body is no longer able to serve our needs....
—*Roy E. Davis*

Whatsoever that be within us that feels, thinks, desires, and animates, is something celestial, divine, and consequently, imperishable....

—*Aristotle*

Nothing is eternal but the laws of God.... —*Allan Kardec*

When we leave this plane of experience, I think we graduate to the next phase of our ongoingness of life itself. And we continue by stages. For example, in the first grade we didn't have to know everything perfectly, but we had to know enough to get into the second grade, and so on from there, building on what we learned. That's my picture of what immortality is all about.... —*H. Frederick Vogt*

Immortality is the belief in the worthlessness and nothingness of this life.... —*Ludwig A. Feuerback*

I am a better believer, and all serious souls are better believers, in immortality than we can give grounds for....The blazing evidence of immortality is our dissatisfaction with any other solution.... —*Ralph W. Emerson*

Immortality is the great world of light that lies behind all human destinies....

—*Henry W. Longfellow*

Journey

H e that will not sail until all dangers are over, will never put to sea.... —*Thomas Fuller*

Do you know....Where you are....On your journey?... —*Deng Ming-Dao*

Don't be afraid to take a big step if one is indicated. You can't cross a chasm in two small jumps.... —*David L. George*

If you want to go east, don't go west....

—*Ramakrishna*

Whenever I prepare for a journey I prepare for death. Should I never return; all is in order. This is what life has taught me.... —*Katherine Mansfield*

Whether we know it or not, we are all on a journey beyond belief....

—*Roger Walsh*

The path to God is not an easy one. You have to make your mind and intellect absolutely pure.... —*Papa Ramdas*

Every part of an element separated from its mass desires to return to it by the shortest way....

—*Leonardo Da Vinci*

The true path is through the sky and so has no landmarks and no description. All described paths are but tracing on the earth the shadow of one who has gone in the sky....It is a difficult, a heartbreaking path. None can tread it to the end who does not want it more than he wants any other thing....

—*Krishnaprem*

You do not travel the pilgrim's path alone, forsaken, or unaided. He who sent you is still with you. He has not left you alone.... —*Elinor MacDonald*

What a long journey! What a lot of trouble! Especially considering that I was there all the time.... —*Kuleki*

To reach the port of heaven, we must sail sometimes with the wind and sometimes against it—but we must sail, and not drift, nor lie at anchor....

—*Oliver W. Holmes*

It is strange that though all must tread the path of life, so few know whither they are going! We wander from cradle to the tomb, yet know not our true destination which is not the tomb but rather the discovery of our "Super-Self."...
    —*Pierre Schmidt*

If you don't see the path that meets your eye how will your feet know the way?...   —*Shitou*

The last laps of all paths are the same—surrender of the ego....
    —*Ramana Maharshi*

Two roads diverged in a wood, and I—I took the one least traveled by, and that has made all the difference....
    —*Robert Frost*

It is not enough to know the way; we must travel it....   —*Alice H. Rice*

One can only make progress on the spiritual path if one is prepared to give up all one's attachments....
    —*Annamalai Swami*

When you go on a pilgrimage, it directs the mind towards God. But remember—God is within....   —*Yoga Swami*

The distance is nothing: it is only the first step that is difficult....
    —*Marie A. du Deffand*

There is no glimpse of the light without walking the path. You can't get it from anyone else, nor can you give it to anyone. You take whatever steps seem easiest for you, and as you take a few steps it will be easier to take a few more....
    —*Peace Pilgrim*

Do not follow a path. Follow your own footsteps. Your path will create itself....
    —*Paul Williams*

The real voyage of discovery consists not in seeking new landscapes but in seeing with new eyes....—*Marcel Proust*

The path is smooth that leadeth onto danger....   —*William Shakespeare*

Not I, not anyone else, can travel that road for you. You must travel it yourself....   —*Walt Whitman*

There is no such thing as a spiritual journey; what there is, is a spiritual awakening....   —*Anonymous*

Buddha left a road map, Jesus left a road map, Krishna left a road map, Rand McNally left a road map. But you still have to travel the road yourself....
    —*Stephin Levine*

The spiritual journey is individual, highly personal. It can't be organized or regulated. It isn't true that everybody should follow one path. Listen to your own truth....   —*Ram Dass*

Like the sharp edge of a razor, the sages say, is the path. Narrow it is, and difficult to tread....
    —*The Upanishads*

You are constantly being sent signs from the universe about what path to take....   —*Sanaya Roman*

Genuine beginnings begin within us, even when they are brought to our attention by external opportunities....
    —*William Bridges*

To journey hopefully is better than to arrive....   —*Chinese proverb*

A tree as big around as you can reach starts with a small seed; a journey of a thousand miles begins with a single step....   —*Lao-tzu*

Life is a pilgrimage where man drags his feet along the rough and thorny road....There is no stopping-place in this pilgrimage....When the road ends, and the Goal is gained the pilgrim finds that he has traveled only from himself to himself.... —*Sathya Sai Baba*

The life of man is a journey that must be traveled, however bad the roads or the accommodations....
—*Oliver Goldsmith*

What we call the beginning is often the end and to make our end is to make the beginning. The end is where we start from.... —*T. S. Eliot*

True progress quietly and persistently moves along without notice....
—*Francis de Sales*

For a small reward a man will hurry away on a long journey, while for eternal life many will hardly take a single step.... —*Thomas à Kempis*

Wide is the gate, and broad is the way, that leads to destruction, and many there be who go that way, because straigth is the gate, and narrow is the way, which leads to life, and few there be that find it.... —*Jesus*

Let us watch well our beginnings, and the results will manage themselves....
—*Alex Clark*

There is a path to walk on, there is walking being done, but there is no traveler. There are deeds being done, but there is no doer....
—*Gautama Buddha*

The spiritual path is one of falling on your face, getting up, brushing yourself off, turning and looking sheepishly at God and then taking the next step....
—*Aurobindo*

Transformation is a journey without a final destination....
—*Marilyn Ferguson*

The path of the seeker is full of pitfalls and temptations, and the seeker must walk it alone with God. I would recommend that you keep your feet on the ground and your thoughts at lofty heights.... —*Peace Pilgrim*

The journey is in yourself. You travel along the highways of the inner world. Without inner movement it is impossible to bring forth anything....The inner journey must never be without direction.... —*Darwin Gross*

Two persons may be traveling side by side in the same direction with perhaps even a common destination. Yet both may be marching on variant paths. How is this possible? If one is marching uphill and the other downhill then they are traveling in dissimilar dimensions and are only side by side for a short length of time.... —*Shantidasa*

What is the use of going over the old track again?...You must make tracks into the unknown....
—*Henry D. Thoreau*

The world stands aside to let anyone pass who knows where he is going....
—*David S. Jordan*

The longest journey is the journey inward.... —*Dag Hammarskjöld*

People who are far from God think they are very near to Him, when they take a few steps to approach him....
—*Francois Fenelon*

What is the path? Everyday life is the path.... —*Nansen*

A fool beholds only the beginnings of his works, but a wise man taketh heed to the end....
—*Anonymous*

He travels the fastest who travels alone....
—*Rudyard Kipling*

The spiritual quest is a journey without distance. You travel from where you are right now to where you have always been. From ignorance to recognition....
—*Anthony de Mello*

You speak of paths as if you were somewhere and the Self somewhere else and you had to go and attain it. But in fact the Self is here and now and you are it always....
—*Ramana Maharshi*

Long is the road from conception to completion....
—*Jean B. Moliere*

The first step is what counts: First beginnings are hardest to make and as small and inconspicuous as they are potent in influence, but once they are made, it is easy to add to the rest....
—*Aristotle*

To take a journey of a thousand miles, you have to begin with the first step from the place where you stand; the romantic description of the journey and the things the body sees on the way and the description of the scenery are of no use unless you lift your foot and take the first step....
—*Vimala Thakar*

Any path is only a path, and there is no affront, to oneself or to others, in dropping it if that is what your heart tells you....
—*Carlos Castaneda*

It is good to have an end to journey towards; but it is the journey that matters in the end....
—*Ursula LeGuin*

From of old there were not two paths. "Those who have arrived" all walked the same road....
—*Zenrin*

Sometimes, mistakes or unforeseen circumstances can knock our roads so far off-course that it might be easier and more productive to change our destinations....
—*Lois Wolfe-Morgan*

If you do not know the way, seek where His footprints are....
—*Rumi*

We think we must climb to a certain height of goodness before we can reach God. But He says not, "At the end of the way you may find me." He says, "I am the Way; I am the road under your feet, the road that begins just as low down as you happen to be."...
—*Helen Wodehouse*

Weary the path that does not challenge....
—*Hosea Ballou*

You will never stub your toe standing still. The faster you go, the more chance of stubbing your toe, but the more chance you have of getting somewhere....
—*Charles F. Kettering*

The magnetic needle always points toward the north, and hence the sailing vessel does not lose her course. So long as the heart of man is directed towards God, he cannot be lost in the ocean of worldliness....
—*Ramakrishna*

For thirty years I went in search of God, and when I opened my eyes at the end of this time, I discovered that it was really He who sought for me....
—*Bayazid al-Bistami*

Where there is no road, a new road must be trodden....
—*Joseph Hurwitz*

To travel hopefully is better than to arrive, and the true success is labor....
—*Robert L. Stevenson*

In order to know what lies on the road ahead, it might be well to question those travelers who are making their way back.... —*Anonymous*

Let no one be deluded that a knowledge of the path can substitute for putting one foot in front of the other.... —*M. C. Richards*

Many roads lead to God. Travel any one of them you like and I'm sure you'll come within God's reach.... —*Claud H. Foster*

The happiest journey is not made with downcast eyes which see only tired, dusty feet. It is made with uplifted sight to appreciate the visible panorama, and with imagination to understand its significance and to picture what may be beyond.... —*Edward B. Newill*

One step makes the next one easier; that is the excellence of the spiritual journey. At each step, your strength and confidence increase and you get bigger and bigger installments of Grace.... —*Sathya Sai Baba*

No two human beings have made, or ever will make, exactly the same journey in life.... —*Arthur Keith*

As long as you are outside the door, a good portion of the journey is behind you.... —*Scandinavian saying*

The road to pleasure is downhill and very easy, so that one does not walk but is dragged along; the way of self-control is uphill, toilsome no doubt, but exceedingly profitable.... —*Philo*

The true way goes over a rope which is not stretched at any great length, but just over the ground. It is more designed to make people stumble than to be walked on.... —*Franz Kafka*

The man who is strong, who has resolved to find the unknown path, takes with utmost care every step. He utters no idle word, he does no unconsidered action, he neglects no duty or office however homely or however difficult.... —*Mabel Collins*

There is no road too long to the man who advances deliberately and without undue haste; there are no honors too distant to the man who prepares himself for them with patience.... —*Jean La Bruyere*

And how, you ask, are we to walk the spiritual path? We answer: say little, and love much; give all; judge no man; aspire to all that is pure and good.... —*White Eagle*

Know the universe itself as a road, as many roads, as roads for traveling souls.... —*Walt Whitman*

As we progress along the spiritual path we meet with the tests of our apprenticeship. Before each step forward there is always the testing time. When it arrives, if we do not falter, and, above all, do not think that it is evil, or that we have done something wrong, or that we are suffering from an injustice, we find it is all good.... —*Henry T. Hamblin*

There is a well-worn road which is pleasing to the senses and gratifies worldly desires, but leads to nowhere. And there is a less traveled path, which requires purifications and relinquishments, but results in untold spiritual blessings.... —*Peace Pilgrim*

At the beginning of the spiritual path, we are like children whose only real knowledge of themselves is a reflection cast in a mirror.... —*Rick Fields*

My path hitherto has been like a road through diversified country, now climbing high mountains, then descending into the vales. From the summits I saw the heavens; from the vales I look up at the heights again....
—*Henry D. Thoreau*

You must dare to disassociate yourself from those who would delay your journey....Leave, depart, if not physically, than mentally. Go your own way, quietly, undramatically, and venture toward trueness at last....
—*Vernon Howard*

To set one's face in the right direction, and then simply travel on, will in time bring one into the realization of the highest life that can even be conceived of—it is the secret of all attainment....
—*Ralph W. Trine*

God leaves man free to choose his road; so much the worst for him if he takes the wrong one; his pilgrimage will be all the longer....   —*Allan Kardec*

I would rather walk with God in the dark then go alone in the light....
—*Mary G. Brainard*

Joy

The world is not a hell. It is all bliss when ego and likes and dislikes die away....   —*Sivananda*

The lucky folks are the ones who get to do things they enjoy doing....
—*Jerome Kern*

One joy scatters a hundred griefs....
—*Chinese proverb*

Joy is the serious business of Heaven....
—*C. S. Lewis*

I cannot believe that the inscrutable universe turns on an axis of suffering; surely the strange beauty of the world must somewhere rest in pure joy....
—*Louise Bogan*

To pursue joy is to lose it....
—*Alexander Maclaren*

Spirit is never somber. Weeping with the afflicted does not help. It may create a point of contact, but it does not bring a remedy. Joy is the antidote for sorrow....   —*Paramananda*

Real joy comes not from ease or riches or from the praise of men, but from doing something worthwhile....
—*W. T. Grenfell*

Joy is not in things, it is in us....
—*Charles Wagner*

Within your own house dwells the treasury of joy; so why do you go begging from door to door?...
—*Sufi saying*

Joy comes not through possession or ownership but through a wise and loving heart....   —*Jack Kornfield*

All days are one long laugh, all nights one joy, all life one opulence and affluence....   —*S. Nazir*

Joy is the happiness of love—love aware of its own inner happiness. Pleasure comes from without, and joy comes from within, and it is, therefore, within reach of everyone in the world....
—*Fulton J. Sheen*

To get the full value from joy you must have someone to divide it with....
—*Mark Twain*

If you have a long face and a chip on your shoulder, if you are not radiant with joy and friendliness, if you are not filled to overflowing with love and goodwill for all beings....one thing is certain: you do not know God....
—*Peace Pilgrim*

The best way to show gratitude to God is to accept everything with joy. A joyful heart is the inevitable result of a heart burning with love....
—*Mother Teresa*

Rejoice in your strength, rejoice in your talents and powers, rejoice in the wonders of your own nature. For there is far more in you than you ever dreamed....　—*Christian D. Larson*

Joys are our wings; sorrows our spurs....
—*Jean Paul Richter*

Even if you put all the pleasures of the entire world together in one great heap, they say that the ultimate bliss that each individual soul is destined to attain, even one little portion of that bliss, far outweighs the total pleasure that this world is capable of giving....
—*Chidananda*

The soul sings all the time, joy and sweetness are her garments....
—*Abraham Kook*

Ancient Egyptians believed that upon death they would be asked....two questions and their answers would determine whether they could continue their journey in the afterlife. The first question was, "Did you bring joy?" The second was, "Did you find joy?"...
—*Leo Buscaglia*

The secret is, discover the fountain of joy within; that is a never-failing, ever-full, ever-cool fountain, for it arises from God....　—*Sathya Sai Baba*

We all carry it within us: supreme strength, the fullness of wisdom, unquenchable joy. It is never thwarted and cannot be destroyed. But it is hidden deep, which is what makes life a problem....　—*Huston Smith*

Joy is the fruit of the spirit....
—*New Testament*

True enjoyment cannot be expressed in words....　—*Jean J. Rousseau*

The less you can enjoy, the poorer and scantier yourself; the more you can enjoy, the richer and more vigorous....
—*John K. Lavater*

People are always good company when they are doing what they really enjoy....
—*Samuel Butler*

All who would win joy must share it; happiness was born a twin....
—*George Byron*

Great joy....is apt to be silent, and dwells rather in the heart than on the tongue....　—*Henry Fielding*

He who enjoys doing and enjoys what he has done is happy....
—*Johann W. Goethe*

Shared joy is double joy....
—*Swedish proverb*

Lack of joyfulness in our daily tasks brings fatigue, distress and body destroying toxins....　—*Cheryl Canfield*

All the world is searching for joy and happiness, but these cannot be purchased for any price in any marketplace, because they are virtues that come from within....
—*Lucille R. Taylor*

Where there is joy and poverty, there is neither greed and avarice....
—*Francis of Assisi*

There are some people who have the quality of richness and joy in them and they communicate it to everything they touch. It is first of all a physical quality; then it is a quality of the spirit....
—*Thomas C. Wolfe*

Joy follows when our inmost selves imprint their energy on passing events....We see such joy about us in those who are able to work, even at humdrum tasks, with grace of heart and mind.... —*David Seabury*

It is fun to keep focused on the vision of our perfection. It's fun to deal in Reality instead of playing games. And it's fun to see people's light and not their lampshades.... —*Ruth Hanna*

Joy is an elation of spirit—of a spirit which trusts in the goodness and truth of its own possessions.... —*Seneca*

How could one know God and not be joyous?... —*Peace Pilgrim*

The happy man is....the man who, without any direct search for happiness, inevitably finds joy as an added bonus in the act of forging ahead and attaining the fullness and finality of his own self.... —*Teilhard de Chardin*

Joy is more divine than sorrow, for joy is bread and sorrow is medicine....
—*Henry W. Beecher*

Joy consumes time more quickly, not so grief. When men are in joy, time passes fast; when they are in grief, it moves slow.... —*Sathya Sai Baba*

Joy is the echo of God's life within us....
—*Joseph Marmion*

There's only one reason why you're not experiencing bliss at this present moment, and it's because you're thinking or focusing on what you don't have.... —*Anthony de Mello*

Joy of life seems to arise from a sense of being where one belongs....All the discontented people I know are trying sedulously to be something they are not, to do something they cannot do....
—*David Grayson*

Joy is....to will what God wills, to want what He wants.... —*Meister Eckhart*

Joy is very infectious; therefore, be always full of joy.... —*Mother Teresa*

Joy is the feeling of grinning inside....
—*Melba Colgrove*

Judgement

Every man has a right to be valued at his best moment....
—*Ralph W. Emerson*

To judge is to see clearly, to care for what is just and therefore to be impartial, more exactly, to be disinterested, more exactly still, to be impersonal..... —*Henri F. Amiel*

Judge a tree from its fruit, not from the leaves.... —*Euripides*

Virtually all people are a mixture of good and bad. It is very rare to find someone wholly good or wholly bad. If you have to come into contact with a lot of people, try to make yourself aware of their good points and don't dwell on their bad points....
—*Annamalai Swami*

Prejudice does not think logically. It does not ask why, and remains on the deceptive surface. The mark of the sage is the lack of prejudice, that of a fool, the lack of thought....
—*Hans-Ulrich Rieker*

Whoever undertakes to set himself up as a judge of Truth and Knowledge is shipwrecked by the laughter of the gods....   —*Albert Einstein*

Judgement always rests in the past, for past experience is the basis on which you judge. Judgement becomes impossible without the past, for without it you do not understand anything....
—*A Course In Miracles*

Judgements are beliefs about the past that lead us away from the here-and-now....   —*Anonymous*

Duty largely consists of pretending that the trivial is critical....   —*John Fowles*

When the need to be right is a driving force instead of just a preference, it is very heavy baggage....   —*Judith Sills*

You should not say it is not good. You should say you do not like it, and then, you know, you're perfectly safe....
—*James M. Whistler*

We turn to using quantities when we can't compare the qualities....
—*Marvin Minsky*

When you pass judgement on your essence, who is doing the judging? The answer is, some part of you that is not your essence: your opinions, your thoughts, your habits, your fears....
—*Paul Williams*

Judge a man by his questions rather than by his answers....   —*Voltaire*

As we persist in judging one another by what we appear to be, we are all taking part in a great masquerade....
—*Joel Goldsmith*

The judgement of God shall turn topsy-turvy the judgements of men....
—*Edward F. Garesche*

You judge by human standards, I judge no one....   —*Jesus*

The less harshly we judge ourselves, the more accepting we become of others....   —*Harold Bloomfield*

All that glitters is not gold....
—*John Dryden*

Judging others will avail you nothing and injure you spiritually. Only if you can inspire others to judge themselves will anything worthwhile have been accomplished. When you approach others in judgement they will be on the defensive. When you are able to approach them in a kindly, loving manner without judgement they will tend to judge themselves and be transformed....   —*Peace Pilgrim*

No man can judge another, because no man knows himself....
—*Thomas Browne*

Examine the contents of the bottle, not the bottle....   —*The Talmud*

Constantly I am having to fight and overcome my prejudices because I realize that first impressions and judgements are often misleading....
—*Harvey Day*

Man measures everything by his own experiences; he has no other yardstick....
—*Dorothy L. Sayers*

We do not judge men by what they are in themselves, but what they are relatively to us.... —*Ann S. Swetchine*

Actions will be judged according to intentions.... —*Mohammed*

It is wrong, it is sinful, to consider some people lower than ourselves.... —*Mohandas Gandhi*

Wisdom is not to be found in making divisions and comparisons.... —*Maitreya*

Men are not to be judged by their looks, habits and appearances; but by the character of their lives and conversations, and by their works.... —*Roger L'Estrange*

All general judgements are loose and imperfect.... —*Michel Montaigne*

Every person's map of the world is as unique as their thumbprint. There are no two people alike. No two people who understand the same sentence the same way....So in dealing with people you try not to fit them to your concept of what they should be.... —*Milton Erickson*

While man judges another from his own moral standpoint, the wise man looks also at the point of view of another.... —*Hazrat Inayat Khan*

In judging of others a man laboreth in vain....How seldom we weigh our neighbor in the same balance with ourselves.... —*Thomas à Kempis*

Observe things as they are and don't pay attention to other people.... —*Huang Po*

Appearances often are deceiving.... —*Aesop*

Foolish men imagine that because judgement for an evil is delayed, there is no judgement.... —*Thomas Carlyle*

We judge ourselves by what we feel capable of doing, while others judge us by what we have already done.... —*Henry W. Longfellow*

Human nature is so constituted, that we see and judge better in the affairs of others more than in our own.... —*Terence*

The soul's impurity consists in bad judgements, and purification consists in producing right judgements, and the pure soul is one which has right judgements.... —*Epictetus*

We must never undervalue any person.... —*Francis de Sales*

I have never for one instant seen clearly within myself. How then would you have me judge the deeds of others?... —*Maurice Maeterlinck*

God casts no soul away, unless it casts itself away. Every soul is its own judgement.... —*Jakob Böhme*

It is much more ennobling to the human spirit to let people judge themselves than to judge them.... —*Stephen R.Covey*

You may judge a flower or a butterfly by its looks, but not a human being....(Only) fools judge men by their outside.... —*Rabindranath Tagore*

Everything that exists in the world does so independently of your opinion about it.... —*Wayne Dyer*

The thought of judgement, criticism and condemnation must, in time, operate against the one who sets it into motion.... —*Ernest Holmes*

To prove yourself right is just another way to prove another person wrong....
—*Anonymous*

When you judge people, you have no time to love them.... —*Mother Teresa*

The Great Way is not difficult—just cease to cherish opinions....
—*Third Zen Patriarch*

Great Spirit, grant that I may not judge my neighbor until I have walked a mile in his moccasins....
—*American Indian prayer*

Withhold judgement and criticism. The human way is to judge in haste the actions of others, but the divine way is to remain quiet and loving....
—*White Eagle*

Thankfulness is an antidote to judgement.... —*Michael Exeter*

Judge not, and you shall not be judged; condemn not and you shall not be condemned; forgive, and you shall be forgiven.... —*Jesus*

Enjoy your life without comparing it with that of others....
—*Marquis de Condorcet*

The superior man does not set his mind either for or against anything....
—*Confucius*

We should hesitate to pronounce judgement on the conduct of.... eminent men, lest we fall into the common error of condemning what we do not understand.... —*Quintilian*

We are all wise when we admonish others, and yet we know not when we trip ourselves.... —*Euripides*

It is a sin to call a person a sinner....
—*Vivekananda*

When you demand justice for yourself, you demand it for the whole race. If you allow yourself to be dominated, brow-beaten or cheated by others without inward or outward protest, you are condoning deceit and trickery. You are in league with it....
—*Prentice Mulford*

One man's word is no man's word; we should quietly hear both sides....
—*Johann W. Goethe*

There is a criterion by which you can judge whether the thoughts you are thinking and the things you are doing are right for you. The criterion is: Have they brought you inner peace?...
—*Peace Pilgrim*

Judgement consists not in seeing through deceptions and evil intentions, but in being able to awaken the decency dormant in every person....
—*Eric Hoffer*

The perfect way is difficult for those who pick and choose. We should not like, nor should we dislike, and all will become clear... —*Sen Ts'an*

Kindness/ Gentleness

Life is not so short but that there is always time enough for courtesy....
—*Ralph W. Emerson*

Kindness costs nothing....
—*Irish proverb*

There is no strength that compares to that of gentleness.... —*Anonymous*

Civility costs nothing and buys everything.... —*Mary W. Montagu*

The motto of a gentle man might well be, "I must never force things."...
—*Adrian van Kaam*

Always meet petulance with gentleness, and perverseness with kindness. A gentle hand can lead even an elephant by a hair. Reply to thine enemy with gentleness. Opposition to peace is sin....
—*Zoroaster*

True kindness presupposes the faculty of imagining as one's own the suffering and joys of others....
—*André Gide*

One can always be kind to people about whom one cares nothing....
—*Oscar Wilde*

The greatest things in life are the ordinary, everyday humanities: Speaking kindly to people, speaking kindly of people, doing kindness for people....
—*Fred Van Amburgh*

What wisdom can you find that is greater than kindness?...
—*Jean J. Rousseau*

One kind word can warm three winter nights....
—*Oriental saying*

Kindness in words creates confidence. Kindness in thinking creates profoundness. Kindness in giving creates love....
—*Lao-tzu*

Gentleness is not a quality exclusive to women....
—*Helen Reddy*

Nobody appears inferior to us when our heart is kindled with kindness....
—*Hazrat Inayat Khan*

Kind words can be short and easy to speak but their echoes are truly endless....
—*Mother Teresa*

If you stop to be kind, you must swerve often from your path....
—*Mary Webb*

Speak kindly today; when tomorrow comes you will be in practice....
—*Proverb*

It is nature's kindness that we do not remember past births....
—*Mohandas Gandhi*

Kindness is the root of righteousness. Kindness is the enemy of cruelty, harshness, rudeness. It softens the heart. It opens the door to heaven....
—*Sivananda*

Let us be kinder to one another....
—*Aldous Huxley*

Be straightforward, yet mild; gentle, yet dignified; strong, but untyrannical; energetic, but not arrogant; tolerant, yet stern; mild, yet firm....
—*Shu King*

Kindness is the mightiest practical force in the universe....
—*Charles F. Dole*

The highest form of wisdom is kindness....
—*The Talmud*

Let us open up our natures, throw wide the doors of our hearts and let in the sunshine of good will and kindness....
—*Orison S. Marden*

The best portion of a good man's life is his little, nameless, unremembered acts of kindness....
—*William Wordsworth*

Gentleness can only come when we think of God's greatness. Because we forget Him, our pride raises its head....
—*Papa Ramdas*

Kindness is the beginning and the end of the law....
—*Hebrew proverb*

I suspect to pass through life but once. If therefore there be any kindness I can show, or any good thing I can do to my fellow-being, let me do it now, and not defer or neglect it, as I shall not pass this way again.... —*William Penn*

Kindness is gladdening the hearts of those who are traveling in the dark with us.... —*Henri F. Amiel*

Paradise is open to all kind hearts.... —*Pierre de Beranger*

Kind words are the music of the world. They have a power which seems to be beyond natural causes, as if they were some angel's song which had lost its way and come to earth.... —*Frederich W. Faber*

You cannot do a kindness too soon, for you never know how soon it will be too late.... —*Ralph W. Emerson*

Kindness is a language the dumb can speak and deaf can hear.... —*Christian Bovee*

Kindness is a golden chain by which society is bound together.... —*Johann W. Goethe*

A kind heart is a fountain of gladness, making everything in its vicinity freshen into smiles.... —*Washington Irving*

A word of kindness is seldom spoken in vain.... —*George Prentice*

Kindness means doing a lot of little things kindly and always, not just a big thing now and then.... —*Neville Hobson*

He who is kind and courteous to strangers thereby shows himself a citizen of the world.... —*Anonymous*

Kindness is the sunshine in which virtue grows.... —*Robert Ingersoll*

It is the weak who are cruel. Gentleness can only be expected from the strong.... —*Leo Rosten*

The cheapest of all things is kindness, its exercise requiring the least possible trouble and self-sacrifice.... —*Samuel Smiles*

It is a duty to cultivate kindness.... —*Aaron Halevi*

Kindness works simply and perseveringly....Hence it is the furthest reaching and the most effective of all forces.... —*Albert Schweitzer*

We may scatter the seeds of courtesy and kindness about us at little expense.... —*Jeremy Bentham*

When kindness has left people, even for a few moments, we become afraid of them, as if their reason had left them.... —*Willa Cather*

Gentleness is a divine trait: nothing is so strong as gentleness and nothing so gentle as real strength.... —*Ralph Sockman*

The great mind knows the power of gentleness.... —*Robert Browning*

We cannot be just unless we are kind-hearted.... —*Luc de Clapiers Vauvenargues*

To cultivate kindness is a valuable part of the business of life.... —*Samuel Johnson*

Kindness in ourselves is the honey that blunts the sting of unkindness in another.... —*Walter Lander*

I often wonder why people do not make more of the marvelous power there is in kindness. It is the greatest lever to move the hearts of men that the world has ever known....
—*Andrew Chapman*

Don't repay a kindness; pass it on....
—*Proverb*

A more glorious victory cannot be gained over another man than this, that when the injury began on his part, the kindness should begin on ours....
—*John Tillotson*

Let me be a little kinder, let me be a little blinder to the faults of those around me.... —*Edgar A. Guest*

One kind word wins more willing service than a hundred harsh orders or stern reproofs.... —*Jean P. Camus*

Kindness has taken a bad rap in many ways, being associated with weakness or meekness or labels like "goody-goody." But true kindness comes from strength, and is full of life....
—*Bo Lozoff*

No act of kindness is ever wasted; like a boomerang, kindness eventually finds its way back to its sender....
—*Anonymous*

Loving kindness is greater than laws....
—*The Talmud*

Wherever there is a human being there is an opportunity for kindness....
—*Seneca*

Thoughtfulness, the kindly regard for others, is the beginning of holiness....
—*Mother Teresa*

The greatness of man can nearly always be measured by his willingness to be kind.... —*Michel Simon*

Kindness is wisdom....
—*Philip J. Bailey*

He that is kind is free, though he is a slave; he that is evil is a slave, though he be a king.... —*Augustine*

Kindness begets kindness: this is a law that knows no exceptions....
—*Papa Ramdas*

In a gentle way you can shake the world.... —*Mohandas Gandhi*

Laughter

Humor is not a trick, not jokes. Humor is a presence in the world—like grace—and shines on everybody.... —*Garrison Keillor*

The sound of laughter is like the vaulted dome of a temple of happiness....
—*Milan Kundera*

Laughter is the jam on the toast of life. It adds flavor, keeps it from being too dry and makes it easier to swallow....
—*Diane Johnson*

You never see a vain person with any sense of real humor. If he had, he couldn't be vain....
—*Julian P. Johnson*

What soap is to the body, laughter is to the soul.... —*Yiddish proverb*

Life is a joke, but God is laughing with us, not at us....
—*Swami Beyondananda*

Humor brings insight and tolerance....
—*Agnes Repplier*

The enduring love is the love that laughs.... —*George J. Watham*

Laughter can be more satisfying than honor; more precious than money; more heart cleansing than prayer.... —*Harriet Rochlin*

Laugh and be well.... —*Matthew Green*

Good work and joyous play go hand in hand. When play stops, old age begins. Play keeps you from taking life too seriously.... —*George Byron*

Jokes are an admirable instrument for reducing tensions.... —*Robert Mueller*

If you wish to glimpse inside a human soul and get to know a man....just watch him laugh. If he laughs well, he's a good man.... —*Fyodor Dostoyevsky*

The joy of joys is the person of light but unmalicious humor.... —*Emily Post*

Time spent laughing is time spent with the gods.... —*Japanese proverb*

Laughter is a great soul cleanser.... —*Virginia Sale*

We should tackle reality in a slightly jokey way, otherwise we miss its point.... —*Lawrence Durrell*

Humor makes one's problems seem trivial.... —*E. A. Peel*

Laughter is the shortest distance between two people.... —*Victor Borge*

A keen sense of humor helps us to overlook the unbecoming, understand the unconventional, tolerate the unpleasant, overcome the unexpected, and outlast the unbearable.... —*Billy Graham*

Don't forget the recipe of making three people laugh every day.... —*Edgar Cayce*

Fun, frivolity, merriment, are the things essential to the normal mind, as rain is necessary to the flowers....There is always something to laugh about every day, even if it is only about yourself.... —*Fred Van Amburgh*

If you go to bed at night and think about your day and you haven't laughed very much, then you must jump out of bed and go do something fun.... —*Marlo Morgan*

Laugh if you are wise.... —*Martial*

Laughing cheerfulness throws the light of day on all the paths of life.... —*Jean Paul Richter*

He deserves paradise who makes his companions laugh.... —*Koran*

All men laugh more or less, but those who laugh the most are the ones who live the longest and enjoy the best results.... —*David Gunston*

A good laugh is sunshine in a house.... —*William M. Thackeray*

Wholesome laughter is welcome relaxation, when it is not at anyone's expense.... —*Eknath Easwaran*

If you would find fun, live gratefully. Throw yourself into some great cause or issue and seek to boost it towards realization.... —*John H. Crome*

Laughter is the closest thing to the grace of God.... —*Karl Barth*

Laughter is the brush that sweeps away the cobwebs of the heart.... —*Mort Walker*

The love of truth lies at the root of much humor....　　—*Robertson Davies*

If everything goes wrong, just laugh! Just let it have its fling, let it go; but keep your vision upon God, and know that all will come right....
　　—*White Eagle*

Seriousness shows itself more majestic when laughter leads the way....
　　—*Heinrich Heine*

A person without a sense of humor is like a wagon without springs–jolted by every pebble in the road....
　　—*Henry W. Beecher*

Never trust a God who doesn't dance....
　　—*Friedrich W. Nietzsche*

God is the creator of laughter that is good....　　—*Philo*

Honest good humor is the oil and wine of a merry meeting, and there is no jovial companionship equal to that where the jokes are rather small and the laughter abundant....
　　—*Washington Irving*

Good humor is the health of the mind; sadness is its poison....
　　—*Leszczynski Stanislaw*

Men show their character in nothing more clearly than by what they think laughable....　　—*Johann W. Goethe*

If you cannot laugh at yourself, do not laugh at others....
　　—*Julie Sneyd*

The laughter of man is the contentment of God....　　—*Johann Weiss*

Laugh and the world laughs with you; weep and you weep alone....
　　—*Ella Wheeler Wilcox*

Laughter has something in it common with the ancient words of faith and inspiration; it unfreezes pride and unwinds secrecy; it makes men forget themselves in the presence of something greater than themselves....
　　—*G. K. Chesterton*

Laughter is a universal bond that draws all men together....　　—*Nathan Ausubel*

Laughter lifts us over high ridges and lights up dark valleys in a way that makes life so much easier. It is a priceless gem, a gift of release and healing direct from Heaven....
　　—*Alan Cohen*

The greatest prayer you could ever pray would be to laugh every day. For when you do, it elevates the vibratory frequency within your being such that you could heal your entire body....
　　—*Ramtha*

A day without laughter is a lost day....
　　—*Robert Muller*

Get into the habit of laughing; too many of us have forgotten how to laugh. As people grow older, they sometimes forget that they ever laughed. It is a part of their childhood that they can no longer remember....
　　—*Maxwell Maltz*

Laughter is a tonic, the relief, the surcease for pain....
　　—*Charles S. Chaplin*

A man isn't poor if he can still laugh....
　　—*Raymond Hitchcock*

Laughter relieves pain. You can only laugh when you are relaxed and the more relaxed you are the less pain you feel....　　—*Andrew Matthews*

Laughter is inner jogging....
　　—*Norman Cousins*

Humor is a bit like Mary Poppins' sugar—it helps the medicine go down. A little bit of humor allows people to think about very difficult subjects....
—*James Fadiman*

Why wait for heaven? Have fun now....Let's choose to be like the angels, who fly freely because they take themselves lightly....   —*Ruth Hanna*

Don't take yourself so seriously. Laugh and play. It's not the end of the world if something doesn't go right....
—*Sanaya Roman*

The person who knows how to laugh at himself will never cease to be amused....   —*Shirley MacLaine*

In laughter there is always a kind of joyousness that is incompatible with contempt or indignation....   —*Voltaire*

Learn to thrill yourself....Make everything bright and beautiful about you. Cultivate a spirit of humor. Enjoy the sunshine....   —*Baird Spalding*

Laughter is a tranquilizer with no side effects....   —*Arnold Glasow*

People who do not know how to laugh are always pompous and self- conceited....   —*William M. Thackeray*

Lesson

The hardest lesson I had to learn was to believe in myself....
—*Robert G. Allman*

The one eternal lesson for us all is how better we can love....
—*Henry Drummond*

There are many lessons to be learned and scales to be balanced. The laws of the universe cannot be altered for one's convenience. Humanity must learn to accept everything that life offers as a learning experience....   —*Peace Pilgrim*

Learning is a very painful experience. It requires humility from people at an age where the natural habitat is arrogance....   —*May Sarton*

If there is one lesson that history teaches us, it is that wealth and power, pride and prestige, are not only transitory but even illusory....
—*Robert Mueller*

The hardest and most important lesson we have to learn is that cheerfulness is our greatest virtue and that the happiest we'll ever be is while we are helping someone else....
—*Arthur E. Yensen*

That person who has not learned the lesson of saying "no" will remain wretchedly weak throughout life....
—*Anonymous*

The biggest lesson I learned from that experience [*21 days in a liferaft*] was that if you have all the fresh water you want to drink and all the food you want to eat, you ought never to complain about anything....
—*Eddie Rickenbacker*

Love is the Law of God. You live that you may learn to love. You love that you may learn to live. No other lesson is required of man....
—*Mikhail Naimy*

Every stone that bruises the pilgrim's foot will teach him a lesson. Every lesson will yield a pearl....
—*Elinor MacDonald*

All lessons are but the outer, a way of arriving at a conclusion. If the conclusion is not reached, or the aim sought is not attained, the lessons become driftwood, extra baggage, nothing.... —*Baird Spalding*

What we have to learn first is "how to unlearn."... —*Richard E. Burton*

Real learning comes about when the competitive spirit has ceased....This is true not only of competition with others, but competition with yourself as well.... —*J. Krishnamurti*

To learn is to change. Education is a process that changes the learner.... —*George Leonard*

Just as a child goes to school day after day, learning lessons, gathering experiences and passing from grade to grade, so do we in our greater soul-life come here to earth many times, learning lessons, gathering experience, and passing from one social grade to another.... —*Irving C. Cooper*

It is given to the world to learn one great divine lesson, the lesson of absolute selflessness. The saints, sages and saviors of all time are they who have submitted themselves to this task, and have learned and lived it.... —*James Allen*

The chief lesson I have learned in a long life is the only way to make a man trustworthy is to trust him; and the surest way to make him untrustworthy is to distrust him and show your mistrust.... —*Henry Stimson*

They can conquer who believe they can. He has not learned the first lesson of life who does not every day surmount a fear.... —*Ralph W. Emerson*

Having learnt the lesson from a past mistake, simply forget the mistake and you will forge ahead smoothly.... —*Homi Kharas*

Some of the best lessons we ever learn, we learn from our mistakes and failures. The error of the past is the wisdom and success of the future.... —*Tryon Edwards*

The greatest lesson I learned during my long life was to mind my own business.... —*Bernard M. Baruch*

The lesson that most of us on this voyage never learn, but can never quite forget, is that to win is sometimes to lose.... —*Richard M. Nixon*

Our bravest and best lessons are not learned through success, but through misadventure.... —*Amos B. Alcott*

There is no shortcut to life. To the end of our days, life is a lesson imperfectly learned.... —*Harrison E. Salisbury*

The universe is a medium in which evolvement can take place. It is a school where people will eventually develop into the image and likeness of God. It will exist as long as a school is needed. Only in earth life can certain lessons be learned.... —*Peace Pilgrim*

Life

Life is going forth, death is a returning home.... —*Lao-tzu*

The waking life is just a long dream which keeps our attention away from what we really are.... —*Annamalai Swami*

Life is a gift from God, an unlimited series of opportunities to find the good in ourselves and others. There is good in everything, if we are willing to see it.... —*Alan Cohen*

What is the sense of our life, what is the sense of the life of any living thing?...I answer: He who feels that his own life or that of his fellow-beings is senseless is not only unhappy, but hardly capable of living.... —*Albert Einstein*

Life is a moment-to-moment happening, any attempt to possess it, save it, or store it, is to lose the present moment.... —*A Spiritual Warrior*

Life is the only game where the object of the game is to figure out what the rules are.... —*Tom Seeley*

Life should be lived as a play.... —*Plato*

Life is a great school for the development of character, and all, through strife and struggle, vice and virtue, success and failure, we are slowly but surely learning the lessons of wisdom.... —*James Allen*

Life has been described in many ways, as a journey, a game, a battle, an adventure.... —*Norman V. Peale*

Life is a journey from the cradle to the grave and beyond, and back to the cradle and on from life to life. Each life is like a day in school. We learn a few of life's lessons each time we come back to earth, and in time we shall learn them all.... —*Amber M. Tuttle*

Life is made of marble and mud.... —*Nathaniel Hawthorne*

Life is pretty simple: You do some stuff. Most fails. Some works. You do more of what works.... —*Tom Peters*

The aim of life is to be fully born, though its tragedy is that most of us die before we are thus born.... —*Erich Fromn*

Life is coming to form and death is coming into the formless. Life is not separate from death; death is not separate from life. It is one phenomenon.... —*Ormond McGill*

In the final analysis, earth-life is a joke. Do not regard it seriously. All your problems stem from seeing life in a solemn manner. One hundred years from now you'll be chuckling at your so-called somberness. Lighten up!... —*Anonymous*

Life is full of giving and taking. If the giving is more than the taking, then by just that much the individual rises towards a higher life.... —*Julian P. Johnson*

Life is a compound of bitter and sweet, and to expect it to be all of either is futile.... —*Alice H. Rice*

Live your life each day as you would climb a mountain. An occasional glance toward the summit keeps the goal in mind, but many beautiful scenes are to be observed from each new vantage point.... —*Harold V. Melchert*

Life is a bridge. Cross over it, but build no house on it.... —*American Indian proverb*

All I really need to know about how to live and what to do and how to be I learned in kindergarten. Wisdom was not at the top of the graduate-school mountain, but there in the sandpile at Sunday School.... —*Robert Fulghum*

We are always getting ready to live, but never living.... —*Ralph W. Emerson*

Each man must look to himself to teach him the meaning of life. It is not something discovered: it is something molded.... —*Antoine De Saint-Exupery*

Life is an unfoldment, and the further we travel the more truth we can comprehend.... —*Hypatia*

Life is a do-it-with-God, do-it-for-others, do-it-to-yourself program....
—*Denis Waitley*

It is impossible to live pleasurably without living wisely, well and justly, and impossible to live wisely, well and justly without living pleasurably....
—*Epicurus*

When you're not afraid to die, life becomes much more meaningful....
—*Barbara Harris*

Life is good and is always trying to do us a good turn if we will only allow it to do so.... —*Henry T. Hamblin*

Life seems to be a series of crises that have to be faced.... —*Helen Hayes*

The earth-life is a tiny moment in eternity with much after and before. A tiny moment in eternity and yet it's so important.... —*Peace Pilgrim*

Human life is only an endless illusion.... —*Blaise Pascal*

What is life? It is a flash of a firefly in the night. It is a breath of a buffalo in the wintertime. It is as the little shadow that runs across the grass and loses itself in the sunset....
—*Isapwo Muksika*

Mortal life seems to be the unhappy interruption of our natural state of being. When we pass on, we're continuing our lives forward. Life is life eternal.... —*George Anderson*

Life is a voyage—a great mystical journey.... —*Daniel Brinkley*

If life were eternal, all interest and anticipation would vanish. It is uncertainty which lends it fascination.... —*Yoshida Kenko*

Life is not about limitation, it's about options.... —*Brooke Knapp*

Life just is. You have to flow with it. Give yourself to the moment. Let it happen.... —*Jerry Brown*

Strange is our situation upon earth. Each of us comes for a short visit, not knowing why, yet sometimes seeming to a divine purpose....
—*Albert Einstein*

Life is really simple. What we give out, we get back.... —*Louise L. Hay*

All the world's a stage, and all the men and women merely players; they have their entrances and exits; and one man in his time has many parts....
—*William Shakespeare*

It is a pity that the words "spiritual life" were ever invented, for they have caused so much confusion. For, in truth, there is only life—everyday life—which is simply what is at every moment.... —*Robert Powell*

Life is a play. It's an intricate board game. It contains a certain amount of surprise, joy, depression, grief, adventure, and tragedy.... —*Bob Morley*

What is life? A madness. What is life? An illusion, a shadow, a story....
—*Pedro Calderon*

Let each man think himself an act of God, his mind a thought, his life a breath of God.... —*Phillip J. Bailey*

The life which is unexamined is not worth living.... —*Plato*

Life, like any other exciting story, is bound to have painful and scary parts, boring and depressing parts, but it's a brilliant story, and it's up to us how it will turn out in the end.... —*Bo Lozoff*

No one can control life but everyone can be in charge of their reaction to it.... —*Anonymous*

Life is always forcing us to compromise.... —*Jawaharlal Nehru*

The art of living does not consist in preserving and clinging to a particular mood of happiness, but in allowing happiness to change its form without being disappointed by the change.... —*Charles L. Morgan*

One word frees us from the weight and pain of life; that word is love.... —*Sophocles*

Man is not made to understand life, but to live it.... —*George Santayana*

Love says: "I am everything." Wisdom says: "I am nothing." Between the two my life flows.... —*Jack Kornfield*

To fear love is to fear life.... —*Bertrand Russell*

Life is like hot iron, ready to pour. Choose the mold, and life will burn it.... —*William Buck*

Life is a pure flame, and we live by an invisible Sun within us.... —*Thomas Browne*

The great tragedy of life is not that men perish, but that they cease to love.... —*Somerset Maugham*

All the arts are apprenticeship. The big art is life.... —*M. C. Richards*

Life is a battle—you must enter into it fully, and do what needs to be done. You cannot shrink from your duty. Life presents difficult, sometimes horrendous, situations, unwelcome tasks, and obstacles of every sort. Despite this harsh reality, you must resolutely go forward.... —*Piero Ferrucci*

Life is no thing or state of a thing, but a continuous movement or change.... —*S. Radhakrishnan*

Life itself turns out to be nothing more or less than a giant Rorschach test.... —*U. S. Anderson*

If we but knew how short is the earth life in comparison with the whole, we would be less troubled with the difficulties of the earth life than we are troubled now with the difficulties of one of our days.... —*Peace Pilgrim*

Every man's life is a plan of God.... —*Horace Bushnell*

The real test of a happy life is to see how much pain and loss and frustration can be endured and absorbed without spoiling the joy of it.... —*Rufus M. Jones*

Naked and empty-handed you came here; empty handed and naked you depart. Results?—nothing: simply treading the wheel.... —*Julian P. Johnson*

Pain and death are part of life. To reject them is to reject life itself.... —*Havelock Ellis*

Life is like that, one stitch at a time, taken patiently, and the pattern will come out all right, like the embroidery.... —*Oliver W. Holmes*

Be fixed, be firm, be steadfast, for life is too short to shift to and fro. The stickers are the successes. The failures flit. We cannot step in after we step out. Life will not wait....
—*Fred Van Amburgh*

Life's supreme adventure is the adventure of living. Life's greatest achievement is the continual remaking of yourself so at last you do know how to live....   —*Winfred Rhodes*

Life is too brief to waste even one moment in useless regret or vain expectation....   —*Dorothy Strange*

The man who has no inner life is the slave of his surroundings....
—*Henri F. Amiel*

Life is not a matter of holding good cards, but playing a poor hand well....
—*Robert L. Stevenson*

Life is like a game of cards. The hand that is dealt you represents determinism; the way you play it is free will....   —*Jawaharlal Nehru*

For a long time it had seemed to me that life was about to begin—real life. But there was always some obstacle in the way, something to be got through first, some unfinished business, time still to be served, a debt to be paid. At last it dawned on me that those obstacles were my life....
—*Alfred D'souza*

Life teaches us to be less harsh with ourselves and with others....
—*Johann W. Goethe*

Life is difficult. This is a great truth, one of the greatest truths. It is a great truth because once we see this truth, we transcend it....   —*M. Scott Peck*

Human life may be reverently compared to an opera. God is the author of the music, and He gives each person the part he is to take....
—*George H. Hepworth*

Life will give you what you ask of her if only you ask long enough and plain enough....   —*E. Nesbit*

Life is a glass given us to fill....
—*William A. Brown*

The world is a great stage on which God displays His many wonders....
—*Francis Sales*

Life is tension. Without tension, there could be no life. Too little tension or too much tension interferes with the process of life in the same way a string of a guitar interferes with the melody when it is either too loose or too tight....
—*Bruno Geba*

Only a life lived for others is a life worthwhile....   —*Albert Einstein*

Life vibrates. It does not move....
—*Vimala Thakar*

Life breaks us all. There's not one of us who can stand up to life by ourselves. If we try, we're going to stumble....
—*Max Cleland*

Life is more than just trying to get everything; life is learning not to be attached to anything....   —*Anonymous*

Life is a flower of which love is the honey....   —*Victor Hugo*

Life is like the shadow of a bird in flight....   —*The Talmud*

I have found that if you love life, life will love you back....
—*Arthur Rubinstein*

Life is a journey from impurity to purity, from hatred to cosmic love, from death to immortality, from slavery to freedom, from imperfection to perfection, from pain to eternal bliss, from diversity to unity, from ignorance to eternal wisdom, and from weakness to strength....

—*Sivananda*

As you watch it, your life turns to dust....

—*Kabir*

Life is a campaign against foes, it is a battle with obstacles, temptations, hardships and limitations. These foes are within man and so the battle has to be incessant and perpetual....

—*Sathya Sai Baba*

Life is one-way, its law is the same for all, it moves only forwards....

—*Paul Tournier*

Life can be pulled by goals just as surely as it can be pushed by drives....

—*Victor Frankl*

Life is a series of surprises....

—*Ralph W. Emerson*

Life is a dream for the wise, a game for the fool, a comedy for the rich, a tragedy for the poor....

—*Shalom Aleichem*

He who has a why to live can bear with almost any how....

—*Friedrich W. Nietzsche*

The greatest use for life is to spend it for something that will outlast it....

—*Henry James*

Whoever refuses to take risks pays the penalty of loss of life in one form or another....

—*Alexis Carrel*

Life is not first lived and then understood; it is poorly lived till understood....

—*George A. Gordon*

Life is a fragment, a moment between two eternities....

—*William E. Channing*

The true meaning of life is to plant trees, under whose shade you do not expect to sit....

—*Nelson Henderson*

Life's a voyage that's homeward bound....

—*Herman Melville*

The mystery of life is that everybody dies, but nobody believes they will. It's only when we understand and accept this inevitability that we really begin living....

—*Bernie Siegal*

Life is the childhood of our immortality....

—*Johann W. Goethe*

Life's but a walking shadow, a poor player that struts and frets his hour upon the stage and then is heard no more: it is a tale told by an idiot, full of sound and fury, signifying nothing....

—*William Shakespeare*

The sense of living is joy enough....

—*Emily Dickinson*

Life is a one-way street. No matter how many detours you take, none of them leads back....

—*Isabel Moore*

The aim of life is to live, and to live means to be aware, joyously, drunkenly, serenely, divinely aware....

—*Henry Miller*

The meaning of life is the road, not the goal....

—*Arthur Schnitzler*

There is no cure for birth and death save to enjoy the interval....

—*George Santayana*

Life is ours to be spent, not to be saved....

—*D. H. Lawrence*

To live is the rarest thing in the world; most people exist, that is all....
—*Oscar Wilde*

Life is what happens while we're busy making other plans....   —*John Lennon*

The longer I live the more beautiful life becomes....   —*Frank L. Wright*

Life resembles the Olympic games; a few men strain their muscles to carry off the prize; others bring trinkets to sell to the crowd for a profit; and some there are who seek no further advantage than to look at the show and see how and why everything is done....
—*Michel Montaigne*

Life is like stepping on a boat which is about to set sail and sink....
—*Suzuki Roshi*

Life demands from you only the strength you possess....
—*Dag Hammarskjöld*

There is more to life than increasing its speed....   —*Mohandas Gandhi*

No man enjoys the true taste of life but he who is ready and willing to quit it....
—*Seneca*

Life is a long preparation for something that never happens....   —*William B. Yeats*

Life is not truly Life while the thought of death can still disturb it....
—*Karlfried G. Durckheim*

The art of living is not in eliminating but in growing with troubles....
—*Bernard M. Baruch*

The purpose of life is like a horizon; the further one advances, the farther it recedes....   —*Hazrat Inayat Khan*

Whittled down to a few words, Life can be summed up in the following: Love God, trust God—serve Life, trust Life....
—*Henry T. Hamblin*

Every man's life is a fairy tale, written by God's fingers....
—*Hans Christian Andersen*

The play is enlivened by the presence of trouble-makers. They are necessary to lend zest to the play—there is no fun without them....   —*Ramakrishna*

Real life is, to most men, a long second-best, a perpetual compromise between the ideal and the possible....
—*Bertrand Russell*

All life is an experiment. The more experiments you make the better....
—*Ralph W. Emerson*

Life is either a daring adventure or nothing. Security does not exist in nature, nor do the children of men as a whole experience it. Avoiding danger is no safer in the long run than exposure....   —*Helen Keller*

Life is really simple, but men insist on making it complicated....
—*Confucius*

Life would be dull and colorless but for the obstacles that we have to overcome and the fights we have to win....
—*Jawaharlal Nehru*

The great victories of life are oftenest won in a quiet way, and not with alarms and trumpets....
—*Benjamin Cardozo*

Life is learning which rules to obey, which rules not to obey, and the wisdom to tell the difference between the two....   —*Anonymous*

There are two ways to slice easily through life: to believe everything or to doubt everything. Both ways save us from thinking.... —*Alfred Korzybski*

Whether you think life is worth living or not, you will have to live it. There's no escape, no oblivion around the corner....Life must be lived, but of course you can decide on what level you will live it. That is, if you know enough and are prepared to make the right effort.... —*J. B. Priestley*

Life goes on—never the same—but onward, spiraling, expanding, and growing—always an adventure....
—*Margaret Pounders*

Life was never meant to be a struggle; just a gentle progression from one point to another, much like walking through a valley on a sunny day....
—*Stuart Wilde*

It's a funny thing about life; if you refuse to accept anything but the best, you very often get it....
—*Somerset Maugham*

Life can only be understood backwards. It must be lived forwards....
—*Sören Kierkegaard*

The purpose of life is a life of purpose.... —*Robert Byrne*

One person who has mastered life is better than a thousand persons who have mastered only the contents of books, but no one can get anything out of life without God....
—*Meister Eckhart*

Individual existence is a rope which stretches from the infinite to the finite and has no end and no commencement, neither is it capable of being broken....
—*Mabel Collins*

Life holds no mystery. From the very beginning, as man of today understands the beginning, life has been complete. There is nothing man can add to life, but there is much for man to enjoy.... —*Frater Achad*

If there is a sin against life, it consists perhaps not so much in despairing of life as in hoping for another life and in eluding the implacable grandeur of this life.... —*Albert Camus*

To be where we are, and to become what we are capable of becoming, is the only end in life....
—*Robert L. Stevenson*

Life is not something to be lived through: it is something to be lived up to. It is a privilege, not a penal servitude of so many decades on earth.... —*William G. Jordan*

Age and youth look upon life from the opposite ends of a telescope; to the one it is exceedingly long, to the other exceedingly short....
—*Henry W. Beecher*

The whole world is a comedy to those that think, a tragedy to those that feel....
—*Horace Walpole*

Life is a quarry, out of which we are to mold and chisel and complete a character.... —*Johann W. Goethe*

If you harvest the strength to impose your own terms upon life, you must accept the terms it offers you....
—*T. S. Eliot*

There must be more to life than having everything.... —*Maurice Sendak*

Life is an error-making and error-correcting process.... —*Jonas Salk*

One of the most tragic things....about human nature is that all of us tend to put off living. We are dreaming of some magical rose garden over the horizon—instead of enjoying the roses that are blooming outside our windows today....
—*Dale Carnegie*

We do not understand that life, before all definitions of it, is a drama of the visible and the invisible....
—*Maurice Nicoll*

To live is to know what counts in your life....   —*Martin Grey*

Accept every event in your life as natural, whether it is life, death, birth, marriage, goings or comings. Accept everyone. Do not argue. Do not question. Do not doubt. Do not judge. You will find that each step will lead on to another one, and when you start living this way there will be a great rejoicing in the heavens because a prodigal son or daughter is beginning to return home....   —*Ronald Beesley*

The end of life is to be like God....
—*Socrates*

Life is neither a good or an evil; it is simply a place where good and evil exist....   —*Seneca*

Life has no boundaries....
—*Ben Weininger*

Learn this great secret of life: What people call interruption or disturbance to their routine is just as much a part of living as the routine. To split life into two parts, one called routine and the other called interruption, is to be caught between them....
—*Vernon Howard*

The principal business of life is to enjoy it....   —*Samuel Butler*

The greatest abundance is gained by not falling into the whirlpool of life....
—*Lakshmana*

The mystery of life is not a problem to be solved, it is a reality to be lived....
—*Van der Leeuw*

The chess board is the world, the pieces the phenomena of the universe, the rules of the game are what we call the laws of Nature. The player on the other side is hidden from us. We know that his play is always fair, just and patient. But also we know, to our cost, that he never overlooks a mistake, or makes the smallest allowance for ignorance....
—*Thomas H. Huxley*

I count all that part of my life lost which I spend not in communion with God, or in doing good....
—*John Donne*

Life resembles the banquet of Damocles; the sword is ever suspended....
—*Voltaire*

Your living is determined not so much by what life brings to you as by the attitude you bring to life; not so much by what happens to you as by the way your mind looks at what happens....
—*John H. Miller*

The great tragedy of life is that man demands a return or reward for all that he does, either in money, or praise....
—*Henry T. Hamblin*

Life wants to give us the best, but you must make application for it, you must work for it in the unseen....
—*Anonymous*

Life is a series of tests, but if you pass your tests you'll look back upon them as a good experience....
—*Peace Pilgrim*

Life begins for anyone when that individual refuses to be a victim of any delimiting experience: disease, accident, poverty, family pressure, marriage dilemma, neglect. Whatever the curse, if you will not take it, or accept the role fate seems to offer, you can never become a mental cripple and nothing can hold you back....
—David Seabury

Life is like a library owned by an author. In it are a few books which he wrote himself, but most of them were written for him....   —Harry E. Fosdick

Light

A candle never loses anything when it lights another candle....
—Anonymous

To keep a lamp burning we have to keep putting oil into it....
—Mother Teresa

Dwelling in the light, there is no occasion at all for stumbling, for all things are discovered in the light....
—George Fox

Experience is a dim light, which only lights the one who bears it....
—Louis-Ferdinand Celiné

A man who moves with the earth will necessarily experience days and nights. He who stays with the sun will know no darkness....   —Nisargadatta

If you enter a dark place with a lamp, light falls on everyone who is near you. You don't have to tell people, "I have a light" because they will all be aware of its presence....   —Annamalai Swami

In the light there are no secret things. The sun reveals all hidden truths. There are no mysteries in God....
—The Aquarian Gospel

The greater the darkness, the more power the light has by contrast. If you light a candle in a totally darkened room, the candle has an almost shattering effect upon the darkness....
—Ron Watson

A man may wreck himself utterly in self-pleasure—may debase his whole nature, as it seems—yet he fails of becoming the perfect devil, for there is still the spark of divine light within him....   —Mabel Collins

There is no darkness if you face the sun....   —Amar Jyoti

Truly, it is in darkness that one finds the light, so when we are in sorrow, then this light is nearest to all of us....
—Meister Eckhart

God's body is Light....
—Zarathustra

Woe to the man who seeks to shed a brilliant light in a place where people want to keep in darkness and shadow....
—Benedetto Croce

You must not think of the light of the sun as the true Light of God. It is a reflection of the true Light. That other Light, that we can neither know nor comprehend, is so subtle, so highly potent that, for us, and even for many creatures of the spirit world who are far more advanced than we, it is darkness....   —Omraam M. Aivanhov

There are two ways of spreading light: to be the candle or the mirror that reflects it....   —Edith Wharton

Light is the symbol of truth....
—*James Russell Lowell*

You can visualize God's light each day and send it to someone who needs help. Your divine nature must reach out and touch the divine nature of another. Within you is the light of the world, it must be shared with the world....
—*Peace Pilgrim*

Keep your face to the sunshine and you cannot see the shadow....
—*Helen Keller*

The sun is always shining. Even though clouds may come along and obscure the sun for a while, the sun is always shining. The sun never stops shining. And even though the earth turns, and the sun appears to go down, it really never stops shining....
—*Louise L.Hay*

In order to cause a shadow to disappear you must shine a light upon it....
—*Anonymous*

I am like the man in Plato's Allegory of the Cave who knew that his chief task was to turn the prisoners round so that they could face in the direction of the sun. The sun would do the rest....
—*Charles Bennett*

Do you not seek a light, ye who are surrounded in darkness....
—*Dhammapada*

A sensible man would remember that the eyes may be confused in two ways, and for two reasons—by a change from light to darkness, or from darkness to light. He will consider that the same will happen with the soul....
—*Plato*

What is meant by light? To gaze with undimmed eyes on all darkness....
—*Nikos Kazantzakis*

The light of truth gives particular offense to certain peoples who are accustomed to darkness. Offering them light is like introducing a ray of sunshine into a nest of owls: it only serves to hurt their eyes and make them squawk....
—*Denis Diderot*

Lead me from the unreal to the real! Lead me from darkness to light....
—*The Upanishads*

It is better to light one small candle than to curse the darkness....
—*Confucius*

They who have light in themselves will not revolve as satellites....
—*Seneca*

Suppose a neighbor should desire to light a candle at your fire, would it deprive your flame of light, because another profits by it?...
—*Robert Lloyd*

Light and darkness cannot exist at the same time. When you bring in light, darkness must fly; no matter what darkness it is, it must fly. So that is the power of light....
—*Chidananda*

In the light there are no mysteries, no hidden things, everything is revealed; only in darkness are things concealed....
—*Anonymous*

There is no object so foul that intense light will not make it beautiful....
—*Ralph W. Emerson*

A cave that has been dark a thousand years is illuminated the instant a lamp is lit....
—*Sevakram*

Give light and the darkness will disappear of itself....
—*Erasmus*

When you think everything is hopeless, a little ray of light comes from somewhere....
—*German proverb*

There is not enough darkness in all the world to put out the light of even one small candle.... —*Robert Alden*

The secret of the sun's splendor and the star's glory is in the ability to scatter light. The true secret of man's real helpful influence is when he can scatter sunlight by day and starlight by night.... —*Fred Van Amburgh*

A light for one is a light for a hundred.... —*The Talmud*

The spiritual world is one single spirit who stands like unto a light behind the bodily world and who, when any single creature comes into being, shines through it as through a window. According to the size and kind of the window, less or more light enters the world.... —*Aziz Nasafi*

Let the light penetrate the darkness until the darkness shines and there is no longer any division between the two.... —*Hebrew proverb*

As far as we can discern, the sole purpose of human existence is to kindle a light in the darkness of mere being.... —*Carl Jung*

He who is worshiped as Light Inaccessible is not light that is material, the opposite of which is darkness, but light absolutely simple and infinite in which darkness is infinite light.... —*Nicholas of Cusa*

It isn't more light we need, it's putting into practice what light we already have.... —*Peace Pilgrim*

Only the light which we have kindled in ourselves can illuminate others.... —*Arthur Schopenhauer*

It takes only a little light to dispel much darkness.... —*Anonymous*

The light of a candle is useful when it precedes you; it is useless when it trails behind.... —*Bahya Ben Asher*

Light, even though it passes through pollution, is not polluted.... —*Augustine*

Little

L ife is made up not of great sacrifices or duties, but of little things, in which smiles, and kindnesses, and small obligations, given habitually are what win and preserve the heart and secure comfort.... —*Humphry Davy*

Little drops of water, little grains of sand, make the mighty ocean and the pleasant land.... —*Julia A. Fletcher Carney*

We ourselves feel that what we are doing is just a drop in the ocean. But if that drop was not in the ocean, I think the ocean would be less because of that missing drop. I do not agree with the big way of doing things.... —*Mother Teresa*

The hardest thing you have to do: The mundane, the routine, the unrecognized tasks of life.... —*Judith Sills*

The happiness of life is made up of minute fractions—the little soon-forgotten charities of a kiss or a smile, a kind look, a heartfelt compliment and the countless infinitesimals of pleasurable and genial feeling.... —*Samuel T. Coleridge*

Practice yourself, for heaven's sake, in little things; and thence proceed to greater.... —*Epictetus*

The power of little things to give instruction and happiness should be the first lesson in life, and it should be inoculated deeply....
—Russell H. Conwell

Blessed is the man who can enjoy the small things, the common beauties, the little day-by-day events; sunshine on the fields, birds on the bough, breakfast, dinner, supper, the daily paper on the porch, a friend passing by. So many people who go afield for enjoyment leave it behind them at home.... *—David Grayson*

Little things are infinitely more important.... *—Arthur C. Doyle*

It is by studying little things that we attain the great art of having as little misery and as much happiness as possible.... *—Samuel Johnson*

Most of the critical things in life, which become the starting points of human destiny, are little things....
—Robert Smith

Who despises small things shall become poor.... *—Apocrypha: Ben Sira*

Small deeds done are better than great deeds planned.... *—Peter Marshall*

Too often we underestimate the power of a touch, a smile, a kind word, a listening ear, an honest compliment, or the smallest act of caring, all of which has the potential to turn a life around....
—Leo Buscaglia

Little self-denials, little honesties, little passing words of sympathy, little nameless acts of kindness, little silent victories over favorite temptations— these are the silent threads of gold which, when woven together, gleam out so brightly in the pattern of life that God approves.... *—Frederic W. Farrar*

Drop by drop, the measure is filled....
—Old Testament

Has the thought ever struck your intellectual roundhouse that life is made up of little things—that quiet people who are always doing the little things often accomplish the most....
—Fred Van Amburgh

Blessed are the unimportant, as much as the important....
—Saul Chernihovsky

Rule number one: Don't sweat the small stuff. Rule number two: It is all small stuff.... *—Robert Elliot*

The things that count most in life are usually the little things that cannot be counted.... *—Bernard Meltzer*

Good things, when short, are twice as good.... *—Baltazar Gracian*

Learn the great art of being small....
—Joseph Brennen

Little things are indeed little, but to be faithful in little things is a great thing....
—Augustine

The first springs of great events, like those of great rivers, are often mean and little.... *—Jonathan Swift*

Big doesn't necessarily mean better. Sunflowers aren't better than violets....
—Edna Ferber

Trifles make perfection....
—Michelangelo

Little things affect little minds....
—Benjamin Disraeli

What lies behind us and what lies before us are tiny matters compared to what lies within us....
—Ralph W. Emerson

It is the greatest of all mistakes to do nothing because you can only do little. Do what you can....   —*Sydney Smith*

Little by little does the trick....
                              —*Aesop*

Sometimes when I consider what tremendous consequences come from little things....I am tempted to think there are no little things....
                        —*Bruce Barton*

The beginnings of all things are small....
                              —*Cicero*

A man who cannot tolerate small ills can never accomplish great things....
                        —*Chinese proverb*

Most people would succeed in small things if they were not troubled by great ambitions....
                  —*Henry W. Longfellow*

We shut our eyes to the beginnings of evil because they are small, and in this weakness lies the germ of our defeat....
                        —*Henri F. Amiel*

The Godly nature does not need to be sated with trivial items and petty praises. Already it contains whatever is needed to sustain itself....
                          —*Shantidasa*

You have to begin with little things, and when you have proved God in small experiences, and God has proven you, you will be ready to launch out in larger ventures of faith....
                      —*Henry T. Hamblin*

The spirit of delight comes in small ways....   —*Robert L. Stevenson*

The importance of little things. This is true but so also is the unimportance of great things—sooner or later....
                        —*Samuel Butler*

When one understands that the great things of the world and of life consist of a combination of small things, and that without this aggregation of small things the great things would be nonexistent, then he begins to pay careful attention to those things which he formerly regarded as insignificant....
                          —*James Allen*

Trivial words or gestures are apt to reveal an individual far more than his studied poses and utterances....
                      —*Jawaharlal Nehru*

A multitude of small delights constitutes happiness....
                      —*Charles Baudelaire*

Loneliness

The person who tries to live alone will not succeed as a human being. His heart withers if he doesn't answer another heart. His mind shrinks away if he hears only the echoes of his own thoughts and finds no other inspiration....   —*Pearl Buck*

Man's loneliness is but his fear of life....
                        —*Eugene O'Neill*

Man is never alone....His existence and feelings are individual and collective at one and same time....   —*Eliphas Levi*

When you live in constant communion with God, you cannot be lonely....
                          —*Peace Pilgrim*

Loneliness and feelings of being unwanted is the most terrible poverty....   —*Mother Teresa*

The hardest thing for a person to bear is not a dressing-down or beating, but loneliness, ostracism....   —*Ru Zhijuan*

What loneliness is more lonely than distrust?...   —*George Eliot*

The deepest need of man is the need to overcome his separateness, to leave the prison of his aloneness....
—*Erich Fromm*

We not only have to die alone; we also, save for a few close associates, have to live alone....   —*Henry L. Mencken*

In cities, no one is quiet but many are lonely; in the country, people are quiet but few are lonely....
—*Geoffrey F. Fisher*

Are you lonely, O my brother? Share your little hand with another! Stretch your hand to one unfriended and your loneliness is ended....
—*John Oxenham*

Leave the public roads, and walk in unfrequented paths....   —*Pythagoras*

We all have to cross the stream alone....
—*Bhai Sahib*

Being alone is a markedly different experience than being lonely....
—*Clark E. Moustakas*

The worst loneliness is not to be comfortable with yourself....
—*Mark Twain*

There is no loneliness if one is satisfied with oneself....   —*Hans-Ulrich Rieker*

There is none more lonely than the man who loves only himself....
—*Abraham Ibn Esra*

Loneliness is the desire for someone; being alone is contentment....
—*Tom Seeley*

Loneliness is the way by which destiny endeavors to lead man to himself....
—*Hermann Hesse*

The eternal quest of the individual human being is to shatter his loneliness....   —*Norman Cousins*

Loneliness vanishes completely in the Stillness....   —*Paul Brunton*

Loneliness can only truly be conquered by those who appreciate solitude....
—*Anonymous*

Never fear being alone, because you never are....   —*Rod McKuen*

Seldom can a heart be lonely, if one seeks one lonelier still....
—*Francis R. Havergal*

There is no loneliness like the loneliness of a great crowd....
—*Fred Van Amburgh*

People who cannot bear to be alone are generally the worst company....
—*Albert Guidon*

There is only one thing that all people possess equally. This is their loneliness....   —*Hyemeyohsts Storm*

Love

The salvation of man is through love and in love....
—*Victor Frankl*

Love is the great solvent of all difficulties, all problems, all misunderstandings....   —*White Eagle*

The path of love and the path of insight lead into the same garden....
—*Stephen Mitchell*

Tell me who you love, and I'll tell you who you are.... —*Creole proverb*

Ordinary love based on the physical affinity is a source of misery both to the lover and the loved. But Divine Love based on the feeling of spiritual oneness is sublime. It is a source of pure bliss. Here you love another not because he is a relation of yours, but because you and he are one in Spirit....
—*Papa Ramdas*

Love is greater than faith, because the end is greater than the means....(Love) is greater than charity, again, because the whole is greater than the part....
—*Henry Drummond*

The passion we call love is the misguided belief that one person is somehow different from another person.... —*Anonymous*

The absence of love in our lives is what makes them seem raw and unfinished.... —*Ingrid Bengis*

A crowd is not company, faces are but a gallery of pictures and talk but a tinkling of cymbals where there is no love.... —*Francis Bacon*

To love is to place our happiness in the happiness of another....
—*Gottfried Leibnitz*

Love is the end of the struggle. When you have got love, your struggle ceases.... —*Papa Ramdas*

Only the loving ones find love and they never have to reach for it....
—*Sunyata*

As long as we see our fellow men as merely human, we shall be doomed to disappointment and disillusionment. It is only when we glimpse potentialities of the divine beneath the weakness of the flesh that we truly love....
—*Alice H. Rice*

When we love, we see the infinite in the finite. We find the Creator in the creation....True love is a dazzling revelation of the immortality of the soul.... —*Eliphas Levi*

The nearest way to God leads through love's open door....
—*Angelus Silesius*

If love does not know how to give and take without restrictions, it is not love, but a transaction that never fails to lay stress on a plus and a minus....
—*Emma Goldman*

Love of body or skin is passion. Love of God is....devotion. It is pure love. It is love for love's sake. It is divine....
—*Sivananda*

Love grows by service....
—*Charlotte P. Gilman*

That's all non-violence is—organized love.... —*Joan Baez*

We are not made to love only one or two individuals. We have the immense capacity to be in love with everyone....
—*Eknath Easwaran*

When we love, we lose ourselves, and conversely when we have lost ourselves....we become capable of inexhaustible love.... —*Stephen Larsen*

The only way you can ever hope to be loved is to stop asking for it and start giving it; you get love only when you give it to others.... —*Dale Carnegie*

Try to radiate your love equally to all people instead of just a few. Try to feel that the whole world is your Self, your God. Try to see the Self in all people. Spread your love in all directions as an act of worship and surrender, because everything in the world is a manifestation of God....   —*Annamalai Swami*

Infantile love follows the principle: I love because I am loved. Mature love follows the principle: I am loved because I love....   —*Erich Fromm*

Love is strong as death....Many waters cannot quench love, neither can the floods drown it....   —*Old Testament*

He who loves another tries truly to understand the other....
                   —*Harry A. Overstreet*

They do not love who do not show their love....   —*William Shakespeare*

The remedy of all blunders, the cure of blindness, the cure of crime, is love....
                   —*Ralph W. Emerson*

Only love can be divided endlessly and still not diminish....
                   —*Anne Morrow Lindbergh*

To live without loving is not really to live....   —*Jean B. Moliere*

If only you could love enough you would be the happiest and most powerful being in the world....
                   —*Emmet Fox*

When we come to the last moment of this lifetime, and we look back across it, the only thing that's going to matter is "What was the quality of our love?"...
                   —*Richard Bach*

There is no right or wrong. There is only love....   —*Carol Chapman*

Love and compassion are necessities, not luxuries. Without them humanity cannot survive....   —*Dalai Lama*

There is a love like a small lamp, which goes out when the oil is consumed; or like a stream which dries up when it doesn't rain. But there is a love like a mighty spring gushing up out of the earth; it keeps flowing forever, and is inexhaustible....   —*Isaac of Ninveveh*

The conclusion is always the same: love is the most powerful and still the most unknown energy of the world....
                   —*Teilhard de Chardin*

Love knows no pain....
                   —*Meister Eckhart*

If you love one person more than another this is not true love; it is an attachment created by desire. To love all things equally....is true love....
                   —*Saradamma*

The path of love is rugged, thorny and precipitous. It is a razor path....It can only admit one....   —*Sivananda*

It is possible that a man can be so changed by love as hardly to be recognized as the same person....
                   —*Terence*

Take away love and our earth is a tomb....   —*Robert Browning*

Don't fall into the trap that there is only one special person that you are able to love. Instead, try to develop the expectation that the world is full of people that you can love and that can love you....   —*Ken Keyes, Jr.*

Love is the power of God that binds two souls and makes them one; there is no power on earth that can dissolve that bond....   —*The Aquarian Gospel*

To love means never to be afraid of the windstorms of life....
—*Elisabeth Kubler-Ross*

When the satisfaction or the security of another person becomes as significant to one as one's own satisfaction or security, then the state of love exists....
—*Harry S. Sullivan*

In real love you want the other person's good. In romantic love you want the other person.... —*Margaret Anderson*

The more we forget ourselves in giving to others, the better we can understand what love really means....
—*J. Donald Walters*

Love has no errors, for all errors are the want of love.... —*William Law*

A genuine caring love is like a tree that is mature. It does not get uprooted by every passing wind of feeling or change. It develops with time a strong root structure. It sends out sturdy branches. It can survive dry spells....
—*Larry Christenson*

No human love affair can substitute for the divine one.... —*Gerald G. May*

To be able to say how much you love is to love but little.... —*Petrarch*

Love is but the discovery of ourselves in others, and the delight in the recognition.... —*Alexander Smith*

Love does not survive neglect. Once planted, it must be carefully tended if it is to grow.... —*Alice H. Rice*

Love is the free exercise of choice. Two people love each other only when they are quite capable of living without each other but choose to live with each other.... —*M. Scott Peck*

Love, the magician, knows this little trick whereby two people walk in different directions yet always remain side by side.... —*Hugh Prather*

Love is an incurable disease. No one who catches it wants to recover, and all its victims refuse a cure.... —*Ibn Hazim*

It's not unusual for love to remain a lifetime. It's passion that doesn't last....
—*Tom Robbins*

Falling in love is exhilaration about the future.... —*Robert C. Solomon*

When you are in love with someone, you do indeed see them as divine....
—*Alan Watts*

Perfect love means to love the one through whom one becomes happy....
—*Sören Kierkegaard*

Love....like a lively flame and burning torch forces its way upwards and securely passes through all things....
—*Thomas à Kempis*

Love is the expression of an ancient need, that human desire was originally one and whole and the desire and the pursuit of the whole is called love....
—*Aristophanes*

Love is a medicine for the sickness of the world; a prescription often given, too rarely taken....
—*Karl A. Menninger*

Love means to commit oneself without guarantee, to give oneself completely in the hope that our love will produce love in the loved person. Love is an act of faith, and whoever is of little faith is of little love.... —*Erich Fromm*

Love is a product of habit....
—*Lucretius*

When love comes, reason flees hastily away....   —*Ferid Ed-dim Attar*

The first step to unselfish love is the recognition that our love may be deluded. We must first of all purify our love by renouncing the pleasure of loving as an end in itself....
—*Thomas Merton*

There is no path greater than love. There is no law higher than love. And there is no goal beyond love. God and love are identical....
—*Meher Baba*

You want to be loved because you do not love; but the moment you love, it is finished, you are no longer inquiring whether or not somebody loves you....
—*J. Krishnamurti*

To love is to return to a home we never left, to remember who we are....
—*Sam Keen*

Love is the energizing elixir of the universe, the cause and effect of all harmonies....   —*Rumi*

We are shaped and fashioned by what we love....   —*Johann W. Goethe*

Born at the banquet of the gods, Love has of necessity been eternally in existence, for it springs from the intention of the Soul towards its best, towards the Good; and as long as the Soul has been—Love has been....
—*Plotinus*

Instead of allowing yourself to be unhappy, just let your love grow as God wants it to grow. Seek goodness in others. Love more persons more. Love them more impersonally, more unselfishly, without thought of return. The return, never fear, will take care of itself....   —*Henry Drummond*

Pure love is a willingness to give, without a thought of receiving anything back in return....
—*Peace Pilgrim*

It is love which binds the universe together and sustains it. Without love it would be nothing more than a collection of inert matter....
—*Saradamma*

The more one loves the nearer he approaches to God, for God is the spirit of infinite love....
—*Ralph W. Trine*

All things work together for good to them that love God....   —*Paul of Tarsus*

He who loves brings God and the world together....   —*Martin Buber*

Love one human being purely and warmly, and you will love all....
—*Jean Paul Richter*

Love gives; love never withdraws. Love warms and frees the will of man, so he may receive his own inheritance and make his own decisions....
—*Elsie Morgan*

Love cures. It cures those who give it and it cures those who receive it....
—*Karl A. Menninger*

The only genuine love worthy of the name is unconditional....
—*John Powell*

As a mother even at the risk of her own life protects her only son, so let a man cultivate goodwill without measure among all beings. Let him suffuse the whole world with thoughts of love, unmixed with any sense of difference or opposed interests....
—*Gautama Buddha*

Every part of our personality that we do not love will become hostile to us....
—*Robert Bly*

To heal is to touch with love that which we previously touched with fear....
—*Stephen Levine*

Love is a mysterious divine glue that unites the hearts of all....
—*Sivananda*

Love makes every space sacred and every moment meaningful....
—*Barbara De Angelis*

Immature love says, "I love you because you love me." Mature love says, "I love you whether you love me or not."...
—*Shantidasa*

If you can justify everything that everyone in the universe does and find no fault with anyone; see good in everything and everyone–*that* is truly expressing LOVE....
—*James B. Schafer*

Without love one lacks the warmth and emotions which create life, youth and beauty. He is like a stagnant pond compared with a flowing, babbling, laughing brook. He depresses the life force in those around him instead of radiating sunshine to all who come near him....
—*Leon DeSeblo*

We don't love qualities, we love persons, sometimes by reason of their defects as well as their qualities....
—*Jacques Maritain*

While I don't ask you to save the world, I do ask you to love those with whom you sleep, share the happiness of those you call friend, engage those among you who are visionary, and remove from your life those who offer you despair and disrespect....
—*Nikki Giovanni*

Love is not selective, desire is selective; with love there are no strangers....
—*Anonymous*

All true love is grounded on esteem....
—*George Buckingham*

One word frees us of all the weight and pain of life: that word is love....
—*Sophocles*

There can be no excess to love....
—*Ralph W. Emerson*

When love and skill work together, expect a masterpiece.... —*John Ruskin*

Love in the making sees faults, but forgives them. Love in its grand fulfillment never sees any faults; hence it has nothing to forgive....
—*Papa Ramdas*

Love should be as natural as living and breathing.... —*Mother Teresa*

No disguise can long conceal love where it is, nor feign it where it is not.... —*Francois La Rochefoucauld*

Love consists in this, that two solitudes protect and touch and greet each other.... —*Rainer M. Rilke*

Love cannot stay at home; a man cannot keep it to himself. Like light, it is constantly traveling. A man must spend it, must give it away....
—*Alexander Macleod*

Love cannot endure indifference. It needs to be wanted. Like a lamp, it needs to be fed out of the oil of another's heart, or its flame burns low.... —*Henry W. Beecher*

Love doesn't make the world go 'round. Love is what makes the ride worthwhile.... —*Franklin P. Jones*

The most important word that's ever been invented is the word love....
—*Gary Busey*

Love is never lost. If not reciprocated it will flow back and soften and purify the heart.... —*Washington Irving*

Man's love of God is identical with his knowledge of Him....
—*Maimonides*

Love makes burdens lighter, because you divide them. It makes joys more intense, because you share them. It makes you stronger, so that you can reach out and become involved with life in ways you dared not risk alone....
—*Arthur Gordon*

Love conquers all things; let us surrender to love.... —*Virgil*

Love is the nature of God, He can do no other: Thus, to be God, love at each moment.... —*Angelus Silesius*

Reality is not clearly and immediately apprehended, except by those who have made themselves loving, pure in heart and poor in spirit....
—*Aldous Huxley*

People who do not experience self-love have little or no capacity to love others.... —*Nathaniel Branden*

Love is space and time measured by the heart.... —*Marcel Proust*

At the center of non-violence stands the principle of love....
—*Martin L. King, Jr.*

To love for the sake of being loved is human, but to love for the sake of loving is angelic....
—*Alphonse de Lamartine*

Love is an act of endless forgiveness....
—*Peter Ustinov*

Love is when each person is more concerned for the other than for one's self.... —*David Frost*

God is love, and he that has learnt to live in the Spirit of love has learnt to live and dwell in God....
—*William Law*

If you would be loved, love and be lovable.... —*Benjamin Franklin*

Love is the strongest force the world possesses, and yet it is the humblest imaginable.... —*Mohandas Gandhi*

Love can be its own reward....
—*Arnold Lobel*

Put love into the world and heaven with all its beauties and glories becomes a reality. Not to love is not to live, or to live a living death. The life that goes out in love to all is the life that is full, and rich, and continually expanding in beauty and in power....
—*Ralph W. Trine*

In love, respect should come first and ardor second.... —*Robert Benson*

Love is patient and kind; love is not jealous or conceited or proud; love is not ill-mannered, or selfish or irritable; love does not keep a record of wrongs. Love is not happy with evil, but is happy with the truth. Love never gives up: its faith, hope and patience never fail. Love is eternal.... —*Paul of Tarsus*

Love, and do what thou wilt....
—*Augustine*

Love turns one person into two; and two into one.... —*Isaac Abravanel*

Bitterness imprisons life; love releases it. Bitterness paralyzes life; love empowers it. Bitterness sours life; love sweetens it. Bitterness sickens life; love heals it. Bitterness blinds life; love anoints its eyes....   —*Harry E. Fosdick*

Love knows no rule....

—*St. Jerome*

Love requires no defense and bears no need to prove itself. It knows that it is lovable, and all that comes from love must be lovable, too....   —*Alan Cohen*

Happiness comes more from loving than being loved....   —*J. E. Buckrose*

To love is the most important thing in life. But what do we mean by love? When you love someone because that person loves you in return surely that is not love. To love is to have that extraordinary feeling of affection without asking anything in return....
—*J. Krishnamurti*

Love brings to life whatever is dead around us....   —*Franz Rosenzweig*

Love does not make you weak because it is the source of all strength, but it makes you see the nothingness of the illusionary strength on which you depended before you knew it....
—*Leon Bloy*

We love because it's the only true adventure....   —*Nikki Giovanni*

Love doesn't just sit there, like a stone; it has to be made, like bread, remade all the time, made new....
—*Ursula K. LeGuin*

Let us love each other more, and we shall have a feeling of spaciousness....
—*Raphael of Bershad*

A man or a woman will fall in love with you because of the way they feel about themselves when they are with you....
—*Ellen Kreidman*

True love will always commit itself and engage in lasting ties; it needs freedom only to effect its choice, not for its accomplishment....   —*Carl Jung*

Love rules without rules....
—*Italian saying*

Among those who dwell in that world above there is no disagreement; all have one purpose; there is one mind, one feeling in them all; for the spell which binds them one to another is Love....   —*Hermes*

Love is the holy bond that holds all worlds together....
—*Julian P. Johnson*

If we seek to be loved—if we expect to be loved—this cannot be accomplished; we will be dependent and grasping, not genuinely loving....   —*M. Scott Peck*

Respect is love in plain clothes....
—*Frankie Byrne*

He who knows nothing loves nothing. He who can do nothing understands nothing. He who understands nothing is worthless. But he who understands also loves, notices, sees....   —*Paracelsus*

A mind might ponder its thoughts for ages and not gain so much self-knowledge as the passion of love shall teach in a day....   —*Ralph W. Emerson*

Absence is to love what wind is to fire; it puts out the little and kindles the great....   —*Roger de Busy-Rabutin*

In love is found the secret of divine unity....   —*The Zohar*

Every man loves what he is good at....
—*Thomas Shadwell*

A single atom of the love of God in a heart is worth more than a hundred thousand paradises....
—*Bayazid al-Bistami*

The love we give away is the only love we keep.... —*Elbert Hubbard*

Love is clarity....Decisions made from love will bring even greater clarity....
—*Maya Sarada Devi*

You must expand your love to as wide a circle as possible.... —*Sathya Sai Baba*

A man doesn't learn to understand anything unless he loves it....
—*Johann W. Goethe*

Love is not bargaining; it is not give and take. It is a spontaneous merging of souls.... —*Papa Ramdas*

True love demands nothing, seeks nothing for its own, but desires only to give. If we love God and our neighbor we desire only to give, to serve, to pour out all that we have at the feet of Life....
—*Henry T. Hamblin*

It is only the souls that do not love that go empty in this world....
—*Robert Benson*

Love is union with somebody or something outside oneself, under the condition of retaining the separateness and integrity of one's own self....
—*Erich Fromm*

Teach only Love for that is what you are.... —*Gerald Jampolsky*

We love people because they have loving thoughts of us, not because they are beautiful.... —*Robert Collier*

There is no difficulty that enough love will not conquer; no disease that enough love will not heal; no door that enough love will not open; no gulf that enough love will not bridge; no wall that enough love will not throw down; no sin that enough love will not redeem.... —*Emmet Fox*

All love is Divine. Let it never be said that physical or romantic love is less than God's Love, for ideas cannot be apart from their source....
—*Alan Cohen*

I will love you no matter what. I will love you if you are stupid, if you slip and fall on your face, if you do the wrong thing, if you make mistakes, if you behave like a human being—I will love you no matter what....
—*Leo Buscaglia*

As a human being related to all living beings, we must be first related to ourselves. We cannot understand, love and welcome others without first knowing and loving ourselves....
—*Jean Klein*

People think love is an emotion. Love is good sense.... —*Ken Kesey*

Start learning to love God by loving those whom you cannot love. The more you remember others with kindness and generosity, the more you forget yourself, and when you forget yourself completely, you find God....
—*Meher Baba*

Above all things, love yourself....
—*Pythagoras*

A loving person lives in a loving world. A hostile person lives in a hostile world: everyone you meet is a mirror....
—*Ken Keyes, Jr.*

That all things are possible to him who believes, that they are less difficult to him who hopes, that they are easier to him who loves, and still more easy to him who perseveres in the practice of these three virtues....
—*Brother Lawrence*

Reason is not what directs love....
—*Jean B. Moliere*

The love in your heart wasn't put there to stay—Love isn't love until it's given away.... —*Anonymous*

While God awaits for the temple to be built of love, men bring stones....
—*Rabindranath Tagore*

Love makes all hard hearts gentle....
—*George Herbert*

Someday, after mastering the wind, the waves, and the tides, we shall harness for God the power of love, and then, for the second time in history, man will have discovered fire....
—*Teilhard de Chardin*

Sex wants to possess its beloved, even to enslave her. Love is willing to let her stay free.... —*Paul Brunton*

Love and lust cannot exist at the same time.... —*Tom Seeley*

Those that go searching for love only make manifest their own lovelessness. And the loveless never find love, only the loving find love, and they never have to seek for it.... —*D. H. Lawrence*

When the power of love replaces the love of power, man will have a new name: God.... —*Sri Chinmoy*

Love is our highest word and the synonym for God....
—*Ralph W. Emerson*

For love is victorious in attack, and invulnerable in defense. Heaven arms with love those who it would not see destroyed.... —*Lao-tzu*

To love anyone is nothing else than to wish that person good....
—*Thomas Aquinas*

Love is the biggest eraser there is. Love erases even the deepest imprinting because love goes deeper than anything.... —*Louise Hayes*

If God is love, the more we can understand the nature of love and put that understanding into practice, the more God-like will be our experience....
—*Reginald Armor*

Love is not just another attitude. Many people think the opposite of fear is love. But love is actually what we are. It is a step beyond attitude. It is a shift in consciousness.... —*Michael Exeter*

Divine Love is distinguished from human love in this supremely important particular: it is free from partiality.... —*James Allen*

If our hearts go all out in love to all with whom we come in contact, we inspire love, and the same ennobling and warming influences of love always return to us....If you would have all the world love you, you must first love all the world.... —*Ralph W. Trine*

Love is a fruit in season at all times, and within the reach of every hand....
—*Mother Teresa*

To love is to release God's storehouse of golden treasure. If we love we cannot help giving, and to give is to gain, and the law of love is fulfilled....
—*Baird Spalding*

I am realizing every day that the search for truth is vain unless it is founded upon love. To injure a single human being is to injure those divine powers within us, and thus the harm reaches not only that one human being, but with him the whole world....
—*Mohandas Gandhi*

The purpose of life is to learn to love—as we evolve we learn to love and learn to be loved.... —*Shirley MacLaine*

He who comes to do good knocks at the gate; he who loves finds the gate open.... —*Rabindranath Tagore*

Love is not blind. Lust is blind. If love is blind, God is blind.... —*Gordon Palmer*

Love that has nothing but beauty to keep it in good health, is short lived....
—*Erasmus*

To love all alike is distinctly a divine quality.... —*Papa Ramdas*

Love is the reduction of the universe to a single being.... —*Victor Hugo*

Meditation

We spend a great deal of time telling God what we think should be done, and not enough time waiting in the stillness for God to tell us what to do.... —*Peace Pilgrim*

Meditation provides a way of learning how to let go. As we sit, the self we've been trying to construct and make into a nice, neat package continues to unravel.... —*John Welwood*

Keeping God in your mind as everything around you becomes meditation.... —*Ramana Maharshi*

The purpose of meditation practice is not enlightenment; it is to pay attention even at extraordinary times, to be of the present, nothing-but-in-the-present, to bear this mindfulness of now into each event of ordinary life....
—*Peter Matthiessen*

Meditation is simplicity itself. One is to just let go, nothing special is supposed to happen.... —*A Spiritual Warrior*

Meditation is silence. If you realize that you really know nothing, then you will be truly meditating. Such truthfulness is the right soil for silence. Silence is meditation.... —*Yoga Swami*

Meditation needs an awake mind not an unconscious one....Meditation is not something that should be done in a particular position at a particular time. It is an awareness and an attitude that must persist throughout the day....
—*Annamalai Swami*

Meditation is not some strange technique that we have to learn with great effort and difficulty....Whatever we accomplish in this world we accomplish through the power of concentration, which is nothing but meditation....Above all, meditation stills the wandering mind and establishes us forever in a state of peace....
—*Muktananda*

This is the only way....to explain existence, to overcome sadness and grievances, to banish death and misery, to find the right path, to realize Nirvana—it is correct meditation....
—*Gautama Buddha*

Meditation helps keep us from identifying with the "movies of the mind."... —*Joan Borysenko*

Spiritual meditation is the pathway to Divinity. It is a mystic ladder which reaches from earth to heaven, from error to Truth, from pain to peace. Every saint climbed it; every sinner must sooner or later come to it....
—*James Allen*

Before embarking on important undertakings, sit quietly, calm your senses and thoughts, and meditate deeply. You will then be guided by the great creative power of Spirit....
—*Paramahansa Yogananda*

Meditation is not a means to an end. It is both the means and the end....
—*J. Krishnamurti*

There is no ill in life that cannot be cured by right meditation....True meditation gives us, as it were, wings for flight to a higher realm and thus detaches us from terrestrial fetters....
—*Paramananda*

If you can't meditate in a boiler room, you can't meditate.... —*Alan Watts*

Contemplation is to knowledge what digestion is to food—the way to get life out of it.... —*Tryon Edwards*

Meditation is that exercise of the mind by which it recalls a known truth....
—*George Horne*

The mind turned outward results in thoughts and objects. Turned inwards it becomes itself the Self....
—*Ramana Maharshi*

No great work has been ever produced except after a lone interval of still and musing meditation....
—*Walter Bagehot*

Contemplation places us in a purity and radiance which is far above our understanding.... —*John Ruysbroeck*

We become contemplatives when God discovers Himself in us....
—*Thomas Merton*

Real meditation is already radical activity. It is understanding....And when understanding has become observation, reflection, insight, radical cognition, then the state of consciousness itself is meditation....
—*Da Free John*

Seek in reading and thou shalt find in meditation; knock in prayer and it shall be opened in contemplation....
—*John of the Cross*

Those who are striving for knowledge will not get very far on the highway of life unless some time is given to meditation and contemplation; meditation on the past, that mistakes may not be repeated—contemplation on the future, that the learning and experience of today may be profitably applied to tomorrow....
—*Fred Van Amburgh*

Meditation applies the brakes to the mind.... —*Ramana Maharshi*

Contemplation for an hour is better than formal worship for sixty years....
—*Mohammed*

Meditation is a valuable exercise, but eventually you have to open up your eyes and look around....
—*Dan Millman*

Some hours of the day should be set apart for meditation so that the work in which we would be engaged during the other hours may be done as a spontaneous and blissful outflow of Eternal Reality dwelling in us....
—*Papa Ramdas*

Meditation is a rich and powerful method of study for anyone who knows how to examine his mind....the greatest men make it their occupation....It is the occupation of the Gods....
—*Michel Montaigne*

Arise in the midst of the night and commune with thy God. The ego will be crushed and things will be revealed to thee thou didst not know before and thy path in life will be made smooth....
—*Koran*

Through meditation, the Higher Self is seen....   —*Bhagavad-Gita*

The practice of reflective meditation, which consists in holding certain ideas in the mind long enough to enable them to form emotional connections, tends to break up the crust of habit and to create a new will....
—*Walter M. Horton*

Contemplation is for man the end of human life....   —*St. Thomas*

Stop talking, stop thinking, and there is nothing you will not understand. Return to the root and you will find Meaning....   —*Seng-ts'an*

Prayer is speaking to God. Meditation is listening. Trust tranquility....
—*Shirley MacLaine*

In contemplation it is the principle—namely God—which is sought....
—*Pope St. Gregory I*

Stop thinking that meditation is anything special. Stop thinking altogether....   —*Surya Singer*

There is only one meditation—the rigorous refusal to harbor thoughts. To be free from thoughts is itself meditation....   —*Nisargadatta*

Meditation is simply seeing reality and acknowledging it with bare honesty. Which means ultimately....we stop relying on every form of external authority. That's very revolutionary....
—*Bo Lozoff*

Do you know what one feels in meditation? The mind becomes like a continuous flow of oil—it thinks one object only, and that is God. It does not think of anything else....
—*Ramakrishna*

The spirit of meditation is the combating of self-willed thinking—it is a combat against the weight of one's feelings....   —*Hakuin*

Meditation is not a matter of trying to achieve ecstasy, spiritual bliss or tranquility, nor is it attempting to be a better person. It is simply the creation of a space in which we are able to expose and undo our neurotic games, our self-deceptions, our hidden fears and hopes....   —*Chögyam Trungpa*

Whoever is not very humble can never draw profit from contemplation....
—*Teresa of Avila*

What is meditation? It is the suspension of thoughts....   —*Ramana Maharshi*

Words are but the shell; meditation is the kernel....   —*Bahya Ibn Paquda*

The contemplative life is the life that puts thought above action, the invisible above the visible....   —*Cuthbert Hall*

Meditating means bringing the mind back to something again and again. Thus, we all meditate, but unless we direct it in some way, we meditate on ourselves and on our own problems, reinforcing our self-clinging....
—*Yeshe Dorje*

A meditator keeps his mind open every second. He is constantly investigating life, investigating his own experience, viewing existence in a detached and inquisitive way. Thus, he is constantly open to truth in any form, from any source, and at any time....
—*Henepola Gunartana*

There is no necessity for a technique or formula for meditation. Inner feeling, or inner knowing, is the Silent Voice of inspiration....
—*Walter Russell*

It were better to live one single day in the pursuit of understanding and meditation, than to live a hundred years in ignorance and restraint....
—*Gautama Buddha*

Mind

Minds, like bodies, will often fall into a pimpled, ill-conditioned state from mere excess of comfort....
—*Charles Dickens*

There is no misery or suffering outside your own mind because the whole world is nothing but a projection of your mind.... —*Annamalai Swami*

I find, by experience, that the mind and the body are more than married, for they are most intimately united; and when one suffers, the other sympathizes.... —*Philip Chesterfield*

Mind is only thoughts. The more easily you can be without thoughts, the nearer you are to a direct experience of Self. To make the mind die you must deprive it of thoughts....
—*Lakshmana*

Mind is nothing tangible upon which you can place your finger, as mind is not a thing. Mind is a process which the Self (you, as consciousness) uses to produce thoughts.... —*Ormond McGill*

The thoughts within our mind are in our power to control, but few ever exercise their freedom to control them, and instead are witness to an endless parade of fantasy, concepts and illusions.... —*A Spiritual Warrior*

The mind is the commander-in-chief and the senses are the armed forces. Hence, control of the mind is control (or victory) over the senses. If one's feet are covered with leather shoes, the entire world is covered with leather....
—*Yoga Vasistha*

There is only one means to control one's mind, that is to destroy thoughts as soon as they arise....
—*The Upanishads*

It's the nature of the mind to always change its mind....
—*Stephen H. Wolinsky*

The mind is an instrument which can be used by either the self-centered nature or the divine nature....
—*Peace Pilgrim*

Only the mind is capable of error....
—*A Course In Miracles*

Whenever you jettison false notions from the mind you make room for reality to enter.... —*Anonymous*

Breath is the bridge which connects life to consciousness, which unites your body to your thoughts. Whenever your mind becomes scattered, use your breath as a means to take hold of your mind again.... —*Thich Nhat Hanh*

When your mind stops racing, it is naturally kind instead of rude, naturally loving instead of selfish....
—*Eknath Easwaran*

The beginning of wisdom is to know the imperfection of one's own mind. If a man recognizes its weakness, he will not use it as a means to answer important questions.... —*Epictetus*

The human mind....is incapable of thinking rightly. It thinks from the point of view of error and limitation, instead of from the point of view of Truth and limitless power....In order to be free one must reverse his thoughts, learning to think from the Universal Mind, instead of from the finite mind....
—*Henry T. Hamblin*

Some minds remain open long enough for the truth not only to enter but to pass on through by way of a ready exit without pausing anywhere along the route.... —*Elizabeth Kenny*

The average mind is like a pool of water violently agitated by windstorms: storms of passion, of desires, of duties to be done, of a hundred demands upon one's time, of restless hurrying to-and-fro, of irritations, anxieties, worries, and a thousand other ills of the mind. Concentration is the cure....
—*Julian P. Johnson*

The chief characteristic of the mind is to be constantly describing itself....
—*Henri Focillon*

The human mind likes a strange idea as little as the body likes a strange protein and resists it with a similar energy....
—*W. H. Beveridge*

Little minds are interested in the extraordinary; great minds in the commonplace.... —*Elbert Hubbard*

If you give your mind your full, detached attention, you begin to understand the futility of all mental activities. Watch the mind wandering here and there, seeking out useless or unnecessary things or ideas which will ultimately only create misery for itself....
—*Annamalai Swami*

One must first discipline and control one's own mind. If a man can control his own mind he will find the way to Enlightenment, and all wisdom and virtue will naturally come to him....
—*Gautama Buddha*

As every divided kingdom falls, so every mind divided between many studies confounds and saps itself....
—*Leonardo da Vinci*

The mind is the mischief-maker. It jumps from doubt to doubt; it puts obstacles in the way. It weaves a net and gets entangled in it. It is ever discontented; it runs after a hundred things and away from another hundred.... —*Sathya Sai Baba*

Conquer the mind, and you conquer the world.... —*Nanak*

Nothing contributes so much to tranquilize the mind as a steady purpose.... —*Mary Wollstonecraft*

What we call a mind is nothing but a heap or collection of certain perceptions.... —*David Hume*

We should take care not to make the intellect our God.... —*Albert Einstein*

Where there is an open mind, there will always be a frontier....
—*Charles Kettering*

The mind unlearns with difficulty what has long been impressed on it....
—*Seneca*

Men allow their minds to become shackled in many ways—by self-pity, by anxiety, by self-interest, by lust, by greed.... —*Norman V. Peale*

Man's mind stretched by a new idea never goes back to its original dimension.... —*Oliver W. Holmes*

Your mind is your predicament. It wants to be free of change, free of pain, free of the obligations of life and death.... —*Dan Millman*

We are caught in the prison of the mind. If we are to escape we must recognize that we are in prison. If we think we are free, then no escape is possible.... —*George I. Gurdjieff*

If you were to practice keeping your mind motionless at all times with the object of not creating any thought, the result would be no dualism, no dependence upon others, and no attachment; if you would allow all matters to take their own course throughout the day as if you were too ill to bother, without the specific to be known or unknown to others, with a mind like a block of stone that mends no holes, then the universal law would deeply impregnate your understanding.... —*Huang Po*

Small minds cannot handle great themes.... —*St. Jerome*

There is nothing wrong with God's creation. Misery and suffering only exist in the mind.... —*Ramana Maharshi*

A closed mind is an enigma, indeed. Nothing ever goes in—but odd things are forever coming out.... —*Lawrence Dunphy*

Our minds have unbelievable power over our bodies.... —*André Maurois*

The mind is, without a doubt, unsteady and difficult to curb, but it can be controlled through practice and dispassion.... —*Bhagavad-Gita*

Empty your mind. Become still, and everything will happen of its own accord. There is really nothing you have to do. Just be still.... —*Robert Adams*

What is done by the mind is action, what is done by the body is not action....The physical body achieves nothing, on the other hand, the mental body gets results.... —*Yoga Vasistha*

To the mind that is still, the whole universe surrenders.... —*Chuang Tse*

If you are always thinking about worldly things your mind becomes dirty. From a spiritual point of view the mind is like a mirror; it is only useful when it is clean.... —*Saradamma*

What a superb thing it would be if we were big enough in mind to see no slights, accept no insults, cherish no jealousies and admit into our heart no hatred.... —*Elbert Hubbard*

Mind no longer appears as an accidental intruder in the realm of Matter. We are beginning to suspect that we ought rather to hail it as the creator and governor of the realm of Matter. Not, of course, our individual minds, but the Mind in which the atoms, out of which our individual minds have grown, exist as Thought.... —*James Jeans*

Only the receptive open mind can receive. Even the Sun's light cannot come in through closed windows.... —*J. Abelson*

If there's no desire in the mind, there's no mind at all. The mind is like a rockpile. Take all the rocks away and there is no pile....   —*Satchidananda*

Could one....remove the top of the most conventional individual's head and see the forbidden and obscene thoughts that constantly stream through the mind, one would be appalled....
—*Abraham Myerson*

Mind alone is neither moral nor immoral, any more than your automobile. It is a machine as truly as your car....   —*Julian P. Johnson*

The mind is an instrument for communication, for practical purposes. The mind cannot grasp the truth. The Self witnesses the mind, but the mind cannot catch hold of the Self....The mind can only work with some name or form or image. If you give this up, the mind will be helpless....
—*Nisargadatta*

Great minds have purpose; others have wishes. Little minds are tamed and subdued by misfortunes, but great minds rise above them....
—*Washington Irving*

The causes of all poverty are in the mind, and when these are removed abundance fills the life to overflowing. This does not mean the acquisition of great wealth, but something far better in every way....   —*Henry T. Hamblin*

The mind detached is of such nobility that what it sees is true, what it desires befalls and its behests must be obeyed....   —*Avicenna*

One should use the mind in such a way that it be free from any attachment....
—*Diamond Sutra*

Mind is the deadliest of foes, but the most useful of servants. When it turns wild and gets out of control, it heads for certain destruction. When properly awakened and controlled, there is no limit to what the mind can do....
—*Charan Singh*

Narrow minds think nothing right that is above their own capacity....
—*Francois La Rochefoucauld*

The immature mind hops from one thing to another; the mature mind seeks to follow through....
—*Harry A. Overstreet*

The man who has acquired the power of keeping his mind filled with the thoughts which uplift and encourage, the optimistic thought, the cheerful, hopeful thought, has solved one of the great riddles of life....
—*Orison S. Marden*

Our minds possess by nature an insatiable desire to know the truth....
—*Cicero*

A weak mind is like a microscope, which magnifies trifling things, but cannot receive great ones....
—*Philip Chesterfield*

When my mind is all made up to be miserable, I stop to consider; and I am convinced that not the world nor the people in it, but only my mind can make me miserable—or happy....
—*Fred Van Amburgh*

Our minds are like our stomachs, they are whetted by the change of their food, and variety supplies both with fresh appetite....   —*Quintilian*

Memory, of all the powers of the mind, is the most delicate and frail....
—*Ben Johnson*

The mind is like a strolling street dog. You are eating out of garbage cans. You who are heir to immortal glory, divine blessedness—why are you picking up these little droppings and trying to fill yourself?...
—*Sivananda*

The mind's highest good is the knowledge of God, and the mind's highest virtue is to know God....
—*Baruch Spinoza*

Curiosity is, in great and generous minds, the first passion and the last....
—*Samuel Johnson*

The pure mind which is the source of all things, shines forever with the radiance of its own perfection....
—*Huang Po*

The best way to promote the clearness of our mind, is by showing its faults; as when a stream discovers the dirt at the bottom, it convinces us of the transparency and purity of the water....
—*Alexander Pope*

The mind has to be still, not made still. Effort only leads to a rigid mind. When it realizes the futility of effort to penetrate to reality, the mind becomes still....
—*L. C. Soper*

A mind always determined has always a determined walk. A mind always weak, shifting, vacillating, and uncertain, makes a shuffling, shambling, uncertain gait....
—*Prentice Mulford*

Mind control is not one's birthright. The successful few owe their success to their perseverance....
—*Ramana Maharshi*

The Infinite has left us free to experience whatsoever we desire to create through our minds....
—*Raymond C. Barker*

A closed mind is a dying mind....
—*Edna Ferber*

There is no state of mind, however simple, which does not change every moment....
—*Henri Bergson*

Our minds are like crows. They pick up everything that glitters, no matter how uncomfortable our nests get with all that metal in them....
—*Thomas Merton*

The intellect....is the link that joins us to God....
—*Maimonides*

The cessation of the mind's waves is liberation....
—*Patanjali*

The "inner voice" is not always reliable, as much depends upon the purity of one's mind....
—*Shantidasa*

Instead of wanting to look at the back of the moon, remote from our lives, we can try to look at the back of our own minds....
—*J. B. Priestley*

The mind is a dangerous weapon, even to the possessor, if he knows not discreetly how to use it....
—*Michel Montaigne*

Man alone is the architect of his destiny. The greatest revolution in my generation is that human beings, by changing the inner attitudes of the mind, can change the outer aspects of their lives....
—*William James*

Wisdom entereth not into a malicious mind....
—*Francois Rabelais*

"Thoughtlessness" is to see and to know all things with a mind free from attachment....
—*Hui-Neng*

Man's minds perceive second causes, but only prophets perceive the action of the First Cause....
—*Rumi*

The human spirit is so great that no man can express it; could we rightly comprehend the mind of man nothing would be impossible to us upon the earth....
—*Paracelsus*

The mind that wishes to behold God must itself become God.... —*Plotinus*

All that is comes from the mind; it is based on the mind, it is fashioned by the mind.... —*The Pali Canon*

If your mind is empty, it is always ready for anything; it is open to everything. In the beginner's mind there are many possibilities; in the expert's mind there are few....
—*Shunryu Suzuki*

Every passion, every emotion, has its effect upon the mind. Every change of mind, however slight, has its effect upon the body....
—*Hazrat Inayat Khan*

Calmness of mind does not mean you should stop your activity. Real calmness should be activity itself....
—*Ram Dass*

It is not the body that is ill, but the mind.... —*S. Weir Mitchell*

The mind is said to be two-fold: the pure and also the impure; impure by union with desire—pure when from desire completely free....
—*The Upanishads*

Mind is consciousness which has put on limitations. You are originally unlimited and perfect. Later you take on limitations and become the mind....
—*Ramana Maharshi*

The mind grows narrow in proportion as the soul grows corrupt....
—*Jean J. Rousseau*

In the sky there is no distinction of east and west; people create distinctions out of their own minds and then believe them to be true....
—*Gautama Buddha*

Excitement exhausts the mind, and leaves it withered and sterile....
—*Francois Fenelon*

Man's mind is his essence; he is where his thoughts are....
—*Nahman Bratzlav*

The function of the mind is thinking; when you think, you keep your mind, and when you don't think, you lose your mind....That is how a man becomes a great man.... —*Mencius*

Minds are not conquered by force, but by love and highmindedness....
—*Baruch Spinoza*

The attainment of the one-pointedness of the mind and the senses is the best of austerities. It is superior to all religious duties.... —*Sankaracharya*

Praise be God who has given us a mind that cannot be satisfied with the temporal.... —*Nicholas of Cusa*

The mind is a useful servant, but a very bad master.... —*Julian P. Johnson*

The mind of the sage being in repose becomes the mirror of the universe. The repose of the sage is not what the world calls repose. His repose is the result of his mental attitude. All creation could not disturb his equilibrium: hence his repose....
—*Chuang Tse*

The mind has a way of being drawn away by passing fancy....The mind is the enchanter, the usurper who has established sovereignty over you....
—*Sathya Sai Baba*

Mind is thought. Thought means emotions, hopes, memory. Erase the emotions, good or bad, erase hope and disappointments, erase the memory, and the mind will be stilled....
—*Deepa Kodikal*

The mind denies that which it cannot understand. In valuing the mind as much as we do, we have a tendency to deny mystery, to deny the spiritual....
—*Rachel N. Remen*

Only the just man enjoys peace of mind....   —*Epicurus*

A pure mind in a chaste body is the mother of wisdom and deliberation....
—*Jeremy Taylor*

Chastity is a mind that is completely free from all image-making, all the pictures, sensations, which thought has built in its search for pleasure through sex. Then you will find an abundance of energy....   —*J. Krishnamurti*

The sound body is a product of the sound mind....   —*George B. Shaw*

The mind flows along the course of wisdom or of ignorance, in whatever direction you make it flow....
—*Yoga Vasistha*

Our minds are finite, and yet even in these circumstances of finitude we are surrounded by possibilities that are infinite, and the purpose of human life is to grasp as much as we can of that infinitude....   —*Alfred N. Whitehead*

A tamed mind brings happiness....
—*Dhammapada*

The perfect man's mind is like a mirror. It grasps nothing; it refuses nothing. It receives, but does not keep....   —*Chuang Tse*

Anything the human mind can believe, the human mind can achieve....
—*Napoleon Hill*

Purity of mind and idleness are incompatible....   —*Mohandas Gandhi*

The husbandman deals with land; physicians and trainers with the body; the wise man with his own Mind....
—*Epictetus*

We are, through our mental conditions, always drawing things to us good and bad, beneficial or injurious, pleasant or disagreeable....   —*Prentice Mulford*

Your mind may be likened to an incubator which provides the proper conditions for thoughts to grow. It matters not the thought, be it positive or negative, if concentrated upon sufficiently, it will flourish....
—*Shantidasa*

I believe that the mind has the power to affect groups of atoms and even tamper with the odds of atomic behavior, and that even the course of the world is not predetermined by physical laws but may be altered by the uncaused volition of human beings....
—*Arthur Eddington*

Make up your mind you can't—and you're always right....   —*Bob Goddard*

It is the mind that maketh good or ill, that maketh wretch or happy, rich or poor....   —*Edmund Spenser*

Everything that has happened to you has come about because you first saw it happening in your mind's eye....
—*Howard Sherman*

When you have learned to control your mind in the face of disturbances, then your mind has acquired one-pointedness....   —*Patanjali*

The secret of strength lies in the quiet mind.... —*Grace Cooke*

When everything has its proper place in our minds, we are able to stand in equilibrium with the rest of the world.... —*Henri F. Amiel*

In the province of the mind, what one believes to be true either is true or becomes true.... —*John Lilly*

As soon as the mind perceives differences, it awakens desire, grasping and....suffering....If the mind could remain undisturbed by differences and distinctions, the concept of an ego would die away.... —*Asvaghosa*

It is impossible for you to receive that which your mind refuses to accept.... —*Ernest Holmes*

The marvel of the living mind is that when it is illumined it can move into uncharted territories. It is enabled to take this step not out of reaction to the hurts of the past, but through the miracle of liberation from them.... —*Indira Gandhi*

Have a happy state of mind, a state that is untouched by the events of life.... —*Paramahansa Yogananda*

The mind is like a fire which is fueled by thoughts and desires. If there are no thoughts or desires, then the fire of the mind will die out.... —*Lakshmana*

Little minds are too much hurt by little events. Great minds understand all of them, and remain undisturbed.... —*Francois La Rochefoucauld*

The mind is like the body—the less its possessor is aware of it the more easy it's working.... —*Pearl S. Buck*

If men could regard the events of their lives with more open minds, they would frequently discover that they did not really desire the things they failed to obtain.... —*André Maurois*

Though we may not always realize it, it is the mind, not external events, that drives our constant state of urgency and restlessness... —*Eknath Easwaran*

Great spirits have always encountered violent opposition from mediocre minds.... —*Albert Einstein*

Most of the difficulties arise in your daily life if you do not have proper control over your mind. For instance, if a man does evil to you, instantly you want revenge, to extract tooth for tooth, tit for tat policy; to return anger for anger. Every reaction of evil shows that the mind is not under control. By anger one loses his energy.... —*Robert Collier*

Mind will never select a new course of action, unless a new force enters into it from without itself. Otherwise, it will go on indefinitely doing exactly what it has been trained to do. Mind does not want to do differently from what it has become accustomed. It resents innovation. It dislikes change.... —*Julian P. Johnson*

The more accurately we search into the human mind, the stronger traces we everywhere find of the wisdom of Him who made it.... —*Edmund Burke*

By annihilating desires you annihilate the mind.... —*Claude A. Helvetius*

When the mind is stilled, when the intellect is stilled, that is called the highest state by the wise.... —*The Upanishads*

Miracles

W hat....is a miracle? Nothing more or less than this: a highly illumined soul, one who has brought his life into harmony with the higher spiritual laws.... —*Ralph W. Trine*

Whatever a righteous man wishes is approved by God. Whatever a righteous man writes, God signs, and it is an everlasting testament....
—*Eliphas Levi*

Miracles are natural and involuntary, and should not be under conscious control.... —*A Course In Miracles*

Miracles are instantaneous; they cannot be summoned, but they come of themselves, usually at unlikely moments and to those who least expect them....
—*Katherine A. Porter*

All God's angels come to us disguised....
—*James Russell Lowell*

A miracle is what happens when you are going from one point to another in your life and suddenly you are at your destination without taking what you thought were the necessary steps....
—*Ron Smothermon*

True miracles are created by men when they use the courage and intelligence that God gave them....
—*Jean Anouilh*

To me every hour of the light and dark is a miracle, every cubic inch of space is a miracle.... —*Walt Whitman*

Miracles only happen to people who believe in them.... —*Anonymous*

There are only two ways to live your life. One is as though nothing is a miracle. The other is as though everything is a miracle....
—*Albert Einstein*

Miracles only work through your own faith. Where there is no faith there can be no miracle. So he who wants to perform a miracle can only do so by the power of faith. From this it is evident that the matter rests entirely with you.... —*Papa Ramdas*

Yes, it is true, I am a miracle. I am a miracle like a tree is a miracle, like a flower is a miracle. Now, if I am a miracle, can I do a bad thing? I can't, because I am a miracle, I am a miracle.... —*Pablo Casals*

To be a miracle worker you do not have to get a doctoral degree, become a minister, eat a particular food, or be able to meditate for long hours. All you need to do is to begin to see beauty in your life and those around you....
—*Alan Cohen*

The man who does not believe in miracles surely makes it certain that he will never take part in one....
—*William Blake*

You shall know the truth and the truth shall make you free. This is true in everything. Once you really know, the thing is accomplished, the miracle wrought.... —*Henry T. Hamblin*

To create miracles, you have to be very clear about what it is you want. By acting forthright and acting as if you have already obtained the object or condition that you desire, you create such a powerful energy that the Universal Law gives you what you want.... —*Stuart Wilde*

A miracle implies interfering with nature. Anyone on the path of self-realization finds that he slowly acquires certain powers by which he can perform small miracles. But these are to be shunned....　　*—Deepa Kodikal*

A miracle is an event which creates faith. Frauds deceive. An event which creates faith does not deceive; therefore it is not a fraud, but a miracle....
　　　　　　　　—George B. Shaw

A miracle cannot prove what is impossible; it is useful only to confirm what is possible....　　*—Maimonides*

To aim to convert a man by miracles is a profanation of the soul....
　　　　　　　　—Ralph W. Emerson

What we cannot do, God in us can do. What seems impossible to us is possible with God....　　　*—Martha Smock*

Where there is great love there are always miracles. Miracles rest not so much upon faces or voice or healing power coming to us from afar off, but in our own perceptions being finer....
　　　　　　　　—Willa Cather

The place where light and dark begin to touch is where miracles arise....
　　　　　　　　—Robert A. Johnson

We are miracles. Each of us is an absolute astonishment. So whether you believe in miracles or not, we still are. We still partake of "miracledom."...
　　　　　　　　—Ruby Doe

A coincidence is a small miracle where God chose to remain anonymous....
　　　　　　　　—Heide Quade

Miracles are signs not to them that believe, but to them that disbelieve....
　　　　　　　　—Thomas Aquinas

A miracle is no argument to one who is deliberately, and on principle, an atheist....　　　*—John H. Newman*

If angels come not to minister unto us it is because we do not invite them, it is because we keep the door closed through which they might otherwise enter....　　　*—Ralph W. Trine*

A miracle is never lost. It may touch many people you have not even met, and produce undreamed changes in situations of which you are not even aware....　　*—A Course In Miracles*

Self-sacrifice is the real miracle out of which all the reported miracles grew....
　　　　　　　　—Ralph W. Emerson

You are always wanting miracles; but God sows miracles by handfuls under your feet, and yet you still have men who deny their existence....
　　　　　　　　—Allan Kardec

Moderation

Those who know when they have enough are wealthy....The silken cord running through the chain of all virtues is moderation....
　　　　　　　　—Fred Van Amburgh

Everything that exceeds the bounds of moderation has an unstable foundation....　　　　　　*—Seneca*

An addiction is measured not by what an individual does, but by what he or she cannot do....　　*—Jay Rohrlick*

If you don't have enough you won't be happy. Neither are you happy if you have too much. It is those who have enough but not too much who are the happiest....　　*—Peace Pilgrim*

A man can find satisfaction with enough.... —*Keri Hulme*

Extremes, though contrary, have like effects. Extreme heat kills, and so extreme cold; extreme love breeds satiety, and so extreme hatred....
—*George Chapman*

If a man oversteps the limits of moderation, he pollutes his body and mind. To be god-like is to be natural; to be natural is to follow Nature...(i.e., to keep) within the limits set by instinct and reason.... —*Inazo Nitobe*

If you have too much of anything, you cannot know yourself....
—*Bhagavan Das*

Moderation is the only virtue. The other so-called virtues are virtuous only insofar as they are joined with moderation.... —*Charlton Ogburn, Jr.*

Good sense avoids all extremes, and requires us to be soberly rational....
—*Jean B. Moliere*

Nonviolent extremes endure; a sober moderation stands secure....
—*Charles Alleyn*

There is a mean in everything. Even virtue itself has its sated limits, which, not being strictly observed, it ceases to be virtue.... —*Horace*

He knows to live who keeps the middle state.... —*Alexander Pope*

The choicest pleasures of life lie within the ring of moderation....
—*Martin Tupper*

There should be balance in all our actions; to be either extreme or luke-warm is equally bad....
—*Hazrat Inayat Khan*

He who wants to do everything will never do anything....
—*André Maurois*

Neither great poverty nor great riches will hear reason.... —*Henry Fielding*

To go beyond the bounds of modera-tion is to outrage humanity. The greatness of the human soul is shown by knowing how to keep within proper bounds....There are two equally danger-ous extremes—to shut reason out, and not to let nothing in....
—*Blaise Pascal*

Every excessive power wears itself out.... —*Johann G. Herder*

All extremes are error. The reverse of error is not truth but error still. Truth lies between these extremes....
—*Richard Cecil*

You will go most safely in the middle....
—*Ovid*

The greatest flood has soonest ebb; the sorest tempest, the most sudden calm; the hottest love, the coldest end....
—*Socrates*

The true boundary of man is mod-eration.... —*Owen Felltham*

All excess brings on its own punishments....Moderation is the inseparable companion of wisdom....
—*Charles C. Colton*

There should be moderation in all things.... —*Apocrypha: Aristeas*

Moderation in temper is always a virtue; but moderation in principle is always a vice.... —*Thomas Paine*

A wise man will carefully avoid excess, lest he give the impression of haughtiness.... —*Maimonides*

An excess of sorrow is as foolish as profuse laughter; while, on the other hand, not to mourn at all is insensitivity....   —*Seneca*

Temperance is moderation in the things that are good and total abstinence from the things that are foul....   —*Frances E. Willard*

There is a proper measure in all things, certain limits beyond which and short of which right is not to be found....Who so cultivates the golden mean avoids the poverty of a hovel and the envy of a palace....   —*Horace*

Extreme views are never just; something always turns up which disturbs the calculations founded on their data....   —*Tancred*

Moderate desires constitute a character fitted to acquire all the good which the world can yield....   —*Timothy Dwight*

An excess of courtesy is discourteous....
                    —*Japanese proverb*

To go beyond is as bad as to fall short....
                    —*Chinese proverb*

Keep the golden mean between saying too much and too little....
                    —*Publilius Syrus*

Money

Money is a wonderful thing, but it is possible to pay too high a price for it....   —*Alexander Bloch*

To possess money is very well; it may be a valuable servant; to be possessed by it, is to be possessed by the devil, and one of the meanest and worst kind of devils....   —*Tryon Edwards*

The poorest man in the world is he who has nothing but money....
                    —*John D. Rockefeller*

If money be not thy servant, it will be thy master. The covetous cannot so properly be said to possess wealth, as that it may be said to possess him....
                    —*Francis Bacon*

Empty pockets never held anyone back. It's only empty heads and empty hearts that do it....   —*Norman V. Peale*

Preoccupation with money is the great test of small natures, but only a small test of great ones....
                    —*Nicolas de Chamfort*

Money is human happiness in the abstract: he, then, who is no longer capable of enjoying human happiness in the concrete devotes his heart entirely to money....   —*Arthur Schopenhauer*

Where there is money, there is fighting....   —*Marian Anderson*

Money destroys human roots wherever it is able to penetrate, by turning desire for gain into the sole motive....
                    —*Simone Weil*

For money, people sell their soul....
                    —*Sophocles*

As long as money is our servant it works for us, the moment it becomes master we work for it....
                    —*Alice H. Rice*

Money is in some respects like fire—it is a very excellent servant but a terrible master....   —*P. T. Barnum*

Money attracts egotism and irresistibly leads to its misuse....
                    —*Albert Einstein*

Money was meant to be our servant. But when we depend on servants too much they gradually become our masters....   —*Philip Slater*

To have enough is good luck, to have more than enough is harmful. This is true of all things, but especially money....   —*Chuang Tse*

Whoever desires money never has enough of it, there always seems to be lack, and more never seems to be quite enough....   —*Anonymous*

Money is a bottomless sea, in which honor, conscience, and truth may be drowned....   —*Kozlay*

Money will come to you when you are doing the right thing....
                —*Michael Philips*

Money often costs too much....
                —*Ralph W. Emerson*

The golden age only comes to men when they have forgotten gold....
                —*G. K. Chesterton*

Money can help you to get medicines, but not health. Money can help you to get soft pillows, but not sound sleep. Money can help you to get material comforts, but not eternal bliss. Money can help you get ornaments, but not beauty....   —*Sivananda*

Gold is a fool's curtain, which hides all his defects from the world....
                —*Owen Felltham*

Money can buy the husk of things, but not the kernel. It brings you food but not appetite, medicine but not health, acquaintances but not friends, servants but not faithfulness, days of joy but not peace or happiness....
                —*Henrik Ibsen*

Make money your God, it will plague you like the devil....
                —*Henry Fielding*

There are two laws known by spiritual teachers everywhere, and in all ages, which must be at all times obeyed, for most dire consequences follow their disregard or violation....That on no account a charge be demanded for revealing spiritual truths and that all money received by the teacher be regarded as God's and used accordingly....   —*Henry T. Hamblin*

Happiness cannot be bought; indeed, money has very little to do with it....
                —*William S. Ogden*

It's good to have money and the things that money can buy, but it's good, too, to check up once in a while and make sure you haven't lost the things that money can't buy....
                —*George H. Lorimer*

The greedy search for money or success will almost always lead men into unhappiness. Why? Because that kind of life makes them depend upon things outside themselves....
                —*André Maurois*

Superfluous wealth can buy superfluities only. Money is not required for one necessity of the soul....
                —*Henry D. Thoreau*

I can't afford to waste my time making money....   —*Louis Agassiz*

Money is the cause of good things to a good man, and evil things to a bad man....   —*Philo*

If someone thinks that when he or she makes a million dollars, he or she will be happy, that person is a very great fool....   —*Leo Buscaglia*

Starting out to make money is the greatest mistake in life. Do what you have a flair for doing, and if you are good enough at it money will come....
—*William Rootes*

The love of money is the mother of all evil.... —*Phocylides*

All love has something of blindness in it, but the love of money especially....
—*Robert South*

He who loves money never has money enough; he who loves wealth never has profit enough.... —*Ecclesiastes*

Money never made a man happy yet, nor will it. There is nothing in its nature to produce happiness. The more a man has, the more he wants. Instead of filling a vacuum, it makes one....
—*Benjamin Franklin*

The darkest hour of any man's life is when he sits down to plan how to get money without earning it....
—*Horace Greeley*

The only problems money can solve are money problems....
—*Jay W. Forrester*

Money is two steps removed from happiness.... —*David G. Myers*

Money spent on ourselves may be a millstone about the neck; spent on others it may give us wings like eagles.... —*Roswell D. Hitchcock*

If money is your hope for independence you will never have it. The only real security that a man can have in the world is a reserve of knowledge, experience, and ability....
—*Henry Ford*

Money is like manure, of very little use except to be spread....
—*Francis Bacon*

Money breeds insensitiveness....
—*Aldous Huxley*

When a fellow says it ain't the money but the principle of the thing, it's the money.... —*Artemus Ward*

That man is admired above all men who is not influenced by money....
—*Cicero*

Nothing that is God's is obtainable by money.... —*Tertullian*

Accumulated money brings misery to the owner. Keep money flowing....
—*Papa Ramdas*

Nature

Nature is but a name for an effect whose cause is God....
—*William Cowper*

Nature is always generous and kind even though we may not always like her ways.... —*Julian P. Johnson*

Man masters nature not by force but by understanding.... —*Jacob Bronowski*

Nature provides exceptions to every rule.... —*Margaret Fuller*

Nature is a volume of what God is the author.... —*Moses Harvey*

Nature does nothing uselessly....
—*Aristotle*

In nature nothing creates itself and nothing destroys itself....
—*Maria Montessori*

Nature is always trying to adjust itself and, in that adjustment, destruction also plays an important part....
—*Papa Ramdas*

Nature is an endless combination and repetition of a very few laws. She hums the old well-known air through innumerable variations....
—*Ralph W. Emerson*

Nature never leaps toward what she will eventually bring about....
—*Johann W. Goethe*

We do not see nature with our eyes, but with our understanding and our hearts....   —*William Hazlitt*

Repetition is the only form of permanence that nature can achieve....
—*George Santayana*

Nature is our mother. Because we live cut off from her, we get sick....
—*Thich Nhat Hanh*

What one has achieved can be attained by another. This is the grand law of Nature....   —*Sivananda*

Nature is the signature of God....
—*Coqosh Auh-Ho-Oh*

The law's of God's Nature are written on Nature's face; but it takes whole lifetimes of intense research by the ablest scientists to decipher one now, one again....   —*J. Abelson*

Nature is one grand cosmic book describing the power and majesty of God....   —*John A. O'Brien*

Every spring Nature writes a fresh, new chapter in the Book of Genesis....
—*Anonymous*

Nature is visible thought....
—*Heinrich Heine*

Nature's intent is neither food, nor drink, nor clothing, nor comfort, nor anything else in which God is left out. Whether you like it or not, whether you know it or not, secretly nature seeks, hunts, tries to ferret out the track on which God may be found....
—*Meister Eckhart*

Nature has devised a grand plan leading toward perfection. Life itself is one lengthy march to such an ideal using death as the process by which the tainted and the imperfect are recycled into another more enduring form....
—*Shantidasa*

There is no other door to knowledge than the door nature opens; there is no other truth except the truths we discover in nature....
—*Luther Burbank*

Whether man is disposed to yield to nature or to oppose her, he cannot do so without a correct understanding of her language....   —*Jean Rostand*

Nature uses as little as possible of everything....   —*Johannes Kepler*

Nature always takes her time. Great oaks don't become great overnight. They also lose a lot of leaves, branches and bark in the process of becoming great....   —*Andrew Matthews*

Nature is constantly seeking to show man that he is his own best friend, or his own worst enemy. Nature gives man the option on which he will be to himself....   —*William G. Jordan*

Leave all things to take their natural course, and do not interfere....
—*Lao-tzu*

We cannot fail in following nature....
—*Michel Montaigne*

Nature does not complete things. She is chaotic. Man must finish, and he does so by making a garden and building a wall....   —*Robert Frost*

He who understands nature walks with God....   —*Edgar Cayce*

If you only sit and reflect on the wonders of nature, you will gradually begin to feel that everything happens by divine will and power....   —*Papa Ramdas*

There is no trifling with nature; it is always true, dignified, and just; it is always in the right, and the faults and errors belong to us. Nature defies incompetence, but reveals its secrets to the competent, the truthful, and the pure....   —*Johann W. Goethe*

Nature, to be commanded, must be obeyed....   —*Francis Bacon*

Nature, in her indifference, makes no distinction between good and evil....
—*Anatole France*

Nature is a light, and by looking at Nature in her own light we will understand her. Visible Nature can be seen in her visible light; invisible Nature will become visible if we acquire the power to perceive her in her inner light....   —*Paracelsus*

Nature has some perfections, to show us that she is the image of God; and some imperfections to show us that she is only His image....
—*Blaise Pascal*

Everything in nature contains all the powers of nature. Everything is made of one hidden stuff....
—*Ralph W. Emerson*

Nature is man's teacher. She unfolds her treasure to his search, unseals his eye, illumes his mind, and purifies his heart....   —*Alfred B. Street*

Nature always springs to the surface and manages to show what she is. It is vain to stop or try to drive her back. She breaks through every obstacle, pushes forward, and at last makes for herself a way....   —*Nicolas Boileau*

I follow nature as the surest guide, and resign myself, with implicit obedience, to her sacred ordinances....   —*Cicero*

If I were to name the three most precious resources of life, I would say books, friends and nature; and the greatest of these, at least the most constant and always at hand, is nature....   —*John Burroughs*

All nature in its myriad forms of life is changeable, impermanent, unenduring. Only the informing Principle of nature endures. Nature is many, and is marked by separation. The informing Principle is One, and marked by unity....   —*James Allen*

Nature and wisdom always say the same....Never does nature say one thing and wisdom another....   —*Juvenal*

Our Mother, the earth, is in the middle, made round like an egg, and has all good things in herself, like a honeycomb....   —*Trimalchio*

Nature has no beginning and no end. Everything in it acts upon everything else, everything is relative, everything is at once effect and cause, acting and reacting on all sides....
—*Ludwig Feuerbach*

Nature never deserts the wise and pure....   —*Hartley Coleridge*

When a man digs a grave and there buries deep his ugly thoughts, when a man spades up a garden of kindly feelings, he is working with nature....
—*Fred Van Amburgh*

Nature has neither kernel nor shell; she is everything at once....Nature knows no pause in progress and development, and attaches her curse on all inaction....
—*Johann W. Goethe*

Nature is avariciously frugal; in matter, it allows no atom to elude its grasp; in mind, no thought or feeling to perish. It gathers up the fragments that nothing is lost.... —*David Thomas*

Nature never makes any fuss, and yet it does everything.... —*Lao-tzu*

You could cover the whole world with asphalt, but sooner or later green grass would break through....
—*Ilya Ehrenburg*

The laws of nature are just, but terrible. There is no weak mercy in them. Cause and consequence are inseparable and inevitable.... —*Henry W. Longfellow*

The grand show is eternal. It is always sunrise somewhere; the dew is never all dried at once; a shower is forever falling; vapor is ever rising....
—*John Muir*

Nature speaks in symbols and signs....
—*John G. Whittier*

Nature has placed mankind under the government of two sovereign masters, pain and pleasure.... —*Jeremy Bentham*

Nature is the most thrifty thing in the world; she never wastes anything; she undergoes change, but there is no annihilation—the essence remains....
—*Thomas Binney*

Nature never deceives us; it is always we who deceive ourselves....
—*Jean J. Rousseau*

No man can violate Nature's laws and escape her penalties....
—*Julian P. Johnson*

Nature is no spendthrift, but takes the shortest way to her ends....
—*Ralph W. Emerson*

Nature gives to every time and season some beauties of its own; and from morning to night, as from the cradle to the grave, is a succession of changes so gentle and easy we can scarcely mark their progress.... —*Charles Dickens*

In the whole realm of nature there is nothing purposeless, trivial or unnecessary.... —*Maimonides*

Nature seems reluctant to reveal her secrets to the intellectually arrogant....
—*Harold Burr*

It is not true that equality is a law of nature. Nature has no equality. Its sovereign law is subordination and dependence....
—*Luc de Clapiers Vauvenargues*

Nature cannot be hastened. The bloom of a flower opens in its own proper time.... —*Paul Brunton*

Nothing/ Emptiness

God made everything out of nothing.... —*Paul Valery*

"Blessed is the man who expects nothing, for he shall never be disappointed" was the ninth beatitude....
—*Alexander Pope*

Your nothingness is the miraculous essence of God....
—*A Spiritual Warrior*

God is nothingness. God is just Being. There is nothing to see, nothing to tell. It is just nothingness. And yet this nothing is total bliss. Bliss Divine....
—*Deepa Kodikal*

When you have reduced yourself to nothing—when your "self" has disappeared—when you have become nothing, then you are yourself God. The man who is nothing knows God, for God is nothing. Nothing is everything....
—*Yoga Swami*

There is nothing to do. Just be. Do nothing. Be. No climbing mountains and sitting in caves. I do not even say 'be yourself' since you do not know yourself. Just be....
—*Nisargadatta*

Nothing is necessary except God....
—*Joseph de Maistre*

The truth is that everything and nothing are the same and that we are both. You are not your body and your body is contained within you....
—*Ron Smothermon*

Seeing into nothingness—this is the true seeing, the eternal seeing....
—*Shen Hai*

Nothing is void of God; He Himself fills his work....
—*Seneca*

Become envious of anyone lower than you. You must become very small. In fact you must become nothing. Only a person who is nobody can abide in the Self....
—*Ramana Maharshi*

When nothing is sure, everything is possible....
—*Margaret Drabble*

All my life I believed I was somebody. But then one strange day came when I realized that I knew nothing, yes, I knew nothing. And so words became void of meaning....
—*Ezra Pound*

To be empty, completely empty, is not a fearsome thing; it is absolutely essential for the mind to be unoccupied; to be empty, unenforced, for then only it can move into unknown depths....
—*J. Krishnamurti*

Everything is the nature of no thing....
—*Parmenides*

Death and emptiness are the firm ground upon which life walks....
—*Alan Watts*

The game is not about becoming somebody, it's about becoming nobody....
—*Ram Dass*

After I realized I knew nothing—I realized that I knew everything....
—*Werner Erhard*

Out of emptiness arises compassion....
—*Buddhist saying*

It takes a long time to understand nothing....
—*Edward Dahlberg*

When one does nothing, nothing is left undone....
—*Hindu saying*

Among the great things which are to be found among us, the being of nothingness is the greatest....
—*Leonardo da Vinci*

Only when we are nothing do we become everything....
—*Nancy D. Potts*

Born from nothingness, man goes back to nothingness....
—*Seneca*

Nothing is better than something....
—*Hari Dass*

I am not what I am, and I am what I am not....
—*Jean-Paul Sartre*

To be able to do away with a thing, that is to say, to fling it into nothingness, nothingness would have to exist; and, if it exists, under whatsoever form, it is no longer nothingness....
—*Maurice Maeterlinck*

God is nothing....
—*St. Dionysius*

One of thine attributes is pure nothingness, which belongeth unto thee and unto the world in its entirety. If thou acknowledge thy nothingness, He will increase thee with His being....
—*Shaykh Ahmad al'Alawi*

This then is the sum of great knowledge for a man to know that by himself he is nothing.... —*Augustine*

It is only because the sage does nothing that he can do everything.... —*Lao-tzu*

Many people are afraid to empty their minds lest they may plunge into the Void. They do not know that their own Mind is the Void.... —*Huang Po*

That you may have pleasure in everything, seek pleasure in nothing. That you may know everything, seek to know nothing. That you may possess all things, seek to possess nothing. That you may be everything, seek to be nothing.... —*John of the Cross*

Ideas come from space. This may seem astonishing and impossible to believe, but it is true. Ideas come from out of space.... —*Thomas Edison*

Do not vainly lament but realize that nothing is permanent and learn from it the emptiness of life....
—*Gautama Buddha*

Become nothing before God....
—*Sören Kierkegaard*

When you demand nothing of the world, nor of God, when you want nothing, expect nothing, then the Supreme State will come to you uninvited and unexpected....
—*Nisargadatta*

God fills the place men call space. There is no place that God is not, for God is All.... —*James B. Schafer*

Nothing is brought into this world and nothing can be taken....
—*Nityananda*

Only he has become so free from self as to be equally content to be annihilated, is fit to enter into the Infinite....
—*James Allen*

I'm Nobody! Who are you? Are you—Nobody—Too? Then there's a pair of us? Don't tell!... —*Emily Dickinson*

Heaven and earth do nothing, yet there is nothing they do not accomplish....
—*Chuang Tse*

Know that the world, although appearing as substantial, has nothing substantial in it: it is a void, being merely an appearance created by the images and vagaries of the mind....
—*Yoga Vasistha*

Have your mind like unto space....
—*D. T. Suzuki*

Emptiness is perhaps the greatest wealth one can possess, for it provides the arena for adventure, discovery and creativity.... —*Peter Oppenheimer*

At the bottom of the modern man there is always a great thirst for self-forgetfulness, self-distraction....and therefore he turns away from all these problems and abysses which might recall to him his own nothingness.... —*Henri F. Amiel*

God dwells in the nothing-at-all that was prior to nothing....
—*Meister Eckhart*

The more that holy men advance in contemplation, the more they despise what they are, and know themselves to be nothing, or next to nothing....
—*Gregory the Great*

Power is emptiness and nothingness, as all definitions of your self melt away, and you neither begin nor end....
—*Maya Sarada Devi*

We maintain, and it is the evident truth, that the Supreme is everywhere and yet nowhere....It is precisely because there is nothing within the One that all things are from it....
—*Plotinus*

Put three grains of sand inside a vast cathedral, and the cathedral will be more closely packed with sand than space is with stars....   —*James Jeans*

The grace of God supplies the void....
—*Francis de Sales*

Brahma is the Void, the Ancient Void of the spirit....   —*The Upanishads*

Positively, the best thing a man can do is nothing, and, next to that, perhaps, good works....   —*Charles Lamb*

He is nowhere who is everywhere....
—*Seneca*

The Hebrew word "I" consists of the same letters as the word for "nothing."...   —*Anonymous*

I dissolved into the Emptiness, and discovered it was filled with Love....
—*Dom Bede Griffiths*

Great things can be reduced to small things, and small things can be reduced to nothing....   —*Chinese proverb*

Sitting quietly, doing nothing, everything is achieved....   —*Zen saying*

All matter is created out of some imperceptible substratum....nothingness, unimaginable and undetectable. But it is a peculiar form of nothingness out of which all matter is created....
—*Paul Dirac*

Nothingness is the building blocks of the universe....   —*J. A. Wheeler*

Anytime you are willing to experience the void it is available....
—*Ken Wilber*

Everything is emptiness and form is condensed emptiness....
—*Albert Einstein*

Form is emptiness and emptiness is form....   —*Shunryu Suzuki*

I have noticed that when one paints one should think of nothing: everything then comes better....
—*Raphael*

This is real liberation: to know that you are nothing. All your knowledge, including yourself, is liquidated—then you are liberated....   —*Nisargadatta*

Things are entirely what they appear to be—and behind them....there is nothing....   —*Jean Paul Sartre*

The real is empty: and the empty is real....   —*Tao saying*

Emptiness is most powerful. It is all pervading. When the mind becomes still, you experience that emptiness within you.. Empty yourself and realize the truth....   —*Papa Ramdas*

Old Age

The dead might as well try to speak to the living as the old to the young.... —*Willa Cather*

We grow old as soon as we cease to love and trust.... —*Louise H. de Choiseul*

Our true age can be determined by the ways in which we allow ourselves to play.... —*Louis Walsh*

The worst thing about being seventy-five years old is being treated as a seventy-five-year-old.... —*Norman Cousins*

Futility, pessimism, frustration, living in the past, are not only characteristic of "old age"; they contribute to it.... —*Maxwell Maltz*

In accepting aging, we need to accept death.... —*Annie Dorsey*

Many blessings do the advancing years bring with them.... —*Horace*

Nothing is more futile than a frantic clinging to life beyond its natural span.... —*Alice H. Rice*

The brain is the organ of longevity.... —*George A. Sacher*

We have aspects of ourselves hidden deep within, waiting to blossom in our later years.... —*Ken Dychtwald*

Up to one's last breath, one may retain the simple joys of childhood, the poetic ecstasies of the young man, the enthusiasms of maturity. Right to the end, one may intoxicate one's spirit with flowers, with beauty and with smiles.... —*Eliphas Levi*

Old age is not a disease—it is strength and survivorship, triumph over all kinds of vicissitudes and disappointments, trials and illnesses.... —*Maggie Kuhn*

It gives me great pleasure to converse with the aged. They have been over the road that all of us travel and know where it is rough and difficult and where it is level and easy.... —*Plato*

Honor age; even an old, blind man may lead you to a rainbow.... —*American Indian saying*

The great secret of all old people is that you really haven't changed in seventy or eighty years. Your body changes, but you don't change at all, and that, of course, causes great confusion.... —*Doris Lessing*

The objective is to live a full life, not just a long one. Survival into old age requires only good luck, whereas living enough demands character.... —*Seneca*

We grow old more through indolence than through age.... —*Christina of Sweden*

Youth is so full of doubts and fears and needs that harass and worry constantly, but which happily largely disappear with the passing years.... —*Charles F. Potter*

Growing old should be a rich summation of experience, not a decay.... —*Constance Warren*

We age, not by years, but by events and our emotional reactions to them.... —*Arnold A. Hutschnecker*

A man is not old until regrets take the place of dreams.... —*John Barrymore*

Old as I am in age, I have no feeling that I have ceased to grow inwardly or that my growth will stop at the dissolution of my flesh....
—*Mohandas Gandhi*

When a man acts wisely, he grows old slowly. When he acts unwisely, he grows older and older every day and in every way.... —*Fred Van Amburgh*

Old age is not a time of life. It is a condition of the body. It is not time that ages the body, it is abuse that does.... —*Herbert M. Shelton*

Old age is the climbing of a mountain. The higher you get, the more tired and breathless you become. But your view becomes much more extensive....
—*Ingmar Bergman*

To know how to grow old is a masterpiece of wisdom, and one of the most difficult chapters in the great art of living.... —*Henri F. Amiel*

Age does not depend upon years, but upon temperament and health. Some men are born old and some men grow so.... —*Tryon Edwards*

Thoughts of death pile up to an astonishing degree as the years increase. Willy-nilly, the aging person prepares himself for death. That is why I think that nature herself is already preparing for the end.... —*Carl Jung*

To me, old age is always fifteen years older than I am....
—*Bernard M. Baruch*

Each part of life has its own pleasures. Each has its own abundant harvest, to be garnered in season. We may grow old in body, but we need never grow old in mind and spirit....No one is as old as to think he cannot live one more year.... —*Cicero*

He who would pass his reclining years with honor and comfort, should, when young, consider that he may one day become old, and remember when he is old that he has once been young....
—*Joseph Addison*

Some people never seem to grow old. Always active in thought, always ready to adopt new ideas, they are never chargeable to fogeyism. Satisfied, yet ever dissatisfied, settled, yet ever unsettled, they always enjoy the best of what is, and are the first to find the best of what will be....
—*William Shakespeare*

Young souls look for happiness, older ones for peace, calm, and equilibrium.... —*Paul Brunton*

If wrinkles must be written upon our brows, let them not be written upon the heart. The spirit should not grow old.... —*James Garfield*

Too many of us grow old before we grow up.... —*Sonya Friedman*

When one finds company in himself and his pursuits he cannot feel old, no matter what his years may be....
—*Amos B. Alcott*

The older men grow the more they realize that it is only by putting the focus of their activities in some movement or activity greater than their individual ego, that they can attain peace and security in old age....
—*Walter B. Wolf*

Those who love deeply never grow old; they might die of old age, but they die young.... —*Arthur W. Pinero*

A graceful and honorable old age is the childhood of immortality.... —*Pindar*

Senility is not confined to old age....you do not have to be old; you simply have to have a rigid mind....
—*Eknath Easwaran*

As for old age, embrace it and love it....The gradually declining years are among the sweetest in a man's life....
—*Seneca*

To resist the frigidity of old age one must combine the body, mind and the heart. And to keep these in parallel vigor one must exercise, study and love.... —*Charles de Bonstetten*

If you have peace of mind, contentment, old age is no unbearable burden. Without that, both youth and age are painful.... —*Sophocles*

Youth is the age to receive instruction, middle age to make use of it, and old age to impart it to others....
—*Pythagoras*

Wisdom is found in the old, and discretion comes with great age....
—*Old Testament*

Knowledge is a comfortable and necessary retreat and shelter for us in advanced age, and if we do not plant it while young, it will give us no shade when we grow old....
—*Philip D. Stanhope*

For the ignorant, old age is winter; for the learned, old age is the harvest....
—*Yiddish saying*

Nothing is inherently and invincibly young except spirit. And spirit can enter a human being perhaps better in the quiet of old age and dwell there more undisturbed than in the turmoil of adventure.... —*George Santayana*

It is a rare and difficult attainment to grow old gracefully and happily....
—*Lydia Child*

Don't be ashamed of your grey hair! Wear it proudly, like a flag. You are fortunate, in a world of vicissitudes, to have lived long enough to wear it....Grow old eagerly, triumphantly....
—*William L. Phelps*

It is magnificent to grow old, if one keeps young.... —*Harry E. Fosdick*

Anyone who keeps the ability to see beauty never grows old....
—*Franz Kafka*

The spiritual eyesight improves as the physical eyesight declines.... —*Plato*

Don't complain about growing old— many people don't have that privilege.... —*Earl Warren*

For the man who has lived for the body, old age is decay; for the man who has lived for the spirit it is an apotheosis (exaltation).... —*Jean Delay*

No wise man ever wished to be younger.... —*Jonathan Swift*

We grow neither better or worse as we get old, but more like ourselves....
—*May L. Becker*

At sixty a man has passed most of the reefs and whirlpools. Excepting only death, he has no enemies left to meet....that man has awakened to a new youth.... —*George Luks*

To live long it is necessary to live slowly.... —*Cicero*

Grow old with me! The best is yet to be.... —*Robert Browning*

You don't get old from living a particular number of years: you get old because you have deserted your ideals. Years wrinkle your skin, renouncing your ideals wrinkles your soul. Worry, doubt, fear and despair are the enemies which slowly bring us down to the ground and turn us to dust before we die....　　　—*Douglas MacArthur*

I used to think that eighty was a very old age, but now that I am ninety-one I don't think so anymore. There are times I feel like a boy. As long as you are able to admire and to love, you are young....　　　—*Pablo Casals*

Old age is the most unexpected of all things that happens to a man....
　　　—*Leo Tolstoy*

That man never grows old who keeps a child in his heart....
　　　—*Richard Steele*

Neurosis is always linked with an inability to evolve. The adult who cannot accept growing old, or the old person who cannot accept his old age, or accepts it grudgingly, 'because he's got to,' is in the same difficulty, blocked in his evolution against the stream of life....　　　—*Paul Tournier*

We are not limited by our old age; we are liberated by it....　　—*Stu Mittleman*

The older I grow, the more apt I am to doubt my own judgement and to pay more respect to the judgement of others....　　　—*Benjamin Franklin*

Let your old age be childlike, and your childhood like old age; that is, so that neither may your wisdom be with pride, nor your humility without wisdom....　　　—*Augustine*

A man is getting old when he walks around a puddle instead of through it....　　　—*R. C. Ferguson*

Enjoy the seasons of life....Each season of life is wonderful if you have learned the lessons of the season before. It is only when you go on with lessons unlearned that you wish for a return....
　　　—*Peace Pilgrim*

No matter how old you get, if you can keep the desire to be creative, you're keeping the manchild alive....
　　　—*John Cassavetes*

A man is always startled when he hears himself seriously called an old man for the first time....　　　—*Oliver W. Holmes*

So long as you are learning, you are not growing old. It's when a man stops learning that he begins to grow old....
　　　—*Joseph Hergesheimer*

Old age can be the greatest time of your life....　　　—*Napoleon Hill*

Some men are born old, and some never seem so. If we keep well and cheerful we are always young, and at last die in youth, even when years would count us old....　　—*Tryon Edwards*

In your old age you will complete for the glory of God the tower of your soul that you began to build in the golden days of your youth....　　—*Mother Teresa*

The ignorant think less clearly as they age, the wise more clearly as they grow older....　　　—*The Talmud*

There is no finer or more fitting way to spend time during the evening years of life than turning the mind toward reflection and then stilling it in the Silence....　　　—*Paul Brunton*

Oneness

The whole universe is one whole; there is interaction between all things, but not determinism....
—*Plotinus*

If the doors of perception were cleansed, everything would appear to man as it is, infinite....
—*William Blake*

Oneness is experienced from within. Oneness lives within....
—*Iris Belhayes*

Seeing difference is ignorance. We are all one....   —*Sankara*

There are no others.....
—*Ramana Maharshi*

For him who sees him-Self in every self, in everything, there is no longer left any perplexity, doubt, sorrow, fear....   —*The Upanishads*

There does not exist 'another' except the one pure, formless consciousness....
—*Yoga Vasistha*

A single Spirit fills infinity. It is that of God, whom nothing limits or divides, who is everywhere entire and nowhere confined....   —*Eliphas Levi*

There is no boundary between subject and object, self and no-self, seer and seen....the subject and object always turn out to be one....   —*Ken Wilber*

Nothing is born, nothing is destroyed. Away with your dualism, your likes and dislikes. Every single thing is just One Mind....   —*Huang Po*

In the deeper reality beyond space and time, we may be all members of one body....   —*James Jeans*

All things are connected like to blood that connects us all. Man did not weave the web of life, he is merely a strand in it....   —*Chief Seattle*

When through concentration (drawing to a center) we have brought our forces into one point of power, we have contacted God in silence, we are one with him, and hence one with all power....   —*Baird Spalding*

Nothing less than becoming one with the universe will suffice....
—*Morihei Uyeshisba*

Everything in the universe is connected, everything is osmosis. You cannot separate any part from the whole; interdependence rules the cosmic order....   —*Taisen Deshimaru*

I am part of all that I have met....
—*Homer*

Life and death are one, even as the river and the sea are one....
—*Kahlil Gibran*

When man is at one, God is at one....
—*The Zohar*

All life is one. The world is one home. All are members of one human family. All creation is an organic whole. No man is independent of this whole. Man makes himself miserable by separating himself from others. Separation is death. Unity is eternal life....
—*Sivananda*

The True doctrine of omnipresence is that God reappears with all His parts in every moss and cobweb....
—*Ralph W. Emerson*

God is an artist par excellence. He has painted the picturesque universe on the screen of His own immutable and glowing Spirit. So He is the painter and the painted....　　*—Papa Ramdas*

When the oneness of the totality of things is not recognized, then ignorance as well as particularization arises....　　　　　*—Ashvaghosa*

We are already one. But we imagine that we are not. And what we have to recover is our original unity. What we have to be is what we are....
　　　　　　—Thomas Merton

I see God in everything....I recognize my oneness with all mankind and my oneness with God....　　*—Peace Pilgrim*

The whole is One....I guard the original One, and rest in harmony with externals....　　　　　*—Chuang Tse*

He drew a circle that shut me out— heretic, rebel, a thing to flout. But love and I had the wit to win: we drew a circle and took them in....
　　　　　　—Edwin Markin

If you would find the highest, the fullest, and the richest life....then do away with the sense of separativeness of your life from the life of God. Hold to the thought of your oneness....
　　　　　　—Ralph W. Trine

Survival is the second law of life. The first is that we are all one....
　　　　　—Joseph Campbell

All are really one....　　*—Black Elk*

We are members of one great body....
　　　　　　　—Seneca

There is one truth and one goodness penetrating and governing all things....
　　　　　—Giordano Bruno

In order to become conscious of the presence of abundance you need only become conscious of the presence of God. You need only become conscious of the Oneness of God. You have to know that Cause and Effect is One....
　　　　　—James B. Schafer

It is one thing to preach oneness, but if it is not fully understood and lived, then what is preached becomes an empty gesture....　　*—David Manners*

All humanity is one undivided and indivisible family....
　　　　　—Mohandas Gandhi

The one is here, there and everywhere; there is not a pin-hole where this one will not be found....　　*—Nityananda*

All life is one. Differences are super- ficial. They are only in the outer; they are only in the body. But one great common Consciousness dwells as the Reality within all names and forms, with all creatures, not only all human beings, in all creatures....
　　　　　　—Ramanujan

When we try to pick out anything by itself, we find it hitched to everything else in the universe....　　*—John Muir*

Not on my authority, but on that of truth, it is wise for you to accept the fact that all things are one....
　　　　　　—Heraclitus

There is no other side. There are only levels of apprehension, a single incom- prehensibly vast universe....
　　　　　　—Arthur Ford

All creatures seek after unity; all multiplicity struggles toward it—the universal aim of all life is always this unity....　　*—Johannes Tauler*

When, to a man who understands, the Self has become all things, what sorrow, what trouble can there be to him who once beheld that oneness....
—*The Upanishads*

Do you think that God is only in your heart? You should be able to recognize Him in every garden, in every forest, in every house, and in every person....
—*Shems Tabriez*

When a person abstains from doing wrong to any creature, in thought, word, or deed, he is said to attain to the state of oneness with God....
—*Mahabharata*

God is one. And he that is one is nameless; for he does not need a name, since he is alone....All things have been derived from One....   —*Hermes*

There is inherent in man a longing and tendency towards wholeness, and only when this longing is stilled is his negative state of tension wiped out and neutralized....   —*Gerhard Adler*

Realize that each soul is related to you. When you recognize that everyone is part of you, you will find you cannot withdraw from another....
—*Elsie Morgan*

All is One....
—*Xenophanes*

All souls are one. Each is a spark of the original soul, and this soul is inherent in all souls....   —*Hasidic saying*

The drop poured into the ocean is the ocean....All is one and one is all in all....
—*Meister Eckhart*

The universe in its entirety is nothing but one individual being....
—*Maimonides*

One in All. All in One—if only this is realized. No more worry about your not being perfect....   —*Seng-ts'an*

There is only one power that is active in every one of us and that is God....It is the one power that pervades the whole universe that is responsible for all activities and movements in the universe....   —*Papa Ramdas*

It does not matter what name you attach to it, but your consciousness must ascend to the point through which you view the universe with your God-centered nature. The feeling accompanying this experience is that of complete oneness with the Universal Whole. One merges into a euphoria of absolute unity with all life....
—*Peace Pilgrim*

You are the prison-house, you are the prisoner and you are the one who imprisons yourself....   —*Vimala Thakar*

That which exists is one; sages call it by various names....   —*Vedic saying*

What the principle of oneness teaches us is that no matter how hard we try to act otherwise, we are all equals....
—*Anonymous*

The chain which makes us one, is to honor the one God....   —*Philo*

If a man sees himself become one with the One, he has in himself a likeness of the One, and if he passes out of himself, as an image to its archetype, he has reached the end of his journey....
—*Plotinus*

Unity is convertible with eternity, for there cannot be more than one Eternal God....   —*Nicholas of Cusa*

All life is one—God is on our side....
—*Elbert Hubbard*

If one contemplates the things in mystical meditation, everything is revealed as one.... —*The Zohar*

No man lives unto himself; for every living thing is bound by cords to every other living thing....
—*The Aquarian Gospel*

In reality there are not two. There is only One.... —*Ramakrishna*

We go on believing we are separate. We are not—not even for a single moment. Drop the idea of separation—and the fear of death disappears. If you become one with the whole, you will live forever. You will go beyond birth and death.... —*Rajneesh*

See all things in one....
—*Jeremy Taylor*

The One is invisible: It cannot be seen. The One is inaudible: It cannot be heard. The One is Inapprehensible: It cannot be grasped.... —*Lao-tzu*

The heavens and the heavens of heavens together with the depths of the earth constitute one unit, one world, one being.... —*Abraham Kook*

One and God make a majority....
—*Frederick Douglass*

No man is an island, entire of itself; every man is a piece of the continent, a part of the main.... —*John Donne*

Keep cool, it will be all one a hundred years hence.... —*Ralph W. Emerson*

A mysterious bond of brotherhood makes all men one....
—*Thomas Carlyle*

Through drying one person's tears you are drying the whole world's tears. In making one lame person walk, you are helping every lame person throughout the universe....because the Group is never separated, and always works through the contribution of each member to the whole.... —*Ronald Beesley*

It's fearful to know we're connected to everything in the universe, because we're responsible....
—*Glenda Taylor*

The drop of water is only weak when it is removed from the ocean; replace it and it is as powerful as the ocean....If a portion of one unit excludes itself from the whole, it makes no difference to Principal Being, but it makes a vast difference to the unit. The ocean is not conscious of the removal of a drop of water, but the drop is very conscious of the ocean when it is returned....
—*Baird Spalding*

I believe that if one man gains spiritually the whole world gains with him and, if one falls, the whole world falls to that extent...
—*Mohandas Gandhi*

The universe is a single life comprising one substance and one soul....
—*Marcus Aurelius*

This is one of the most important factors in the development of man, the recognition—profound and complete recognition—of the law of universal unity and coherence....
—*Mabel Collins*

There is no man alone, because every man is a microcosm, and carries the whole world about him....
—*Thomas Browne*

As ridiculous as it seems for the lone wave to see itself as separate from the ocean, is it not equally ridiculous for the individual to close his eyes to his true connection to the Infinite....

—*Meredith L. Young*

The moment a person realizes his oneness with the Infinite Spirit he recognizes himself as a spiritual being, and no longer a physical, material being.... —*Ralph W. Trine*

Look upon all and everything as images of One, namely God....

—*Sathya Sai Baba*

He who in his own soul perceives the Supreme Soul in all beings, and acquires equanimity towards all of them, attains the highest bliss....

—*Manu*

Order

Order is never observed; It is disorder that attracts attention because it is awkward and intrusive....

—*Eliphas Levi*

Confusion is a word we have invented for an order which is not....

—*Henry Miller*

The only way whereby you can replace disorder with order is for you to become "at-one" in consciousness with the Divine Order....

—*James B. Schafer*

There is no chance, and no anarchy in the universe. All is system and gradation. Every god is there sitting in his ~here.... —*Ralph W. Emerson*

A secret force is at work trying to carry out a plan—a moral, spiritual plan to bring order out of the seeming chaos of creation.... —*Paramahansa Yogananda.*

Order is heaven's first law....

—*Alexander Pope*

The art of progress is to preserve order amid change and to preserve change amid order.... —*Alfred N. Whitehead*

Nature goes her own way, and all that to us seems an exception is really according to order....

—*Johann W. Goethe*

Order means light and peace, inward liberty and free command over one's self; order is power....

—*Henri F. Amiel*

Though we can't always see it at the time, if we look upon events with some perspective, we see things always happen for our best interests. We are being guided in a way better than we know ourselves.... —*Satchidananda*

The law and order which we find in the universe are most easily described and....explained in the language of idealism.... —*James Jeans*

I believe in God....who reveals Himself in the orderly harmony of the universe.... —*Albert Einstein*

You are a part of the universe, no less than the stars and the trees, and you have a right to be here. And whether it is clear to you or not, no doubt the universe is unfolding as it should....

—*Desiderata*

Everything that happens happens as it should, and if you observe carefully, you will find this to be so....

—*Marcus Aurelius*

Every man is where he is by the law of his being; the thoughts which he has built into his character have brought him there, and in the arrangement of his life there is no element of chance....
—*James Allen*

Chance is a word void of sense; nothing can exist without cause.... —*Voltaire*

Good order is the foundation of all things.... —*Edmund Burke*

Nothing happens at random, but everything from reason and necessity....
—*Leucippus*

To a sensible man, there is no such thing as chance.... —*Ludwig Tieck*

There is nothing that happens by chance in our universe. Everything unfolds according to higher laws—everything is regulated by divine order.... —*Peace Pilgrim*

Order is the sanity of the mind, the health of the body, the peace of the city, the security of the state. As the beams to a house, as the bones to a body, so is order to all things....
—*Robert Southey*

Any power capable of creating the world and overseeing the orderly process of evolution must know exactly where it is going and how it intends to get there. Its course cannot possibily be altered by any one of the finite minds it has created.... —*U. S. Anderson*

It is a rare life that remains orderly even in private.... —*Michel Montaigne*

In the presence of eternal order, disorder is essentially transitory. In the presence of absolute order, which is the will of God, disorder is only relative....
—*Eliphas Levi*

Beauty is absent where order is lacking.... —*Philo*

What comfort, what strength, what economy there is in order....To know where one is going and what one wishes—this is order; to keep one's word and one's engagements—again order....to discipline one's habits, one's efforts, one's wishes; to organize one's life, to distribute one's time....all this belongs to and is included in the word order.... —*Henri F. Amiel*

The world is not to be put in order, the world is order incarnate. It is for us to put ourselves in unison with this order.... —*Henry Miller*

Chaos demands to be recognized and experienced before letting itself be converted into a new order....
—*Hermann Hesse*

Order is intelligent, well-organized motion.... —*Anonymous*

Pain

Do not consider painful what is good for you.... —*Euripides*

The cup of pain, though it burns your lips, has been fashioned from the clay which the Potter has moistened with his own sacred tears....
—*Arabian saying*

Pain is a blessing in disguise. Pain is an eye-opener. Pain is your silent teacher. Pain will turn your mind toward God....
—*Sivananda*

What annoyances are more painful than those of which we cannot complain?... —*Marquis de Custine*

Sometimes pain and illness is not meant to be removed. You can't second-guess God. Rather than praying for it to go away, it's often wiser to pray that you learn as much from it as you possibly can.... —*Stephen Levine*

Pain is your teacher; pain is there for a reason... —*Satchidananda*

Nothing happens to any man which he is not formed by nature to bear.... —*Marcus Aurelius*

There is no pain like a bleeding heart.... —*Jane C. Turell*

In intense pain, a point is reached where it is indistinguishable from its opposite, pleasure. This is indeed so, but a few have the heroism or the strength to suffer to such a far point.... —*Mabel Collins*

The horror of pain is a rather low instruct and....if I think of human beings I've known and of my own life....I can't recall any case of pain which didn't on the whole, enrich life.... —*Malcolm Muggeridge*

Pain is no longer pain when it is past.... —*Margaret Preston*

God whispers to us in our pleasures, speaks in our conscience, but shouts in our pains: it is a megaphone to rouse the deaf world.... —*C. S. Lewis*

Though we may not always be able to avoid pain, we can choose how much we suffer.... —*Judy Tatelbaum*

Illness is the doctor to whom we pay most heed: to kindness, to knowledge we make promises only: pain we obey.... —*Marcel Proust*

The means by which certain pleasures are gained brings pains many times greater than the pleasures.... —*Epicurus*

With the help of a thorn in my foot, I spring higher than anyone with sound feet.... —*Sören Kierkegaard*

So long as you can sweeten another's pain, life is not in vain.... —*Helen Keller*

Much of your pain is self-chosen. It is the bitter potion by which the physician within you heals your sick self.... —*Kahlil Gibran*

Pain interferes with making plans by undermining interest in anything that's not immediate.... —*Marvin Minsky*

The purpose of pain is not to punish but to teach.... —*Elinor MacDonald*

We are a feelingless people. If we could really feel, the pain would be so great that we would stop all the suffering.... —*Julian Beck*

Pain is only triggered by another person when there is already pain within you.... —*Sanaya Roman*

The whole purpose of letting pain be pain is precisely this: to let go of pain. By entering into it, we see that we are strong enough and capable enough to move through it. We find out that it ultimately has a gift for us.... —*Matthew Fox*

Every pain in man is the result of some fear of lack, some belief in limitation. God can be the author only of good. Man suffers through his ignorance of his Oneness with God.... —*Craig Carter*

Do not try to drive pain away by pretending it is not real. If you seek serenity in oneness, pain will vanish of its own accord.... —*Seng ts'an*

When you cling to pain you only succeed in pouring more salt on the wound.... —*Anonymous*

People have a need to feel their pain. Very often pain is the beginning of a great deal of awareness. As an energy center it awakens consciousness....
—*Arnold Mindell*

Miseries, though belonging to the world of dreams, are of a certainty painful, and do not vanish until we cease dreaming....
—*Srimad Bhagavatam*

There is no pain quite like that of a broken heart. But a broken heart is an open heart. When we allow ourselves to be broken, a gentle transformation takes place.... —*Douglas Bloch*

Pain can be a doorway that takes us into the attic of spiritual inspiration....
—*Richard Moss*

Life breaks us all, and we heal stronger in the broken places....
—*Friedrich W. Nietzsche*

The pangs of pain, of failure, in this mortal lot, are the birth-throes of transition to better things. We are separated for a time by the indifference of space and our blindness which particularizes and isolates us. But in us is a longing for unity.... —*John E. Boodin*

Seek not outside yourself, for all pain comes simply from a futile search for what you want, insisting where it must be found.... —*A Course In Miracles*

There will be pain in your spiritual growth until you will to do God's will and no longer need to be pushed into it.... —*Peace Pilgrim*

Pain confers spiritual insight, a beauty of outlook, a philosophy of life....
—*Louis E. Bisch*

When the body is in pain, a distorted area of awareness is crying out to the rest of awareness for help....
—*Deepak Chopra*

One often learns more from ten days of agony than from ten years of contentment.... —*Merle Shain*

It is ironic that man should feel such a painful void inside of himself when he lives in a world of so many things which fill the air with sound, light and smog, but which apparently cannot fill the heart of men.... —*John Powell*

Pain is the outcome of sin....
—*Gautama Buddha*

If we want to be without any sort of pain, we must first ascertain the cause of pain. A little consideration will make it clear to us that the root cause of all sorrow is the mistaken identification of the Self with the body....
—*Chandrasekhara Bharati*

One of the greatest pains to human nature is the pain of a new idea....
—*Walter Bagehot*

When the mind is in tune with God, we shall be above the pains of the world.....
—*Papa Ramdas*

Change is painful when we attach our happiness to outer circumstances....
—*Jesse Jennings*

Even though he causes pain to his patient by applying certain remedies, the physician is not taken to be the cause of the suffering because in the final analysis he has produced the good that was sought after....
—*Mrigendra Agama*

The world is so constructed that, if you wish to enjoy its pleasures, you must also endure its pains. Whether you like it or not, you cannot have one without the other....
—*Brahmananda*

The mass of men lead lives of quiet desperation....
—*Henry D. Thoreau*

No man desires to see the light which illumines the spaceless soul until pain and sorrow and despair have driven him away from the life of ordinary humanity. First he wears out pleasure; then he wears out pain—till, at last, his eyes become incapable of tears....
—*Mabel Collins*

The cure for pain is in the pain....
—*Rumi*

The pain and suffering that comes to us has a purpose in our lives—it is trying to teach us something. We should look for its lesson....
—*Peace Pilgrim*

Pain is neither intolerable nor ever-lasting....It is the power of the soul to maintain its own serenity....
—*David Grayson*

Man suffers from pain and calls it evil, yet in reality it may be growing pains of the Spirit—the changing of the body into a finer and more spiritual substance....
—*Henry T. Hamblin*

Pain is telling us something is wrong, that we need to behave differently, that what hurts must be fixed....
—*Ernie Larson*

Your pain is the breaking of the shell that encloses your understanding....
—*Kahlil Gibran*

There are only two ways to live. If a man will not listen to his own inner wisdom, he will have to listen to his own inner pain. He can choose either teacher....
—*Vernon Howard*

Illness does not just happen to people with no reason. Often it is a message that a change is needed on some level of your life. And to resolve the illness, it may be necessary to understand and respond to that message....
—*Michael Volen*

Pain is not, like joy, an end in itself. It is often the result of mistakes, conscious or unconscious, and carries with it self-condemnation, regret, remorse....
—*Alice H. Rice*

If you are pained by any external thing, it is not this thing that disturbs you, but your own judgement about it. It is in your power to erase this judgement now. If anything in your own nature gives you pain, you are who hinders you from correcting your opinion....
—*Marcus Aurelius*

With proper understanding, the pain and the pleasure are the same. Both are lessons. In such a light, pain becomes pain no more. One who understands the world in the proper way will see the pain is there as a necessity, something to be risen above....
—*Satchidananda*

Past

There is nothing you can do about the past except forget it. There is a great deal, however, that you can do about the present and the future....
—*Joel Goldsmith*

Dwell not on the past. Use it to illustrate a point, then leave it behind. Nothing really matters except what you do now in this instant of time....
—*Eileen Caddy*

Anyone who limits her vision to memories of yesterday is already dead....　　　　—*Lillie Langtry*

In the carriages of the past you can't go anywhere....　　　—*Maksim Gorky*

The past and the unknown do not meet at any point; they cannot be brought together by any act whatsoever; there is no bridge to cross over nor a path that leads to it....　　　—*J. Krishnamurti*

Every journey into the past is complicated by delusions, false memories, false naming of real events....
—*Adrienne Rich*

Make it a rule of life never to regret and never to look back. Regret is an appalling waste of energy; you can't build on it; it's only good for wallowing in....　　　—*Katherine Mansfield*

Finish every day and be done with it. You have done what you could. Some blunders and absurdities no doubt crept in; forget them as soon as you can....　　　—*Ralph W. Emerson*

What is done, is done....
—*William Shakespeare*

Too many people live with mistakes they've made in their pasts. They stay locked in the same unsatisfying jobs, marriages, friendships and habits they developed at a time when they might not have had an idea what was best for them....　　　—*Lois Wolfe Morgan*

Rather than cursing the past, bless it....
—*Wayne Dyer*

Of all sad words of tongue or pen the most saddest are: "What might have been."...　　　　—*Anonymous*

It is when a man begins to live in the past, the good old days, that the boat begins to drift downstream, eventually coming to rest in stagnant waters....
—*Frank Case*

We should have no regrets. We should never look back. The past is finished. There is nothing to be gained by going over it....　　　—*Rebecca Beard*

Why wish for the privilege of living your past life again? You begin a new one every morning....　—*Robert Quillen*

God has no power over the past except to cover it with oblivion....
—*Pliny the Elder*

Let the lessons of life's errors sink in, but time spent in vain regret is one hundred percent wasted. To regret is to resurrect your mistakes. Any man is liable to make mistakes, but only a silly man will try to resurrect them....
—*Fred Van Amburgh*

The past is present in the future....
—*Louis L. Mann*

Guilt and sin are only a fear of the past....　　　—*Charles P. Curtis*

Regrets are caused by a misuse of memory....The man who broods over the past can never master the difficulties of today. Every wise man learns to forget. He does not allow himself to become a slave to his memory....　　—*Herbert Casson*

The present contains nothing more than the past, and what is found in the effect was already in the cause....
—*Henri Bergson*

No man having put his hand to the plow and looking back is fit for the kingdom of heaven....   —*Jesus*

The past is only yesterday's dream....   —*Tom Seeley*

Let us not raise the ghost of the past....   —*Papa Ramdas*

The present is the living sum-total of the whole Past....   —*Thomas Carlyle*

The past is a bucket of ashes....   —*Carl Sandburg*

Nothing changes more constantly than the past; for the past that influences our lives does not consist of what actually happened but of what men believe happened....   —*Gerald W. Johnson*

That deed is not well done that one regrets when it is done....   —*Gautama Buddha*

Those who cannot remember the past are condemned to repeat it....   —*George Santayana*

You can never plan the future by the past....   —*Edmund Burke*

A good memory is one trained to forget the trivial....   —*Clifton Fadiman*

Even God cannot change the past....   —*Agathon*

With God nothing is imposssible, God can change even the past....   —*Sevakram*

Look at the past like a bullet. Once it's fired it's finished....   —*Catherine Bauby*

We crucify ourselves between two thieves: regret for yesterday and fear of tomorrow....   —*Fulton Oursler*

Patience

How poor are they that have not patience! What wound did ever heal but by degrees?...   —*William Shakespeare*

Flowers do not force their way with great strife. Flowers open to perfection slowly in the sun....Don't be in a hurry about spiritual matters. Go step by step, and be very sure....   —*White Eagle*

Never think that God's delays are God's denials. Hold on; hold fast; hold out. Patience is genius....   —*Comte de Buffon*

The first proof of a well-ordered mind is to be able to pause and linger with itself....   —*Seneca*

In any contest between power and patience, bet on patience....   —*Anonymous*

It is necessary to work patiently with others, all the time....If you have patience with people, they will slowly change....   —*Chögyam Trungpa*

Patience is a bitter plant but its fruit is always sweet....   —*Persian saying*

There is no way to push the river; equally you cannot hasten the harvest....   —*Ralph Blum*

The virtue of patience is the one which most assures us of perfection....   —*Francis de Sales*

The power of patience, which has been called the grace of God, lies largely in the fact that it usually wins where force fails....   —*Alice H. Rice*

Patience is a particular requirement. Without it you can destroy in an hour what it might take you weeks to repair.... —*Charlie W. Shedd*

All human errors are impatience....
—*Franz Kafka*

Patience conquers everything in the end.... —*Paramananda*

Perhaps there is only one cardinal sin: impatience. Because of impatience we were driven out of Paradise, because of impatience we cannot return....
—*W. H. Auden*

Adversity borrows its sharpest sting from our impatience.... —*George Horne*

We are impatient people. We want everything immediately....We don't know how to to wait.... —*Ken Olson*

The philosophy of waiting is sustained by all the oracles of the universe....
—*Ralph W. Emerson*

There is as much difference between genuine patience and sullen endurance, as between the smile of love, and the malicious gnashing of the teeth....
—*William S. Plumer*

Patience and diligence, like faith, remove mountains.... —*William Penn*

There is no escape from the rule that we must do many, many little things to accomplish even just one big thing. This gives me patience when I need it most.... —*James Q. DuPont*

Slow down and the thing you are chasing will come around and catch you.... —*Zen saying*

Patience is the best remedy for every trouble.... —*Plautus*

We shall sooner have the fowl by hatching the egg than by smashing it....
—*Abraham Lincoln*

Hope and patience are two sovereign remedies for all, the surest reposals, the softest cushions to lean on in adversity.... —*Robert Burton*

One must know how to sail with a contrary wind and to tack until one meets a wind in the right direction....
—*Fortune de Felice*

Impatience in any manner is a sign of weakness. So, to be free from it, submission to God's will in all things is the way.... —*Papa Ramdas*

The slower you go, the farther you will be.... —*Russian proverb*

Learn to pause....or nothing worthwhile will catch up to you.... —*Doug King*

Patience is so like fortitude that she seems either her sister or her daughter.... —*Aristotle*

Everything comes if a man will only wait.... —*Tancred*

There is no great achievement that is not the result of patient working and waiting.... —*Josiah Holland*

Patience and tenacity of purpose are assets of infinitely greater value than cleverness. There is great strength in patiently waiting. The sun, having set, comes up. The tide ebbs, but always flows in again.... —*Fred Van Amburgh*

With time and patience the mulberry leaf becomes a silk gown....
—*Oriental proverb*

Never cut what you can untie....
—*Joseph Joubert*

A patient man cannot be irritated even a bit. Patience helps a man in the conquest of temper. Patience gives immense strength.... —*Sivananda*

It is not necessary for all men to be great in action. The greatest and sublimest power is often simple patience.... —*Horace Bushnell*

Everything comes in time to those who can wait.... —*Francois Rabelais*

Patience is power. Patience is not an absence of action; rather, it is "timing"; it waits on the right time to act, for the right principles and in the right way.... —*Fulton J. Sheen*

Stumbling is the fruit of haste.... —*Arabian saying*

When you are patient, you take the time to immerse yourself in joy of the moment which is denied to those who hurry.... —*Donald Curtis*

To go faster, you must slow down.... —*John Brunner*

Be patient toward all that is unsolved in your heart....and try to love the questions themselves.... —*Rainer M. Rilke*

Be patient in your striving; be persistent in your expectations.... —*Anonymous*

To know how to wait is the great secret of success.... —*Xavier de Maistre*

Patience can't be acquired overnight. It is just like building up a muscle. Every day you need to work on it.... —*Eknath Easwaran*

Patience is a gift that God only gives to those He loves.... —*African proverb*

Only those who have the patience to do simple things perfectly will acquire the skill to do difficult things easily.... —*Johann von Schiller*

It is because men cannot hold to patience that they fail to achieve anything. Else there is no other reason for failure.... —*Turiyananda*

We rush through life so fast that we don't even know the flowers are there.... —*Dale Evans Rogers*

Patience and fortitude conquer all things.... —*Ralph W. Emerson*

Whoever is out of patience is out of possession of his soul.... —*Francis Bacon*

In America, an hour is forty minutes.... —*German proverb*

Ask too much and it shall not be given to you; knock too loudly and it shall not be opened unto you; seek impatiently and you shall not find.... —*Will Durant*

There is nothing so bitter, that a patient mind cannot find some solace for it.... —*Seneca*

If I were asked what single qualification was necessary for one who has care of children, I should say patience—patience with their tempers, with their understandings, with their progress.... —*Francois Fenelon*

If I have ever made any valuable discoveries, it is owing more to patient attention than to any other talent.... —*Isaac Newton*

Patience gives you the power to practice; practice gives you the power that leads you to perfection.... —*Yogi Bhajan*

Patience strengthens the spirit, sweetens the temper, stifles anger, extinguishes envy, subdues pride, bridles the tongue, restrains the hand, and tramples upon temptation....
—*George Horne*

Patience is but lying to and riding out the gale.... —*Henry W. Beecher*

Patience and delay achieve more than force and rage.... —*Jean La Fontaine*

Patience and silence go together....
—*Paramananda*

The conflict of patience is such that the vanquished is better than the vanquisher.... —*Euripides*

He who is slow to answer has great understanding.... —*Old Testament*

All things come round to him who will but wait.... —*Henry W. Longfellow*

Have patience with all the world, but first of all with yourself....
—*Francis de Sales*

There is no road too long to the man who advances deliberately without undue haste; no honors too distant to the man who prepares himself for them with patience.... —*Jean La Bruyere*

Patience is strength....
—*Anonymous*

Do you have the patience to wait until your mud settles, and the water is clear? Can you remain unmoving till the right action arises by itself?...
—*Lao-tzu*

You must grow in patience when you meet with great wrongs, and they will be powerless to vex your mind....
—*Leonardo da Vinci*

You are not defeated until you lose your patience.... —*Robert Schuller*

True patience simply means having absolute confidence in God....
—*Anonymous*

Of all the qualities of an excellent character, patience is enough for us....
—*Michel Montaigne*

Patience and tolerance are handmaidens. They walk down the path of life, hand—in—hand. They are not separate entities, so to speak. They are one.... —*Frater Achad*

Apply discipline to your thoughts when they become anxious over the outcome of a goal. Impatience breeds anxiety, fear, discouragement and failure. Patience creates confidence, decisiveness and a rational outlook, which eventually leads to success....
—*Brian Adams*

Patience is passion tamed....
—*Lyman Abbott*

What is patience but an equanimity which enables you to rise superior to the trials of life?... —*William Osler*

Our patience will achieve more than our force.... —*Edmund Burke*

A man who is master of patience is master of everything else....
—*Lord Halifax*

Nothing great is created suddenly, any more than a bunch of grapes or a fig. If you tell me that you desire a fig. I answer you that there must be time. Let the tree first blossom, then bear fruit, then ripen.... —*Epictetus*

Patient waiting is often the highest way of doing God's will....
—*Jeremy Collier*

Impatience....is one of our greatest sufferings. To realize how foolish it is to become impatient, try turning your watch ahead, or tear a few sheets off the calendar in your efforts to advance time....　　　　*—James Mangan*

To know how to wait is the great secret of success....　　*—Joseph M. de Maistre*

Patience is all the strength a man needs....　　　　*—Sathya Sai Baba*

The man who can wait indefinitely can wear down the strength of the most belligerent opposition, for in the end a forgiving spirit disarms an opponent, and wins his reluctant admiration....
　　　　　　　—Alice H. Rice

To lose patience is to lose the battle....
　　　　　　—Mohandas Gandhi

Patience means waiting without anxiety....　　　　*—Francis de Sales*

There are before you countless opportunities that can be built into a big success, but it is a mistake to expect to see your corn come up the day after you plant it....　　*—Fred Van Amburgh*

The greater our hurry, the longer the way; the greater our patience, the sooner we reach the goal....
　　　　　　　—German proverb

Peace/Harmony

The home is the empire! There is no peace more delightful than one's own fireplace....　　　*—Cicero*

At the heart of the cyclone tearing the sky....is a place of central calm....
　　　　　　　—Edwin Markham

Peace will come when each of us goes within, and realizes that we are all equal aspects of God; then we can sit together in harmony with no necessity to compare personal views....
　　　　　　—A Spiritual Warrior

Peace is difficult to attain for those whose mind is centered on the body....
　　　　　　　—Nityananda

Neither money, nor worldly possessions, neither science nor authority, will bring you the sweet rest of paradise, at which you can arrive only by the noble knowledge of the higher self....　　　　　*—Jakob Böhme*

To the peaceful a house is like a forest and to the restless even a forest is like a crowded city. To one who is at peace, the entire world is a peaceful forest. To one who is restless with a thousand thoughts, it is an ocean of sorrow....
　　　　　　　—Yoga Vasistha

For peace of mind, resign as general manager of the universe....
　　　　　　—Larry Eisenberg

Peace is a costly privilege—to be fought for, attained and won. It comes only from a conquered mind....
　　　　　　　—Paul Brunton

Peace comes not from doing, but from undoing; not from getting, but from letting go....　　*—Satchidananda*

Peace exists when you have nothing to prove, or stated differently, when you have no self to prove....
　　　　　　　—Vernon Howard

The conflict of opposites gives birth to harmony....　　*—William Gibson*

Harmony seldom makes a headline....
　　　　　　　—Silas Bent

We should have much peace if we would not busy ourselves with the sayings and doings of others....
—*Thomas à Kempis*

Harmony seeks nothing outside of itself. It is what ought to be; it is the expression of right, order, law and truth; it is greater than time and represents eternity....   —*Henri F. Amiel*

If you are inwardly free from fighting, no one will be able to start a fight with you....   —*Anonymous*

Harmony means absence of conflict; it means stillness and silence, peace and tranquility....   —*Ramesh Balsekar*

Discord is rife in the outward world, but unbroken harmony holds sway at the heart of the universe....
—*James Allen*

Undisturbed peace of mind is attained by the cultivation of friendliness toward the happy, compassion for the unhappy, delight in the virtuous, and indifference in the evil....   —*Patanjali*

Humanity can only improve as people improve. When you have improved your life, you can inspire those around you to want to improve their lives. Remember that a few in harmony with God's will are more powerful than multitudes out of harmony....
—*Peace Pilgrim*

Like water, we are truest to our nature in repose....   —*Cyril Connolly*

A happy person is not his own enemy, does not carry on an endless war with his soul. We may be fiercely at odds with the wrongs of the world around us. But inside ourselves, near the core, if we are happy, we are at peace....
—*Lewis B. Smedes*

All the frictions, all the uncertainties, all the ills, the sufferings, the fears, the forebodings, the perplexities of life come to us because we are out of harmony with the divine purpose of things. They will continue to come as long as we so live. Rowing against the tide is hard and uncertain....
—*Ralph W. Trine*

What is dangerous about tranquilizers is that whatever peace of mind they bring is packaged peace of mind. When you buy a pill and buy peace with it, you get conditioned to cheap solutions instead of deep ones....   —*Max Lerner*

In the gates of eternity the black hand and the white hand hold each other with equal clasp....
—*Harriet Beecher Stowe*

We fluctuate long between love and hatred before we arrive at tranquility....
—*Heloise*

He is happiest, be he king or peasant, who finds his peace at home....
—*Johann W. Goethe*

Never be in a hurry; do everything quietly and in a calm spirit. Do not lose your inward peace for anything whatsoever, even if your whole world seems upset....   —*Francis de Sales*

What all men are after is some form, or perhaps only some formula, of peace....
—*Joseph Conrad*

If there is to be peace it will come through being, not having....
—*Henry Miller*

That man attains peace who, abandoning all desires, moves about without longing, without the sense of mine and without egoism....
—*Bhagavad-Gita*

The thirst for objects is the greatest enemy of peace. Desire causes distraction of various sorts....The mind will be ever restless and hanker after the objects. When this thirst dies, man enjoys peace.... *—Sivananda*

Where there is peace and meditation, then there is neither anxiety nor doubt.... *—Francis of Assisi*

God is peace, His name is peace, and all is bound together in peace....
—The Zohar

When everything is in its right place within us, we ourselves are in balance with the whole work of God....
—Henry F. Amiel

From the cradle to his grave a man never does a single thing which has any first and foremost object save to secure peace of mind, spiritual comfort, for himself.... *—Mark Twain*

If you really want peace of mind and inner calm, you will get it. Regardless of how unjustly you have been treated, or how unfair the boss has been, or what a mean scoundrel someone has proved to be, all this makes no difference to you when you awaken to your mental and spiritual powers....
—Joseph Murphy

Nothing can bring you peace but yourself. Nothing can bring you peace but the triumph of principles....
—Ralph W. Emerson

Peace is rarely denied to the peaceful....
—Johann von Schiller

Slowly, painfully, I have learned that peace of mind may transform a cottage into a spacious manor hall; the want of it can make a regal park an imprisoning nutshell....
—Joshua L. Liebman

Peace is when time doesn't matter as it passes away.... *—Maria Schell*

As long as a man thinks he can do something by himself, so long he shall find no peace.... *—Arjun*

The world is not in need of saving, it is perfect in itself—it is not a mess to be fixed up. It is harmonious and whole, and it is our responsibility to harmonize with it, not change it....
—A Spiritual Warrior

Peace is the happy, natural state of man; war, his corruption, his disgrace.... *—James Thomson*

Riches bring anxiety; wisdom gives peace of mind.... *—Ibn Gabirol*

I was glad I was born, glad I suffered so, glad I did make big blunders, glad to enter peace.... *—Vivekananda*

Peace rules the day where reason rules the mind.... *—Wilkie Collins*

Each one has to find his peace from within. And peace to be real must be unaffected by outside circumstances....
—Mohandas Gandhi

A happy life consists in tranquility of mind.... *—Cicero*

Peace of mind is worth any price it demands.... *—Gayatri Devi*

Few find inner peace but this is not because they try and fail, it is because they do not try....When your life is governed by the divine nature instead of the self-centered nature you have found inner peace.... *—Peace Pilgrim*

Peace is not absence of war, it is virtue, a state of mind, a disposition for benevolence, confidence, justice....
—Baruch Spinoza

Peace cannot suddenly descend from the heavens. It can only come when the root causes of trouble are removed....
—*Jawaharlal Nehru*

It is only after a man has rid himself of all pretense, and taken refuge in mere unembellished existence, that he is able to attain peace of mind....
—*Arthur Schopenhauer*

Five great enemies to peace inhabit us: avarice, ambition, envy, anger and pride. If those enemies were to be banished, we would infallibly enjoy perpetual peace....　　　—*Petrarch*

I learned that it is possible for us to create light, sound and order within us no matter what calamity may befall us in the outer world....　　—*Helen Keller*

Peace of mind is that mental condition in which you have accepted the worst....
—*Lin Yutang*

When a man finds no peace within himself it is useless to seek it elsewhere....　　—*Francois La Rochefoucauld*

If you only knew the peace there is in accepted sorrow....
—*Madame Guyon*

To be at one with God is to be at peace....Peace is to be found only within, and unless one finds it there he will never find it at all. Peace lies not in the external world. It lies within one's own soul....　　—*Ralph W. Trine*

The life of inner peace, being harmonious and without stress, is the easiest type of existence....
—*Norman V. Peale*

Nothing contributes more to peace of mind than to have no opinions whatever....　　—*Georg C. Lichtenberg*

Perfect peace can dwell only where all egotism has disappeared....
—*Gautama Buddha*

To insure peace of mind, ignore the rules and regulations....
—*William Feather*

Peace is the most priceless possession of man. It is the sign of a virtuous character....　　—*Sathya Sai Baba*

Peace can reign only where there is no disturbance, and disturbance is due to thoughts that arise in the mind....
—*Ramana Maharshi*

Our work for peace must begin within the private world of each of us....
—*Dag Hammarskjöld*

The peace which results from social comfort, passing gratification, or worldly victory is transitory in nature, and is burned up in the heat of fiery trial....only the selfless heart can know the Peace of Heaven....　　—*James Allen*

Peace is in that heart in which no wave of desire of any kind arises....This eternal peace is your real existence—it is not a state or truth to be attained but to be realized; because you are ever That....　　—*Papa Ramdas*

Whoever lives in the spirit lives in perennial peace. It is a happy peace, a smiling peace, but he is not lost in it. He is aware also of the suffering which exists around him and the world at large....　　—*Paul Brunton*

I realize that God is always at peace. Even when God is expressing excitement as a storm at sea, God is still at peace....　　—*William Curtiss*

Peace is better than a fortune....
—*Francis de Sales*

The first rule is to keep an untroubled spirit. The second is to look things in the face and know them for what they are.... —*Marcus Aurelius*

Everyone thirsts for peace, but few people understand that perfect peace cannot be obtained as long as the inner soul is not filled with the presence of God.... —*Anandamayi Ma*

As long as you have no equanimity and can still feel the sting of insult, you have not attained to the state where you can connect your thoughts with God.... —*Isaac of Acre*

There can never be peace between nations until there is first known that true peace which....is within the souls of men.... —*Black Elk*

People look in vain places for peace. They seek it in the world outside, in places, people, ways, activities....but there is no peace found this way. They are looking in the wrong direction, and the longer they look the less they find what they are looking for.... —*Meister Eckhart*

Nothing we ever get, see, taste, smell, touch, hear, or think about, is going to bring us the peace we really seek.... —*Bo Lozoff*

To win true peace, a man needs to feel directed, pardoned, and sustained by a supreme power.... —*Henri F. Amiel*

Peace cannot be kept by force. It can only be achieved by understanding.... —*Albert Einstein*

No matter how turbulent the storm might be, there is an 'eye' at the center of the hurricane where all is calm and still.... —*Donald Curtis*

Inner peace is not found by staying on the surface of life, or by attempting to escape from life through any means. Inner peace is found by facing life squarely, solving its problems, and delving as far beneath the surface as possible to discover its verities and realities.... —*Peace Pilgrim*

A peaceful mind is your most precious capital.... —*Sivananda*

Peace is important, for God's name is Peace.... —*Midrash Tahama*

The first step to bringing peace into the world is to realize the peace that already dwells within you.... —*Anonymous*

Perfection

Your basic nature is that of perfection....Life works perfectly, naturally, when you are willing to let it. When you try, you are not letting it be naturally perfect.... —*Ron Smothermon*

There can never be a perfect world because the world is always a creation of an imperfect mind. A perfect object cannot be made by such an imperfect tool.... —*Ramana Maharshi*

God is perfection itself, not an effort at perfection.... —*Nisargadatta*

The perfect way is difficult for those who pick and choose. We should not like or dislike, only then will all become clear.... —*Seng Ts'an*

The perfect man employs his mind as a mirror. It grasps nothing: It refuses nothing. It receives, but doesn't keep. Thus he can triumph over matter, without injury to himself.... —*Lao-tzu*

Everything has its own perfection, be it higher or lower in the scale of things; and the perfection of one is not the perfection of another....
—*John H. Newman*

This is perfect, that is perfect; from perfection, perfection comes; take away perfection from perfection. Perfection remains.... —*Haidakhan Aarati*

To imagine oneself perfect fixes the idea of perfection in the invisible mind substance, and the mind forces at once begin the work of bringing forth perfection.... —*Charles Fillmore*

No one ever approaches perfection except by stealth, and unknown to themselves.... —*William Hazlitt*

This is the very perfection of man, to find out his own perfection....
—*Augustine*

To seek perfection in property or health or character is not a worthy human goal; nor is it a proper cause of pride and glory for man; the knowledge of God is the only true wisdom, and the sole perfection man should seek....
—*Maimonides*

We can never attain perfection while we have an affliction for any imperfection.... —*Francis de Sales*

Every perfect life is a parable invented by God.... —*Simone Weil*

Life is perfect exactly the way it is; no one ever said perfection must be consistent.... —*Shantidasa*

The pursuit of perfection often impedes progress.... —*George Will*

Don't you see that it's all perfect?...
—*Neem Karoli Baba*

When people reach the highest perfection, it is nothing special, it is their normal condition.... —*Hindu saying*

The demand for perfection on the physical plane can be your worst enemy.... —*Emmanuel*

The quest for perfection is a curse....
—*Melvyn Kinder*

Perfection is eternal....
—*Charles Secretan*

Only in the deepest silence of the night the stars smile and whisper among themselves: vain is this (human) seeking: unbroken perfection is over all....
—*Rabindrinath Tagore*

If we accept God as perfect, we must admit a perfect universe and Cosmic scheme. If, however, we do not accept a belief in a perfect universe, then we have to accept an imperfect Creator....
—*Henry T. Hamblin*

We are part of a design which fits all its parts together perfectly....
—*C. Alan Anderson*

They are the perfect men who, being such, out of the greatness of their loving hearts, make themselves small to slave continuously to make the imperfect ones perfect also....
—*Sufi saying*

Be ye perfect, even as your Father which is in Heaven is perfect....
—*Jesus*

It is reasonable to have perfection in our eye that we may advance toward it, though we know it can never be reached.... —*Samuel Johnson*

In and with all your imperfections, YOU are perfect.... —*Sunyata*

You already are your perfect Self. It is only a matter of recognition. There never was, is, or will be more perfection that you are at this perfect moment....　　　*—David Manners*

The search for perfection—which is a search for divinity—is nothing more than the failure to accept our existence the way it is....　　*—Bernadette Roberts*

Perfection is not attained at that point at which nothing can be added, but at that point at which nothing can be taken away....　　　*—Bud Wilkenson*

Perfection consists not in doing extraordinary things, but in doing ordinary things extraordinarily well. Neglect nothing; the most trivial action may be performed to God....
　　　—Angelique Arnauld

Everything, by an impulse of its own nature, tends toward perfection....Everything is at its best and most perfect when in the condition intended for it by the First Cause....　*— Dante Alighieri*

Ultimate perfection does not include any action or good conduct, but only knowledge....　　　*—Maimonides*

If you consistently do your best, the worst won't happen....　　*—B. C. Forbes*

Aim at perfection in everything, though in most things it is unattainable....
　　　—Philip Chesterfield

A man ought to live always in perfect holiness....　　　*—Plato*

It is only imperfection that complains of what is imperfect. The more perfect we are the more....quiet we become toward the defects of others....
　　　—Francois Fenelon

Perfection is attained by slow degrees; it requires the hand of time....　*—Voltaire*

The perfect man desires tranquility....
　　　—Philo

This is moral perfection: to live each day as though it were the last; to be tranquil, sincere....
　　　—Marcus Aurelius

The man with insight enough to admit his limitations comes nearest to perfection....　　*—Johann W. Goethe*

When you aim for perfection, you discover it's a moving target....
　　　—George Fisher

Nothing gives a man a sense of failure so often as an overdeveloped sense of perfection....　　*—George S. Odiorne*

Perfection is immutable, but for things imperfect, to change is to perfect them....　　　*—Owen Felltham*

People who seek perfection in their lives are setting themselves up for failure....　　　*—Anonymous*

Behind this world of unreality and seeming imperfection is the Perfect World of Reality, the perfect expression of the Divine Idea....The perfect man already IS, and as this Truth is revealed so is he brought into manifestation....
　　　—Henry T. Hamblin

On the one hand evil is necessary for good, for were the imperfections not felt, there would be no striving after perfection....　　*—Giordano Bruno*

Perfection consists in one thing alone, which is doing the will of God....
　　　—Vincent de Paul

When a thing bores you, do not do it. Do not pursue fruitless perfection....
　　　—Eugene Delacroix

Perfection means a state in which all your senses and passions are under control and you are absolute master of your own self. Perfection does not mean a realm, but a state of existence, a level of enlarged consciousness where we come into tune with the infinite....
—*Abhedananda*

Perfection....of all the ways to reach it, the first is humility; the second is humility; the third, humility....
—*Augustine*

God gave man the power of reason, which makes man capable of perfection....
—*Maimonides*

The image of perfection is the sun and if you adapt him as your model, if, like him, you think of nothing but bringing light, warmth and life to all creatures, then you will really work your own transformation....
—*Omraam M. Aivanhov*

Perseverance

W e have many second chances in life, sometimes even tenth chances. Let no man give up hope till the last breath is drawn....
—*Charles F. Potter*

Perseverance is a great element of success. If you only knock long enough and loud enough at the gate, you are sure to wake up somebody....
—*Henry W. Longfellow*

Austere perseverance, harsh and continuous, may be employed by the least of us and rarely fails of its purpose, for its silent power grows irreversibly greater with time....
—*Johann W. Goethe*

The difference between perseverance and obstinacy is that one comes from a strong will and the other from a strong won't....
—*Henry W. Beecher*

Do not be afraid to demand great things of yourself. Powers which you never dreamed you possessed will leap to your assistance....
—*Orison S. Marden*

In the confrontation between the stream and the rock, the stream always wins—not through strength but by perseverance....
—*H. Jackson Brown*

What can a man not accomplish if he will but master the secret of steadfast perseverance....
—*Alice H. Rice*

Continuous effort—not strength or intelligence—is the key to unlocking our potential....
—*Liane Cordes*

Not in rewards, but in the strength to strive, the blessing lies....
—*John T. Trowbridge*

The drops of rain make a hole in the stone, not by violence, but by often falling....
—*Lucretius*

It's not the size of the dog in a fight, it's the size of the fight in the dog....
—*Kit Raymond*

I hold to the doctrine that with ordinary talent, and extraordinary perseverance, all things are attainable....
—*Thomas Buxton*

The block of granite which was an obstacle in the pathway of the weak becomes a stepping stone in the pathway of the strong....
—*Thomas Carlyle*

No rock is so hard but that a little wave may beat admission in a thousand years....
—*Alfred L. Tennyson*

Press on! A better fate awaits you....
—*Victor Hugo*

That which we persist in doing becomes easier—not that the nature of the task has changed, but our ability to do it has increased....
—*Ralph W. Emerson*

I know of no more encouraging fact than the unquestionable ability of man to elevate his life by conscious endeavor....
—*Henry D. Thoreau*

Great people are just ordinary people with an extraordinary amount of determination....
—*Robert Schuller*

Perseverance is the ability to follow through on an idea long after the mood has passed....
—*Anonymous*

If you persevere in reaching out into the Invisible, then outward work and labor cease to be anxious toil, and you are able to accomplish far more, with less effort than ever before....
—*Henry T. Hamblin*

If you must begin then go all the way, because if you begin and quit, the unfinished business you have left behind begins to haunt you all the time....
—*Chögyam Trungpa*

I think and think for months and years. Ninety-nine times the conclusion is false. The hundredth time I am right....
—*Albert Einstein*

Times of growth are beset with difficulties....But these difficulties arise from the profusion of all that is struggling to attain form. Everything is in motion: Therefore, if one perseveres there is a prospect of great success....
—*I Ching*

The constant dripping of water wears away the stone....
—*Sufi saying*

Flinch not, neither give up or despair, if thou dost not invariably succeed in acting from right principles....
—*Marcus Aurelius*

Endure and persist; this pain will turn to your good by and by....
—*Ovid*

Steady perseverance alone will tame your mind, and it is only through a tamed mind that you can experience God....
—*Sathya Sai Baba*

Decide what you want, decide what you are willing to exchange for it. Establish your priorities and go to work....
—*H. L. Hunt*

One of the simplest things about all facts of life is that to get where you want to go, you must keep on keeping on....
—*Norman V. Peale*

When luck is running against you, that is the time to play harder, to cinch up your belt, pluck up your courage, smile, and be unafraid....
—*U. S. Anderson*

Do what you can, with what you have, where you are....
—*Theodore Roosevelt*

Let me tell you the secret that has led me to my goal. My strength lies solely in my tenacity....
—*Louis Pasteur*

There is no royal road to anything. One thing at a time, and all things in succession. That which grows slowly, endures....
—*Josiah Holland*

Perseverance is more prevailing than violence; and many things which cannot be overcome when they are together yield themselves up when taken little by little....
—*Plutarch*

Persistent people begin their success where others end in failure....
—*Edward Eggleston*

Persistence has performed greater things than ambition and ability. If you lack persistency where you are, you will lack grit where you go....
—*Fred Van Amburgh*

It is persistence that gives the one who uses it an actual mathematical edge on his fellows. He is making the laws of chance work for him....
—*Douglas Lurton*

Nothing in the world can take the place of persistence. Talent will not; nothing is more common than unsuccessful men with talent. Genius will not; unrewarded genius is almost a proverb. Education will not; the world is filled with educated derelicts. Perseverance and determination alone are omnipotent....
—*Calvin Coolidge*

Never give in. Never, never, never, never. In nothing great or small, large or petty—never give in except to convictions of honor and good sense....
—*Winston Churchill*

Victory belongs to the most persevering....
—*Napoleon Bonaparte*

Take up one thing and do it, and see the end of it, and before you have seen the end, do not give up. Those who only take a nibble here and a nibble there will never attain anything....
—*Vivekananda*

Great works are performed, not by strength, but by perseverance. He that shall walk with vigor, three hours a day, will pass in seven years, a space equal to the circumference of the globe....
—*Samuel Johnson*

We will either find a way or make one....
—*Hannibal*

There are two ways of attaining an important end—force and perseverance. Force falls to the lot of a privileged few, but austere and sustained perseverance by the insignificant—its silent power grows irresistible with time....
—*Ann S. Swetchine*

Perseverance is the essence of success. The diamond is the product of the charcoal sticking and hardening sufficiently long....
—*Anonymous*

The characteristic of heroism is its persistency. All men have wandering impulses, fits and starts....But when you have chosen your part, abide by it, and do not weakly try to reconcile yourself with the world....
—*Ralph W. Emerson*

Success depends upon staying power. The reason for failure in most cases is lack of perseverance....
—*James R. Miller*

One cannot achieve anything lasting in this world by being irresolute....
—*Mohandas Gandhi*

The man who persists in knocking will succeed in entering....
—*Moses Ibn Ezra*

Pessimism

No one has ever been able to convince me that optimism is not preferable to pessimism....
—*Robert Mueller*

The minute you identify with, "it's difficult," that's what your experience has got to be....
—*Stephen H. Wolinsky*

The pessimist....is seldom an agitating individual. His creed breeds indifference to others, and he does not trouble himself to thrust his views upon the unconvinced.... —*Agnes Repplier*

The pessimist tells us that the thorns outlive the roses, and this is true, but a sharp prick from a thorn teaches us to use more care in gathering roses.... —*Fred Van Amburgh*

The optimist keeps his eye on the doughnut; the pessimist can only see the hole.... —*Anonymous*

The optimist is right. The pessimist is right. The one differs from the other as the light from the dark. Yet both are right. Each is right from his own particular point of view, and this point of view is the determining factor in the life of each. It determines as to whether it is a life of power or of impotence, of peace or of pain, of success or of failure.... —*Ralph W. Trine*

The worst walls are the ones you find in your way. The worst walls are the ones you put there—you build yourself. Those are the high ones, the thick ones, the ones with no doors.... —*Ursula K. LeGuin*

When people are depressed they are also pessimistic.... —*Martin E. P. Seligman*

Each one of us has a way of deceiving himself.... —*André Gide*

Watch what people are cynical about, and one can often discover what they lack.... —*Harry E. Fosdick*

I never think of the negative. All obstacles can be overcome.... —*Donald Trump*

If there seem to be negative attributes of a situation and one positive aspect, we must seize on that one thing, bless it, hold to it with determination, meditate upon it, be grateful for it, exaggerate it, and glorify it.... —*Alan Cohen*

You can't raise positive people on negative feedback.... —*Gerald Jampolsky*

Everything we shut our eyes to, everything we run away from, everything we deny, denigrate or despise, serves to defeat us in the end. What seems nasty, painful, evil, can become a source of beauty, joy and strength, if faced with an open mind.... —*Henry Miller*

Man is not naturally a cynic; he wants pitifully to believe in himself, in his future, in his community and in the nation of which he is a part.... —*Louis Bromfield*

A cynic can chill and dishearten with a single word.... —*Ralph W. Emerson*

Pessimists are second-rate people. They do not believe in life. Pessimism is just an excuse for their cowardice. All they want is to drag you down and appease their own feelings of mediocrity and fear.... —*U. S. Anderson*

Our negative thoughts are like black wings covering the sun. When we think too many of them, we find ourself living in a world of darkness and gloom.... —*Elinor MacDonald*

Never think a defeatist thought....Never lose faith! God's will is bound to prevail in the end.... —*Peace Pilgrim*

We can destroy ourselves by cynicism and disillusion just as effectively as by bombs.... —*Kenneth Clark*

A cynic is not merely one who reads bitter lessons from the past; he is one who is prematurely disappointed in the future.... —*Sydney J. Harris*

A pessimist is very gloomy and depressed, lazy and lethargic. Cheerfulness is unknown to him. He infects others. Pessimism is an epidemic and infectious disease. A pessimist cannot succeed in the world.... —*Sivananda*

When it is dark enough you can see the stars.... —*Charles A. Beard*

The world is moving so fast these days that the man who says it can't be done is generally interrupted by someone doing it.... —*Harry E. Fosdick*

Pessimism likes to build walls where optimism builds bridges....
—*Anonymous*

A pessimist is a man who thinks everybody as nasty as himself, and hates them for it....
—*George B. Shaw*

Those who sneer habitually at human nature, and affect to despise it, are among its worst and least pleasant samples.... —*Charles Dickens*

Cynics are only happy in making the world as barren to others as they made it for themselves....
—*George Meredith*

When the outlook is steeped in pessimism, I remind myself, "Two and two still make four, and you can't keep mankind down for long."...
—*Bernard M. Baruch*

A cynic is just a man who found out when he was about ten that there wasn't any Santa Claus, and he's still upset.... —*James G. Cozzens*

A pessimist sees only the dark side of the clouds, and mopes; a philosopher sees both sides and shrugs; an optimist doesn't see the clouds at all—he's walking on them.... —*D. O. Flynn*

Cynicism is, after all, simply idealism gone sour.... —*Will Herberg*

Pessimism is mental disease....It means illness in the person who voices it, and in the society which produces that person.... —*Upton Sinclair*

Away with pessimism! Let us work at whatever is pure, whatsoever is constructive, and not parade our failings and our sins....
—*Wilfred T. Grenfell*

A cynic is a man who knows the price of everything, and the value of nothing.... —*Oscar Wilde*

The only deadly sin I know is cynicism.... —*Henry L. Stimson*

The pessimist, by virtue of his limitations, is making his own hell, and in the degree that he makes his own hell is he helping to make one for all mankind.... —*Ralph W. Trine*

There is no sadder sight than a young pessimist.... —*Mark Twain*

A skeptic is a person who, when he sees the handwriting on the wall, claims it is a forgery.... —*Morris Bender*

Both the optimist and the pessimist are right, but as different as light is from darkness.... —*Anonymous*

How you think when you lose determines how long it will be until you win.... —*David Schwartz*

Possessions

Possessions are generally diminished by possession....
—*Friedrich W. Nietzsche*

If we could put material things into their proper place, and use them without being attached to them, how much freer we would be. Then we wouldn't burden ourselves with things we don't need....
—*Peace Pilgrim*

Remember that only that to which you have developed the attitude of ownership can be snatched away from you....
—*Ormond McGill*

If a man's happiness is due to outer causes and external possessions, then a man devoid of possessions should have no happiness whatever. Does real experience show this? No....
—*Ramana Maharshi*

The moment you have a desire to possess something is the exact moment you enter into the first phase of enslavement to it....
—*Anonymous*

The sense of possession is a great obstacle to the realization of God. Attachment to any external object narrows our vision, fosters egotism and gives rise to the false notion that we are separate from God....
—*Papa Ramdas*

Trying to satisfy one's desires with possessions is like putting out a fire with straw....
—*Confucius*

Whatever there be on the surface of the earth—property, gold, cattle, good health—none of these truly satisfy man. Tranquility arises from this understanding....
—*Tibetan saying*

Some day people will learn that material things do not bring happiness....
—*Charles P. Steinmetz*

Complete possession is proved only by giving. All you are able to give possesses you....
—*André Gide*

No possession is gratifying without a companion to share it....
—*Seneca*

Of what can we be sure, except that whatever we have will soon be gone?...
—*Yoga Vasistha*

Possessions are mere transient effects that come when they are required, and after their purpose has been served, pass away....
—*James Allen*

You may possess things, but you must not be possessed by them....
—*Aurobindo*

When you don't have possessions, you don't constantly live to acquire and protect them....
—*Marlo Morgan*

Unnecessary possessions are unnecessary burdens. If you have them, you will have to take care of them....
—*Peace Pilgrim*

Possession of material riches, without inner peace, is like dying of thirst while bathing in a lake. If material poverty is to be avoided, spiritual poverty is to be abhorred. For it is spiritual poverty, not material lack, that lies at the core of all human suffering....
—*Paramahansa Yogananda*

It is the preoccupation with possession, more than anything else, that prevents men from living freely and nobly....
—*Bertrand Russell*

Property has its duties as well as its rights....
—*Thomas Drummond*

With the great part of rich people, the chief employment of riches consists in the parade of riches.... —*Adam Smith*

Every time we think we have really taken possession of something, the truth is we have completely lost it....
—*Alan W. Watts*

Self-mastery is a far greater possession than the possession of earth goods. If we do not possess ourselves, we may possess all the fine things of life and be unable to use them to any advantage....
—*Paramanananda*

Material possessions are oftentimes a hindrance toward attaining higher consciousness. They take a cunning delight in becoming one's master while appearing as a benevolent slave....
—*Shantidasa*

Our most valuable possessions are those which can be shared without lessening—those which, when shared, multiply. Our least valuable possessions, on the other hand, are those which, when divided, are diminished....
—*William H. Danforth*

The emptiness of life cannot be satisfied by filling ourselves with possessions, although many people try.... —*Anonymous*

The rich man is not one who is in possession of much, but one who gives much.... —*John Chrysostom*

Attachment to material things is a sign of inferiority, because the more a man cares for the things of this world, the less does he understand his destiny; his disinterestedness, on the contrary, proves that he has arrived at a wider and clearer view of the future....
—*Allan Kardec*

You possess only whatever will be not lost in a shipwreck.... —*El-Ghazali*

You give but little when you give of your possessions. It is when you give of yourself that you truly give....
—*Kahlil Gibran*

All the possessions of mortals are mortal.... —*Metrodorus*

Do not cultivate too much attachment to things of the world, which appeal to carnal desires and sensual thirsts. A moment comes when you have to depart empty-handed, leaving all you have laboriously collected and proudly called your own.... —*Sathya Sai Baba*

The wise man carries his possessions with him.... —*Bias of Priene*

A life spent, however victoriously, in securing the necessaries of life is no more than an elaborate furnishing and decoration of apartments for the reception of a guest who is never to come.... —*A. E. Housman*

Man was created to serve God and to cleave to Him, not to accumulate wealth and erect buildings which he must leave behind.... —*Ibn Ezra*

I carry all my possessions with me....
—*Cicero*

It is possible to own too much. A man with one watch knows what time it is; a man with two watches is never quite sure.... —*Lee Segall*

How is it possible to find real happiness in those things which, by their very nature, must pass away?...
—*James Allen*

We only possess what we renounce; what we do not renounce escapes from us.... —*Simone Weil*

What does not belong to you does not have the power to disturb you....

—*Anonymous*

We try to acquire so many things of the world, but find no peace in them. When your mind is flitting from object to object....it lives in a state of restlessness which is itself misery. After possession of an object, comes care and anxieties; after a loss, grief and pain....

—*Papa Ramdas*

Property is the greatest cause of human troubles....

—*Seneca*

He who is enslaved with the sole desire for material possessions here will continue to be enslaved even after he can no longer retain his body....

—*Ralph W. Trine*

People have had to make up for their spiritual impoverishment by accumulating material things. When spiritual blessings come, material blessings seem unimportant....As long as we desire material things this is all we receive, and we remain spiritually impoverished....

—*Peace Pilgrim*

Power

Y ou gain power over another person in one of two ways: by winning his heart or by breaking his spirit....

—*Anonymous*

Love of money often makes a man a coward, but love of power always makes a man a brute. It is the most degrading love of all. Love of material well-being seldom hurts others, but love of power and glory always does....

—*Lin Yutang*

As wealth is power, so all power must infallibly draw wealth to itself by some means or other....

—*Edmund Burke*

Achievement gives power, but renunciation gives still more power....

—*Hazrat Inayat Khan*

If you make power and fame your goal, even if you attain them, you will find that they don't bring you what you thought they would—it's an empty experience....

—*Dean Ornish*

Power will intoxicate the best hearts, as wine the strongest heads. No man is wise enough, nor good enough to be trusted with unlimited power....

—*Charles C. Colton*

If any man is rich and powerful he comes under the law of God by which the higher branches must take the burning of the sun, and shade those that are lower; by which the tall trees must protect the weak plants beneath them....

—*Henry W. Beecher*

Anyone entrusted with power will abuse it if not also animated with the love of truth and virtue, no matter whether he be a prince, or one of the people....

—*Jean La Fortaine*

Because men are everywhere corruptible and always corrupted, no man or group of men can be trusted with too much power and indeed with no power at all which is not balanced or checked by the power of other men....

—*J. V. Langmead Casserlay*

Authority poisons everyone who takes authority on himself....

—*Vladimir I. Lenin*

Don't fight forces. Use them....

—*Buckminster Fuller*

Force is as pitiless to the man who possesses it, or thinks he does, as it is to its victims; the second it crushes, the first it intoxicates. The truth is, nobody really possesses it.... —*Simone Weil*

Authority has always attracted the lowest elements of the human race....
—*P. J. O'Rourke*

Power should not be concentrated in the hands of so few, and powerlessness in the hands of so many....
—*Maggie Kuhn*

You have much more power when you are working for the right thing than when you are working against the wrong thing.... —*Peace Pilgrim*

Authority without wisdom is like a heavy axe without an edge, fitter to bruise than polish....
—*Anne Bradstreet*

Nobody has a right to arbitrary and despotic power. No, nobody, not even God. Nobody is the absolute master of anybody else.... —*Eliphas Levi*

Power is sweet, it is a drug, the desire for which increases with habit....
—*Bertrand Russell*

Force is no remedy....
—*John Bright*

The lust for power, for dominating others, inflames the heart more than any other passion.... —*Tacitus*

You only have power over people as long as you don't take everything from them. But when you've robbed a man of everything, he's no longer in your power—he's free again....
—*Alexander Solzhenitsyn*

Power is much more easily manifested in destroying than in creating....
—*William Wordsworth*

Power resides not in aggressiveness, but in conscious choice....
—*Stephanie Rhea*

The leader who controls others by fear will find that the control is reactive and temporary.... —*Stephen R. Covey*

Desire for power acts like puffs of air which may blow out the lamp....that is being carefully tended....
—*Sivananda*

Power undirected by high purpose spells calamity.... —*Theodore Roosevelt*

Power without wisdom falls of its own weight.... —*Horace*

This is the secret of power....to rein in, with unfaltering will, the dark steed of desire.... —*James Allen*

Where love reigns, there is no will to power; and where the will to power is paramount, love is lacking. The one is but the shadow of the other....
—*Carl Jung*

Those who have been once intoxicated with power....even but for one year, never can willingly abandon it....
—*Edmund Burke*

Power is the attempt to produce any effect, and to succeed....
—*William Hazlitt*

Into the hands of every individual is given a marvelous power for good or evil—the silent, unconscious, unseen influence of his life. This is simply the constant radiation of what man really is, not what he pretends to be....
—*William G. Jordan*

Patience and gentleness is power....
—*Leigh Hunt*

The measure of man is what he does with power....
—*Pittacus*

All progress and infinite power is in every man's nature, only it is barred in and prevented from taking its proper course. If anyone can take the bar off, in rushes nature....
—*Vivekananda*

You must yield up power over everyone....
—*Pantanjali*

The seeds of godlike power are in us still: Gods we are, Bards, Saints, Heroes, if we will....
—*Matthew Arnold*

Power always corrupts; absolute power absolutely corrupts. All great men are bad....
—*Lord Acton*

I have never been able to conceive how any rational being could propose happiness to himself from the exercise of power over others....
—*Thomas Jefferson*

No one is fit to be trusted with power. No one....
—*C. P. Snow*

No master cared a rap for occult powers for he has no need for them in his daily life....
—*Ramana Maharshi*

To know the pains of power, we must go to those who have it; to know its pleasures, we must go to those who are seeking it: the pains of power are real, its pleasures imaginary....
—*Charles C. Colton*

Power is far from being desirable in itself, that it sometimes ought to be refused, and sometimes to be resigned....
—*Cicero*

If power is what you want and you think you want it for the service of humanity, don't trust your thinking too much....
—*Fritz Kunkel*

Abusive power demonstrates itself by knocking down doors that are best unlocked with a key....
—*Anonymous*

Of all men's miseries the bitterest is this, to know so much and to have control over nothing....
—*Herodotus*

People want to demonstrate power, and that is a sickness even God cannot cure. It is beyond curing, and they call it "spiritual ego." When a man becomes a little spiritual and people start loving him and respecting him, giving him things, bowing to him, well, that's where the problem starts....
—*Yogi Bhajan*

It is a strange desire that seeks power over others while losing power over oneself....
—*Francis Bacon*

Grim experience taught men that power is poisonous to its possessors; that no dynasty and no class can exclusively control the engines of power without ultimately confusing their public interest with the public well-being....
—*Harold J. Laski*

You shall have joy, or you shall have power, said God; you shall not have both....
—*Ralph W. Emerson*

Beware of dissipating your powers; strive constantly to concentrate them....
—*Johann W. Goethe*

Never underestimate the power of a loosely knit group working for a good cause....Their power is beyond their numbers....
—*Peace Pilgrim*

Those in power only want to perpetuate it.... —*William O. Douglas*

Power exercised with violence has seldom been of long duration, but temperance and moderation generally produce permanence in all things....
—*Frederick Langbridge*

The wrong sort of people are always in power because they would not be in power if they were not the wrong sort of people.... —*Jon Wynne-Tyson*

Right and truth are greater than any power.... —*Benjamin Whichcote*

Power gradually extirpates from the mind every humane and gentle virtue....and the greater the powers, the more dangerous the abuse....
—*Edmund Burke*

Occult powers are heaps of rubbish....
—*Ramakrishna*

Power may be justly compared to a great river; while kept within its bounds it is both beautiful and useful; but when it overflows its banks, it is too impetuous to be stemmed; it bears down all before it, and brings destruction and desolation wherever it comes.... —*Andrew Hamilton*

Power is of two kinds. One is obtained by the fear of punishment and the other by the art of love. Power based on love is a thousand times more effective and permanent than the one derived from fear of punishment....
—*Plutarch*

Why settle for little powers, when you can have God?... —*Hilda Charlton*

Power is a Dead Sea fruit. When you achieve it, there is nothing there....
—*George Macdonald*

Power is a dangerous thing to handle, even in religion.... —*Joseph R. Sizoo*

A man who possesses wealth possesses power; but it is a power to do evil as well as good.... —*Angel S. Roe*

In this world there are two forces: the sword and the spirit. The spirit has always conquered the sword....
—*Napoleon Bonaparte*

The true secret of power lies in keeping one's connection with the God who worketh all things.... —*Ralph W. Trine*

Power without love becomes brutal; love without power is insipid and weak.... —*Robert A. Johnson*

He is most powerful who has power over himself.... —*Seneca*

Possession of powers causes intoxication of mind. He who possesses powers always misuses them. He wants to command, control and domineer over others. It is very difficult to renounce position and power....
—*Sivananda*

Every type of power besides being a means is at the same time an end—at least for those who aspire to it....
—*Milovan Djilas*

The love of power is the love of ourselves.... —*William Hazlitt*

The only prize much cared for by the powerful is power. The prize of the general is not a bigger tent, but command.... —*Oliver W. Holmes*

Power flows to the man who knows how.... —*Elbert Hubbard*

Power is poison....
—*Henry Adams*

We cannot avoid using power, cannot escape the compulsion to afflict the world, so let us, cautious in diction and mighty in contradiction, Love powerfully.... —*Martin Buber*

From the summit of power men no longer turn their eyes upward, but begin to look about them....
—*James Russell Lowell*

The love of power may be as dominant in the heart of a peasant as of a prince.... —*J. T. Headly*

Power entraps even when it is used to do good.... —*Ram Dass*

To get power over is to defile. To possess is to defile.... —*Simone Weil*

Power is not happiness....
—*William Godwin*

Those who are in the highest places and have the most power, have the least liberty, because they are the most observed.... —*John Tillotson*

The lust for power is not rooted in strength but in weakness....
—*Erich Fromm*

Power always sincerely, conscientiously, believes itself right....Power must never be trusted.... —*John Adams*

Those who have seized power, even for the noblest of motives, soon persuade themselves that there are good reasons for not relinquishing it. This is particularly likely to happen if they believe themselves to represent some immensely important cause....
—*Bertrand Russell*

Unlimited power is apt to corrupt the minds of those who possess it....
—*William Penn*

Power buries those who would wield it.... —*The Talmud*

Personal power lies in taking responsibility for yourself, not in assuming the responsibilities of other people....
—*Anonymous*

It is impossible to reign innocently....
—*Antoine Saint-Just*

Even in a righteous cause, force is a fearful thing....
—*Johann von Schiller*

Power, like a desolating pestilence, pollutes whatever it touches....
—*Percy B. Shelley*

There is no more contemptible poison than power over one's fellow men....
—*Maksim Gorky*

As for men in power, they are so anxious to establish the myth of their infallibility that they do the utmost to ignore truth.... —*Boris Pasternak*

Experience constantly proves that every man who has power is impelled to abuse it.... —*Charles de Secondat*

It is not power itself, but the legitimation of the lust for power, which corrupts absolutely....
—*Richard H. Crossman*

A man is possessed of limited powers and is miserable; he wants to expand his powers so that he may be happy. But consider if it will be so; if with limited perceptions one is miserable, with extended perceptions the misery must increase proportionally....
—*Ramana Maharshi*

The truth is that all men having power ought to be mistrusted....
—*James Madison*

The love of power comes from a lack of the most important power, that of living a life of eternity with every creature.... —*Aaron D. Gordon*

Power intoxicates men. It is never voluntarily surrendered. It must be taken from them.... —*James F. Byrnes*

As long as....power exists there will always be rulers and ruled, masters and slaves, exploiters and exploited.... —*Mikhail A. Bakunin*

All persons possessing a portion of power ought to be strongly and awfully impressed with an idea that they act in trust, and that they are to account for their conduct in that trust to the one great Master, Author, and Founder of society.... —*Edmund Burke*

He is the best of men who dislikes power.... —*Mohammed*

Real power has fullness and variety. It is not narrow like lightning, but broad like light.... —*Roswell D. Hitchcock*

He who does not desert his principles when threatened with the loss of every earthly thing, even to the loss of reputation and life, is the man of power.... —*James Allen*

True power is the falling away of individual identity.... —*Maya Sarada Devi*

Unlimited power is worse for the average person than unlimited alcohol; and the resulting intoxication is more dangerous.... —*William L. Phelps*

There is no stronger test of a man's character than power and authority, exciting as they do every passion, and discovering every latent vice.... —*Plutarch*

The heart declines when power mounts to the head.... —*Henry Hurwitz*

The human mind is prone to pride even when not supported by power; how much more, then, does it exalt itself when it has support.... —*Pope Gregory I*

The aspirant to knowledge should beware of occult powers. Even if they come and court him of their own accord, he should reject them.... —*G. V. Sabbaramayya*

Power directed by guilt has seldom been directed to any good end or useful purpose.... —*Tacitus*

No one with absolute power can be trusted to give it up even in part.... —*Louis D. Brandeis*

Power is strength and the ability to see yourself through your own eyes and not through the eyes of another. It is being able to place a circle of power at your own feet and not take power from someone else's circle.... —*Agnes Whistling Elk*

Prayer

Joy and thankfulness are the secret ingredients to all successful prayer.... —*Anonymous*

The one who prays and the one to whom prayers are addressed are one and the same.... —*Yoga Swami*

Many times the words of our prayer are in conflict with the real desires of our heart. We pray for one thing when really we want something else.... —*Charles L. Allen*

Prayer is a perpetual stillness of the heart, a surrendering to yourself as the aspect of God within you. Prayer is not beseeching an entity outside us for favors, but acknowledging the presence of God with us....
—*A Spiritual Warrior*

Communicating with God is a deep inner knowing that God is within you and around you. God "speaks" through the still small voice within....
—*Peace Pilgrim*

Spiritual favors are not always to be looked for, and not always to be relied upon.... —*Amelia Barr*

Prayer is not an old woman's idle amusement. Properly understood and applied, it is the most potent instrument of action.... —*Mohandas Gandhi*

A simple prayer for the soul's journey is: "I will to will Thy will." Such a simple form of prayer is proper, it seems, on almost any occasion.... —*Ralph Blum*

It is a travesty to pray daily "Thy kingdom come" and then do nothing to help bring it to pass.... —*Alice B. Rice*

When we pray to God we must be seeking nothing—nothing....
—*Francis of Assisi*

God hears no more than the heart speaks; and if the heart be dumb, God will certainly be deaf....
—*Thomas B. Brooks*

There are moments when, whatever be the attitude of the body, the soul is on its knees.... —*Victor Hugo*

The most powerful form of energy one can generate is prayer. Prayer, like radium, is a luminous and self-generating form of energy.... —*Alexis Carrel*

You can't pray a lie....
—*Mark Twain*

The right way to pray for the answer to all your problems is to feel and know that the In-dwelling God knows only the answer.... —*Joseph Murphy*

Do our prayers come true? The answer lies in the way we pray. Let's pray in a way that our prayers are true....
—*Ainsky Meares*

Let us not pray to be sheltered from dangers but to be fearless in facing them. Let us not beg for the stilling of the pain but for the heart to conquer it.... —*Rabindranath Tagore*

The man who prays longest and loudest....is either trying to convince others or he is trying to convince himself.... —*Fred Van Amburgh*

More tears are shed over answered prayers than unanswered ones....
—*Teresa of Avila*

Prayer is a state of continual gratitude.... —*John of Kronstadt*

The only thing worth praying for is light.... —*Elinor MacDonald*

Prayer is a ladder on which thoughts mount to God....
—*Abraham J. Heschel*

Prayer is the spirit speaking truth to Truth.... —*Philip Bailey*

Rejoice evermore. Pray without ceasing. In everything give thanks; for this is the will of God.... —*Paul of Tarsus*

You pray in your distress and in your need; would that you might pray also in the fullness of your joy and in your days of abundance....
—*Kahlil Gibran*

The prayer of power is not reaching toward anything above or around or beneath. It is knowing that you are one with all there is. It is an understanding that the substance of your being is the one and only substance there is in the universe.... —*H. B. Jeffery*

No cry that goes up from the depths of a sincere heart goes up in vain, and if your prayer is fashioned aright, it will be answered by the god in your own heart.... —*Paul Brunton*

A heart-felt prayer is not recitation with the lips. It is a yearning from within which expresses itself in every word, every act, nay every thought of man.... —*Mohandas Gandhi*

A single grateful thought towards heaven is the most complete prayer....
—*Minna von Barnbelm*

Nothing is too small a subject for prayer, because nothing is too small to be the subject of God's care....
—*Henry T. Hamblin*

To pray....is to desire; but it is to desire what God would have us desire. He who desires not from the bottom of his heart, offers a deceitful prayer....
—*Francois Fenelon*

God is not a cosmic bell-boy for whom we can press a button to get things....
—*Harry E. Fosdick*

Pray as if it all depends on God, but work as if it all depends upon you....
—*George W. Carver*

If we are holding anyone in condemnation as a human being, good or bad, just or unjust, we have not made peace with our brother and we are not ready for the prayer of communion with the Infinite.... —*Joel Goldsmith*

Truth is what prays in man, and a man is continually at prayer when he lives according to truth....
—*Emanuel Swedenborg*

When you pray do not imitate the hypocrites: they love to say their prayers standing up in the temples and street corners for people to see them....they have had their reward. But when you pray, go to your own private room and pray to your Father in secret and you will be rewarded.... —*Jesus*

The simple heart that freely asks in love, obtains.... —*John G. Whittier*

The journey of prayer is nothing more or less than a gradual awakening to the reality of recognizing what is already there.... —*Delia Smith*

Prayer as a means to effect a private end is theft and meanness. It supposes dualism in nature and consciousness. As soon as the man is one with God he will not beg. He will then see prayer in all action.... —*Ralph W. Emerson*

In prayer it is better to have a heart without words than words without a heart.... —*John Bunyan*

Complaint is the largest tribute heaven receives.... —*Jonathan Swift*

We, ignorant of ourselves, beg often our own harms, which the wise powers deny us for our good....
—*William Shakespeare*

Do not pray for yourself: you do not know what will help you....
—*Johann W. Goethe*

Prayer is exhaling the spirit of man and inhaling the spirit of God....
—*Edwin Keith*

The most important part of prayer is what we feel, not what we say....
—*Peace Pilgrim*

The inward sighs of humble penitence rise to the ear of heaven, when pealed hymns are scattered to the common air.... —*Joanna Baillie*

Prayer is like the turning-on of an electric switch. It does not create the current; it simply provides a channel through which the electric current may flow.... —*Max Handel*

When you make prayer a moment of truth in your life, the heavens open in response.... —*Anonymous*

I have been driven many times to my knees by the overwhelming conviction that I had nowhere to go....
—*Abraham Lincoln*

Prayer is not flight; prayer is power. Prayer does not deliver a man from some terrible situation; prayer enables a man to face and to master a situation.... —*William Barkley*

Prayer! I couldn't live without it; I would have died a thousand times if it had not been for my chance to talk it over with God, and gain strength in it from Him.... —*Dale Evans Rogers*

Most people when they pray, talk to God rather than with Him. They don't take the time to listen, in deep inner silence, for His answer....
—*J. Donald Walters*

So many times we pray for gifts and favors when we should be praying for the strength to work and the patience to wait.... —*Fred Van Amburgh*

Our prayers should be for a sound mind and a healthy body.... —*Juvenal*

Prayer, if not the very gate of heaven, is the key to let us into its holiness and joys.... —*John Wesley*

The great thing is to pray, even if it be in a vague and inarticulate fashion....
—*John W. Strutt*

If you would have God hear you when you pray, you must hear Him when he speaks.... —*Thomas Brooks*

God punishes us mildly by ignoring our prayers and severely by answering them.... —*Richard J. Needham*

Pray to God, at the beginning of all thy works, that so thou mayest bring them all to a good ending.... —*Xenophon*

Direct all your prayers to one thing only, that is, to conform your will perfectly to the Divine will....
—*Teresa of Avila*

To pray for a bodily cure and nothing more is a limited and limiting procedure. Pray also to be enlightened as to why this sickness fell upon you....
—*Paul Brunton*

Prayer is nought but a rising desire of the heart unto God by withdrawing of the heart from all earthly things....
—*Walter Hilton*

The greatest prayer is patience....
—*Gautama Buddha*

There is a very high rung only one man in a generation can reach: that of having learned all the wisdom, then praying like a child....
—*Mendel of Rymanov*

There is no prayer so blessed as the prayer which asks for nothing....
—*Oswald J. Simon*

The time of business does not with me differ from the time of prayer....
—*Brother Lawrence*

Through prayer we work the world of Cause....
—*Henry T. Hamblin*

Prayer is not verbal. It is from the heart. To merge into the Heart is prayer....
—*Ramana Maharshi*

The fewer the words the better prayer....
—*Martin Luther*

Prayers should be the key of the day and the lock of the night....
—*English proverb*

We often want one thing and pray for another, not telling the truth even to the gods....
—*Seneca*

I have resolved to pray more and pray always; to pray in all places where quietness inviteth, in the house, on the highway and on the street, and know no street or passage in the city that may not witness that I have not forgotten God....
—*Thomas Browne*

The way you learn how to pray is to simply start praying....
—*Shantidasa*

Every thought of God is prayer....
—*Rahel L. Varnhagen*

The deepest words of the heart find expression in secret prayer....
—*George Rees*

Prayer does not change God, but changes him who prays....
—*Sören Kierkegaard*

Prayer is the most perfect and most divine action that a rational soul is capable of. It is of all other actions and duties the most indispensably necessary....
—*F. Augustine Baker*

He prays best who does not know that he is praying....
—*St. Anthony*

We should never pray to God that He may grant what we desire, but that His will may be accomplished in us....
—*St. Nilus*

Prayer is not a vain attempt to change God's will: it is a filial desire to learn God's will and to share it. Prayer is not a substitute for work: it is the secret spring and indispensable ally of all true work....
—*George Buttrick*

We are always telling God what he can do for us, but to many of us it rarely occurs to ask God what we can do for Him....
—*John Powell*

To truly pray is to use the law of polarity. Prayer is praise, thus lifting the mind from fear, separation, censure and condemnation to oneness, sameness and completion....
—*Sue Sikking*

True prayer is not begging or beseeching, it is right knowing. It is not a matter of trying to make something happen, but of becoming aware of that which already is. It is not a time to say "Please" but to say "Thank you."...
—*Elinor MacDonald*

What men usually ask God for when they pray to God is, that two and two may not make four....
—*Russian proverb*

It is an immature concept to think of prayer for personal gain. It takes from one the responsibility of the conditions of one's life. Everything in creation is based on universal laws. Cause and effect work perfectly in accordance with this law. Yet mankind attempts to escape the hurt brought on by his disobedience to higher law by praying to God to violate His own laws....
—*Cheryl Canfield*

Prayer must be neutral if it is to be effective; once you lose your neutrality by asking for results, prayer becomes impotent. —*Anonymous*

Prayer is a force as real as terrestrial gravity.... —*Alexis Carrel*

To pray to God for things—health, money, houses, companionship—would be to look upon him as a servant whom you can command to obey your wish.... —*Joel Goldsmith*

Many people are praying for mountains to be moved when all they need to do is climb them.... —*Anonymous*

Prayer is always acceptable to God when dictated by the heart, for the intention is everything in His sight; and the prayer of the heart is preferable to one read from a book, however beautiful it may be, if read with the lips rather than with the thought.... —*Allan Kardec*

We cannot approach prayer as we do everything else in our push-button, instant society. There are no prayer pills.... —*Janie Gustafson*

Prayer needs no speech. It is in itself independent of any sensuous effort. But it must be combined with the utmost humility.... —*Mohandas Gandhi*

The highest prayer is not one of faith merely, it is demonstration.... —*Mary Baker Eddy*

You pray to what you love; for true, whole prayer is nothing but love.... —*Augustine*

Prayer is conversation with God.... —*Josippon*

More things are wrought by prayer than the world dreams of.... —*Alfred L. Tennyson*

Only in prayer do we achieve that complete and harmonious assembly of body, mind and spirit, which gives the frail human reed its unshakable strength.... —*Alexis Carrel*

Supply does not come through prayer. It comes as a result of an attitude of faith, a condition of mind and heart, in which the Invisible is depended upon solely for all things necessary, instead of upon the visible and earthly. Prayer in the form of begging and beseeching God to kindly answer our requests is not capable of producing supply in itself.... —*Henry T. Hamblin*

If you ask of God, He gives you what you ask, but if you dare to live Him, God gives Himself and all that you would have asked for.... —*Aurobindo*

When I pray, my heart is in my prayer.... —*Henry W. Longfellow*

Prayer is not an easy way of getting what we want, but the only way of becoming what God wants us to be.... —*Studdert Kennedy*

In the foothills of the Himalayas....one hears the prayer: "Oh Lord, we know not what is good for us. Thou knowest what it is. For it we pray."... —*Harry E. Fosdick*

People often say to me: "Pray for me." And I think to myself: Why ever do ye go out? Why not stop at home and mine your own treasure? For indeed the whole truth is native in you.... —*Meister Eckhart*

Prayer is a concentration of positive thoughts.... —*Peace Pilgrim*

In the life of the Indian there is only one inevitable duty—the duty of prayer—the daily recognition of the Unseen and Eternal. His daily devotions were more necessary to him than daily food....   —*Ohiyesa*

Our prayers should be for blessings in general, for God knows best what is good for us....   —*Socrates*

Prayer is the contemplation of the facts of life from the highest point of view....
            —*Ralph W. Emerson*

Our prayers should be burning words coming forth from the furnace of a heart filled with love....
            —*Mother Teresa*

He who prays without knowing what he prays does not pray....
            —*Maimon Ben Joseph*

Pride

There is perhaps not one of our natural passions so hard to subdue as pride. Disguise it, struggle with it, stifle it, mortify it as much as one pleases, it is still alive, and will every now and then peep out and show itself....   —*Benjamin Franklin*

Proud people breed sorrows for themselves....   —*Emily Brontë*

The man who claims he is something special does so because he knows that he is not. It is the inferior man who is always ambitious....
            —*Ormond McGill*

The sun will set without your assistance....   —*The Talmud*

When a proud man hears another praised, he thinks himself injured....
            —*English proverb*

Humility does not strive; that's all pride knows how to do....   —*Anonymous*

Too much learning makes one proud. One must bend one's head....realizing the limitations of reason. It can only take you to the gate and it has to be left behind when you enter the realm of the Spirit. You have to unlearn what you have learnt and become as simple and guileless as a child....
            —*Papa Ramdas*

Pride is the mask of one's own faults....
            —*Hebrew saying*

The intelligent man who is proud of his intelligence is like the condemned man who is proud of his large cell....
            —*Simone Weil*

Outside show is a poor substitute for inner worth....   —*Aesop*

Pride is ignorance. A little possession of....wealth, beauty, strength or intelligence intoxicates a man....
            —*Sivananda*

We are rarely proud when we are alone....   —*Voltaire*

The opposite of pride is not humility. The opposite of pride is shame....
            —*Robert Schuller*

Of all the causes which conspire to blind man's erring judgement, and mislead the mind, what the weak head with strongest bias rules, is pride....
            —*Alexander Pope*

Pride alone fastens onto good, to the end that it shall perish....   —*Augustine*

When pride cometh, then cometh shame; but with the lowly is wisdom....
—*Old Testament*

The worst man is the one who sees himself as the best.... —*Arabian saying*

The highest and most lofty trees have the most reason to dread the thunder....
—*Charles Rollin*

False pride is an all-consuming vice. Personal pride is a virtue....
—*Fred Van Amburgh*

Be very slow to believe that you are wiser than all others; it is a fatal but common error. Where one has been saved by a true estimate of another's weakness, thousands have been destroyed by the false appreciation of their own strength....
—*Charles C. Colton*

Pride is a vice, which pride itself inclines every man to find in others, and to overlook in himself....
—*Samuel Johnson*

Evil can have no beginnings, but from pride; nor any end, but from humility.... —*William Law*

He who places implicit confidence in his genius will find himself some day utterly deflated and deserted....
—*Benjamin Disraeli*

Whoever has in his heart so much as a rice-grain of pride cannot enter into Paradise.... —*Mohammed*

All the other vices flee God; pride alone rises up against Him.... —*Boethius*

A proud man is always hard to be pleased, because he hath too great expectations from others....
—*Richard Baxter*

The beginning of the pride of man is to fall from God....for pride is the beginning of all sin: he that holdeth it, shall be filled with maledictions, and it shall ruin him in the end....
—*Old Testament*

God cannot be realized if there is the slightest trace of pride....
—*Ramakrishna*

The cause of bigness has prevented proper thinking.... —*Louis Brandeis*

Whosoever shall exalt himself shall be abased; and he that shall humble himself shall be exalted.... —*Jesus*

Staring up to admire your own halo creates a pain in the neck....
—*Harold Coffin*

When the proud man thinks he is humble his case is hopeless....
—*Thomas Merton*

If you are discouraged, it is a sign of pride, because it shows you trust in your own powers.... —*Mother Teresa*

Whenever you hear someone inflating his ego by speaking of his good works, walk away quickly and do not encourage him any more....
—*Ronald Beesley*

Pride and conceit were the original sin of man.... —*Alain Lesage*

The most difficult secret for a man to keep is his opinion of himself....
—*Marcel Pagnol*

Pride is a negative virtue; it exists to glorify humility.... —*Sivananda*

Pride has no more value than a cock crowing on a dung heap....
—*Anonymous*

A proud man is seldom a grateful man, for he never thinks he gets as much as he deserves....   *—Henry W. Beecher*

Principle

This is an eternal and fundamental principle, inherent in all things, in every system of philosophy, in every religion and in every science. There is no getting away from the law of love. It is feeling that imparts vitality to thought. Feeling is desire, and desire is love. Thought impregnated with love becomes invincible....   *—Charles Haanel*

If you focus on principles, you empower everyone who understands those principles to act without constant monitoring, evaluating, correcting or controlling....   *—Stephen R. Covey*

There is only one Principle, and this is Good. There is no principle of evil. If there were a principle of evil, evil would be positive and not negative, and therefore could never be overcome, because it would be eternal and unchanging....   *—Henry T. Hamblin*

A fad lives its life in a few weeks; a philosophy lives through generations and centuries; a principle, forever.... *—William G. Jordan*

Once possessed of the principle, it is equally easy to make forty or forty thousand applications of it.... *—Ralph W. Emerson*

Principles are like seeds; they are little things which do much good, if the mind that receives them has the right attitudes....   *—Seneca*

Most people would prefer to fight for their principles than live up to them.... *—Anonymous*

Search for a rock, a principle, and having found it, get it under your feet and stand erect upon it, until at last, immovably fixed upon it, you succeed in defying the fury of the waves and storms of selfishness....   *—James Allen*

If the principle is right, the details will take care of themselves.... *—Napoleon Bonaparte*

Back of every noble life there are principles which have fashioned it.... *—George H. Lorimer*

Where true principles lack, the results are imperfect....   *—Henry Madathanas*

God is the principle behind everything that exists today. The principle behind a thing is Spirit; and Spirit is Omnipotent, Omnipresent and Omniscient. God is one Mind that is both the direct and the directing cause of all the good that we see about us.... *—Baird Spalding*

Rely on principles.... *—Epictetus*

He who floats with the current, who does not guide himself according to higher principles, who has no ideal, no convictions—such a man is....a thing moved, instead of a living and moving being—an echo, not a voice.... *—Henri F. Amiel*

It is easier to produce ten volumes of philosophical writings than to put one principle into practice.... *—Leo Tolstoy*

Principle is a passion for truth and right.... *—William Hazlitt*

Many men do not allow their principles to take root, but pull them up every now and then, as children do the flowers they have planted, to see if they are growing.... —*Henry W. Longfellow*

A new principle is an inexhaustible source of new ideas....
—*Luc de Clapiers Vauvenargues*

The moment you use a principle, it will work for you whether it is a principle of mathematics or of the mind....
—*Sue Sikking*

The Principle is an infinity which nothing can augment or diminish....
—*Chuang Tse*

Old cranks have practiced all their lives, just as old saints have likewise practiced all their lives. They just practiced different life principles....
—*John Powell*

One must not make even principles so set that one cannot alter them....
—*Hazrat Inayat Khan*

He who merely knows right principles is not equal to him who loves them....
—*Confucius*

When a society is perishing, the wholesome advice to give to those who would restore it is to recall it to the principles from which it sprang....
—*Pope Leo XIII*

We have always found that, if the principles were right, the area over which they were affected did not matter. Size is only a matter of the multiplication table....
—*Henry Ford*

Principles have achieved more victories than horsemen or chariots....
—*W. M. Paxton*

Principles are like a seed in the ground, they must continually be visited with heavenly influences or else your life will be a barren field....
—*Thomas Traherne*

An unprincipled life is a tragic waste indeed.... —*Sivananda*

The more clearly a principle is understood by the intellect, the more inexcusable is the neglect to put it into practice.... —*Allan Kardec*

A problem which is not met with higher principles will simply create another problem. It cannot happen otherwise.... —*Vernon Howard*

Principles are eternal....
—*William J. Bryan*

No single principle can answer all of life's complexities....
—*Felix Frankfurter*

Nothing can bring you peace but the triumph of principles....
—*Ralph W. Emerson*

There are principles which govern our life—they are the principles of Life. If our life is lived according to these principles all is well, and harmony reigns in place of vexation and struggle.... —*Henry T. Hamblin*

All that there is to the making of a successful, happy, and beautiful life, is the knowledge and application of a few simple, root principles....
—*James Allen*

Principles don't die. They aren't here one day and gone the next. They can't be destroyed by fire, earthquake or theft. Principles are deep, fundamental truths, classic truths....
—*Stephen R. Covey*

Problems

Anyone can carry his burden, however heavy, until nightfall. Anyone can do his work, however hard, for a day. Anyone can live sweetly, patiently, lovingly and purely until the sun goes down.... —*Lucy Cornellssen*

Problems are messages....
—*Shakti Gawain*

Mountains are removed by first shoveling away the small stones....
—*Anonymous*

If you have a problem, take the matter to God in prayer, and visualize it in God's hands. Then leave it, knowing it is in the best possible hands, and turn your attention to other things....
—*Peace Pilgrim*

We....have no need to solve or figure out a solution to the problem of life. The manifestation is not a problem to figure out; it has no solutions, because it contains no problems; it has no answers, for it contains no questions....
—*A Spiritual Warrior*

Don't hope for a life without problems. An easy life results in a judgemental and lazy mind.... —*Kyong Ho*

Behind every dark happening, behind every difficulty, there is a hidden blessing.... —*White Eagle*

You are yourself your biggest problem. You cannot hand it over to anyone else, be he savior or master, and escape from it, except in delusive imagination or in erroneous belief.... —*Paul Brunton*

Stand back from the mountain of problems, refuse to acknowledge that they are yours, and they will dissolve and disappear before your eyes....
—*Annamalai Swami*

When a child encounters something he does not want, he has all kinds of maneuvers to avoid it, such as crying, hiding or fighting....Unless we are taught to face our problems directly and work through them, the pattern of avoidance will be repeated....it can be a natural, accepted way to act....
—*Tarthang Tulku*

You have no problems, though you think you have....
—*A Course In Miracles*

Every problem contains within itself the seeds of its own solution....
—*Stanley Arnold*

Man needs difficulties; they are necessary for health.... —*Carl Jung*

Most problems do not stand alone but are only smaller parts of larger problems.... —*Marvin Minsky*

The second assault on the same problem should come from a totally different direction.... —*Tom Hirshfield*

Those who in this world have the courage to try and solve in their own lives new problems of life, are the ones who raise society to greatness....
—*Rabindranath Tagore*

The problems of the world, AIDS, cancer, nuclear war, pollution, are, finally, no more soluble than the problem of a tree which has borne fruit: the apples are overripe and they are falling—what can be done? Nothing can be done, and nothing needs to be done....
—*David Mamet*

We are all faced with a series of great opportunities brilliantly disguised as impossible situations....
—*Charles R. Swindoll*

Troubles are usually the brooms and shovels that smooth the road to a good man's fortune.... —*St. Basil*

When everything seems to be going against the wind, remember that the airplane takes off against the wind, not with it.... —*Henry Ford*

Suicide is no release from one's problems....All your problems and troubles are in your thinking; so you can see that by losing your body you can't lose your problems, for they are not physical.... —*James B. Schafer*

What appears to you to be a misfortune is not always such; for the good which it is destined to work out is often greater than the seeming evil....
—*Allan Kardec*

Each problem has hidden in it an opportunity so powerful that it literally dwarfs the problem. The great success stories were created by people who recognized a problem and turned it into an opportunity.... —*Anonymous*

Don't fight your problem. Know that there is a solution.... —*Joseph Murphy*

Obstacles are a natural part of life, just as boulders are a natural part of the course of the river. The river does not complain or get depressed because there are boulders in its path....
—*I Ching*

Whatever your problem, no matter how difficult, you can release spiritual power sufficient to solve your problem. The secret is—pray and believe....
—*Norman V. Peale*

Mistake, error is the discipline through which we advance....
—*William E. Channing*

Everywhere you trip is where the treasure lies.... —*Norman Lear*

Never solve a problem from its original perspective.... —*Charles C. Thompson*

The worst thing in your life may contain seeds of the best. When you see crises as an opportunity, your life becomes not easy, but more satisfying.... —*Joe Kogel*

Every mistake is your best teacher. One has to evolve through sins and mistakes. They are inevitable....
—*Sivananda*

Every crucial experience can be regarded as a setback—or the start of a new kind of development....
—*Mary R. Rinehart*

All of your problems and difficulties are the instruction of life, pointing out to you where you are wrong, where you are lacking in wisdom and understanding, where you need to change so that you can open yourself to a greater degree of good than you have yet experienced.... —*Elinor MacDonald*

Trouble is where you make it....
—*John A. Schindler*

Some people wish for a life of no problems, but I would never wish such a life for any of you. What I wish for is the great inner strength to solve your problems meaningfully and grow. Problems are learning and growing experiences.... —*Peace Pilgrim*

Man's problem in the last analysis is man himself.... —*Robert Lynd*

If there is a problem in your life that you would solve, do not set your will to work on it. You will conquer this problem in the end, not by fighting it, but by understanding it. The reason it exists in the first place is because of the lack of understanding....
—*U. S. Anderson*

Every problem faced, even if it can't be solved satisfactorily, is a moral victory; it strengthens your character and makes future problems easier to tackle....
—*Harvey Day*

A man cannot help going wrong and making mistakes as long as he is ignorant of his true nature....
—*Paramananda*

Anyone who proposes to do good must not expect people to roll stones out of his way, but must accept his lot calmly if they even roll a few more on it....
—*Albert Schweitzer*

Grapple with each new difficulty as it comes up. Wrestle with it till you down it, if it takes until the break of day. Get on top of every difficulty that comes your way. Otherwise, it will get on top of you....
—*Archer Brown*

There are two ways of meeting difficulties: you alter the difficulties, or you alter yourself to meet them....
—*Phyllis Bottome*

Regard setbacks as a challenge to greater success, not as a reason for failure. The full scope of our ability and ingenuity is usually only called forth by problems....
—*R. J. Heathorn*

A good many gifted people would accomplish more in life if thorns grew on laurels, so they would be harder to rest upon....
—*Rush Middlecombe*

If it hurts, you're doing it wrong. If you insist—it's going to hurt you even more. It will not stop hurting until you alleviate the cause....
—*Arlin C. Hauser*

The first problem for all of us....is not to learn, but to unlearn....
—*Gloria Steinem*

Recognizing a problem is the first step to solving it....Some problems cannot be solved but you can make peace with them....
—*Sonya Friedman*

Problems cannot be solved with words, but only through experience....
—*Alice Miller*

The man who has no more problems to solve is out of the game....
—*Elbert Hubbard*

Every adventure creates its own particular set of difficulties. You cannot protect yourself from problems by living a cautious life, but you may die of boredom....
—*Robert Schuller*

The wonderful thing about having problems is that they give us something obvious to work on....anything that causes us to contact God is a blessing....
—*Walter Starcke*

Difficulties, like work, are blessings in disguise....To the healthy man, difficulties should act as a tonic. They should open us to greater exertion. They should strengthen our willpower....
—*B. C. Forbes*

Every human being is a problem in search of a solution....
—*Ashley Montagu*

A problem is not solved, a disease not spirited away by denying that it exists....
—*Paul Brunton*

To every disadvantage there is a corresponding advantage....
—*Clement Stone*

The best way to solve a complex problem is to break it into pieces and solve it one piece at a time....
—*Anonymous*

The average man takes life as a trouble. He is in a chronic state of irritation at the whole performance. He does not learn to differentiate between troubles and difficulties, usually, until some real trouble bowls him over. He fusses about pinpricks until a mule kicks him. Then he learns the difference....
—*Herbert Casson*

Superficiality is the curse of our age. The doctrine of instant satisfaction is a primary spiritual problem....
—*Richard Foster*

The significant problems we face cannot be solved at the same level of thinking which created them....
—*Albert Einstein*

Life affords no higher pleasure than that of surmounting difficulties, passing from one step of success to another.... —*Samuel Johnson*

There is no problem unless you create one.... —*Gayatri Devi*

It is not the obstacle itself, but the thoughts about the obstacle that dismay us.... —*Eastern proverb*

Difficulties are the things that show what men are....The greater the difficulty, the more glory in surmounting it. Skillful pilots gain their reputation from storms and tempests....
—*Epictetus*

The burden becomes light which is cheerfully borne.... —*Ovid*

There is no such thing as a problem without a gift for you in its hands. You seek problems because you need their gifts.... —*Richard Bach*

We only think when we are confronted with a problem.... —*John Dewey*

It makes no difference how deeply seated may be the trouble, how hopeless the outlook, how muddled the tangle, how great the mistake. A sufficient realization of love will dissolve it all.... —*Emmet Fox*

How many problems have you got? They are problems of your own making, because you refuse to allow the spirit life to enter in partnership with our earthly life.... —*Ronald Beesley*

We can magnify our problems and we can minimize them....
—*Paramananda*

All the greatest and most important problems of life are fundamentally insoluble....They can never be solved, but only outgrown.... —*Carl Jung*

When life gives you lemons, make lemonade.... —*Esco Brown*

When you get into a tight place and everything goes against you till it seems as though you could not hold on for one minute longer, never give up then, for that is just the place that the tide will turn.... —*Harriet Beecher Stowe*

The tribulations of life are trials or expiations; happy are those who bear them without murmuring, for great will be their reward....
—*Allan Kardec*

Most of our problems are test questions.... —*Henry S. Haskins*

Life is a wonderfully complex problem for the individual, until, someday, in a moment of illumination, he awakens to the great realization that he can make it simpler—never quite simple, but always simpler.... —*William G. Jordan*

Do not be intimidated by problems. A problem is not a problem, only a challenge to be surmounted. Defiantly hoist your sails and sail into the prevailing wind. There are no storms sufficient to scuttle a ship when a positive attitude is taken....
—*Shantidasa*

A problem is a chance for you to do your best.... —*Duke Ellington*

The solution to the problem of the day is the awakening of the consciousness of humanity to the divinity within....
—*Hazrat Inayat Khan*

To be resentful of a problem only makes it heavier; to recognize and appreciate it always makes it lighter....
—*Anonymous*

Personal problems are never solved by dwelling on them, but always by forgetting them in serving a larger interest.... —*Sahajananda*

Each has his own problems to work out. Each must work out his own problems. Each must grow the insight that will enable him to see what the causes are that have brought the unfavorable conditions, and to set into operation forces that will bring about a different set of conditions....
—*Ralph W. Trine*

Progress is the mother of problems....
—*G. K. Chesterton*

Misfortunes are great, but human beings are even greater than misfortune.... —*Rabindranath Tagore*

What is it that troubles you? Death? Or because your foot has stumbled on the earth? There is no man who has never stumbled.... —*Schemuel Ha-Nagid*

If you can get people to see the comic side of their tragedy, you can also get them to look at solving their problems.... —*James Fadiman*

The longer we dwell on our misfortunes, the greater is their power to harm us.... —*Voltaire*

Need and struggle are what excite and inspire us.... —*William James*

There is no height to which you cannot climb; no difficulty which you cannot overcome; no failure which cannot be retrieved; no disease which cannot be healed....The difficulties and problems of life become like rungs on the ladder for each one raises us up higher....
—*Henry T. Hamblin*

Trust would settle every problem now.... —*A Course In Miracles*

If a great problem is set before you, this merely indicates that you have the great inner strength to solve a great problem.... —*Peace Pilgrim*

Helping others is the best way to rid yourself of your own troubles....
—*Edgar Cayce*

You may ponder internally over your personal problems and try to seek guidance, but it may be only wasting your energy to think over the problems of others.... —*Maharaj C. Singh*

All your problems arise because you have defined and therefore limited yourself. When you do not think yourself to be this or that, all conflict ceases.... —*Nisargadatta*

Misfortune is never mournful to the soul that accepts it; for such do always see that in every cloud is an angel's face.... —*Eusebius Hieronymus*

The best years of your life are the ones in which you decide your problems are your own. You don't blame them on your mother, the ecology or the President. You realize that you control your own destiny.... —*Albert Ellis*

To walk against adversity, to bring forth the inner strength, to cope with the problems of life, to walk against the wind of life and push against it makes you breathe hard and gives you strength.... —*Hilda Charlton*

Whenever a problem appears in our experience, it is because we are strong enough to meet it successfully and overcome it. It is not there to punish us.... —*Elinor MacDonald*

If all misfortunes of mankind were cast into a public stock, in order to be equally distributed among the whole species, those who now think themselves the most unhappy would prefer the share they already possess.... —*Socrates*

Troubles are often the tools by which God fashions us for better things.... —*Henry W. Beecher*

Prosperity

P rosperity, alas! is often but another name for pride.... —*Lydia H. Sigourney*

Prosperity is more of an ordeal than adversity, especially sudden prosperity.... —*Yiddish proverb*

It is very difficult for the prosperous to be humble.... —*Jane Austen*

Prosperity is only an instrument to be used, not a deity to be worshipped.... —*Calvin Coolidge*

What the world regards as prosperity often hides the most poignant sorrows.... —*Allan Kardec*

It is a mistake to think that it is only in the sunshine of prosperity one can find happiness. Rare and beautiful blessings blossom "in that holy ground where the shadows fall."... —*Alice H. Rice*

All sunshine makes the desert.... —*Arabian proverb*

We are corrupted by prosperity.... —*Tacitus*

Everything in the world may be endured, except only a succession of prosperous days.... —*Johann W. Goethe*

In prosperity, when the stream of life flows in accordance with our wishes, let us diligently avoid all arrogance, haughtiness and pride.... —*Cicero*

Prosperity is a feeble reed.... —*Daniel d'Ancheres*

Prosperity destroys fools and endangers the wise.... —*Henry Bohn*

We become wiser in the midst of adversity; it is prosperity that takes away righteousness.... —*Seneca*

Pride waxes in prosperity, nor is it easy to bear good fortune with equal mind.... —*Ovid*

Prosperity is a great teacher; adversity is a greater.... —*William Hazlitt*

Prosperity can change man's nature; and seldom is anyone cautious enough to resist the effects of good fortune....
—*Quintas C. Rufus*

Adversity is sometimes hard upon a man, but for one man who can stand prosperity, there are a hundred that will stand adversity....
—*Thomas Carlyle*

Nothing is harder to direct than a man in prosperity; nothing more easily managed than one in adversity....
—*Plutarch*

No man knows of what stuff he is made until prosperity and ease try him....
—*A. P. Gouthey*

One is never more on trial than in the moment of excessive good fortune....
—*Lewis Wallace*

The mind that is much elevated with prosperity, and cast down by adversity, is generally abject and base....
—*Epicurus*

This is the law of prosperity: When apparent adversity comes, be not cast down by it, but make the best of it, and always look forward for better things, for conditions more prosperous....
—*Ralph W. Trine*

Purpose

We are all designed for a specific purpose; we all have something for which each of us, and each of us alone, is responsible....
—*Naomi Stephan*

The real purpose of the world is to use it to correct your unbelief....
—*A Course In Miracles*

The only useful purpose of this birth is to turn within and realize. There is nothing else to do....
—*Ramana Maharshi*

Those who have failed to work toward the truth have missed the purpose of living.... —*Gautama Buddha*

Learn to get in touch with silence within yourself and know that everything in this life has a purpose....
—*Elisabeth Kubler-Ross*

The purpose of life....is to live it, to taste experience to the utmost, to reach out eagerly and without fear for newer and richer experience.... —*Eleanor Roosevelt*

Where there is purpose there is ego. Play is no purpose. It gives joy. Play itself is the purpose. No object is to be gained by playing.... —*Papa Ramdas*

Life is everlasting. Everything that happens in your life has a purpose....
—*George Anderson*

The purpose of life is to unlearn what has been learned and to remember what has been forgotten....
—*Sufi saying*

Man has come here with a definite purpose. Life is not meant merely for eating, drinking and procreating....
—*Sivananda*

The purpose of life is to acquaint man with himself.... —*Ralph W. Emerson*

Strong lives are motivated by dynamic purposes.... —*Kenneth Hildebrand*

Nothing contributes so much to tranquilizing the mind as a steady purpose-point on which the soul may fix its intellectual eye....
—*Mary W. Shelley*

A man without a purpose is like a ship without a rudder....Have a purpose in life, and having it, throw into your work such strength of mind and muscle as God has given you....
—*Thomas Carlyle*

To have a purpose that is worthwhile, and that is steadily being accomplished, that is one of the secrets of a life that is worth living....
—*Herbert Casson*

A life without purpose is a languid drifting thing. Every day we ought to renew our purpose, say to ourselves: this day let us make a sound beginning, for what we have hitherto done is nought. Our improvement is in proportion to our purpose....
—*Thomas à Kempis*

The purpose of man's life is not happiness, but worthiness....
—*Felix Adler*

There is no road to success but through a clear strong purpose. Nothing can take its place....A purpose is the eternal condition of success....
—*Theodore Munger*

The great and glorious masterpiece of man is to know how to live to purpose....   —*Michel Montaigne*

Fixedness of purpose is at the root of all successful efforts, whether in things worldly or spiritual....
—*James Allen*

Purpose is what gives life meaning....
—*Charles Parkhurst*

I finally learned that my main purpose was to have no purpose, to learn how to give up effort....   —*Joanna Field*

Happiness is the meaning and the purpose of life, the whole aim and end of human existence....   —*Aristotle*

What men want is not talent; it is purpose; in other words, not the power to achieve, but the will to labor....
—*Edward Bulwer-Lytton*

The human heart refuses to believe in a universe without a purpose....What are the aims which are at the same time duties? They are the perfecting of ourselves and the happiness of others....
—*Immanuel Kant*

Firmness of purpose is one of the most necessary sinews of character, and one of the best instruments of success....
—*Philip D. Stanhope*

The true purpose is to see things as they are, to observe things as they are, and to let everything go as it goes....
—*Shunryu Suzuki*

Man's destined purpose is to conquer old habits, to overcome the evil in him and to restore good to its rightful place....   —*Mohandas Gandhi*

When a man does not know what harbor he is heading for, no wind is the right wind....   —*Seneca*

You have a purpose only as long as you are not complete; until then, completeness, perfection, is the purpose. But when you are complete in yourself, fully integrated within and without, then you enjoy the universe; you do not labor at it....   —*Nisargadatta*

Clear purpose is half of the struggle....
—*Sevakram*

Divine purpose for us is learning to live in harmony with God's will....When you know your part in the scheme of things, in the Divine Plan, there is never a feeling of inadequacy. You are always given the resources for any situation, any obstacle. There is no strain; there is always security....
—*Peace Pilgrim*

Your sole business in life is to attain God-realization. All else is useless and worthless....   —*Sivananda*

Man is not born to solve the problems of the universe, but to find out what he has to do; and to restrain himself within the limits of comprehension....
—*Johann W. Goethe*

There is no defeat save your own inherent weakness of purpose....
—*Richard Pape*

Relationship

T he easiest relationship for me is with 10,000 people. The hardest is with one....   —*Joan Baez*

A relationship is like a garden. If it is to thrive it must be watered regularly. Special care must be given, taking into account the seasons as well as any unpredictable weather. New seeds must be sown and weeds must be pulled....   —*John Gray*

So many persons think divorce a panacea for every ill, who find out, when they try it, that the remedy is worse than the disease....
—*Dorothy Dix*

Loves which change are passing whims....   —*Eliphas Levi*

Too many people are more concerned with what they can get out of marriage than with what they can give to it....
—*Elinor MacDonald*

The difficulty with relationships is that they blur boundaries that are used to determine who we really are....
—*Anonymous*

In order for a relationship to be really successful in the widest sense of the term, you have to want God more than you want your partner....
—*Stephen Levine*

Couples who love each other can communicate a thousand things without ever once talking.... —*Chinese proverb*

When we enter into any relationship with the premise that we are empty and the other person will fill us in, we are sure to fail. We can only win when we proceed from wholeness....
—*Alan Cohen*

If you would learn the secret of right relations look only for the divine in people and things, and leave the rest to God....   —*J. Allen Boone*

Love is a drama of contradictions....
—*Franz Kafka*

The fact that one is married by no means proves that one is a mature person....   —*Clara Thompson*

There is no way to take the danger out of human relationships....
—*Barbara G. Harrison*

It is only when we no longer compulsively need someone that we can have a real relationship with them....
—*Anthony Storr*

The most satisfying relationships are intimate. They enable us to be known and accepted as we truly are. A friend is someone with whom you feel comfortable being yourself....
—*David G. Myers*

You can't lose when you simply appreciate and grow from a relationship....
—*Wayne Dyer*

Associations formed in this earth life are not necessarily for the duration of the life span. Separation takes place constantly, and as long as it takes place lovingly not only is there no spiritual injury, but spiritual progress may actually be helped.... —*Peace Pilgrim*

Love is mutually feeding each other, not living on another like a ghoul....
—*Bessie Head*

In almost every marriage there is a selfish and unselfish partner. A pattern is set up and soon becomes inflexible, of one person always making the demands and one person always giving away.... —*Iris Murdoch*

A successful marriage is an edifice that must be rebuilt daily....
—*André Maurois*

Relationship is a mirror into which your inner being gets reflected....
—*Vimala Thakar*

Human love is often the encounter of two weaknesses.... —*Francois Mauriac*

Two persons who love each other are in a place more holy than the interior of a church.... —*William L. Phelps*

Individuals seeking relationships are often attempting to get another to fill up their emptiness....
—*Stephen H. Wolinsky*

Lovers dream in courtship, but in wedlock awake.... —*Alexander Pope*

The best friend is likely to acquire the best wife, because a good marriage is based on the talent for friendship....
—*Friedrich W. Nietzsche*

The essential ingredients for relationship are affection and commitment....
—*Robert A. Johnson*

It is easier to live through someone else than to become complete yourself....
—*Betty Friedan*

No man can be friends with a woman he finds attractive. He always wants to have sex with her. Sex is always out there. Friendship is ultimately doomed and that is the end of the story....
—*Nora Ephron*

Pity the selfishness of lovers: it is brief; a forlorn hope; it is impossible....
—*Elizabeth Bowen*

A man falls in love through his eyes, a woman through her ears....
—*Woodrow Wyatt*

In every union there is a mystery....
—*Henri F. Amiel*

If a relationship is built on 'what am I getting?' all is lost.... —*Ossie Davis*

There is so much you cannot understand in human relationship; often you have to endure what seems to be injustice. But those....who can take the long view, can always tell you that all crooked places will be made straight and all injustice will be righted....
—*White Eagle*

Marriage is a rooted thing, a growing and flowering thing that must be tended faithfully.... —*Donald C. Peattie*

The married state is....the completest image of heaven and hell we are capable of receiving in this life....
—*Richard Steele*

The inner progressiveness of love between two human beings is a most marvelous thing; it cannot be found by looking for it or by passionately wishing for it. It is sort of Divine accident....
—*Hugh Walpole*

There are only two valid reasons to get married. One is for the care and raising of children....The only other valid reason....is for the friction....
—*M. Scott Peck*

Life is a series of relationships—being together and separating....
—*JoAnn Kelley Smith*

Marriage is a box to put your love in. It can hold it safe and warm forever, the door closed against all evil. Or it can be a cage. The box is of your own making.... —*Mary Williams*

The notion of marrying for love is one of the most pathological experiments that a civilized society has ever imagined, namely, the basing of marriage, which is lasting, upon romance, which is a passing fancy....
—*M. Denis DeRougemont*

It is impossible to love and be wise at the same time.... —*Francis Bacon*

Now we will feel no rain for each of us will be shelter for the other. Now we will feel no cold for each of us will be warmth for the other. Now there will be no more loneliness for each of us will be companion to the other. There is only one life before us and our seasons will be long and good....
—*Apache Wedding Blessing*

Marry, and with luck it may go well. But when a marriage fails, then those who marry live at home in hell....
—*Euripides*

Ending a relationship on the physical level is not failing, anymore than someone dying represents a failure, although it certainly ends the physical relationship.... —*Wayne Dyer*

Neither husband nor wife has any rights; they have only the privilege of giving, but they have no right to demand anything of the other....
—*Joel Goldsmith*

When our marriages no longer inspire enthusiasm....it is because the sacred is missing in our lives.... —*Mark Gerzon*

Deceive not thyself by overexpecting happiness in a married state....
—*Thomas Fuller*

For one human being to love another: that is perhaps the most difficult of our tasks.... —*Rainer M. Rilke*

In all our struggles with relationships, we learn there is a point where we release others to a pattern of their own making.... —*Carol W. Parrish-Harra*

No relationship can provide everything needed for the complete experience of being yourself.... —*David Viscott*

Relationships fail because of unfulfilled expectations, and the greater the expectation, the more likely the failure.... —*Anonymous*

The consuming desire of most human beings is deliberately to plant their whole life in the hands of some other person. I would describe this method of searching for happiness as immature....
—*Quentin Crisp*

There are no snares more dangerous than those which lurk under the guise of duty or the name of relationship....
—*Cicero*

Our primary relationship is really with ourselves....Our relationships with other people constantly reflect exactly where we are in the process....
—*Shakti Gawain*

Almost all our relationships begin and most of them continue as forms of mutual exploitation, a mental or physical barter, to be terminated when one or both parties run out of goods....
—*W. H. Auden*

When two people marry and give all their love to each other they are building a wall around themselves. They have no love left for God or the Self....
—*Saradamma*

Love is an ideal thing, marriage is a real thing. A confusion of the real with the ideal never goes unpunished....
—*Johann W. Goethe*

The secret of forming a successful relationship is for both parties to win....
—*John Gray*

Sometimes dignity in a marriage can best be preserved when the partners separate before all love dies—in order to work on their individual problems and in order not to hurt each other any more than they already have....
—*Sara Kay Cohen*

Even positive relationships are easily subject to fracture....
—*Robert Schuller*

Seldom or never does a marriage develop into an individual relationship smoothly and without crisis. There is no birth of consciousness without pain....
—*Carl Jung*

In the face of the relationship with God, all other relations dwindle into nothing....the question of any domestic relationship....cannot arise....
—*Papa Ramdas*

If we did not look to marriage as the principle source of happiness, fewer marriages would end in tears....
—*Anthony Storr*

The false promise is that another person giving you love will solve your problems, make you happy, give you security you desire, make you feel good about yourself....
—*Jordan & Margaret Paul*

The reality is that all relationships inevitably will be dissolved and broken....
—*James Lynch*

The purpose of a relationship is not for two incomplete people to become one, but rather for two complete people to join together for the greater glory of God....
—*Marianne Williamson*

A marriage is like a long trip in a tiny rowboat; if one passenger starts to rock the boat, the other has to steady it; otherwise, they will go to the bottom together....
—*David Reuben*

Chains do not hold a marriage together. It is threads, hundreds of tiny threads which sew people together through the years....
—*Simone Signoret*

I believe that we should wise up and recognize that a marriage is a small business and that married couples are business partners....
—*David Hopkinson*

Love does not consist in gazing at each other, but in looking outward in the same direction....
—*Antoine de Saint-Exupery*

Sometimes we may find that our partner continues to seek satisfaction in ways that we cannot live with. Nevertheless, when we decide to go our own way we still have a choice as to how we separate. We can separate with bad feelings, blaming the other's faults and unacceptable behavior. Or we can separate with forgiveness, love and understanding....　　　*—Peter Russell*

Relationships are not always easy. Misunderstandings happen. They cannot be healed by dwelling on hurts, but by turning to the consciousness of love and understanding. Love heals all wounds....　　　*—Norma Hawkins*

All of life is relationship....
　　　　　　　—Swami Rama

Is not marriage an open question, when it is alleged, from the beginning of the world, that such as are in the institution wish to get out, and such as are out wish to get in....
　　　　　　　—Ralph W. Emerson

When two people get close to each other, there is generally an explosion in their lives. Most of the recrimination between quarreling lovers and spouses involves the collision of power and love....　　　*—Robert A. Johnson*

Some people spend much less time picking a life partner than they spend picking out a car. They just drift into these relationships by this thing we call love....　　　*—Peace Pilgrim*

It is not the lack of love but lack of friendship that makes unhappy marriages....　　　*—Friedrich W. Nietzsche*

There is no relationship that is more important than your relationship with yourself—it affects all others and everything that you do in life....
　　　　　　　—Sharon Garell

Your most important relationship is with yourself; most people form relationships to avoid themselves....
　　　　　　　—Anonymous

The highest love a person can have for you is to wish for you to evolve into the best person you can be. No one owns you, no matter what your relationship....　　　*—David Viscott*

Don't attempt to perpetuate a relationship by contract....Try to avoid any situation in which you or anyone else is obligated....You wouldn't get good value when the individual no longer wants to be involved....
　　　　　　　—Harry Browne

Powerful relationships arise when two centered individuals commit themselves to unconditionally love one another and to support each other's growth toward full potential....
　　　　　　　—Thomas Crum

If a relationship is ever going to work....we must surrender to each other. If you look up surrender in Webster's you will find that the first definition says, "To give up possession of or power over." Thus, surrender in a relationship would mean to give up possession of the power over each other....　　　*—Stewart Emery*

People think that their possessions, their family, their marriage and natural life are terribly important. They are not! We cannot serve two masters. We can only serve one force, the one life. God must come first. We can still serve the secondary side of our nature, but primarily it must be the expression of a spiritual nature....　　　*—Ronald Beesley*

If love is the foundation of a happy marriage, good manners are the walls and roof....　　　*—Clarita de Forceville*

The greatest of all arts is the art of living together....Every man who is happily married is a successful man even if he has failed in everything else....   *—William L. Phelps*

Relationships fail because people try to change one another, thereby altering the chemistry that brought them together in the first place....   *—Anonymous*

This is the only soil in which love can possibly grow. "We're gonna make it together!"...   *—John Powell*

The most empowering relationships are those in which each partner lifts the other to a higher possession of their own being....   *—Teilhard de Chardin*

When two loving minds are united in a single purpose there is a mighty mental force generated which will unfailingly accomplish the purpose....   *—Leon DeSeblo*

The self-centered person tests all things by the question, "Am I getting in marriage the happiness which I deserve?" And yet it is unfair without an accompanying one: "Am I giving in marriage the best that is possible for me to give?" Two persons thinking of each other's happiness will find themselves sharing a rich store of durable satisfactions....   *—Leland F. Wood*

Many people are greatly enslaved by what we term ties of relationship. It is well, however, for us to remember that our true relatives are not necessarily those who are connected with us by ties of blood. Our truest relatives are those who are nearest akin to us in mind, in soul, in spirit....   *—Ralph W. Trine*

No other person can bring us happiness if she or he does not possess it herself or himself. The romantic urge to seek in a second individual that which neither of the two has, can never find successful fulfillment....   *—Paul Brunton*

Relationships are like a dance, with visible energy racing back and forth between the partners....   *—Colette Dowling*

Only independent people can choose to remain in a relationship. Dependent people remain out of necessity. The most mature level of love exists only in the face of free choice. Therefore, loving can be experienced and enjoyed only to the extent that the participants are able to maintain themselves independently....   *—Aaron Stein*

You must first have a good relationship with yourself before you can have a good relationship with others. You have to feel worthwhile and acceptable in your own eyes. The more independent you are, the better you'll be able to connect and relate with others....   *—Gary Emery*

Relationships are only as alive as the people engaging in them....   *—Donald B. Ardell*

You do not possess any other human being, no matter how close that other may be. No husband owns his wife; no wife owns her husband; no parents own their children. When you think you possess people there is a tendency to run their lives for them....   *—Peace Pilgrim*

If you want your relationship to last, never, never, never, ever threaten the relationship itself....   *—Anthony Robbins*

The greater the fundamental differences between two persons are the more difficult it is to establish a fully personal relationship between them, but also the more worthwhile the relationship will be if it can be established and maintained....
—*John Macmurray*

I do my thing, and you do your thing. I am not in this world to live up to your expectations, and you are not in this world to live up to mine. You are you and I am I. If by chance we find each other, it's beautiful. If not, it can't be helped....
—*Fritz Perls*

Relationships are part of a vast plan for our enlightenment....
—*Marianne Williamson*

In healthy relationships, people view one another as unique, one-of-a-kind individuals; there is no attempt to control, to be a caretaker, to create a dependency....
—*Shantidasa*

As travelers meet by chance on the way, so does man meet a wife, children, relatives, and friends; let him therefore be in the world and yet separate from it....
—*Srimad Bhagavatam*

Religion

True religion must awaken in us a sense of joy....
—*Paramananda*

The poverty of all religions has been their inability to make God real to their devotees....
—*Julian P. Johnson*

There is no such thing as God of one religion and God of another. We have made distinctions through our ignorance....
—*Papa Ramdas*

Every true faith began with something very good, but as they get old they become encrusted with dogma....
—*Peace Pilgrim*

Religions and dogmas keep one looking for God....God is not external to us; no looking or searching is necessary—one need only abide within the consciousness of their realization of God's presence....
—*A Spiritual Warrior*

Do you think that you can find God by worshipping another? You do such silly, stupid things—offering flowers and lighting candles! Do you think that you can find God by giving bribes?...
—*Yoga Swami*

All our religious systems are only the works of intellectual children....
—*Jakob Böhme*

What cannot be followed out in day-to-day practice cannot be called religion....
—*Mohandas Gandhi*

Where all religions meet is the realization in no mystical sense, but in the most worldly and everyday sense, that GOD IS EVERYTHING, AND EVERYTHING IS GOD....
—*Ramana Maharshi*

The religious man always thinks that his zeal for making converts is a virtue. It is not a virtue at all, but a vice, because this zeal is due to his egoism....
—*Lakshmana Sarma*

All the religion we have is the ethics of one or another holy person....
—*Ralph W. Emerson*

Religion should unite men everywhere; instead it sunders and separates them. Religion has proved a razor among men, when it should have healed all their wounds....
—*Abdul Baha*

Pure religion....is this, to help the fatherless and widows in their affliction, and to keep unspotted from the world.... —*Paul of Tarsus*

Religion is a bridge to the spiritual—but the spiritual lies beyond religion. Unfortunately, in seeking the spiritual we may become attached to the bridge rather than crossing over it.... —*Prabhushri*

For true worship, only God and the human soul are necessary. It does not depend upon times, or seasons, or occasions. Anywhere and at any time God and man in the bush may meet.... —*Ralph W. Trine*

Too much religion kills God, the God in Man; enslaves him to superstition, instead of bringing him Freedom from all fear.... —*Bhagavan Das*

No religion can be built on force.... —*George Sand*

Religion does not blithely promise some sort of no-trouble, no-problem, no-poverty world; but rather a spirit, a power, an enthusiasm that endows everyone with the ability to overcome any and all of it.... —*Norman V. Peale*

Religion is doing; a man does not merely think his religion or feel it, he "lives" his religion as much as he is able, otherwise it is not religion but fantasy or philosophy.... —*George I. Gurdjieff*

Any system of religion that has anything in it that shocks the mind of a child cannot be a true system.... —*Thomas Paine*

Forms are but symbols; we should never rest in them, but make them the stepping stones to the good to which they point.... —*Nathaniel Emmons*

The followers of different religions quarrel about truth because they have never experienced it. Most of them don't even try to experience it; they are much happier quarrelling, fighting and killing each other.... —*Lakshmana*

It is good to be born in a church, but it is bad to die there. It is good to be born a child, but bad to remain a child. Churches, ceremonies, symbols are good for children; but when the child is grown up, he must burst, either the church or himself....The end of all religion is the realization of God.... —*Vivekananda*

God is not imprisoned or caged within the four walls of temples or other religious places. He fills the universe and lives in devotees' hearts.... —*Shirdi Sai Baba*

For a truly religious man nothing is tragic.... —*Ludwig Wittgenstein*

A maker of idols is never an idolater.... —*Chinese proverb*

Any religion in which a man is good—and unbigoted—is a good religion for him and should be held in esteem.... —*Caroline Duerr*

The humble, meek, merciful, just, pious, and devout souls are everywhere of one religion; and when death has taken off the mask, they will know one another.... —*William Penn*

What we need in religion is not new light, but new sight, not new paths, but new strength to walk in the old ones.... —*Tryon Edwards*

True religion and virtue give a cheerful and happy turn to the mind.... —*Joseph Addison*

Religions become corrupted when leaders are assigned to explain God's will to people instead of showing them how to find this direction within themselves....   —*James Redfield*

Doing good to others is the highest religion....   —*Sivananda*

A religion that is without joy is really no religion at all....   —*Anonymous*

The true worship of God is not a prostration of man in blind delirium; on the contrary....it is profound peace, the tranquility which arises from perfect order....   —*Eliphas Levi*

Religion is always man-made. It cannot therefore be the whole truth. It is a good thing for the ordinary and outside man, but surely it will never bring him to the Gates of Gold....   —*Mabel Collins*

If a religion does not teach love, respect, and regard for others, it cannot be the religion of humanity....
—*Muktananda*

Your religion is where your love is....
—*Henry D. Thoreau*

The spiritual is not religious. A religion is dogma, a set of beliefs about the spiritual and a set of practices which rise out of those beliefs....
—*Rachel N. Remen*

Religion is a mental faculty which, independent of, nay, in spite of sense and reason, enables man to apprehend the Infinite under different names and under different disguises....
—*Max Muller*

The consciousness of God in the soul of man is the essence, indeed the sum and substance of all religions....
—*Ralph W. Trine*

Religion, wherever it exists, spreads over the whole of life. One cannot take it up as one takes up golf—by giving it a couple of afternoons a week. That kind of amateur religion is not religion. Religion is either the whole of one's life, or else it is not religion, no matter how much fuss is made over it....
—*Gregory Vlastos*

The religions we call false were once true....   —*Ralph W. Emerson*

A sage once said: "It is good to be born into a church, but it is bad to die in a church," which meant that while we are born into a religion, we have no choice about it. As we grow up and expand in wisdom we should be tolerant and our love and sympathy and understanding should go beyond the borders of our own religion....
—*Chidananda*

Religion is not an end in itself. One's union with God is the ultimate goal....
—*Peace Pilgrim*

Religion, in one way or another, has always been with us. Religion will continue to always be with us. What needs to be discarded and thrown away is the ecclesiastical rubbish which binds us to religion instead of God....
—*Shantidasa*

There is only one religion, though there are a hundred versions of it....
—*George B. Shaw*

No religion has a monopoly on spirituality....   —*Anonymous*

Religion is nothing else but love of God and man....   —*William Penn*

In matter of religion, it is very easy to deceive a man, and very hard to undeceive him....   —*Pierre Bayle*

I maintain that Faith is a pathless land, and you can approach it by any path whatsoever, by any religion, by any sect....
—*J. Krishnamurti*

Never hurt the feelings of others. Speak the truth. Do not kill any sentient beings. Cultivate such divine virtues as humility, courage, forgiveness, tolerance and compassion. Love all, be kind to all. Be good, do good. Be charitable. Purify the heart. Serve humanity. Share what you have with others....Love thy neighbor as thyself....These, indeed, constitute the essentials of all religions....
—*Sivananda*

Men never do evil so completely and cheerfully as when they do it with religious conviction....
—*Blaise Pascal*

Difference of religion breeds more quarrels than differences of politics....
—*Wendell Phillips*

Many religions claim that theirs is the only path to the Truth....But God never made an agreement with any of these religions. All religions are of fairly recent origin, but God has existed since the beginning of time. He could not have signed a contract with any religious founder saying, "You are my exclusive salesman."...
—*Muktananda*

Religion without mystery ceases to be religion....
—*William T. Manning*

Religion is regarded by the common people as true, by the wise as false, and by the rulers as useful....
—*Seneca*

It is more important to create a safer, kinder world than to recruit more people to the religion that happens to satisfy us....
—*Dalai Lama*

The religion of love is apart from all religions....
—*Rumi*

The religion of each is the attainment of his soul's desire. When he is on the path of that attainment he is religious. When he is off the path he is impious....
—*Hazrat Inayat Khan*

Religion is not so much man's attempt to know God as his attempt to know himself....
—*Stuart Holroyd*

The great turmoil in the religions is caused by the spirit demanding superiority. Faith is not dying in the West. It is merely moving inside....
—*Anthony Padovano*

God has no religion....
—*Mohandas Gandhi*

Unselfishness is the only real religion....
—*Israel Zangwill*

There is a diversity of religious doctrines, but there is only one Religion....
—*Leo Tolstoy*

What counts is not creed but conduct....
—*Sarvepalli Radhakrishnan*

When a man is on a low cultural level, he can satisfy his spiritual needs with outward religious observances; but as he becomes more highly developed, he wants to grasp the spirit of religion....
—*Nahman Krochmal*

My father considered a walk among the mountains as the equivalent of churchgoing....
—*Aldous Huxley*

Religion, any religion, is the inner experience of the individual....There is no such distinction as true and false religion, for every man's religion is for him true and genuine....
—*Julian P. Johnson*

The first and last lesson of religion is, "The things that are seen are temporal; the things that are not seen are eternal."...
—Ralph W. Emerson

What the world craves today is a more spiritual and less formal religion....
—John D. Rockefeller, Jr.

True religion needs neither arms nor fingers for its use; it is all spirit and heart....
—Moses Mendelssohn

So long as you have a creed, you have no God....
—Vivekananda

All the disharmony of the world caused by religious differences is the result of man's failure to understand that religion is one, truth is one, God is one: how can there be two religions....
—Anonymous

Science without religion is lame, religion without science is blind....
—Albert Einstein

Different creeds are but different paths to reach the Almighty....
—Ramakrishna

Like the bee gathering honey from different flowers, the wise man accepts the essence of different Scriptures and sees only the good in all religions....
—Srimad Bhagavatam

We have just enough religion to make us hate, but not enough to make us love one another....
—Jonathan Swift

The only religion is conscience in action....
—Henry O. Lloyd

All belief that does not render us more happy, more free, more loving, more active, more calm, is, I fear, an erroneous and superstitious belief....
—John K. Lavater

Religion is not what is grasped by the brain, but a heart grasp....
—Mohandas Gandhi

Religion is to be used as a stepping stone to God but it must never be used as a tower to hold one aloft from others. We are all cells in the body of humanity. When anyone attempts to isolate another, they only isolate themselves more....
—Peace Pilgrim

The object of religion is that the soul should serve God, not that God should serve the soul....
—Robert Benson

Every religion is good that teaches man to be good....
—Thomas Paine

Religious teaching in the past has dealt mainly with preparing man for the next world. This is of course of the utmost importance, but we should not allow it to blind us to the fact that there is a Power that can make this life perfect also....
—Henry T. Hamblin

Religion is a man's total reaction upon life....
—William James

My religion is very simple. My religion is kindness....
—Dalai Lama

Religion is not knowledge but a direction of the heart....
—Rainer M. Rilke

The highest aim of religion....is not to condemn and to destroy, but to fulfill....
—Raymond C. Knox

Religion holds a man back from the path, prevents his stepping forward, for various very plain reasons. First, it makes the vital mistake of distinguishing between good and evil....
—Mabel Collins

Religion is a personal relationship with God.... —*William Temple*

Truth, in matters of religion, is simply opinion that has survived.... —*Oscar Wilde*

Common men talk bagfuls of religion but act not a grain of it, while the wise man speaks little, but his whole life is a religion acted out.... —*Ramakrishna*

A man's religion is the truth he lives habitually, subconsciously and consciously.... —*Benjamin Leeming*

What is religion? That which is never spoken.... —*Henry D. Thoreau*

Religion in its true sense is the most joyous thing the human soul can know, and when the real religion is realized, we will find it to be an agent of peace, of joy, and of happiness, and never an agent of gloomy, long-faced sadness.... —*Ralph W. Trine*

It is certainly no part of religion to compel religion.... —*Tertullian*

Religion presents few difficulties to the humble; many to the proud; insuperable ones to the vain.... —*Augustus & Julius Hare*

Religion is something which every individual must work out for himself; and we cannot call ourselves religious until through our life we prove the reality of God and the reality of our own soul.... —*Paramananda*

The time is now come when we must choose between creeds and the Brotherhood of Man. Creeds are but the conjuring of man.... —*Baird Spalding*

God builds His temple in the heart on the ruins of churches and religions.... —*Ralph W. Emerson*

Temples are not to be built for Him with stones piled on high; God is to be concentrated in the breast of each.... —*Seneca*

Religions were never designed to unite man. They were supposed to unite man and God. They failed in both because they never realized that in the unity of human being, God is born.... —*Babu Rao Patel*

One can become so attached to the outward symbols and structure of religion that one forgets its original intent—to bring one closer to God.... —*Peace Pilgrim*

Saints

Saints have a habit of saying that they feel themselves to be no better than the vilest sinners, and they are right. Scoundrels and saints stand equal in the opposite pans of one and the same balance.... —*Eliphas Levi*

When a saint does something holy there's nothing surprising about it.... —*Yuliya Voznesenskaya*

Saints are the great teachers of the loving-kindness and fascination with God.... —*Evelyn Underhill*

A person remains ordinary as long as he is led by the mind: but freed from the mind, he becomes a great saint.... —*Nityananda*

A man does not have to be an angel to be a saint.... —*Albert Schweitzer*

The heroes, the saints and sages—they are those who face the world alone.... —*Norman Douglas*

The beginning of saintliness is killing of egoism. The end of saintliness is Eternal Life. The key to saintliness is chastity. The light of saintliness is universal love.... —*Sivananda*

Saints are not saints by chance, nor by choice, but by necessity–because there is a hunger in their souls which cannot be satisfied by anything less than the divine.... —*Nancy Pope Mayyorya*

There are no external signs to mark out a God–realized saint. He does not grow a horn. But he is always full of bliss. He is happy under all conditions.... —*Papa Ramdas*

A man may have never entered a church or a mosque, nor performed any ceremony; but if he realizes God within himself, and is thereby lifted above the vanities of the world, that man is a holy man, a saint, call him what you will.... —*Vivekananda*

Saints are simply men and women who have fulfilled their natural obligation, which is to approach God.... —*Evelyn Waugh*

He whom God has touched will always be a being apart: he is, whatever he may do, a stranger among men; he is marked by a sign.... —*Ernest Renan*

Whoever fights ceaselessly against his own selfishness and strives to supplant it with all-embracing love is a saint, whether he live in a cottage or in the midst of riches and influence; or whether he preaches or remains obscure.... —*James Allen*

The true saint goes in and out amongst the people and eats and sleeps with them and buys and sells in the market and marries and takes part in social intercourse, and never forgets God for a single moment.... —*Abu Sa'id Ibn*

The wonderful thing about saints is that they were human. They lost their tempers, got hungry, scolded God, were egotistical or testy or impatient in their turns, made mistakes and regretted them. Still they went on doggedly blundering toward heaven.... —*Phyllis McGinley*

Every Saint has the same message to give and the same teachings to impart. No Saint, no perfect Master, comes into this world to create a religion, to divide people, to set one nation against another or one religion against another. They come only to show us the Way which leads back to our original Home.... —*Charan Singh*

Even saints who engage in no outward work bestow, through their thoughts and holy vibrations, more precious benefits on the world than can be given by the most strenuous humanitarian activities of unenlightened men.... —*Paramahansa Yogananda*

A saint is like a tree. He does not call anyone, neither does he send anyone away. He gives shelter to whoever cares to come.... —*Anandamayee Ma*

Saints seek neither recognition nor fame. Like the sun, their very being is their greatness.... —*The Mountain Path*

Saints are like big steamships which not only cross the ocean themselves but carry many passengers to the other shore.... —*Ramakrishna*

A saint is a golden chain, in which each saint is a separate link, united to the next by faith, works, and love.... —*Symeon, the New Theologian*

A child has no real knowledge of the attainments of an adult. An ordinary adult cannot understand the attainments of a learned man. In the same way, an educated man cannot yet understand the experiences of enlightened saints....   —*El-Ghazali*

Pioneers have to tread a lonely road. It is so in order that they may stand out as great, solitary figures, which act as landmarks to guide those who come after them. What is exceptional today, becomes the commonplace of tomorrow....   —*Henry T. Hamblin*

Saintship is the exclusive possession of those who have either worn out or never had the capacity to sin....   —*Elbert Hubbard*

All good men are saints....   —*Francois Fenelon*

The creed of the saint is to make the most of life, and to make the best of it....   —*Edwin H. Chapin*

The saint is he who bears enmity to no living creature. There is but one Spirit: he has no enemy....   —*Dadu*

If we ask of the saints how they achieved spiritual effectiveness, they are only able to reply that, insofar as they did it themselves, they did it by love and prayer....   —*Evelyn Underhill*

Only the saints are truly happy. The pity of our lives is that we are not all saints....   —*Leon Bloy*

The saints of God are sealed inwardly with faith, but outwardly with good works....   —*John Boys*

The saintlier the man, the deeper went his desire to remain inconspicuous and anonymous....   —*Sheldon Cheney*

Why were saints, saints? Because they were cheerful when it was difficult to be cheerful, patient when it was difficult to be patient, and because they pushed on when they wanted to stand still, and kept silent when they wanted to talk; and were agreeable when they wanted to be disagreeable. That was all. It was quite simple and always will be....   —*Anonymous*

Patience in calamity, mercy in greatness, fortitude in adversity; these are the self-attained perfections of great saints....   —*Hitopodesa*

A saint is a very simple man: when he walks, he walks; when he talks, he talks and that's all. He doesn't think while listening, daydream while walking, see while touching. That is very hard. That is why he is a saint....   —*Sujata*

Many of the insights of the saint stem from his experience as a sinner....   —*Eric Hoffer*

The saint hath no fear, because fear is the expectation either of some future calamity or the eventual loss of some object of desire, whereas the saint is the son of his time: he has no future that he should fear anything....   —*Junayd*

One cannot expect to become a saint without paying the price, and the price is much renunciation, much temptation, much struggle and persecution, and all sorts of sacrifice....   —*Mother Teresa*

The holiest men are not always those who commit the fewest faults, but those who have the most courage, most love, and the most free spirit; those who make the heartiest effort for conquering self....   —*Jean N. Grou*

The whole life of a saint should be one great continual prayer....   —*Origen*

The work of great Masters or Saints is to take people up and out of this world....The Saints come to take people to their eternal home....
—*Julian P. Johnson*

Every prophet and every saint hath a way, but it leads to God: all the ways are really one....
—*Rumi*

The first characteristic of a Saint is that he is calm and tranquil, and bears like a diamond the buffets of misfortune....
—*Tukaram*

Sainthood is not just the negation of human life. Saints have been kings, artisans, preachers, doctors, priests, painters, poets....
—*Jacques Maritain*

The saints of God are known by three signs: their thought is of God, their dwelling is with God, and their business is in God....
—*Attar*

The saints are the sinners who keep on trying....
—*Robert L. Stevenson*

The glory alike of the saint, the sage, and the savior is this—that he has realized the most profound lowliness, the most sublime unselfishness....He gives, yet never thinks of receiving; he works without regretting the past or anticipating the future, and never looks for a reward....
—*James Allen*

Great sages and saints have set certain rules for us to follow. If we followed those rules we shall know what is right and what is wrong so that we may avoid certain things....
—*Papa Ramdas*

The greatest saints avoided the company of men as much as possible, and chose to live with God in secret....
—*Thomas à Kempis*

Search/
Look Within

Nothing gives rest but the sincere search for truth....
—*Blaise Pascal*

When you go in search of honey you must expect to be stung by bees....
—*Kenneth Kauda*

There is no search or goal possible, we are spiritually free and united in oneness with the absolute....The search is the ego's looking for itself, an illusory game of hide and seek....
—*A Spiritual Warrior*

Life refuses to yield up or to display its sublimest secret to the slothful. If you wish to discover the depth of its meaning, why then, you must break up the fallow ground and prepare to search for it, and the place to seek it is within....
—*Pierre Schmidt*

It is foolish to seek for God outside of oneself. This will result either in idolatry or skepticism....
—*Toyohiko Kagawa*

Be a lamp unto your own feet; do not seek outside yourself....
—*Gautama Buddha*

The search for God is always futile because God can never be found, ever, simply because God has never been lost....
—*Anonymous*

When ye leave off seeking you will experience that there was never anything to seek for. You were only seeking to lose something, when you went forth so vigorously in search....
—*Sunyata*

People are looking for something and cannot seem to find it. They say they want more but cannot describe what that more is. This essentially is a spiritual quest.... —*James W. Jones*

You search for God, and seek to find Him here. Or you seek to find Him there. Why need you look in the corners of the room when He entirely fills the room.... —*Ormond McGill*

If you can find the God inside yourself, you can find the God inside everybody.... —*Stephen Levine*

There is only one temple, and that is the temple of yourself. And to find God you have to know this temple of yourself. There is no other temple. No one can save you.... —*Yoga Swami*

If we pursue spiritual illumination, it will fade away. If we separate ourselves from God as the doer, we become the searcher, always haunted and always trying to find the ultimate Reality. We neither seek it nor look for it, for all we want is here, now.... —*Paul Twitchell*

We have all to return to the source. Every human being is seeking its source and must one day come to it. We must come from the Within; we have gone outward; now we must return inward.... —*Ramana Maharshi*

Science cannot solve the ultimate mystery of Nature. And it is because in the last analysis we ourselves are part of the mystery we are trying to solve.... —*Max Planck*

The great blessings of mankind are within us, and within our reach; but we shut our eyes and, like people in the dark, fall short of the very thing we search for without finding it.... —*Seneca*

Remember, you cannot abandon what you do not know. To go beyond yourself you must know yourself.... —*Nisargadatta*

A humble knowledge of thyself is a surer way to God than a deep search after learning.... —*Thomas à Kempis*

We must seek God in error and forgetfulness and foolishness.... —*Meister Eckhart*

Looking for God is like seeking a path in a field of snow; if there is no path and you are looking for one, walk across it and there is your path.... —*Thomas Merton*

You never know yourself till you know more than your body.... —*Thomas Traherne*

The most excellent and divine counsel, the best and most profitable advertisement of all others, but the least practiced, is to study and learn how to know ourselves. This is the foundation of wisdom and the highway to whatever is good.... —*Pierre Charron*

Look within for your answers. Your divine nature—your inner light—knows all the answers.... —*Peace Pilgrim*

Look within. Within you is the hidden God. Within you is the immortal Soul. Within you is the inexhaustible spiritual treasure. Within you is the ocean of bliss. Look within for the happiness which you have sought in vain.... —*Sivananda*

What we are looking for is what is looking.... —*Francis of Assisi*

Look within. Within is your fountain of good.... —*Marcus Aurelius*

If you want to understand others, look into your own heart....
—*Johann von Schiller*

If a man happens to find himself....he has a mansion which he can inhabit with dignity all the days of his life....
—*James Michener*

When one is a stranger to oneself then one is estranged from others too....
—*Anne Morrow Lindbergh*

Men do not know themselves, and therefore they do not understand the things of their inner world. Each man has the essence of God and all the wisdom and power of the world in himself....
—*Paracelsus*

People do not know and they do not want to know themselves....
—*Matthew Kelty*

What lies behind us and what lies before us are tiny matters compared to what lies within us....
—*Oliver W. Holmes*

The final mystery is oneself....When one has weighed the sun in the balance, and measured the steps of the moon and mapped out the seven heavens star by star, there still remains oneself....
—*Oscar Wilde*

Riches and power may vanish because they are outside ourselves. Only that which is within can we call our own....
—*Hazrat Inayat Khan*

Until we lose ourselves there is no hope of finding ourselves....
—*Henry Miller*

Look within: It can't be found by seeking, but only seekers will find it....
—*Bo Lozoff*

At the end of all religious paths there is the quest 'Who am I?' Until that question is satisfactorily answered no one can claim to know what the truth is or what God is. The ultimate instruction in all religions should therefore be 'Know thyself.'...
—*Lakshmana*

The seekers of the light are one....
—*Samuel Longfellow*

You have to leave the city of your comfort and go into the wilderness of your intuition. What you discover will be wonderful. What you discover will be yourself....
—*Alan Alda*

When a man's fight begins within himself, he is worth something....
—*Robert Browning*

How can you come to know yourself? Never by thinking; always by doing....
—*Johann W. Goethe*

He who knows others is wise. He who knows himself is enlightened....
—*Lao-tzu*

Withdraw into yourself and look. And if you do not find yourself beautiful as yet, do as the creator of a statue that is to be made beautiful; he cuts away here, he smoothes there, he makes this line lighter, this other purer, until he has shown a beautiful face upon the statue....
—*Plotinus*

Look at your own life. Has it become overly complex? Have you found yourself burdened by too many possessions or responsibilities? Take a deep breath and ask yourself: "What steps can I take to reduce the clutter so that I may live simply and joyously?"...
—*Douglas Bloch*

The important thing is not to stop questioning....
—*Albert Einstein*

The greatest virtue of man lies in his ability to correct his mistakes and continually to make a new man of himself....   —*Wang Yang Ming*

Cherish that which is within you, and shut off that which is without; for much knowledge (of outward things) is a curse....   —*Chuang Tse*

All life is from within out. This is something that cannot be reiterated too often. The springs of life are all from within....   —*Ralph W. Trine*

He that knows himself knows how to strengthen his weakness, and the wise man conquers everything, even the stars in their courses....
—*Baltazar Gracian*

The most important things ever said to us are said by our inner selves....
—*Adelaide Bry*

In each of us there is a king. Speak to him and he will come forth....
—*Danish proverb*

You have everything. You are the whole world. Why? Because the kingdom of God is within you. Then why do you want to run about and beg?...
—*Yoga Swami*

To study ourselves is to forget ourselves....   —*Dogen-zenji*

Man should turn his gaze within in order to begin that most marvelous of all explorations, since happiness comes only from within....
—*Pierre Schmidt*

As we go deeper within ourself we are less inclined to notice outer happenings....   —*Paramananda*

The most difficult thing in life is to know yourself....   —*Thales*

Nothing will make us so charitable and tender to the faults of others, as by self-examination, thoroughly to know our own....   —*Francois Fenelon*

The sole concern of learning is to seek one's original heart....   —*Mencius*

Look within. Seek the Self. There will be an end of the world and its miseries....The enquiry "Who am I?" is the only method of putting an end to all misery and ushering in supreme Beatitude....   —*Ramana Maharshi*

Learn God, and thou shall know thyself....   —*Martin Tupper*

The simplest questions are the most profound. Where were you born? Where is your home? Where are you going? What are you doing?...
—*Richard Bach*

Most people are standing on a mountain of gold looking at a pile of silver in the distance....   —*Anonymous*

If you know him by whom you were made, you will know yourself....
—*Sextus, the Pythagorean*

The search must begin in our bosom: Who am I?...   —*Rufus Jones*

The world is ready to give up its secrets if we only know how to knock, how to give it the necessary blow....
—*Vivekananda*

No one who has not a complete knowledge of himself will ever have a true understanding of another....
—*Friedrich Von Novalis*

Deep within himself man seeks a meaning for his life, and tries to fulfill himself in accordance with that meaning....   —*Victor Frankl*

Don't waste time hunting for the pot of gold at the foot of the rainbow. Better see what a little digging will accomplish right where you stand. Your pot of gold is probably under your own feet....
—*Fred Van Amburgh*

When you meet someone not as good as you are, look within and examine your own self.... —*Confucius*

The precept, "Know yourself," was not solely intended to obviate the pride of mankind, but likewise that we might understand our own worth....
—*Cicero*

The final proof that we have really found God is that all the discordant elements in our life fall into place and we are at peace....
—*William A. Brown*

What you are trying to find out is what you already are.... —*Nisargadatta*

The path to the source of your and the world's being is not without. You have to go within yourself. 'Seek within and know thysel;f' these secret and sublime hints come to us wafted from the breath of Rishis (wise men) through the dust of ages.... —*Papa Ramdas*

Seek ye first the kingdom of God, and his righteousness, and all things will be added unto you.... —*Jesus*

The highest and most profitable learning is the knowledge of ourselves.... —*Thomas à Kempis*

Resolve to be thyself; and know that he who finds himself, loses his misery....
—*Matthew Arnold*

Look inward, and in a flash you will conquer the Apparent and the Void....
—*Seng-ts'an*

The height of all philosophy is to know thyself; and the end of this knowledge is to know God.... —*Francis Quarles*

Do not search in distant skies for God. In man's own heart is He found....
—*Shinto saying*

Whoever knows the All but fails to know himself lacks everything....
—*Gospel of Thomas*

Man lives with himself....and doesn't know himself. "Know thyself" means: devote time each day to studying yourself....ferreting out your weakness, working at self-improvement, purifying your immortal soul....
—*Israel S. Lipkin*

No man should ever grope outside of his best self to find God. He should always seek the God who is speaking to him in his best self....
—*Harry E. Fosdick*

God works in us from within outwards.... —*Jan Van Ruysbroeck*

Next to the knowledge of God nothing is so precious as the knowledge of Self.... —*Jean N. Grou*

In one's search for God, one cannot reach God until one has made a great effort, until one becomes obsessed with the thought of God alone and until one has given up all attachments and relationships.... —*Saradamma*

All our interior world is reality—and that perhaps more so than our apparent world.... —*Marc Chagall*

People try to find out about things which are outside of them before they try to find out "Who am I?"...
—*Ramana Maharshi*

Try to enter your inner treasure-house and you will see the treasure-house of heaven.... —*Isaac of Syria*

If a man knows himself, he shall know God.... —*Clement of Alexandria*

To the man who hesitated to embark on the spiritual quest for fear of effort and renunciation, the Master said: "How much effort and renunciation does it take to open one's eyes and see?"... —*Anthony de Mello*

Men who know themselves are no longer fools, they stand on the threshold of the Door of Wisdom.... —*Havelock Ellis*

From heaven descended the precept "Know Thyself."... —*Juvenal*

What is lost shall be found, though not always in the same place.... —*Janis J. Kinens*

Do not seek to follow in the footsteps of men of old; seek what they sought.... —*Basho*

Every man is engaged in searching for something lost. Life is the chance afforded him to recover the peace and the joy he has lost.... —*Sathya Sai Baba*

If you search in deep water only, you will find the pearl. If you keep to the shore, you will find broken shells only.... —*Sivananda*

"The pursuit of happiness" is responsible for a good part of the ills and miseries of the modern world.... —*Malcolm Muggeridge*

Many millions search for God and find Him in their hearts.... —*Sikh proverb*

In the search for truth there are certain questions that are not important. Of what material is the universe constructed? Is the universe eternal? Are there limits or not to the universe? What is the ideal form of organization for human society? If a man were to postpone his search and practice for Enlightenment until such questions were solved, he would die before he found the path.... —*Gautama Buddha*

Oh, my God, how does it happen....that Thou art so great and yet nobody finds Thee, that thou callest so loudly and nobody hears Thee, that Thou art so near and nobody feels Thee, that Thou givest Thyself to everybody and nobody knows Thy name.... —*Hans Denck*

If we know that God is forever right where we are, we shall not be reaching out in every direction for Him.... —*Ernest Holmes*

If you want to be found, stand where the seeker seeks.... —*Sidney Lanier*

If you know that fundamentally there is nothing to seek, you have settled your affairs.... —*Rinzai*

The way to God is but one step, the step out of yourself.... —*Abu Said of Mineh*

There is no creature in existence who is not looking for God but each one understands this in his own way.... —*Omraan M. Aivanhov*

Man is the reflection of God; but the reflection cannot exist without the object reflected; so man must know what God is, if he would know himself. This has been the search down the ages and this search must be made by every individual for himself; there is no one who can answer this question for another.... —*Paramananda*

Why are you looking for God up there? He is here, here!...   *—Niffari*

It is everyone's duty to search and search until he finds within himself some point of goodness....
—Rabbi Nachman

The search for happiness is the search for God, although very few people understand this great truth....
—Elinor MacDonald

For thirty years I went in search of God, and when at the end of that time I opened my eyes, I discovered that it was he who had been looking for me....
—Bayezid Bistami

I want to know how God created this world. I am not interested in this or that phenomenon. I want to know His thoughts, the rest are details....
—Albert Einstein

Oh friend, where are you going? Where have you come from, and what are you supposed to do? You belong to the supreme Truth, but you have forgotten your origin. Now is the time to get back on the main road...   *—Muktananda*

We have what we seek. It is there all the time, and if we give it time it will make itself known to us....
—Thomas Merton

All search is vain, until we begin to perceive that wisdom is within ourselves....then we may know the sun is rising, that the morning is breaking for us....   *—Vivekananda*

In truth, we seek God outside of ourselves until we make the great Discovery—which is that our heart is the sanctuary where the Lord of the universe dwells in all His glory....
—Papa Ramdas

No one can know God who has not first known himself. Go to the depths of the soul, the secret place....to the roots, to the heights, for all that God can do is focused there....   *—Meister Eckhart*

No man can know himself as he is, and all the fullness of his nature, without also knowing God....
—Theodore Munger

Who am I? Where have I come from? Where am I going?—are not questions with an answer but questions that open us up to new questions which lead us deeper into the unspeakable mystery of existence....   *—Henri Nouwen*

I know well what I am fleeing from but not what I am in search of....
—Michel Montaigne

The heavens are still; no sound. Where then shall God be found? Search not in distant skies; in man's own heart He lies....   *—Shao Yung*

We go here, there, to this place, to that one, always looking for the happiness that is there inside....   *—Satchidananda*

Secreted and hidden in the heart of the world and in the heart of man is the light which can illuminate all life, the future and the past. Shall we not search for it?...   *—Mabel Collins*

Ask and it shall be given unto you; seek and ye shall find; knock, and it shall be opened unto you....For every one that asks, receives; and he that seeks, finds; and to him that knocks it shall be opened....   *—Jesus*

We must not cease from exploration and the end of all our exploring will be to arrive where we began and to know the place for the first time....
—T. S. Eliot

Look well into yourself; there is a source of strength which will always spring up if you will always look there.... —*Marcus Aurelius*

Why does a man go out to look for God? It is your own heart beating, and you do not know, you were mistaking it for something outside.... —*Vivekananda*

We seek satisfaction in the baubles of the world, yet we discover no satisfaction at all, but only disappointment and despair. Finding no solace anywhere, we at last turn to Reality where alone true satisfaction may be found.... —*Henry T. Hamblin*

Where do you go in search of God? He is with you.... —*Kabir*

To the possession of the Self the way is inward.... —*Plotinus*

No matter how much we seek, we never find anything but ourselves.... —*Anatole France*

Lord....I went round the streets and squares of the city of this world seeking thee; and I found thee not, because in vain I sought without for him, who was within myself.... —*Augustine*

Self-Esteem

He who undervalues himself is justly undervalued by others.... —*William Hazlitt*

The lower our self-esteem, the more we're attracted to our opposite, and the higher our self-esteem, the more we are attracted to another like ourselves.... —*Marilyn vos Savant*

If you lose self-esteem, you are losing far more than you realize.... —*Elinor MacDonald*

A person is in hell who has lost his self-esteem.... —*Robert Schuller*

Confidence holds the world and nourishes all. How can a baby thrive if it has no confidence in its mother? How can a lover gain pleasure if he does not trust his beloved?... —*Tripura Rahasya*

Self-esteem stems from positive beliefs about yourself; it does not depend upon the approval of another person.... —*Anonymous*

Keeping the other fellow talking about himself and knowing that you are controlling the situation can do wonders to bolster your self-confidence.... —*L. F. Mules*

Self-confidence is a good thing to develop, after you are sure you have something to be confident about.... —*Fred Van Amburgh*

Skill and confidence are an unconquered army.... —*George Herbert*

In quietness and confidence shall be your strength.... —*Old Testament*

When you love who you are, there is no thing unconquerable, no thing unreachable.... —*Ramtha*

I have an everyday religion that works for me. Love yourself first and everything else falls into place.... —*Lucille Ball*

It is difficult to make a man miserable while he feels he is worthy of himself and claims kindred to the great God who made him.... —*Abraham Lincoln*

The person who has no respect for himself cannot be relied upon to be courteous toward others....
—*Charles E. Garman*

Esteem by others or self-esteem, which is better?...The more you depend on others for esteem, the less you are self-sufficient....
—*Lao-tzu*

Genuine self-love is the greatest protection against dependent relationships....
—*Robert Coleman*

He that respects himself is safe from others; he wears a coat of mail that none can pierce....
—*Henry W. Longfellow*

Unless we are in love with ourselves, we have no love to offer anyone else....
—*Walter Starcke*

If you don't like yourself, you can't be happy....
—*Dennis Wholey*

We are worthwhile simply because we are, irrespective of any work we may produce....
—*Margaret Stortz*

Don't say you like the way you are....You haven't seen anything yet....
—*Eric Butterworth*

The divinity that shapes your destinies is not a mighty person molding you as a potter molds his clay, but a Mighty Divine Power—within and all around you, and around and in all substance—which is yours to use as you will. If you do not realize this you cannot have any confidence in yourselves....
—*Baird Spalding*

That kind of life is most happy which affords us the most opportunities of gaining our own esteem....
—*Samuel Johnson*

Don't let the opinions of other people determine the image you have of yourself. There is no need to feel either appreciated or understood. Be even-minded. What you think about yourself is everything. What others think about you has no value at all, unless you choose to give it value....
—*Shantidasa*

It is a psychological fact that man always conforms to the image he holds of himself. Change his image and you change his actions, his reactions, his environment, his world....
—*Jack Holland*

The biggest secret of self-esteem is this: Begin to appreciate other people more, show respect for any human being merely because he is a child of God and therefore a "thing of value."...
—*Maxwell Maltz*

Lack of confidence is not the result of difficulty; the difficulty comes from lack of confidence....
—*Seneca*

Self-esteem is the result of the relationship that you have with yourself....the thoughts and attitudes you have of yourself....
—*Phil Laut*

Do not imagine that any one can have true faith in God who has not faith in himself....
—*Paramananda*

Without self-respect and self-esteem, surrender is weakness....
—*Sevakram*

Those with low self-esteem do not know what they want out of life. They have lived protected, restricted, perhaps indulged or abused lives....The person with a healthy self-view knows how to fend for himself....
—*Marsha Sinetar*

As soon as you trust yourself you will learn to live.... —*Friedrich von Schiller*

You must see God inside of you before you recognize it in another human being.... —*Ma Jaya Sati Bhagavati*

Self-respect is the noblest garment with which a man may clothe himself, the most satisfying elevating feelings with which the mind can be inspired.... —*Samuel Smiles*

Above all things, revere yourself.... —*Pythagoras*

Believe in yourself; feel that you are able to dominate your surroundings. Resolve that you will be master and not the slave of circumstances.... —*Orison S. Marden*

If I am not for myself, who will be for me?... —*Hillel*

Self-esteem cannot be sought as an end in itself but must come as a by-product of meeting standards of excellence—taking pride in work....learning about life and imparting that wisdom.... —*Aaron Wildavsky*

Your self-confidence will improve when you realize who you are. You are God's child, and capable of acting that way.... —*Peace Pilgrim*

The biggest obstacle to happiness is lack of self-esteem. People who lack an internal sense of self-value, self-respect and self-worth become very ego-centric.... —*Robert Schuller*

The triumph of personal achievement is found in feeling good about yourself.... —*Wess Roberts*

A man cannot be comfortable without his own approval.... —*Mark Twain*

There is overwhelming evidence that the higher the level of self-esteem, the more likely one will treat others with respect, kindness, and generosity.... —*Nathaniel Branden*

How can we send the highest love to others if we do not have it for ourselves?... —*Prentice Mulford*

Everyone stamps his own value on himself. The price we charge for ourselves is given us. Man is made great or little by his own will.... —*Johann von Schiller*

Whenever an inferiority complex exists, there is a good reason for it. There is always something inferior there.... —*Carl Jung*

No man who is occupied in doing a difficult thing, and doing it very well, ever loses his self-respect.... —*George B. Shaw*

Nobody holds a good opinion of a man who has a low opinion of himself.... —*Anthony Trollope*

For a man to achieve all that is demanded of him he must regard himself as greater than he is.... —*Johann W. Goethe*

A man can stand a lot as long as he can stand himself.... —*Axel Munthe*

Putting someone else high upon a pedestal is just another way of putting yourself down.... —*Anonymous*

The man who makes everything that leads to happiness depend upon himself, and not upon other men, has adopted the very best plan for living happily.... —*Plato*

Selfishness

It is the ignorant man who seeks his own ends at the expense of the greater whole. It is the ignorant man, therefore, who is the selfish man. The truly wise man is never selfish....
—Ralph W. Trine

Selfish people are, by definition, those whose activities are devoted to bringing themselves happiness. Yet....these selfish people are far less likely to be happy than those whose efforts are devoted to making others happy....
—Bernard Rimland

As a man goes down in self, he goes up in God.... —George B. Cheever

Selfish persons are incapable of loving others, but they are not capable of loving themselves either.... —Erich Fromm

The hardest victory is the victory over self.... —Aristotle

If you always seek your own advantage, what is the use of remaining among men? A selfish man frustrates every chance to make all beings rejoice....
—Tibetan saying

Self-love and love of the world would constitute hell.... —Emanuel Swedenborg

Look in the mirror every day, for if scars of selfishness or pride are in the heart, they will grow into lines on the face. Watch closely....
—Etu Inagaki Sugimoto

Every act of selfishness or thought of selfishness makes us attached to something, and immediately we are made slaves.... —Vivekananda

If you live only for yourself you are always in immediate danger of being bored to death with the repetition of your own views and interests....
—Walter B. Wolfe

A selfish man is always miserable. He has neither peace nor happiness....
—Sivananda

Any idea that is built on selfishness will disturb your mind.... —Satchidananda

I perceived the entirely self-centered life as not worth living. If what you are doing will not benefit others besides yourself, it is not worth doing....
—Peace Pilgrim

Selfishness is the great enemy of peace. Selfishness walks by itself and no one walks with it.... —Blackfeather

The strongest barrier to faith is selfishness.... —Joseph Baron

No man is more cheated than the selfish man.... —Henry W. Beecher

It is almost impossible to reason with someone who is basically selfish....
—Akbarali H. Jetha

Selfishness keeps man blind through life....Life is a misery for the man who is absorbed in himself....
—Hazrat Inayat Khan

Self-love cannot endure to see itself; it would die of shame and vexation! If by chance it gets a glimpse, it at once places itself in some artificial light, as to soften the full hideousness and find some comfort.... —Francois Fenelon

The reason why lovers and their mistresses never tire of being together is that they are always talking of themselves....
—Francois La Rochefoucauld

When a man's soul is clouded with selfishness in any or every form, he loses the power of spiritual discrimination, and confuses the temporal with the eternal, the perishable with the permanent, mortality with immortality, and error with Truth....
—*James Allen*

The force of selfishness is as inevitable and as calculable as the force of gravitation....   —*George S. Hillard*

The trouble is that we are self-centered, and no effort of the self can remove the self from the center of its own endeavor....   —*William Temple*

The disease we all have and that we have to fight against all our lives is, of course, the disease of self....
—*Sherwood Anderson*

No one, I am convinced, can be happy who lives only for himself....
—*James M. Brown*

The more self is indulged the more it demands and, therefore, of all the men the selfish are the most discontented....
—*Benjamin Franklin*

We are more troublesome to ourselves than anyone else is to us....
—*Francis de Sales*

Self-interest is but the survival of the animal in us. Humanity only begins for man with self-surrender....
—*Henri F. Amiel*

We feel and weigh soon enough what we suffer from others; but how much others suffer from us, of this we take no heed....   —*Thomas à Kempis*

The root of all discontent is self-love....
—*James F. Clarke*

The great enemy of the soul is not trial but sadness, which is the bleeding wound of self-love....
—*William Ullathorne*

Selfishness is the only real atheism....
—*Israel Zangwill*

The man who works for self, or thinks that his business is being run for his personal benefit, or who expects other people to help him, can never become a success. His very attitude toward life keeps away all possibilities of such a thing; it dams up the channel through which good and abundance can flow....
—*Henry T. Hamblin*

Selfishness is a negative virtue; it exists to glorify selflessness....   —*Sivananda*

Virtue and wisdom are sublime things; but if they create pride and a consciousness of separateness from the rest of humanity in the mind of man, then they are only the snakes of self(ishness) reappearing in a finer form....A man who becomes selfish isolates himself, grows less interesting and less agreeable to others....   —*Mabel Collins*

Poverty wants some things, luxury many, avarice all things....
—*Abraham Cowley*

The best way of saving oneself a lot of trouble in life is to pay very little heed to one's interests...   —*Joseph Joubert*

The smaller the man and the woman, the more dwarfed and dwindling their natures, the more they pride themselves upon their "exclusiveness." Anyone can be exclusive. It comes easy. It takes and it signifies a large nature to be universal, to be inclusive....
—*Ralph W. Trine*

Inferiors revolt in order that they may be equal, and equals that they may be superior. Such is the state of mind which creates revolutions....
—*Aristotle*

Selfishness is not living as one wishes to live, it is asking others to live as one wishes to live.... —*Oscar Wilde*

The covetous man cannot so properly be said to possess wealth, as that may be said to possess him....
—*Francis Bacon*

Selfish striving is at the root of all the world's suffering.... —*James Allen*

Master pride and dame vanity have mingled and given birth to an ogre named "selfishness."... —*Shantidasa*

Greed is the chief officer of passion. Wherever there is greed, there is passion; and where there is passion, there is greed almost invariably. The understanding gets clouded, the intellect gets perverted, and the memory gets confused by passion and greed.... —*Sivananda*

Avarice increases with the increasing pile of gold.... —*Juvenal*

The covetous man lives as if the world were made altogether for him, and not he for the world; to take in everything and part with nothing....
—*Robert Smith*

The lust of avarice has so fully seized upon mankind that their wealth seems rather to possess them, than they possess their wealth.... —*Pliny*

To greed, all nature is insufficient. Avarice is so insatiable that it is not in the power of abundance to contest it....
—*Seneca*

Avarice in old age is foolish; for what can be more absurd than to increase our provisions for the road the nearer we approach our journey's end?...
—*Cicero*

The covetous man heaps up riches, not to enjoy but to have them; he starves himself in the midst of plenty....
—*John Tillotson*

The very heart and root of sin is an independent spirit. We erect the idol self and not only wish others to worship, but worship it ourselves....
—*Richard Cecil*

Covetousness, by greediness of getting more, deprives itself of the true end of getting; it loses the enjoyment of what it had got.... —*Thomas Sprat*

The selfish man suffers more from his selfishness than he from whom that selfishness withholds some important benefit.... —*Ralph W. Emerson*

The avaricious man is like a barren sandy ground of the desert which sucks in all the rain and dew with greediness, but yields no fruitful herbs or plants for the benefit of others.... —*Zeno*

The weaknesses of our age is our apparent inability to distinguish our needs from our greeds....
—*Don Robinson*

Little souls wish you to be unhappy. It aggravates them to have you joyous, efficient and free....It gives their egos wings if yours are clipped. You can ruin your life in an hour by listening to their puerile opinions.... —*David Seabury*

The very heart and root of sin is an independent spirit. We erect the idol self and not only wish others to worship, but worship it ourselves....
—*Richard Cecil*

God does not chastise us really, for we chastise ourselves. We cut ourselves off from the Universal Life and its abundance, by acting in a personal and selfish, acquisitive way, instead of a universal way....
—*Henry T. Hamblin*

Personality, separateness, selfishness are one and the same, and are the antithesis of wisdom and divinity. By the unqualified surrender of personality, separateness and selfishness cease, and man enters into the possession of his divine heritage....
—*James Allen*

Half the harm that is done in the world is due to people who want to feel important.... —*T. S. Eliot*

As long as man persists in wanting to be the hub and center of his own existence he will, in fact, continue to revolve round something exterior to himself, and forever be tossed hither and thither....
—*Omraam M. Aivanhov*

A man is called selfish, not for pursuing his own good, but for neglecting his neighbor's.... —*Richard Whatly*

The selfish man can stand up to his chin in water and still be thirsty....
—*Anonymous*

It is from selfishness that everything evil proceeds. Study all the vices, and you will see that selfishness is at the bottom of them all. Combat them as you will, you will never succeed in extirpating them until, attacking the evil in it root, you have destroyed the selfishness which is their cause. Let all your efforts tend to this end; for selfishness is the veritable social gangrene.... —*Allan Kardec*

Self-Realization

Man is self-realized when the Spirit realizes that man is One with God, and conducts himself in all his experiences in conformity with that self realization....God and man are one.... —*Frater Achad*

We know what we are, but know not what we may be....
—*William Shakespeare*

Self-realization is nothing but seeing God literally. Our greatest mistake is that we think of God as acting symbolically and allegorically, instead of practically and literally....You must get rid of the idea that you are yet to realize the Self. You are the Self here and now.... —*Ramana Maharshi*

The awareness of being the witness of everything is the secret of self-realization.... —*Sathya Sai Baba*

Realization is self-evident. It shines by its own light.... —*Papa Ramdas*

Realizations are personal, one cannot borrow or have the same realization as another person, nor can one take the same path....With realization, spirit abides in itself. Communion is within the whole, freedom is its essence. The absolute is, and I never was separate....
—*A Spiritual Warrior*

Self-realization means I am completely full, I don't want to know anything, I don't require anything at all now....
—*Nisargadatta*

There's only one corner of the universe you can be certain of improving: that's your own self.... —*Aldous Huxley*

Earth is the theatre on which we play the game of life. It is the stage where we struggle to attain the supreme beatitude of life. It is the field in which we prepare ourselves for Self-realization....   —*Papa Ramdas*

One cannot get a true feeling about God from the study of books....books, Scriptures and science appear as mere dirt and straw after the realization of God....   —*Ramakrishna*

Human life has been given to you for the sole purpose of realizing the Self. If you die without realizing the Self your life has been wasted. Death can come at any time....   —*Annamalai Swami*

Why speak of Self-realization in the future? It is here and now—only the veil that hides it has to be destroyed....
                   —*Anandamayi Ma*

What is worship? To realize reality....
                   —*Ansari*

It is only by forgetting yourself that you draw nearer to God....
                   —*Henry D. Thoreau*

The Higher Self is realized not by doing something, but by refraining from doing anything, by remaining still and being simply what one really is....
                   —*G. V. Subbaramayya*

If there is a thing easiest of all it is the attainment of self-realization; because one is not required to do anything for it. Is there anything easier than remaining without doing anything?...
                   —*Gopala Swamy*

Man's ultimate aim is the realization of God, and all of his activities—social, religious—have to be guided by the ultimate aim of the vision of God....
                   —*Mohandas Gandhi*

Self-realization is not a matter of withdrawal from a corrupt world or narcissistic contemplation of oneself. An individual becomes a person by enjoying the world and contributing to it....   —*Francine Klagsbrun*

No one can tell us in truth that we can never know ourselves. It simply isn't true. We can not but know ourselves....
                   —*Iris Belhayes*

At the point of realization there is no ego. That's when the shadow realizes it's a shadow....   —*Satchidananda*

Self-realization is real religion, all the rest is only preparation—hearing lectures, or reading books, or reasoning, is merely preparing the ground; it is not religion....   —*Vivekananda*

This above all: to thine own self be true....   —*William Shakespeare*

The Self is hidden in the deepest cave of the heart....   —*The Upanishads*

The realized man finds himself in others—they are not different from himself. With wise men he is wise, but with ignorant men he becomes ignorant, with children he will play and with the learned he will be scholarly....   —*Ramana Maharshi*

Those who attain Self-realization on earth live a twofold existence. Conscientiously performing their work in the world, they are yet immersed in an inward beatitude....   —*Yukteswar*

Self-realization means that we have been consciously connected with our Source of being. Once we have made this connection then nothing can go wrong....   —*Paramananda*

No action is more fascinating than the action of self-transformation. Nothing on earth can compare with its drama or its value.... —*Vernon Howard*

Before we can change others, we must first change ourselves. This is a case of where charity really does begin at home, and by beginning to cleanse ourselves of those fears and dreads, uncertainties, wishful thinking, might be's and maybe's, we come to a complete acceptance of spiritual realization.... —*Ronald Beesley*

The man or woman who realizes God has everything and lacks nothing. Having this, one desires nothing further; he cannot be shaken by the heaviest burden of sorrow. Life cannot threaten such a person; all it holds is the opportunity to love, to serve, and to give.... —*Eknath Easwaran*

What stands between a man and his Self-realization is metaphysical ignorance; and the ultimate goal....is the elimination of that ignorance.... —*Amaury de Reincourt*

When we have realized God in all His fullness and perfection, then we have no difficulties and no obstacles in life. We adjust our life according to the conditions and circumstances in which God places us. We have no reason to grumble, complain or feel unhappy at any time.... —*Papa Ramdas*

No one is ever away from his Self and therefore everyone is in fact Self-realized; only—and this is a great mystery—people do not know this and want to realize the Self. Realization consists only in getting rid of the false idea that one is not realized. It is not anything new to be acquired.... —*Ramana Maharshi*

Who stands already on heaven's topmost dome needs not to search for ladders.... —*Rumi*

For realization, effort is needed but grace is also required, and grace is more important.... —*Lakshmana*

Self-Reliance

Pray to God but continue to row the boat to shore.... —*Russian proverb*

No one can build his security upon the nobleness of another person.... —*Willa Cather*

Once you really know that nobody can take from you what is really yours, you stop trying to protect it.... —*Theodora Wells*

Don't believe anyone who promises to help you. No one will help you because no one can. Another may point the way, but you have to do the walking.... —*Yoga Swami*

You are your own physician. You are your own savior and redeemer. Nobody can give you freedom. You will have to tread the spiritual path yourself. Rely on your own self-exertion. Teachers and books can only help you to a certain extent... —*Sivananda*

He who is being carried does not realize how far the next town is.... —*African proverb*

It is easy to be independent when all behind you agree with you, but the difficulty comes when nine-hundred and ninety-nine of your friends think you wrong.... —*Wendell Phillips*

Do not seek from another, or you will be estranged from self....
　　　　　　　　　—Dongshan

Only those means of security are good, are certain, are lasting, that depend on yourself and your own vigor....
　　　　　　　—Niccolo Machiavelli

Never play another person's game. Play your own....　　　*—Andrew Salter*

The only person I control in the entire world is me....　　　*—Ralph Stayer*

Self-reliance as commonly understood is ego-reliance and it worsens bondage. Reliance on God alone is true self-reliance....　　　*—Ramana Maharshi*

The individual must be self-reliant and, in a sense, self-sufficient, or else he goes down....　　*—Luther Burbank*

Remember this point well. No one can save another. You will have to depend upon yourself alone....　　*—Sivananda*

Everyone can raise himself, but only by his own actions....　*—Nahman Bratzlav*

You must rely upon yourself. The influence of a saint may give you a push on the spiritual path, but you have to tread the path yourself....
　　　　　　　　—Ramcharandas

If another drinks, does it quench your thirst? If another eats, does it appease your hunger? If another sleeps, does it rest you? Who, then, shall develop your understanding?...　*—Gautama Buddha*

A man is best off if he is thrown upon his own resources, and can be all in all to himself, and Cicero goes so far as to say that a man who is in this condition cannot fail to be happy....
　　　　　　　—Arthur Schopenhauer

The man who is self-reliant, always says: "No one can realize my possibilities for me, but me; no one can make me good or evil but myself." He works out his own salvation, financially, socially, mentally, physically, and morally. Life is an individual problem that man must solve for himself....　　*—William G. Jordan*

Even in the common affairs of life, in love, friendship, and marriage, how little security have we when we trust our happiness in the hands of others....
　　　　　　　　—William Hazlitt

Mankind has a way of proclaiming self-reliance in a loud voice, but seldom is the dependency upon a higher force for every breath ever mentioned....　　　*—Anonymous*

My true being, the essence of my nature, myself, remains inviolate and inaccessible to the world's attacks....
　　　　　　　　—Henri F. Amiel

No person can save another....
　　　　　　　　—Joyce C. Oates

You can depend upon no man, upon no friend, but on him who depends upon himself. Only he who acts beneficially towards himself will act so towards others....　　　*—John K. Lavater*

Society everywhere is in conspiracy against the manhood of every one of its members....Self-reliance is an aversion....　　　*—Ralph W. Emerson*

They can conquer who believe they can....　　　　　　*—Virgil*

There is no virue greater than self-reliance. The possession of this important quality is a *sine qua non* for all aspirants who search after Truth....　　　　　*—Sivananda*

Believe your strength....Learn to repeat endlessly to yourself. "It all depends on me."...
—*André Gide*

The man who makes everything that leads to happiness depend upon himself, and not upon other men, has adopted the very best plan for living happily....
—*Plato*

Help thyself, and God will be there....
—*George Herbert*

Nature has not said to me, "Be not poor," still less, "Be rich." She calls out to me, "Be independent."...
—*Sebastien Chamfort*

In the last resort everyone is his own authority....
—*Lakshmana Sarma*

The strongest man in the world is he who stands most alone....
—*Henrik Ibsen*

Self-help is the capacity to stand on one's legs without anybody's help...
—*Mohandas Gandhi*

It is not the greatness of man's means that makes him independent, so much as the smallness of his wants....
—*William Cobbett*

God helps those who help themselves....
—*Benjamin Franklin*

Heaven never helps the man who will not act....
—*Sophocles*

Rely upon yourself, trust yourself, and others will trust you unquestioningly....For the self-helping man, all doors are flung open....
—*Fred Van Amburgh*

You must live within yourself and depend on yourself, always tucked up and ready for a start....
—*Henry D. Thoreau*

No bird soars too high, if he soars with his own wings....
—*William Blake*

Self-reverence, self-knowledge, self-control, these three alone lead to sovereign power....
—*Alfred L. Tennyson*

Every tub must stand on its own bottom....
—*Charles Macklin*

God gives food to every bird, but he does not throw it into the nest....
—*Hindu saying*

Why do you look at me? Look at your own self. Why do you listen to me? Listen to your own self....trust in your own inner voice....
—*Peace Pilgrim*

I have ever held it a maxim, never to do through another what it was possible for me to do myself....
—*Charles Montesquieu*

Self-reliance is only a part of the picture. When we carry it to the extreme, we cut ourselves off from others and from the nourishment we need from them....
—*Melvyn Kinder*

If you will only help yourself, God will help you....
—*Mathurin*

To blame society for one's own deficiency is like blaming the pillow for the headache one suffers....
—*Sathya Sai Baba*

There is no use whatsoever trying to help people who do not help themselves. You cannot push anyone up a ladder unless he is willing to climb himself....
—*Andrew Carnegie*

Self-reliance and self-respect are about as valuable commodities as we can carry in our pack through life....
—*Luther Burbank*

God only helps when men can help no more....　　*—Johann von Schiller*

Reliance on one's apparent self leads to ruin. To presume to be all knowing is extremely harmful. Self-reliance or self-confidence means faith in the higher self....　　*—Turiyananda*

The strength whereby God saves is the strength that is our own....
—Israel Zangwill

True self-reliance does not mean reliance on one's physical strength; it means reliance on something mightier, something which is less perishable....It means trusting in the spiritual....
—Paramananda

Self-confidence without self-reliance is as useless as a cooking recipe without food. Self-confidence sees the possibilities of the individual; self-reliance realizes them. Self-confidence sees the angel in the unhewn block of marble; self-reliance carves it out for himself....
—William G. Jordan

The old saying that "God help him who helps himself" is true in more senses than one. It is true in the sense that the Higher Aid seems to refuse to come to the assistance of one who is not willing to strike out for himself and do his best....　　*—William W. Atkinson*

Service

Service is the rent we pay for our place on earth....　　*—Anonymous*

Great opportunities to help others seldom come, but small ones surround us daily....　　*—Sally Koch*

When a blind man carries a lame man, both are able to go forward....
—Swedish proverb

Often we can help each other most by leaving each other alone; at other times we need the hand-grasp and the word of cheer....　　*—Elbert Hubbard*

To bring joy to one heart with love—is better than a thousand litanies....
—Sufi saying

We cannot actually help others; we can only love, share, encourage and set an example by which others can learn to help themselves....
—A Spiritual Warrior

He is the greatest man who is the servant of all....　　*—Sivananda*

If you make your mind pure, you automatically help everyone in the world because each person will receive a cleansing and healing measure of your own purity....　　*—Annamalai Swami*

Trying to help the world without knowing yourself will be just like a blind man trying to treat the diseases of the eyes of others. First, clear your own eyes....　　*—Ramana Maharshi*

If you hear that a sick man is in need of hot soup, I counsel you to wake up from your ecstasy and warm the soup for him. Leave God to serve God; find Him and serve Him in His members; you will lose nothing by the change....
—John Ruysbroeck

It is the individual who is not interested in his fellow man who has the greatest difficulties in life and provides the greatest injury to others. It is from among such individuals that all human failures spring....
—Alfred Adler

Life is best spent in alleviating pain, assuaging distress, and promoting peace and joy. The service of man is more valuable than what you call "service to God." God has no need of your service. Please man, you please God.... —*Sathya Sai Baba*

Small service is true service....The daisy, by the shadow that it casts, protects the lingering dewdrop from the sun.... —*William Wordsworth*

It is true that if we look after others, God will look after us—and do a lot better job of it than we can....
—*Arthur E. Yensen*

Desire to sow no seed for your own harvesting; desire only to sow that seed, the fruit of which shall feed the world. You are a part of the world; in giving it food you feed yourself....
—*Mabel Collins*

One of the things I keep learning is that the secret of being happy is doing things for other people....
—*Dick Gregory*

It is plain that we exist for our fellow men.... —*Albert Einstein*

The way you begin to change the world is through service.... —*Martin L. King, Jr.*

The highest service is, after getting for yourself the knowledge of the Divine, to share with others that knowledge and rouse in their hearts devotion for and faith in God.... —*Papa Ramdas*

The leader is a servant....
—*Max De Pree*

At the heart of silence is prayer. At the heart of prayer is faith. At the heart of faith is life. At the heart of life is service.... —*Mother Teresa*

Good works are valuable only as a means of becoming free. They do good to the doer, never to any other....
—*Vivekananda*

The leader is chief servant of the tribe.... —*Mohammed*

He who has seen, known and realized most fully the truth of the identity of all selves in the one Self, he is the greatest and most free and willing servant.... —*Bhagavan Das*

There is nothing small in the service of God.... —*Francis de Sales*

The motive, if you are to find inner peace, must be an outgoing motive. Service, of course, service. Giving, not getting. Your motive must be good if your work is to have good effect. The secret of life is being of service....
—*Peace Pilgrim*

Joy can be real only if people look upon their life as a service, and have a definite object in life outside themselves and their personal happiness....
—*Leo Tolstoy*

Certain is it that the memories which afford us the greatest satisfaction are those of when we served others rather than when others served us....
—*R. MacDonald Ladell*

Service of God consists in what we do to our neighbor.... —*Leo Baeck*

Service rendered as a gift or love-offering to Life: work that is engaged in, not for self or for profit, but as an act of love and service, these bring the doer a harvest of blessings....When we serve and when we give, we open ourselves to receive life's richest blessings, its greatest prizes, and its most enduring success....
—*Henry T. Hamblin*

Proclaim yourself solemnly and joyfully, "Servant of God."...
—*Samuel Hirsch*

You can't live a perfect day without doing something for someone who will never be able to repay you....
—*John Wooden*

The more you care about others, the more confidently you act. There is nothing you cannot do, no defeat you cannot survive, no fear you cannot overcome, when you are concentrated heart and soul in helping others....
—*Robert O'Brien*

God has so constituted our nature that we cannot be happy unless we are, or think we are, the means of good to others.... —*Erskine Mason*

The greatest service we can do for another is to help him help himself. To help him directly might be weakening, though not necessarily. It depends entirely upon circumstances. But to help one to help himself is never weakening, but always encouraging and strengthening, because it leads him to a larger and stronger life....
—*Ralph W. Trine*

The great happiness in life is not to donate but to serve....
—*Louis Brandeis*

Doing nothing for others is the undoing of ourselves....
—*Horace Mann*

All other pleasures and possessions pale into nothingness before service which is rendered in a spirit of joy....
—*Mohandas Gandhi*

If you would find greater joy in life, attempt to serve and please someone every day.... —*John H. Crowe*

Get outside yourself. Stress causes people to turn into themselves and focus on their own problems. Try something for someone else. Or find something other than yourself and your accomplishments to care about....
—*Donald Tubesing*

No one has ever risen to the real stature of spiritual maturity until they have found it finer to serve someone else than to serve themselves....
—*Anonymous*

Through our willingness to help others we can learn to be happy rather than depressed.... —*Gerald Jampolsky*

The best way for one to serve the world is to win the egoless state. If you are anxious to help the world but think you cannot do so by attaining the egoless state, then surrender to God all the world's problems along with your own.... —*Ramana Maharshi*

Who hath not served cannot command.... —*John Florio*

What do we live for if not to make the world less difficult for each other....
—*George Eliot*

The superior man....is eyes for the blind, strength for the weak, and a shield for the defenseless. He stands erect by bending above the fallen. He rises by lifting others....
—*Robert Ingersoll*

No one is useless in this world who lightens the burdens of it for another....
—*Charles Dickens*

Love lies in service. Only that which is done not for fame or name, nor for appreciation or thanks of those for whom it is done, is life's service....
—*Hazrat Inayat Khan*

He who wishes to secure the good of others has already secured his own....
—*Confucius*

For though I be free from all men, I have made myself servant unto all, that I might gain the more....
—*Paul of Tarsus*

There is no lonely pilgrim on the way to light. Men only gain the heights by helping others gain the heights....
—*The Aquarian Gospel*

Little kindnesses....will broaden your heart and slowly you will habituate yourself to helping your fellow man in many ways.... —*Zadik*

It is not what we see and touch or that which others do for us which makes us happy; it is that which we think and feel and do, first for the other fellow and then for ourselves....
—*Helen Keller*

SERVICE. A beautiful word fallen upon bad days.... —*Claude McKay*

This only is true service—to forget oneself in love towards all, to lose oneself in working for the whole....
—*James Allen*

To be a servant of God is man's greatest boast.... —*Philo*

The way that lies at the foundation of positive change, the way I see it, is service to a fellow human being....
—*Lech Walesa*

The test of real service of God is that it leaves behind it the feeling of humility.... —*Israel Baal Shem Tov*

Service is like a burning candle: it lights the path for others while consuming itself.... —*Anonymous*

To live is not to live for one's self alone; let us help one another.....
—*Menander of Athens*

He only does not live in vain who employs his wealth, his thought, his speech to advance the good of others....
—*Hindu proverb*

Do all the good you can, by all the means you can, in all the ways you can, in all the places you can, all the times you can, to all the people you can, as long as you can.... —*John Wesley*

All service of God must be performed with gladness and zest, otherwise it is not perfect.... —*The Zohar*

The most acceptable service of God is doing good to man....
—*Benjamin Franklin*

Service to a just cause rewards the worker with more real happiness and satisfaction than any other venture of life.... —*Carrie C. Catt*

The worst days of darkness through which I have passed have been greatly alleviated by throwing myself with all my energy into some work relating to others.... —*James A. Garfield*

He that is greatest among you shall be your servant.... —*Jesus*

If your loyalty is to your family, you are a servant of the family; if it is to God, you are a servant of God....
—*Sathya Sai Baba*

Men resemble the gods in nothing so much as in doing good to their fellow creatures.... —*Cicero*

He who does not know about service knows even less about Mastership....
—*Tirmizi*

The value of all service lies in the spirit in which you serve and not in the importance or magnitude of the service. Even the lowliest task or deed is made holy, joyous, and prosperous when it is filled with love....
—*Charles Fillmore*

We may serve God by digging with the hands or by talking friendly with our neighbor....   —*Robert Benson*

Give service priority in your life over all the other superficial things that customarily clutter human life....
—*Peace Pilgrim*

Let service be the motto of your life—service not for the petty self, not for name or fame, not for your own low satisfactions, but service for the spontaneous joy which it yields you....
—*Papa Ramdas*

I am the servant of servants....
—*Krishna*

I slept and dreamt that life was joy. I awoke and saw that life was service. I acted and behold, service was joy....
—*Rabindranath Tagore*

There is nothing you cannot do, no defeat you cannot survive, no fear you cannot overcome, when you are concentrated heart and soul in helping others....   —*Robert O'Brien*

I can't help thousands. I can help only the one who stands before me....
—*Mother Teresa*

We need to be needed. Service to others can give us a new purpose in life....
—*Abbe Pierre*

No one has learned the meaning of living until he has surrendered his ego to the service of his fellow man....
—*Walter B. Wolfe*

It is one of the most beautiful compensations of this life that no man can sincerely try to help another without helping himself....Serve and thou shall be served. If you love and serve men, you cannot, by any hiding or stratagem, escape the remuneration....   —*Ralph W. Emerson*

Service does not mean making other people lazy, nor does it require us to assume individual responsibility for other people's lives: neither does service require us to interfere....Service needs wisdom more than any other talent, and it is this question of wisdom that each individual must decide for himself....   —*Ronald Beesley*

Always try to serve others. Don't even call it helping, call it service because you are benefitted by that. If a man begs from you and you give him something, you shouldn't think you are helping him. Instead, he is helping you....   —*Satchidananda*

One of the great underlying principles governing our life is service. Most of us have to work, but do we serve? Do we work in a spirit of service? Do we work for Life and our fellows? Or do we merely work for self, in order to make a living?...   —*Henry T. Hamblin*

Perhaps the greatest service any man performs is not in the importance of his work, but in the release of his inner powers. He makes a greater gift to his fellow men in becoming a freed spirit than by a score of scientific discoveries or hundreds of works of art....
—*David Seabury*

The purpose of life is to increase the warm heart. Think of other people. Serve other people sincerely. No cheating....   —*Dalai Lama*

Down in their hearts, the wise men know this truth: the only way to help yourself is to help others....
—*Anonymous*

Men exist for mutual service....
—*Marcus Aurelius*

Service without humility is selfishness and egotism....   —*Mohandas Gandhi*

They serve God well, who serve his creations....   —*Caroline Norton*

Silence

W hat is it that stands higher than words? Action. What is it that stands higher than action? Silence....
—*Francis of Assisi*

Blessed is the man who, having nothing to say, abstains from giving us worldly evidence of the fact....
—*George Eliot*

There is silence when you realize that there is nothing to gain and nothing to lose....   —*Yoga Swami*

The still mind of the sage is a mirror of heaven and earth—the glass of all things....   —*Chuang Tse*

What a strange power there is in silence....   —*Ralph W. Emerson*

Nothing is so good for any ignorant man as silence; and if he was sensible of this he would not be ignorant....
—*Saadi*

When the oak is felled the whole forest echoes with its fall, but a hundred acorns are sown in silence by an unnoticed breeze....   —*Thomas Carlyle*

True silence really means going deep within yourself to that place where nothing is happening, where you transcend time and space. You go into a brand new dimension of nothingness. That's where all the power is. That's your real home. That's where you really belong, in deep Silence where there is no good or bad, no one trying to achieve anything. Just being, pure being....Silence is the ultimate reality....   —*Robert Adams*

If the mind can get quiet enough, something sacred will be revealed....
—*Helen Tworkov*

Silence gives us a new way of looking at something....   —*Mother Teresa*

As long as someone cries out "Oh God! Oh God!" be sure that he has not found God, for whoever has found him becomes still....   —*Ramakrishna*

Silence is one of the hardest arguments to refute....   —*Josh Billings*

The absence of language simply makes the presence of silence more apparent....   —*Max Picard*

Silence is often the highest form of praise. To praise a flawless pearl is to deprecate it....   —*Judah of Kfar*

Be silent that the Lord who gave thee language may speak....
—*Divani Shamsi Tabriz*

There is silence, the child of love, which expresses everything, and proclaims more loudly than the tongue is able to do....   —*Vittorio Alfieri*

The truest communication with God is absolute, total silence; there is not a single word in existence that can convey this communication....
—*Bernadette Roberts*

To be in mental quiet is to observe the mind's own nature....   —*Lao-tzu*

Silence has a wonderful creative power. Make a study of the lives of great men. They conceive an idea but they do not go out and shout it to the world; they think silently and work quietly until they realize their ideal....
    —*Paramananda*

God will not enter into your heart until it is empty and still....   —*Paul Brunton*

He (the American Indian) believes profoundly in silence—the sign of a perfect equilibrium. Silence is the absolute poise or balance of the body, mind and spirit....   —*Ohiyesa*

A fool cannot be silent....
    —*Greek proverb*

Silence is the element in which great things fashion themselves together....
    —*Thomas Carlyle*

Silence is as full of potential wisdom and wit as the unhewn marble of great sculpture....   —*Aldous Huxley*

Do not even listen, simply wait. Do not even wait, be quiet, still and solitary. The world will freely offer itself to you to be unmasked, it has no choice, it will roll in ecstasy at your feet....
    —*Franz Kafka*

Be silent and safe—silence never betrays you....   —*John B. O'Reilly*

Silence is the language God speaks, and everything else is a bad translation....
    —*Thomas Keating*

A periodical decree of silence is not a torture but a blessing....
    —*Mohandas Gandhi*

Any trial whatever that comes to you can be conquered by silence....
    —*Abbot Pastor*

Avoid action, and keep the silence; all the rest is commentary....   —*Lich-tse*

Be content to feed on ecstasy, for stillness is the perfect likeness of divinity....
    —*Marpa*

It is easier to be altogether silent than not to exceed in words....
    —*Thomas à Kempis*

It is as important to cultivate your silence—power as it is your word—power....   —*William James*

Go placidly amid the noise and the haste, and remember what peace there may be in silence....   —*Max Ehrmann*

Silence is the cornerstone of character....   —*American Indian saying*

I like the silent church, before the service begins, better than preaching....
    —*Ralph W. Emerson*

The most silent people are generally those who think most highly of themselves....   —*William Hazlitt*

We all have within us a center of stillness surrounded by silence....
    —*Dag Hammarskjöld*

We need to find God, but we cannot find Him in noise, in excitement. See how nature, the trees, the flowers, the grass grow in deep silence. See how the stars, the moon, and the sun move in silence....   —*Mother Teresa*

True silence is the rest of the mind, and is to the spirit what sleep is to the body, nourishment and refreshment....
    —*William Penn*

Listen in the silence....Listen and you shall hear God speak....The chamber of silence is man's divine self. It is there that man meets man's God....
—Frater Achad

There is no explanation quite so effective as silence....   —Alfred A. Montapert

Silence fertilizes the deep place where personality grows. A life with a peaceful center can weather all storms....
—Norman V. Peale

Nothing in all creation is so like God as stillness....   —Meister Eckhart

The necessity of inward stillness has appeared clearly to my mind. In true silence strength is renewed, the mind is weaned from all things save as they may be enjoyed in the divine Will....
—John Woolman

He can never speak well who knows not how to hold his peace....   —Plutarch

We need a reason to speak, but none to keep silent....   —Pierre Nicole

Verily, he who speaks noble truths, and gives utterance to the Word of God, observes the vow of silence. Silence is restraint of speech....
—Srimad Bhagavatam

Silence is becoming to the wise and even more so to the fool....
—The Talmud

Silence is the language of the Real....
—Sunyata

It is better to be silent, or to say things of more value than silence....
—Pythagoras

Silence is a true friend who never betrays....   —Confucius

The world would be happier if men had the same capacity to be silent that they have to speak....
—Baruch Spinoza

There are silent depths in the ocean which storms that lash the surface into fury never reach....   —Orison S. Marden

Silence and meditation are the rungs on which one climbs to the Higher Worlds....   —Harry Sackler

The only language able to express the wholeness of truth is silence. Silence is our eternal speech. Silence is ever speaking. It is a perennial flow of language which is interrupted by speaking....   —Ramana Maharishi

Everything that does us good is so apt to do us harm too, that it is a strong argument for men to be quiet....
—Lord Halifax

Silence of the sewn-up lips is no silence. One may achieve the same result by chopping off one's tongue, but that too would not be silence. He is silent who, having the capacity to speak, utters no idle word....
—Mohandas Gandhi

The spiritual teachers of humanity, who have attained the peak of inner development, are said to be in eternal Silence, using their mental powers only when necessary to communicate with earthly men....   —Mouni Sadhu

Life teaches us silently while men utter their instruction in loud voices....
—Paul Brunton

An inability to stay quiet, an irritable desire to act directly, is one of the most conspicuous failings of mankind....
—Walter Bagehot

Silence is more eloquent than words....
—*Thomas Carlyle*

Let silence be your general rule; or say only what is necessary and in few words....
—*Epictetus*

We can do more work in the silence than we can by moving the lips and letting the mouth make a continuous noise. That interferes with our own thinking as well as with other people's. There is a stillness in a thinker's mind; there is a quietness in a thinker's presence, where even words are entirely unnecessary....
—*Ronald Beesley*

Silence is wisdom's best reply....
—*Euripides*

Rumors and slander are answered best with silence....
—*Ben Jonson*

There is one thing we can always do, no matter what things appear before us. We can mentally stand still, very undemanding, and determine to let the infinite nature of God unfold itself in our lives....
—*Margaret Stortz*

Silence is the language of God: it is also the language of the heart....
—*Sivananda*

A happy life must be to a great extent a quiet life, for it is only in an atmosphere of quiet that true joy can live....
—*Bertrand Russell*

The highest thoughts are those least dependent on language....
—*John Ruskin*

The first virtue is to restrain the tongue. He approaches nearest the gods who knows how to be silent, even though he is in the right....
—*Cato*

Power rests in tranquility....
—*Richard Cecil*

The ancient sentence said, "Let us be silent for so are the gods." Silence is a solvent that destroys personality, and gives us leave to be great and universal....
—*Ralph W. Emerson*

Silence is a healing for all ailments....
—*Babylonian Talmud*

Concentrated power is silence. Diffused power is noise....When you reach the place of silence in mind, you have reached the place of power, the place where all is one....
—*Baird Spalding*

The most important thing is silence....We cannot place ourselves directly in God's presence without imposing upon ourselves interior and exterior silence....
—*Mother Teresa*

Silence is the essential condition of happiness....
—*Heinrich Heine*

Speech is silver, silence is golden; speech is human, silence is divine....
—*German proverb*

As there are silent depths in the ocean which the fiercest storm cannot reach, so there are silent, holy depths of the heart of man which the storm of sin and sorrow can never disturb. To reach this silence and to live consciously in it is peace....
—*James Allen*

God is a word, an unspoken word....
—*Meister Eckhart*

Prayer begins by talking to God, but it ends by listening to Him. In the face of Absolute Truth, silence is the soul's language....
—*Fulton J. Sheen*

Silence has a regenerative power of its own. It is always sacred. It always returns you home....
—*Barbara De Angelis*

Silence is man's chief learning....
—*Palladas*

The more you talk about It, the more you think about It, the further from It you go. Stop talking, stop thinking, and there is nothing you will not understand.... —*Seng–Ts'an*

If you have difficulty finding your place in the life pattern try seeking in receptive silence....Still your mind and listen to the urging of the higher will....
—*Peace Pilgrim*

Simplicity

The ability to simplify means to eliminate the unnecessary so that the necessary may speak....
—*Hans Hofmann*

The price we pay for the complexity of life is too high.... —*Jean Baudrillard*

Our purpose in life is to realize the Self. It is an easy matter to get a little food and find somewhere congenial to live and meditate. Once we have achieved this we should have no further interest in the world and its problems....
—*Annamalai Swami*

Purity and simplicity are the two wings with which man soars above the earth and all temporary nature....
—*Thomas à Kempis*

How much there is in the world I do not want.... —*Socrates*

It does not matter whether one paints a picture, writes a poem, or carves a statue—simplicity is the mark of a master-hand.... —*Elsie De Wolfe*

We have very little, so we have nothing to be preoccupied with. The more you have, the more you are occupied, the less you give. But the less you have, the more free you are.... —*Mother Teresa*

Life itself can be very simple, it is we who insist on making life complicated.... —*Anonymous*

How soon will you realize that the only thing you don't have is the direct experience that there's nothing you need that you don't have.... —*Ken Keyes, Jr.*

Nothing is better than simplicity....
—*Walt Whitman*

The greatness of simplicity comes in no small way, from an appreciation of truth and beauty....
—*Fred Van Amburgh*

The average man is apt to attempt more than he can accomplish, to seek to acquire more than he needs and to exhaust himself in senseless competition.... —*Alice H. Rice*

A simple life is its own reward....
—*George Santayana*

There is nothing to chase after. We can go back to ourselves, enjoy our breathing, our smiling, ourselves, and our beautiful environment....
—*Thich Nhat Hanh*

People don't want simplicity, they want something complicated....
—*Lakshmana*

The simplification of life is one of the steps to inner peace. A persistent simplification will create an inner and outer well-being that places harmony in one's life. For me this began with the discovery of the meaninglessness of possessions beyond my actual and immediate needs.... —*Peace Pilgrim*

A man who has gained access to Divinity, he has simplified his whole life....
—*Paramananda*

Simple living will help you to control thoughts. If you lead a simple life, you have only very few wants and you will have to think a little only....
—*Sivananda*

Simplicity, simplicity, simplicity! I say let your affairs be as one, two, three and not a hundred or a thousand....We are happy in proportion to the things we can do without....
—*Henry D. Thoreau*

Few things are needed to make a wise man happy; nothing can make a foolish man content, and that is why most men are miserable....
—*Francois La Rochefoucauld*

The art of simplicity is simply to simplify....Simplicity avoids the superficial, penetrates the complex, goes to the heart of the problem, and pinpoints the key factors. Simplicity does not beat around the bush. It does not take winding detours. It follows a straight line to the objective. Simplicity is the shortest distance between two points....
—*Wilferd Peterson*

If you wish to give happiness, do not multiply possessions, but reduce wants. It is not the man who has too little, but the man who craves more, that is poor...
—*Seneca*

To live a life of faith in utter dependence upon God is very simple. It is the simplest life possible. It is the only life entirely free from the complications which afflict all those who depend upon human effort and finite wisdom. But while it is simple, it is far from easy....
—*Henry T. Hamblin*

You lose the very life you seek when you wallow in stupid luxuries. You don't need nine-tenths of the things you scramble for. Don't be afraid to have nothing. Happiness is not what you have, but who you are. You are already who you need to be....
—*Diogenes*

Half the confusion in the world comes from not knowing how little we need....I live more simply now, and with more peace....
—*Richard Byrd*

Very little is needed to make a happy life....
—*Ptolemy*

Voluntary simplicity involves both inner and other conditions. It means singleness of purpose, sincerity and honesty within, as well as avoidance of exterior clutter, of many possessions irrelevant to the chief purpose of life....
—*Richard Gregg*

Life is not complex. We are complex. Life is simple and the simple thing is the right thing....
—*Oscar Wilde*

Nothing is more simple than greatness, indeed, to be simple is to be great....
—*Ralph W. Emerson*

Simplicity is making the journey of this life with just baggage enough....
—*Charles D. Warner*

Simple style is like white light. It is complex but its complexity is not obvious....
—*Anatole France*

Possessions, outward success, publicity, luxury—to me these have always been contemptible. I believe that a simple and unassuming manner of life is best for everyone, best both for the body and the mind....
—*Albert Einstein*

If you would imitate Nature, you should take her simplicity for your model....   —*Michael Sendivogius*

Less is more....
—*Robert Browning*

Simplicity, of all things, is the hardest to be copied....   —*Richard Steele*

Simplicity of life is the true secret of happiness. Unhampered experience of joy which lies within comes out of simplicity. Your life should never be complicated with too many things....
—*Chidananda*

He who is satisfied with the simple needs of his nature, refusing the superfluous delights of the world, will not be tempted by any seductions....
—*Huai Nan Tzu*

I have lived long enough to learn how much there is I can really do without....He is nearest to God who needs the fewest things....   —*Socrates*

The more complicated life becomes, the more people are attracted to simple solutions....   —*James Reston*

Simplicity lies concealed in this chaos, and it is only for us to discover it....
—*Augustin Fresnel*

The simple wealth of nature is food and shelter....   —*Philo*

In character, in manners, in style, in all things, the supreme excellence is simplicity....   —*Henry W. Longfellow*

The art of art, the glory of expression and the sunshine of the light of letters, is simplicity....   —*Walt Whitman*

Simplicity is the peak of civilization....
—*Jessie Sampter*

God, indeed, is not in want of anything, but the wise man is in want of God alone. He therefore, who is in want of few things, and those necessary, emulates him who is in want of nothing....
—*Sextus, the Pythagorean*

The more we have the less we own....
—*Meister Eckhart*

If everyone would take only according to his needs and would leave the surplus to the needy, no one would be rich, no one poor, no one in misery....
—*St. Bernard*

There is no way to fake simplicity....
—*Anonymous*

The higher the truth the simpler it is....
—*Abraham Kook*

The really great of the earth are always simple. Pomp and ceremony, popes and kings, are toys for children....
—*Heinrich Heine*

Blessed are the simple, for they shall have much peace....
—*Thomas à Kempis*

I am bound to praise the simple life, because I have lived it and found it good....   —*John Burroughs*

The only simplicity that matters is the simplicity of the heart....
—*G. K. Chesterton*

The simplified life is a sanctified life, much more calm, much less strife. Oh, what wondrous truths are unveiled—projects succeed which had previously failed. Oh, how beautiful life can be, beautiful simplicity....   —*Peace Pilgrim*

Simplicity is the nature of great souls. They live and serve as incense burners....   —*Papa Ramdas*

Smile

A smile is ever the most bright and beautiful with a tear upon it....
—*Walter S. Landor*

The unselfish effort to bring cheer to others will be the beginning of a happier life for ourselves.... —*Helen Keller*

We can not open our hearts to give out cheer without more cheer rushing in to takes its place.... —*Alice H. Rice*

The knowers of truth....are happy and smiling all the time... —*Yoga Vasistha*

The greatest of all virtues is to be cheerful.... —*Robert L. Stevenson*

Some people are too tired to give you a smile. Give them one of yours, as no one needs a smile so much as one who has none to give.... —*Frank I. Fletcher*

The secret of divine omnipotence resides in the eternal smile....
—*Eliphas Levi*

If in our daily life we can smile, if we can be peaceful and happy, not only we, but everyone will profit from it. This is the most basic kind of peace work.... —*Thich Nhat Hanh*

Smiles are like pebbles cast into the water. The ripples spread and spread....
—*Fred Van Amburgh*

We shall never know all the good that a simple smile can do....
—*Mother Teresa*

The world belongs to the cheerful....The soul's highest duty is to be of good cheer.... —*Ralph W. Emerson*

All life is like a mirror. Smile at it and it smiles back at you. I just put a big smile on my face and everyone smiles back....
—*Peace Pilgrim*

The cheerful live longest in years and afterwards in our regards. Cheerfulness is the offshoot of goodness....
—*Christian Bovee*

The true source of cheerfulness is benevolence. The soul that perpetually overflows with kindness and sympathy will always be cheerful....
—*Parke Godwin*

Real hearty, healthy smiles bring down blood pressure and make for a long life. I think when humor disappears humans are also finished....
—*Frantisek Dostal*

There are two kinds of smiles, genuine and artificial. Very often we put on smiles, but the heart does not smile, only the lips and face take part in it. This is not a real smile. When the heart is filled with joy, it is reflected on the face as a smile. It is a natural outflow of joy.... —*Papa Ramdas*

A wise man laughs and smiles through his eyes....The smile and laughter through the eyes influence people tremendously. No energy leaks if you smile through the eyes.... —*Sivananda*

Every time a man smiles, and much more when he laughs, it adds something to his fragment of life....
—*Laurence Sterne*

When we learn to smile at life, we shall find that the problems we encounter dissolve.... —*Donald Curtis*

Cheerfulness is as natural to the heart of a man in strong health as color is to his cheek.... —*John Ruskin*

The mind that is cheerful and present will have no solicitude for the future, and will meet the bitter occurrences of life with a smile....   —Horace

Those who bring sunshine into the lives of others cannot keep it from themselves....   —James M. Barrie

Let no day then pass that ye do not speak a cheery and encouraging word to someone....   —Edgar Cayce

You find yourself refreshed by the presence of cheerful people. Why not make earnest effort to confer that pleasure on others? Half the battle is gained if you never allow yourself to say anything gloomy....   —Lydia Child

I have often been asked what I thought was the secret of Buddha's smile. It is—it can only be—that he smiled at himself for searching all those years for what he already possessed....
          —Paul Brunton

If you force yourself to smile, you'll end up laughing. You will be cheerful because you smile....   —Kenneth Goode

The grandest of things are achieved with a light heart: allow your soul to smile....   —Shirley MacLaine

You have not fulfilled every duty unless you have fulfilled that of being cheerful and pleasant....   —Charles Buxton

If you're not using your smile, you're like a man with a million dollars in the bank and no checkbook....   —Les Giblin

Grin and bear it. You can lighten a problem's weight if you brighten up and smile. There is more power to a punch delivered in high spirits than one delivered in low spirits....
          —Douglas Fairbanks

Be cheerful always. There is no path but will be easier traveled, no load but will be lighter, no shadow on the heart and brain but will lift sooner for a person of determined cheerfulness....
          —A. A. Willits

If you can smile here and now with only that which is presently available, then life is lived to the fullest....
          —Narayana

Cheerfulness is the great lubricant of the wheels of life. It lightens labor, diminishes difficulties, and mitigates misfortunes....   —Alfred A. Montapert

The burden of the self is lightened when I laugh at myself....
          —Rabindranath Tagore

There are those who suffer greatly and they go their way full of suffering. But if they meet someone whose face is bright with laughter, he can quicken them with gladness....   —Martin Buber

If good people would make their goodness agreeable, and smile instead of frowning in their virtue, how many would they win to the good cause....
          —James Usher

Of cheerfulness....the more it is spent, the more of it remains....
          —Ralph W. Emerson

True humor springs not more from the head than from the heart. It is not contempt; its essence is love. It issues not in laughter, but in still smiles, which lie far deeper....   —Thomas Carlyle

Mirth is like a flash of lightning that breaks through a gloom of clouds and glitters for a moment; cheerfulness keeps up a kind of daylight in the mind, and fills it with a steady and perpetual serenity....   —Joseph Addison

The gloomy soul aggravates misfortune, while a cheerful smile often dispels those mists that portend a storm....
—*Lydia Sigourney*

In speaking of others always be calm and cheerful....   —*Teresa of Avila*

My religion of life is always be cheerful....   —*George Meredith*

The mind that is cheerful will have no concern for the future, and will meet the bitterness of life with a smile....
—*Horace*

A fool raises his voice when he laughs, but a wise man smiles quietly....
—*Ben Sirach*

Let no one ever come to you without leaving better and happier....to children, to the poor, to all who suffer and are lonely, give always a happy smile....
—*Mother Teresa*

Cheerfulness and content are great beautifiers and are faithful preservers of youthful looks....   —*Charles Dickens*

Smiles are contagious....Watch how quickly someone responds to you when you are smiling at them. We are all spiritually unified in a joyous universe....
—*Norma Hawkins*

Nature intended you to be the fountain-spring of cheerfulness....and not the monument of despair and melancholy....   —*Arthur Helps*

A cheerful friend is like a sunny day, which sheds its brightness on all around....   —*John Lubbock*

Cheerfulness is a friend of grace; it puts the heart in tune to praise God....
—*John Watson*

Solitude

You find in solitude only what you take to it....   —*Juan R. Jimenez*

A solitude is an audience-chamber with God....   —*Walter S. Landor*

The best of all is to Be alone to experience one's soul in Silence. To be nakedly alone, unseen, is better than anything in the world, a relief like death. To Be—alone—is one of life's greatest delights....   —*Sunyata*

Solitude is strength; to depend on the presence of the crowd is weakness. The man who needs a mob to nerve him is much more alone than he imagines....
—*Paul Brunton*

A man attached to desire cannot get solitude, wherever he may be; a detached man is always in solitude....
—*Ramana Maharshi*

The more powerful and original a mind, the more it will incline towards the religion of solitude....
—*Aldous Huxley*

The pain of leaving those you grow to love is only the prelude to understanding yourself and others....
—*Shirley MacLaine*

Solitude is bearable only with God....
—*André Gide*

Solitude, if rightly used, becomes not only a privilege but a necessity. Only a superficial soul fears to fraternize with itself....   —*Alice H. Rice*

Companions be content to forsake, for solitude is president of the divine assembly....   —*Marpa*

Very few things keep their charm in solitude; and if the solitude is absolute and complete, everything turns irretrievably to ashes....
—*Fernando Savater*

Solitude can be frightening because it invites us to meet a stranger we think we may not want to know—ourselves....
—*Melvyn Kinder*

Inside myself is a place, where I live all alone, and that's where you renew your springs that never dry up....
—*Pearl S. Buck*

Nowhere can a man find a quieter or more untroubled retreat than in his own soul.... —*Marcus Aurelius*

Solitude is fine when you are at peace with yourself and have something definite to do.... —*Johann W. Goethe*

Quiet minds cannot be perplexed or frightened but go on in fortune or misfortune at their own private pace like the ticking of a clock during a thunderstorm.... —*Robert L. Stevenson*

Conversation enriches the understanding, but solitude is the school of genius.... —*Edward Gibbon*

No man will unfold the capacities of his own intellect who does not at least checker his life with solitude....
—*Thomas De Quincey*

You will easily get illumination in solitude. Solitude has its charms. Prepare yourself for life in seclusion....
—*Sivananda*

Only when one is connected to one's own core is one connected to others. And, for me, the core, the inner spring, can best be refound through solitude....
—*Anne Morrow Lindbergh*

Solitude is often a way into the inner source, a way into our own hearts, God's heart, and the hearts of others....
—*Matthew Fox*

Solitude takes away the cataracts and we get a glimpse of the world as God sees it.... —*Thomas M. MacDonald*

I find it wholesome to be alone the greater part of the time. To be in company, even with the best, is soon wearisome and dissipating. I love to be alone.... —*Henry D. Thoreau*

Only in complete loneliness do we learn the true meaning of the words: know thyself! For only then do we stand before our own true selves....
—*Hans-Ulrich Rieker*

Pioneers have to tread a lonely road. It is so in order that they may stand out as great, solitary figures, which act as landmarks to guide those who come after them.... —*Henry T. Hamblin*

Through silence, solitary practice, and simple living, we begin to fill the empty reservoir.... —*David A. Cooper*

Solitude is not out to deceive anyone; it does not pretend or embellish; it has nothing to hide and invents nothing. It is completely naked and without adornment; it knows nothing of shows or the applause which poisons the mind. It has God as sole witness of its life and actions.... —*Petrarch*

No time is ever wasted that is spent in wordless solitude.... —*Anonymous*

Our language has wisely sensed the two sides of being alone. It has created the word loneliness to express the pain of being alone. And it has created the word solitude to express the glory of being alone.... —*Paul Tillich*

Religion is what the individual does with his own solitariness. It runs through three stages, if it evolves to its final satisfaction. It is the transition from God the void to God the enemy, and from God the enemy to God the companion.... —*Alfred N. Whitehead*

Inspiration makes solitude anywhere.... —*Ralph W. Emerson*

A man should not seek to see himself in running water, but in still water. For only what is itself still can impart stillness into others.... —*Chuang Tse*

Solitude is the highest stage. Only in solitude can man attain....union with the eternal God.... —*Nahman Bratzlav*

Solitude gives birth to the original in us.... —*Thomas Mann*

Every pious man should seek retirement and seclusion, and should only in case of necessity associate with others.... —*Maimonides*

Solitary trees, if they grow at all, grow strong.... —*Winston Churchill*

Man cannot survive without air, water and sleep. Next in importance comes food. And close on its heels, solitude.... —*Thomas Szasz*

A man alone is either a saint or a devil.... —*Richard E. Burton*

To live a spiritual life we must first find the courage to enter into the desert of loneliness and change it by gentle and persistent efforts into a garden of solitude.... —*Henry J. Nouwen*

It is good to be solitary, for solitude is difficult; that something is difficult must be a reason the more for us to do it.... —*Rainer M. Rilke*

Even in paradise, it is good to be alone.... —*Jewish proverb*

A wise man is never less alone than when he is alone.... —*Jonathan Swift*

Against the love of pleasure, effective beyond all else is solitude. For he who puts out of sight the things that are worldly loses the desire for them.... —*Moses H. Luzzatto*

Settle yourself in solitude, and you will come upon God in yourself.... —*Teresa of Avila*

A certain degree of solitude seems necessary to the full growth and spread of the highest mind.... —*Friedrich von Novalis*

All humans are frightened of their own solitude. But only in solitude can we learn to know ourselves, learn to handle our own eternal aloneness.... —*Han Suyin*

I was never less alone than when by myself.... —*Edward Gibbon*

One of the greatest necessities in America is to discover creative solitude.... —*Carl Sandburg*

Only in solitude do we raise our hearts to the Heart of the Universe.... —*Miguel de Yunamunojugo*

Many teachers praise love as the highest of virtues; I, however, place solitude higher than love....Motionless detachment makes a man superlatively Godlike.... —*Meister Eckhart*

It is well to be alone. It fertilizes the creative impulse.... —*Max Nordau*

At bottom, we live spiritually alone.... —*Heinrich Heine*

Without solitude there can be no real people....The measure of your solitude is the measure of your capacity for communion.... —*John Eudes*

Rest is more perfect than movement, and for the sake of rest the individual things are moved.... —*Marsilio Ficino*

Solitude, though it may be silent as light, is like light, the mightiest of agencies; for solitude is essential to man. All men come into this world alone; all leave it alone.... —*Thomas De Quincey*

Blessed are the solitary....for you shall find the Kingdom; because you came from it, and you shall go there again.... —*Gospel of Thomas*

A religious man is a man who is Alone—not lonely, you understand, but Alone—with no theories or dogmas, no opinion, no background; he is alone and enjoying it.... —*J. Krishnamurti*

The chief support for purity of the heart is love of solitude.... —*Bahya*

The happiest of all lives is a busy solitude.... —*Voltaire*

Men fear silence as they fear solitude, because both give them a glimpse of the terror of life's nothingness.... —*André Maurois*

We must reserve a little back-shop, all our own, entirely free, wherein to establish our true liberty and principle retreat and solitude.... —*Michel Montaigne*

Solitude is the nurse of enthusiasm, and enthusiasm is the parent of genius.... —*Isaac D'Israeli*

There is no true solitude except interior solitude.... —*Thomas Merton*

In solitude, where we are LEAST alone... —*George Byron*

Nowhere can you retire with more quietness or more freedom than within your own spirit....Constantly give yourself to this retreat, and renew yourself.... —*Marcus Aurelius*

It takes solitude, under the stars, for us to be reminded of our eternal origin and our far destiny.... —*Archibald Rutledge*

Great minds are like eagles, and build their nest in some lofty solitude....A man can be himself only so long as he is alone, and if he does not love solitude, he will not love freedom, for it is only when he is alone that he is really free.... —*Arthur Schopenhauer*

It is easy in the world to live after the world's opinion; it is easy in solitude to live after your own; but the great man is he who, in the midst of a crowd, keeps with perfect sweetness the independence of solitude.... —*Ralph W. Emerson*

Little do men perceive what solitude is; and how far it extends. For a crowd is not company, and faces are but a gallery of pictures, and talk but a tinkling cymbal, where there is no love....Whosoever is delighted in solitude is either a wild beast, or a god.... —*Francis Bacon*

They are never alone that are accompanied with noble thoughts.... —*Philip Sidney*

Solitude is to the mind what fasting is to the body, fatal if it is too prolonged, and yet necessary.... —*Luc de Clapiers Vauvenargues*

Solitude makes us tougher toward ourselves and tenderer toward others and in both ways improves our character....
—*Friedrich W. Nietzsche*

Should you band together the legs of two birds with a short rope an interesting phenomenon will take place. Each bird will hamper the other during their attempts to fly. Both birds will remain grounded. The same analogy can be applied to spiritual matters. Self-realization is a solitary affair in which each pilgrim must travel unhindered, alone....
—*Shantidasa*

Solitude is not to be found in forests only. It can be had even in towns and the thick of worldly occupation....
—*Ramana Maharshi*

I never found the companion that was so companionable as solitude. I am for the most part more lonely when I go abroad among men than when I stay in my chambers....
—*Henry D. Thoreau*

Be able to be alone. Lose not the advantage of solitude, and the society of thyself, nor be only content, but delight to be alone and single with Omnipresence....
—*Thomas Browne*

You cannot build a character in a solitude; you need a formed character to stand a solitude....
—*Austin O'Malley*

When you have closed your doors, and darkened your room, remember never to say that you are alone, for you are not alone; God is within, and your genius is within....
—*Epictetus*

Solitude is a discipline....essential for those who would acquaint themselves with God and be at peace....
—*E. Herman*

Eagles fly alone; sheep herd together....
—*Sufi saying*

It would do the world good if every man in it would compel himself occasionally to be absolutely alone. Most of the world's progress has come out of such loneliness....
—*Bruce Barton*

In this business of life, I have a silent partner, God, who gives me complete freedom to run this partnership and make it successful....Most importantly, I must be still....and affirm what I need, and then listen from within for an answer....
—*Ronnie Fisher*

The best thinking has been done in solitude. The worst has been done in turmoil....
—*Thomas A. Edison*

Spirituality is not to be learned by flight from the world, by running away from things, or by turning solitary and going apart from the world. Rather, we learn an inner solitude wherever or with whomsoever we may be. We must learn to penetrate things and find God there....
—*Meister Eckhart*

Speech

Listen to all the conversations of our world between nations as well as those between couples. They are, for the most part, dialogue of the deaf....
—*Paul Tournier*

They that govern the most make the least noise....
—*John Selden*

True eloquence consists in saying all that need be said and no more....
—*Francois La Rochefoucauld*

Once a word has been allowed to escape, it cannot be recalled....
—*Horace*

In speech, we can only speak fragments of the truth, thus all speech misses the point; at best it is the partial expression of the inner feeling, but it can never grasp the totality of our heart—thus speech mostly divides, and rarely unites....　　　*—A Spiritual Warrior*

If you propose to speak, always ask yourself—Is it true, is it necessary, is it kind?...　　　*—Gautama Buddha*

If you stop talking and stop thinking, there will be nothing you do not understand....　　　*—Paul Twitchell*

Those who speak with discretion are respected by mankind, as the sun, emerging from the shadows, by its rays creates great warmth....
—Tibetan saying

To talk without thinking is to shoot without aiming....　　*—English proverb*

When the mouth stumbles, it is worse than the foot....　*—West African proverb*

The instant you speak about a thing, you miss the mark....　　*—Zen saying*

A talkative person runs himself into great inconveniences by babbling out his and other's secrets....
—John Ray

Speech is a mirror of the soul; as a man speaks, so he is....　　*—Publilius Syrus*

The mouth speaks from the heart. It is impossible for man to conceal himself. In every act, word, or gesture, he stands revealed as he is, and not as he would have himself appear to be....
—Ernest Holmes

Talk doesn't cook rice....
—Chinese proverb

One should speak what is true; one should speak what is sweet; one should not speak what is true if it is not sweet or what is sweet if it is false; this is the ancient law....　　　*—Manu*

An enormous amount of energy is wasted by excessive talking. The energy that is spent talking should be carefully and vigilantly conserved and utilized for spiritual practices and in divine contemplation. The organ of speech distracts the mind considerably. A talkative man cannot dream of having peace even for a short time....
—Sivananda

We cannot talk about atoms in ordinary language....　　*—Werner Heisenberg*

Speak to everyone in accordance with his level of understanding....
—Sufi saying

One of the things that keep us at a distance from perfection is, without doubt, our tongue....　*—Francis de Sales*

Not that which goeth in at the mouth defileth a man, but that which cometh out of the mouth, this defileth him....
—Jesus

Nature has given us two ears, two eyes, and but one tongue, to the end that we should hear and see more than we speak....　　　*—Epictetus*

The less you speak the less you err....
—Solomon Ibn Gabirol

The best way to cut your problems in half is to learn how to keep your mouth closed....　　　*—Anonymous*

Speak soft and sweet; sympathize with suffering and loss and ignorance; try your best to apply the salve of smoothing words and timely succor....
—Sathya Sai Baba

The less men think, the more they talk.... —*Charles Montesquieu*

He who tells the truth says almost nothing.... —*Porchia*

Do you wish men to speak well of you? Then never speak well of yourself.... —*Blaise Pascal*

The man who findeth God loseth his speech.... —*Mohammed*

If you can't say good and encouraging things, say nothing. Nothing is often a good thing to say, and always a clever thing to say.... —*Will Durant*

Speech is of time; silence of eternity.... —*Thomas Carlyle*

Man has great power of speech, but the greater part thereof is empty and deceitful.... —*Leonardo da Vinci*

Keep your remarks brief, otherwise the complete plan of your thoughts will seldom be grasped. Before you reach the conclusion, the listener will have forgotten the beginning and the middle.... —*Horace*

We are ruined by foolish speech and saved by silence.... —*Hindu saying*

There is nothing in the world better for the perfection of the soul than the curbing of speech.... —*Shmuel Agnon*

He who knows Tao does not care to speak of it; and he who is ever willing to speak of it does not know it.... —*Lao-tzu*

The more you speak of yourself, the more you are likely to lie.... —*Johann G. Zimmerman*

It is easier to talk than to hold one's tongue.... —*Greek proverb*

Speech is a God-given form peculiar to man, and must not be employed for that which is degrading.... —*Maimonides*

Discretion in speech is more than eloquence.... —*Francis Bacon*

The sage does not talk, the talented ones talk, and the stupid ones argue.... —*Kung Tingan*

Happiness is speechlessness.... —*George W. Curtis*

A man's defeat lies in his tongue.... —*Persian proverb*

When speech is controlled, the eyes speak; the glance says what words can never say.... —*Hazrat Inayat Khan*

Be in no hurry to speak.... —*Old Testament*

Talkative people listen to no one, for they are ever speaking. And the first evil surrounding those who do not know the meaning of silence is that they hear nothing.... —*Epictetus*

A dog is not considered a good dog because he is a good barker. A man is not considered a good man because he is a good talker.... —*Chuang Tse*

Speech is the small change of silence.... —*George Meredith*

They always talk who never think.... —*Matthew Prior*

He who speaks becomes silent before the Divine Essence.... —*Jili*

An egotist will always speak of himself, either in praise or censure, but a modest man ever shuns making himself the subject of his conversation.... —*Jean La Bruyere*

Speech is a faculty given to man to conceal his thoughts....
—*Alexander Talleyrand*

Do not trust all who talk smoothly. Listen much and speak little....
—*Robert Benson*

Talk that does not end in any kind of action is better suppressed altogether....
—*Thomas Carlyle*

Let a fool hold his tongue and he will pass for a sage. I have often regretted my speech, never my silence....
—*Publilius Syrus*

He who says he knows—shun; he who thinks he knows—listen; he who says he doesn't know—follow....
—*Chinese proverb*

Undisciplined talk means an undisciplined mind....   —*Art Linkletter*

We say little when we talk about ourselves....   —*Anonymous*

Spirituality

In the spiritual life, all paths lead to the same place....
—*Satchidananda*

Once spirit was God, then it became man....   —*Friedrich W. Nietzsche*

Our spiritual being is here to experience the process of life, not hold it stagnant, or try to control and possess it....Our spirit cannot be free if it is desirous of controlling life, or if it is attached to the results of its actions....
—*A Spiritual Warrior*

No one who hasn't experienced for himself at least something of the nature and joys of the spiritual life can have any valid opinion on the subject....
—*Krishnaprem*

We will never be spiritual until we give up trying, and become aware that we already are spiritual....
—*Walter Starcke*

The man who has no inner life is a slave of his surroundings, as the barometer is the obedient servant of the air....
—*Henri F. Amiel*

The material world, which has been taken for a world of blind mechanism, is in reality a Spiritual world seen very partially and imperfectly. The only real world is the Spiritual world....
—*J. B. S. Haldane*

Are we not all divine? Are we not all made for a higher life?...
—*Mother Teresa*

In order to make spiritual progress you must be patient like a tree and humble like a blade of grass....
—*Lakshmana*

Spirituality does not "separate" you from the world; it allows you to connect with All There Is, and that includes your life here....   —*Iris Belhayes*

The spiritual life is the way of walking with God instead of walking alone....
—*Elinor MacDonald*

In our spiritual development we are often required to pull up roots many times and to close many chapters in our lives until we are no longer attached to any material thing and we can love all people without any attachment to them....
—*Peace Pilgrim*

Life in the world and life in the spirit are not incompatible....
—*The Upanishads*

The universe is a more spiritual entity than we thought. The real fact is that we are in the midst of a spiritual world which dominates the material....
—*Bhagavan Das*

Whatever can't be done in the physical can be done in the spiritual. And in direct proportion as man recognizes himself as spirit, and lives accordingly, is he able to transcend in power the man who recognizes himself merely as material....
—*Ralph W. Trine*

The eternity of the spirit does not begin after death....but is, like God, always present....
—*Moses Hess*

Whatever draws the mind outward is unspiritual and whatever draws the mind inward is spiritual....
—*Ramana Maharshi*

We do not grasp that we are invisible....We do not understand that life, before all definitions of it, is a drama of the visible and invisible....
—*Maurice Nicoll*

We have been too content with allocating the high places of spirituality to the few names of a far-off past, and with assigning the muddy depths to humanity in general. We forget our own divine nature....
—*Paul Brunton*

We are not here for the sake of possession, or of power, or of happiness, but we are here to transfigure the divine out of human spirit....
—*Walter Rathenau*

While the body perishes the Spirit is immortal. We are here to realize we are spirit....
—*Papa Ramdas*

Spirituality is like a bird: if you hold on to it tightly, it chokes, and if you hold it loosely, it escapes....
—*Israel Lipkin*

Spiritual achievement costs much, though never as much as it is worth....
—*Evelyn Underhill*

There is no reality except the one contained within us....
—*Hermann Hesse*

Spirit is the real and eternal; matter is the unreal and temporal....
—*Mary Baker Eddy*

By having reverence for life, we enter into a spiritual relation with the world....By practicing reverence for life we become good, deep and alive....
—*Albert Schweitzer*

Zen does not confuse spirituality with thinking about God while one is peeling potatoes. Zen spirituality is just to peel the potatoes....
—*Alan Watts*

There are no plains in the spiritual life; we are either going uphill or coming down....
—*Fulton J. Sheen*

A soul, because of its heavenly origin, will no more be satisfied with worldly luxuries than a princess can be with a peasant for a husband, though he bring her everything on earth....
—*Isaac Hanina*

The spiritual life does not demand that we give up everything. We give up nothing, but we fill everything with the richness of feeling....
—*Paramananda*

Only spiritual values can bring light and joy....
—*Alexis Carrel*

Facts as facts do not always create a spirit of reality, because reality is a spirit....
—*G. K. Chesterton*

The spiritual life is constituted in a very few words and a very great inclination to God.... —*Mother Marguerite*

The soul is a stranger in this world.... —*Bahya*

If there is one thing fundamental to the life of the spirit it is the absence of force.... —*Harold Laski*

The majority of men live without being thoroughly conscious that they are spiritual beings.... —*Sören Kierkegaard*

He who believes himself to be far advanced in the spiritual life has not made a good beginning.... —*Jean P. Camus*

We are not human beings having a spiritual experience. We are spiritual beings having a human experience.... —*Teilhard de Chardin*

Spiritual life and secure life do not go together; to save oneself one must struggle and take risks.... —*Ignazio Silone*

Don't make the excuse that man is only human. With all the force of the truth that is in us, we say, we know, that man is divine.... —*White Eagle*

To fully understand the meaning of spirit, we must accept one direct principle, and that is—life is indestructible. It cannot be destroyed. It can change form and its rate of living consciousness; it can be transmuted, and its frequency changed to higher and lower levels, but it cannot be destroyed.... —*Ronald Beesley*

The spirit of man is inseparable from the Infinite, and can be satisfied with nothing less than the Infinite.... —*James Allen*

If you wish to progress spiritually, do not reject things you do not understand. You build up a mental block this way. It is not healthy to reject things you do not understand. Simply put them aside for the present.... —*Peace Pilgrim*

Our spiritual life is a life of dependence on God.... —*Mother Teresa*

Real spirituality is not up in the clouds—it is down on earth, here and now. Deep spirituality is seeing God every day in the common things, and showing God your appreciation by doing common tasks.... —*Fred Van Amburgh*

Man is a vessel of the Spirit....Spirit is the voyager who, passing through this land of man, bids the human soul to follow it to the Spirit's purely spiritual destination.... —*Erich Heller*

Spiritual victory is a living force. It reaches out and touches all who come within its magnetic field, transforming each and every thing it contacts. When this happens to be a human mind, it is lifted above physical bondage, conquering tragic odds and finding joy despite the presence of pain.... —*David Seabury*

We are born into a world of nature; our second birth is into a world of spirit.... —*Bhagavad-Gita*

Spiritually, man is a giant. Spiritually, there is nothing impossible for man to accomplish. Godman never becomes defeated. Therefore, keep the mental soil well-tilled and your harvest shall be great.... —*Frater Achad*

Spirituality is the process of getting our minds off ourselves and back on God.... —*Anonymous*

The great truth is that man is a spiritual being, who brings with him a life to unfold, a power to release, a love to express, and a veritable kingdom of heaven to outpicture. He doesn't begin life empty, but as a dynamic spiritual potentiality.... —*Eric Butterworth*

Spirit is strong but flesh is weak, so weak sometimes it even overpowers the strong spirit 'which knows all truth.'.... —*H. P. Blavatsky*

The spirit is an inward flame; a lamp the world blows upon but never puts out.... —*Margot Asquith*

Spirit is the life of God within us.... —*Teresa of Avila*

The first sign of spirituality is cheerfulness.... —*Anonymous*

We make for ourselves, in truth, our own spiritual world.... —*Henry F. Amiel*

The grand secret of humanity is its inability to perceive its own spiritual character. Mankind is nothing less than miniature gods in the unfolding. When the ancient masters bid their students "To know thyself," they were merely guiding them to this sacred knowledge.... —*Shantidasa*

Four thousand volumes of metaphysics .will not teach us what the spirit is.... —*Voltaire*

Just as a candle cannot burn without fire, men cannot live without a spiritual life.... —*Gautama Buddha*

If the windows of your spirit are dirty and streaked, covered with matter foreign to them, then the world as you look out of them will be dirty and streaked and out of order....Go wash your windows.... —*Ralph W. Trine*

You are going to develop a new kind of love, not physical but spiritual. That is not true love. Physical love is attachment. Spiritual love is born of oneness with the spirit....Therefore, rise up and declare that you are the immortal Spirit.... —*Papa Ramdas*

Fearlessness is the first requisite of the spiritual life.... —*Mohandas Gandhi*

The physical body is a temple. Take care of it. The mind is energy. Regulate it. The spirit is the projection. Represent it.... —*Yogi Bhajan*

The divine essence itself is love and wisdom.... —*Emanuel Swedenborg*

No man who has lived through a temporary spiritual experience is ever likely to forget it. His days will be haunted until he sets out to seek ways and means of repeating it.... —*Paul Brunton*

Spiritual life cannot force out of anyone more than the person wishes to put into it.... —*Gayatri Devi*

Your spirit is everything; your body is a garment that rots, and nothing more.... —*Allan Kardec*

Success

Personal success, business success, built upon materialism alone, are empty shells concealing....saddened lives.... —*George R. White*

Success can make you go one of two ways. It can make you a prima donna, or it can smooth the edges, take away the insecurities, let the nice things come out.... —*Barbara Walters*

If you would have a successful life, less and less try to make things happen and more and more just let things happen.... —*Ormond McGill*

Some of the world's greatest feats were accomplished by people not smart enough to know they were impossible.... —*Doug Larson*

Do your job naturally because you like it and success will take care of itself.... —*Norman V. Peale*

Every worthwhile accomplishment, big or little, has its stages of drudgery and triumph; a beginning, a struggle, and a victory.... —*Anonymous*

Success is how high you bounce when you hit bottom.... —*George Patton*

He has achieved success who has lived well, laughed often and loved much; who has enjoyed the trust of pure women, the respect of intelligent men and the love of little children; who has filled his niche and accomplished his task; who has left the world better than he found it.... —*Bessie A. Stanley*

If people are highly successful in their profession they lose their senses. Sight goes. They have no time to look at pictures. Sound goes. They have no time to listen to music. Speech goes. They have no time for conversation. They lose their sense of proportion.... —*Virginia Woolf*

Success is more dangerous than failure. The ripples break over a wider coastline.... —*Graham Greene*

The logic of worldly success rests on fallacy: the strange error that our perfection depends on the thoughts and opinions and applause of other men.... —*Thomas Merton*

God doesn't require us to succeed, he only requires that you try.... —*Mother Teresa*

No illusion is more cruel than the illusion that great success and huge money buy you immunity from the common ills of mankind.... —*Larry McMurtry*

Success is....a series of glorious defeats.... —*Mohandas Gandhi*

Success doesn't always bring the anticipated sense of fulfillment. For some, success evokes a sense of disillusionment.... —*Melvyn Kinder*

Life is a mixture of successes and failures. May you be encouraged by your successes and strengthened by your failures. As long as you never lose faith in God, you will be victorious over any situation you face.... —*Peace Pilgrim*

The secret of the truly successful....is that they learned very well early in life how not to be busy. They saw through the adage....that anything worth doing is worth doing well. The truth is, many things are worth doing only in the most slovenly, halfhearted fashion possible, and many things are not worth doing at all.... —*Barbara Ehrenreich*

If you hit every time, the target is too near or too big.... —*Tom Hirshfield*

The real demon is success—the anxieties engendered by this quest are relentless, degrading, corroding. What is worse, there is no end to the escalation of desire.... —*Marya Mannes*

Success makes life easier. It doesn't make living easier.... —*Bruce Springsteen*

Success cannot mean the accumulation of inert matter.... —*Martin Gray*

Success makes men rigid and they tend to exalt stability over all the other virtues.... —*Walter Lippmann*

Success is going from one failure to the next without a loss of enthusiasm.... —*Winston Churchill*

My formula for success? It is very simple. I am merely a man who knows how to enlist in his service better men than himself.... —*Andrew Carnegie*

This is the secret of success—an unfaltering faith, and a wisely directed purpose.... —*James Allen*

People seldom see the halting and painful steps by which the most insignificant success is achieved.... —*Annie Sullivan*

Never talk about failure. There is no such thing. Even for those who are in the grave—for they shall have another chance....If you have gone down to failure's door, you may accend to success by retracing your steps.... —*James B. Schafer*

People are often intoxicated by success; they put their trust in their destiny, and pay in the end for their former successes by severe reverses, which greater prudence would have enabled them to avoid.... —*Allan Kardec*

Success is not to be gained by a blind and slavish following of anyone's rules or advice, our own any more than any other person's. There is no royal road to success—no patent process by which the unsuccessful are to be magically transformed....Rules and advice may greatly assist—and they undoubtedly do this—but the real work must be accomplished by the individual. He must carve out his own destiny.... —*William W. Atkinson*

Success can corrupt; usefulness can only exalt.... —*Dimitri Mitropoulos*

Success seems to be largely a matter of hanging on after others have let go.... —*William Feather*

Wealth, notoriety, place and power are no measure of success whatever.... —*William Danforth*

Success is to be measured not so much by the position that one has reached in life as by the obstacles which he has overcome while trying to succeed.... —*Booker T. Washington*

You must not expect to reap success from sowing the seed of failure. Nor should you look for a lot when you have given only a little.... —*Fred Van Amburgh*

A lot of successful people are risk-takers. Unless you are willing to do that, to have a go, to fail miserably, and have another go, success won't happen.... —*Phillip Adams*

Many people dream of success. To me, success can only be achieved through repeated failure and introspection. In fact, success represents the one percent of your work which results only from the ninety-nine percent that is called failure.... —*Soichiro Honda*

The truth is that all of us attain the greatest success and happiness possible in this life whenever we use our native capacities to their greatest extent.... —*Smiley Blanton*

Always bear in mind that your own resolution to success is more important than any other one thing.... —*Abraham Lincoln*

Your greatest triumphs are not in winning, but in rising again after every fall.... —*Anonymous*

Success in life has been achieved when all that one wants is finely balanced by all that one needs.... —*Sufi saying*

Put your heart, mind, intellect and soul even into your smallest acts. This is the secret of success.... —*Sivananda*

Most people are quitters. This is wonderful news for those of us who decide to be successful. It means that if we stick to what we are doing, we will, in a very short time, be ahead of the multitudes.... —*Andrew Matthews*

Whether you think you will succeed or not, you are right.... —*Henry Ford*

Success is not a harbor but a voyage with its own perils to the spirit. The game of life is to come up a winner, to be a success, or to achieve what we set out to do. Yet there is always the danger of failing as a human being....
—*Richard M. Nixon*

Successful people are not gifted; they just work hard—then succeed on purpose.... —*G. K. Neilson*

Success is a series of right thoughts put into action.... —*Fred Van Amburgh*

To laugh often and much; to win the respect of intelligent people and the affection of children; to earn the appreciation of honest critics and endure the betrayal of false friends; to appreciate beauty; to find the best in others; to leave the world a bit better....to know even one life has breathed easier because you lived. This is to be successful.... —*Ralph W. Emerson*

Try not to become a man of success. Rather become a man of value....
—*Albert Einstein*

The difference between a successful man and an unsuccessful one is this: the former keeps going when he is tempted to give up in spite of the temptation to become depressed and discouraged, while the latter gives up, slackens his efforts because he gives way to depression and discouragement.... —*Henry T. Hamblin*

Success has made failures of many men.... —*Cindy Adams*

The secret of all success is commitment. No one has ever received, gained, or accomplished anything in life without first being deeply committed to it....
—*Alan Cohen*

Success is to rise from the illusion of pursuit to the disillusion of possession.... —*Elbert Hubbard*

The secret of success in life is known only to those who have succeeded....
—*John C. Collins*

The most important single ingredient in the formula of success is the knack of getting along with people....
—*Theodore Roosevelt*

A wise man will make more opportunities than he finds.... —*Francis Bacon*

The secret of success lies in living for the sake of others.... —*Papa Ramdas*

The hopeful man sees success where others see failure, sunshine where others see shadows and storm....
—*Orison S. Marden*

The secret of success is constancy of purpose.... —*Benjamin Disraeli*

If you think you can do something, you have a much better chance for success than if you wish you could....
—*Tom Kubistant*

Why should we be in such desperate haste to succeed, and in such desperate enterprises? If a man does not keep pace with his companions, perhaps it is because he hears a different drummer....
—*Henry D. Thoreau*

The surest way to miss success is to miss the opportunity....
—*Philarete Charles*

The greedy search for money or success will almost always lead men into unhappiness. Why? Because that kind of life makes them depend upon things outside themselves....
—*André Maurois*

One magic formula for successful and enthusiastic living is stated in six powerful words: "Find a need and fill it!" Every enterprise that has achieved success has been predicated on that formula....
—*Norman V. Peale*

The great secret of success is to go through life as a man who never gets used up....
—*Albert Schweitzer*

Never stop being creative. The more you practice, the more creative you become. Creativity spells success....
—*Alden James*

He that would make sure of success should keep his passion cool, and his expectations low....
—*Jeremy Collier*

Success is full of promise till men get it; and then it is last year's nest from which the birds have flown....
—*Henry W. Beecher*

Along with success comes a reputation for wisdom....
—*Euripides*

I measure success by how well I sleep at night. If I am at peace with my God and myself, I fall asleep easily. If sleep comes hard, then I know the day has been a perfect failure....
—*Rod McKuen*

The great secret of the highly successful life is....to infuse the mental and physical with the spiritual; in other words, to spiritualize all, and so to raise all to the highest possibilities and powers....
—*Ralph W. Trine*

There are three primary principles essential to the success of any venture. They are simple, but important: 1. Determine your objectives. 2. Analyze the obstacles in your way. 3. Learn how to overcome your obstacles....
—*Dick Carlson*

There are no secrets to success. It's the result of preparation, hard work, learning from failure....
—*Colin L. Powell*

The talent of success is nothing more than doing what you can do well, without a thought of fame....
—*Henry W. Longfellow*

Personal success is never static. It usually comes in small steps leading to other small steps that lead to broader achievement....
—*Wess Roberts*

Progress in the spiritual path as well as success in the world, is impossible if you do not cultivate this cardinal virtue of keeping your word....
—*Sivananda*

If we believe in the necessity of trying to win over others, we will also believe in the need for wearisome scheming....
—*Vernon Howard*

The difference between failure and success is doing a thing nearly right and doing it exactly right....
—*Edward Simmons*

What people call an overnight success is generally the result of years of intensive preparation....   —*Anonymous*

The key to success is to feel your "work" is "play."...   —*Michael Korda*

The trouble with most of us is that we envy the success of others. We oftentimes fail to get our share of success because we spend so much time trying to get the other fellow's share....
          —*Fred Van Amburgh*

The common idea that success spoils people by making them vain, egotistic, and self-complacent is erroneous; on the contrary it makes them, for the most part humble, tolerant, and kind. Failure makes people bitter and cruel....
          —*Somerset Maugham*

Self-trust is the first secret of success....
          —*Ralph W. Emerson*

The surest way not to fail is to determine to succeed....   —*Richard Sheridan*

Success is knowing that because of you, the world is a little better....
          —*Michael Sneyd*

I believe the true road to preeminent success in any line is to make yourself master of that line....
          —*Andrew Carnegie*

Success truly is the result of good judgement. Good judgement is the result of experience, and experience is often the result of bad judgement....
          —*Anthony Robbins*

Great successes never come without risks....   —*Flavius Josephus*

Success comes from finding meaning in life—in spite of loss....
          —*Barbara Hansen*

Experience shows that success is due less to ability than to zeal. The winner is he who gives himself to his work, body and soul....   —*Charles Buxton*

Success is not a matter of position or possession. It is a frame of mind. It is the satisfying feeling of a life spent in a worthwhile way, and a feeling of service rendered....   —*Stephen M. Paulson*

We can do anything we want to do if we stick with it long enough....
          —*Helen Keller*

The toughest thing about success is that you've got to keep on being a success....
          —*Irving Berlin*

Success does not consist in never making blunders, but in never making the same one the second time....
          —*Henry W. Shaw*

The line between failure and success is so fine that we scarcely know when we pass it: so fine that we are often on the line and don't know it. How many a man has thrown up his hands at a time when a little more effort, a little more patience, would have achieved success....   —*Elbert Hubbard*

Hope is the great power that can move you to success. Why? Because when a man expects to win he does not hold anything back, but he gives his project all that he's got....   —*Norman V. Peale*

When a man has put a limit on what he will do, he has put a limit on what he can do....   —*Charles M. Schwab*

Winning is making a total commitment to something you believe in—regardless of the outcome....   —*Joseph Paterno*

A man may be outwardly successful all his life long, and die hollow and worthless....   —*Henry W. Beecher*

Suffering

Sorrow cannot be conquered by bitterness and resentment. You must accept your loss, turn from it as from a closed door....　　　*—James G. Gilkey*

Sorrow makes a man think of God.... Every man from king to peasant has a certain amount of sorrow. Even in cases where it seems absent, it is only a time factor that makes you think so—sooner or later it comes....One man may not question sorrow or God at the first blow but he is likely to do so at the fifth blow. We have taken this vehicle in order to know our real state....
　　　—Ramana Maharshi

All that is not of the Will of God is out of accord with the true Harmony....And nothing that is not in harmony with the Divine order is of any use to you—it does but increase and prolong your suffering....　　*—Henry T. Hamblin*

We are healed of suffering only by experiencing it to the full....
　　　—Marcel Proust

It is because human loves are narrow and confined and mingled with selfishness that they cause suffering. No suffering can result from that Love which is so absolutely pure that it seeks nothing for itself....　　*—James Allen*

Half our sorrows come from setting exalted standards for people and then breaking our hearts when they fail to live up to them....　　*—Alice H. Rice*

The hardships of life are not sent by an unkind destiny to crush, but to challenge....　　*—Sam E. Roberts*

All....suffering can be avoided by realizing that God is the only reality. You are the manifestation of God, a spiritual being emanating from the one and only source, which is God. Your spirit is eternal—you live, breathe and have your being in God. You cannot be separated from God, for God is the totality and the only reality—God "is," nothing else is....
　　　—A Spiritual Warrior

Suffering in any form has as its primary object to impel people to turn towards the Path of Love.....
　　　—Julian P. Johnson

To become the spectator of one's own life is to escape the suffering of life....
　　　—Oscar Wilde

God never punishes. Punishment is always self-inflicted. We bring suffering on ourselves by our wrong actions. If we are conscious that God is acting through us, we never do any wrong. We do wrong only when we forget God....　　*—Papa Ramdas*

Sorrow is a gentle teacher, and reveals many things that would be hard to understand....　　*—Anna Brown Lindsay*

You suffer from yourself alone; no one compels you....　　*—Gautama Buddha*

If you come to see with clarity that the world is only a projection of the mind, you will transcend all suffering....
　　　—Subramania Bharati

Suffering is not an evil, it is the consequence and nearly always the remedy of evil....　　*—Eliphas Levi*

The suffering that comes to us has a purpose....It is trying to teach us something. We should look for its lesson....　　*—Peace Pilgrim*

Life is truly known only to those who suffer, lose, endure adversity and stumble from defeat to defeat....
—*Ryszard Kapuscinski*

Suffering gives us the impetus to escape from our self-limiting ignorance. If God did not send these gifts of suffering and misery, many people would be content to live their whole lives alienated from God and ignorant of their true nature....
—*Annamalai Swami*

Sorrow makes us all children again, destroys all differences of intellect. The wisest knows nothing....
—*Ralph W. Emerson*

Sorrow and suffering give opportunities for growth. Disappointment opens doors to wider fields....
—*Elizabeth Gray Vining*

Sorrow is a kind of rust of the soul, which every new idea contributes in its passage to scour away....
—*Samuel Johnson*

When troubles will come, they are always temporary—nothing lasts forever....
—*Aryeh Kaplan*

Man suffers because of his craving to possess and keep forever things which are essentially impermanent....
—*Alan Watts*

There is no bitterness in life, but what man of earth HAS BROUGHT UPON HIMSELF....
—*Frater Achad*

We humans, not God, create pain and suffering....
—*Mother Teresa*

When there is no longer a cyclone, there is no longer an eye. So the storms, crises and sufferings of life are a way of finding the eye....
—*Bernadette Roberts*

Sorrow washes the eyes with the tears of more perfect understanding....
—*Fred Van Amburgh*

When a man suffers, he ought not to say, "That's bad! That's bad!" Nothing that God imposes upon man is bad....
—*Hasidic saying*

Suffering....we owe to it all that is good in us, all that gives value to life; we owe to it pity, we owe to it courage, we owe to it all the virtues....
—*Anatole France*

To live is to suffer; that we suffer is, at least in large part, our own fault; there is a way to eliminate suffering; the way is open to all; the way to eliminate suffering is to eliminate attachment....
—*William Gerber*

If you know the purpose of suffering—to burn up your ego—you'll even rejoice in it. Suffering is a way of purification. You heat your mind and body to transform it, burning out the undesirable impurities. Just as gold ore is repeatedly heated and cooled to raise its purity, all individuals are purified by the heat of suffering. So accept suffering as it comes....
—*Satchidananda*

God is in all humans, but all humans are not in God; that is the reason they suffer....
—*Ramakrishna*

Suffering turns the mind towards God. Suffering infuses mercy in the heart and softens it. Suffering strengthens. Suffering produces dispassion....Therefore, suffering is a blessing in disguise. It is the best thing in this world....
—*Sivananda*

Trouble and suffering are often extremely useful, because many people will not bother to learn the Truth until driven to do so by sorrow and failure....
—*Emmet Fox*

Suffering has a redeeming quality. Pain and repetition are fixative agents....
—*Irina Tweedie*

When someone beats a rug with a stick, he is not beating the rug–his aim is to get rid of the dust from the veil of I-ness and that dust will not leave all at once. With every cruelty and every blow, it departs little by little, from the heart's face, sometimes in sleep and sometimes in wakefulness.... —*Rumi*

We are never ripe till we have been made so by suffering....
—*Henry W. Beecher*

Man cannot remake himself without suffering. For he is both the marble and the sculptor.... —*Alexis Carrel*

Wisdom comes alone through suffering.... —*Aeschylus*

If you see suffering all around you, it is just a reflection of your own inner suffering. If you want to alleviate suffering, go to the root cause which is the suffering inside yourself....
—*Annamalai Swami*

If you are out of harmony through ignorance, you suffer somewhat; but if you know better and are still out of harmony, then you will suffer a great deal. Suffering pushes you toward obedience to God's will.... —*Peace Pilgrim*

Suffering is caused by desire; desire can be eradicated.... —*Gautama Buddha*

I do not want to die without leaving a record of my belief that suffering can be overcome. For I do believe it. What must one do?...One must submit. Do not resist. Take it. Be overwhelmed. Accept it fully. Make it a part of life. Everything in life that we really accept undergoes a change. So suffering must become Love.... —*Katherine Mansfield*

You add just as much suffering to the world when you take offense as when you give offense.... —*Anonymous*

Know how sublime a thing it is to suffer and be strong....
—*Henry W. Longfellow*

Suffering is separation and separativeness. And suffering is the primary fact for individual life.... —*Da Free John*

Sorrow is a fruit; God does not allow it to grow on a branch that is too weak to bear it.... —*Victor Hugo*

All the frictions, all the uncertainties, all the ills, the sufferings, the fears, the forebodings, the perplexities of life come to us because we are out of harmony with the divine order of things....So long as there is a violation of laws, so long disease and suffering will result.... —*Ralph W. Trine*

It is difficult to make a man miserable while he feels he is worthy of himself and claims kindred to the great God who made him.... —*Abraham Lincoln*

The path of sorrow, and that path alone, leads to the land where sorrow is unknown; no traveler ever reached that blessed abode who found not thorns and briers on his road....
—*William Cowper*

Spiritual suffering is a contradiction in term-symbols; spirit does not suffer; suffering is not spiritual....
—*Sunyata*

To be born is to suffer; to grow old is to suffer; to die is to suffer; to be tied to what is not loved is to suffer; to endure what is distasteful is to suffer. In short, all the results of individuality, of separate self-hood, necessarily involve pain or suffering.... —*Subhadra Bhikshu*

Suffering is a cleansing fire that chars away triviality and restlessness....
—*Louis E. Bisch*

It may serve as a comfort to us, in all our calamities and afflictions, that he that lost anything and gets wisdom by it, is a gainer by the loss....
—*Roger L'Estrange*

Suffering is the surest means of making us truthful to ourselves....
—*Jean Sismondi*

The soul that is without suffering does not feel the need of knowing the ultimate cause of the universe. Sickness, grief and hardships are all indispensable elements in the spiritual ascent....
—*Anandamayi Ma*

No man has affliction enough that is not matured and ripened by it, and made fit for God by that affliction....
—*John Donne*

The more you move towards the goal, all sorrow will cease. Even if there is sorrow, you will become impervious to it. It will not touch you. There will be an inner strength created within you where even sorrow will not have a meaning for you. You will smile even at misfortune and suffering....
—*Chidananda*

Experience is the extract of suffering....
—*Arthur Helps*

People wail aloud that they are suffering and they are destitute, but very few turn away from the sources of their suffering and destitution....
—*Yoga Vasistha*

Tragedy is in the eye of the observer and not in the heart of the sufferer....
—*Ralph W. Emerson*

Every tunnel has its end....
—*Comte de Saint Germaine*

Sorrow is to fall away from God....
—*John of Kronstadt*

Suffering is a very expensive school to attend, but most people learn in no other way....
—*Anonymous*

No substance can be rendered perfect without a long suffering. Great is the error of those who imagine that the philosophers' stone can be hardened without first having been dissolved....
—*Henry Madathanas*

All neurosis is an attempt to avoid legitimate suffering....
—*Carl Jung*

We blame others for our sorrows and misfortunes, not perceiving that we ourselves are the creators of our world....
—*Hazrat Inayat Khan*

In spite of warnings, admonitions, advice, and appeals that he should not submerge himself in the trivial and the transitory, man is still drawn towards misery by defects in his understanding....
—*Sathya Sai Baba*

The whole human race is so miserable and above all so blind that it is not conscious of its own miseries....
—*Comenius*

The cause of all our sufferings is in ourselves alone, not outside....Suffering turns men toward their Creator....
—*Ramana Maharshi*

Love your suffering. Do not resist it, do not flee from it. Give yourself to it. It is only your aversion that hurts, nothing else....
—*Hermann Hesse*

Earth has no sorrow that Heaven cannot heal....
—*Thomas More*

You are not here to cry about the miseries of the human condition, but to change them when you find them not to your liking through joy, strength and vitality that is within you.... —*Seth*

Only one-fourth of the sorrow in each man's life is caused by outside uncontrollable elements; the rest is self-imposed by failing to analyze and act with calmness.... —*George Jackson*

Suffering should lend man to self-inspection.... —*Adolph Buchler*

Affliction preaches awakening. Affliction is the villain who cruelly says to the sufferer, "I shall recruit hope for you, all right." But as it always is in life, he who has to play the villain is never appreciated.... —*Sören Kierkegaard*

To repel one's cross is to make it heavier.... —*Henri F. Amiel*

Some people think that all the world should share their misfortunes, though they do not share in the sufferings of anyone else.... —*Achille Poincelot*

Sorrow, like rain, makes roses and mud.... —*Austin O'Malley*

We are like thirsty souls running away from a spring of fresh water. We run away from that which would bring us what we are seeking. No wonder we have miseries....Miseries come because we do not listen to the voice within.... —*Paramananda*

The way that will relieve your woes on the physical plane will also take you to the highest spiritual realizations. And the way is simple. No resistance.... —*Thaddeus Golas*

A man who suffers before it is necessary suffers more than is necessary.... —*Seneca*

If you are distressed by anything external, the pain is not due to the thing itself but to your estimation of it, and this you have the power to revoke at any moment.... —*Marcus Aurelius*

To be unhappy is only half the misfortune—to be pitied is misery complete.... —*Arthur Schnitzler*

Do not close your eyes before suffering. Find ways to be with those who are suffering by all means, including personal contact and visits....By such means, awaken yourself and others to the reality of suffering in the world.... —*Gautama Buddha*

Man has ever risen nearer to God by altar-stairs of pain and sorrow.... —*Alfred Adler*

If you train yourself to rejoice in suffering, if you think that everything is done by God for one's own betterment and uplift, if you welcome pain as a messenger of God to make you remember Him....then pain will not be pain anymore. Suffering will not be suffering anymore.... —*Sivananda*

Although the world is full of suffering, it is full also of the overcoming of it.... —*Helen Keller*

All worldly pursuits have but one unavoidable and inevitable end, which is sorrow: acquisitions end in dispersion; buildings, in destruction; meetings, in separation; births, in death.... —*Milarepa*

As long as you identify yourself with the body-mind, you are vulnerable to sorrow and suffering.... —*Nisargadatta*

Suffering is a journey which has an end.... —*Matthew Fox*

If you bear the cross unwillingly, you make it a burden, and load yourself more heavily....If you cast away one cross, you will certainly find another, and perhaps heavier....

—*Thomas à Kempis*

God sends us nothing that is too hard or too painful to bear. He proportions all to our strength and abilities. Our trials are suited to our needs as the glove to the hand of the wearer....

—*Alphonsus Liguori*

Sorrow, borne with resentment and bitterness, isolates the soul not only from God, but from her own fellows....

—*Robert Benson*

The more the diamond is cut, the brighter it sparkles; and what seems hard dealing, there God has no end in view but to perfect His people....

—*Thomas Guthrie*

Men suffer all their life long, under the foolish superstition that they can be cheated. But it is impossible for a man to be cheated by anyone but himself....

—*Ralph W. Emerson*

Take sorrow out of your heart, for it is the sister of divided purpose and violent anger.... —*Shepherd of Hermas*

Every time you ascribe your suffering to a source outside your mind you not only perpetuate your hurt, but you divest yourself of the power that God gave you to create a loving and rewarding life.... —*Alan Cohen*

Never to suffer would have been never to have been blessed....

—*Edgar A. Poe*

The diamond cannot be polished without friction, nor man perfected without trials.... —*Confucius*

Men are chained to that which causes suffering because they desire to be so, because they love their chains, because they think their little dark prison of self is sweet and beautiful, and they are afraid that if they desert that prison they will lose all that is real and worth having.... —*James Allen*

Suffering is a device to turn one's thoughts in the direction of God....

—*Sufi saying*

At first one passes some time in suffering from things which seem to come from other persons, or from circumstances outside oneself. Gradually one finds a great part (or all) one's troubles are in oneself.... —*Don J. Chapman*

We are enticed and led astray by our own lusts and the deceitfulness of our own hearts, but the Spirit makes use of the misery which we encounter, so that through our suffering, disappointment and disillusionment we may at length turn toward God.... —*Henry T. Hamblin*

Out of suffering have emerged the strongest souls; the most massive characters are seared with scars....

—*Edwin H. Chapin*

There is no virtue in suffering. In itself, suffering has no value or reward. This is contrary to what confused people like to believe, for suffering fills a place inside them which would feel empty if it were not agitated by pain....

—*Vernon Howard*

To realize that one's creation necessitates one's suffering, that suffering is one of the greatest of God's gifts, is almost to reach a mystical solution of the problem of evil.... —*J. W. Sullivan*

Suffering bravely borne brings inner unfoldment.... —*Paramananda*

Paradoxical as it may seem, God means to not only to make us good, but to make us also happy, by sickness, disaster and disappointment....
—*Cyrus A. Bartol*

Three ways are open to a man who is in sorrow. He who stands on a normal rung weeps, he who stands higher is silent, but he who stands on the topmost rung converts his sorrow into song....
—*Kotzker*

Tears are the best gift of God to suffering man....
—*John Keble*

The ills from which we are suffering have had their seat in the very foundation of human thought....
—*Teilhard de Chardin*

It has done me good to be somewhat parched by the heat and drenched by the rain of life....
—*Henry W. Longfellow*

God washes the eyes by tears until they behold the invisible land where tears shall come no more....
—*Henry W. Beecher*

Without suffering, happiness cannot be understood. The ideal passes through suffering like gold through fire. The heavenly kingdom is attained through effort....
—*Fyodor Dostoyevsky*

All troubles and suffering contain the hidden seeds of good....To shake the mind into wakefulness, God at times sends pain and disease. They serve to open up the eyes to the unrealities of this earthly life....
—*Sivananda*

Suffering is due entirely to clinging or resisting; it is a sign of unwillingness to move on, to flow with life....
—*Nisargadatta*

The greatest of all crosses is self. If we die in part every day, we shall have but little to do on the last. These little daily deaths will destroy the power of the final dying....
—*Francois Fenelon*

Surrender

If one surrenders completely, there will be no one left to ask questions....Surrender can never be regarded as complete as long as the devotee wants this or that from God....
—*Ramana Maharshi*

How seek the way which leadeth to our wishes? By renouncing our wishes. The crown of excellence is renunciation....
—*Hazif Divan*

Nothing relinquished is lost; everything finds its true balance, its equilibrium, in God....
—*Elsie Morgan*

Really, you don't lose anything by renouncing. Instead you become owner of the entire world. A homeless man can claim every home as his own. A pocketless man can thrust his hand into every pocket....
—*Satchidananda*

When water surrenders to the flow of the river it reaches the ocean, so also must we surrender in order to reach our Source....
—*Anonymous*

We must be willing to get rid of the life we've planned, so as to have the life that is awaiting us....The old skin has to be shed before the new one is to come....
—*Joseph Campbell*

Surrender is the secret. I take in God with my inward breath and try to give myself up completely, completely, with my outward breath....
—*Nancy Pope Mayorga*

He that will not surrender himself to God's grace has to suffer worries without end, while the devotee that cultivates the attitude of surrender is free from cares, and therefore happy, even now.... —Lakshmana Sarma

You can find God if you will only seek—by obeying divine laws, by loving people, by relinquishing self-will, attachments, negative thoughts and feelings. And when you find God it will be in the stillness. You will find God within.... —Peace Pilgrim

There was a day when I died....to George Muller, his opinions, preferences, tastes and will—died to the world, its approval or censure—died to the approval or blame even of my brethren and friends—and since then I have studied only to show myself approved unto God.... —George Muller

Spiritual maturity lies in the readiness to let go of everything. The giving up is the first step. But the real giving up is in realizing that there is nothing to give up, for nothing is your own.... —Nisargadatta

I finally learned that my main purpose was to have no purpose, to learn how to give up effort....But why had I been so slow in discovering that by relinquishing I could produce riches.... —Joanna Field

Everything belongs to the man who wants nothing. Having nothing, he possesses all things in life, including life itself. Nothing will be denied the man who denies himself. Having chosen to be utterly solitary he now comes into possession of the most utterly social fact in the universe, the kingdom of God.... —E. Stanley Jones

Whosoever shall seek to save his life shall lose it; and whosoever shall lose his life shall find it.... —Jesus

To be free, to be able to stand up and leave everything behind—without looking back. To say Yes.... —Dag Hammarskjöld

Only he who has become so free from self as to be equally content to be annihilated is fit to enter into the Infinite.... —James Allen

God can only help you if you surrender to God.... —Saradamma

If we surrender to God we do not have to make any choices at all.... —Papa Ramdas

Giving up something in the hope of getting something else in its place is not really giving up.... —U. G. Krishnamurti

Who are you who go about to save them that are lost? Are you saved yourself? Do you know that who would save his own life must lose it? Are you one of the "lost"? Be sure, very sure, that each one of these can teach you as much as, probably more than, you can teach them.... —Edward Carpenter

Renunciation means giving up one's attachment to the things of the world, an attachment based on the wish to possess them.... —Arthur Deikman

What prevents us from total surrender is also the cause of our other troubles. It is our selfish will.... —Piero Ferrucci

There is a way that we can live happily in this miserable world. That way is to give our minds to God.... —Jnanasambandhar

It is the very attempt to have power which makes us powerless. And it is the abandonment of all attempts to have power which blends us with cosmic power, which conquers all....
—*Vernon Howard*

Surrender and all will be well. Throw all responsibility on God. Do not bear the burden....If one surrenders to God, there will be no cause for anxiety. Nothing will affect you....God never forsakes one who has surrendered....
—*Ramana Maharshi*

When surrender is complete, everything is God. Everything that happens is then His action. In that state there is peace, harmony and an absence of thoughts.... —*Annamalai Swami*

The thing we surrender to becomes our power.... —*Ernest Holmes*

Surrendering yourself to God is giving up what you can't keep in order to realize what you can't lose.... —*Shantidasa*

Resignation, surrender or living His Will—they are practically one and the same—As long as the mind is dominant, there's no surrender. There's no living in the Will of the Father, there's no elimination of the ego....
—*Charan Singh*

A completely renounced person has no want at all. And the minute he stops wanting anything, he has his Self....
—*Satchidananda*

The Master gives himself up to whatever the moment brings.... —*Lao-tzu*

If you realize what the real problem is—losing yourself, giving yourself to some higher end....you realize that this itself is the ultimate trial....
—*Joseph Campbell*

What God requires of us, what Life demands of us, is that we surrender ourselves and all that we have, inwardly, in love to the Whole: that we should dedicate our all to service, in love to our fellow man.... —*Henry T. Hamblin*

Surrender does not denote any change in the external mode of life, but a right attitude toward it.... —*Papa Ramdas*

When a man is able to regard his own life as part of a whole....he will no longer struggle in order to obtain anything for himself. This is the surrender of personal rights.... —*Mabel Collins*

In order to let go of something, first you must know what it is....
—*Nisargadatta*

When you surrender to God and agree to be guided from within—life becomes an adventure into the un-known....
—*Anonymous*

Surrender is the most difficult thing in the world while you are doing it; and the easiest when it is done....
—*Bhai Sahib*

Until one is committed, there is hesitancy, the chance to draw back, always ineffectiveness. Concerning all acts of initiative (and creation), there is one elementary truth the ignorance of which kills countless ideas and splendid plans: That the moment one definitely commits oneself, then providence moves too....
—*Johann W. Goethe*

Some people are so immersed in the workings of the ego that they haven't the faintest idea what is meant by subordinating it to another principle. To them the ego is the beginning and the end, the sum of all existence....
—*U. S. Anderson*

Renouncing the world is not enough. It is the invisible things that must be surrendered—the will, the character, everything.... —*Irina Tweedie*

Energy arises from surrender to God. Energy comes from the heart expanding. A small, closed heart—no energy.... —*Sathya Sai Baba*

The true meaning of....surrender is the complete wearing away of the ego-sense, which is individuality.... —*Lakshmana Sarma*

There is a world of difference between submitting to a Divine Will from sullenness and submitting to it knowing that God is Supreme Wisdom; and that someday we will know all that happened, happened for the best.... —*Fulton J. Sheen*

If your mountain will not move, surrender it to God. He will either move it or show you how to turn it into a mine or a monument.... —*Robert Schuller*

To die—for this into the world you came. Yes, to abandon more than you ever conceived as possible: All ideals, plans—even the very best and most unselfish—all hopes and desires.... —*Edward Carpenter*

When opportunity for self-surrender arises, seize it. You will discover the secret in what you had hitherto tried to avoid; indeed, you will find even more.... —*Thomas à Kempis*

Man is too often afraid to surrender. He thinks he will lose something; but one never loses when he gives himself absolutely to God.... —*Turiyananda*

We must empty ourselves to be filled with God. Even God cannot fill what is full.... —*Mother Teresa*

Surrender is giving oneself up to the original cause of one's being. Do not delude yourself by imagining this source to be some God outside oneself. One's source is within oneself. Give yourself up to it.... —*Ramana Maharshi*

By the surrender of self all difficulties are overcome, and there is no error in the universe but the fire of inward sacrifice will burn it up like chaff; no problem, however great, but will disappear like a shadow under the searching light of self-abnegation.... —*James Allen*

Self-surrender is the surrender of all concern. It cannot be done, but it happens spontaneously when you realize your true nature. Verbal self-surrender, even accompanied by feeling, is of little value and breaks down under stress.... —*Nisargadatta*

Surrender refreshes and regenerates. Failure to surrender strains and wearies. Behind every genuine surrender lives a faith fulfilled; behind every failure to surrender lies confidence betrayed.... —*Piero Ferrucci*

There is no way of making a person true unless he gives up his own will. In fact, apart from complete surrender of the will, there is no traffic with God.... —*Meister Eckhart*

Yes God! Yes God! Yes, yes and always yes.... —*Nicolas de Cusa*

The only real surrender is that in which the poise is undisturbed by any adverse circumstance, and the individual, amidst every kind of hardship, is resigned with perfect calm to the will of God.... —*Meher Baba*

If you want to be given everything, give up everything.... —*Lao-tzu*

The great thing is to resign all your interests and pleasures and comfort and fame to God. He who unreservedly accepts whatever God may give him in this world—humiliation, trouble and trial from within or from without—has made a great step towards self-victory.... —*Francois Fenelon*

This surrender of my life to God has never meant that I was turning my back on the world—rather that I was interesting myself in it in a wider and deeper way.... —*Paul Tournier*

There is no loss in total, unreserved self-surrender. It is not at all a bad bargain. It is a mighty gain indeed.... —*Sivananda*

One must realize that no physical or mental effort can take one to God. One must give up, mentally and physically, all idea of reaching God and one must finally throw oneself at God's feet and let him do whatever He wishes with you. When there is complete physical and mental self-surrender, then God's grace takes you to the goal.... —*Saradamma*

When our motive is right, and when our heart is pure, our eye single, and our faith in God—that is, when we cast ourselves utterly and completely upon the inner, sustaining Providential Power of the Universe—then God cannot fail us, something must happen.... —*Henry T. Hamblin*

Surrender can take effect only when it is done with full knowledge as to what real surrender means.... —*Ramana Maharshi*

Surrender does not mean inaction. Surrender is action done on the Divine plane... —*Papa Ramdas*

It is our emptiness and lowliness that God needs and not our plenitude.... —*Mother Teresa*

Teacher

The teacher treads the way; on every span of ground he leaves his footprints clearly cut, which all can see and be assured that he, their master went that way.... —*The Aquarian Gospel*

First, teach a person to develop to the point of his limitation and then—pfft!—break the limitation.... —*Viola Spolin*

Good teaching is one-fourth preparation and three-fourths theatre.... —*Gail Godwin*

All a teacher can do is to put our feet on a path and point the way. No teacher, living or past, can give us the actual understanding of truth. It is wholly dependent upon the individual to make his way to truth.... —*Paul Twitchell*

I have learned silence from the talkative, tolerance from the intolerant and kindness from the unkind. I should not be ungrateful to those teachers.... —*Kahlil Gibran*

No teaching, no theorizing, no philosophizing, no rules of conduct or life will take the place of actual experience.... —*Edward Carpenter*

Learning is a good thing, but in the end it availeth not. Experience, not learning, leads to wisdom and the bliss of immortality... —*William Blake*

The words of the great teachers and guides of humanity are streams of power and light.... —*Mouni Sadhu*

Divine knowledge is realized, not taught.... —*Shirdi Sai Baba*

It is seldom that we go beyond our teachers.... —*Darcy Maxwell*

He who wishes to teach us a truth should not tell it to us, but simply suggest it with a brief gesture.... —*José Ortega y Gasset*

We teachers can only help the work going on, as servants wait upon a master.... —*Maria Montessori*

Teachers are of two breeds, those who teach us how to be, and those who teach us how not to be.... —*Anonymous*

Teaching is like climbing a mountain.... —*Fawn M. Brodie*

We are all teachers; and what we teach is what we learn, and so we teach it over and over again until we learn.... —*A Course In Miracles*

The men who have gone before us have taught us how to live and how to die. We are the heirs of the ages.... —*Sidney Dark*

Your own self is your ultimate teacher. The outer teacher is merely a milestone. It is your inner teacher that will walk with you to the goal, for he is the goal.... —*Nisargadatta*

Much learning will not teach understanding.... —*Heraclitus*

The wise man is always a student. He is ever eager to learn. He never poses to be a teacher....A man of little learning and little understanding is ever eager to teach. He wants to take up the role of preceptor. He is not eager to learn.... —*Sivananda*

The years teach much which the days never know.... —*Ralph W. Emerson*

In all ancient teaching the first demand at the beginning of the way to liberation was: Know thyself.... —*George I. Gurdjieff*

It is nothing short of a miracle that the modern methods of instruction have not yet entirely strangled the holy curiosity of inquiry.... —*Albert Einstein*

A good teacher must be able to put himself in the place of those who find learning hard.... —*Eliphas Levi*

A guru is like a fire; stand too close and you'll get burnt; stand too far away and you won't get heat.... —*Tibetan proverb*

You are your own best teacher.... —*Warren Bennis*

True teaching liberates the student from his teacher. He will find the teacher within himself. This will not make him arrogant or egotistical; rather, he will have a deep sense of humility, as we should when we face the Great Reality.... —*Ernest Holmes*

The teacher, however great, can never give his knowledge to the pupils....although....he can kindle the light if the oil is in the lamp.... —*Hazrat Inayat Khan*

The real purpose of teachers, books and teachings is to lead us back to the kingdom of God within ourselves..... —*Joel Goldsmith*

You will find something more in the woods than in books. Trees and stones will teach you that which you can never learn from masters.... —*St. Bernard*

If you wish to know the road up the mountain, ask the man who goes back and forth on it.... —*Zenrin*

The teacher is really yourself. You have created a teacher to wake you up. The teacher would not be here if you were not dreaming about the teacher....
—*Robert Adams*

We are all teachers of one another during our earthly pilgrimage, some greater teachers than others, but nevertheless, all teachers....
—*Anonymous*

The best teacher is always heart to heart silence.... —*Ramana Maharshi*

A bus driver is the best example of a guru. He is totally involved in taking you to a destination, but he is uninvolved with you as well. His job is to pick you up and to deliver you....
—*Yogi Bhajan*

When God is our teacher, we come to think alike.... —*Xenophon*

The teacher can show you the way. The teacher can inspire you. The teacher can try to give you a little bit of enthusiasm and courage. But you will have to keep your feet yourself on every rung of the spiritual ladder. The teacher cannot do it for you.... —*Gurudev*

Our teachers come in surprising packages. They are not always loving persons in our life. Our greatest teacher may be the person who brings out the worst in us.... —*Shirley Briggs*

All the great spiritual teachers have denied themselves personal luxuries, comforts and rewards, have abjured temporal power, and have lived and taught the limitless and impersonal Truth.... —*James Allen*

A person seeking to escape from prison would be wise to seek the advice of someone who has escaped from that prison; a person seeking God would be wise to seek someone who has found God.... —*Shantidasa*

A teacher affects eternity; he can never tell where his influence stops....
—*Henry Adams*

Give a man a bowl of rice and you feed him for the day; teach a man to grow rice and you feed him for a lifetime....
—*Chinese proverb*

By learning you will teach; by teaching you will learn.... —*Latin aphorism*

There is no reason for us to intentionally impoverish ourselves by not inviting the wisdom of great sages into our lives.... —*Ravi Ravindra*

I give people what they want, so eventually they'll want what I have to give....
—*Shirdi Sai Baba*

No books or gurus can awaken us. They are but signposts. If we study signposts; we can go in the direction pointed to. We should not ignore teachers and books; they show us the way....
—*David Manners*

Gurus and teachers only show the spiritual path, remove doubts and give some inspiration. You are the redeemer....You have to tread the spiritual path yourself.... —*Sivananda*

Every man I meet is my superior in some way. In that, I learn from him....
—*Ralph W. Emerson*

A teacher is one who communicates out of personal experience to someone who is interested in learning....
—*Vimala Thakar*

The best teacher is the one who suggests rather than dogmatizes, and inspires his listener with the wish to teach himself....
—*Edward Bulwer-Lytton*

We all have a [*silent*] teacher from another plane who instructs us and sometimes there are more than one. There are no accidents in the Divine Plan nor does God leave us unattended....
—*Peace Pilgrim*

Every person of learning is finally his own teacher....
—*Thomas Paine*

The teacher who is attempting to teach without inspiring the pupil with desire to learn is hammering on cold iron....
—*Horace Mann*

It is said that someone who acts as an enemy toward you is your best teacher....
—*Dalai Lama*

Teachers and teachings are forms, and ultimately you must go beyond forms....
—*Ram Dass*

For the true student, everything that happens in daily life is a test....
—*Karlfried G. Durckheim*

A real teacher has no teaching. He merely apprises you of the fact that you are no different from himself, the Self. You are already that! What is there to teach? You are already free! The ultimate truth is that there is no teacher, no teaching, and no student....
—*H. W. L. Poonja*

It is the supreme art of a teacher to awaken joy in creative expression and knowledge....
—*Albert Einstein*

To teach another is the best way to learn for yourself....
—*Tryon Edwards*

Too much dependence on another person—even if it be a guru—develops an inferiority complex, a feeling of unworthiness or of weakness....
—*Paul Brunton*

The teaching which is written on paper is not the true teaching. Written teaching is a kind of food for the brain....
—*Shunryu Suzuki*

Teachers can only bring the food; we must eat it to be nourished....
—*Vivekananda*

The true teacher will never stand as the interpreter of truth for another. The true teacher is the one whose endeavor is to bring the one he teaches to a true knowledge of himself and hence his own interior powers that he may become his own interpreter....
—*Ralph W. Trine*

Books are....the most patient of teachers....
—*Charles L. Eliot*

When a teacher allows himself to develop a personality which will carry him to success with his students and audiences, then he is running into problems: he has lost truth....
—*Paul Twitchell*

He teaches who gives, and he learns who receives....
—*Ralph W. Emerson*

What nobler employment or more valuable to the state than that of the man who instructs the rising generation....
—*Cicero*

When the pupil is ready, the teacher will appear....
—*Zen saying*

I hear and then I forget; I see and sometimes I remember; I do and then I understand....
—*Chinese proverb*

The fundamental requirements for meeting a genuine Sat Guru (true teacher) are humility, love, and freedom from the bonds of creeds....
—*Julian P. Johnson*

Doctrine should be such as should make men in love with the lesson, and not with the teacher....
—*Francis Bacon*

The Guru (teacher) is the person who discovers that you have fallen into a wrong road that leads into further and further darkness. For he knows the right road and he is full of love for all who strive to escape the travails of the night, without lamps to light their steps.... —*Sathya Sai Baba*

You teach best what you most need to learn.... —*Richard Bach*

The true teacher defends his pupils against his own personal influence....
—*Amos B. Alcott*

Teaching is lighting a lamp and not filling a bucket.... —*Frank Crane*

Be with the world, but be not of it. Worldly duties are not ties. The world is the best teacher....
—*Sivananda*

The greatest teacher can do no more than walk the way of Truth for himself, and point it out to you; you yourself must walk it for yourself....
—*James Allen*

An impatient man cannot be a teacher.... —*Hillel*

The best teachers of humanity are the lives of great men....
—*Orson S. Fowler*

God said: you must teach, as I taught, without a fee.... —*The Talmud*

The first teacher is the mother; then the next teacher is the father; then the environment; and then God....
—*Yogi Bhajan*

If the teacher doesn't have a sense of humor, something vital is probably missing.... —*James Fadiman*

Any attempt to share an experience would be a very weak dilution of the original experience. A peasant cannot begin to understand the royal life just because he has chanced to catch a momentary glimpse of a king....
—*Anonymous*

We learn to do something by doing it. There is no other way....What we can best learn from good teachers is how to teach ourselves better.... —*John Holt*

When a teacher ceases to learn he ceases to teach. Such a one becomes rigid and fixed—a signpost, perhaps, but not a teacher.... —*Emmanuel*

Not the greatest master can go even one step for his disciple; in himself he must experience each stage of developing consciousness. Therefore, he will know nothing for which he is not ripe....
—*De Lubicz*

It is the function of God's teachers to bring true learning to the world. Properly speaking, it is unlearning that they bring, for that is "true learning" in the world.... —*A Course In Miracles*

Learning is not the accumulation of knowledge. Learning is movement from moment to moment....
—*J. Krishnamurti*

There is one teacher—God himself. We are all pupils.... —*Hazrat Inayat Khan*

Teacher, teach thyself first. Lecturer, lecture to thyself first. Reformers, reform thyself first. Physician, heal thyself first....   —*Sivananda*

In the school of life, everything that happens to you is a teaching, and everyone is your teacher. Think of your experiences as coded messages that are saying, "There is something that you have to learn in order to grow and to expand."...   —*Douglas Bloch*

Men learn while they teach....
                                        —*Seneca*

Earth School may be likened to a great feast in which every known food is made available for sampling and each individual is encouraged to select his own diet....
                          —*Meredith L. Young*

In teaching there should be no class distinctions....   —*Confucius*

There is no teaching until the pupil is brought into the same state or principle in which you are; a transformation takes place, he is you and you are he....
                          —*Ralph W. Emerson*

It is always safe to learn, even from our enemies....   —*Charles C. Colton*

A false teacher cannot even think of urging others toward self-dependence, for he has never found it himself....If you want to know how to find gold, ask a man who has found gold....
                            —*Vernon Howard*

The art of teaching is the art of assisting discovery....   —*Mark Van Doren*

Experience is the best of schoolmasters, only the school-fees are heavy....
                            —*Thomas Carlyle*

To teach is to learn twice....
                            —*Joseph Joubert*

The wisest mind hath something yet to learn....   —*George Santayana*

Seeing much, suffering much, and studying much are the pillars of learning....   —*Benjamin Disraeli*

If the life of a teacher does not measure up to his or her teachings, the teacher is a charlatan....   —*Anonymous*

Nature is the universal teacher. Whatever we cannot learn from the external appearance of Nature, we can learn from her spirit. Both are one....
                            —*Paraceslus*

Thoughts

When we think thoughts...we make thought forms....
                            —*Max Freedom Long*

Thoughts are our enemy. When we are free of thoughts, we are naturally blissful. The gap between thoughts is our true state, it is the real Self. Get rid of thoughts, be empty of them, be in a state of perpetual thoughtlessness....
                            —*Ramana Maharshi*

Do you know that every moment of your life you're creating through thought? You create your own inner conditions; you're helping create the conditions around you....
                            —*Peace Pilgrim*

All things are thought; all life is thought activity. The multitudes of beings are but phases of the one great thought made manifest. Lo, God is Thought, and Thought is God....
                            —*The Aquarian Gospel*

The most lively thought is still inferior to the dullest sensation....

—*David Hume*

If your thoughts are active, and your activities rushed, then you cannot be fully alive and conscious in the moment. Only if your thoughts are quiet and your heart at peace, can you be fully attentive and aware of the unfolding moment....

—*A Spiritual Warrior*

Everyone creates through thought; some people create lack from abundance and others create abundance from lack.... —*Shantidasa*

Nowhere in all the world is there anything solid and real. We tread on thought, our bodies are made of thought, and the whole world is but thought.... —*Krishnaprem*

Nobody can tell you how to think, unless you permit him to do so. Herein lies your greatest glory....and (up to now) one of your greatest sources of trouble.... —*Elinor MacDonald*

One's own thought is one's world. What a person thinks is what he becomes—That is the eternal mystery. If the mind dwells within the supreme Self, One enjoys undying happiness....

—*The Upanishads*

Of all the hard facts of science....I know of none more solid and fundamental than the fact that if you inhibit thought (and persevere), you come at length to a region of consciousness below or behind thought....a realization of an altogether vaster self than that to which we are accustomed....

—*Edward Carpenter*

As soon as you have made a thought, laugh at it.... —*Lao-tzu*

Thoughts of strength both build strength from within and attract it from without. Thoughts of weakness actualize weakness from within and attract it from without....

—*Ralph W. Trine*

What concerns me is not the way things are, but rather the way people think things are.... —*Epictetus*

Creative thinking may simply mean the realization that there is no particular virtue in doing things the way they have always been done....

—*Rudolph Flesch*

You are continuously radiating a mental energy which affects everything and everyone around you....

—*Annamalai Swami*

Thought is a kind of opium; it can intoxicate us, while still wide awake; it can make transparent the mountains and everything that exists....

—*Henri F. Amiel*

Time is of no account with great thoughts. They are as fresh today as when they first passed through their authors' minds, ages ago....

—*Samuel Smiles*

We know what a person thinks not when he tells us what he thinks, but by his actions.... —*Isaac Bashevis Singer*

Just as we walk without thinking, we think without thinking....

—*Marvin Minsky*

Energy follows thought. You actually become what you think....

—*Lynne Namka*

Everything you think vibrates through your body.... —*Bobbie Probstein*

Trying to understand the workings of the universe in terms of linear thought and verbal concepts is a little like trying to see an enormous mural by Michelangelo in the dark with a single dull ray of a flashlight!... —*Ramesh Balsekar*

People who are able to do their own thinking should not allow others to do it for them.... —*Elbert Hubbard*

All that we are is the result of what we have thought; it is founded upon our thoughts, it is made up of our thoughts. If a man speaks or acts with an evil thought, pain follows him, as the wheel follows the foot of the ox that draws the carriage....If a man speaks or acts with a pure thought, happiness follows him, like a shadow that never leaves him.... —*Gautama Buddha*

Nothing is good or bad, but thinking makes it so.... —*William Shakespeare*

A man is what he thinks about all day long....Great men are they who see that the spiritual is stronger than any material force, that thoughts rule the world.... Nothing in the universe is so solid as a thought.... —*Ralph W. Emerson*

Thoughts are there because you think....Thinking is not your nature. Your nature is unalloyed happiness.... —*Ramana Maharshi*

A great many people think they are thinking—when they are really rearranging their prejudices and superstitions.... —*Edward R. Murrow*

Change your thoughts and you change your world.... —*Norman V. Peale*

Every thought you have contributes to truth or to illusion; either it extends the truth or multiplies illusions.... —*A Course In Miracles*

Thoughts are the fathers of deeds. You cannot achieve success or happiness in the world unless you have thoughts that are conducive to happiness or success.... —*Robert Collier*

Figuratively, thought makes giants out of pygmies, and often turns giants into pygmies. History is filled with accounts of how thought has made weak men strong and strong men weak, and we see evidence of its workings around us constantly.... —*Claude Bristol*

We are all living is a vast ocean of thought. Thoughts are forces....They have form, quality and substance.... —*Ralph W. Trine*

Every thought that crops up in the mind is in itself a test to see what one's reaction will be.... —*Nityananda*

Each thought, each feeling and desire, which is not spiritual in nature weighs us down like a frost on the branches of a tree in winter.... —*Omraam M. Aivanhov*

Woe unto the man or woman who suffers from mental indigestion. For it is as the farmer who sows various varieties of seed in the same rows. What would be the crop to come forth? So it is with man's thinking. Find the choice seed and plant it in deep furrows with love. Nurture them with patience and sincerity and there can be no lack, no want, no limitation.... —*Frater Achad*

Thought sees beauty; emotion feels it.... —*Theodore Parker*

Let a prince be guarded with soldiers, attended by counselors, and protected by a fort, yet if his thoughts disturb him, he is miserable.... —*Plutarch*

Thought is a mirror: it shows man the ugliness and the beauty within him....
—*Moses Ibn Ezra*

The power of thought is a mental dynamic of enormously powerful energy. It has been responsible for the soaring of humankind to the heights of achievement, and likewise for the sinking of man to the depths of degradation.... —*Shantidasa*

If we hold our thoughts on worldly, material things and refuse to think of that which is higher and subtler, then our faith in the Unseen will inevitably diminish.... —*Paramananda*

Thought is invisible nature; nature, visible thought.... —*Heinrich Heine*

Make yourselves nests of pleasant thoughts. None of us yet know, for none of us have been taught in early youth, what fairy palaces we may build of beautiful thought—proof against all adversity.... —*John Ruskin*

Always think of what you have to do as easy, and it will become so....
—*Emile Cove*

If we only knew deeply, absolutely, that our smallest act, our smallest thought, has such far-reaching effects; setting forces in motion; reaching out to the galaxy; how carefully we would act and speak and think. How precious life would become in its integral wholeness.... —*Irina Tweedie*

A neurotic thought pattern repeats itself with monotonous regularity.....
—*Thomas Troward*

How did man get out of the Kingdom of God? How did he lose his place in it? By his negative thinking....
—*Robert A. Russell*

The effect of living within a society oftentimes confuses and complicates our stream of thought. It makes people forget who they really are by causing them to be obsessed with what they are not.... —*Lao-tzu*

All that is wrong, is wrong as thinking makes it such.... —*Francis Bacon*

There are no limitations in what you can do except the limitation of your own mind as to what you cannot do. Don't think you cannot. Think that you can.... —*Darwin P. Kingsley*

Think like a man of action, and act like a man of thought.... —*Henri Bergson*

Negative thinking will always lead to failure and nervous prostration; but positive faith—positive thinking—will lead you towards happy, healthy and abundant living.... —*Albert E. Cliffe*

If you realized how powerful your thoughts are, you would never think a negative thought. They can have a powerful influence for good when they're on the positive side, and they can and do make you physically ill when they're on the negative side.... —*Peace Pilgrim*

Our thoughts reverberate in our bodies.... —*Thomas Allen*

Every morning pull yourself up to your full height and stand tall. Then think tall—think big, elevated thoughts. Then go out and act tall. Do that and joy will flow to you.... —*William Danforth*

Thought impregnated with love becomes invincible.... —*Charles Haanel*

Man is a plant which bears thoughts, just as a rose tree bears roses and an apple tree bears apples....
—*Antoine F. D'Olivet*

Of all the known forms of energy, thought is the most subtle, the irresistible force. It has always been operating; but, as far as the great masses of the people are concerned, it has been operating blindly, or, rather, they have been blind to its mighty power, except in the cases of a few here and there....
—*Ralph W. Trine*

To stop thinking is as if one wanted to stop the wind....   —*Chinese proverb*

When I want to think things more pleasant, I close the cupboards of my mind revealing the more unpleasant things of life, and open the cupboards containing the more pleasant thoughts. If I want to sleep, I close up all the cupboards of my mind....
—*Napoleon Bonaparte*

If you don't catch....thoughts as they rise, they sprout, become plants and, if you still neglect them, they grow into great trees....If you can be so indifferent to it that it doesn't sprout or flourish, you are well on the way to escaping from the entanglements of the mind....
—*Annamalai Swami*

Thought is neither good or bad, but like any other force, the use of it determines its character....
—*Ernest Holmes*

Nothing erases unpleasant thoughts more effectively than concentration on pleasant ones....   —*Hans Selye*

The thoughts you think will irradiate you as though you are a transparent vase....   —*Maurice Maeterlinck*

Let no man imagine that he has no influence. Whoever he may be, and wherever he may be placed, the man who thinks becomes a light and a power....   —*Henry George*

If your thoughts center round the body, you will have worries about pains and illnesses, real or imaginary; if they are centered on riches, you will be worried about profit and loss, tax and exemptions, investment and insolvency; if they roam round fame, then you are bound to suffer from the ups and downs of scandal, calumny and jealousy....   —*Sathya Sai Baba*

While we stop to think, we often miss our opportunity....   —*Publilius Syrus*

You are today where your thoughts have brought you; you will be tomorrow where your thoughts take you....
—*Anonymous*

Misery is due to the great multitude of discordant thoughts that prevail in the mind. If all thoughts be replaced by one single thought, there will be no misery....   —*Ramana Maharshi*

I have always thought the actions of men the best interpreters of their thoughts....   —*John Locke*

Our thought is the key which unlocks the doors of the universe....
—*Samuel M. Crothess*

By space the universe embraces me and swallows me up like an atom; by thought I embrace the universe....
—*Blaise Pascal*

We become what we think about most of the time....   —*Earl Nightingale*

Negative thoughts are the world's most communicable disease....
—*Gene E. Clark*

We never do anything well till we cease to think about the manner of doing it....
—*William Hazlitt*

He who is in harmony with Nature hits the mark without effort and apprehends the truth without thinking....
—*Confucius*

When thoughts arise, then do all things arise. When thoughts vanish, then do all things vanish....　—*Huang Po*

Every good thought you think is contributing its share to the ultimate result of your life....　—*Grenville Kleiser*

The way we are going to think tomorrow depends largely on what we are thinking today....　—*David L. Brown*

We are all much more influenced by the thought-forces and mental states of those around us and of the world at large than we have even the slightest conception of....　—*Ralph W. Trine*

Time

To realize the unimportance of time is the gate of wisdom....
—*Bertrand Russell*

Time, whose tooth gnaws away at everything else, is powerless against the truth....　—*Thomas Huxley*

He is the best teacher who makes the best use of his time and that of his pupils. For time is all that is given by God in which to do the work of improvement....　—*Emma H. Willard*

Time can be your joyous friend in the experience of spiritual being; or time can be your dreaded foe that dissolves illusions, breaks your attachments, and destroys your life....
—*A Spiritual Warrior*

Every day is a god, each day is a god, and holiness holds forth in time....
—*Annie Dillard*

Time is not a line, but a series of now-points....　—*Taisen Deshimaru*

In reality, killing time is only the name for one of the multifarious ways by which Time kills us....　—*Osbert Sitwell*

You will never 'find' time for anything. If you want time you must make it....
—*Charles Buxton*

When there is a stain, and nothing will remove it—time will take it away....
—*William Buck*

Know the true value of time! Snatch, seize, and enjoy every moment of it. No idleness, no laziness, no procrastination. Never put off until tomorrow what you can do today....
—*Philip Chesterfield*

Time is an illusion of this earth life....
—*Peace Pilgrim*

Everything is flowing. The Great River of Time takes everything with it, and nothing in this world remains unchanged or stabilized....
—*Mouni Sadhu*

Time is what we want most, but what alas! we use worst....　—*William Penn*

We talk about saving time and killing time when actually we can't do either. We have no choice but to spend it at a constant and flowing rate....
—*Michael LeBeouf*

Those who make the worst use of their time are the first to complain of its shortness....　—*Jean La Bruyere*

We never shall have any more time. We have, and we have always had, all the time there is.... —*Arnold Bennett*

One who is afraid of time becomes a prey of time. But time itself becomes a prey of that one who is not afraid of it.... —*Nisargadatta*

Time is what keeps the light from reaching us. There is no greater obstacle to God than time.... —*Meister Eckhart*

Time is the chief ingredient in judgement.... —*William Feather*

Time is a sort of river of passing events, and strong is its current; no sooner is a thing brought to sight than it is swept by and another takes its place, and this too will be swept away.... —*Marcus Aurelius*

There is no time after time, but there is eternity above time.... —*Paul Tillich*

Time swallows up everything except character; this is the only thing it cannot touch.... —*Paramananda*

Time heals griefs and quarrels, for we change and are no longer the same persons.... —*Blaise Pascal*

A hundred years of living is but a transient moment, the length of which resembles only a spark struck with stone.... —*Chang Po-tuan*

Time is change, transformation, evolution.... —*Isaac L. Peretz*

Time makes more converts than reason.... —*Thomas Paine*

Time is a kindly god....
—*Sophocles*

How you spend your time is more important than how you spend your money. Money mistakes can be corrected, but time is gone forever.... —*David Norris*

If the eons that comprise the lifetime of Earth were compressed into the span of a single year....recorded history would occupy the last 30 seconds of the last day of the year.... —*Carl Sagan*

Time is short, eternity is long.... —*John H. Newman*

Time is a circus always packing up and moving away.... —*Ben Hecht*

When a man sits with a pretty girl for an hour, it seems like a minute. But let him sit on a hot stove for a minute— and it's longer than any hour. That's relativity.... —*Albert Einstein*

We have time enough if we will use it aright.... —*Johann W. Goethe*

Time and patience will remedy every evil.... —*Max Lilienthal*

Time is the teacher most sublime....Time was but created to destroy.... —*Moses Ibn Ezra*

Time is the greatest of all tyrants. As we go on toward age, he taxes our health, limbs, faculties, strength and features.... —*John Foster*

Let a man fix his mind on the reality and, having done this, he will transcend time.... —*Mahabharata*

Time is your greatest advisor. Time will tell you if you can waste your life in illusion and fantasy thoughts, dwelling over past regrets, and future apprehensions. Just ask time, and time will point out that there are no survivors.... —*A Spiritual Warrior*

Time is an unwholesome physician, for it deceives the patient daily with the expectation of the future....
—*Marsilo Ficino*

Waste of time is the most extravagant and costly of all expenses....
—*Theophrastus*

Many situations can be clarified by the passing of time....   —*Theodore I. Rubin*

The great rule of moral conduct is, next to God, to respect time....
—*John K. Lavater*

Our time is a very shadow that passes away....
—*Apocrypha: Wisdom of Solomon*

Time is too slow for those who wait, too swift for those who fear, too long for those who grieve, too short for those who rejoice; but for those who love, time is eternity....   —*Henry Van Dyke*

Time....moves slowly to him whose employment is to watch its flight....
—*Samuel Johnson*

Time heals what reason cannot....
—*Seneca*

The timeless knows the time, the time does not know the timeless....
—*Nisargadatta*

Time is the same for pauper and priest....   —*The Talmud*

Truth

Truth is the exact opposite of the evidence of the senses. It ever declares the perfection of God and all his works....   —*Henry T. Hamblin*

There are no new truths, but only truths that have not been recognized....
—*Mary McCarthy*

Everything that is true is beautiful. The only vanity under the sun is error and falsehood. Even pain and death are beautiful because they are the work which purifies and the transfiguration which delivers....   —*Eliphas Levi*

Truth is as impossible to be soiled by any outward touch, as the sunbeam....
—*John Milton*

The only way into truth is through one's own annihilation; through dwelling a long time in a state of extreme and total humiliation....
—*Simone Weil*

Seek truth first and you may eventually find comfort. Seek comfort at the expense of truth and you may be a patsy for those who are all too willing to leave your wallet and your heart empty....   —*David G. Myers*

Truth will always win in a free and open encounter....   —*Richard Rorty*

Striving is an obstacle....All the time you are doing spiritual practices, the Truth is standing before you, smiling at you....   —*H. W. L. Poonja*

Many men boast of being in possession of Truth who are continually swayed by grief, disappointment, and passion, and who sink under the first little trial that comes along....   —*James Allen*

Fiction reveals truths that reality obscures....   —*Jessamyn West*

The opposite of a fact is falsehood, but the opposite of one profound truth may very well be another profound truth....
—*Neils Bohr*

Truth does not reveal itself in the chatter of conversation, nor can it be coaxed to betray its secrets upon a printed page. Truth speaks only in the deep stillness of silence....
—*Shantidasa*

Truth can never change its nature, whereas untruth is always changing....
—*Tripura Rahasya*

The Truth is one. The rest is illusion....Truth is betrayed by the first attempt at articulation....
—*Yoga Swami*

Truth cannot be your monopoly: it is for the good of all.... —*Vivekananda*

What does it matter how one comes by the truth so long as one pounces upon it and lives by it.... —*Henry Miller*

If you seek the plain truth, be not concerned with right and wrong. The conflict between right and wrong is the sickness of the mind.... —*Taoist saying*

"Be true to yourself" is the highest truth.... —*A Spiritual Warrior*

There are very few human beings who receive the truth complete and staggering by instant illumination. Most of us acquire it fragment by fragment, on a small scale, by successive developments, cellularly, like a laborious mosaic.... —*Anais Nin*

The truth is sort of mysterious and sometimes has nothing to do with facts.... —*Oliver Sacks*

Why shouldn't truth be stranger than fiction? Fiction, after all, has to make sense.... —*Mark Twain*

The ritual of him who has seen the Truth is above anger and kindness, infidelity and religion.... —*Rumi*

I believe that in the end the truth will conquer.... —*John Wycliffe*

No truth remains as truth the moment it is given expression. It becomes a concept.... —*Nisargadatta*

Truth consists in being aware of WHAT IS without thinking about it, relying on spontaneity for such action as may be necessary in the circumstances of the present moment.... —*Ramesh Balsekar*

It is because of the Divine Spirit within us that we seek truth: it is because of the Divine Spirit without us that there is truth to discover.... —*Lily Dougall*

No truth is rigid in its form, no fact is absolute, and no situation can be expressed in dogmatic form. Only half of life can be reasoned. The other half must be creatively experienced....
—*David Seabury*

What is Truth? A difficult question; but I have solved it for myself by saying that it is what the "voice within" tells you.... —*Mohandas Gandhi*

There is no need to seek Truth; only stop having views.... —*Seng-ts'an*

If I held Truth in my hand, I should let it go, for the joy of pursuing it is greater than that of finding it....
—*William Hamilton*

If you want Truth as badly as a drowning man wants air, you will realize it in a split-second.... —*The Upanishads*

Every great advance in natural knowledge has involved the absolute rejection of authority.... —*Thomas Huxley*

Truth is too simple for us; we do not like those who unmask our illusions....
—*Ralph W. Emerson*

Men occasionally stumble over the truth, but most of them pick themselves up and hurry off as if nothing ever happened....
—*Winston Churchill*

Truth is always the same, in spite of the difference in the language employed by those who expound it. God does not change, the Law remains the same, and Principle is always unaltered and unalterable.... —*Henry T. Hamblin*

Truth has never been—can never be—contained in one creed....
—*Mrs. Humphry Ward*

In the mountains of truth, you never climb in vain....
—*Friedrich W. Nietzsche*

The way of truth is like a great road. It is not difficult to know it. The evil is only that men will not seek it....
—*Menicus*

The realization of Truth is brought about by perception, and not in the least by ten millions of acts....
—*Sankara*

Truth is tough. It will not break, like a bubble, at a touch....you may kick it about all day like a football, and it will be round and full at evening....
—*Oliver W. Holmes*

Every man seeks for the truth, but God only knows who has found it....
—*Philip Chesterfield*

If you seek truth, you will not seek to gain a victory by every possible means; and when you have found the truth, you need not fear being defeated....
—*Epictetus*

The truth is always the strongest argument.... —*Sophocles*

Hardly one in ten thousand will have the strength of mind to ask himself seriously and earnestly, "Is that true?"...
—*Arthur Schopenhauer*

Truth does not change; if truth were to change, truth would not be truth....
—*Anonymous*

Truth is not introduced into the individual from without, but was within all the time.... —*Sören Kierkegaard*

Truth is always paradoxical....
—*Henry D. Thoreau*

There are many truths of which the full meaning cannot be realized until personal experience has brought it home....
—*John S. Mill*

Whenever a man or a woman shuts himself or herself to the entrance of truth on account of intellectual pride, preconceived opinions, prejudices, or for whatever reason, there is a great law which says that truth in its fullness will come to that one from no source....
—*Ralph W. Trine*

The truth is more important than facts.... —*Frank L. Wright*

We know the truth; not only by reason, but also by the heart....
—*Blaise Pascal*

A lively, disinterested, persistent liking for truth is extraordinarily rare....
—*Henri F. Amiel*

Whatever is only almost true is quite false, and among the most dangerous of errors; being quite so near truth, it is more likely to lead astray....
—*Henry W. Beecher*

You shall know the truth and the truth shall make you free.... —*Jesus*

It is easier to perceive error than to find truth, for the former lies on the surface and is easily seen, while the latter lies in the depth, where few are willing to search for it.... —*Johann W. Goethe*

Because God lives within you, then truth lives within you.... —*Albert E. Cliffe*

Self is the denial of Truth. Truth is the denial of self. As you let self die, you will be reborn in Truth. As you cling to self, Truth will be hidden from you.... —*James Allen*

To love the truth is to refuse to let oneself be saddened by it.... —*André Gide*

The man who finds a truth lights a torch.... —*Robert Ingersoll*

Truth will always triumph; do not doubt this in the least.... —*Sathya Sai Baba*

There is nothing so powerful as truth and nothing so strange.... —*Daniel Webster*

Truth is the pearl without price. One cannot obtain truth by buying it—all you can do is to strive for spiritual truth and when one is ready, it will be given freely.... —*Peace Pilgrim*

I cannot comprehend how any man can want anything but the truth.... —*Marcus Aurelius*

The name of God is Truth.... —*Hindu saying*

Truth is incontrovertible. Panic may resent it; ignorance may deride it; malice may distort it; but there it is.... —*Winston Churchill*

Truth conquers all.... —*Latin proverb*

The fundamental truths are all men's property. Whether or not we live by them, we all know them, with deep instinctiveness.... —*J. Donald Adams*

We must be true inside, true to ourselves, before we can know a truth that is outside us.... —*Thomas Merton*

Tis strange—but true; for truth is always strange, stranger than fiction.... —*George Byron*

Truth is a jewel which should not be painted over; but it may be set to advantage and shown in good light.... —*George Santayana*

The language of truth is unadorned and simple.... —*Marcellinus Ammianus*

Truth and love are two of the most powerful things in the world; and when they both go together they cannot easily be withstood.... —*Ralph Cudworth*

Without error there could no such thing as Truth.... —*Chinese proverb*

Every truth passes through three stages before it is recognized. In the first it is ridiculed, in the second it is opposed, in the third it is regarded as self-evident.... —*Arthur Schopenhauer*

There is an inmost center in all of us where Truth abides in fullness.... —*Robert Browning*

Truth is never realized by the weak.... —*Ramakrishnananda*

Truth is not only the fulfillment of our own being; it is that by which things outside of us have an existence.... —*Confucius*

Emancipation from error is the condition of real knowledge....
—*Henri F. Amiel*

The greatest and noblest pleasure which men can have in this world is to discover new truths; and the next is to shake off old prejudices....
—*Frederick the Great*

Truth, like light, blinds. Falsehood, on the contrary, is a beautiful twilight that enhances every object....
—*Albert Camus*

Accept the truth; whatever the source....take the pearls from the sea, the gold from the dust, and the roses from amidst the thorns....
—*Emmanuel*

The deepest truths are the simplest and the most common....
—*Frederick Robertson*

He who would claim to have all the truth and the only truth is a bigot, a fool, or a knave.... —*Ralph W. Trine*

Truth exists, only falsehood has to be invented.... —*Georges Braque*

He who loves the Truth and subdues his whole being to the love of Truth shall find it.... —*Bhagavad-Gita*

Nothing is too amazing to be true....
—*M. Faraday*

A man who seeks truth will never find it. Truth is in what IS and that is the beauty in it.... —*Sunyata*

The truth does not have to utter a word; it is just there. It speaks of itself; it is the open book of the scripture of life. It is like the light of the sun....
—*Vilayat I. Khan*

Truths turn into dogma the moment they are disputed....
—*G. K. Chesterton*

Sit down before fact as a little child, be prepared to give up every preconceived notion, follow humbly wherever and to whatever abyss nature leads, or you shall learn nothing....
—*Thomas Huxley*

Never to have seen the truth is better than to have seen it and not acted upon it.... —*Anonymous*

The plain truth is too simple for the seeker of complexity, who is looking for things he cannot understand....
—*Hazrat Inayat Khan*

There is no God higher than Truth....
—*Mohandas Gandhi*

The truth is men have lost their belief in the Invisible....it is no longer a worship of the Beautiful and Good, but a calculation of the Profitable....
—*Thomas Carlyle*

An intimate truth is also a universal truth.... —*John Cournos*

Truth is something you stumble into when you think you're going someplace else.... —*Jerry Garcia*

Truth is a diamond that scratches every other stone.... —*Shantidasa*

To live in the presence of great truths and eternal laws—that is what keeps a man patient when the world ignores him and calm and unspoiled when the world praises him....
—*Honoré de Balzac*

The exact contrary of what is generally believed is often the truth....
—*Jean La Bruyere*

Once we imagine that we have grasped the truth of life, the truth has vanished, for truth cannot become anyone's property, the reason being that truth is life, and for one person to think that he possesses all truth is a manifest absurdity.... —*Alan W. Watts*

A truth that's told with bad intent beats all the lies you can invent.... —*William Blake*

Truth is the center of the circle.... —*Abraham Ibn Ezra*

Truth does not change because it is, or is not, believed by a majority of the people.... —*Giordano Bruno*

Every truth we see is one to give to the world, not to keep to ourselves alone.... —*Elizabeth C. Stanton*

Truth makes the face of that person shine who speaks and owns it.... —*Robert South*

We must never throw away a bushel of truth because it happens to contain a few grains of chaff.... —*Arthur Stanley*

The simplest questions are the hardest to answer.... —*Northrop Frye*

Truth is our most common synonym for God and can carry only one message: the standard of God. Truth cannot be qualified as bad truth, better Truth or good Truth. Truth is just Truth! It never changes.... —*James B. Schafer*

Nature has planted in our minds an insatiable longing to see the truth.... —*Cicero*

Truth is like light; you must be accustomed to it gradually; otherwise it dazzles you.... —*Allan Kardec*

We cannot get hold of the truth with a logical mind....Truth cannot be encompassed by facts.... —*Darwin Gross*

The city of truth cannot be built on the swampy ground of skepticism.... —*Albert Schweitzer*

Truth always expresses itself with the greatest simplicity.... —*Pierre Schmidt*

The deepest truth blooms only from the deepest love.... —*Heinrich Heine*

Though the sages speak in diverse ways, they express one and the same Truth.... —*Srimad Bhagavatam*

Truth by her own simplicity is known.... —*Robert Herrick*

I arrived at Truth, not by systematic reasoning and accumulation of proofs but by a flash of light which God sent into my soul.... —*Al-Ghazali*

To seek for the truth, for the sake of knowing the truth, is one of the noblest objects a man can live for.... —*Dean Inge*

He who is not true himself will not see the truth.... —*Paracelsus*

Hard are the ways of truth, and rough to walk.... —*John Milton*

The measure of a man's truth is the measure of his love, and Truth is far removed from him whose life is not governed by Love.... —*James Allen*

Man can live his truth, his deepest truth, but cannot speak it.... —*Archibald MacLeish*

Know the truth and you will know its Master.... —*Shem Tob Falaquera*

Truth may be stretched, but cannot be broken, and always gets above falsehood, as oil does above water....
—*Miguel de Cervantes*

The greatest friend of truth is Time, her greatest enemy is Prejudice, and her constant companion is Humility....
—*Charles C. Colton*

When once we KNOW the Truth, no one can take it away from us. We have entered into the Eternal....When we KNOW the Truth....we enter into Reality: we see things as they are in God, and not as they falsely appear to the senses. All problems are solved, and all our questions answered; or, rather, they are transcended, and we find there are no problems to be solved and no questions to be answered, simply because we KNOW....
—*Henry T. Hamblin*

We forget that Truth is self-sufficient and self-sustaining and does not require human hand to protect it....
—*Paramananda*

Truth that has merely been learned is like an artificial limb, a false tooth, a waxen nose, it adheres to us only because it is put on. But truth acquired by thought of our own is like a natural limb, it alone belongs to us....
—*Arthur Schopenhauer*

Truth has no degrees. The sea has the same level at its greatest depth as that point where it touches the shore....
—*Douglas Meador*

Whoever undertakes to set himself up as a judge in the field of Truth and Knowledge is shipwrecked by the laughter of the gods.... —*Albert Einstein*

There is no negotiation with truth....
—*Ferdinand Lassalle*

The way to combat noxious ideas is with other ideas! The way to combat falsehoods is with truth....
—*William O. Douglas*

Truth is not to be found by anybody who has not got an abundant sense of humility. If you would swim on the bosom of the ocean of Truth you must reduce yourself to zero....
—*Mohandas Gandhi*

To love God and love the truth are one and the same.... —*Silvio Pellico*

Truth has no special time of its own. Its hour is now—always....
—*Albert Schweitzer*

Spiritual truth should not be sold, lest the seller be injured spiritually. You lose any spiritual contact the moment you commercialize it. Those who have the truth would not be packaging it and selling it, so anyone who is selling it really does not possess it....
—*Peace Pilgrim*

A truth does not become greater by repetition.... —*Maimonides*

War

When the rich wage war, it's the poor who die....
—*Jean-Paul Sartre*

The cannon thunders....limbs fly in all directions....one can hear the groans of victims and the howling of those performing the sacrifice....it's Humanity in search of happiness....
—*Charles Baudelaire*

If it's natural to kill why do men have to go into training to learn how?...
—*Joan Baez*

We seem always ready to pay the price for war. Almost gladly we give our time and our treasure—our limbs and even our lives—for war. But we expect to get peace for nothing.... —*Peace Pilgrim*

Minds are conquered not by arms, but by love and magnanimity.... —*Baruch Spinoza*

The most disadvantageous peace is better than the most just war.... —*Erasmus*

Can anything be more ridiculous than that a man has a right to kill because he dwells on the other side of the water, and because his prince has a quarrel with mine, although I have none with him.... —*Blaise Pascal*

When people talk about war I vow with all beings to raise my voice in the chorus and speak of original peace.... —*Robert Aiken*

We are mad not only individually, but nationally. We check manslaughter and isolated murders, but what of war and the much-vaulted crime of slaughtering whole people.... —*Seneca*

In peace, sons bury their fathers; in wars, fathers bury their sons.... —*Herodotus*

It takes twenty years or more of peace to make a man; it takes only twenty seconds of war to destroy him.... —*Baudouin I*

All wars are wars among thieves who are too cowardly to fight and therefore induce the young members of the world to do the fighting for them.... —*Emma Goldman*

To oppose something is to maintain it.... —*Ursula K. LeGuin*

Fighting is like champagne. It goes to the heads of cowards as quickly as of heros. Any fool can be brave on a battlefield when it's be brave or else be killed.... —*Margaret Mitchell*

I hate war as only a soldier who has lived it can, only as one who has seen its brutality, its futility, its stupidity.... —*Dwight D. Eisenhower*

I have known war as few men now living know it. Its very destructiveness on both friend and foe has rendered it useless as a means of settling international disputes.... —*Douglas MacArthur*

The best general is the one who never fights.... —*Sun Tzu*

War is the child of pride, and pride the daughter of riches.... —*Jonathan Swift*

You can no more win a war than you can win an earthquake.... —*Jeannette Rankin*

War is nothing more than the continuation of politics by other means.... —*Carl von Clausewitz*

The first and most imperative necessity in war is money, for money means everything else—men, guns, ammunition.... —*Ida Tarbell*

During war we imprison the rights of man.... —*Jean Giraudoux*

Kill a man and you are a murderer. Kill millions and you are a conqueror.... —*Jean Rostand*

The most persistent sound which reverberates through man's history is the beating of war drums.... —*Arthur Koestler*

War prefers its victims young.... —*Sophocles*

A "just war" is a contradiction in terms....   —*John Quinn*

There is a war going on at the present moment. What does it signify? It signifies that several millions of sleeping people are trying to destroy several millions of other sleeping people. They would not do this, of course, if they were awake....   —*George I. Gurdjieff*

He who is the author of war lets loose the whole contagion of hell and opens a vein that bleeds a nation to death....   —*Thomas Paine*

Nothing....marks man's unreason as positively as war. Indeed, what folly to kill one another for interests often imaginary....   —*Mary W. Montagu*

I find war detestable, but even more detestable are those who praise war without participating in it....   —*Romain Rolland*

Anyone who has ever looked into the glazed eyes of a soldier dying on the battlefield will think hard before starting a war....   —*Otto von Bismarck*

War: first, one hopes to win; then, one expects the enemy to lose; then, one is satisfied that he too is suffering; in the end, one is surprised that everyone has lost....   —*Karl Kraus*

Even fighting in self defense is wrong, though it is higher than fighting in aggression. There is no "righteous", indignation because indignation comes from not recognizing sameness in all things....   —*Vivekananda*

You cannot qualify war in harsher terms than I will. War is cruelty, and you cannot refine it....   —*William Sherman*

War would end if the dead could return....   —*Stanley Baldwin*

Wars are not fought for territory, but for words. Man's deadliest weapon is language. He is as susceptible to being hypnotized by slogans as he is to infectious diseases....   —*Arthur Koestler*

War's a profanity, because let's face it, you've got two opposing sides trying to settle their differences by killing as many of each other as they can....   —*Norman Schwarzkopf*

War is only a cowardly escape from the problems of peace....   —*Thomas Mann*

To my mind, to kill in war is not a whit better than to commit ordinary murder....   —*Albert Einstein*

The world does not encourage a perfectly rational army, because a perfectly rational army would run away....   —*G. K. Chesterton*

There never was a time when, in my opinion, some way could not be found to prevent the drawing of a sword....   —*Ulysses S. Grant*

War is the greatest of all crimes; and yet there is no aggressor who does not color his crime with the pretext of justice....   —*Voltaire*

Wars will exist until that distant day when the conscientious objector enjoys the same reputation and prestige that the warrior does today....   —*John F. Kennedy*

Armament is an important factor in war, but not the decisive factor....Man, not material, forms the decisive factor....   —*Mao Tse-tung*

The first casualty when war comes is truth....   —*Hiram Johnson*

Patriotism is a kind of religion; it is the egg from which wars are hatched....
—*Guy de Maupassant*

The greatest curse that can be entailed on mankind is a state of war....
—*Sydney Smith*

The appalling thing about war is that it kills all love of truth....
—*Georg Brandes*

Every gun that is made, every warship launched, every rocket fired, signifies in the final sense a theft from those who are hungry and are not fed, those who are cold and not clothed....
—*Dwight D. Eisenhower*

Every war is a national misfortune....
—*Helmuth von Moltke*

They wrote in the old days that it is sweet and fitting to die for one's country. But in modern war there is nothing sweet and fitting in your dying. You will die like a dog for no good reason....
—*Ernest Hemingway*

Worse than war is the fear of war....
—*Seneca*

Preparation for war is a constant stimulus to suspicion and ill will....
—*James Monroe*

War is the unfolding of miscalculations....
—*Barbara Tuchman*

There is no such thing as an inevitable war. If war comes it will be from the failure of human wisdom....
—*Bonar Law*

War is fear cloaked in courage....
—*William Westmoreland*

There will be no veterans of World War III....
—*Walter Mondale*

War should belong to the tragic past, to history; it should find no place on humanity's agenda for the future....
—*John Paul II*

We hear war called murder. It is not: it is suicide....
—*Ramsay MacDonald*

The human race is a family. Men are brothers. All wars are civil wars....
—*Adlai Stevenson*

If war no longer occupied men's thoughts and energies, we would, within a generation, put an end to all serious poverty throughout the world....
—*Bertrand Russell*

To fight and conquer in all our battles is not supreme excellence; supreme excellence consists in breaking the enemy's resistance without fighting....
—*Sun Tzu*

If sunbeams were weapons of war, we would have had solar energy long ago....
—*George Porter*

The most important wars in history were the result of trivial causes....
—*Fred Van Amburgh*

Wars can be prevented just as surely as they can be provoked, and we who fail to prevent them must share in the guilt of the dead....
—*Omar Bradley*

War is an instrument entirely inefficient toward redressing wrong; and multiplies, instead of indemnifying losses....
—*Thomas Jefferson*

Wars do not end wars....
—*Henry Ford*

Older men declare war. But it is youth that must fight and die....
—*Herbert Hoover*

Why is there war? The real problem is immaturity. With real maturity war would be impossible. It would never be considered as a solution of problems between men.... —*Peace Pilgrim*

War is not an adventure. It is a disease. It is like typhus.... —*Antoine de Saint-Exupery*

The guns and the bombs, the rockets and the warships, all are symbols of human failure.... —*Lyndon B. Johnson*

Sometime they'll give a war and nobody will show.... —*Carl Sandburg*

If there is anything in which earth more than any other, resembles hell, it is its wars.... —*Albert Baines*

War is delightful to those who have had no experience of it.... —*Erasmus*

Wars occur because people prepare for conflict, rather than peace....War can be abolished forever by providing clothing, food, and housing, instead of bombers, destroyers and rockets.... —*Trygve Lie*

Patriotism is the passion of fools and the most foolish of passions.... —*Arthur Schopenhauer*

Men will fight and die without knowing what they are fighting and dying for.... —*Douglas MacArthur*

War is low and despicable, and I had rather be smitten to shreds than participate in such doings. Such a stain upon humanity should be erased without delay.... —*Albert Einstein*

To call war the soil of courage and virtue is like calling debauchery the soil of love.... —*George Santayana*

It would be true to say that no one believes that war pays.... —*Norman Angell*

No amount of treaties can be relied on to prevent war, so long as the nations continue to have and exercise the unrestricted right of arming themselves against each other.... —*Robert Cecil*

War. There is no solution for it. There is never a conqueror. The winner generates such hatred that he is ultimately defeated.... —*Michel Simon*

War is nothing but a duel on a larger scale.... —*Carl von Clausewitz*

The grim fact is that we prepare for war like precious giants and for peace like retarded pygmies.... —*Lester Pearson*

Peace remains the hope of the wise, but war is the history of men.... —*Charles de Gaulle*

Give me the money that has been spent in war, and I will clothe every man, woman and child in an attire of which kings and queens would be proud. I will build a school house in every valley over the whole earth.... —*Charles Sumner*

War is nothing less than a temporary repeal of the principles of virtue.... —*Robert Hall*

War is that mad game the world so loves to play.... —*Jonathan Swift*

War is death's feast.... —*George Herbert*

Patriotism is a beautiful thing, it is well to love my country, but why should I love my country more than I love others? If I love my own and hate others, I show my limitations.... —*Ralph W. Trine*

War is a contagion....
—*Franklin D. Roosevelt*

Peace is the happy natural state of man; war is corruption and disgrace....
—*James Thomson*

War is the science of destruction....
—*John S. C. Abbot*

Wars are not "acts of God." They are caused by man, by man-made institutions, by the way in which man has organized society. What man has made, man can change....
—*Frederick M. Vinson*

War is that condition which uses man's best to man's worst....
—*Harry E. Fosdick*

War settles nothing....
—*Dwight D. Eisenhower*

Wealth

Two of the hardest things to accomplish in this world are to acquire wealth by honest effort and having gained it, to learn how to use it properly....
—*Elmer H. Bobst*

Wealth is conspicious, but poverty hides....
—*James Reston*

When you pile up riches, fear and anxiety are also piling up in proportion....
—*Sathya Sai Baba*

Most of the rich people I've known have been fairly miserable....
—*Agatha Christie*

There is no wealth but life....That country is the richest which nourishes the greatest number of noble and happy human beings....
—*John Ruskin*

The imperishable, inexhaustible wealth is the spiritual wealth. No thief can plunder this. He who has this wealth is the richest man....even if he is clad in rags, even if he has nothing to eat. He is the King of Kings. All other wealthy persons in the world are verily poor. They are beggers despite their material possessions....
—*Sivananda*

The God of this century is wealth. To succeed one must have wealth. At all costs one must have wealth....
—*Oscar Wilde*

We cannot hope to possess other true riches than those we already bear within us, and we should use them and not neglect them, but they are....so familiar to us that they no longer appear of any value....
—*Pierre Schmidt*

No one has had the courage to memorialize his wealth on his tombstone. A dollar sign would not look good there....
—*Corra M. Harris*

Surplus wealth is a sacred trust which its possessor is bound to administer in his lifetime for the good of the community....
—*Andrew Carnegie*

Wealth acquired through an insecure lifestyle that is marred by uncertainty, instability and excessive efforts is no wealth at all....
—*Tom Seeley*

No man can tell whether he is rich or poor by turning to his ledger. It is the heart that makes a man rich. He is rich according to what he is, not according to what he has....
—*Henry W. Beecher*

The longer I live, the more I grow in the opinion that it is useless to pile up wealth....
—*Francoise de Maintenon*

The more wealth, the more worry....
—*Hillel*

The fountains are with the rich, but they are no better than a stagnant pool till they flow in streams to the laboring people.... —*Catherine M. Sedgwick*

This is surely a short cut to wealth. If one wants nothing he has everything.... —*Julian P. Johnson*

Wealth and happiness do not dwell together. Rare is that wealthy man who does not have rivals and enemies who scandalize him.... —*Yoga Vasistha*

Real riches consist not in the abundance of goods but in the paucity of wants.... —*Alfred Marshall*

Man's greatest wealth is to live on a little with contented mind; for a little is never lacking.... —*Julius Caesar*

A poor person who is unhappy is in a better position than a rich person who is unhappy because the poor person has hope. He thinks money would help.... —*Jean Kerr*

A man's true wealth hereafter is the good he does in this world to his fellow-man.... —*Mohammed*

A stingy person will always be poor, a generous person always rich.... —*Anonymous*

The idea of hoarding money for the selfish satisfaction of being considered rich is pretty good proof that you cannot appreciate the magic influence of a beautiful sunset.... —*Fred Van Amburgh*

Most rich people do not know how poor they really are.... —*Shantidasa*

Wealth is affliction disguised as good.... —*Bahya*

Wealth beyond a certain amount cannot be used, and when it cannot be used, then it becomes a hindrance rather than an aid, a curse rather than a blessing.... —*Ralph W. Trine*

Even if one possessed the wealth of the whole world, but had no love for God, that man would be poor.... —*Chidananda*

The greatest wealth is to live content with little, for there is never want where the mind is satisfied.... —*Lucretius*

Who trusts in his riches shall fall.... —*Old Testament*

Riches harden the heart faster than boiling water an egg....from poverty our own power can save us, from riches only divine grace.... —*Ludwig Boerne*

As wealth is power, so all power must infallibly draw wealth to itself by some means or other.... —*Edmund Burke*

Wealth is not a deterrent to self-realization or to true happiness, if enjoyed with a feeling of detachment....To enjoy wealth with a feeling of attachment is to be always aware that wealth is not permanent, as also that, by itself, it is not the giver of true happiness and eternal peace.... —*Deepa Kodikal*

Wealth is the diploma of slavery....A great fortune is a great slavery.... —*Seneca*

Every man is rich or poor according to the proportion between his desires and his enjoyments.... —*Samuel Johnson*

The wealth of a man is the number of things which he loves and blesses, which he is loved and blessed by.... —*Thomas Carlyle*

You are like a traveler who comes and goes. You accumulate wealth and take pride in your riches. But when you leave, you take nothing with you. You came into the world with your fists clenched, but when you go, your hands will be open....　　　*—Kabir*

Wealth is like sea-water; the more we drink, the thirstier we become....
　　　　　—Arthur Schopenhauer

The only thing wealth does for some people is to make them worry about losing it....　　　*—Comte de Rivarol*

All amassing of wealth or hoarding of wealth above and beyond one's legitimate needs is theft....
　　　　　—Mohandas Gandhi

To try to extinguish the desire for riches with money is like trying to quench a fire with butterfat....　*—Hindu saying*

Riches are apt to betray a man into arrogance....　　*—Joseph Addison*

Great wealth can be like a huge sledge hammer in one's hand—you try to touch gently with it, you cannot, it smashes at every touch....
　　　　　—Gerald Heard

Ill-gotten wealth is never stable....
　　　　　—Euripides

Real wealth is the soul in repose....
　　　　　—Samuel Hoffenstein

Riches do not consist in the possession of treasure, but in the use made of them....　　*—Napoleon Bonaparte*

Who is rich? He who rejoices in his lot....　　　*—Tonna Ben Zona*

Riches are not forbidden, but the pride of them is....　*—John Chrysostom*

Riches do not delight so much with their possession, as torment us with their loss....　　*—Samuel Gregory*

Without a rich heart, wealth is an ugly beggar....　　*—Ralph W. Emerson*

The problem of our age is the proper administration of wealth, so that the ties of brotherhood may still bind together the rich and poor in harmonious relationship....
　　　　　—Andrew Carnegie

The one who has come into the realization of the higher life no longer has a desire for the accumulation of enormous wealth, anymore than he has a desire for any other excess....
　　　　　—Ralph W. Trine

No wealth in the world can help humanity forward, even in the hands of the most devoted worker in this cause....　　*—Albert Einstein*

To whom can riches give repute or trust, content or pleasure, but to the good and just....　*—Alexander Pope*

Riches prick us with a thousand troubles in getting them, as many cares in preserving them, and yet more anxieties in spending them, and with grief in losing them....　　*—Jean P. Camus*

Very few men acquire wealth in such a manner as to receive pleasure from it....
　　　　　—Henry W. Beecher

The rich who only use their wealth for selfish purposes are sowing the seeds of eventual poverty. All that is not given is lost....　　　*—Shantidasa*

The desire to gain wealth and the fear to lose it are our chief breeders of cowardice and propagators of corruption....
　　　　　—William James

There is nothing so characteristic of narrowness and littleness of soul as the love of riches; and there is nothing more honorable or noble than indifference to money....   —*Cicero*

The riches that you should strive to amass are not fields or factories, bungalows or bank balances, but wisdom and experience of oneness with the grandeur of the Universe and the force that runs it without a hitch....
                    —*Sathya Sai Baba*

Wealth is like a viper, which is harmless if a man knows how to take hold of it; but if he does not, it will twine round his hand and bite him....
                    —*St. Clement*

If we foster our attention on what we have rather than what we lack, a very little wealth is sufficient....
                    —*Francis Johnson*

One of the main reasons wealth makes people unhappy is that it gives them too much control over what they experience. They try to translate their own fantasies into reality instead of tasting what reality itself has to offer....
                    —*Philip Slater*

To have a tranquil mind, a clean, calm, conscientious purpose, a few true friends, good health, a happy home, a sufficient amount saved to guarantee against any embarrassment from want, means that you are wealthy....
                    —*Fred Van Amburgh*

The advantages of wealth are greatly exaggerated....   —*Amasa L. Stanford*

Of all the riches that we hug, of all the pleasures we enjoy, we can carry no more out of this world than out of a dream....   —*James Bonnell*

Wealthy men are generally insolvent and arrogant; their possession of wealth affects their understanding; they feel as if they have every good thing that exists; wealth becomes a sort of standard for everything else, and therefore they imagine there is nothing it cannot buy....   —*Aristotle*

Men who think they possess their wealth are on the contrary completely possessed by it....
                    —*Ralph W. Trine*

A rich man is nothing but a poor man with money....   —*W. C. Fields*

To be rich is not the end, but only a change of worries....   —*Epicurus*

Let us not envy some men their accumulated riches; their burden would be too heavy for us; we would not sacrifice, as they do, health, quiet, honor and conscience, to obtain them....
                    —*Jean La Bruyere*

That man is rich whose pleasures are the cheapest....   —*Henry D. Thoreau*

The best and safest way of getting wealth is to work for it....
                    —*Queen Elizabeth of Rumania*

He is richest who is content with the least, for content is the wealth of nature....   —*Socrates*

He is poor who is dissatisfied; he is rich who is contented with what he has; and he is richer who is generous with what he has....   —*James Allen*

Wealth has never given happiness but has often hastened misery....
                    —*Martin F. Tupper*

The amassment of wealth is one of the worst species of idolatry, no idol more debasing....   —*Andrew Carnegie*

It is neither wealth or splendor, but tranquility and occupation, which gives happiness.... —*Thomas Jefferson*

People with material wealth and enjoyments do not generally feel the necessity to think of God....Man depends upon wealth and glory–the so-called good things for his joy. They are illusive. The joy you receive from them is a flicker. Next second the light is gone and you are enveloped in the darkness.... —*Papa Ramdas*

Wisdom

W isdom is the end attained, the prize which has been offered. God gives it to those who deserve it, nobody brings it with them at birth.... —*Eliphas Levi*

The heart of a wise man lies quiet like still water.... —*Cameroonian proverb*

Wisdom is not gained by traveling afar, but by standing still; not by thought, but by the absense of thought.... —*Anonymous*

The wisest man simply has nothing to say. He realizes that all thoughts, words and acts and even enlightenment are only relative....The very wisest spiritual soul knows for a fact that he is ignorant and understands nothing, for his knowledge is relative unto a higher reality.... —*A Spiritual Warrior*

The sage has no creed of his own; and the reason is that he is egoless.... —*Lakshmana Sarma*

Wisdom never kicks at the iron walls it can't bring down.... —*Olive Schreiner*

Wisdom lies neither in fixity nor in change, but in the dialectic between the two.... —*Octavio Paz*

Though a man be learned if he does not apply his knowledge, he resembles the blind man, who, lamp in hand, cannot see the road.... —*Tibetan saying*

The greatest wisdom is not to be wise.... —*Catherine Willoughby*

The only competition worthy a wise man is with himself.... —*Anna B. Jameson*

The beginning of wisdom is the beginning of supernatural power.... —*Paracelsus*

Who is a wise man? He who learns from all men.... —*The Talmud*

With wisdom we flourish and live. Without it we wither and die. With wisdom, years can keep us young in heart and mind. Without it we grow old. With wisdom we can be strong and know no fear. Without it we become weak and frightened.... —*Dore Schary*

Wisdom is to see the miraculous in the common.... —*Ralph W. Emerson*

All human wisdom is summed up in two words–wait and hope.... —*Alexandre Dumas*

Wisdom gives praise liberally and makes promises discreetly.... —*Shantidasa*

The art of being wise is the art of knowing what to overlook.... —*William James*

True wisdom consists in not departing from nature and in molding our conduct according to her laws....   —*Seneca*

Our knowledge is a little island in a great ocean of non-knowledge....
    —*Isaac Bashevis Singer*

The more I know, the more I realize I don't know....   —*Albert Einstein*

Wise are they who have learned the truths: Trouble is temporary. Time is tonic. Tribulation is a test tube....
    —*William A. Ward*

The wise man is never surprised by death: he is always ready to depart....
    —*Jean La Fontaine*

Wisdom is like gold ore, mixed with stones and dust....   —*Moses Ibn Ezra*

Wisdom is the principal thing; therefore get wisdom: and with all thy getting, get understanding....
    —*Old Testament*

The Delphic oracle said I was the wisest of all the Greeks. It is because that I alone, of all the Greeks, know that I know nothing....   —*Socrates*

The ignorant work for their own profit; the wise work for the welfare of the world....   —*Bhagavad-Gita*

When you have gained true wisdom, you will find that good fortune should not be gloated over, nor bad fortune grieved over....   —*Sathya Sai Baba*

The way of the sage is to act but not compete....   —*Lao-tzu*

The only thing that we can know is that we know nothing and that is the highest flight of human wisdom....
    —*Leo Tolstoy*

A wise man feels he is not so wise; otherwise, he is not wise....
    —*Fred Van Amburgh*

To understand all makes us very tolerant....   —*Madam de Staël*

All true wisdom is only learned far from the dwellings of men, out in the great solitudes, and is to be attained through suffering....   —*Igjugarjuk*

Many men can utter words of wisdom, few men can practice it themselves....
    —*Hitopadesa*

Wisdom will never be noticed since it always resides in order, calmness, harmony and peace....   —*Eliphas Levi*

Wisdom is knowledge of God. Wisdom comes by intuition. It far transcends knowledge....   —*Ralph W. Trine*

By rousing himself, by earnestness, by restraint and control, the wise man makes for himself an island which no flood can immerse....   —*Dhammapada*

The sage must distinguish between knowledge and wisdom. Knowledge is of things, acts and relations. But wisdom is of God alone; and, beyond all things, acts, and relations, it abides forever. To become one with God is the only wisdom....   —*The Upanishads*

In every heart there dwelleth a sage; only man will not steadfastly believe it....   —*Wang Yang Ming*

Wise company will make thee also wise....   —*Sufi saying*

The end of learning is to know God, and out of that knowledge to love him....   —*John Milton*

Wisdom is not in words, it is in understanding.... —*Hazrat Inayat Khan*

Wisdom denotes the pursuing of the best ends by the best means.... —*Frances Hutcheson*

Aim for wisdom. If you become poor it will be wealth for you; if you become rich it will adorn you.... —*El-Zubeir*

Wisdom is ofttimes nearer when we stoop than when we soar.... —*William Wordsworth*

The fruit of wisdom is peace.... —*Chinese proverb*

The wise man is he who knows the relative value of things.... —*William R. Inge*

The most certain sign of wisdom is continual cheerfulness; her state is like that of things in the regions above the moon, always clear and serene.... —*Michel Montaigne*

Wisdom does not attain completeness except through the living of life.... —*Rabindranath Tagore*

He who learns the rules of wisdom, without conforming to them in his life, is like a man who labors in his field, but did not sow.... —*Saadi*

The learning and knowledge that we have is, at the most, but little compared with that of which we are ignorant.... —*Plato*

If we desire wisdom we must seek for it, work for it, and pray for it. We must patiently strive for the wisdom that we desire and then we must pass it out to others who are also seeking wisdom.... —*Amber M. Tuttle*

Pain is the father, and love is the mother, of wisdom.... —*Ludwig Borne*

Cleverness is not wisdom.... —*Euripides*

All wish to possess knowledge, but few, comparatively speaking, are willing to pay the price.... —*Juvenal*

The wise man realizes how little he knows; it is the foolish person who imagines that he knows everything.... —*Jawaharlal Nehru*

The truly wise make no plans, and therefore require no wisdom.... —*Chuang Tse*

The wise man thinks about his troubles only when there is some purpose in doing so; at other times he thinks about other things.... —*Bertrand Russell*

Divine wisdom is inexhaustible; the limitation is only in the receptive faculty of the form.... —*Henry Madathanas*

It is knowledge that ultimately gives salvation.... —*Mohandas Gandhi*

Great wisdom consists in not demanding too much of human nature, and yet not altogether spoiling it by indulgence.... —*Lin Yutang*

The truly wise are anonymous; they do not display wisdom for the benefit or admiration of others.... —*Anonymous*

Discrimination is the mark of wisdom.... —*Bhikkhu Pesala*

The wisest man preaches no doctrines; he has no scheme; he sees no rafter, not even a cobweb, against the heavens. It is a clear sky.... —*Henry D. Thoreau*

From the errors of others a wise man corrects his own.... —*Publilius Syrus*

Wisdom is the child of experience....
—*John F. Kennedy*

Humility, unostentatiousness, non-injury, forgiveness, simplicity, purity, steadfastness, self-control; this is declared to be wisdom; what is opposed to this is ignorance....
—*Bhagavad-Gita*

The wise man endeavors to shine in himself; the fool to outshine others....
—*Joseph Addison*

Is there not one true coin for which all things ought to be exchanged?—and that is wisdom....   —*Plato*

Remind yourself that all men assert that wisdom is the greatest good, but that there are few who strenuously endeavor to obtain this greatest good....
—*Pythagoras*

A man's wisdom is his best friend....
—*William Temple*

Wisdom begets humility....
—*Abraham Ibn Ezra*

The attempt to combine wisdom and power has only rarely been successful and then only for a short time....
—*Albert Einstein*

Fruitless is the wisdom of him who has no knowledge of himself....   —*Erasmus*

A wise man hears one word and understands two....   —*Yiddish saying*

Wisdom, properly used, is a remedy for every ill; but when misdirected, becomes an incurable disease....
—*Bahaya*

To know that which before us lies in daily life is the prime wisdom....
—*John Milton*

The surest sign of a man of the highest wisdom is that he is unattracted by the pleasures of the world, for in him even the subtle tendencies have ceased. When these tendencies are strong, there is bondage; when they have ceased, there is liberation....
—*Yoga Vasistha*

The price of wisdom is above rubies....
—*Old Testament*

Wisdom amazes all that is sensible of her, but is herself not amazed at anything....   —*Apollonius of Tyana*

Not to know certain things is a great part of wisdom....   —*Hugo Grotius*

Who is wise? He that learns from everybody....   —*Benjamin Franklin*

Fools scatter about their many attributes, the wise keep such within; a piece of straw floats upon the surface of water, a precious gemstone sinks to the bottom. Therefore, it is best to disregard the seen and concentrate upon the unseen. Only within the latter may riches be found....
—*Ancient Greek parable*

Wisdom is meaningless until your own experience has given it meaning....
—*Bergen Evans*

Wisdom does not rub off from one to another. Enlightenment is a do-it-yourself project....   —*Shantidasa*

Make wisdom your provision from youth to old age, for it is more certain support than all other possessions....
—*Diogenes*

The beginning of wisdom is the definition of words....   —*Socrates*

Wisdom is not communicable. The wisdom which a wise man tries to communicate always sounds foolish. Knowledge can be communicated, but not wisdom. One can find it, live it, be fortified by it, do wonders through it, but one cannot communicate and teach it....   —*Hermann Hesse*

Wisdom....may be summed up in four words: to know, to will, to love, and to do what is true, good, beautiful and just....   —*Eliphas Levi*

We are wiser than we know....   —*Ralph W. Emerson*

The falling drops of water will in time fill a water-jar. Even so the wise man becomes full of good, although he may gather it little by little....   —*Dhammapada*

The wisest man is generally he who thinks himself the least so....   —*Nicolas Boileau*

Wisdom will not dwell in a body enslaved by evil....   —*Apocrypha: Wisdom of Solomon*

One cannot have wisdom without living life....   —*Dorothy McCall*

To find God is but the beginning of wisdom, because then for all our lives we have to learn His purpose with us and to live our lives with Him....   —*H. G. Wells*

Wisdom is usually acquired at the cost of great pain....   —*Harold S. Kushner*

Wisdom lifts the poor man's head, and sets him among princes....   —*Apocrypha: Ben Sira*

It is not wise to be wiser than necessary....   —*Philippe Quinault*

He is a miserable man who knows all things and does not know God; and he is happy who knows God, even though he knows nothing else....   —*Augustine*

Even wisdom has to yield to self-interest....   —*Pindar*

It is characteristic of wisdom not to do desperate things....   —*Henry D. Thoreau*

The wise man lives after the image of God and is not guided by the ways of the world. And he who imitates the image of God will conquer the stars....   —*Paracelsus*

The wisdom of the world is foolishness with God....   —*Paul of Tarsus*

The truly learned man is he who understands that what he knows is but little in comparison with what he does not know....   —*Arabian saying*

Knowledge is power, but only wisdom is liberty....   —*Will Durant*

Wisdom is the soul's natural food....   —*Jacob Anatoli*

If then you do not make yourself equal to God, you cannot apprehend God; for like is known by like....   —*Hermes*

There are two classes of the wise; the men who serve God because they have found him, and the men who seek him because they have not found him....   —*Richard Cecil*

Wisdom comes from disillusionment....   —*George Santayana*

Wisdom is like fire: a little enlightens, too much of it can burn....   —*Moses Ibn Ezra*

A physician is not angry at the intemperance of a mad patient, nor does he take it ill to be insulted by a man in fever. Just so, should a wise man treat all mankind as a physician treats a patient, and look upon it only as sick and irresponsible.... —*Seneca*

Mere silence is not wisdom, for wisdom consists in knowing when and how to speak and when and where to keep silent.... —*Jean P. Camus*

Wisdom saves, not sentimentality....
—*Vernon Howard*

Wisdom is knowing which bridge to burn and which to cross over....
—*Anonymous*

Words

When old words die out on the tongue, new melodies break forth from the heart....
—*Rabindranath Tagore*

Because the truth cannot be accurately conveyed in words, it is pointless to query one man's opinion of the truth with another collection of words....
—*Ramana Maharshi*

Words do not reach beyond the mind....
—*Nisargadatta*

No human words can ever express that which we call Truth, Spirit, or God. Yet those who have trodden the path of search before us have left some traces of their experiences in the sacred scriptures of all the religions of the world.... —*Mouni Sadhu*

Words are employed to conceal ideas....
—*French saying*

The six greatest words on earth are: "Control thyself!"—Cicero; "Know thyself!"—Socrates; "Give thyself!"—Jesus....
—*Anonymous*

Words are not as satisfactory as we should like them to be, but, like our neighbors, we have got to live with them and must make the best and not the worst of them.... —*Samuel Butler*

You should always keep your word. All the setbacks in life come only because you don't keep your word....
—*Sivananda*

One word frees us of all the weight and pain of life: that word is love....
—*Sophocles*

We are held accountable for the very words which we speak....By our words we are justified or condemned....
—*Ernest Holmes*

Be careful what you say when you talk with words....for words are made of syllables and syllables are made of air....
—*Carl Sandburg*

Harsh and bitter words serve no useful purpose and only exhibit weakness....
—*Shantidasa*

Words can be a power for good—or they can be a power for evil....
—*James G. Keller*

We have too many high sounding words, and too few actions that correspond with them.... —*Abigail Adams*

A thousand words will not leave so deep an impression as one deed....
—*Henrik Ibsen*

Words, like glasses, obscure everything which they do not make clear....
—*Joseph Joubert*

We should believe only in deeds; words go for nothing everywhere....
—*Fernando Rojas*

Words are, of course, the most powerful drug used by mankind....
—*Rudyard Kipling*

False words are not only evil in themselves, but they infect the soul with evil....
—*Plato*

Mere words cannot be relied upon. Overdependence on them leads to bad results....
—*I Ching*

One word can be canceled by another....
—*The Talmud*

Monks and scholars should accept my word not out of respect, but upon analyzing it as a goldsmith analyzes gold, through cutting, melting, scraping and rubbing it....
—*Gautama Buddha*

Do not say a little in many words, but a great deal in a few....
—*Pythagoras*

Now if these words are helpful to you, put them into practice. But if they aren't helpful, then there's no need for them....
—*Dalai Lama*

The more a writer rambles, the less a reader remembers. Facts require few words....You have noticed that the more limbs on a tree, the smaller the fruit on the branches. The more words, the less wisdom....
—*Fred Van Amburgh*

By your words you will be justified; and by your words you will be condemned....
—*Jesus*

We should have a great many fewer disputes in the world if words were taken for what they are, the signs of our ideas only, and not for the things themselves....
—*John Locke*

One person who has mastered life is better than a thousand persons who have only mastered the contents of books, but no one can get anything out of life without God....
—*Meister Eckhart*

Words cannot describe everything. The heart's message cannot be communicated in words....
—*Ekai*

All words are pegs to hang ideas on....
—*Henry W. Beecher*

The word once spoken flies beyond recall....
—*Aesop*

Let thy words be few when in the midst of many....
—*Teresa of Avila*

Words are like leaves, and where they most abound, much fruit of sense is rarely found....
—*Alexander Pope*

Words are but the shadows of thoughts and feelings....
—*Hazrat Inayat Khan*

Try saying "war" or "cancer" or "money" ten thousand times, and you will find that your whole mood has been changed and colored by the associations connected with the word. Similarly, the name of God will change the climate of your mind. It cannot do otherwise....
—*Prabhavananda*

There is no choice of words for him who clearly sees the truth....
—*Ralph W. Emerson*

There are too many who are content to learn words by heart, and to put words in the place of experience. No one can understand these things unless he has experienced them himself....
—*Carl Jung*

A very great part of the mischiefs that vex this world arises from words....
—*Edmund Burke*

The words of a man who practices austerity of speech cannot cause pain to others. His words will bring cheer and solace to others. His words will prove beneficial to all.... —*Sivananda*

A word to the wise is sufficient....
—*Terence*

Words do not express thoughts very well. They always become a little different immediately after they are expressed, a little distorted, a little foolish....
—*Hermann Hesse*

Never utter an ugly word....
—*Levi Joshua*

The tongue of man is a twisty thing, there are plenty of words there of every kind.... —*Homer*

Words and magic were in the beginning one and the same thing, and even today words retain much of their magical power.... —*Sigmund Freud*

God is wordless....
—*Paul Twitchell*

Words are the most powerful thing in the universe....Words are containers. They contain faith, or fear, and they produce after their kind....
—*Charles Capps*

A hasty, sarcastic word....can quickly undo or offset many advances toward good. Seldom is anyone won by being nagged, irritated, or belittled....
—*James G. Keller*

Men of few words are the best men....
—*William Shakespeare*

One kind word has more power within it than a dozen ultimatums....
—*Anonymous*

Our words are useless unless they come from the bottom of the heart....
—*Mother Teresa*

Everyone hears only what he understands.... —*Johann W. Goethe*

Words form the thread on which we string our experiences....
—*Aldous Huxley*

Without knowing the force of words, it is impossible to know men....
—*Confucius*

Words cannot describe one's spiritual experience.... —*Papa Ramdas*

Hold firmly to your word....
—*Maimonides*

Much wisdom often goes with the fewest words.... —*Sophocles*

Words are deceptive little devils. Words promise much, yet provide so little. They often confuse and confine our limits of expression; they are not where the pulsating rhythm of truth may be found.... —*Shantidasa*

The more words, the more foolishness.... —*Judah Lev Mordecai*

Strong and bitter words indicate a weak cause.... —*Victor Hugo*

Every word you say has a vibration that brings you what you have and what you need. So be very careful when you speak a word, because one word spoken can make and mar the destiny of the being.... —*Yogi Bhajan*

Words are merely the vehicle on which thoughts ride.... —*James R. Adams*

Judge your words before you utter them.... —*The Talmud*

Positive words possess power. Words vibrate according to their character and nature. A negative word depresses, discourages and weakens us if we use it and dwell upon it....
—*Henry T. Hamblin*

Spiritual experience cannot be described in words. Language is imperfect....
—*Sivananda*

If man would practice sending forth words of Life, Love, Harmony, Peace and Perfection, he would in a short time be unable to utter an inharmonious word.... —*Baird Spalding*

Every word carries a vibration that sent out, comes back. A cutting word destroys what a sweet word heals. One spoken word can make or mar the destiny of a being. When heart is put into a word, the word encompasses the totality of love and brings love back. When a word is without heart, it is cold and empty and will bring back cold and emptiness.... —*Cheryl Canfield*

Gentle words calm tense situations, but harsh words cut like whips....
—*Leland F. Wood*

Words are things, and a small drop of ink, falling like dew upon a thought, produces that which makes thousands, perhaps millions, think....
—*George Byron*

Words should be scattered like seed: no matter how small the seed may be, if it has found favorable ground, it unfolds its strength.... —*Seneca*

Where wisdom is perfect, there the words are few.... —*Chinese proverb*

Kind words produce their own image in men's souls; and what a beautiful image it is.... —*Blaise Pascal*

Short words are best....
—*Winston Churchill*

The great man does not think beforehand of his words that they may be sincere....he simply speaks and does what is right.... —*Menicus*

The finest words in the world are only vain sounds, if you cannot comprehend them.... —*Anatole France*

Work

No task guarantees to protect us from stressful situations, or from people with different views....
—*Eknath Easwaran*

Work is the keystone of a perfect life. Work and trust in God....
—*Woodrow Wilson*

It is not what we do that has importance, but rather how well we do it....
—*A Spiritual Warrior*

If you are called to be a streetsweeper, you should sweep streets even as Michelangelo painted, or Beethoven composed music, or Shakespeare wrote poetry.... —*Martin L. King, Jr.*

Work is not man's punishment. It is his reward and his strength, his glory and his pleasure.... —*George Sand*

When our inner self connects to our work and our work to our inner self, the work knows no limit, for the inner self knows no limit.... —*Matthew Fox*

When I work, I leave my body outside the door, the way the Moslems take off their shoes before they enter a mosque.... —*Pablo Picasso*

Work is the grand cure of all the maladies and miseries that ever beset mankind.... —*Thomas Carlyle*

It is not hard work that is dreary; it is superficial work....
—*Edith Hamilton*

All work is empty save when there is love. And when you work with love you bind yourself to yourself, and to one another, and to God....
—*Kahlil Gibran*

The test of a vocation is the love of the drudgery it involves....
—*Logan P. Smith*

I would be content with any job, however thankless, in any quarter, however remote, if I had the chance of making a corner of the desert blossom and a solitary place glad.... —*Lord Tweedsmuir*

It is important to know that words don't move mountains. Work, exacting work moves mountains....
—*Danilo Dolci*

It does not matter what your work is on the earth. What does matter is that you do your work with all your heart and with all your strength and all your mind.... —*White Eagle*

The desire of one man to live on the fruits of another's labor is the original sin of the world.... —*James O'Brien*

The longest-lived men give the longest hours to work.... —*Fred Van Amburgh*

One of the symptoms of an approaching nervous breakdown is the belief that one's work is terribly important....
—*Bertrand Russell*

There is a condition or circumstance that has a greater bearing upon the happiness of life than any other. What is it?...something to do; some congenial work. Take away the occupation of all men and what a wretched world it would be.... —*John Burroughs*

The difference between work and play is only a matter of attitude. Work, fully done, is play.... —*Gerald G. May*

Without work all life goes rotten....
—*Albert Camus*

The wise prove, and the foolish confess, by their action, that a life of employment is the only life worth leading....
—*William Paley*

It is the experience of those who have tried it, that working from a sense of duty, working for the work's sake, working as a service, instead of for a living, or to make money, or in order to hoard up wealth, brings blessings into the life.... —*Henry T. Hamblin*

There is a criterion by which you can ascertain whether or not your work on earth is over. The criterion is: Are you still alive? If you are, there is still more work for you to do.... —*Shantidasa*

We work to become, not to acquire....
—*Elbert Hubbard*

Work that produces unnecessary consumer junk and weapons of war is wrong and wasteful. Work that is built upon false needs or unbecoming appetites is wrong and wasteful. Work that deceives or manipulates, that exploits or degrades is wrong and wasteful. Work that wounds the environment or makes the world ugly is wrong and wasteful....
—*Theodore Roszak*

The supreme accomplishment is to blur the line between work and play....
—*Arnold Toynbee*

If you wish to work properly, you should never lose sight of two great principles: first, a profound respect for the work undertaken, and second, a complete indifference to its fruits. Thus only can you work with the proper attitude....
—*Brahmananda*

Work is man's greatest function. He is nothing, he can do nothing, achieve nothing without working....
—*J. M. Cowan*

Employment is nature's physician, and it is essential to human happiness....
—*Galen*

Work keeps at bay three great evils: boredom, vice and need....
—*Voltaire*

Work is the true elixir of life. The busiest man is the happiest man....
—*Theodore Martin*

We can be truly successful only in the work to which we have been called. The work is not ours, it is God's, and we are privileged to be worked through by God....How foolish, then, for anyone to think and proclaim that he has a certain work to do for God. God may have a certain work to do through him, that is if he is sufficiently humble, but that is quite a different thing....
—*Henry T. Hamblin*

When we use our hands effectively, our hearts are most at peace....
—*Akira Yoshizawa*

The secret of being miserable is to have leisure to bother about whether you are happy or not. The cure for it is occupation....
—*George B. Shaw*

Work silently....Work is worship. When there is joy in the work itself, why do you want the fruit of it? Make work itself worship. That is possible only when you surrender to God and allow him to work through you. It means absence of ego-sense...
—*Papa Ramdas*

To work alone thou hast the right, but never the fruits thereof. Be thou neither actuated by the fruits of action, nor be thou attached to inaction....
—*Bhagavad-Gita*

Work, especially good work, becomes easy only when desire has learnt to discipline itself....
—*Rabindranath Tagore*

Occupation is one great source of enjoyment. No man, properly occupied, was ever miserable....
—*Letitia Landon*

Nothing is more likely to help a person overcome or endure troubles than the consciousness of having a task in life....
—*Victor Frankl*

Have thy tools ready; God will find thee work....
—*Charles Kingsley*

Divide your tasks into three categories: essential, important and trivial, and forget about the trivial....
—*Donald Tubesing*

The more you advance toward God, the less He will give you worldly duties to perform....
—*Ramakrishna*

If I had five hours to chop down a tree, I'd spend the first four hours sharpening the axe....
—*Abraham Lincoln*

Work is love made visible....
—*Kahlil Gibran*

A vision without work is but a dream; a work without a vision is drudgery, alas; a vision and a work is the hope of the world....
—*Anonymous*

Work and love—these are the basics. Without them there is neurosis....
—*Theodore Reik*

The sum of wisdom is that the time is never lost that is devoted to work....
—*Ralph W. Emerson*

Hard work doesn't give people heart attacks. Hard work itself can be good for you....　　—*Dean Ornish*

Men seldom die of hard work; activity is God's medicine....
—*Robert S. MacArthur*

There is no honest and true work, carried along with constant and sincere purpose that ever really fails....
—*William G. Jordan*

The Masterword which is the 'Open Sesame' to every portal....the true philosopher's stone....is work....
—*William Osler*

Work of your own free will, not from duty. We have no duty. The world is just a gymnasium in which we play; our life is an eternal holiday....
—*Vivekananda*

One of the most durable satisfactions in life is to lose one's self in one's work....
—*Harry E. Fosdick*

God intends no man to live in this world without working; but it seems to me no less evident that He intends every man to be happy in his work....
—*John Ruskin*

Everyone has been made for some particular work, and the desire for that work has been put into his heart....
—*Rumi*

I have found no secret of success but hard work....　　—*Edward Turner*

Excellence is never granted to man but as the reward of labor....
—*Joshua Reynolds*

Without labor nothing prospers....
—*Sophocles*

True happiness comes to him who does his work well....True happiness comes from the right amount of work for the day....　　—*Lin Yutang*

We have too many people who live without working, and we have altogether too many who work without living....
—*Charles R. Brown*

In work, do what you enjoy....
—*Lao-tzu*

I can think of no greater hardship, no greater rebuke, than having nothing to do....　　—*Fred Van Amburgh*

Idleness and lack of occupation are the best things in the world to ruin the foolish....　　—*John Chrysostom*

What is our work? Our only work here is to seek God, or do such work that will enable us to realize God....
—*Papa Ramdas*

Thank God every morning when you get up that you have something to do which must be done, whether you like it or not....　　—*Charles Kingsley*

It doesn't matter what you do—as long as you do it with love....
—*Mother Teresa*

The mintage of wisdom is to know that rest is rust, and that real life is love, laughter and work....
—*Elbert Hubbard*

Every calling is great when greatly pursued....　　—*Oliver W. Holmes*

Whatever your occupation while in your physical body, remember it is a form of service. However humble or even humdrum your work may be to you, it is your special appointment, and through your work on earth you can make your contribution to the happiness of all....   —*White Eagle*

Happiness, I have discovered, is nearly always a rebound of hard work....
                    —*David Grayson*

If people knew how hard I work to get my mastery, it would not seem so marvelous after all....   —*Michelangelo*

Blessed is he who has found his work; let him ask no other blessedness. He has a work, a life-purpose; he has found it, and it will follow him....
                    —*Thomas Carlyle*

If you choose a job that you like you will never have to work a day in your life....   —*Confucius*

The reward for work well done is the opportunity to do more....
                    —*Jonas Salk*

Few persons realize how much of their happiness is dependent upon their work, upon the fact that they are busy and not left to feed upon themselves....Blessed is the man who has some congenial work, some occupation in which he can put his heart, and which affords a complete outlet to all the forces that are in him....
                    —*John Burroughs*

While the unwise work for the fruit of their actions, the wise offer all results of their actions to Me....   —*Bhagavad-Gita*

If you work at what you love to do you can't help but have love flowing through you....   —*Shantidasa*

Your job in the scheme of things is unique and designed especially for you. Your job is something you will be happy doing....You can begin to do your job in life by doing all the good things you feel motivated toward, even though they are just little things....
                    —*Peace Pilgrim*

The occupation you choose in life must be the thing you love to do—the thing you can put your whole being into. Never engage in anything as a permanent activity, or a life-work that you do not love with the fullness of your love....   —*James B. Schafer*

Only the work that is impersonal can live; the works of the self are both powerless and perishable. Where duties, howsoever humble, are done without self-interest, and with joyful sacrifice, there is true service and enduring work. Where deeds, however brilliant and apparently successful, are done from love of self, there is ignorance of the Law of Service, and the work perishes....   —*James Allen*

In our time a secret manifesto is being written. It is the longing to know our authentic vocation in the world, to find the work and the way of being that belongs to each of us....
                    —*Theodore Roszak*

The majority work to make a living; some work to acquire wealth or fame, while a few work because there is something within them which demands expression....Only a few truly love it....   —*Edmund B. Szekely*

Work and thou canst not escape the reward....The reward of a thing well done is to have done it....
                    —*Ralph W. Emerson*

Each individual soul is destined to fulfill some mission on this earth plane, his life being patterned according to his stage of evolution. The path that he must travel in order to fulfill his duties will be burdensome or free from pain and worry in the degree that the individual understands and obeys the laws of his being.... —*Thurman Fleet*

No man is born into the world whose work is not born with him....
—*James Russell Lowell*

You have come into the world to work. You must always be eager to work. The one who is idle is like a dead man. You have come to this world to live, not to die.... —*Babaji*

The fruit derived from labor is the sweetest of all pleasure....
—*Luc de Clapiers Vauvenargues*

Each of us has something within us that needs to be expressed. It may be the desire to play an instrument, paint landscapes, climb mountains, or grow prize-winning chrysanthemums. Whatever that desire is, it comes from our heart and reflects our own unique gifts and abilities.... —*G. Jean Anderson*

The labor of the body relieves us from the fatigues of the mind; and it is that which forms the happiness of the poor.... —*Francois La Rochefoucauld*

Work is not always required of man. There is such a thing as sacred idleness.... —*George Macdonald*

It is the ambition of many to live without working. What they desire is a parasitic life, in which they take everything, but give nothing in return. This is against the principle of Life, and those who try to act in this manner bring a blight upon themselves....
—*Henry T. Hamblin*

The man who does not work for the love of work but only for the money is not likely to make money nor to find much fun in life....
—*Charles M. Schwab*

There is plenty of advancement in any work! Whether you are shining shoes or administering laws, or what!...
—*Edgar Cayce*

God sells us all things at the price of labor.... —*Leonardo da Vinci*

To live in the world or to leave it depends on the will of God. Therefore, work, leaving everything to Him. What else can you do?... —*Ramakrishna*

If our work is not truly beneficial, it is best to cease. Cause and effect works in the physical realms, but also in our own lives.... —*Sevakram*

The surest sign of a person of the highest wisdom is that he or she is unattracted by the pleasures of the world...even the subtle tendencies have ceased.... —*Yoga Vasistha*

Worry

Worry is a useless mulling over of things we cannot change. Worry is not concern, which would motivate you to do everything possible in a situation.... —*Peace Pilgrim*

Worry is seldom necessary....Worry sprinkles salt in the wound and sand in your mental machinery....
—*Fred Van Amburgh*

Worry is spiritual short sight. Its cure is intelligent faith.... —*Paul Brunton*

When we are upset, about 90 percent of the upset is related to our past and has nothing to do with what we think is upsetting us.... —*John Gray*

Worry kills a man. It destroys his hope of life. It is a canker or cancer that slowly eats away at man. It wears you out. Do not worry over the past....Do not worry about things which are likely to happen; so often they really do not.... —*Sivananda*

Mental problems feed on the attention you give them. The more you worry about them, the stronger they become. If you ignore them, they lose their power and finally vanish.... —*Annamalai Swami*

Worry is a state of mind based on fear.... —*Napoleon Hill*

Worry is the interest which we pay on trouble before it comes, and we attract trouble every time we worry about it.... —*Albert E. Cliffe*

The reason why worry kills more people than work is that more people worry than work.... —*Robert Frost*

Worry is an infirmity; there is no virtue in it. Worry is spiritual nearsightedness; a fumbling way of looking at little things and magnifying their value.... —*Anna Brown Lindsay*

We can always get along better by reason and love of truth than by worry of conscience and remorse.... —*Baruch Spinoza*

Happy is the man who has broken the chains which hurt the mind, and has given up worrying once and for all.... —*Ovid*

The sovereign cure for worry is prayer.... —*William James*

Worry is responsible for more disease than all the germs that exist on the face of the earth.... —*Thurman Fleet*

The art of resting the mind and the power of dismissing from it all care and worry is probably one of the secrets of energy in our great men.... —*J. Hadfield*

Any negative state, like worry, is like your shadow. If you run away, it pursues, but by standing still you see that it has no movement except that which you give it by running away.... —*Vernon Howard*

The worst thing you can possibly do is worrying and thinking about what you could have done.... —*Georg C. Lichtenberg*

There is nothing that wastes the body like worry, and one who has any faith in God should be ashamed to worry about anything whatsoever.... —*Mohandas Gandhi*

There are two days of the week upon which and about which I never worry—two carefree days kept sacredly free from fear and apprehension. One of these days is yesterday....And the other day....is tomorrow.... —*Robert J. Burdette*

The more we worry—the more we have something to worry about.... —*Tom Seeley*

Worry is like a microscope. It makes every little misery look huge. We can use a telescope, and see far away into life. We shall see much, but worry we shall hardly notice. We shall find it so small.... —*Nicholas Rodney*

What, me worry?... —*Alfred E. Newman*

Worries cannot be willed away by consciously refusing to acknowledge them—they must be pulled up by the roots and examined in the light, not pushed deeper into the unconscious where they only do darker mischief by disguising themselves in some bizarre manner....   —*Sydney J. Harris*

Some of your grief you have cured, and the sharpest you have survived; but what torments of pain you endured from evil that never arrived....
—*French proverb*

We abuse our bodies and fill our minds with mental pictures of fear and worry and then find it difficult to understand why we have suffered from a nervous breakdown....   —*Harold Sherman*

Worry is the cause of most of the distempers of the mind and the body. Remove worry by steadfast faith in the constant thought of God....
—*Papa Ramdas*

The more we worry, the more we hurry and the man in a hurry has reason to worry—a vicious circle....
—*Fred Van Amburgh*

It is not work that kills man; it is worry. Work is healthy and you can hardly put more upon a man than he can bear; but worry is the rust upon the blade....
—*Henry W. Beecher*

Activity is a great antidote for sitting around and worrying....
—*Margo Howard*

I am an old man and have had many troubles, most of which never happened....   —*Mark Twain*

We little realize the number of human diseases that are begun or are affected by worry....   —*Walter C. Alvarez*

Worry brings fear and fear is crippling....Know that there is a power greater than yourself within you, orchestrating your every encounter and guiding you in the right direction....
—*Susan Smith Jones*

Worry is a thin stream of fear trickling through the mind. If encouraged, it cuts a channel into which all other thoughts are drained....
—*Arthur S. Roche*

When you worry about the problems of tomorrow, you are creating unhappiness for yourself today....
—*Shantidasa*

If, instead of worrying over our own misfortunes, we think ourselves more fortunate than many, many others, we are loving God....   —*Meher Baba*

Worry affects the circulation, the heart, the glands, the whole nervous system....
—*Charles Mayo*

To tremble before anticipated evils, is to bemoan what thou hast never lost....
—*Johann W. Goethe*

Worry is a word that I don't allow myself to use....
—*Dwight D. Eisenhower*

Worry never robs tomorrow of its sorrow; it only saps today of its strength....
—*A. J. Cronin*

There is no use worrying about things over which you have no control, and if you have control, you can do something about it instead of worrying....
—*Stanley C. Allyn*

Worry never righted a wrong, dried a tear or lifted a burden. On the contrary, it has slain tens of thousands....
—*Alfred A. Montapert*

Nothing is so wretched or foolish as to anticipate misfortunes. What madness is it to be expecting evil before it comes....
—*Seneca*

Do not worry about tomorrow; it will have enough worries of its own. There is no need to add to the troubles each day brings....
—*Jesus*

There is no annoyance so great as the annoyance which is composed of many trifling, but continuous worries....
—*Francis de Sales*

Don't take tomorrow to bed with you....
—*Norman V. Peale*

Inability to tell good from evil is the greatest worry of man's life....
—*Cicero*

Faith means not worrying....
—*John Dewey*

Don't worry about tomorrow: who knows what may befall you this day....
—*The Talmud*

To worry continually is the most efficient prayer for getting what you don't want....
—*Shantidasa*

Worry is worship to the wrong god....
—*Jack Exum*

Worries do not belong to you. It is your own fault if you assume that they are yours....
—*Ramana Maharshi*

Worry throws "faith in God" out the window....
—*Anonymous*

One who has abandoned everything is not agitated by worry: if wind can sway the branches of a tree, it cannot be called immovable....
—*Yoga Vasistha*

Live only for the moment, worry not, there is no past or future—only now. Worry brings discomfort and pain. It is the downfall of your being....
—*Archie Canfield*

How often are you worrying about the present moment? The present moment is usually all right. If you're worrying, you're either agonizing over the past which you should have forgotten long ago, or else you're apprehensive over the future which hasn't even come yet. We tend to skip over the present moment which is the only moment God gives any of us to live....
—*Peace Pilgrim*

There is nothing to worry about. It is all God and His play. Clouds sweep over the sky: they appear and disappear; but the sky remains unaffected. So also the things of the world—its sorrows and its joys—they come and go: but we are eternal Changeless Existence, full of peace and bliss. We are the witness of a gigantic cinema show....
—*Papa Ramdas*

Inspiring Books from Blue Dove Press

Never to Return
A Modern Quest for Eternal Truth
by Sharon Janis
Softcover   330pp. $16.95   ISBN: 1-884997-29-5

> *"...In a larger sense, this memoir is a dialogue between Indian spirituality and Western psychology. The question that Janis answers in her memoir is: 'Can a westerner come to know Indian spirituality and flourish in its depths, even when it is alien to western ways of knowing?' She answers with a resounding 'Yes.'"* — **Publishers Weekly**

> *"...Never to Return is a beautiful and poignant spiritual odyssey that is equally provocative and touching, informative and enlightening, humorous and heartbreaking. Sharon Janis writes with an admirable clarity, and her lightness of spirit in the face of adversity is exemplary for us all."*
> — **Joseph Chilton Pierce**, author of *Crack in the Cosmic Egg*

This highly acclaimed memoir is both a real-life spiritual adventure and a rare and intimate glimpse into a modern-day search for eternal truth.

Raised an atheist, author Sharon Janis survived a painful and dysfunctional childhood with a strength, independence, and curiosity that awakened in her a voracious spiritual hunger. Eventually, her search would take her to an Indian monastery, where she lived for ten years.

Janis has a natural gift for story-telling. Her engagingly humorous and touching personal anecdotes address some of the most delicate topics of human existence: the power and vulnerability of the mind, devotion, death, humility, justice, grace and ultimately, the intimacy between the individual and his or her God.

Peace Pilgrim's Wisdom

A Very Simple Guide
Compiled by Cheryl Canfield
Softcover   224 pp. $14   ISBN: 1-884997-11-2

"It is considered the highest level of enlightenment to simply 'walk as you talk'— Peace Pilgrim lived out this message. Indeed, she is my hero."— **Dr. Wayne Dyer**, author of *Your Erroneous Zones* and *Your Sacred Self*

"There is no doubt that she was letting God write the script of her life, every moment of the day." — **Gerald Jampolsky**, author of *Love is Letting Go of Fear*

"I am one of many who have admired and emulated the life and wisdom of Peace pilgrim. Here is an American saint who transcended all national, religious, or sectarian bonds to communicate love, understanding and integrity. Her life was her teaching."— **Dan Millman**, author of *Way of the Peaceful Warrior*

Peace Pilgrim was a genuine American saint who for 28 years, from 1953 to 1981, walked in faith across North America. Her vow was *"to remain a wanderer until mankind learned the way of peace. Walking until given shelter and fasting until given food."* Penniless, she owned only what she carried, little more than the clothes on her back, a comb and a toothbrush. She walked many thousands of miles as a witness for both inner and outer peace, inspiring people to work for peace in their own lives. Many lives were transformed by her compelling example.

Designed as a study guide, *Peace Pilgrim's Wisdom*, divides her words into 19 sections to help us assimilate these powerful truths into our own lives.

Cheryl Canfield spent much time with Peace Pilgrim and is one of the five compilers of *Peace Pilgrim – Her Life and Work in Her Own Words*, which currently has over 400,000 copies in print.

The Wisdom of James Allen
5 Classic Works Combined into One
by James Allen
Edited by Andy Zubko
Softcover 384 pp. $7.95 ISBN: 1-889606-00-6

Little is known of James Allen, the mysterious contemplative Englishman who chose a quiet life of voluntary poverty, spiritual self-discipline, and simplicity during the 19th and early 20th centuries. Influenced by the writings of Leo Tolstoy, Allen came to realize that devoting one's life to making money and engaging in frivolous activities is a meaningless way to live.

At age 38, Allen retired with his wife, to a small cottage in southwestern England to devote the remainder of his life to quiet, thoughtful writing.

Allen's best-known book, the spiritual classic *As a Man Thinketh*, has sold steadily over the decades inspiring thousands and thousands of readers to a life of quiet dignity, self-discipline, and contemplation.

This valuable little volume combines four more James Allen books into one exquisite, gift-sized edition. In addition to *As a Man Thinketh*, are: *The Path to Prosperity*, *The Mastery of Destiny*, *The Way of Peace*, and *Entering the Kingdom*.

Excerpt from the foreword:

"I looked around upon the world, and saw that is was shadowed by sorrow and scorched by the fierce fires of suffering. And I looked for the cause...And I dreamed of writing books which would help men and women ...to find within themselves the source of all success, the source of all happiness...and now I send forth these books into the world on a mission of healing and blessedness, knowing they cannot fail to reach the homes and hearts of those who are waiting and ready to receive them."

Collision with the Infinite
A Life Beyond the Personal Self
by Suzanne Segal

Softcover   170pp. $14.00   ISBN: 1-884997-27-9

"...Segal describes the profound spiritual experience of the egoless state...Many have tried to do what Segal does, but none have achieved such clarity in the task."-- **Publishers Weekly**

"This is an extraordinary account of the experience of selflessness..."—**Joseph Goldstein**, author of *The Experience of Insight*

"...an amazingly honest, fascinating, and vivid account of one woman's awakening to her essential emptiness—and her eventual discovery, through much pain and fear, that as emptiness-fullness it is freedom *from pain and fear...this awakening is available, right now and just as one is, to all who dare to look in at the infinite..."*—**Douglas Harding**, author of *On Having No Head*

"...To anyone interested in the subject, I would say, 'Read this book!'"—**Ramesh S. Balsekar**, author of *Consciousness Speaks*

One day, in the early 1980's, a young American woman, Suzanne Segal, stepped onto a bus in Paris. Suddenly and unexpectedly, she found herself egoless, stripped of any sense of personal self. Struggling for years to make sense of her mental state, she consulted therapist after therapist. Eventually, she turned to spiritual teachers, coming at last to understand that this was the egoless state, that elusive consciousness to which so many aspire— the Holy Grail of so many spiritual traditions.

Written in a spare, unpretentious style, this book is Suzanne Segal's own account of what such a terrifying event meant to her when it crashed into her everyday life.

The Play of God
Visions of the Life of Krishna
by Devi Vanamali
Softcover   416 pp. $19.95   ISBN: 1-884997-07-4

"Krishna's biography is an exceptional introduction to the Indian worldview. This is going to become a classic text which opens many doors —doors historical, cultural and spiritual."
— **Publishers Weekly**

"Highly recommended as a fresh and readable presentation, in English, of the life and meaning of Krishna."
— **Library Journal**

"This is a valuable treasure to be cherished."
— **Swami Chidananda**
President of the Divine Life Society, Rishikesh

The Play of God is the account of a spiritual phenomenon. It describes the extraordinary manifestation of the Eternal in the realm of time that occurred in Krishna, the playful and enchantingly beautiful Deity who embodies the highest truths of India's spiritual vision.   Readers will find here powerful visions of God as child, playmate, friend, and teacher. What is evoked here is not a religion of moral law and stern obligation, but a spirituality of joy and true desire, love and beauty, contemplation and inner awakening.

Never before has the complete life of Krishna been told in a way that is so engaging and understandable, yet so faithful to the ancient epics of India. The life of Krishna stretches our conception of Divinity and lifts our minds to a higher spiritual plane as we contemplate the unlimited joy of the Eternal appearing to us in a form combining beauty, strength, and astounding playfulness. Spiritual seekers of all traditions will find faith in these pages.

Dr. Robert Powell's Nisargadatta Maharaj Trilogy

The Ultimate Medicine
As Prescribed by Sri Nisargadatta Maharaj
Edited by Robert Powell, Ph.D.
Softcover   240 pp. $14   ISBN: 1-884997-09-0

The Nectar of Immortality
Sri Nisargadatta Maharaj's Discourses on the Eternal
Edited by Robert Powell, Ph.D.
Softcover   208 pp. $14   ISBN: 1-884997-13-9

The Experience of Nothingness
Sri Nisargadatta Maharaj's Talks on Realizing the Infinite
Edited by Robert Powell, Ph.D.
Softcover   166 pp. $14   ISBN: 1-884997-14-7

*"Sri Nisargadatta Maharaj hardly needs an introduction any longer to lovers of the highest wisdom. Known as a maverick Hindu sage, Nisargadatta is now generally acknowledged to rank with the great masters of **advaita** teachings, such as Sri Ramana Maharshi...,Sri Atmananda...,and the more recently known disciple of the Maharshi, Poonjaji... "*— **Robert Powell**

"...Sri Nisargadatta Maharaj is my greatest teacher. His words guide my writing, speaking, and all my relationships..."
— **Dr. Wayne Dyer**, author of *Your Sacred Self*

Sri Nisargadatta Maharaj (1897-1981), one of the most important spiritual preceptors of the twentieth century, lived and taught in a small apartment in the slums of Bombay, India. A realized master of the Tantric Nath lineage, Maharaj had a wife and four children whom he supported for many years by selling inexpensive goods in a small booth on the streets outside his tenement.

In the tradition of Ramana Maharshi, he shared the highest Truth of nonduality, in his own unique way, from the depths of his own realization.

The Swami Ramdas Trilogy from Blue Dove Press

In Quest of God
The Saga of an Extraordinary Pilgrimage
by Swami Ramdas
Preface by Eknath Easwaran
Foreword by Ram Dass (Richard Alpert)
Softcover   190 pp. $10.95 ISBN: 1-884997-01-5

This is the tale of a remarkable pilgrimage. Walking in a God-intoxicated state of total surrender to the divine will, Swami Ramdas traveled the dusty roads of India as a penniless monk. This narrative, told with a keen wit, contains many inspiring accounts of how his pure love transformed many he encountered who at first behaved harshly toward him.

In the Vision of God Volume 1
The Continuing Saga of an Extraordinary Pilgrimage
by Swami Ramdas
Softcover   288 pp. $14.95 ISBN: 1-884997-03-1

Beginning where *In Quest of God* leaves off, this chronicle of Swami Ramdas' pilgrimage is comparable to such famous classics as *The Way of the Pilgrim* and Brother Lawrence's *The Practice of the Presence of God.*

In the Vision of God Volume 2
The Conclusion to the Saga of an Extraordinary Pilgrimage
by Swami Ramdas
Softcover   280 pp. $14.95 ISBN: 1-884997-05-8

In this final volume the story of Swami Ramdas' pilgrimage concludes with the end of his wanderings and relates how he settled down in an ashram created for him by his many devotees. This became more than a center for spiritual aspirants, but also a vehicle to help the needs of the local people.

The Lights of Grace
Catalog
from
Blue Dove Press

It is the mission of Blue Dove to make available and promote the messages, lives, and examples of saints and sages of all religions and traditions, as well as other spiritually-oriented works. We do so both by publishing inspirational books and tapes, and distributing the works of other publishers which also provide tools for inner growth.

The *Lights of Grace* catalog is the culmination of our efforts to date. From Saint Teresa of Avila to Milarepa, the Tibetan yogi, we have assembled an inspired collection of spiritual literature at its most diverse and best.

Great saints tend to transcend any single sect, regardless of the path they themselves have chosen. Their perspective is universal. It is our belief that people who have gone beyond the constraints and conditioning of the ego and have realized God, the Self, inner peace, *moksha*—call it what you will—are a tremendous resource for the entire planet. We believe that reading about and studying their lives, messages and examples is of great assistance on our own spiritual path. At Blue Dove, we are committed to contributing to the spiritual unfoldment of all. Blue Dove Press is not affiliated with any particular path, tradition, or religion.

To order contact:
Blue Dove Press
4204 Sorrento Valley Blvd. Suite K
San Diego, CA 92121
Phone: (619)623-3330
FAX: (619)623-3325
Orders: (800)691-1008
E-Mail: bdp@bluedove.com
Website:www.bluedove.com